Innovations in Cryptocrime and Financial Fraud

Leo S.F. Lin
Charles Sturt University, Australia

IGI Global
Scientific Publishing
Publishing Tomorrow's Research Today

Vice President of Editorial — Melissa Wagner
Director of Acquisitions — Mikaela Felty
Director of Book Development — Jocelynn Hessler
Production Manager — Mike Brehm
Cover Design — Jose Rosado

Published in the United States of America by
IGI Global Scientific Publishing
701 East Chocolate Avenue
Hershey, PA, 17033, USA
Tel: 717-533-8845 | Fax: 717-533-7115
Website: https://www.igi-global.com E-mail: cust@igi-global.com

Library of Congress Cataloging-in-Publication Data
Names: Lin, Leo S. F. editor http://id.loc.gov/rwo/agents/no2024125689
Title: Innovations in cryptocrime and financial fraud / [edited by] Leo S.F Lin.
Description: Hershey, PA : IGI Global Scientific Publishing, [2026] | Includes bibliographical references and index. | Summary: "This book aims to ignite crucial discussions within the academic and research communities by presenting a range of perspectives on the intersections of crime, technology, security, and finance"-- Provided by publisher.
Identifiers: LCCN 2025009728 (print) | LCCN 2025009729 (ebook) | ISBN 9798337306759 hardcover | ISBN 9798337306766 paperback | ISBN 9798337306773 ebook
Subjects: LCSH: Commercial crimes http://id.loc.gov/authorities/subjects/sh85028935 | Computer crimes http://id.loc.gov/authorities/subjects/sh85029492 | Cryptocurrencies http://id.loc.gov/authorities/subjects/sh2018001347 | Fraud http://id.loc.gov/authorities/subjects/sh85051619
Classification: LCC HV6768 .I534 2026 (print) | LCC HV6768 (ebook) | DDC 364.16/8--dc23/eng/20250514
LC record available at https://lccn.loc.gov/2025009728
LC ebook record available at https://lccn.loc.gov/2025009729

British Cataloguing in Publication Data
A Cataloguing in Publication record for this book is available from the British Library.

Editorial Advisory Board

Table of Contents

Detailed Table of Contents

This chapter examines the emerging trends between cryptocurrencies, financial crimes, and cybercrimes. While cryptocurrencies promote transaction efficiency, the decentralized and anonymous features give rise to ample opportunities for financial crimes, such as Initial Coin Offering (ICO) fraud, cross-chain money laundering, and crypto-enabled financial crimes (e.g., crypto thefts). Cryptocurrencies also facilitate the avenue of cybercrime through cyber-dependent crimes (e.g., crypto ransomware), cyber-enabled crimes (e.g., crypto scams), and online illicit cryptomarkets. Along with financial loss, victims' psychological and social harms are further exacerbated by forensic complexities. Networked approaches are recommended to prevent and mitigate the harms, which are composed of nodal and interoperable engagement between criminal justice systems, financial institutions, and technological companies. The findings underscore the importance of ongoing research and adaptive regulations against evolving conundrums posed by cryptocurrency-related financial crimes.

This chapter explores the Janus Paradox, of dematerialization, highlighting the inherent tension and pronounced duality of crime and justice; anonymity and traceability, regulation and privacy, profit and loss, individual rights, and collective responsibilities; technology and social repercussions; and the risks and opportunities offered by the digital ecosystem. The chapter also examines the role of technology as both a positive catalyst for security advancement and a negative instrument of cybercriminal enterprise, in an ever-evolving threat environment. Selected case studies shed light on current and emerging challenges posed by cybercrime, cryptocrime, economic fraud, and identity theft. The chapter further outlines technological and strategic response emphasizing policy recommendations to strengthen government, corporate, and private security. Finally, the chapter underscores the importance of cyber literacy, secure infrastructure, robust regulatory measures, and digital tools as vital instruments for enhancing resilience in the digital age.

This systematic review explored cryptocurrency-related crime and the role of community education in mitigating these threats using PRISMA guidelines. The study synthesised evidence from 20 high-quality studies (2008–2025) obtained from databases including Scopus, Web of Science, IEEE Xplore, the Australian Institute of Criminology, and Google Scholar. The review revealed key cryptocurrency-enabled crimes, such as phishing, ransomware, identity theft, romance fraud, market manipulation, and gambling scams, that exploit the decentralised and anonymous nature of cryptocurrencies, resulting in financial losses worldwide. Increasing awareness and community education are fundamental in reducing exposure through methods such as targeted training, strong security practices (including two-factor and multi-factor authentication), source verification, and prompt reporting of suspicious activities. The review further indicated the necessity of building trust through risk management practices, technological expertise, and a regulatory framework to enhance community resilience.

The quickly advancing development of artificial intelligence (AI) and rapidly spreading cryptocurrencies established a modern environment for both legal developments and illegal practices. The analysis explores AI-related crime activities in cryptocurrencies through a study of AI technologies that assist and combat various crypto-based criminal operations. This paper investigates AI-driven crimes which include fraud alongside money laundering and cyberattacks and evaluates the dual capabilities of AI between criminal execution and prevention functions. This paper explains the ethical and legal risks of AI implementations in cryptocurrency crimes and provides recommendations for present and future research to tackle emerging threats.

Blockchain technology offers transformative potential for disaster response and management in Small Island Developing States (SIDS), which are particularly vulnerable to disasters or face heightened disaster risks due to geographic isolation and limited resources. By providing a decentralized, immutable, and transparent ledger, blockchain technology facilitates secure data sharing, streamlines disaster logistics, and enhances emergency aid distribution, fostering resilience in disaster-prone regions. However, risks of cryptocrime, such as money laundering and smart contract exploits, can undermine its benefits. This chapter examines blockchain's applications in disaster logistics, community identification, and resource allocation, highlighting its role in reducing fraud and building trust. This study proposes the Blockchain Response Efficacy Model (BREM) to assess the efficiency, transparency, and fraud risks associated with SIDS. Through case studies and literature analysis, this chapter offers insights to strengthen disaster resilience while mitigating cryptocrime vulnerabilities.

This chapter delves into the revolutionary emergence of Decentralized Finance (DeFi), its potential to revolutionize, and its vulnerabilities. Based on blockchain technology, DeFi bypasses conventional financial intermediaries through smart contracts to execute lending, trading, and other economic activities. The permissionless aspect of DeFi increases financial inclusion worldwide, especially for the unbanked and underbanked. Yet, this openness also exposes DeFi platforms to threats such as vulnerabilities in smart contracts, oracle manipulation, flash loan attacks, and governance attacks. Case studies like the Poly Network hack, Mango Markets manipulation, and Squid Game token rug pull illustrate these risks. The research covers technology innovations such as smart contract audits, formal verification, decentralized oracles, and AI-based threat detection to strengthen DeFi's future. It also examines how regulatory sandboxes and decentralized identification solutions can balance innovation and regulation.

This chapter explores the intersection of cryptocurrency crime and artificial intelligence (AI), highlighting both the threats posed by AI-driven cybercriminal activities and the potential of AI-based countermeasures. Cybercriminals increasingly leverage AI for money laundering, fraud, market manipulation, ransomware attacks, and identity theft, exploiting vulnerabilities in smart contracts and decentralized finance (DeFi) platforms. Conversely, AI is a powerful tool for combating these threats, aiding in blockchain analysis, anomaly detection, and Anti-Money Laundering (AML) enforcement. Advanced machine learning models enhance Know Your Customer (KYC) protocols and enable predictive crime prevention by analyzing transactional patterns. Additionally, this chapter examines challenges such as regulatory loopholes, adversarial AI, and jurisdictional complexities. The future implications of AI in financial crime prevention, including the role of quantum computing and emerging financial technologies, are also discussed.

This chapter reviews techniques for detecting and preventing card-not-present (CNP) fraud, which has escalated due to the rise in online transactions and the COVID-19 pandemic. It evaluates methods like machine learning, behavioral analytics and risk-scoring, highlighting their integration for effective fraud detection. Key findings indicate that traditional methods remain relevant, while advanced technologies, such as artificial intelligence, significantly enhance detection accuracy. The chapter emphasizes collaboration across sectors to combat CNP fraud and explores future research aimed at enhancing fraud detection, user experience, and ethical data usage, ultimately contributing to safer digital transactions.

With the rapid advancement of technology and the proliferation of online transactions, internet fraud has emerged as a significant global issue. The increasing reliance on digital platforms for personal, financial, and business transactions has made individuals and organizations vulnerable to various forms of cybercrime. The need to address internet fraud has never been more urgent to safeguard personal security, protect organizational integrity, and maintain consumer trust in online services. The study aims to explore the different types of internet fraud, examine the factors responsible for its rise, analyze the methods used by cybercriminals, and evaluate the broader impact of such fraudulent activities. The chapter also highlights emerging threats in internet fraud, role of AI in fraud detection and challenges in combating internet fraud in India. This study adopts a qualitative approach. Data from existing research, real-world examples are analyzed to offer a comprehensive understanding of the topic.

Deepfake is a technology that enables the creation and manipulation of audio, video, and images, often leading to falsified content. Youths, as major social media users, are especially vulnerable to its risks. This study aims to explore the impact of deepfakes on social platforms and methods to counter misinformation. It covers the history and evolution of deepfakes, their potential for harm, and current detection techniques. Deepfakes have been used to spread misinformation, damage reputations, and manipulate public opinion, challenging societal trust and unity. Legal and policy frameworks, along with technological solutions like AI detection tools and platform-level safeguards, are being developed to address this growing threat. The paper underscores the importance of responsible content creation, awareness, and collaborative strategies to detect, prevent, and regulate deepfakes in the digital era.

Technological advancements and changing legislative frameworks have had a notable impact on the important milestones and problems that have marked the development of cryptocurrencies in India. The increasing need for alternative investments and the population's penchant for technology have propelled the acceptance of cryptocurrencies. The Supreme Court of India's 2020 ruling to reverse the Reserve Bank of India's restriction on cryptocurrency transactions was a turning point that rekindled interest in digital assets. In spite of this, efforts to write comprehensive laws are ongoing, and the regulatory landscape is still unsettled. Although investors find the decentralised and secure transactions that cryptocurrencies enable enticing, worries about market instability, privacy, and misuse still exist. Notwithstanding the potential for growth in the Indian cryptocurrency industry and the several areas in which blockchain applications are being used, institutional and individual investors encounter difficulties as a result of unclear regulations.

Cryptocurrencies have revolutionized traditional finance by providing decentralized payment methods and disrupting global solutions. However, the increasing prevalence of cryptocrime threatens financial market security and public confidence. This study, "The Ripple Effect," examines the financial damage caused by crypto-attacks on global payment networks and the regulatory complexities arising from deceitful cryptocurrency activity. It also examines the economic impact of cryptocrime, affecting individuals, organizations, and countries. The chapter highlights the financial threats that span across global markets and the regulatory barriers governments and organizations face. The fight against crypto crime requires international cooperation, sophisticated legal frameworks, and innovative blockchain analytical tools. The study emphasizes the need for transparency initiatives, education programs, and robust communication methods to restore trust within the crypto community.

Preface

INTRODUCTION

In the rapidly evolving digital age, where technological innovations promise unprecedented efficiency and connectivity, they also cast long shadows of vulnerability and exploitation in different spaces. Innovations in Cryptocrime and Financial Fraud emerges as a timely exploration into this duality, dissecting how cutting-edge tools such as cryptocurrencies, artificial intelligence (AI), blockchain, decentralized finance (DeFi), and financial technology (FinTech) are reshaping not only legitimate economic landscapes but also the underworld of crime and fraud. This book compiles multidisciplinary perspectives from researchers, academics, and practitioners to illuminate the intricate ways in which these technologies enable illicit activities, from money laundering and cyber extortion to sophisticated scams and market manipulations. At its core, this volume addresses the intersection of crime and technology, highlighting emerging threats like AI-driven deepfakes, ransomware powered by crypto, and exploits in smart contracts, while also proposing countermeasures through regulatory frameworks, forensic advancements, and educational initiatives. By weaving together case studies, theoretical analyses, and practical recommendations, the book provides a comprehensive overview of cryptocrime, a term encapsulating crime involving cryptocurrencies and broader financial fraud amplified by digital tools, underscoring the need for adaptive strategies in an era where innovation outpaces oversight.

The target audience for this book is broad and multifaceted, reflecting the interdisciplinary nature of cryptocrime and financial fraud. Primarily, it serves researchers and academics in fields such as cybersecurity, criminology, emergency management, computer science, economics, and law, who seek in-depth analyses and empirical insights to advance scholarly work. Practitioners in law enforcement, financial institutions, and regulatory agencies will find practical value in the proposed frameworks, detection strategies, and case studies that inform real-world applications, from forensic investigations to policy development. Policymakers and government officials grappling with legislative responses to digital threats will benefit from the discussions on ethical AI governance, cross-border challenges, and adaptive regulations. Additionally, the book appeals to industry professionals in FinTech and blockchain sectors, who must navigate risks while innovating, as well as educators and students pursuing degrees in information technology, finance, or criminal justice. By catering to this diverse group, the volume fosters collaboration across silos, encouraging a holistic approach to combating these pervasive issues.

CHAPTER OVERVIEW

Chapter 1, "Understanding the Evolving Landscape of Financial Crimes and Cybercrimes Using Cryptocurrencies," sets the foundational tone for the book by mapping out the symbiotic relationship between cryptocurrencies and criminal enterprises. Its importance cannot be overstated, as it dissects emerging trends like ICO fraud, cross-chain money laundering, and crypto-enabled cybercrimes such as ransomware and scams, which exploit the decentralized anonymity of digital currencies. Through highlighting the psychological and social harms inflicted on victims and the forensic hurdles in tracing these activities, the chapter underscores the urgent need for networked collaborations among criminal justice systems, financial institutions, and tech companies. This analysis not only contextualizes the broader cryptocrime ecosystem but also advocates for adaptive regulations and ongoing research to mitigate harms.

Chapter 2, "The Janus Paradox: Cybercrime and Cryptocurrency in the Digital Age," is pivotal for its exploration of the inherent dualities in digital ecosystems, framing cybercrime as a "Janus Paradox" where technology serves both as a shield and a sword. Its importance stems from case studies on cryptocrime, economic fraud, and identity theft, which illustrate tensions like anonymity versus traceability and profit versus loss, while proposing policy recommendations for government, corporate, and private sectors. By emphasizing cyber literacy, secure infrastructure, and robust regulations, the chapter contributes to building resilience against evolving threats and fosters a balanced approach to technological advancement that prioritizes societal repercussions.

Chapter 3, "Combating Misinformation and Global Nations' False Narratives Through Education: Mitigating Cryptocurrency-Related Crime," stands out for its systematic review of crypto-enabled crimes like phishing, ransomware, and scams, synthesizing evidence from diverse sources to advocate community education as a frontline defense. Its significance lies in promoting awareness through training, security practices, and regulatory frameworks, which build trust and resilience against misinformation-fueled threats. This chapter underscores education's role in risk management, making it a key resource for empowering communities and policymakers to foster a safer cryptocurrency ecosystem through proactive, evidence-based strategies.

Chapter 4, "Artificial Intelligence and Crime Linked to Cryptocurrencies," is critical for its comprehensive study of AI's role in both perpetrating and preventing crypto-related crimes, including fraud, money laundering, and cyberattacks. Its value lies in evaluating AI's dual capabilities, ethical risks, and legal implications, while offering recommendations for future research to address emerging threats. This chapter enriches the book by bridging technological analysis with policy insights, emphasizing the need for balanced AI implementations that enhance prevention without enabling criminal exploitation, thus contributing to a more secure cryptocurrency environment.

Chapter 5, "Combating Cryptocrime and Fraud in Small Island Developing States' Disaster Management: A Blockchain-Based Framework," proposes the Blockchain Response Efficacy Model (BREM) to leverage blockchain for secure aid distribution while mitigating risks like money laundering in disaster-prone regions. Its importance is in highlighting blockchain's transformative potential for resilience in SIDS through case studies and literature, offering insights to reduce fraud and build trust. This chapter is vital for demonstrating how technology can fortify disaster management against cryptocrime, providing actionable frameworks for policymakers in resource-limited settings.

Chapter 6, "Decentralized Finance (DeFi) and the Rise of Financial Exploits, Challenges and Opportunities," delves into DeFi's revolutionary promise and perils, analyzing threats such as smart contract vulnerabilities and flash loan attacks via case studies such as the Poly Network hack. Its significance rests in advocating innovations like audits, decentralized oracles, and AI threat detection, alongside regulatory sandboxes, to enhance security and inclusion. This chapter is essential for guiding the sustainable evolution of DeFi, ensuring it empowers the unbanked without becoming a breeding ground for exploits.

Chapter 7, "Artificial Intelligence in the Cryptocurrency Ecosystem: Crime Mechanisms, Detection Strategies, and Legal Perspectives," contrasts AI-driven threats such as ransomware and market manipulation with countermeasures, including anomaly detection and predictive prevention. The intersection of AI and cryptocurrency crime is thoroughly examined, addressing regulatory loopholes, adversarial AI, and future implications like quantum computing, making it a cornerstone for legal and technological strategies. This chapter advances the field by promoting AI as a tool for AML and KYC, fostering proactive defenses in an ecosystem rife with jurisdictional complexities.

Chapter 8, "A Comprehensive Review of Techniques for Detecting and Preventing Card-Not-Present (CNP) Fraud," is indispensable for its evaluation of methods like machine learning and behavioral analytics amid the surge in online fraud post-COVID. By emphasizing sectoral collaboration and future research on ethical data use, the chapter highlights how integrating traditional and AI-driven approaches enhances detection accuracy. Its contribution lies in promoting safer digital transactions, providing practical insights for financial institutions and researchers to combat CNP fraud effectively in an increasingly e-commerce-dependent world.

Chapter 9, "A Critical Analysis of Fraud Cases on the Internet," offers a qualitative deep dive into types of internet fraud, factors driving its rise, and AI's role in detection, with a focus on challenges in India. Its significance stems from analyzing real-world examples and emerging threats, evaluating cybercriminals' methods and impacts on trust. Through emphasizing the urgency of addressing online vulnerabilities, the chapter provides a comprehensive understanding essential for safeguarding personal and organizational integrity in a digitally reliant society.

Chapter 10, "A Study on Deepfake Dangers in the Digital Age Social Media Misinformation and the Youth at Risk," emphasizes youths' vulnerability to deepfakes on social platforms and the need for detection techniques, legal frameworks, and awareness. Its importance lies in tracing deepfakes' evolution and harms, such as misinformation and reputation damage, while proposing collaborative strategies for regulation. This chapter is vital for preserving societal trust, equipping readers with tools to counter manipulative content in an era of AI-generated falsehoods.

Chapter 11, "Cryptocurrency in India: Technological Growth and Regulatory Challenges," traces India's crypto journey, from the Supreme Court's 2020 ruling to ongoing legislative uncertainties, stressing growth drivers like technological adoption and concerns over volatility and misuse. Its value is in analyzing blockchain applications amid privacy worries, offering insights for investors and regulators. As India navigates this unsettled landscape, the chapter is key for understanding how clear regulations can unlock potential while mitigating risks in one of the world's largest emerging markets.

Chapter 12, "The Ripple Effect: Assessing the Impact of Crypto Crime on Global Financial Systems," examines how the rapid spread of cryptocurrency-related crime has generated profound challenges for financial security and stability worldwide. It analyzes the ways in which deceitful activities within digital currencies disrupt global payment networks, erode public trust, and cause cascading economic harm to individuals, institutions, and entire nations. In exploring these issues, the study underscores the urgent need for coordinated international strategies, advanced blockchain forensic techniques, and comprehensive legal frameworks.

CONCLUSION

In conclusion, *Innovations in Cryptocrime and Financial Fraud* stands as a seminal contribution to the fields of cybersecurity, criminology, and financial regulation, synthesizing diverse perspectives to illuminate the shadowy underbelly of digital innovation. By dissecting threats and proposing multifaceted solutions, this book not only maps the current terrain of cryptocrime but also charts pathways for resilience and ethical advancement. It impacts the field by fostering multidisciplinary dialogue, empowering stakeholders to anticipate and counter evolving risks, and ultimately contributing to a more secure, inclusive digital future where technology serves humanity without being subverted by malice. As the pace of innovation accelerates, this volume serves as a beacon, urging continued vigilance and collaboration to safeguard the integrity of our global financial systems.

Leo S.F. Lin
Charles Sturt University, Australia

Chapter 1
Understanding the Evolving Landscape of Financial Crimes and Cybercrimes Using Cryptocurrencies

Milind Tiwari
https://orcid.org/0000-0002-5948-1828
Charles Sturt University, Australia

You Zhou
https://orcid.org/0000-0002-9255-5403
Monash University, Australia

ABSTRACT

This chapter examines the emerging trends between cryptocurrencies, financial crimes, and cybercrimes. While cryptocurrencies promote transaction efficiency, the decentralized and anonymous features give rise to ample opportunities for financial crimes, such as Initial Coin Offering (ICO) fraud, cross-chain money laundering, and crypto-enabled financial crimes (e.g., crypto thefts). Cryptocurrencies also facilitate the avenue of cybercrime through cyber-dependent crimes (e.g., crypto ransomware), cyber-enabled crimes (e.g., crypto scams), and online illicit cryptomarkets. Along with financial loss, victims' psychological and social harms are further exacerbated by forensic complexities. Networked approaches are recommended to prevent and mitigate the harms, which are composed of nodal and interoperable engagement

DOI: 10.4018/979-8-3373-0675-9.ch001

between criminal justice systems, financial institutions, and technological companies. The findings underscore the importance of ongoing research and adaptive regulations against evolving conundrums posed by cryptocurrency-related financial crimes.

INTRODUCTION

Distributed Ledger Technology (DLT), commonly referred to as blockchain technology, is often acknowledged as a disruptive innovation due to its potential to transform businesses. Its potential resides in significantly reducing settlement time and costs, offering real-time transaction settlements, and eliminating the need for central intermediaries (World Economic Forum, 2016). For example, blockchain technology has demonstrated its capability to transform international trade by streamlining and automating the document-verification process (Chuah, 2022). The ability of blockchain to offer such benefits has driven its extensive adoption, highlighting its increasing significance for national economies. A notable case is Australia, where it is utilized in finance, professional services, and the retail sector (Smith, 2020).

Blockchain technology has diverse applications across sectors, such as education, finance, healthcare, and tourism. However, among its prominent and widely recognized applications is the facilitation of digital currencies (Catalini & Gans, 2017; Sureshbhai et al., 2020; Tapscott & Tapscott, 2017; Tiwari et al., 2019). Digital currencies, which can be managed via the use of electronic software or hardware wallets and operate within blockchain-based decentralized systems, are referred to as cryptocurrencies (Teichmann & Falker, 2021). The extensive use and adoption of cryptocurrencies can be understood from the capitalization of the global cryptocurrency market, which was estimated to be three trillion US dollars in 2022 (Mackenzie, 2022). Such a surge in the prominence of cryptocurrencies has facilitated new avenues for financial crimes. Such offenses can be attributed to pseudo-anonymity, low cost, transactional irrevocability, and low barriers to entry associated with cryptocurrencies (Durrant & Natarajan, 2019; Kethineni & Cao, 2020; Trozze et al., 2021). Examples of such offenses include, but are not limited to, hacking, initial coin offering (ICO) scams, Ponzi schemes, market manipulation, money laundering, sanctions evasion, tax fraud, theft, malware, and other types of fraudulent activities (Gandal et al., 2018; Kamps & Kleinberg, 2018; Reynolds & Irwin, 2017; Teichmann & Falker, 2021; Trozze et al., 2022).

Stuhlmiller (2013) highlights the significance of pseudo-anonymity offered by cryptocurrencies, coupled with the lack of regulatory oversight, to be pivotal in their use for unlawful purposes. Similarly, Turner and Irwin (2018) direct attention to the challenges posed by pseudo-anonymity and the untraceability issues associated with cryptocurrencies. While it is often argued that such features provided by cryptocurrencies are exploited to obscure the true source of income and the identity of users, the degree to which cryptocurrencies genuinely afford anonymity remains a debatable subject (Androulaki et al., 2013; Reid & Harrigan, 2013).

Reynolds and Irwin (2017) examined the debate surrounding the anonymity of online transactions conducted through cryptocurrencies like Bitcoin and the capacity of law enforcement agencies to track such transactions back to the user's real-life identity. Their findings revealed that analyzing the transaction history of an actor via the cryptocurrency exchange, where submission of identification documents is mandatory, can be used to identify and prosecute illicit actors. Nevertheless, they emphasized that the effectiveness of this is subject to strict adherence to Customer Due Diligence (CDD) and Know Your Customer (KYC) regulations by cryptocurrency exchanges. Effective compliance with and effective implementation of these regulations would enable law enforcement agencies to leverage the collected data to link transactions to their rightful owners. The importance of collecting and verifying the provided customer information has prompted the development of KYC verification systems using the DLT, which focuses on reducing costs as well as enhancing the ability to verify the provided information to combat money laundering (Moyano & Ross, 2017; Park & Youm, 2021). Subsequently, in recent times, the necessity of monitoring trends among institutional investors conducting operational due diligence on cryptocurrencies has gained prominence (Scharfman, 2022).

While much of the academic literature has directed attention towards anonymity offered by cryptocurrencies, it has also explored the use of cryptocurrencies in committing a range of financial crimes (Braaten & Vaughn, 2019; Dawes Centre for Future Financial Crime, 2021; Durrant & Natarajan, 2019; Gandal et al., 2018; Grobys, 2021; Kamps & Kleinberg, 2018; Teichmann & Falker, 2021; Trozze et al., 2021; Trozze et al., 2022). For example, Teichmann and Falker (2021), examined the money laundering typologies used by money launderers to exploit cryptocurrencies for laundering illicit funds. Similarly, Dawes Centre for Future Financial Crime (2021) attributed pump-and-dump schemes, ransomware, and money laundering using Bitcoin ATMs to be the most profitable and feasible cryptocurrency-based crimes. Trozze et al. (2022) concluded that Ponzi schemes/high-yield investment program schemes and initial coin offering (ICOs) scams are the most discussed forms of cryptocurrency fraud. Consequently, efforts have been made towards detecting and mitigating financial crimes involving the use of cryptocurrencies (Farrugia et al., 2020; Gandal et al., 2018; Grobys, 2021; Kamps & Kleinberg, 2018; Park & Youm, 2021; Rognone et al., 2020; Shi et al., 2019; Sureshbhai et al., 2020).

This includes scholarly efforts made to deepen the understanding of financial crimes within the cryptocurrency domain, recognizing its potential to inform criminological perspectives on cybercrime, and grey economies, as well as its interpretation for social and financial lives, lived in a blend of on/offline (Mackenzie, 2022). Notable initiatives taken in this direction include the application of the convenience theory of white-collar crime to cryptocurrency crime litigations to understand dimensions facilitating the perpetration of cryptocurrency offenses (Braaten & Vaughn, 2019) and the examination of characteristics of cases contributing towards successful cryptocurrency-based financial crime prosecution (Trozze et al., 2021).

While attention has been given to cryptocurrencies, concentrating on their use in illegal activities, such as money laundering, and the factors contributing to their misuse, anti-money laundering (AML) legislation to address the issue remains underdeveloped (Teichmann & Falker, 2021). For example, it was not until 2017 that Australia's AML/CTF Act of 2006 was extended to regulate cryptocurrency exchanges, requiring them to implement CDD/KYC regulations to mitigate money laundering risks (Smith, 2020). Despite such regulations, cryptocurrency exchanges have been misused to undertake money laundering.

This study aims to review the characteristics of cryptocurrency-related financial crimes, focusing on their conceptual foundations, emerging trends, connections with cybercrimes, and the associated harms along with potential mitigation strategies. The rest of this chapter is structured as follows: The next section provides a comprehensive examination of blockchain technology and its implications within the crypto asset ecosystem. It begins with an overview of blockchain, including a discussion of its core concepts and diverse applications. Following this, the chapter dives into financial crime trends associated with crypto assets, with a particular focus on a notable crime that gained prominence in the late 2010s: ICO fraud. This segment explores the concept of Initial Coin Offerings (ICOs), the fraudulent opportunities they present, and the common patterns observed in some of the well-documented cases of ICO fraud. Subsequently, the chapter broadens its scope to examine other emerging financial crime trends, focusing on issues such as money laundering and cybercrime that have arisen alongside the growth of crypto assets. The connections between cryptocurrencies and cybercrimes are further examined to provide interdisciplinary insights into the intertwined dynamics between financial and cybercrime. Finally, psychological and social harms and multifaceted harm mitigation methods are also reviewed. The findings of the current chapter underscore the ongoing regulatory and research commitment to enhance financial resilience and online safety in the era marked by the growing prevalence of cryptocurrencies.

OVERVIEW OF BLOCKCHAIN

The blockchain technology can be touted as one of the significant technological advancements of the 21st century. At its core, a blockchain can be described as a digital ledger that is both decentralized and distributed among participants in a peer-to-peer network (Underhill, 2018). Conceptually, it can be understood as a text file that records events, such as transactions, on the basis of consensus among network participants, thus eliminating the need for an intermediary. In terms of structure, a blockchain is composed of a series of blocks, with each block storing a record of transactions that have occurred in the network (Turner & Irwin, 2018). These transactions are collected into blocks, which are then added to the existing chain through a cryptographic process known as the proof of work (Sullivan & Burger, 2017), a mathematical procedure utilized to verify and validate transactions before they are added as new blocks of transactions in the blockchain. This computational process, known as mining, is undertaken by network nodes called miners. Once a transaction is mined, it produces a solution known as a hash. This process is illustrated further in Figure 1 below using three blockchains, where each hash is compared to its counterpart in the other blockchains. Each hash is verified by comparing it with the corresponding hashes in other blockchains. In the scenario presented, when the hashes are consistent in each blockchain, they are deemed as valid.

Figure 1. Example of working blockchain network (modified from concept by Lee (2017))

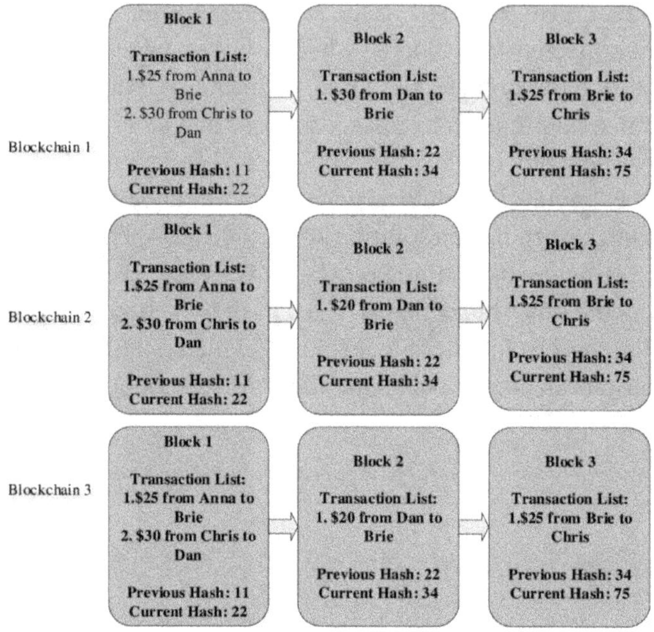

Figure 1: Example of Working Blockchain Network (modified from concept by Lee (2017))

In the real application of a blockchain, a much larger number of blockchains exist that are distributed across the network, thus commonly referred to as 'distributed ledger technology' (DLT). Similarly, in the above Figure 1, hashes are represented as two-digit numbers, whereas they are actually longer and more complex. Finally, the previous hash of each block matches the current hash of the preceding block, thus providing an additional layer of verification. Therefore, each block incorporates information from earlier blocks in addition to current information, with the integrity and authenticity of each component being verified against prior records (Mansfield-Devine, 2017). Furthermore, when a new transaction or event takes place on the blockchain, the ledger gets updated simultaneously for all participants in the network (Underhill, 2018). Each participant of the network possesses a copy of the ledger, and any updates are reflected in their respective individual ledger through cryptographic verification to ensure accuracy and security (Sullivan & Burger, 2017). As a result, when an error arises, as depicted in Figure 2 below, the resulting hash will not match the hash in other blockchains, resulting in a chain of invalidated blocks in that chain. For instance, if a hacker alters the amount value in Block 2 of Blockchain 1, the resulting hash produced will be distinct from the corresponding hash in other blockchains, thus rendering the entire blockchain invalid. Consequently, it is not possible for a hacker to successfully modify a single blockchain without detection, as the rest of the network will be able to identify the corrupted data.

Figure 2. Hacker attempting to modify block 2 of blockchain 1

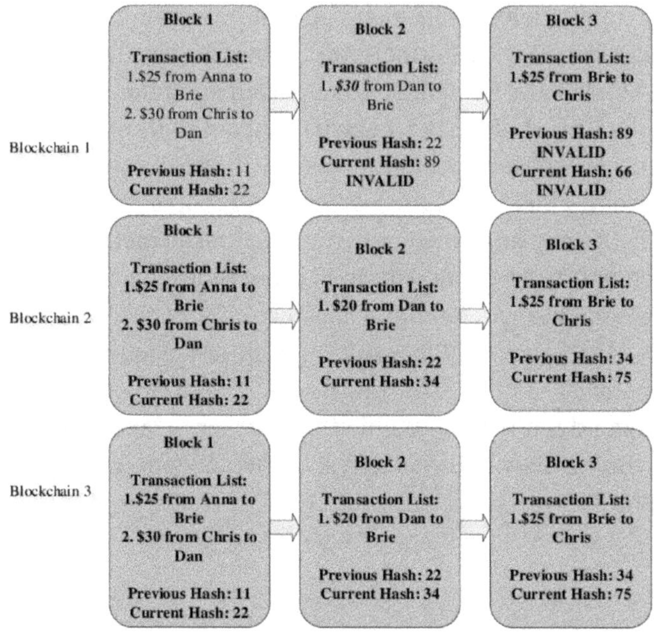

Figure 2: Hacker attempting to modify Block 2 of Blockchain 1

From an access perspective, blockchain can be broadly classified into two main types: public (open) and private (closed) blockchain networks. Private blockchains operate as restricted systems that require authorization for network access, thus limiting participation to entities considered to be trustworthy. On the contrary, public blockchains are permissionless, facilitating public participation by simply installing and running the required software and hardware infrastructure (SEC, 2018).

Bitcoin is a prominent example of a public blockchain implementation – a digital currency enabling peer-to-peer transactions without the need for financial intermediaries. Furthermore, anyone with the required software and hardware infrastructure can participate in validating transactions on the Bitcoin blockchain (SEC, 2018). It is critical to note that Bitcoin is just one of the many cryptocurrencies employing blockchain technology, with numerous other alternatives.

Nakamoto (2008), in his work, introduced the concept of a digital currency operating on the blockchain without traditional financial institutions. The proposed system employed digital signatures for coin authentication and required an immutable transaction record to prevent double-spending. Furthermore, such a system is protected against attacks, given that the majority of network participants oppose such actions. This framework laid emphasis on collective interest over individualism and consensus-based decision-making instead of hierarchical control, thus using participant networks for event validation.

Consequently, some of the key attributes of a blockchain network include a decentralized structure and the use of cryptography. The distinct nature of the technology emerges from its reliance on participant networks in place of centralized intermediaries, universal accessibility, and transparency of transaction records. Moreover, the implementation of cryptographic security for validating transactions facilitates numerous applications (Tapscott & Tapscott, 2017). While understanding the fundamental infrastructure and the functioning of blockchain is critical, it is equally important to examine its diverse applications across various sectors and current implementation status.

Uses of Blockchain Technology and Current Implementation

The blockchain technology and its applications extend far beyond cryptocurrencies (Abad-Segura et al., 2021; Abid et al., 2024; Ahlawat & Tripathi, 2021; Akinrotimi, 2020; Al Shamsi et al., 2023; Mansfield-Devine, 2017). For instance, the human resource department can leverage it to enhance the recruitment process by having access to verified, tamper-proof information of candidates (Catalini & Gans, 2017; Tapscott & Tapscott, 2017). The data of job applicants can be stored in virtual databases for HR professionals to search when seeking qualified candidates. Moreover, individuals would maintain control over their personal information, choosing whether to grant or deny access to specific details (Tapscott & Tapscott, 2017).

Corporate financial information can be verified through blockchain-enabled systems accessible through company websites (Ahlawat & Tripathi, 2021). Similar to banking transaction updates, financial information could be provided instantaneously

(Gepp et al., 2018). Such integration would enhance transparency in financial reporting and potentially expose any financial wrongdoing, thus representing significant progress in combating financial statement fraud, which was estimated to cost over USD 1.2 trillion globally in the last decade (Gepp, 2016; Tiwari et al., 2019).

Considering patents and governance around it, blockchain holds tremendous potential in the domain. This is valuable when considering patents, recording timing is critical, and keeping track of multiple components is important (Mansfield-Devine, 2017). Maritime trading systems, which often face numerous supply chain security challenges (Barnes & Oloruntoba, 2005; Chuah, 2022), could benefit substantially from blockchain solutions. Similarly, contractual agreements could employ blockchain technology. Moreover, the technology could also provide opportunities for firms to directly engage with customers for targeted marketing. Consumers would have control over their data, thus preventing unwanted profiling based on their online activities, while selectively granting access to businesses. Such an arrangement would be beneficial for both parties through precise need-matching and reduced marketing costs.

Blockchain can contribute to the verification of product or service quality (Tapscott & Tapscott, 2017), with application in the precious stone industry and the food sector (Abid et al., 2024; Bhat et al., 2025; Knight, 2017). For instance, the technology allows for the authentication of gemstone sources and genuineness by linking each transaction to the previous one. This results in a reduction of dependence on central record-keeping authorities, lowering tracking and data storage expenses (Mansfield-Devine, 2017). From an economic perspective, blockchain offers two primary advantages: reducing authentication costs and decreasing network establishment expenses through the elimination of intermediaries (Catalini & Gans, 2017). Although financial lending without intermediaries could become a standard, such a shift would require regulatory frameworks beyond national boundaries, catering to global approaches (Lagarde, 2017; Smith & Tiwari, 2023; Tiwari et al., 2025a).

Nevertheless, applications of blockchain are evident, as substantiated by its use in large corporations and national governments. For instance, Estonia has employed this technology in its e-Residency initiative (Sullivan & Burger, 2017), giving its citizens control over their identity and electronic records while ensuring protection against data breaches through decentralization. Maersk, in partnership with IBM, has applied blockchain technology to its global trade operations (IBM, 2018). Moreover, Amazon Web Services supports numerous blockchain technologies by providing secure platforms for blockchain application development (AWS, 2018; Roma et al., 2016). These wide-ranging applications highlight blockchain's transformative potential beyond cryptocurrencies and its capacity to revolutionize current business practices.

Initial Coin Offerings (ICOs) and Opportunities for Fraud

Blockchain technology has paved the way for the creation of novel financing opportunities for businesses in the last decade (Tapscott & Tapscott, 2017). As discussed in the last section, the immutability of the blockchain presents an attractive avenue to be considered for fundraising, resulting in the rise of Initial Coin Offerings (ICOs). An ICO, also known as Initial Token Sales (ITS), represents an approach where issuers provide tokens to investors in exchange for either fiat money or established cryptocurrencies. The aim of such a strategy was to accumulate funds for future business development opportunities while simultaneously generating interest and building a user community for upcoming product offerings by an entity (Silverberg et al., 2018; Underhill, 2018). The interest in blockchain technology and its applications, such as ICOs, resulted in broad investor participation.

The interest in the adoption of ICOs for fundraising can be substantiated by the findings of Ernst & Young (2018), who found that 372 ICOs collectively raised a staggering USD 3.7 billion in 2017. Apart from startups employing ICOs as a funding channel, established organizations such as Perth Mint and IAGON launched and planned their own offerings (Garvey, 2018; Harison, 2018). The widespread adoption and interest in ICOs at the time can be attributed to their speed and cost-effectiveness, owing to the lack of need to comply with securities regulations as required in the case of conventional fundraising methods. Furthermore, the innovative nature of blockchain was key in attracting investors to potentially seek substantial returns (Underhill, 2018).

It was argued that investments in ICOs were different from initial public offerings (IPOs) as ownership of tokens acquired through an ICO did not confer ownership rights, unlike shares purchased in an IPO. The process of an ICO began with an announcement on the part of the issuer, followed by marketing of the initiative using company websites and social media platforms, resulting in a time-constrained token offering. The announcement for an ICO would typically include a whitepaper, equivalent to an IPO prospectus, containing project information, token details, investor rights, project timeline, and other key points. However, compared to a prospectus, it was found that whitepapers provided less comprehensive information and did not follow any standardized guidelines (Underhill, 2018).

The diversity offered by ICO projects is reflected in a variety of tokens that were offered. Some tokens allow the holders to access the issuer's existing or upcoming products and services, which are supposed to be funded by proceeds from ICOs (ESMA, 2017). The other types of coins offered through ICOs were meant to facilitate users' utilization of them as normal currencies or to convert them into fiat money (ESMA, 2017; Underhill, 2018). Therefore, the issuer would issue the coins during or immediately after the sale, with the most common method being pre-sale, in which coins were not developed for distribution and would be scheduled for distribution at a later date (Underhill, 2018).

With the increasing focus on applications of blockchain technology and the interest in ICOs, in 2017, the enthusiasm to circumvent securities laws through ICOs was prominent, with not a single ICO registering with the Securities and Exchange Commission in the US. The lack of regulatory clarity around ICOS resulted in confusion for legitimate issuers and provided opportunities for fraudulent activities, including Ponzi schemes, pump-and-dump schemes, pyramid structures, and money laundering (Underhill, 2018).

The prevailing vulnerabilities owing to information gaps and insufficient due diligence were exploited extensively by illicit actors (DeVoe, 2018; Patel, 2017). For example, the inability to audit presented information would provide potential fraudsters for disseminate misleading information to prospective investors. Furthermore, it would allow illicit actors to establish websites with vague information to attract investors, utilizing numerous social media platforms and endorsements from celebrities to draw attention and undertake fraudulent schemes. All this paved the way for countless fraudulent cases, including AriseBank, Benebit, PlexCorps, RECoin, and Diamond Reserve (Tiwari et al., 2019).

These cases presented recurring patterns in fraudulent ICO schemes, with a systematic violation of securities regulations being a predominant characteristic. For example, in the case of AriseBank, the entity offered AriseCoin without proper SEC registration, with its top executive misrepresenting the offering as exempt from SEC regulation (Evans et al., 2018). Similarly, RECoin provided its token offering without SEC registration, while Diamond Reserve made an attempt to bypass regulatory requirements by addressing its offering as an "Initial Member Offer" instead of an investment vehicle (SEC, 2017). PlexCorps addressed its tokens as cryptocurrencies instead of securities, thus attempting to evade the SEC's jurisdiction (SEC, 2017). All of this suggests the pervasiveness of regulatory evasion in fraudulent ICO operations.

Furthermore, these cases also demonstrated a systematic pattern of misrepresentation across numerous communication channels, including fabrication of business relationships and credentials, exaggeration of financial performance, misrepresentation of organizational capacity, concealment of material information, employment of sophisticated legitimacy-building strategies, and misappropriation of investor capital (Tiwari et al., 2019). The noted incidents of fraud in the context of ICOs have emphasized the importance of due diligence and verification of claims before engaging in such investment opportunities. Furthermore, these fraudulent schemes did provide valuable insights for the development of effective regulatory frameworks, investor protection mechanisms, and educational initiatives as the blockchain and cryptocurrency ecosystem continues to evolve. The need for improved measures and improved protection measures is still pertinent in the current landscape. While ICOs represented an early manifestation of financial crime mechanisms in the cryptocurrency ecosystem, the evolving landscape has observed a significant diversification of financial crime typologies extending beyond fraudulent token offerings.

Cryptocurrencies and Evolving Financial Crime Landscape

Apart from ICO frauds (Tiwari et al., 2019), as discussed in the previous section, the rapid growth and increasing sophistication of technologies have engendered a significant evolution in the financial crime landscape (Leuprecht et al., 2023). The increasing use of cryptocurrencies and the emergence of technological infrastructures such as decentralized finance (DeFi) and the metaverse have paved the way for this evolution, posing considerable challenges for law enforcement and regulatory bodies (Tiwari et al., 2025a, 2025b; Zhou et al., 2024). Initially, when considering financial crimes and cryptocurrencies, the focus revolved around the potential of cryptocurrencies to facilitate illicit activities, such as terrorism financing and money laundering, owing to their characteristics of decentralization and pseudonymity (Stuhlmiller, 2013; Teichmann & Falker, 2021; Trozze et al., 2022; Turner & Irwin, 2018).

Consequently, the scope of financial crimes in the context of cryptocurrencies has expanded beyond traditional methodologies. A notable development in this context has been the development of cross-chain crime, which involves the conversion of crypto-assets across different blockchains to conceal their illicit origins – a practice termed "asset-hopping" or "chain-hopping" (Chainalysis, 2022). This is enabled by an increasing number of crypto assets, including privacy coins offering enhanced confidentiality and stablecoins that mitigate volatility concerns. The lack of robust identity verification mechanisms on services facilitating cross-chain and cross-asset transfers has further exacerbated this issue.

Virtual asset service providers (VASPs) such as decentralized exchanges, cross-chain bridges, and cross-swap services are frequently utilized to facilitate cross-asset and cross-chain swaps, thus contributing to separating funds from their illicit source. For example, DEX facilitates the conversion of assets that can be confiscated, such as USDT and USDC, into those that cannot, such as DAI stablecoins, and then further facilitates the conversion into mainstream assets, such as ETH. This can aid in protecting the illicit actors from value fluctuations associated with less popular cryptocurrencies. Similarly, cross-chain bridges can allow for the exchange of tokens across numerous blockchains in an anonymized and decentralized manner, thus presenting an avenue for exploitation. For example, the North Korean Lazarus Group has extensively exploited cross-chain solutions for laundering illicit proceeds (Akartuna & Madelin, 2023).

Apart from the exploitation of new mechanisms to undertake financial crimes, established cryptocurrency-related crimes have also witnessed an evolution in terms of their execution and impact. For instance, ransomware attacks, after declining in 2022, witnessed an increase in 2023, accompanied by an increase in ransom payments and attack complexity. The shift in focus on targeting large organizations for randoms and the proliferation of the Ransomware as a Service Model (RaaS) have allowed all kinds of actors to perpetuate such attacks, thus marking a significant evolution in the way these crimes are undertaken (Chainalysis, 2022, 2024; Graver et al., 2023). Conversion platforms facilitating crypto-to-fiat transactions have emerged as a critical juncture for the integration of illicitly obtained cryptocurrency into the traditional financial system (Transparency International Russia, 2023).

Similarly, cryptocurrency hacking and the theft of funds from crypto platforms continue to remain a significant threat, as substantiated by the ByBit exchange hack (Tidy, 2025). Continuing with the trends observed in the past few years, North Korea-affiliated cybercriminals have continued to be active in cryptocurrency exchange hacking (Chainalysis, 2022, 2024; Graver et al., 2023). Given the numerous concerns associated with sexual violence (Zhou et al., 2022), the utilization of cryptocurrency in enabling crimes such as child sexual abuse material (CSAM), represents a criminal evolution with deep social concerns. This can be attributed to an increase in the adoption of obfuscation measures, such as mixers and privacy coins like Monero, posing significant challenges for law enforcement efforts (Chainalysis, 2024). Furthermore, the growth in sophistication has often been accused of cryptocurrencies being employed to evade sanctions amidst geopolitical conflicts (Tiwari et al., 2024).

Therefore, financial crime typologies have evolved in the context of cryptocurrencies. This transformation stems from the adaptation of traditional crimes to the unique attributes of cryptocurrencies, new typologies (such as cross-chain crimes), and the increasing sophistication of established cryptocurrency-related criminalities. As these criminalities continue to evolve, it becomes pertinent to examine their implications for cybercrimes and the challenges they present.

Cryptocurrencies and Cybercrime

The current study intends to understand the relationships between cryptocurrencies and cybercrimes from three dimensions: 1) crypto and cyber-dependent cybercrime, 2) crypto and cyber-enabled cybercrime, and 3) online illicit cryptomarkets. This typology is developed from the widely accepted cybercrime dichotomy, which classifies cybercrimes into cyber-dependent and cyber-enabled crimes (Brenner, 2007). Cyber-dependent crimes refer to crimes that can only be committed using information and communication technologies (ICTs), while cyber-enabled crimes denote crimes that are facilitated by ICTs (McGuire & Dowling, 2013). Apart from the updated dichotomy, a more complicated criminal phenomenon has arisen along with the rapid expansion of cryptocurrency ecosystems – online illicit markets. The following sections will briefly touch on the three dimensions of crypto-related cybercrimes by reviewing typical cases of each.

Crypto and Cyber-Dependent Cybercrimes: Cryptocurrency Ransomware

Cryptocurrencies, as an increasingly recognized transferable currency, have been exploited by cybercriminals by committing various cyber-dependent crimes, including ransomware, cryptocurrency hacking, cryptojacking (unauthorized crypto mining), and Distributed Denial-of-Service blackmail. Among those crimes, cryptocurrency ransomware, which refers to a type of ransomware attack in which cybercriminals demand payment in cryptocurrency, has gained widespread attention from academia and industry (Cong et al., 2025; Connolly & Wall, 2019; Whelan et al., 2024).

Cryptocurrency facilitates ransomware attacks by providing cybercriminals with a more profitable, more secure, and less traceable payment opportunity (Connolly & Wall, 2019). The embedded characteristics of cryptocurrencies (e.g., decentralization, pseudonymity, and transaction transparency) accurately meet the needs of ransomware perpetrators, who demand payment in ways that can minimize detection risks and maximize financial rewards (Cong et al., 2025; Trozze et al., 2022). Given that decentralized and anonymous transaction systems have significantly complicated digital forensic protocols and law enforcement procedures, ransomware attackers have been furiously operating globally with minimal regulatory oversight (Gómez Hernández et al., 2023).

Moreover, the widespread availability of cryptocurrency infrastructure, such as exchanges, wallets, and mixers, has expanded opportunities for attackers to swiftly and securely convert illicit gains into usable funds (Buil-Gil & Saldaña-Taboada, 2022; Gómez Hernández et al., 2023). The increasing prevalence of ransomware-as-a-service (RaaS) platforms further exacerbates this issue by providing less skilled criminals with opportunities to learn and access sophisticated ransomware tools, boosting the volume and reach of ransomware attacks (Connolly & Wall, 2019).

Recent research also reveals that ransomware operates as an organized crime, with encryption as the key enabler of organizational and reputational management (Cong et al., 2025; Whelan et al., 2024). For example, ransomware operations often resort to cryptocurrencies for distortion, which not only indicates the complexities of criminal activities but also symbolic representations of extra-legal governance, such as internally indoctrinated rules and orders for risk management (Whelan et al., 2024). Cong also found that some ransomware organizations endow ransomware attacks with ethical meanings by apologizing for attacking hospitals and offering an encryptor for free.

Crypto and Cyber-Enabled Crimes: Crypto-Enabled Fraudulent Schemes

Cryptocurrencies have also facilitated various cyber-enabled crimes. Apart from money laundering discussed above, another critical cyber-enabled crime that is highly associated with cryptocurrency is cyber fraud, or, more precisely, crypto-enabled fraudulent schemes. Similar to the emergence of cryptocurrency ransomware, the proliferation of crypto-enabled fraudulent schemes can also be attributed to cryptocurrencies' decentralized and anonymous nature (Bartoletti et al., 2021).

Fraudulent schemes exploiting cryptocurrencies typically encompass investment-centered scams such as Ponzi schemes (Mukherjee et al., 2021), ICO scams (Tiwari et al., 2019), pump-and-dump scams (Trozze et al., 2022), as well as human-centered scams, like online romance scams (Wang & Zhou, 2023), virtual kidnapping (Chang et al., 2023), and health fraud (Zhou et al., 2023). Cryptocurrency exchanges have also been targeted for scam offenses, such as fake apps and phishing websites, which are developed to defraud cryptocurrency investors by transferring fiat currencies to fraudulent cryptocurrencies (Chen et al., 2020; Xia et al., 2020).

Research highlights that the decentralization and anonymity of cryptocurrency transactions complicate tracing stolen funds, thus attracting fraudsters who exploit the limited financial transparency and legal accountability inherent in blockchain-based financial systems (Bartoletti et al., 2021; Patel, 2022). The recently observed crypto-enabled fraudulent schemes already show the explicit exploitation of decentralized and anonymous features, as exemplified by the intersections between crypto investment and online romance scams (Cross, 2024). Such intertwined digital criminality demonstrates the adaptability of fraudsters in leveraging emotional vulnerability manipulation alongside advanced financial transaction technologies (Cross, 2024; Zhou et al., 2023).

Moreover, cryptocurrency scams often exploit social media and online platforms to propagate blockchain-related fraudulent information. For example, studies found that scammers leverage manipulative tactics with complex cryptocurrency knowledge to enhance perceived legitimacy and attract victims (Siu et al., 2022). Promises of high returns often attract victims, but they frequently face challenges in detecting fraudulent schemes due to the technical complexity of blockchain technologies and the persuasive manipulation techniques employed (Holt & Cross, 2024). As a result, the rapid proliferation and innovation in cryptocurrency scams underscore an urgent need for more resilient and adaptive detection mechanisms, public awareness initiatives, and regulatory frameworks to mitigate escalating victimization risks (Barnes, 2018).

Crypto and Online Illicit Markets: The Emergence of Illicit Cryptomarkets

Apart from cyber-dependent and cyber-enabled crimes, cryptocurrencies also promoted the expansion of online illicit markets, harboring a wide range of illicit and criminal industries. Illicit markets had long existed in the terrestrial realm until the recent centuries' flourishing of ICTs, especially the invention of cryptocurrency (Haynie & Duxbury, 2024). Cryptocurrencies have become the dominant transaction currency in most online illicit markets, given their decentralized and anonymous features (Aldridge, 2019).

By current observations, cryptocurrency-empowered online illicit markets have provided services for both terrestrial and digital illegal properties. As for physical illegal property transactions, an accumulated number of studies have found abundant evidence that cryptocurrencies have been exploited by drug vendors who sell illicit substances online via crypto payment (Chawki, 2022; Norbutas, 2018; Rhumorbarbe et al., 2016). Other studies have also found the existence of cryptomarkets for firearms (Holt & Lee, 2023), human trafficking and smuggling (Noval et al., 2023), and counterfeit goods (Soldner et al., 2024).

Meanwhile, recent studies have also discovered the emergence of cryptomarkets that provide products and services for cybercriminals. For instance, Hutchings and Holt (2017) found that stolen data has been trafficked in online illicit markets with the financial intermediaries of cryptocurrencies. Ouellet et al. (2022) extended the research by incorporating network analysis on online stolen data markets. They found that vendor networks remain relatively stable after law enforcement, indicating trends of crime displacement across digital platforms. Besides, cybercrime tutorials and criminal tools have also been provided in online illicit markets, which can be conveniently purchased with either fiat currency or cryptocurrency (HackingRealm, 2024).

Above all, it is clear that cryptocurrencies have reshaped the financial ecosystem of both terrestrial and online criminal industries by enabling more anonymous transaction methods with pseudonymous identities. However, these crypto-related cybercrimes have further challenged cybercrime policing by complicating financial investigation processes. Antecedent studies already revealed the dilemmas of digital forensics in law enforcement, such as data collection, analysis, and storage (Holt & Bossler, 2015). Cybercrimes that involve decentralized and anonymous cryptocurrency transactions have cast another giant conundrum that policing agencies cannot efficiently and independently address. Proactive and networked policing frameworks might be promising for coping with the mounting challenges of crypto-related cybercrimes.

Harms of Victimization and Mitigation Approaches

Apart from financial loss, victims of cryptocurrency-related financial crimes often endure prominent psychological and social suffering. Psychologically, victims frequently experience intense emotional distress, including shame, guilt, and self-blame (Cross, 2015), which are also accompanied by mental health disorders such as anxiety (Wang et al., 2024), depression (Wang et al., 2023), and even suicidal attempts (Cross, 2017). Socially, the stigma associated with victim identities not only leads to withdrawal from personal and professional relationships but also attracts victim-blaming from social networks, exacerbating mental health disorders and impeding emotional recovery (Cross, 2015, 2016).

Victims' vulnerabilities, compounded with technological complexities, have become the leverage maliciously manipulated by perpetrators to gain greater profits (Cross, 2016; Xu et al., 2024; Zhou et al., 2023). The anonymous and decentralized features of cryptocurrencies further exacerbate victims' perceived harms, given the expectations that loss recovery opportunities are limited and perpetrators are untraceable. The sense of hopelessness can deter victims from reporting crimes (Cross et al., 2016). For example, victims who do not know offenders' cryptocurrency payment details are 168% less likely to report the crime to authorities (Holt & Cross, 2024). Given the prominent harms elicited by cryptocurrency-related financial crimes, tailored crime prevention and harm mitigation methods should be implemented.

To mitigate these harms, multifaceted approaches have been proposed in earlier literature. Studies suggest that targeted education and awareness campaigns can inform potential investors and consumers about the risks associated with cryptocurrency investments, as well as the deceptive techniques employed by fraudsters (Kasula, 2024). In addition, regulatory authorities should establish clear regulatory frameworks and risk management mechanisms for cryptocurrency markets, including enforcing anti-money laundering (AML) and know-your-customer (KYC) protocols to deter illicit financial activities (Tiwari et al., 2024). Moreover, introducing specialized victim support services can provide essential psychological and legal assistance, offering timely counseling, personalized financial advice, and specific guidance on crime reporting (Cross, 2015, 2016).

Nevertheless, the responsibility for combating cryptocurrency-related financial crimes should not rest solely with law enforcement agencies. Security networks that facilitate collaboration between criminal justice systems, financial institutions, and technology companies are also vital to developing tools and protocols for detecting and preventing these crimes (Whelan, 2012; Whelan et al., 2024). Finally, broadening ongoing research into the dynamic tactics employed by money laundering perpetrators and cryptocurrency scammers can inform targeted intervention strategies, helping to develop timely and effective policy responses. By implementing these strategies, associated stakeholders can collectively work toward crime prevention and harm mitigation, alleviating the burdens suffered by victims.

LIMITATIONS AND FUTURE STUDIES

While this chapter offers a comprehensive literature review of cryptocurrency-related financial crimes, some limitations must be acknowledged. First, the discussion relies heavily on literature review and case study analysis, which may not capture the extended scope of empirical insights. This methodological limitation restricts the findings' generalizability and indicates a demand for empirical investigations into offenders' tactics and victim experiences. Second, the current analysis is largely dependent on high-profile cases and sources from Western contexts, sparing little contextualized and focused attention on the dynamics from Global South jurisdictions where the prevalence of cryptocurrency is also rising at an alarming rate. Third, criminological theories (e.g., routine activity theory and rational choice theory) have not been profoundly integrated into the analysis, discounting the theoretical foundations for the observed crime patterns.

Future studies may design longitudinal or panel research to examine temporal relationships between financial crimes and blockchain technologies, demonstrating evidence-based insights for the developmental patterns of cryptocurrency-related financial crimes. Besides, more studies are expected from non-Western contexts, investigating the intervening roles of cultural characteristics (e.g., Asian-specific offenders or victims) in the aforementioned crimes. Finally, considering the evolving nature of financial crimes and cybercrimes (Zhou et al., 2024), ongoing research is warranted to advance our understanding of deceptive techniques and the effectiveness of harm mitigation programs.

CONCLUSION

This chapter examines how the technologies of cryptocurrencies have brought new avenues for financial crimes. Although the innovations offer some financial advantages, like increased transaction efficiency and decentralized management, they also contribute to salient digital threats, such as types of financial crimes. The forefront literature review found both novel and adaptive financial crimes and cybercrimes, such as fraudulent initial coin offerings (ICOs), cross-chain money laundering, ransomware attacks, and various cybercrimes. Due to cryptocurrencies' decentralized and anonymous features, these crimes have made regulatory efforts more challenging.

The subsequent discussion demonstrates that cryptocurrency-related financial crimes are not confined to a single approach. Instead, they encompass a constantly evolving range of activities exploiting regulatory gaps, identity verification loopholes, and public confusion about financial technologies. The discussion also highlights how criminals exploit cryptocurrency tools, including mixing services, decentralized exchanges, and privacy coins, to hide transaction trails and evade regulatory detection.

Moreover, cryptocurrencies have influenced cybercrime dynamics. Cyber-dependent crimes, like cryptocurrency ransomware and cryptojacking, have increased due to the challenges of tracking digital payments. Besides, cryptocurrencies have facilitated cyber-enabled crimes, as exemplified by crypto-enabled fraudulent schemes. Online illicit markets have also adopted cryptocurrencies as a prioritized payment method, stimulating the digital trade of both physical and digital illegal goods, such as drugs, weapons, stolen data, and hacking tools. These crypto-related cybercrimes have introduced new obstacles for law enforcement regarding financial investigations. Proactive and networked policing approaches may provide new solutions.

The connection between cryptocurrencies and financial crime is multifaceted and ever evolving. Confronting financial, psychological, and social harms endured by victims, tailored and collaborative mitigation methods are increasingly necessary. Sustained interdisciplinary research and cross-sector collaboration will also be essential in developing effective countermeasures, ensuring that cryptocurrency and blockchain technologies strengthen, rather than undermine, financial resilience and public well-being.

REFERENCES

Abad-Segura, E., Infante-Moro, A., González-Zamar, M. D., & López-Meneses, E. (2021). Blockchain technology for secure accounting management: Research trends analysis [Article]. *Mathematics*, *9*(14), 1631. Advance online publication. DOI: 10.3390/math9141631

Abid, H. M. R., Khan, N., Hussain, A., Anis, Z. B., Nadeem, M., & Khalid, N. (2024). Quantitative and qualitative approach for accessing and predicting food safety using various web-based tools. *Food Control*, *162*, 110471. DOI: 10.1016/j.foodcont.2024.110471

Ahlawat, S., & Tripathi, A. (2021). Blockchain: Implications for accounting and audit practice. In (pp. 9-19). https://doi.org/DOI: 10.1515/9783110702507-002

Akartuna, E. A., & Madelin, T. (2023). *The State of Cross-chain Crime* Elliptic. https://www.elliptic.co/resources/state-of-cross-chain-crime-2023

Akinrotimi, A. O. (2020). Legal Ramifications of Blockchain Technology. In Khan, M. A., Quasim, M. T., Algarni, F., & Alharthi, A. (Eds.), *Decentralised Internet of Things: A Blockchain Perspective* (pp. C1–C1). Springer International Publishing. DOI: 10.1007/978-3-030-38677-1_10

Al Shamsi, M., Smith, D., & Gleason, K. (2023). Space transition and the vulnerabilities of the NFT market to financial crime. *Journal of Financial Crime, ahead-of-print*(ahead-of-print). https://doi.org/DOI: 10.1108/JFC-09-2022-0218

Aldridge, J. (2019). Does online anonymity boost illegal market trading? *Media Culture & Society*, *41*(4), 578–583. DOI: 10.1177/0163443719842075

Androulaki, E., Karame, G. O., Roeschlin, M., Scherer, T., & Capkun, S. (2013). *Evaluating User Privacy in Bitcoin.* Financial Cryptography and Data Security. DOI: 10.1007/978-3-642-39884-1_4

AWS. (2018). *AWS Blockchain Partners: Accelerating your distributed ledger journey*. Retrieved 22 February 2018 from https://aws.amazon.com/partners/blockchain/

Barnes, P., & Oloruntoba, R. (2005). Assurance of security in maritime supply chains: Conceptual issues of vulnerability and crisis management. *Journal of International Management*, *11*(4), 519–540. https://doi.org/https://doi.org/10.1016/j.intman.2005.09.008. DOI: 10.1016/j.intman.2005.09.008

Bartoletti, M., Lande, S., Loddo, A., Pompianu, L., & Serusi, S. (2021). Cryptocurrency scams: Analysis and perspectives. *IEEE Access : Practical Innovations, Open Solutions*, *9*, 148353–148373. DOI: 10.1109/ACCESS.2021.3123894

Bhat, M. A., Rather, M. Y., Singh, P., Hassan, S., & Hussain, N. (2025). Advances in smart food authentication for enhanced safety and quality. *Trends in Food Science & Technology*, *155*, 104800. DOI: 10.1016/j.tifs.2024.104800

Braaten, C. N., & Vaughn, M. S. (2019). Convenience Theory of Cryptocurrency Crime: A Content Analysis of US Federal Court Decisions [Article; Early Access]. *Deviant Behavior*, *21*. Advance online publication. DOI: 10.1080/01639625.2019.1706706

Brenner, S. W. (2007). Cybercrime: Re-thinking crime control strategies. In Jewkes, Y. (Ed.), *Crime online* (pp. 12–28). Willan Publishing.

Buil-Gil, D., & Saldaña-Taboada, P. (2022). Offending concentration on the internet: An exploratory analysis of bitcoin-related cybercrime. *Deviant Behavior*, *43*(12), 1453–1470. DOI: 10.1080/01639625.2021.1988760

Catalini, C., & Gans, J. S. (2017). Some Simple Economics of the Blockchain. *Rotman School of Management Working Paper No. 2874598; MIT Sloan Research Paper No. 5191-16., Available at SSRN:* https://ssrn.com/abstract=2874598. Available at *SSRN*: https://ssrn.com/abstract=2874598

Chainalysis. (2022). *The 2022 Geography of Cryptocurrency Report*. https://go.chainalysis.com/rs/503-FAP-074/images/2022-Geography-of-Cryptocurrency.pdf

Chainalysis. (2024). *The 2024 Crypto Crime Report*. https://documenti.camera.it/leg19/documentiAcquisiti/COM02/Audizioni/leg19.com02.Audizioni.Memoria.PUBBLICO.ideGes.34062.02-04-2024-16-52-36.832.pdf

Chang, L. Y. C., Zhou, Y., & Phan, D. H. (2023). Virtual kidnapping: Online scams with 'Asian characteristics' during the pandemic. In *Cybercrime in the pandemic digital age and beyond* (pp. 109–130). Springer International Publishing., DOI: 10.1007/978-3-031-29107-4_6

Chawki, M. (2022). The Dark Web and the future of illicit drug markets. *Journal of Transportation Security*, *15*(3), 173–191. DOI: 10.1007/s12198-022-00252-y

Chen, W., Guo, X., Chen, Z., Zheng, Z., & Lu, Y. (2020). Phishing scam detection on Ethereum: Towards financial security for blockchain ecosystem. In *International Joint Conference on Artificial Intelligence*, 7, 4456-4462. https://doi.org/DOI: 10.24963/ijcai.2020/621

Chuah, J. (2022). Money Laundering Considerations in Blockchain-based Maritime Trade and Commerce. *European Journal of Risk Regulation*, •••, 1–16. DOI: 10.1017/err.2022.21

Chuah, J. C. T. (2022). Money Laundering Considerations in Blockchain-based Maritime Trade and Commerce. *European Journal of Risk Regulation*, •••, 1–16. DOI: 10.1017/err.2022.21

Cong, W., Harvey, C., Rabetti, D., & Wu, Z. Y. (2025). An anatomy of crypto-enabled cybercrimes. *Management Science*, *71*(4), 3622–3633. Advance online publication. DOI: 10.1287/mnsc.2023.03691

Connolly, L. Y., & Wall, D. S. (2019). The rise of crypto-ransomware in a changing cybercrime landscape: Taxonomising countermeasures. *Computers & Security*, *87*, 101568. DOI: 10.1016/j.cose.2019.101568

Cross, C. (2016). 'They're very lonely': Understanding the fraud victimisation of seniors. *International Journal for Crime. Justice and Social Democracy*, *5*(4), 60–75. DOI: 10.5204/ijcjsd.v5i4.268

Cross, C. (2017). "I've Lost Some Sleep over It": Secondary Trauma in the Provision of Support to Older Fraud Victims. *Canadian Journal of Criminology and Criminal Justice*, *59*(2), 168–197. DOI: 10.3138/cjccj.2016.E11

Cross, C. (2024). Romance baiting, cryptorom and 'pig butchering': An evolutionary step in romance fraud. *Current Issues in Criminal Justice*, *36*(3), 334–346. DOI: 10.1080/10345329.2023.2248670

Dawes Centre for Future Financial Crime. (2021). *Crytpcorrencies and Future Crime*. https://www.ucl.ac.uk/jill-dando-institute/sites/jill-dando-institute/files/ucl_cryptocurrencies_and_future_crime_policy_briefing_feb2021_compressed_1.pdf

DeVoe, R. (2018). *Benebit – The Biggest ICO Exit Scam In History Nets Up to $4 Million*. Coin Bureau. Retrieved 1 February 2018 from https://www.coinbureau.com/ico/benebit-biggest-ico-exit-scam-history-nets-4-million/

Durrant, S., & Natarajan, M. (2019). Cryptocurrencies and Money Laundering Opportunities. In Natarajan, M. (Ed.), *International and Transnational Crime and Justice* (2nd ed., pp. 73–79). Cambridge University Press., https://doi.org/DOI, DOI: 10.1017/9781108597296.012

Ernst & Young. (2018). *Big risks in ICO market: flawed token valuations, unclear regulations, heightened hacker attention and congested networks*. Retrieved 12 February 2018 from https://www.ey.com/Publication/vwLUAssets/ey-research-initial-coin-offerings-icos/$File/ey-research-initial-coin-offerings-icos.pdf

ESMA. (2017). *Press Release: ESMA highlights ICO risks for investors and firms.* European Securities and Markets Authority (ESMA). Retrieved 15 February 2018 from https://www.esma.europa.eu/sites/default/files/library/esma71-99-649_press_release_ico_statements.pdf

Farrugia, S., Ellul, J., & Azzopardi, G. (2020). Detection of illicit accounts over the Ethereum blockchain [Article]. *Expert Systems with Applications, 150*(11), 113318. Advance online publication. DOI: 10.1016/j.eswa.2020.113318

Gandal, N., Hamrick, J. T., Moore, T., & Oberman, T. (2018). Price manipulation in the Bitcoin ecosystem [Article]. *Journal of Monetary Economics, 95*, 86–96. DOI: 10.1016/j.jmoneco.2017.12.004

Garvey, P. (2018). *Blockchain-backed gold: Mint's answer to bitcoin.* The Australian. Retrieved 12 February 2018 via Proquest Database from Gepp, A. (2016). Addressing the problem of financial statement fraud: Better detection through improved models. In *8th Asia-Pacific Interdisciplinary Research in Accounting (APIRA) Conference.*

Gepp, A., Linnenluecke, M. K., O'Neill, T. J., & Smith, T. (2018). Big data techniques in auditing research and practice: Current trends and future opportunities. *Journal of Accounting Literature, 40*(1), 102–115. https://doi.org/https://doi.org/10.1016/j.acclit.2017.05.003. DOI: 10.1016/j.acclit.2017.05.003

Gómez Hernández, J. A., García Teodoro, P., Magán Carrión, R., & Rodríguez Gómez, R. (2023). Crypto-ransomware: A revision of the state of the art, advances and challenges. *Electronics (Basel), 12*(21), 4494. DOI: 10.3390/electronics12214494

Graver, K., Jardine, E., Leosz, E., & Updegrave, H. (2023). *The 2023 Crypto Crime Report.* https://go.chainalysis.com/2023-crypto-crime-report.html

Grobys, K. (2021). When the blockchain does not block: On hackings and uncertainty in the cryptocurrency market. *Quantitative Finance, 21*(8), 1–13. DOI: 10.1080/14697688.2020.1849779

HackingRealm. (2024). *Welcome to HackingRealm!* Retrieved 3 April 2025 from https://hackingrealm.shop/

Harison, E. (2018). *Artificial Intelligence- and Blockchain-Based Decentralized Cloud Systems: The IAGON Way.* Medium. Retrieved 12 February 2018 from https://medium.com/iagon-official/iagon-artificial-intelligence-and-blockchain-based-decentralized-cloud-systems-113269d9c5b9

Haynie, D. L., & Duxbury, S. W. (2024). Online Illegal Cryptomarkets. *Annual Review of Sociology, 50*(1), 671–690. DOI: 10.1146/annurev-soc-090523-052916

Holt, T., & Bossler, A. (2015). (Manuscript submitted for publication). [*Theory and prevention of technology-enabled offenses*. Routledge.]. *Cybercrime*.

Holt, T. J., & Cross, C. (2024). Assessing the Correlates of Cryptofraud Victimization Reporting. *Deviant Behavior*, •••, 1–12. DOI: 10.1080/01639625.2024.2435907

Holt, T. J., & Lee, J. R. (2023). A crime script model of dark web firearms purchasing. *American Journal of Criminal Justice*, *48*(2), 509–529. DOI: 10.1007/s12103-022-09675-8

Hutchings, A., & Holt, T. J. (2017). The online stolen data market: Disruption and intervention approaches. *Global Crime*, *18*(1), 11–30. DOI: 10.1080/17440572.2016.1197123

IBM. (2018). *Maersk and IBM to Form Joint Venture Applying Blockchain to Improve Global Trade and Digitize Supply Chains*. Retrieved 7 February 2018 from https://www-03.ibm.com/press/us/en/pressrelease/53602.wss

Kamps, J., & Kleinberg, B. (2018). To the moon: defining and detecting cryptocurrency pump-and-dumps [Article]. *Crime Science*, *7*(1), 18, Article 18. https://doi.org/DOI: 10.1186/s40163-018-0093-5

Kasula, V. K. (2024). *Awareness of Cryptocurrency Scams* (Doctoral dissertation). University of the Cumberlands.

Kethineni, S., & Cao, Y. (2020). The Rise in Popularity of Cryptocurrency and Associated Criminal Activity. *International Criminal Justice Review*, *30*(3), 325–344. DOI: 10.1177/1057567719827051

Knight, W. (2017). *The Technology Behind Bitcoin Is Shaking Up Much More Than Money*. MIT Technology Review. Retrieved 14 February 2018 from https://www.technologyreview.com/s/604148/the-technology-behind-bitcoin-is-shaking-up-much-more-than-money/

Lagarde, C. (2017). Central Banking and Fintech—A Brave New World? In *Bank of England conference*. International Monetary Fund.

Lee, A. (2017). *Blockchain—A visual explanation*. Medium. Retrieved 15 February 2018 from https://medium.com/@kkomaz/blockchain-a-visual-explanation-afe82d19a234

Leuprecht, C., Jenkins, C., & Hamilton, R. (2023). Virtual money laundering: Policy implications of the proliferation in the illicit use of cryptocurrency. *Journal of Financial Crime*, *30*(4), 1036–1054. DOI: 10.1108/JFC-07-2022-0161

Mackenzie, S. (2022). Criminology towards the metaverse: Cryptocurrency scams, grey economy and the technosocial. *British Journal of Criminology, 62*(6), 1537–1552. DOI: 10.1093/bjc/azab118

Mansfield-Devine, S. (2017). Beyond Bitcoin: Using blockchain technology to provide assurance in the commercial world. *Computer Fraud & Security, 2017*(5), 14–18. https://doi.org/https://doi.org/10.1016/S1361-3723(17)30042-8. DOI: 10.1016/S1361-3723(17)30042-8

McGuire, M., & Dowling, S. (2013). Cyber crime: A review of the evidence. *Summary of key findings and implications.* Home Office Research Report

Moyano, J. P., & Ross, O. (2017). KYC Optimization Using Distributed Ledger Technology [Article; Proceedings Paper]. *Business & Information Systems Engineering, 59*(6), 411–423. DOI: 10.1007/s12599-017-0504-2

Mukherjee, S., Larkin, C., & Corbet, S. (2021). Cryptocurrency ponzi schemes. *Understanding cryptocurrency fraud: The challenges and headwinds to regulate digital currencies, 2*, 111. https://doi.org/DOI: 10.1515/9783110718485-009

Nakamoto, S. (2008). *Bitcoin: A Peer-to-Peer Electronic Cash System.* bitcoin.org. Retrieved 18 February 2018 from https://bitcoin.org/bitcoin.pdf

Norbutas, L. (2018). Offline constraints in online drug marketplaces: An exploratory analysis of a cryptomarket trade network. *The International Journal on Drug Policy, 56*, 92–100. DOI: 10.1016/j.drugpo.2018.03.016

Noval, S. M. R., Jamaludin, A., Saputra, D. D., Munifah, N. F., Raswanti, P. S., & Lestia, S. N., (2023). The fusion of blockchain, pornography and human trafficking in a global digital dragnet that forms the online child sex trafficking. *Russian Law Journal, 11*(5s, 5S), 1–19. DOI: 10.52783/rlj.v11i5s.891

Ouellet, M., Maimon, D., Howell, J. C., & Wu, Y. (2022). The network of online stolen data markets: How vendor flows connect digital marketplaces. *British Journal of Criminology, 62*(6), 1518–1536. DOI: 10.1093/bjc/azab116

Park, K., & Youm, H. Y. (2021). Proposal for Customer Identification Service Model Based on Distributed Ledger Technology to Transfer Virtual Assets [Article]. *Big Data and Cognitive Computing, 5*(3), 19, Article 31. https://doi.org/DOI: 10.3390/bdcc5030031

Patel, D. (2017). *6 red flags of an ICO scam.* TechCrunch. Retrieved 1 February 2018 from https://techcrunch.com/2017/12/07/6-red-flags-of-an-ico-scam/

Reid, F., & Harrigan, M. (2013). An Analysis of Anonymity in the Bitcoin System. In Altshuler, Y., Elovici, Y., Cremers, A. B., Aharony, N., & Pentland, A. (Eds.), *Security and Privacy in Social Networks* (pp. 197–223). Springer New York., DOI: 10.1007/978-1-4614-4139-7_10

Reynolds, P., & Irwin, A. S. M. (2017). Tracking digital footprints: Anonymity within the bitcoin system [Article]. *Journal of Money Laundering Control*, *20*(2), 172–189. DOI: 10.1108/JMLC-07-2016-0027

Rhumorbarbe, D., Staehli, L., Broséus, J., Rossy, Q., & Esseiva, P. (2016). Buying drugs on a Darknet market: A better deal? Studying the online illicit drug market through the analysis of digital, physical and chemical data. *Forensic Science International*, *267*, 173–182. DOI: 10.1016/j.forsciint.2016.08.032

Rognone, L., Hyde, S., & Zhang, S. S. (2020). News sentiment in the cryptocurrency market: An empirical comparison with Forex [Article]. *International Review of Financial Analysis*, *69*(17), 101462. Advance online publication. DOI: 10.1016/j.irfa.2020.101462

Roma, P., Quarre, F., Israel, A., Johnston, M., & Flores, A. (2016). *Blockchain: An Enabler for Life Sciences and Healthcare*. Deloitte. Retrieved 31 January 2018 from https://d1.awsstatic.com/blockchain_assets/deloitte_bc_paper.pdf

Scharfman, J. (2022). Operational Due Diligence on Cryptocurrency and Digital Asset Funds [Article]. *Journal of Alternative Investments*, *24*(3), 44–50. DOI: 10.3905/jai.2021.1.146

SEC. (2017). *SEC V. RECOIN GROUP FOUNDATION, LLC, DRC: COMPLAINT WORLD INC. a/k/a DIAMOND RESERVE CLUB: and MAKSIM ZASLAVSKIY*. US Securities and Exchange Commission (SEC). Retrieved 4 February 2018 from https://www.sec.gov/litigation/complaints/2017/comp-pr2017-185.pdf

SEC. (2018). *SEC V. ARISEBANK, JARED RICE SR., and STANLEY FORD*. US Securities and Exchange Commission (SEC). Retrieved 4 February 2018 from https://www.sec.gov/litigation/complaints/2018/comp-pr2018-8.pdf

Shi, F. B., Sun, X. Q., Gao, J. H., Xu, L., Shen, H. W., & Cheng, X. Q. (2019). Anomaly detection in Bitcoin market via price return analysis [Article]. *PLoS One*, *14*(6), e0218341. Advance online publication. DOI: 10.1371/journal.pone.0218341

Silverberg, K., French, C., & Ferenzy, D. (2018). *Initial Coin Offerings: The Frontier of Financing*. Institute of International Finance. Retrieved 3 March 2018 from https://www.iif.com/system/files/32370132_ico_background_final.pdf

Siu, G. A., Hutchings, A., Vasek, M., & Moore, T. (2022, November). Invest in crypto! In *An analysis of investment scam advertisements found in Bitcointalk. In 2022 APWG symposium on electronic crime research (eCrime)* (pp. 1–12). IEEE.

Smith, M. (2020). A modern approach to regulation: Integrating law, system architecture and blockchain technology in Australia'. *Australian Business Law Review, 48*(5), 460–465. https://sites.thomsonreuters.com.au/journals/2021/01/08/australian-business-law-review-update-vol-48-pt-5/

Smith, M., & Tiwari, M. (2023). The implications of national blockchain infrastructure for financial crime. *Journal of Financial Crime, ahead-of-print*(ahead-of-print). https://doi.org/DOI: 10.1108/JFC-01-2023-0006

Soldner, F., Plum, F., Kleinberg, B., & Johnson, S. D. (2024). From cryptomarkets to the surface web: Scouting eBay for counterfeits. *arXiv preprint arXiv:2406.05021.*

Stuhlmiller, L. (2013). *Mitigating virtual money laundering: An analysis of virtual worlds and virtual currencies* Utica College]. United States -- New York. https://search.proquest.com/docview/1449374093?accountid=26503

Sullivan, C., & Burger, E. (2017). E-residency and blockchain. *Computer Law & Security Review, 33*(4), 470–481. https://doi.org/https://doi.org/10.1016/j.clsr.2017.03.016. DOI: 10.1016/j.clsr.2017.03.016

Sureshbhai, P. N., Bhattacharya, P., & Tanwar, S., & Ieee. (2020). KaRuNa: A Blockchain-based Sentiment Analysis Framework for Fraud Cryptocurrency Schemes. In *2020 Ieee International Conference on Communications Workshops*. Ieee. <Go to ISI>://WOS:000607199300080 DOI: 10.1109/ICCWorkshops49005.2020.9145151

Tapscott, D., & Tapscott, A. (2017). How Blockchain Will Change Organizations. *MIT Sloan Management Review, 58*(2), 10.

Teichmann, F. M. J., & Falker, M. C. (2021). Money laundering via cryptocurrencies - potential solutions from Liechtenstein [Article]. *Journal of Money Laundering Control, 24*(1), 91–101. DOI: 10.1108/JMLC-04-2020-0041

Tidy, J. (2025). *North Korean hackers cash out hundreds of millions from $1.5bn ByBit hack*. BBC. https://www.bbc.com/news/articles/c2kgndwwd7lo

Tiwari, M., Gepp, A., & Kumar, K. (2019). The future of raising finance - a new opportunity to commit fraud: A review of initial coin offering (ICOs) scams. *Crime, Law, and Social Change*. Advance online publication. DOI: 10.1007/s10611-019-09873-2

Tiwari, M., Lupton, C., Bernot, A., & Halteh, K. (2024). The cryptocurrency conundrum: The emerging role of digital currencies in geopolitical conflicts. *Journal of Financial Crime, 31*(6), 1622–1634. DOI: 10.1108/JFC-12-2023-0306

Tiwari, M., Zhou, Y., Ferrill, J., & Smith, M. (2025a). Crypto Crashes: An examination of the Binance and FTX scandals and associated accounting challenges. *The British Accounting Review, 101584*, 101584. https://doi.org/https://doi.org/10.1016/j.bar.2025.101584. DOI: 10.1016/j.bar.2025.101584

Tiwari, M., Zhou, Y., Gilmour, P., & Bernot, A. (2025b). Confronting metacrime: Complexities, enforcement challenges, and regulatory pathways. *Law, Innovation and Technology, 17*(1), 1–18. DOI: 10.1080/17579961.2025.2469347

Transparency International Russia. (2023). *Anonymity for sale: The thriving black market of crypto-to-fiat mules*. https://ti-russia.org/wp-content/uploads/2023/10/epaycrypto_.pdf

Trozze, A., Davies, T., & Kleinberg, B. (2021). Explaining prosecution outcomes for cryptocurrency-based financial crimes [Article; Early Access]. *Journal of Money Laundering Control, 17*. Advance online publication. DOI: 10.1108/JMLC-10-2021-0119

Trozze, A., Kamps, J., Akartuna, E. A., Hetzel, F. J., Kleinberg, B., Davies, T., & Johnson, S. D. (2022). Cryptocurrencies and future financial crime [Review]. *Crime Science, 11*(1), 35, Article 1. https://doi.org/DOI: 10.1186/s40163-021-00163-8

Turner, A., & Irwin, A. S. M. (2018). Bitcoin transactions: A digital discovery of illicit activity on the blockchain. *Journal of Financial Crime, 25*(1), 109–130. https://doi.org/doi:10.1108/JFC-12-2016-0078. DOI: 10.1108/JFC-12-2016-0078

Underhill, J. (2018). *Initial coin offerings: Fraudsters use new technology to perpetrate old schemes*. ACFE Fraud Magazine. Retrieved 31 March 2018 from https://www.fraud-magazine.com/article.aspx?id=4295000887&Site=ACFEWEB

Wang, F., & Zhou, X. (2023). Persuasive schemes for financial exploitation in online romance scam: An Anatomy on Sha Zhu pan ( ) in China. *Victims & Offenders, 18*(5), 915–942. DOI: 10.1080/15564886.2022.2051109

Wang, J., Zhang, L., Xu, L., & Qian, X. (2024). The dynamic emotional experience of online fraud victims during the process of being defrauded: A text-based analysis. *Journal of Criminal Justice, 94*, 102231. DOI: 10.1016/j.jcrimjus.2024.102231

Wang, X., Ma, J., Liang, Y., Ma, L., & Liu, P. (2023). The association between experiences of being defrauded and depressive symptoms of middle-aged and elderly people: A cross-sectional study in China. *Public Health*, *216*, 51–57. DOI: 10.1016/j.puhe.2023.01.002

Whelan, C. (2012). *Networks and national security: dynamics, effectiveness and organisation*. Routlege.

Whelan, C., Bright, D., & Martin, J. (2024). Reconceptualising organised (cyber) crime: The case of ransomware. *Journal of Criminology*, *57*(1), 45–61. DOI: 10.1177/26338076231199793

Whelan, C., Dupont, B., Harkin, D., Martin, J., Miccelli, M., & Villeneuve-Dubuc, M. P. (2024). Expertise integration in cybercrime policing: Exploring civilian career lifecycles. *Deviant Behavior*, •••, 1–18. DOI: 10.1080/01639625.2024.2357810

World Economic Forum. (2016). *The future of financial infrastructure*.

Xia, P., Wang, H., Zhang, B., Ji, R., Gao, B., Wu, L., Luo, X., & Xu, G. (2020). Characterizing cryptocurrency exchange scams. *Computers & Security*, *98*, 101993. DOI: 10.1016/j.cose.2020.101993

Xu, J., Sun, G., Wu, S., Zhu, S., & Zhou, Y. (2024). Understanding health fraud offenders in China: An emotional labour perspective. *Asian Journal of Law and Society*, *11*(1), 54–69. DOI: 10.1017/als.2023.14

Zhou, Y., Tiwari, M., Bernot, A., & Lin, K. (2024). Metacrime and Cybercrime: Exploring the Convergence and Divergence in Digital Criminality. *Asian Journal of Criminology*, *19*(3), 419–439. DOI: 10.1007/s11417-024-09436-y

Zhou, Y., Xu, B., Sun, I. Y., Zhang, Y., & Chang, L. Y. C. (2022). Examining Sexual Crime Severity in China: A General-Specific Model on Sex Offending Against Adults. *Sexual Abuse*, *34*(7), 830–856. DOI: 10.1177/10790632221112656

Zhou, Y., Xu, J., Wu, S., & Zhu, S. (2023). Health Fraud against the Elderly in China: The Perspective of Vulnerability Manipulation. *Victims & Offenders*, *18*(7), 1354–1372. DOI: 10.1080/15564886.2023.2211570

Chapter 2
The Janus Paradox: Cybercrime and Cryptocurrency in the Digital Age

James Patrick Welch
https://orcid.org/0000-0002-3563-1254
Alliance University, India

ABSTRACT

This chapter explores the Janus Paradox, of dematerialization, highlighting the inherent tension and pronounced duality of crime and justice; anonymity and traceability, regulation and privacy, profit and loss, individual rights, and collective responsibilities; technology and social repercussions; and the risks and opportunities offered by the digital ecosystem. The chapter also examines the role of technology as both a positive catalyst for security advancement and a negative instrument of cybercriminal enterprise, in an ever-evolving threat environment. Selected case studies shed light on current and emerging challenges posed by cybercrime, cryptocrime, economic fraud, and identity theft. The chapter further outlines technological and strategic response emphasizing policy recommendations to strengthen government, corporate, and private security. Finally, the chapter underscores the importance of cyber literacy, secure infrastructure, robust regulatory measures, and digital tools as vital instruments for enhancing resilience in the digital age.

INTRODUCTION

The Digital Era's Dual Imperative

The Digital ecosystem calls to mind properties related to the god Janus of ancient Roman religion. Characteristics attributed to Janus, such as beginnings and

DOI: 10.4018/979-8-3373-0675-9.ch002

ends, duality and doorways, passages and transitions parallel our own transition to the technocratic digital world we currently inhabit (Carlisle, 2023, p. 22). On a darker note, the advent and rapid evolution of technologies such as deep learning (DL), natural language processing (NLP), and artificial intelligence (AI) are now coupled with equally rapid levels of rising crime across a hyper-connected digital economy. These advances have transformed the way in which humanity interacts politically, socially, culturally, and economically. The way in which information has been transformed into data points and is created, managed, transmitted, exchanged, and stored has been drastically altered.

The research adopted for the development of this chapter is based largely upon qualitative document analysis. As an empirical foundational base, which clarifies the facts and numbers, there are several digital analytical resources that have served in support of this chapter. Among the most notable are the *2025 crypto crime report* by Chainalysis; the *FBI IC3 2023 Annual Report*, the *2023 Imperva Bad bot report*, the *2024 DBIR data breach investigation report*, the *ENACT 2023 OCI in Africa report*, the *Cyber Ark 2024 Identity Security Threat Landscape report*, the *IOCTA 2024 Report* (the internet organized crime threat assessment); the *iProov 2025 threat intelligence report*, and the *TRM Labs, 2024 Crypto adoption and illicit activities report*. The fact is that this part of the cyber security and intelligence market is well represented by in-depth and well-detailed reports. Peer reviews of journals and resources were consulted in the course of the research, and these are aptly noted and accessible within the body of the chapter text. Alternative academic titles were also used to develop the chapter, and these are presented later in this chapter.

One prominent transformation in the digital era has been dematerialization, where physical assets such as documents, credit cards, and financial transactions are converted into digital formats (Ghernaouti, 2023, pp. 2, 33). While this shift enhances efficiency and accessibility, it also introduces vulnerabilities, such as identity theft, financial fraud, and increased exposure to ransomware attacks. The result is an environment that is rife with opportunity for illicit exploitation and the expansion of criminal enterprise.

The erosion of geographical boundaries and jurisdictional enforcement mechanisms further amplifies these risks, and enforcement efforts, beyond the national level, are fraught with significant challenges. Given the transnational nature of criminal operations, dematerialization serves as a catalyst and inducement for new criminal activity. Criminals benefit from a sense of impunity, and can operate unimpeded, with relative anonymity.

Criminals also benefit in other, less obvious ways. First there is a lack of physical forensic evidence typically found in standard criminal investigations. This drastically reduces the impact of Locard's exchange principle, an observation that emphasizes every contact leaves a trace (Saferstein, 2004, p. 9). Consequently, this lack of direct contact also means that there will be no witnesses, and the victim will most likely be unable to identify the perpetrator.

Increased connectivity and innovation provide a target rich environment for malicious activity. Digital investigations are complex, difficult, and expensive to conduct. The existence of digital paradises, where cybercriminals can operate with relative impunity, due to weak enforcement of cybersecurity laws, lack of international cooperation, or permissive regulations, further exacerbate and contribute to the proliferation of cybercrime. Thus, centralized exchanges, who are closely regulated often transfer their operations to jurisdictions with less stringent oversight, and lax regulation such as the Bahamas, Bermuda, the U.S. Virgin Islands, the Seychelles, the Cayman Islands, or Malta, in a trade-off between customer security and potential benefits (Benson, Turksen, & Adamyk, 2024, p.86). These countries often serve as hubs for ransomware groups, fraudsters, and other cybercriminal activities. Finally, increased cooperation and nexus established between the transnational criminals and terrorist organizations has become increasingly pronounced.

Understanding Financial Crime (FinCrime)

Financial crime encompasses fraudulent financial activities, including money laundering (ML), terrorist financing, and economic fraud. Key definitions of financial crime include:

- **United Kingdom's (U.K.) Financial Conduct Authority (FCA)** defines financial crime as any criminal conduct related to money, financial services, or markets, including fraud, dishonesty, market abuse, and financing of terrorism (Legislation.gov.uk, 2000).
- **The Unites States (U.S.) Legal Definitions**: The U.S. lacks a uniform definition, with agencies like the United States Department of Justice (DOJ). the United States Federal Bureau of Investigation (FBI), and the United States Financial Crimes Enforcement Network (FinCEN), providing varying interpretations. Title 18 of the U.S. Code defines offenses such as money laundering (18 U.S.C. § 1956) and fraud (18 U.S.C. § 1341).
- **Unit21.ai** categorizes FinCrime into fraud, identity theft, market abuse, tax evasion, insider trading, and money laundering (Unit21.ai, n.d.-a.).

Most definitions tend to maintain similar core elements and an addendum of "not limited to." Part of the reasoning and logic behind adopting such "open definitions," can be tied to the evolutionary nature of financial crime. For our purposes, we can synthesize these previous definitions into a more concise paradigm.

Financial crime may, therefore, be generally understood as any illegal act involving the manipulation of financial assets, the misuse of financial instruments, or an associated abuse of financial systems for the purpose of personal gain or criminal intent. Typically, this involves operations focused on the theft of funds, laundering money, or circumventing regulations to obscure the origins of illegally obtained assets using placement, layering, and integration strategies (Lyman, 2018, p.180; Wang & Hsieh, 2024, p. 27). Increased activity and availability in the cryptocurrency sector provide greater opportunities for criminals to launder their illicit funds, while simultaneously reducing risk of traceability. The authors, Wang & Hsieh (2024), extend this aspect of their research, by analyzing money laundering through a criminological lens and creating a useful money laundering Triangle. Their triangular model incorporates routine activities theory, rational choice theory, and control balance theory and then applies these three core criminological models to the placement, layering, and integration phases of money laundering (pp.32, 34–36).

Why This Matters: Global Cybercrime Trends & Regional Impacts

Cybercrime has become a global threat, affecting governments, corporations, and individuals alike. The interconnected nature of the digital economy means that attacks in one region can have cascading effects worldwide. The increasing reliance on digital transactions, decentralized financial systems, and artificial intelligence has made financial institutions and private citizens more vulnerable than ever. The term "decentralized" refers to the fact that there is no intermediary, or central authority, such as a financial institution or bank, to oversee and control transactions. Instead, transactions are conducted directly between parties on a peer-to peer (P2P) basis (Haffke, Fromberger, & Zimmermann, 2020, p. 125; Wang & Hsieh, 2024, p. 26).

Transnational crime, terrorism and armed conflict are all reciprocally intertwined and contribute to political, social, and economic destabilization, Digital tools have become both a resource and force multiplier for international crime and terrorism. There exists an urgent need on the part of national, regional, and international governments, corporations, and individuals to understand and address the growing threats leveraged by cybercrime. Increasingly, decentralized financing (DeFi), coupled with increased reliance and connectivity of digital technology, has been accompanied by an equally proportionate threat of unparalleled dimensions.

At the global level, future trends, developments, and threat vectors are constantly evolving. LSEG threat intelligence (2025) presented four areas of particular concern in their report. These trends include *a marked increase in real-time payments facilities and transnational solutions*; *resilient anti-fraud mechanisms will need to be in place to counter malicious activity*, *robust vendor management systems and identity verification* will be paramount, and *resilience required to ensure uninterrupted smooth supply chain operation and respond to external threats*. Finally, there is an emphasis on a multi-layered approach to customer-supplier relations and the adoption of advanced technology in the fight against malicious actors. By actively leveraging AI, big data and other tools, firms will be better able to respond to emerging threats (Lseg.com, 2025). The report also underscores the Janus Parado principles of this chapter; highlighting the fact that increased leveraging of digital technology channels by businesses simultaneously exposes them to external threats from malicious actors.

Broader Economic and Security Implications

Broader economic and security concerns are also at play. The global financial ecosystem depends on trust and stability, yet cybercrime disrupts markets, erodes consumer confidence, and threatens financial institutions. Transnational criminal networks exploit regulatory gaps, making cooperation among nations essential for cybercrime mitigation. The two major threats facing the European Union in 2023, for instance were the rapid rise of ransomware, and Child sexual exploitation (CSE; Europol, 2024) .

Governments, particularly the executive branch and law enforcement, face an asymmetric battle against those who would exploit the system. Global connectivity provides criminal elements with greater access to a target-rich environment. This large pool of potential targets includes governments, corporations, public services, and private individuals. In other words, no segment of society is immune. The threat extends to all sectors of society particularly those related to national security and the economy.

The irony is that an unbridled zeal for further innovation has led to increased and excessive reliance upon digital technology. Increased connectivity and ubiquity of access provide opportunities for malicious actors and greater vulnerability for stakeholders. Assorted digital devices provide access portals for criminal operations.

Virtual assistant technology, such as Alexa, by Google, Bing's Cortana, or Siri by Apple, and chatbots represent potential portals for illegal activity by overriding the controls using ultrasound (Ghernaouti, 2023. P. 66. 67). The list of potential threat vectors is long and ever-expanding from electric cars to mobile phones, and with the advent of the internet of things technology (IoT), from smart homes to smart cities the threat landscape presents malicious actors with new targets.

Cybercrime has led to a specialization in specific areas of cybercrime and work as part of an organized entity. Greater reliance on digital tools for operational purposes has increased collaboration between the nexus of transnational organized criminal activity (TOCA), and transnational organized terrorist activity (TOTA). Terrorists leverage the services of hackers and other cybercriminal professionals to advance their agendas and achieve their goals. Such services are found in the Darknet frequently referenced as Crimeware-as-a-Service (Caas), Fraud-as-a-service (FaaS), or Access-as-a-service (AaaS) and similar (Ghernaouti, 2023, p.152; Furneaux, 2025 pp. 25, 33–34). This type of service can apply to any number of related criminal service offerings such as Criminal communications and planning exchanges. Consequently, illicit operations are facilitated because of this same dematerialization.

There is no specific "weak link" in the cyber chain, rather the responsibility is shared. The reader is directed to figure 1 below. Vulnerability is spread across three main axes: corporate manufacturers, government institutions, and end users. Nevertheless, a significant share of responsibility for vulnerabilities may be apportioned to technology manufacturers. Prioritizing market competition and innovation over concerns for safety and security can be linked with the failure to provide more robust systems and incorporate security, built in as a core function, or security by design, rather than as an afterthought (Ghernaouti, 2023, p. 23).

Responsibility and Attribution

Governments also share a large part of the responsibility due to their use of outmoded systems, lack of investment in security enhancements, lack of appropriate training, improper vetting of personnel, and the increasing imposition of digital operations in various aspects of governance. Such overreliance upon digital governance creates associated vulnerabilities for users. In this regard, the lack of a plan "B," or back up plan, also presents a significant risk to national safety and security.

Increasingly, responsibility for the perpetuation of intrusions in general, and FinCrime - related attacks, in particular, may be attributed to corporate businesses. Verizon in their informative 2024 Data Breach Investigations Report (2024), found a significant increase in pretexting tactics associated with business email compromise (BEC) accounting for a quarter, or between 24 and 25%, of all financial attacks with a median average loss of $50,000. A significant majority of these intrusions, according to the report, were related directly to employee errors, with nearly five times the amount as seen the year before (Verizon, 2024a). These tactics are detailed more fully under the separate section dedicated to a discussion of BEC.

Finally, the users themselves often provide cybercriminals with the tools they need through shoddy security practices. Sharing personal identifying information (PII) on exposed social media websites, use of outdated systems, and a failure to update security enhancements, are but limited examples of the shortcomings in this regard. The theft of PII by malicious actors represents one of the most common forms of criminal digital activity. In their 2024 Data Breach Investigations Report (DBIR), Verizon noted an astounding 180% increase in the exploitation of vulnerabilities, representing nearly a three-fold increase from the previous year. This was fueled in large part by the ransomware exploits such as MOVEit and other zero-day exploits (Verizon, 2024b).

Figure 1. Digital vulnerabilities

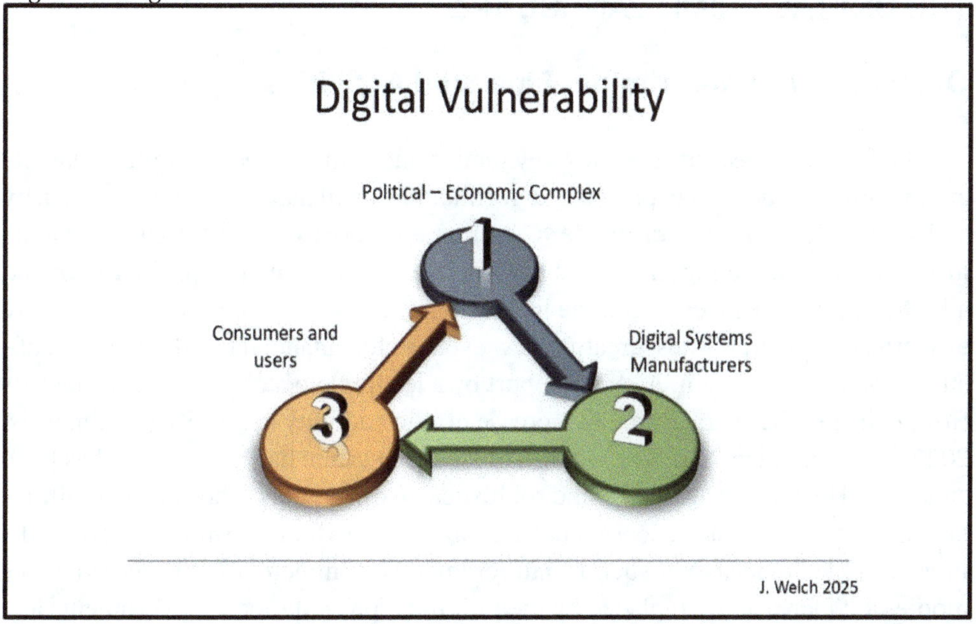

It is also worth underscoring the fact that the aftermarket security industry is a lucrative enterprise, which responds to the complacency and lack of due diligence on the part of digital systems manufacturers. There is no limit to the inventiveness of the malicious actors as evidenced by their recent attacks on computer processors and operating systems themselves. Such innovative attacks were evidenced with the 2018 Meltdown (Intel, and ARM) and Specter (Intel, ARM, and AMD) side-channel attacks, or the more recent iLeakage' attack on Apple products in October 2023. (Kocher, Horn, Fogh, Genkin, Gruss, Haas, Hamburg, Lipp, Mangard, Prescher, Schwarz, & Yarom,2019; Lipp et al., 2018; Toulas, 2025).

There exists an urgent need for governments to impose measures for greater digital security such as enhanced regulatory oversight. This is an imperative that has long been overlooked in the wake of digital utopianism, a desire for endless innovation, and market driven optics. Cybercrime and FinCrime have evolved faster than the responses developed to counter it. Financial cybercrime has already negatively impacted economies around the world and threatens to create even further damage. The deadly terrorist attacks of September 11,2001 on wall street also conveyed a symbolic message, in addition to the tragic loss of life incurred. Today the menace of cybercrime against businesses and banks remains a viable threat of existential proportions.

THE DIGITAL CRIME LANDSCAPE

Overview of Cybercriminal Financial Activities

The following section explores key tactics and crimes used in digital financial exploitation. Cybercrime presents a formidable challenge to financial security and economic stability worldwide. Criminal enterprises exploit digital financial infrastructures, targeting the public and private sector alike. The proliferation and adoption of cryptocurrency and the increasing reliance on digital transactions have exacerbated vulnerabilities, creating new avenues for financial fraud, identity theft, and market manipulation. A recent report by a leading blockchain forensic analysis firm, indicates the average annual increase of illicit activity to be 25%.(Chainalysis, 2025). The traditional *modus operandi* of financial crime has evolved and has been augmented by the advent of new and sophisticated cyber tools. These vulnerabilities have become immediate concerns and pressing priorities for governments worldwide. Physical stakeholder assets, such as fiat, commodity, commercial bank, and fiduciary monies are increasingly replaced by their digital representations. Governments and regulatory bodies are struggling to keep pace with the sophistication of these threats, which continue to evolve at an unprecedented rate.

Crypto Fraud

Crypto is a rapidly growing form of earnings and investment. It is, therefore, unsurprising that illegal activity would inevitably attach itself to such a venture. There currently exists a wide variety of virtual crypto coins, a single unit of which is referred to as a "token." These tokens are then subsequently classified according to three categories of function. These include investment, utility, and currency tokens. Each of these have different applications and use. (Haffke, Fromberger, & Zimmermann, 2020, p. 125–127). There are currently 10,567 crypto currencies in existence as of January 2025 (de Best, 2025).

Where there are investment opportunities and profit to be made, there will be criminals eager to exploit the system (Carlisle, 2023, p.p. 24—25). This is particularly true in the context of a system with global access available for exploitation seven-days-a-week and 24-hours-a-day, This point was echoed serval times by Carlisle's insightful *The Crypto Launderers* (2023), by Furneaux (2025) in his seminal title

There's no Such Thing as Crypto Crime (pp. 37, 56) as well as by Wang & Hsieh (2024) in their informative journal article *Cryptocurrency is New Vogue: a reflection on money laundering prevention* (p.32). Fraudulent investment schemes, exit strategies, pump-and-dump scams, rug pulls, and fake Initial Coin Offerings (ICOs) deceive unsuspecting investors. Cryptocurrency is a primary target for criminal theft.

This threat became abundantly clear with a series of high values, thefts, attacks and extorsion schemes, such as ransomware, which can trace their lineage to two earlier Mt. Gox exchange heists of 2011 and 2014. The first suffered 25,000 BTC stolen, valued at $400,000, followed by a second theft that netted 850,000 BTC, valued at approximately $350 million at the time, but today would be worth billions. This second robbery resulted in the collapse of the exchange and an associated loss of confidence in cryptocurrency. Two years later, in August 2016, another major theft occurred when Bitfinex, a Hong Kong-based exchange, was hacked resulting in a loss of 120,000 bitcoins values at $72 million at the time of the theft. The remaining balance—all but the 25,000 that had been cashed out immediately— sat in an account on the blockchain, for five-and-a-half years without movement. In the interim their net value had increased to $7 billion (Carlisle, 2023, p. xv—xvii). Then, exactly one week ago, as these lines are being written, the largest cryptocurrency theft ever recorded occurred on February 21, 2025. North Korea's Lazarus Group (whom we explore in detail later in this chapter), also known as TraderTraitor, illicitly obtained over 400,000 worth of Ethereum (ETH) and staked ETH (stETH) valued at approximately $1.5 billion from the Dubai-based cryptocurrency exchange Bybit. This is currently the largest recorded crypto theft in history. Strong crisis management from Bybit has helped to stabilize a restless and panic-stricken market (Bratcher, 2025). Nevertheless, ceteris paribus, incidents such as this past week's event underscore the vulnerability of assets such as cryptocurrency and further undermine an already tenuous client confidence in the market.

As a decentralized financial asset, crypto currency is also a medium which criminals can instrumentalize to support, and profit from their illicit activities. All levels of criminal activity are involved from murder-for-hire schemes to money laundering, and from human trafficking to terrorist financing (Wang & Hsieh, 2024, p. 26; Haffke, Fromberger, & Zimmermann, 2020, p. 125). The inherent anonymity of crypto makes it the ideal medium of exchange in the world of illicit affairs.

Romance Scams and Pig Butchering.

Romance scams are one of the most ruthless and insidious forms of fraud that preys on people's vulnerability and naivete. While the tactics related to romance schemes are not new and predate the digital era, their adoption of cryptocurrency as a medium of exchange is (Furneaux, 2025, p. 79). They are a type of fraud where a virtual relationship has been created based upon deception. The perpetrator often procures images from online sources to create a fictive persona and dupe the unwitting and vulnerable victim. This is a long term scheme and often one perpetrator will be conducting multiple such operations simultaneously. This false representation also represents a form of identity theft. This type of tactic is sometimes referred to as catfishing.

The unwitting victim is lured into the trap and provides personal information or is manipulated into sending funds to the scammer. In nearly all cases transfers of funds will be requested in untraceable cryptocurrency, usually Tether (USDT) coins. Sending crypto funds also drastically reduces detection and the unravelling of the fictive plot.

False promises of a joint future; that never materialize are accompanied by increasing requests for larger sums of financial support. For instance, requests related to imaginary visa fees, funds for flight tickets, which are never purchased, and other fictive events such as support for a sick relative. This process has been referred to as "pig butchering," alluding to the Chinese term od "Shā Zhū Pán" of fattening a pig for later slaughter (Carlisle, 2023, 92—93, 95; Furneaux, 2025, pp.76–78, 31–32).

Another facet of this tactic is based on false investment schemes, The scammer convinces the victim to provide ever larger investments, most frequently in cryptocurrency, to fake accounts. and once again there is a relational component involved. Thus, Pig butchering schemes combine traditional investments scams, compounded with elements of psychological and emotional manipulation, usually associated with romance scams (Furneaux, 2025, pp.76–77). Considering that the proceeds derived from pig butchering already amounted to the astronomical sum of $4.4 billion in 2022 according to TRM Labs, this type of fraud represents a grave concern for law enforcement and the justice system (TRM Labs.2023, February 7). There is also another, darker side, to romance scams, however, that have had serious and even fatally tragic consequences, such as suicide by the victims.

As TRM Labs (as cited in Furneaux, 2025, p. 33) underscores, there is a strong correlation between transnational organized criminal activity (TOCA) and romance scam operations, with over half being linked to organized crime syndicates. The tragic irony is that those conducting the scams are often themselves the victims of human trafficking, being held against their will. Call centers, conducting these online fraud operations, are large hubs, where each unit is likely to oversee multiple victims at any given time. Advances in analytics, enhanced forensic investigations, and increased international cooperation among law enforcement agencies have fortunately led to the dismantling of a number of such major organized cybercrime rings.

Global ICM: A Case Study on Pig Butchering

A firsthand case study clearly illustrates the effectiveness of such schemes. In 2023 An investment was made with a company known a Global-ICM, purportedly based in Switzerland. Following the events in this case study, the victim reached out to regulators, notably the Swiss Financial Market Supervisory Authority (FINMA) to report the illicit dealings and was informed that no such society existed in their register.

The scam began with a partnership agreement, proposed, and accepted with their agent who called himself Eric Lewandowski, a Polish national ostensibly located in Dublin Ireland. An investment of €40,000 was made to purchase Bitcoin cryptocurrency. The Bitcoin appeared to rise rapidly and once it peaked at $339,000 for each of the "partners," a cashout was requested. Communications abruptly ended and the site closed.

During phase two of the operation, a certain Alexis Vos, purportedly from the Finance Department of Global ICM subsequently reached out, in response to recent emails from the victim Vos advised that to receive the funds on the account a "swap" fee was necessary. This proved to be merely a further extension of the complex fraud already in progress. Vos provided the bank account, most likely that of a mule, by the name of Rita Theresia, L Billet. The payment was to ensure the release of the blocked funds. Further identifying information was then requested such as a copy of a bank and credit card statements. Luckily, the PII was redacted due to increasing suspicion on the part of the victim.

In November of 2024, the trading platform Atomic Wallet was suggested, An Ethereum (ETH) account was set up and the funds were transferred into the account. Unfortunately, when attempting to cash in the cryptocurrency, Atomic Wallet advised the victim that the deposited coins from Global-ICM were in fact fake and had been most likely minted by Global ICM themselves. This case study is a clear example of the complexity of such schemes.

In such cases, the hapless victims, of this type of fraud, often attempt to reach out to companies, trolling and advertising on social media. These companies often present flashy websites that promise to recover missing investments, but these too are fraudulent scams. Alternatively, companies will contact the victim whose personal details have been divulged sold on the dark web, by the original perpetrator, for yet further exploitation. Furneaux (2025) labels these as "follow-on scams" (p. p.34).

There has been a steady increase in such scams that parallel the growing trend of cryptocurrency fraud. The FBI IC3 unit reported that in 2022 more than $2.5 billion was reported lost by victims (Federal Bureau of Investigation, 2023). Again, education and awareness combined with stronger enforcement and regulatory measures would aid in creating obstacles to this type of fraud. This being said, there is a lack of competence at the local level and police are often unsure how to proceed. A report can be filed but, sadly, often goes no further. Shame and a lack of confidence is the enforcement procedures means that these types of thefts, despite their importance, often go unreported.

Ponzi schemes

Ponzi schemes, the eponymous creation of inveterate fraudster Charles Ponzi, are a classic form of financial deception. Ponzi, an Italian businessman was convicted of fraud in the United States in 1920 (Carlisle, 2023, p. 61, 197; Furneaux, 2025, pp. 29–30; 148–149). Often described colloquially as "borrowing from Peter to pay Paul," these revolving schemes sustain themselves by using funds of new investors to pay earlier investors. Participants are typically enticed and drawn in by their own cupidity and promises of large returns. The funds will be invested for optimal profit with little or no risk involved—though no legitimate investments ever materialize (United States Securities and Exchange Commission, n.d.).

So, it was inevitable that there would be a resurgence of this tactic and indeed the crypto market witnessed a spectacular rise of Ponzi schemes between the years 2012 and 2022. One of the most notable of these high-stake frauds was conducted by an Indian national named Satish Kumbhani, who founded BitConnect in 2016. Kumbhani, selling dreams spun from thin air, wrapped in the illusion of wealth, was able to easily reel in unsuspecting victims. Kumbhani promised that by purchasing BitConnect Coin (BCC) he allegedly created, combined with the adoption of automated trading algorithms, investors could profit from crypto price volatility in the digital marketplace. All the standard elements commonly associated with traditional Ponzi Schemes were present, as were human naivete. The only difference was that the medium of exchange had changed.

These schemes have most likely existed even before Charles Ponzi himself popularized them. Their adaptation to the digital ecosphere should, therefore, not come as a surprise. At the end of the day any crime conducted in the real world will inevitably find its counterpart in one form or another in the virtual realm as well. Related to Ponzi schemes is another devious type of fraud known as pyramid schemes. With a pyramid scheme the goal is to incentivize individual earnings through the recruitment of others. It would appear that the more things change the more they remain the same.

Fake ICOs, Investment Scams, and Inexistent Securities

Initial coin offerings (ICO) are the alleged production of a new crypto offering. These are frequently minted and traded on the Ethereum (ETH) blockchain (Haffke,

Fromberger, & Zimmermann, 2020, p. 127). They became popular following the launch of the Ethereum blockchain in 2015 and the ERC-20 protocol—an initiative to standardize new token creation. Consequently, as a result of this new protocol, thousands of new coins were minted from 2016 onward until fizzling out a year later. It would be an oversight not to mention, in passing, in this context, the rise of stable coins. Stable coins were pegged to fiat currencies such as the dollar or other stable assets. One of the most popular stable coins was the USDC, which was soon joined by others such as Tether. The market share had already grown significantly to $185biliion by 2022 (Carlisle, 2023, p. 145). Current estimates place the number of available stable coins at somewhere between 180 and 190.

Ethereum due to its platform design, and smart contract feature, has a highly transparent blockchain. As a result, there was a call for enhanced privacy and a response came in the form of Tornado Cash, which rapidly became the leading mixer application within the Ethereum ecosphere (Carlisle, 2023, p. 146–147).

The Tempest Surrounding Tornado Cash

Tornado Cash came under the scrutiny of international regulators in 2022, and was sanctioned, but not completely shut down. As explored further in this chapter. The United States Treasury's Office of Foreign Assets Control (OFAC) sanctioned Tornado Cash, for allegedly laundering proceeds worth an astronomical $7billion. This included abetting North Korea's Lazarus group in the amount of $450 million. That same month Dutch authorities arrested Tornado Cash developer Alexey Pertsev, alleging his connection with money laundering. Meanwhile, in the unfolding saga, Roman Storm, one of the founders, was arrested on August 23, 2023, in Washington state. His co-defendant in the same indictment, Roman Semenov, a Russian national remains at large. Both men were charged in the indictment with conspiracy to commit money laundering.

The Netherlands' Oost-Brabant district court eventually sentenced Pertsev to five years and 4 months imprisonment, on May 14, 2024, for allegedly laundering $2 billion in funds. Pertsev was released on bail Friday, February 7, 2025, pending an appeal for his sentence. He was forced to undergo electronic monitoring with an ankle bracelet. Bail was raised through crowd funding efforts, organized by Justice-DAO, and included donations by Vitalik Buterin, founder of Ethereum. Whether Tornado Cash will ever make a revival remains doubtful.

Since Tornado Cash is a decentralized smart contract-based mixer, the protocol itself remains on the Ethereum blockchain and cannot be forcibly shut down. Thus, technically, Tornado Cash is still functional. However, front-end access was restricted, and major DeFi platforms blacklisted Tornado Cash-related addresses to comply with sanctions that had been imposed.

ICO-based Crypto Schemes; Investment Scams, and Inexistent Securities.

An ICO based crypto scheme revolves around the production of fake crypto assets and can also be used within the context of a Ponzi scheme explained, as discussed previously. In technological circles the false minting of initial coin offerings souped with the founders surreptitiously disappearing with investor funds is referred to as a "rug-pull." A flood of ICO offerings, both legitimate and illicit, first manifested on the heels of the spectacular rise in value of Bit coin in 2017 (Carlisle, 2023, p. 60).

This type of operation has dwindled somewhat in significance and is being increasingly replaced by more complex and sophisticated investment fraud such as fake investment schemes or unregistered and inexistent securities (Furneaux, 2025, p. 30; Federal Bureau of Investigation [FBI], 2024, p. 3). As an example of this increase, the FBI Internet Crime Complaint Center (IC3), established in December 2000, has received over eight million complaints to date, with an average rate of 758,000 per year.

The IC3 noted in their 2024 report (2023), that between 2022 and 2023, investment scams rose by $1.26 billion, reaching a total of $4.57 billion in 2023.This amount represents an astronomical 38% increase. Business email compromise (BEC) followed closely in second place with 21,489 complaints and $2.9 billion in reported losses. Tech support scams, closed the gap, coming close behind in third place (Federal Bureau of Investigation, 2024, p.3).

Cross-Chain Swaps, Bridging & Chain Hopping

Crypto bridges, also generically referred to as Cross-chain Bridges or decentralized bridges, relate to a system that allows crypto currency exchange between different block chains. Crypto bridges are based on the smart-contract concept and allow users to transfer their funds seamlessly between different blockchains This innovation provided users with greater flexibility. They could now avoid being obliged to visit centralized exchanges to swap their tokens and could instead exchange their tokens directly between other blockchains (Carlisle, 2023 pp. 150–152).

Attacks on crypto bridges frequently occur as a result of technical issues and a lack of appropriate cyber security measures. Such bridges are a prime target for hackers and other malicious actors, and they have frequently been the victim of high-value hacking and exploits (Furneaux, 2025, p. 22). These bridges are also used by criminal elements to transfer crypto assets from one blockchain network to another.

Chain hopping frequently involves unregulated exchanges (UEXs), occasionally referred to as "Coin Swaps," where the operators take in privacy coins obtained from illicit activity and exchange them, at a profit, for standard cryptocurrency such as bitcoin. One of the advantages of UEX's over other exchanges, from a criminal perspective, is that they do not require identification (Benson et al., 2024, p.81). This serves to obfuscate their illicit origins. These unregulated exchanges are most often located in digital paradises, such as Russia, where there is limited or no regulatory oversight (Carlisle, 2023, p. 80).

Money Laundering via Blockchain

Like all other criminal tactics, techniques, and procedures (TTPs), money laundering also easily transitioned from the real world to the virtual unimpeded. The relative anonymity offered by the digital ecosphere was a clarion call for the criminal underworld. The importance of Bitcoin in money laundering operations cannot be underestimated, however, cybercriminals have complimented their activities by increasingly adding alt coins to their arsenal. (Leuprecht, Jenkins, & Hamilton, 2023, p. 1049). As far as Blockchain activity is concerned the Tron network had the dubious distinction of claiming first place in 2024. The Tron blockchain was responsible in 2024 for $25 Billion in illicit funds, out of a total of $46 Billion, with the remainder of illicit proceeds being attributed to Ethereum and Bitcoin networks (Kelly, 2025).

A well-established paradigm exists for understanding and effectively countering the money laundering process. This model serves as a foundational principle in anti-money laundering (AML) and counter-terrorism financing (CTF) operations. The money laundering process consistently follows three key phases: placement, layering, and integration. During the placement phase, assets such as gift cards, cash deposits, or prepaid cards, can be used to purchase crypto with limited oversight or control. During the layering phase, the assets thus acquired are spread across various non-KYC exchanges to better obfuscate the history of transactions. Finally, when it is time to integrate the ill-gotten assets, the crypto assets are then withdrawn from high-risk jurisdictions, albeit ones with weaker anti-money laundering (AML) controls. This can be accomplished, for example, using crypto debit cards which have been linked to anonymous wallets thus moving assets from the virtual shadow world to the physical realm. Alternatively, assets may also be converted into non-fungible tokens,(NFT's) or any other suitable digital instrument to be later resold in regulated markets.

In a piece of interesting research by Leuprecht, Jenkins, & Hamilton (2023) the authors question the validity of traditional ML model and suggest that the integration phase does not apply to the money laundering process with regard to crypto assets (p.1049). The researchers attribute their hypothesis to the anonymous nature of the asset, limitations imposed as a form of legitimate payment, and finally, its ease of transfer. While this is an interesting hypothesis, its widespread application is dubious given the narrow and limited scope of the research conducted and other well-founded arguments to the contrary.

While banks have served as the outlet for traditional criminal money laundering criminals quickly took advantage of the digital ecosystem to leverage its money laundering potential as well (Carlisle, 2023, p. 25). There currently exists a growing body of research addressing issues of cybercriminality and money laundering. The superbly detailed presentation of past investigations by Andy Greenberg's *Lords of Crypto Crime* (2024) is one of the best in this regard. Greenberg reports on major cryptocurrency money laundering investigations such as Mt. Gox, Silk Road, and Alpha Bay, in both an informative and engaging narrative. Blockchain technology plays a key role in AML forensic investigation efforts. Given the complexity and misconceptions surrounding blockchain technology, it is only fitting that a brief introduction be provided, before delving into its role in money laundering.

To the uninitiated, blockchain technology may seem an inscrutable construct—teetering on the edge of the arcane, if not the outright occult. It is useful, therefore, to present a brief introduction to the technology. The Public ledgers and blockchain, known also known as distributed ledger technology (DLT; Carlisle, 2023, p. 5), serve as the foundation for cryptocurrencies, smart contracts, and non-fungible tokens (NFTs). A blockchain, in its simplest terms, is a decentralized and distributed ledger, consisting of a network of global nodes, which record the transactions occurring in a secure and tamper-free environment (Ghernaouti, 2023, pp.69–70; Greenberg, 2024, p.106). Blockchain technology has forever changed the digital face of online transactions. It is, therefore, important to understand the evolution of this technology.

BACKGROUND AND HISTORICAL EVOLUTION

The history and evolution of the development of the public ledger and blockchain technology traces its origins back long before the advent of the digital ecosphere. Adopting the widest possible interpretation links can be drawn between the blockchain concept and ancient record-keeping systems. The implementation of the actual technology associated with the blockchain, however, required modern computing to support its genesis. True blockchain related research emerged in the 20th century with one of the first noted examples being Leslie Lamport's Byzantine Fault Tolerance (1982). Later adapted to Blockchains consensus mechanisms.

Cryptographic Foundations of Blockchain

Cryptographic research was conducted during the 1970s and 1980s. This research laid the groundwork for the development of later technology such as the blockchain. This was followed by further research in 1991, by Stuart Haber & W. Scott Stornetta, who developed a theoretical framework to timestamp documents, a concept that would later become integral to the blockchain (Hayes, 2014). The story of cryptocurrency and the blockchain is inseparable from the enigmatic and oft-discussed Satoshi Nakamoto.

The Emergence of Bitcoin

Nakamoto first ushered in Bitcoin, in 2008 with the registration of the Bitcoin.org domain name. Nakamoto's highly influential white paper, *A Peer-to-Peer Electronic Cash System*, outlined the principles of decentralized digital currency and set the foundation for Bitcoin. The subsequent launch of Bitcoin cryptocurrency in 2009, was a milestone in the history of digital finance. Bitcoin heralded the advent of the first decentralized blockchain, in contrast to earlier centralized digital cash systems. Whether Satoshi Nakamoto—whose gender-neutral name has fueled speculation—was an individual or a group remains a mystery, further deepened by Nakamoto's sudden and unexplained disappearance. Nakamoto remained active in the development of Bitcoin for only two years, after vanishing without a trace to the present day.

Abundant theories and speculation have surrounded his disappearance. As might be expected, claimants have emerged, and there have been court cases surrounding the Nakamoto title and its related fortune. Deepening the mystery is an untouched wallet holding over one hundred million bitcoins with an estimated value of $50 billion (Carlisle, 2023, pp 3–6;Greenberg, 2024, pp. 27, 31, 48; Furneaux, pp. 5, 139, 140; (Trozze et al., 2022, p.2).

Ethereum and Smart Contracts

Building on Bitcoin's success and its limitations, Vitaly Dmitrievich Buterin, better known simply as Vitalik Buterin developed Ethereum between 2013 and 2015. He introduced the incredibly important concepts of smart contracts and programmable blockchain applications, which were to play a key role in the digital transactions we have today notably with regard to smart contracts. Buterin's Ethereum was first described in a white paper (2014) entitled Ethereum: A *Next-Generation Smart Contract and Decentralized Application Platform. By Vitalik Buterin.* Ethereum developed new innovations, and that story is too long and complex to discuss in the framework of a single chapter. Suffice it to say that it used, Solidity programming language known as *Turing complete language*, a completely different language, from that used by its rivals. Important additional features included an account-based model, and a new blockchain. Though it was not Buterin's main objective, Ethereum offered the first realistic challenger to Bitcoin's relative market monopoly. Also, in contrast to the complexity of Bitcoin's UXTO, or unspent transactions protocol, with Ethereum, the entire liquidity of the account was available for use. It was a decentralized app and also provided users with the technology for creating smart contracts and using decentralized applications (DApps). Ethereum's tokenized engine also permitted the creation of other services and currencies within its blockchain architecture, and is thus, more of a general purpose ledger and not exclusively geared toward financial transactions. Of course, there was a financial component involved and that was manifested in the Ether (ETH) crypto coin. (Carlisle, 2023, pp. 140–155; Furneaux, 2025, pp. 7–14, 51,128–129 The advent of Ethereum was nothing short of revolutionary

Smart Contracts what are they?

Smart contracts are protocols based on automated scripts written in Solidity, a Turing-complete language, which allows a dynamic range of functions other than merely financial transactions. They allow for ownership, transactions, and other rule -based functions with a wide range of potential applications, beyond what Buterin initially proposed. Various applications for smart contracts were proposed, to fulfil cross-sector functions, as referenced in Buterin's initial white paper. Among the potential uses, Buterin suggested applicability in decentralized finance (Defi), government mechanisms, and supply chain tracking, all of which have been subsequently adopted. An important related theoretical proposition woven into Buterin's white paper, the development of DeFi, and the Ethereum blockchain was the development of Decentralized Autonomous Organizations (DAOs). These would represent groups of individuals with common interests and goals who could collectively work together without facing the inherent complexity related to the existing system of administrative requirements and third party intervention (Benson et al., 2024, p. 83; Buterin, 2014, p.1; Carlisle, p. 141; Furneaux, 2025, pp. 7–14).

MONEY LAUNDERING

Factors Facilitating Cryptocurrency-Based Laundering

Cryptocurrencies are an ideal medium for leveraging financial privacy, but, similarly, they provide avenues for illegal activity such as money laundering as well. Using cryptocurrency for money laundering is practical for three distinct reasons, First, there is the fact that users may complete transaction by adopting a pseudonym, or alternatively with near-complete anonymity. Secondly, there is no centralized oversight for controlling the legality of such transactions, and finally, unlike fiat transfers, international cryptocurrency transactions can proceed without being encumbered by regulatory checks and security related restrictions. It is precisely the international reach and global nature of crypto which obfuscate the trail of illicit cash flows and imbue criminals with a sense of impunity (Haffke, Fromberger, & Zimmermann, 2020, pp. 129–130).

There has been a substantial increase in money laundering activity despite the combined efforts of cooperative international law enforcement; various anti-money laundering (AML) initiatives, and countering terrorist financing (CTF) operations. Currently, reporting the actual extent of money laundering is difficult to ascertain (Leuprecht, Jenkins, & Hamilton, 2023, p.1037) . What does exist are those instances where money laundering operations have been dismantled and arrests and seizures have been conducted, but this only relates to a small percentage of all activities. Money laundering is a complex operation and difficult to track and trace. In addition to traditional trade-based fraud, conducted using shell and front companies, criminals leverage privacy coins, tumblers, blockchain-based mixers, and unregulated platforms to obscure illicit transactions (Wang & Hsieh, 2024, p.35). These latter elements will be discussed in detail shortly. While this chapter focuses primarily on AML aspects of cyber fraud, elements of CTF are also strongly interconnected with identical tactics, techniques, and procedures.

Third party decentralized exchanges (DEXs), whether they are crypt to crypto, fiat to crypto, or crypto to fiat, are notorious for money laundering operations (Haffke, Fromberger, & Zimmermann, 2020, p. 128; Chainalysis Team, 2024, "Laundering Activity" section). Mining and mixing services are also used for illegal money laundering services. These latter elements are addressed, separately, later in this chapter. This past year, 2024, marks yet another dark milestone and crypto thefts reached a new high of $2.2 billion, in comparison with 2023. This amount while higher than that in 2023 was substantially lower than in 2021 and 2022 with marked losses of $3.3 and $3.7 billion, respectively. This is related directly to an increased adoption of crypto as an asset, combined with soaring values. Interestingly, the focus of attack vectors has shifted from decentralized systems to centralized services. Of all the various crypto exploits advanced private key compromise, with a rate of 43.8%, stood out as the leading factor is security breaches(Chainalysis Team, 2024) .

Non-KYC Exchanges and Their Role in Money Laundering

Centralized and lightly regulated non-KYC exchanges represent a critical link and gateway between criminal financial profits and DeFi. Due to their anonymity, accessibility, and lack of stringent verification protocols, non-KYC exchanges directly facilitate the movement of illicit funds across fully decentralized and anonymous platforms. The non-KYC exchanges serve a dual function by facilitating both the entry and exit of illicit and untraceable funds (Greenberg, 2024, p. 122; Furneaux, 2025, p. 25).

Sim-Swapping and Its Implications

One next-generation tactic increasingly deployed in conjunction with non-KYC money laundering is known as sim-swapping (Haffke, Fromberger, & Zimmermann, 2020, p. 130). In this procedure criminals convince a mobile phone operator to transfer a victim's number to a sim card under their control. Once the transfer is completed the criminal has direct access to financial information and codes, which are then used to drain the accounts. The illicit funds are then, in turn, processed via one or more non-KYC exchanges. This creates obstacles for law enforcement to track, trace, and eventually recover the illicit funds involved.

Examples of non-KYC activity include the BTC-e Exchange that was eventually shut down after having failed to exercise due diligence, resulting in billions of dollars being laundered. Yet another example worth noting was the events related to the Hydra Marketplace which operated on the darknet/ Hydra Marketplace facilitated money laundering operations of illicit drug proceeds. Finally, tactics such as those adopted by Western industrialized nations sometimes backfire. This has been the case of sanctions imposed on Russia, Venezuela, and North Korea, where sanctions have fueled the expansion of cybercriminality rather than reducing it, Sanctioned states have leveraged non-KYC platforms. to their advantage. to evade sanctions by using ransomware attacks in retaliation. For example, in 2024 North Korea linked hackers stole $1.34 billion.in forty-seven incidents. This represented an increase of 102.88%. intrusions and exploits. Most North Korean exploits re actualized through USDT tokens on the Tron blockchain. These increases indicate improved performance on the part of North Korean hackers and portend greater future threats.

SUMMARY

Non-KYC exchanges offer scope for illegal entities to conduct money laundering operations and present significant challenges to law enforcement in their fights against crypto-enabled money laundering. Potential counter measures might include leveraging crypto exchanges to share customer data for large scale transaction above a specifically defined threshold. The passage of regulatory measures prohibiting interaction between banks and non-KYC exchanges. After all, if the banks are constrained by KYC regulation enforcement, it would make sense that those interacting with them should be as well. Finally, using blockchain analytic forensics to track and trace illicit fund movements from non-KYC platforms could continue to serve as a useful investigative tool. This approach, however, requires constant innovation and evolution as well as establishing the delicate balance between privacy and transparency.

Decentralized Finance (DeFi) Laundering and Exploits

Defi, is a relatively recent development which began around the second half of 2020. MAKERDAO was the first DeFi project and was launched in 2015. DeFi is built upon foundational technologies such as distributed ledger technology (DLT) and blockchain, which provide the infrastructure for decentralized and transparent financial systems (Benson et al., 2024, p. 83). There are numerous advantages related to DeFi. As there is no intermediary involved in the transaction fees are automatically lower. Additionally, the time to process transactions and the complexity of using the system are also reduced. Finally, control of the fund's rests entirely with the end user (Mittal, 2021, "What is decentralized Finance (DeFi)?"). As discussed at the outset of this chapter, the digital ecosphere is marked by an inherent tension, referred to as the *Janus Paradox*. Nowhere is this tension more apparent than in financial transactions, where the demand for financial privacy and anonymity clashes with the need for transparency and traceability (Carlisle, 2023, p. 82).

This paradox is particularly pronounced in financial crime, as DeFi's anonymity facilitates illicit activities such as money laundering. The evolution of money laundering in DeFi mirrors the cumulative structure of the children's tale *This Is the House That Jack Built*. Each element builds upon the last: from blockchain's pseudonymity to mixers and tumblers designed to obscure transactions; CoinJoin enhanced the effectiveness of tumblers; privacy coins (or AECs) further complicated traceability; and physical coin swaps and Bitcoin ATMs introduced yet more innovations that challenged AML and CTF efforts.

Smurfing

One tactic employed by criminals in the context of DeFi, is referred to as "smurfing," whereby substantial amounts of cash procured from illegal activities are broken down into smaller amounts. This tactic is also referred to as "dusting," when used in the context money laundering, and sanctions avoidance or phishing, to mark targets for later attacks, These smaller amounts, always below the $10,000 regulatory threshold, are then deposited into bank accounts by "Smurfs," recruited by the criminal organizations (Wang & Hsieh, 2024, p. 26). In this context, it is also worth noting that regulatory weakness and inadequate oversight are contributing factors to the increasing proliferation of financial crime. For a more in-depth exploration of this strategy please refer to the section on money laundering.

Blockchain Mixers and CoinJoin

Cryptocurrency transactions are recorded on a public ledger known as the blockchain. These transactions can be traced by anyone using the correct tools. For those seeking financial privacy. Whether for licit or illicit purposes, this inherent transparency can pose a challenge.

Blockchain mixers are used to protect crypto transaction history and origins from scrutiny. This is accomplished by pooling the funds of different users shuffling them and then proceeding with an anonymized redistribution. There exist different variants of mixers, each with their own opportunities and risks. Maximum obfuscation can be obtained by channeling illicit funds through a series of mixers and multiple wallets or accounts, rather than a single service provider or wallet and then combining this practice with the mixing of digital and traditional financial instruments as well (Greenberg, 2024, pp. 172–173;Wronka, 2022, p. 86). The overall strength, referred to as "liquidity" of any mixer is a factor of its "anonymity set," or the total number of transactions within a given pool of users (Carlisle, 2023, p. 43).

Blockchain mixers, or tumblers, are terms that describe the same basic functions, that of obfuscating sender/receiver transaction data. These terms are largely used interchangeably, though there is a notable preference for mixers with tumblers being rather informal. For a detailed analysis of methodological differences please refer to table 1 below. They are differentiated solely by their level ofc complexity or implementation, for instance whether applied in centralized or decentralized platforms. Blockchain mixers operate across both publicly accessible networks (Clearnet) and anonymous networks (Dark Web).

Centralized Mixers

Centralized mixers are third party services that take in cryptocurrency, mix it with assets of other users, reshuffles the transaction, and return them as "clean" coins. The potential for attracting money laundering interest is clear in this case. For both licit and illicit use the possibility of delayed payouts and staggered withdrawals helps to avoid attracting suspicion related to large withdrawals. There are appreciable advantages of such systems, however, there are also important drawbacks. Fees on a centralized system are much higher, there is a risk of seizure by authorities, and as with any cryptocurrency environment there is always the risk of leaks or exit scams where the operators, developers, or platform administrators steal the funds and disappear (Greenberg, 2024, pp. 161, 171–172). It is essential to bear in mind that because a system or platform is centralized, it does not automatically infer that it is free from illicit activity. Centralized systems or platforms, while having structured oversight and control, can still be vulnerable to illicit activities such as fraud, money laundering, or hacking. Centralization merely means that control is concentrated in fewer hands, but it does not inherently prevent illegal actions from occurring within the system. This being said, centralized exchanges have far more oversight and regulatory obligations imposed upon them. As a result, many have uprooted operations and transferred their headquarters to more fiscally-friendly environments.

Decentralized Mixers

Decentralized mixers, on the other hand, use either smart contracts or various protocols to conduct their services. The users, both licit and illicit, pool their funds. Like their centralized counterparts, decentralized mixers shuffle funds and reduce traceability. Once again, the funds are redistributed in such a way that sender/receiver origins are obfuscated. The difference here is that when compared with centralized mixers, there is no third party involvement, and hence no single point of failure.

Three examples of decentralized mixers include CoinSwap, Zero Knowledge Mixers, and CoinJoin. Each of these has a different proprietary system, such as coin swapping, furnishing cryptographic proofs, or collective transaction signing, respectively. Advantages include lower fee structures, less risk of seizure by authorities, and the fact there is no third party trust relationship involved (Bick, 2022). The flip side of the crypto coin includes the fact that decentralized mixing is not impervious to forensic tracing. Law enforcement employs advanced analytics to track suspicious transaction patterns. Lastly, decentralized mixing is a more complex system to negotiate and requires a large participant base to be effective.

Criminals adopting this strategy send their funds into a smart contract-based mixer (e.g., Tornado Cash, now largely defunct) that pools transactions and redistributes them in a randomized manner. This makes it virtually (pun intended) impossible to link the sender and receiver. As an example, imagine a hacker who deposits the stolen Ethereum into Tornado Cash, then waits for a period, and finally withdraws smaller amounts to fresh wallets. The potential for money laundering operations to benefit from such a strategy becomes abundantly clear.

Since 2022, sanctions by the U.S. Treasury Department's Office of Foreign Assets Control (OFAC), targeting money laundering operations, have been imposed on various entities, including Blender.io (sanctioned in May 2022) and Tornado Cash (sanctioned in August 2022 and redesignated in November 2022). Entities under such sanctions, are designated on what is referred to as the Specially Designated Nationals (SDN) list, effectively prohibiting U.S. persons from engaging in transactions with these addresses (Unit21, n.d.-b). Consequently, under such a mandate, it is illegal for any US citizen, resident, or company to employ the services of such entities for either depositing or withdrawing crypto (Unit21, n.d.-b).

This back and forth saga between the US Department of Justice and decentralized finance operations, however witnessed surprising turn of events, two years later, when a US appeals court tossed out the sanctions levied by OFAC, citing them as illegal (CyberScoop, 2024; NeosLegal, 2024; Steptoe & Johnson LLP, 2024).

Decentralized mixers threw a cog into the works for law enforcement in their efforts to track and trace illicit funds being laundered. Law enforcement, however, soon found the while mixers obfuscated the individual transactions of holders, senders, recipients, and ultimate beneficial owners (UBOs) of these accounts, the clusters (a group of blockchain addresses) remained visible on the blockchain. This included the addresses used by mixer operators to collect and redistribute the digital assets. Consequently, all funds being sent to the mixer operator's wallet and conversely the funds being transferred from the mixer to the recipients were traceable (Carlisle, 2023, p. 49).Once again, such moves on the part of law enforcement, raised question of balance and contrasted strongly with the respect of financial privacy sought by those using mixer services, licitly and illicitly alike.

Unmixing the Mixers: Case Study

The first blow, in the war on mixers, was delivered in May of 2019, when the third largest mixer, known as Bitmixer.io, was seized by European law enforcement in conjunction with various regulatory agencies. The U.S. FBI; investigation unsurprisingly spearheaded the operation, while Europol coordinated the seizure effort; and the U.S. Department of Justice (DOJ) played a role in the prosecution process. Other agencies involved in the operations included, The U.S. Internal Revenue Service, Criminal Investigation division (IRS-CI), Financial Crimes Enforcement Network (FinCEN), along with various private firms involved in blockchain forensic analysis and working alongside law enforcement (Carlisle, 2023, p. 50). A year later, it was Helix's turn and the DOJ, FBI, IRS-CI, and FinCEN, dismantled that operation as well. The third major strike was delivered in April of 2021 against, a Russian - Swedish national, Roman Sterlingov, the alleged operator of Bitcoin Fog, the last major mixer operation (Carlisle, 2023, p.52).

CoinJoin Obfuscation

Another obfuscation process closely related to mixers and tumblers was known as CoinJoin. When the "house of mixers" began to crumble and fall, it was only logical that a new, and more resilient approach, meant to replace that technology, would make its appearance. The persistent call for privacy was answered by the development of an innovative technology called CoinJoin. CoinJoin is a peer-to-peer decentralized mixing technique that provides similar privacy benefits to those offered by tumblers and mixers. The main difference when compared with mixers and tumblers being that, with CoinJoin, the users retain control and transactions do not require third-party involvement, thus eliminating the single point of failure typically associated with centralized control. The CoinJoin process is notable for enabling users to directly coordinate and mix their funds in a collaborative, transparent, and trustless way.

Following the widespread collapse of mixers and their inherent single-point vulnerability, criminal elements from the dark web rapidly gravitated to CoinJoin platforms. CoinJoin was previously implemented through various tools, like Wasabi Wallet or Samourai Wallet. To render this process even more opaque, Samourai wallet also introduced an application called *Ricochet*, which added an additional intermediary transaction between the already murky sender to receiver operation. The AML operations that impacted Tornado cash, also befell the money laundering practices of CoinJoin platforms. It should come as little surprise, therefore, that Wasabi closed down its operations and Samourai wallet was seized in April 2024, following money laundering accusations and the arrest of its co-founders (Cointelegraph, 2025; Ohtamaa, 2024; United States Attorney's Office, Southern District of New York, 2024) It is important to note that the Wasabi wallet closed of its own initiative and was never charged either criminally or civilly.

While these two market leaders were shut down and put out of business the underlying method of combining Bitcoin transactions to obscure inputs and outputs remains nevertheless, possible Options are available to those seeking this type of anonymity. Advanced users can still manually coordinate CoinJoin transactions without relying on centralized coordinators. There is an active platform called JoinMarket and certain Electrum setups, still accept CoinJoin transactions.

Table 1. Comparative analysis between Mixers, Tumbler's, and CoinJoin

Attribute	Mixer	Tumbler	CoinJoin
Level of Privacy	High particularly when decentralized	Moderate to high depending on the service	High. Transactions are P2P based without trusted intermediary
Management and control	Centralized mixers take temporary control. Decentralized mixers allow more control.	Users lose temporary control to the service	Users maintain full control over their funds throughout
Leve of Centralization	Either centralized or decentralized	Centralized operated by a service provider	Entirely decentralized. No third party involvement

continued on following page

Table 1. Continued

Attribute	Mixer	Tumbler	CoinJoin
Process	Multiple user coins are pooled. Then randomly redistributed	Coins are mixed in a pool with a delayed ransom distribution	Multiparty transactions are combined into a single joint transaction, Rendering tracing more difficult.
Examples	Tornado Cash (Ethereum-based and decentralized); Chipmixer, JoinMarket	Bitcoin Fog, Helix	Wasabi Wallet, Samourai Wallet, JoinMarket

Anonymity Enhanced Currencies (AECs or *Privacy Coins*) *and Transaction Obfuscation*

Privacy Coins offer an alternative to other crypto currencies such as bitcoin and Ethereum. In the never-ending quest for enhanced anonymity, turning to privacy coins became inevitable.

Privacy Coins

CoinJoin largely supplanted mixers and tumblers, and privacy coins or AECs attempted to pick up where CoinJoin left off. These exchanges also support certain privacy enhanced crypto currencies, AECs privacy coins, such as Dash, Zecash (ZEC), or Monero (XMR) which further contributes to the obfuscation of transactions taking place. The standard money laundering protocol, of placement, layering, and integration, also applies in this context regardless of the technology involved. Due to space constraints, this chapter is unable to provide the sort of in-depth discussion and analysis of these coins, and their varied technologies, such as ring signatures, stealth addresses, and zero-knowledge proofs, which would be required. Readers are, therefore directed to Carlisle (2023, pp. 67–71; Furneaux, 2025, pp. 395–399). Interestingly, while writing this chapter and conducting research for this section on private coins, Furneaux also commented on the complexity of reporting on privacy coins given their innovative and revolutionary nature. The legal status of privacy coins varies by country and is subject to change. Different countries have banned or restricted their use due to concerns about anonymity and potential misuse. China, for example, maintains a ban both on initial coin offerings, cryptocurrency trading and mining activities. Since September 2021, The Chinese government declared all cryptocurrency transactions illegal which, in turn provided additional strength to the previous restrictions (Foley, Karlsen, & Putniņš, 2019, p.1799).

Most major centralized exchanges (CEXs) have delisted privacy coins due to AML (Anti-Money Laundering) regulations, criminals have, therefore, turned to

Decentralized Finance (DeFi) platforms where identity verification is weaker. When laundering funds using AECs, criminals convert funds into privacy-focused cryptocurrencies like Monero (XMR) or Zcash (ZEC) before swapping back into mainstream crypto or alternative forms of assets. As an example of this asset conversion process, A fraudster exchanges stolen USDT for wBTC (wrapped Bitcoin), then for XMR, rendering the funds untraceable before converting back. For a comparative analysis relating to the general features, the technical and legal status of different privacy coins, readers are directed to table 2 below.

SUMMARY: COMBATTING DEFI MONEY LAUNDERING

Because of the inevitable surge of illegal activity related to mixer services, mixers have undergone increasing scrutiny and targeting by governments and financial regulators worldwide. Like so many other issues, rights, and responsibilities there have been arguments in support of both sides. One side contends that financial privacy should be a fundamental human right, while the other considers these tools as little more than instruments for the conduct of unimpeded illegal operations, such as extortion payouts, terrorist financing, and laundering the proceeds of illegal activity.

Table 2. Privacy coins features & technology

Name of Coin	Current Legal Status	Core Privacy Features	Technology Utilized
Monero (XMR)	Legal in most jurisdictions; banned in countries like Japan and South Korea due to regulatory concerns.	Ring signatures, stealth addresses, confidential transactions.	CryptoNote protocol.
Zcash (ZEC)	Legal in most jurisdictions; banned in different countries due to regulatory concerns.	zk-SNARKs for shielded transactions; offers both transparent and shielded addresses.	Zero-Knowledge Succinct Non-Interactive Arguments of Knowledge (zk-SNARKs).
Dash (DASH)	Legal in most jurisdictions; some exchanges have delisted it due to regulatory concerns.	Optional PrivateSend feature for transaction mixing; InstantSend for quick transactions.	CoinJoin mixing technique; masternode network.
Grin (GRIN)	Legal in most jurisdictions; subject to regulatory scrutiny due to privacy features.	Confidential transactions, CoinJoin, cut-through for blockchain efficiency.	Mimblewimble protocol.

continued on following page

Table 2. Continued

Name of Coin	Current Legal Status	Core Privacy Features	Technology Utilized
Beam (BEAM)	Legal in most jurisdictions; subject to regulatory scrutiny due to privacy features.	Confidential transactions, mandatory privacy, opt-in auditability.	Mimblewimble protocol.
Verge (XVG)	Legal in most jurisdictions; subject to regulatory scrutiny due to privacy features.	Integration with Tor and I2P to obfuscate IP addresses; optional stealth addressing.	Tor and I2P networks; Wraith Protocol for optional privacy.

Market Manipulation in Financial Systems

In the realm of financial cybercrime, criminals use advanced tools and strategies to exploit systems and manipulate markets. Cybercriminals may rely on infiltration, insider information, digital exchanges, or exploit trading algorithms to achieve their ends. Such exploits are frequently the product of gaps in regulatory oversight. These include Pump-and-Dump schemes, exit strategies, rug pull scams, high-frequency trading (HFT) exploits, cryptocurrency wash trading, front-running attacks, and flash loan manipulations. These tactics often exploit technological or regulatory gaps for financial gain. These activities have become widespread and facilitated by the ability to create new cryptocurrency tokens on blackchins such as Tron, Binance Smart Chain, or even Ethereum (Furneaux, 2025, p.74). For more information on these financial manipulation techniques, refer to Appendix A.

Pump-and-Dump Schemes

Pump-and Dump schemes have long been a feature of financial markets manipulation, particularly in low liquidity and high volatility assets. They are frequently associated with digital assets such cryptocurrencies, smart contracts, and as non-fungible tokens, or NFTs (Carlisle, 2023, p.173). It did not take long for criminals to expand from the traditional financial market attackers to those in the digital eco-sphere. The digital space, with its inherent anonymity, lack of effective regulation, and ease of coordination has contributed to a rise of these criminal tactics.

The strategy behind this particular illegal tactic is to falsely inflate the values of a commodity, asset, or commodity, through price manipulation, with the purpose of increasing investment and the profit that results as a consequence. This is accomplished by artificially inflating the price of a digital asset through misleading statements, coordinated social media campaigns, or fraudulent investment advice. Once the profit margins reach a certain level, the fraudsters sell off their own holdings and disappear.

In the context of cryptocurrency, pump-and-dump schemes have been used in both centralized (CEX) and decentralized (DEX) exchanges. They also appear in NFT market manipulation, meme coin mania, and hyper-driven assets (e.g., DOGE, SHIB, PEPE). Additionally, they have been instrumentalized in illicit markets and darknet finance, particularly in relation to private coins, discussed elsewhere in this chapter. The foreseeable result is an inevitable price crash, leaving the investors empty handed. These types of schemes are most frequently facilitated by unregulated exchanges and are advanced and promoted through the use of social media and online communities. Regulators and law enforcement have had mixed results in tracing privacy coins, though successes have occurred. Both the privacy coin developer and those conducting blockchain forensic analysts continue to struggle under the Janus Paradox of privacy and traceability (Greenberg, 2024, pp. 299–300).

Rug pulls and Exit Schemes

These strategies are little more than a variation on a theme, though their approach is different, the goal and underlying operational methods are quite similar. The simplest form of fraudulent manipulation is that of the exit scam. This is a "hit-and -run, fraudulent scam where the developers offer an asset,—and IOC, for instance, and then disappear with investor funds. At times, this may be the plan, at others it may be a response to authorities closing in on their operation. This type of operation uses similar tactics as other methods such as creating hype about their offering on social media outlets, and warning investors not to miss out on this (imaginary) once-in-a-lifetime opportunity. Rug pulls are a form of exit scam where the developers create a fraudulent crypto project frequently in the form of an NFT, or a token in an initial coin offering A pool for funding is launched. They proceed to attract investors, then suddenly withdraw funds and abandon the project, ultimately disappearing with the proceeds.

Front-Running Attacks

DeFi market manipulation tactics exploit the transparent and automated nature of blockchain transactions, particularly how pending trades are visible before execution. These strategies take advantage of and leverage the inherent financial complexity of the system. A front-running attack is a market manipulation method composed of a complex set of fraudulent financial operations. A full analysis would require an entire chapter to discuss properly. At its most basic level, fraudsters leverage algorithmic trading strategies, gas fee manipulation, and mempool surveillance,

Standard tactics in DeFi market manipulation include Sandwich Attacks, where an attacker strategically places a buy order before, and a sell order after, a large pending trade, exploiting the slippage effect. This manipulation forces the victim to execute their trade at a disadvantageous price, allowing the attacker to profit from the price difference.

Other exploitative techniques include:

- **Transaction Sniffing**, where bots monitor the mempool for profitable trade opportunities.
- **Maximal Extractable Value (MEV) Backrunning**, in which attackers capitalize on price movements caused by prior transactions.
- **Liquidation Sniping**, where attackers force a loan liquidation by artificially moving asset prices.
- **Mempool Surveillance & Exploitation**, where attackers analyze unconfirmed transactions and manipulate execution order for profit.

These techniques rely on algorithmic precision, speed, and access to real-time transaction data, making them inaccessible to average retail traders, while giving bots and well-funded actors a decisive edge in DeFi markets. Individuals who instrumentalize these attacks are typically highly skilled actors with deep technical and financial knowledge. They operate within the gray area of financial manipulation and blockchain exploitation. It is possible to classify such operator into three basic categories: first, there are the technically proficient actors. They may be either individuals or groups. Automated trading bots are created to exploit the Maximal Extractable Value (MEV), The second group operates legally, but unethically. They extract value by instrumentalizing algorithms but avoid directly violating the smart contract rules. The third and final group are directly involved in fraudulent activity. They may use sybil attacks (detailed under the wash trading section), price manipulation, and outright theft.

High-Frequency Trading (HFT)

Cybercriminals exploit trading algorithms, insider information, and digital exchanges to distort financial markets. Many unregulated exchanges engage in cryptocurrency wash trading to artificially inflate trading volumes and attract more users, creating the illusion of a highly liquid market. Sophisticated trading bots conduct rapid buy-sell cycles, in a process known as high-frequency trading (HFT), to manipulate stock and crypto prices in milliseconds. Detection is often avoided given the complexity of automated algorithms. This is both a regulatory and technical issue that requires serious attention.

One of the most well-known HFT exploits was the flash crash of May 6, 2010.A 36 minute exploit which resulted in extreme levels of stock market volatility. The panic that ensued the crash wiped out $1 Trillion in shares before they eventually recovered. Th event was eventually attributed to Navinder Singh Sarao, a British stock market analyst and trader, who was arrested in 2015 by British authorities.

Sarao, using specialized software, was able to place thousands of orders before changing or cancelling them in a practice known as "spoofing," after having created an artificial demand that other traders would be misled in their buying and selling, but which allowed Sarao to profit from the volatility, by buying as the price rose or fell. At his U.S. trial, where he was convicted of one count each of electronic fraud and spoofing, Sarao agreed to pat be $12.8 million to the U.S. government. His sentence was surprisingly lenient with Sarao serving one year of home arrest back in the U.K. Mitigating circumstances were considered, during his sentencing, such as Sarao's autism, his loss of funds to fraudster and his assistance to the government. There was also a view that the sentence imposed had not amply served the interests of justice, nor contributed to deterrence.

Market Manipulation: Wash Trading

Wash trading is yet another deceptive practice in which entities artificially inflate trading volumes with the goal of misleading investors. This is particularly prevalent in unregulated cryptocurrency exchange (UEXs), sometimes referred to as over the-counter markets (OTCs), where platforms or traders execute self-executed transactions to create the illusion of high volume market activity (Carlisle, 2023, pp. 173–174). This generates interest and speculation based on artificially created market manipulation. It is important to underscore the difference between wash trading and Sybil attacks. Were sybil attacks target networks by overwhelming then with fake nodes, the target of wash trading is the financial markets instead.

Wash Trading & Sybil Attacks in DeFi Markets

In decentralized finance (DeFi), wash trading is often facilitated by what are referred to as Sybil attacks. With a Sybil attack artificially created accounts or wallets trade the same funds repeatedly to provide elevated levels of imaginary transaction volume and market legitimacy. These attacks are on a large scale commandeering an entire distributed system through the creation of fake identities or nodes, thus overwhelming the system (Greenberg, 2024, p. 107). Once these manipulated assets peak in price, they can then be cashed out through a compliant exchange. An example of this might be a cybercriminal cycling tokens between different wallets, making it appear as though a portfolio is actively being traded. Whenever an individual moves a sum of tokens, the transactions are clearly visible over the blockchain. Other investors can then be manipulated into believing that this represents an authentic series of events. Sybil attacks exploit the vulnerabilities of distributed systems by overwhelming them with fraudulent identities or nodes (Greenberg, 2024, p. 107). For a deeper dive into how these rather complex attacks work, the readers are directed to the key additional readings section.

NFT Wash Trading & Illicit Sales

In the NFT market, wash trading is used to artificially drive up asset prices or alternatively to launder illicit funds. Criminals may mint or purchase NFTs and then artificially sell and purchase the assets themselves—often across different wallets—to simulate high-value transactions. This tactic establishes a n ostensibly legitimate sales history, allowing illicit funds are them in turn, funneled into reputable exchanges. One example might include a hacker purchasing as NFT from themselves for 100 ETH and falsely presenting it as a high-profile collector's purchase, before cashing out through a trusted marketplace. Such a tactic would, therefore, artificially inflate the value of said asset.

Summary: These types of market manipulations are cleverly designed and also align with other strategic approaches, such as social engineering. They are cleverly designed, and even experienced investors can be easily drawn in. An essential fact to bear in mind is that once these frauds are executed and the perpetrators flee with the misappropriated funds, the story does not end there. They will also go to great lengths to erase any traces and cover their tracks. This makes investigating such crimes highly time-sensitive, with a narrow operational window. Time is of the essence, and the principle of the "golden hour" in criminal investigations should be applied. The longer the delay, the colder the trail becomes. For cross-referential guidance, and comparative analysis of these market manipulation tactics, please, refer to Appendix D.

CYBERCRIMINAL EXPLOITATION OF PII (IDENTITY THEFT & SOCIAL ENGINEERING)

Identity theft and social engineering are closely related. Social engineering is employed as a tactic for obtaining PII. The phenomenon of identity theft has existed long before the arrival of digital technology. The crime remains unaltered, it is merely the procedure and methodology that has changed regarding the digital ecosphere. The pseudonymity and anonymity of the internet have facilitated criminal identity theft since the visuals cues are missing. Additionally, there are far more vectors available to the criminal seeking to steal the identity of their victim.

Identity Theft

Identity theft is nothing new. Traditional tactics have evolved alongside the advent of digital technology, and both represent a major component of financial threats. Like its real world counterpart, identity theft targets victims indiscriminately regardless of demographic characteristics, old or young, urban, or rural, makes no difference to borderless cybercriminals (Allstate Identity Protection, 2017). Identity theft remains a persistent menace regardless of the means of procurement This spike in identity -related criminality has led many companies and organization to develop new approaches to identity verification. The same paradox found in much of the digital industry remains leverage a delicate balance between security needs and user privacy Consequently, both digital identity and document-free verification are projected to become increasingly pervasive moving forward (Andreeva & Abrams, 2024).

Cybercriminals skillfully use social engineering based on psychosocial manipulation, the use of malicious software, intrusion, and redirection to fraudulent websites to lure and defraud unsuspecting victims. Like so many the processes in the bold frontier of digital evolution, there is no universally accepted definition of what constitutes identity theft, and interpretations range from an extremely narrow to an overly broad interpretation. Identity theft has evolved with the advent of digital technology and the ability of cyber criminals to usurp PII has become an issue of urgent global relevance and concern. Criminal tactics are constantly evolving and largely outpace law enforcement efforts to stem the tide of the crime wave. As an indicator of its serious impact, A 2024 report highlighted the fact that over the previous 12 months, 93% of organizations contacted have suffered two or more identity related breaches, and this despite often having robust security measures and practices in place (Cyber Ark 2024).

Access may be achieved either kinetically, or virtually. Two of the most common tactics are those of intrusion and infiltration (Biegelman, 2009, p. xvii). The key to criminal intrusion lies in obtaining access to systems and devices. If there is no access, there can be no crime. Intrusion may be either virtual, for instance the use of trojans, malware or infected files, or physical, for instance theft of a device or installation of a keylogger device. Infiltration, on the other hand, may be either direct, for example via gainful employment, also referred to as the "insider threat," or indirect such as the manipulation, bribing, or blackmailing of employees.

An individual's identity is an important asset. Personal identifying information can be instrumentalized for illicit purposes. These include direct theft and control of the user accounts, misrepresentation, and usurpation of identity for evasion or fraudulent purposes; and system control for botnet incorporation. Stolen identities are sold and traded in the dark net on the deep web (Furneaux, 2025, p.24).

Identity theft is a growing international concern as criminals become increasingly clever and adept at countering system security. It is important to underscore that following the theft of data or PII, criminals will attempt to obliterate any trace of their intrusion. Criminals leverage various tactics such as social engineering to bypass user skepticism and obtain the coveted information.

Phishing, malware, adware, spyware, spam mail, synthetic media, keyloggers, romance scams, pharming, and the growing threats of pretexting and business email compromise (BEC) are just some most common tactics in the criminal toolbox (Ghernaouti, 2023, pp. 124–133; Furneaux, 2025, p.). A cyberattack, whether the goal is to damage, disrupt, or destroy (D3), generally follows the same well-established pattern. Regardless of the methodology, be it phishing or any of its derivative forms, such as fraud, synthetic media, or data exploitation, the primary goal of cyber criminals remains procuring the PII of the chosen victim or organization. Readers are directed to Figure 2 below.

Figure 2. The cyberattack cycle

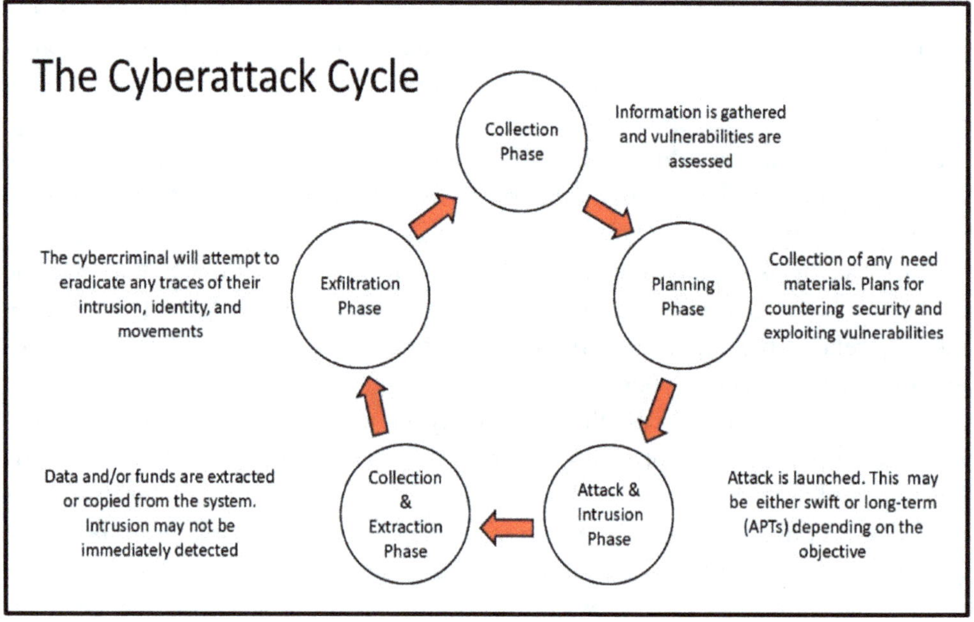

Social Engineering

Social engineering employs various intrusion tactics to exploit human vulnerabilities. Criminals manipulate individuals into revealing sensitive information or performing actions that compromise their security. These tactics often rely on psychosocial manipulation and deception, such as phishing emails, vishing (voice-based fraud), targeted spear-phishing attacks, and romance scams (Ghernaouti, 2023, p.125). Phishing attacks are as varied in approach as they are widespread. Anyone with a computer or cell phone today will be aware of the massive increase in phishing and vishing attempts. The FBI reports that phishing remains the king of the digital jungle when compared with all types of cybercrime reported (Akhgar, Staniforth, & Bosco, 2014, pp. 156–158; Federal Bureau of Investigation, 2024). According to FBI reports 51% of all email scams have their origin in Nigeria, while another 34% originate in other states located in West Africa (Haque, 2024). The FBI reported 298,878 cases of phishing-related attacks topping their list of complaint types, in their Internet crime report 2023 (pp.8, 20).

One of the most popular is known as the advanced fee scam, where an individual is randomly contacted and promised a considerable sum of money in exchange for advancing a fee. The fee is often disguised as tax payments, bribes, or payoffs to release the imaginary funds. These range from the clearly obvious, to more sophisticated attempts.

Another more recent, crypto-related phishing scam, is address poisoning. Scammers rely on the complacency of users not to scrutinize the long alphanumeric crypto transfer addresses and indeed only briefly glance at the beginning and ending portions of the addresses while ignoring the middle. Malicious actors will alter elements in the middle sections of the address, and the outgoing transfer subsequently lands in the scammers account (Furneaux, 2025, p.27).

These types of attacks, as well as those related to extortion and romance scams, originate in developing states, with lax enforcement. Nigeria is most frequently cited as a source in this regard (Haque, 2024). According to the FBI IC3, 2023 report, only the U.S., the U.K., Canada, and India outstrip Nigeria in number of international complaints received. Readers are directed to Figures 2 and 3 below for comparative details. The same report indicated a 10% increase in complaints received for a total of 880,418, representing an estimated potential loss of as much as $12.4 billion.

Figure 3. Top international complaint countries. Public domain statistics FBI IC3

Figure 4. USA, UK, and Canada. Public domain statistics FBI IC3

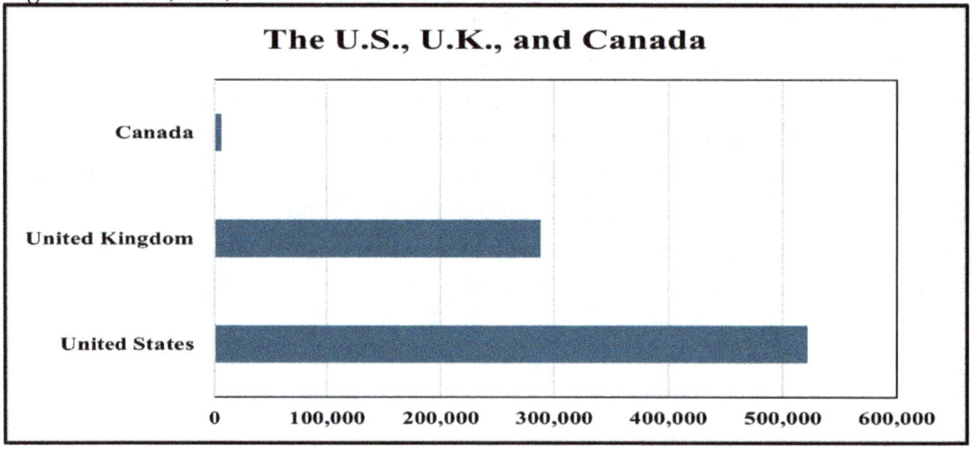

The Special Case of Nigeria

Quite ironically, Nigeria may not top the list of states most involved in cybercriminality, largely outstripped by India the U.S., and the U.K., but nonetheless it retains a reputation as one of the most notorious for such activities. But why? Nigeria has garnered an unenviable reputation, despite not being the most prolific actors involved in cybercriminality, in terms of sheer volume. The state's criminal activities are the confluence of several significant factors. First there is the high visibility of its cybercriminal operations such as the *Nigerian Prince Letters* and the well-documented *419 scams* (advance-fee fraud). Other contributing factors include the sophistication, and international reach of operations such as email phishing, hacking, online fraud, money laundering, and sextortion. These previously underscored causes are further amplified by a lack of stringent enforcement mechanisms, which, in turn, are compounded by the proliferation of significant economic challenges. All these elements contribute to making Nigeria a focal point in the global narrative of cybercrime.

In an insightful and cogent analysis Adebisi Arewa (2019) delves into deeper and more systemic issues that have led to the rise of criminality in Nigeria. Among these Arewa underscores a clear rule of law deficit, which he traces back to as early as 1960— a factor related to the previously highlighted lack of stringent cybercrime enforcement mechanisms. The variables enumerated by Arewa are overlapping and interconnected in nature. Other factors that have directly contributed to the rise of criminality in Nigerian society, according to Arewa, include economic and governance failures, coupled with widespread institutional corruption (Arewa, 2019. Pp. 1133–1134, 1135, 1143). Other contributing factors include demographic characteristics; Nigeria has an exceptionally large population (175 million) outnumbering that of Japan, Russia, and Mexico. As a former British colony, English is widely spoken and serves as an instrument to facilitate international cyberfraud. Nigeria has a large, unemployed, and educated class that have no viable employment opportunities. There has also been an increase in digital literacy within the Nigerian population. Finally, scammers are looked upon as near celebrities in contrast to other regions of the world. (Haque, 2024).

Collectively, these unfavorable conditions have created anomie in Nigerian society, a state of normlessness, a lack of economic development; and a general sense of social impoverishment, compounded by a lack of human growth potential. Positive social development in Nigeria has been undermined Superficial and materialistic criteria have been embodied in "Dorime Culture," itself founded in a misconceived and perverse perceptions of what constitutes Western social success (Eromo Egbejule, 2024). Taken together, these factors contribute to an environment rife for cybercriminality.

On a more positive note, Arewa was writing in 2019, and Nigeria has since transitioned to a more democratic state, under the leadership of its president Bola Ahmed Tinubu, following the 2023 elections. It is worth underscoring the fact that a transition to democratic principles is always fraught with challenges and that society does not change overnight. In recent events Nigeria has become more active in its cracking down on scammer operations. In line with President Tinubu's promises to rid the country of its deeply entrenched systemic corruption, police conducted a massive raid arresting close to 800 suspects in December 2024. The arrest included 124 Chinese nationals as well as 40 Filipinos. Romance scam operations have often been found to be spearheaded by Chinese nationals (Flanagan, 2024).

These staggering figures are literally just the beginning, since, during a recent FBI operation, it was surmised that only 20% of victims reported the crimes (Federal Bureau of Investigation, 2024, p.3). This is understandable if one considers the bureaucratic nature of the reporting mechanisms coupled with the conviction that nothing will or can be done. Additionally, victims may be too ashamed or embarrassed to expose themselves to potential ridicule (Flanagan, 2024). The fact that such fraud attempts persist and that individuals continue to fall prey to such scams underscores the need for greater education, awareness, and enforcement. Each Country on this blacklist seems to have a cybercriminal speciality, be it ransomware, secxtortion, advanced fee schemes, or cyber fraud. The end goal, neverthlessm remais the same—to bilk the unwary and gullible of their life savings.

Deepfakes in Social Engineering

Deepfakes are primarily used to deceive by creating realistic yet fabricated images, audio, or videos. This deception is at the heart of social engineering, which manipulates people's perceptions and trust. For example, deepfakes can impersonate important public figures or company executives to influence the behavior of employees, or spread misinformation, or commit fraud. How effective is this type of social engineering? Initially detection was difficult, though still possible, to the trained eye. However, with the rapid technological evolution being witnessed, the differences have become almost imperceptible, even to experts.

Voice Generated Theft Using Deepfake Technology.

As an example, in March 2019, a vocally-generated deepfake was launched against an employee at a U.K. based, German energy firm .The employee believed that he was speaking on the phone with the CEO. The employee in question was then ordered to transfer the sum of €220,00, or approximately $243,000 at the time, to the account of a Hungarian supplier. Subsequently, the caller attempted further extortion calls, but the employee in question grew suspicious. And refused any further transfer requests. the funds emanating from the initial extortion were rapidly transferred from a bank in Hungary to one in Mexico, and then onward to other locations thus obfuscating the trail (Damiani, 2019).

Impersonation Fraud and Synthetic Media

Phishing attacks discussed previously are certainly one form of impersonation, however, there exist more complex forms which will be explored here. Social engineering attacks rely primarily on technological expertise and duplicity. These approaches are also occasionally augmented by psychological manipulation as well. Synthetic media is also known as *AI-generated media, media produced by generative AI, personalized media, personalized content* and more colloquially as deepfakes. Synthetic media is an umbrella term for the artificial production, manipulation, and modification of data and media created by automated means, especially using AI algorithms. In the cybercriminal context synthetic media has been increasingly used for the purpose of misleading and manipulating individuals

Deepfakes in Social Engineering

Deepfakes are but one form of synthetic media increasingly employed in social engineering attacks, particularly in business fraud, political misinformation, and executive impersonation swindles. While earlier intrusions were less precise and more readily detectable; evolution and technological advances have rendered such differences largely imperceptible. Not only have there been remarkable technological advances, but the tools for developing such attacks are more readily available and more affordable than ever (iProov, 2025, p.5). These developments portend a potential increase in similar attacks in the future. While the topic of this revolutionary technology and its misuse are fascinating; constraints of space do not permit the sort of in-depth analysis it merits. It is possible, nevertheless, and imperative, to speculate on how the future of this technology might be further subtilized for illicit operations including espionage, financial crime and D3 operations. Mission impossible has suddenly become possible and the future is now.

Pretexting

It is an insidious form of high-level social media engineering. The cybercriminal shifts the attack vector from technology to exploiting human vulnerability. The victims are duped using a contrived scenario or false "pretext." In contradistinction to other forms of social engineering the attacker frequently plays to a carefully devised and prearranged script and adopts a persona. This persona may adopt multiple forms ranging from a trusted colleague to a member of HR or the IT staff all the way up to a senior corporate executive. Other examples might include a financial agent such as a broker or bank manager. The only limit is the imagination of the malicious actor involved. The attacker makes full use of a panoply of psychological devices ranging from pressure to sympathy or, alternatively, the exercise of authority. Pretexting relies heavily on deception and little or no technological prowess is required. The goal remains the same as with other forms of social engineering, it is merely the tactics that change. The cybercriminals are seeking PII to either gain system access, or have the victim perform an action, or a series of actions, such as large financial or data transfers.

Synthetic Directors: The Board the that Never was case study.

Regardless of how often this case study is referenced, it never loses interest, given its innovative nature. The events that unfolded lend credence to the axiom "life is stranger than fiction." This particular case study highlight's identity fraud in corporate structures. In January of 2024, a group of deepfake criminals impersonated a UK-based Chief Financial Officer (CFO) and other senior executives using deepfake technology. This operation began with the sending of a phishing link, which the employee in question refused to open. Subsequently, in a change of tactics, an invitation to an encrypted virtual meeting was sent to the same employee. While the meeting included multiple participants, including some from outside the company, all except the victim were impersonations and virtually-generated representations. Investment instructions were provided demanding rapid Swift transfers. The deepfake was so effective that in total fifteen transfers were made by the employee in the amount of $HK200 million, or the equivalent of €28 million. Ironically, despite his reservations, it took the employee over a week to contact corporate headquarters and follow up on the transfers (Agence France-Presse, 2024; Voice of America, 2024). It is useful to note that at least two other similar scams had already previously occurred in Hong Kong.

This case study underscores the evolving nature of cyber threats and the importance of vigilance against sophisticated scams .It further highlights indicates a lack of awareness, training and appropriate security in the financial sector. Countermeasures include the appropriate training of staff and raising awareness related to deepfake technology, establishing specific guidelines and protocols, such as multifactor authentication—particularly in the case of unusual requests and the most obvious measure, that of verifying identities, especially if financial transactions are involved. For an expanded analysis of social engineering threats please refer to **Appendix B**.

Malware-related threats: Data and System Encryption Attacks

Malware encompasses a wide range of malicious software designed to infiltrate, disrupt, damage, or destroy (D3) systems and steal sensitive information. Types of malwares include ransomware, spyware, Trojans, and worms, each having distinct functions and goals within the cybercriminal ecosystem. Two examples of these are ransomware and backdoors. Ransomware is a tactic of remote hijacking or kidnapping a system's access. This criminal strategy represents an increasingly important security threat to both public and private stakeholders alike. Ransomware is an intrusion-based malware that encrypts a victim's data or system and demands payment in exchange for decryption. Ransom payment is almost always demanded in cryptocurrency. For a comprehensive overview of different malware types, their functionality, and notable examples please refer to **Appendix C**.

Ransomware Variants and Techniques

The first historically recorded case of ransomware occurred in 1989, when Dr. Joseph L. Popp, a Harvard university trained evolutionary biologist, infected, and physically mailed out 20,000 copies of his AIDS Trojan, also known as the PC Cyborg Trojan, or the Aids Info Drive. They were so named because Popp had labeled the disks as "AIDS Information– Introductory Diskettes." He distributed these infected floppy disks to subscriber lists of AIDS researchers and organizations, primarily targeting attendees of the World Health Organization (WHO) conference in Stockholm. Additionally, he extended the attack to subscribers of *PS Business World* magazine. The trojan remained dormant, awaiting the system to be rebooted ninety times, before becoming active. After encrypting various files, a message appeared demanding a ransom payment of $189 to the PC Cyborg Corporation at a P.O. box located in Panama for the victim to receive a decryption too in exchange. Popp was caught and arrested at Amsterdam's Schiphol Airport, and extradited to the U.S., but was ultimately found to be mentally incompetent to stand trial, due to his erratic behavior. The underlying motivations of his attack remain forever shrouded in mystery (Carlisle, 2023, p.99;Laffan, 2023; O'Sullivan, 2021).

There is a well-established three step process that occurs within the Ransomware operation. These include infection, encryption (or system lockout), and ransom demand. There are multiple types of ransomwares including Crypto Ransomware, which employs encryption to lock files (e.g., WannaCry, REvil, Maze, LockBit,) and system encryptions such as Locker Ransomware, whereby the entire system or interface, is locked thus preventing the victim from accessing their system, rather than encrypting any files. Cybercriminals encrypt data and demand a cryptocurrency ransom. Corporate blackmail, and personal data ransom demands are common examples of this type of extortion. Ransomware truly came into its own following the advent of Bitcoin, where contactless payments leveraged the pseudonymity of the blockchain to conduct their illicit transactions.

The FBI's IC3 unit emphasized in their most recent report that while ransomware attacks decreased in 2022, there was a sharp upturn in 2023, with 2,825 reported complaints, for an 18% increase since 2023. Reported losses also rose from the previous 2022 level of $.43 million to $59.6 million. The report further noted that here has been a change in tactics as cybercriminals react and adjust to countermeasures (Federal Bureau of Investigation, 2024, p.3). Consequently, multiple ransomware variants are now being deployed against the same victims, along with increased data destruction capability to pressure the victims into compliance.

Table 3. Locker ransomware vs. alternatives

Locker Ransomware vs. Other Types		
Characteristic	**Locker Ransomware**	**Crypto-Ransomware**
Function	Locks users out of their system	Encrypts files without locking the system
Target	Entire device or Operating System	Specific files and data
Recovery Possibility	Sometimes possible through bypass techniques	Requires decryption key
Ransom Note Location	Displayed on the locked screen	Placed in affected directories
Common Variants	Reveton, WinLocker	WannaCry, Ryuk, Conti

Distinct types of ransomware strategies have been developed. Starting with the most basic, there is crypto ransomware which encrypts files in exchange for a ransom payment. Examples of these include WannaCry, REvil, LockBit, and Maz. More complex, yet less common today, when compared with crypto-ransomware, is Locker Ransomware. Locker Ransomware encrypts an entire system's interfaces, preventing system access but does not lock individual files. A more devious tactic is called Double Extortion Ransomware. This strategy applies pressure on the victim, and instrumentalizes a double menace, that if ransom is not met, the data will be released.

Ransomware is also offered, rented, or sold on the Dark Web under the heading of Ransomware-as-a-Service (RaaS). Infecting a system with ransomware can use any of the techniques we have covered in this chapter, ranging from simple phishing attacks to more complex approaches such as synthetic media. Attacks may be virtual or physical in nature. One form of attack that can adopt both physical and digital characteristics is that of backdoors.

Backdoors in Ransomware Attacks

Backdoors are covertly embedded into devices for bypassing security protocols, such as authentication and encryption, to obtain remote system access. Again, this may be conducted either using a physical process, or alternatively via digital intrusion. Backdoors may contain what is referred to as persistence mechanisms. These are ransomware techniques that allow attackers to maintain access to a compromised system despite the victim having paid the ransom demanded. These mechanisms ensure that the malware can reactivate, re-encrypt files, or even provide a backdoor for further, long-term exploitation.

OTHER EXTORTION METHODS

Cybercriminals no longer rely solely on data encryption strategies, such as ransomware, for financial gain. The criminal agenda has evolved to include additional, coercive tactics to maximize financial gains and exert psychological pressure on their victims. Beyond the standard ransomware schemes explored in this chapter, cybercriminals have also adopted a variety of extortion tactics, including the distasteful practices of sextortion and business email compromise (BEC). Both forms of extortion are rooted in psychosocial manipulation, targeting victims' reputation, integrity, and self-worth under extreme pressure. These are deeply personal attacks that can result in grave personal and professional consequences for the victims involved.

Sextortion in Cybercrime

Sextortion involves coercing victims into providing sensitive content, accompanied by threats of exposure. Cybercriminals use deepfake technology, social engineering tactics, and blackmail to exploit individuals. Cryptocurrency payments are frequently demanded to prevent this threatened exposure. One recent report indicates that sextortion scams have rapidly expanded using social media outlets to lure in unwary victims. Generative AI has also played a role in facilitating such tactics by generating plausible scripts and scenarios. There are alternative methods used to coerce the victims into paying extortion demands.

Malicious actors employ webcam blackmail, AI-generated deepfake coercion, and social engineering pressure tactics. The scammer, who may be posing as the opposite gender, approaches a victim, creates an imaginary relationship, and exchanges intimate images (stolen) with the victim to build trust. The victim is then asked to respond in kind, and after doing so becomes the object of extortionate black mail. The fraudster threatens to disseminate the images on social media to friends, family and acquaintances.

An alternative method can be referred to as the "shot-in-the-dark-technique." The scammer sends out a threatening message alleging that they have hacked the victim's system. Intimate activities such as visiting compromising sites have been recorded or tracked, according to the scammer, who then proceeds to threaten the victim with same previously mentioned consequences. This method is less successful since they may approach completely innocent victims who know these alleged accusations to be unfounded. They may be successful, however, in planting a seed of doubt in others.

Scammers often pose as an attractive individual using images copied from social media accounts. Approaches are made on social media sites such as LinkedIn, Tik Tok, Instagram, WhatsApp, Telegram, Meta, and others. There are even training materials and instruction packages available for purchase on the deep web for those interested in undertaking such an unsavory career (Furneaux, 2025, p. 77–78).

Case Study: The Tragic Story of Jodan DeMay

These attacks can have disastrous consequences for the victims ranging from psychological trauma to outright suicide. This was the case of 17-year old Jordan DeMay. In 2002 the youth was caught in the web of a Nigerians sextortion scam, when he shared personally sensitive images with a Nigerian scammer, he believed to be a female. He was then pressured into paying a ransom to prevent public dissemination of the images. While the youth sent $300, he was unable to obtain the remainder. He told the extortionists he would kill himself and they urged him to do so. Tragically, out of hopeless desperation, Jordan died shortly after from a self-inflicted gunshot wound (Eromo Egbejule, 2024; Sherrod, Cory, & Caron, 2023).

The outrage was understandable, and U.S. authorities traced the scammer group to Nigeria and Nigerian authorities made three arrests in the case. An additional three arrests occurred shortly thereafter. Two of the defendants who were brothers; Samuel Ogoshi, age 24, and Samson Ogoshi, age 21, have since been extradited to stand trial in the U.S. They were found guilty on March 25, 2022. The charges ranged across five different counts. Both defendants were charged with conspiracy to sexually exploit minors, conspiracy to distribute child pornography, and conspiracy to commit stalking through the internet, While Samuel Ogoshi was also charged with sexual exploitation and attempted sexual exploitation of a minor resulting in death, The defendants were tried, found guilty and subsequently sentenced to 17.5 years each, accompanied with 5-years of supervised release following release (United States Attorney's Office, Western District of Michigan, 2024).

This group was unfortunately not an isolated case by any means. A malicious Nigerian gang called the "Yahoo Boys" continues to pose a major threat in this nefarious shadow environment. According to a report by the Network Contagion Research Institute (NCRI), These groups offer training to others and perpetuate further attacks. They turn their modest apartments into cybercriminal universities, known as "hustle Kingdoms," providing training to youth as young as 13 years-old (Eromo Egbejule, 2024). A public warning was issued to parents by the FBI regarding a drastic increase in sextortion cases targeting minors reporting that approximately 20% of all cases were currently focused on youth between the ages of 14 and 17.These types of attacks have not been exclusive to Nigeria and other underdeveloped states, have also turned to this disturbingly pernicious form of cybercriminality. Such is the case of the Sakawa boys of Ghana and the Brouters, from the Republic of Côte d'Ivoire to cite but two. In other related events the platform Meta reported closing down 63,000 Nigerian Instagram accounts linked to sextortion operations (Alpert, L.I. 2024).

An important observation is merited. Despite the nonnegligible advantages offered by the digital ecosphere, including anonymity, personal financial privacy and profitable opportunities, there inevitably persists the darker, more nefarious side always waiting in the shadows to take advantage of the system. Once again, the Janus paradox manifests itself.

Business Email Compromise (BEC)

Corporate employees are targeted by criminals using various phishing tactics and deception techniques. BEC is rapidly becoming a major threat vector for global business and organizations. BEC frequently, though not exclusively, targets corporate wire transfers, to commit financial fraud, often leveraging AI-assisted software to bypass security measures. According to the FBI, there has been a change in the strategy relating to BEC scams. Previously the targets were real estate, requests for W2 wage earning information-related requests, compromising vendor emails and gift card supply scams. Currently, criminals have evolved their tactics by having the selected victims transfer funds either to a third party processor, a custodial account, or target a platform directly (Federal Bureau of Investigation, 2024, p.11). For an analysis of data breach vectors the reader is directed to figure 5 below.

Figure 5. Sources of data breaches in BEC

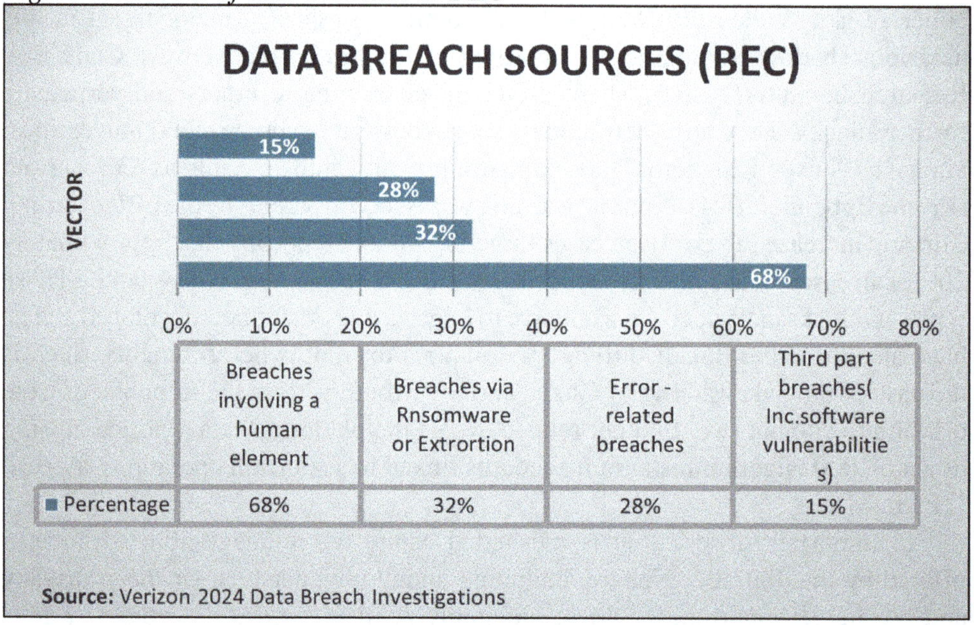

Summary

As ransomware and cyber extortion tactics evolve, criminals continue to refine their methods to maximize financial gain and psychological leverage over their victims. Cybercriminals exploit human weaknesses at the most basic psychological, emotional, and intellectual levels. Criminals increasingly exploit social engineering, financial fraud, and reputational threats to coerce payments. Poor and inattentive security habits and a failure to respect and follow established protocols are also a contributing factor to the success and proliferations of cybercriminal exploitation. The advent of AI -technology has not passed unnoticed by criminal elements who are readily adopting it to their own nefarious ends. Cybercrime is a constantly evolving threat that requires both resilience and dynamic countermeasures. As cybercriminals refine their methods, governments, organizations, and individuals must remain vigilant in implementing protective security measures against financial fraud, identity theft, and extortion schemes, such as those explored here. Understanding these varied extortion strategies is crucial for developing robust counter-fraud defenses and mitigating the risks associated with modern cybercrime.

LAW ENFORCEMENT & POLICY RESPONSES

Challenges in Cybercrime Enforcement

The evolutionary nature of technology renders the work of law enforcement officials extremely difficult. It is an asymmetric game of constant catch-up, with new surprises and challenges at every turn. Increasingly, however, law enforcement has been gaining traction and the tools and knowledge to deal with their wily adversaries. A crucial point, which should be underscored, is the fact that cybercriminality should not be seen as something unfamiliar, exclusive, and divorced from the everyday world of law enforcement and criminal investigation. The well-honed skills and professionalism of real world investigations will stand officers in good stead when dealing with cybercriminality.

A second point emphasized in the literature is the fact that cybercrimes are frequently part of the normal investigation process. There has been some discussion suggesting that rather than developing specialized cyber units within departments, the ideal would be to have officers who specialize within each department, rather than establishing a dedicated service. In other words, digital tools may be just that—instruments used in the furtherance of criminal activities.

Law Enforcement and the Digital Realm: Capabilities in Combatting Digital Crime

The media tends to favor spectacular and problematic headlines rather than positive news. This is encapsulated in the axiom "If it bleeds it leads." Despite the number of gloomy reports there have been successes. These successes have merely been overshadowed by a focus of the negative. The FBI's Recovery Asset Team (RAT) has made outstanding progress coupled with increasing success rates. In 2023 this unit initiated a new tactic known as a Financial Fraud Kill Chain (FFKC). This was applied to 3,008 incidents with a total estimated loss value of $758.05 million. A monetary freeze was imposed on a total of $538.39 million which represents an impressive success rate of approximately 71% (Federal Bureau of Investigation, 2004, P.3).

AI Integration and Technological Tools for Law Enforcement Investigations

AI tools hold out promise for law enforcement at multiple levels, though blind adoption would create unforeseen risks. It is, therefore, essential that the adoption of AI-related law enforcement technology be impartial to built-in bias and robust to defend against intrusion, manipulation, and malicious use. There exist important areas where AI could potentially play a role in enhancing enforcement efforts, notably in financial investigations and AML/CTF operations (Kunju,2023). AI-however should be a tool, like any other, meant to facilitate investigative processes, and not become and end in itself.

Another critical area of concern for law enforcement includes exploring way for dealing with Jurisdictional Gaps. Cross-border transactions and the borderless nature of digital transactions hinder investigations, create unnecessary obstacles for law enforcement intervention, and delay the effective prosecution of cyberfraud. Technological limitations are another area of obvious concern for law enforcement, reduced funding has negatively impacted the ability of agencies and invest in the necessary technology and to update outmoded systems that are no longer secure or effective. Consequently, law enforcement is unable to respond as effectively as it could. The only solution is the provision of adequate funding and technology to stem the decline. Due to this combined lack of both technical expertise and equipment, law enforcement struggles to match comparative cybercriminal sophistication.

Nation-State Advanced Persistent Threat (APT)

APT groups are state-sponsored or state-tolerated cyber units engaged in espionage, sabotage, financial crime, and cyber warfare. There are many active APT groups, however reporting is often highly selective and exhibits a clear Western industrialized state-led bias. States suspected of aiding and abetting such activities, in no specific order, include, China, The United States, Russia, Israel, India, Iran, Pakistan, and many others. While some are specifically oriented towards infiltration, espionage, and the collection of data, others, such as those emanating from sanctioned states, are far more diversified in their operational assignments and mission tasks. They conduct D3 operations often with the support of their host state.

A Nation-State Advanced Persistent Threat (APT) refers to a highly sophisticated and prolonged cyberattack led and conducted a nation-state or state-sponsored group. The goal of these attacks is typically characterized by four features. Firstly, espionage, sabotage, or economic gain, and their distinctive operational strategies combined with the long term aspect of their operations. Secondly, the sophistication of the tools being employed—such attacks often employ highly innovative technologies, zero-day exploits, and custom designed, high-performance malware— usually beyond the reach of everyday cybercriminals. Third, these groups operate within an extremely specific parameters with targets being politically, economically, or militarily motivated. And finally, the aspect of stealth in their attacks and their detection avoidance efforts are unique features which characterize these APTs.

Lazarus Group

A sophisticated North Korean-backed cybercrime syndicate. Lazarus has become a major cyber nemesis for most nations beyond the confines of the Hermit Kingdom. Active since at least 2009, the group, know the moniker of Lazarus, and alternatively "hidden Cobra" (United States Department of Homeland Security), and "Guardians of Peace" (in the context of its attack on Sony Pictures in 2014). is affiliated with North Korea's Reconnaissance General Bureau (RGB)—its main intelligence agency. The group is known as a state sponsored Advanced Persistent Threat (APT). The group is responsible for multiple acts including responsible for cyber espionage, financial theft, and disruptive cyber operations. Thus, they fall well within the D3 strategic classification of damage, disrupt, and destroy. More recently, the Lazarus Group has also been referred to as "TraderTraitor" in some CISA (Cybersecurity & Infrastructure Security Agency) advisories, specifically in their AA22-108A alert (Cybersecurity & Infrastructure Security Agency [CISA], 2022.

Unlike other APT groups, which focus most often on espionage related activities, Lazarus group conducts multifaceted operations, which include an important financial component. This includes both the theft and laundering of the illicit proceeds. Lazurus targets cryptocurrency exchanges, financial institutions, public sector institutions, such as hospitals, DeFi platforms, and wallets. They use BEC, fake job offers, and ransomware to target and infiltrate blockchain connected organizations.

The underlying mission goals of this group appear to be threefold. First, to assist the North Korean regime circumvent sanctions, secondly, to gather intelligence, and finally the destabilization of adversarial financial systems. The persistent, evolving tactics, of this state sponsored APT group, make them a significant threat to global cybersecurity. It is important to note that despite Lazarus group's being physically beyond the jurisdictional boundaries and control of law enforcement and regulators, this does not automatically infer total impunity. An indirect approach can and has been used by enforcement agencies to stem the effectiveness of the group. Thus, the takedown, seizure, and sanctioning of various exchanges, like Tornado Cash, a virtual currency mixer on the Ethereum blockchain, has a direct impact by reducing the number of available outlets for the group to launder their proceeds. Additionally, once effective measures are taken by law enforcement and regulators, other exchanges will be less inclined to follow the same path as an indirect consequence of these deterrence measures (U.S. Department of the Treasury, 2022).

While Lazarus group was chosen as the focus of this particular case study, they are by no means the only group active. Like Lazarus other North Korean APT groups and North Korea's cyber units operate under Bureau 121 of the Reconnaissance General Bureau (RGB). Their cyber activities focus on financial theft, cryptocurrency heists, cyber espionage, and destructive malware.

Efforts to combat attacks by these state-sponsored groups have met with limited success. Part of the failure is due to the ubiquitous obstacles linked to combatting other types of cybercriminality. These include the levels of sophistication exercised by the actors, the jurisdictional limitations for intervention, and efforts on the part of these groups to eliminate any trace of their activities. Greater international interoperability by law enforcement and the intelligence community are required if any measure of success is hoped to be achieved.

Table 4. Nation-state APT characteristics

NATION-STATE APTs	
APT Characteristic	**Lazarus Group's Activity**
State Sponsorship	Backed by the North Korean government, operating under the RGB.
Persistent Operations	Long-term cyber campaigns spanning years, with evolving tactics.
Advanced Capabilities	Uses zero-day exploits, spear-phishing, supply chain attacks, and malware.
Financial & Espionage Motives	Engages in financial theft (crypto heists, bank fraud) and espionage (defense, government hacking).
Stealth & Evasion	Employs custom malware, obfuscation techniques, and false-flag tactics to evade detection.

Table 5. Lazarus group major operations

LAZARUS GROUP CYBER OPERATIONS	
Attack	**Target & Impact**
2009 South Korean Cyber Attacks	Coordinated **DDoS attacks** on government and media websites.
2014 Sony Pictures Hack	Retaliation for *The Interview* movie, involving **data leaks, wiper malware, and threats**.
2016 Bangladesh Bank Heist	Stole **$81 million via SWIFT fraud**, one of the largest cyber bank robberies.
2017 WannaCry Ransomware	**Global ransomware attack**, affecting **hospitals, companies, and infrastructure**.
2020-2024 Cryptocurrency Heists	Lazarus has stolen **over $1 billion in cryptocurrency**, funding North Korea's nuclear capabilities and missile programs.

Balancing Individual Rights and Collective Responsibility

The ethical and legal dimensions of protecting privacy, while attempting to ensure security, are a difficult balance to strike. While one of the primary functions of government is to provide for the safety and security of the public, it cannot do so at the cost of individual rights and freedoms. Striking a balance requires policies that promote collective responsibility while simultaneously safeguarding personal freedoms—a delicate equilibrium that demands continuous assessment and adaptation.

Policy recommendations should emphasize the advancement of transparent governance; the adoption of balanced regulations, and accountability measures to guarantee that government regulation and intervention do not compromise individual freedom. By building public trust through ethical oversight, digital rights management (DRM), and robust legal safeguards, it is possible to achieve a secure and sustainably secure digital environment.

One of these policy initiatives that must be emphasized is far stronger collaboration between the private and public sectors. A clear example of the failure of such partnerships was witnessed with the NSA development of the EternalBlue Exploit. Leaked by the hacker group Shadow Brokers, in 2017, the exploit was weaponized in the malicious WannaCry and Non-Petya ransomware attacks. which targeted both public and private frameworks and systems. The losses related to this attack were estimated at $10 billion. The NSA could well have shared the exploit with Microsoft, but failure to do so, in a timely manner, resulted in creating massive vulnerabilities for millions of systems.

One way of circumventing such failures can be achieved by the adoption of more transparent frameworks such as the Vulnerability Equities Process (VEP). Such frameworks can strike a balance between issue related to national security through the effective and timely sharing of vulnerabilities with software producers. Other policy recommendations in this chapter proposed include promotion and enforcement of patch management practices by regulatory bodies. This is particularly important in sectors related to national safety and security such as finance, defense, healthcare, and energy. International cooperation has been emphasized as a keystone to cybersecurity throughout this chapter and requires no further expansion. Regulating the development and use of cyber weapons, their responsible use, containment, and retirement, should also be a focus of policy development. Counterresponses to the continued persistent threats should also figure as a part of policy implications. This includes improving and refining attribution and effective response strategies. For far too long, rogue regimes have been allowed to operate with relative impunity due to a lack of intelligence and attribution. The persistent problem of limited public awareness, and education should also figure centrally in creative policy development and implementation. Finally, in this non-exhaustive list of policy recommendation, it would be remiss not to underscore the necessity of cyber insurance and effective risk management. All too often responses have been weak and reactive. This only serves to encourage further attacks and exploitation by malicious actors and state sponsored cybercriminals.

Same Page, Same Direction: Effective International Collaboration

The digital ecosphere is based on a global platform and, therefore, requires global approaches and global harmonization. Interorganizational collaboration is not a given, by any means. There are always unforeseen challenges to developing institutional and organizational collaboration. There are the goals of the international order, which must be counterbalanced by respect for the concerns of state sovereignty. Given the global nature of cybercrime and cyberterrorism, these difficulties are compounded. Implementing some sort of international legal frameworks that protect users while preventing abuse is, therefore, inherently fraught with challenges. Compromises will be required.

One of the core elements required for effective global cooperation includes collaborative approaches and finding a common ground from which to move forward. This must occur at multiple levels including executive, judicial, and legislative branches of government. A difficult feat by any measure. One way of establishing a road forward is through enhancing global cooperation through effective partnerships, and bilateral and multilateral agreements. Differences in legal frameworks, regulatory priorities, and jurisdictional limitations create obstacles to effective interoperability and enforcement. Enhancing cross-border collaboration in financial crime investigation and mitigation is essential in the combat against cybercriminality, yet challenges and obstacles continue to hamper success in this direction. The effective implementation of shared intelligence frameworks, and cross-border enforcement agreements, are fundamental to increasing the effectiveness of counter-cybercriminality efforts.

One of the cornerstones to creating a digital ecosystem that creates a safe and welcoming environment for the global population will inevitably require regulatory evolution Regulatory measures could be the topic of an entire volume in their own right; therefore, this chapter will only discuss them briefly. Strengthening compliance and oversight frameworks without hampering access and individual freedoms would be the utopian goal. While much progress has been made, for instance the U.S. AML Act of 1970, and more recently, the EU Sixth Anti-Money-laundering Directive (6AMLI), these initiatives are new, and their effectiveness remains to be seen. In certain case s new regulations are having the desired impact on middlemen such as third party currency exchanges, by impacting money laundering operations, but conversely have proven less effective in curtailing criminal use of cryptocurrency (Leuprecht, Jenkins, & Hamilton, 2023, p. 1036).

It is useful to note in passing that Global regulatory bodies do exist, though they may not be widely known. There is, quite obviously, the United Nations, and its Convention against Transnational Organized Crime and the Protocols Thereto, of 15 November 2000; other global bodies include the Organization for Economic Cooperation and Development (OECD) regulatory body, the Financial Action Task Force (FATF), and the Basel Committee on Banking Supervision (BCBS) (Gonzales, 2023).

While certainly laudable, the level of cooperation and success of these various ventures have produced mixed results. Their record of effectiveness in dealing with cybercrime, financial crime, and cybersecurity threats has not achieved the desired goals This being said, some measure of success has been achieved in areas regarding information sharing, financial regulations, and normative cyber ethics. These successes, however, have often been overshadowed and hampered by the traditional obstacles of gaps in enforcement, dealing with jurisdictional conflicts, and geopolitical tensions, Thus the full potential and impact are rarely achieved.

Areas which stand out as a future challenge to regulatory bodies include the operational aspects and oversight of decentralized exchanges and other technical features of DeFi finance. An inherent feature of the DeFi platform is the lack of a third party intermediary. This factor combined with the pseudonymous nature of Defi's client base, creates enormous, though not insurmountable, challenges for regulatory bodies (Benson, Turksen, & Adamyk, 202, p. 86; Leuprecht, Jenkins, & Hamilton., 2023, p.1037).Other significant areas of regulatory concern include algorithmic trading, market manipulation, and cross-chain bridging .

Corporate responsibility must play a role in enhancing cybersecurity. As mentioned throughout this chapter, corporate manufacturers and developers need to step up and take responsibility for introducing enhanced security in their design and production. Security-by-design must be an imperative—one on an equal footing with the zeitgeist of market concerns and the never-ending demand for innovation.

In the same vein, when considering the role of financial institutions, they too have a key role to play. Financial institutions should be held accountable for enforcing due diligence related to *suspicious activity reports* and *know your customer* obligations (SAR and KYC). Enhanced due diligence (EDD) measures, real-time transaction monitoring, and AI-driven risk assessment tools can also significantly reduce vulnerabilities within the financial sector. The use of technology-driven compliance solutions is one way in which financial institutions can better adapt to regulatory requirements. Regulatory measures are important tools in combatting cybercriminality and AML/CTF money laundering, but if they are ignored, not followed correctly, or properly adhered to, they will have negligible effect. Relatedly, such regulations must also be concise, accessible, and easily understood by those bound by such regulations. Long and tedious documentation, couched in legalese, which obfuscates the underlying principles and guidelines will not increase effectiveness nor ensure effective compliance.

CONCLUSION: STRENGTHENING DIGITAL SECURITY & FINANCIAL CRIME PREVENTION

This chapter has covered various aspects of the Janus paradox as it relates to crypto criminality, and digital fraud. Cryptocrime and digital fraud are extraordinarily complex areas of financial forensic investigation and there are a number of topics and tactics that could not be explored due to constraints of time and space. Topics such as high-yield investment programs, (HYIP) and their related scams, Homunculus computers as backdoor technology, Forex and securities fraud, and the manipulations of flash loans are a few of the topics that remain to be explored (Trozze et al., 2022, p.8). The topics presented, however, should furnish the reader with a solid understanding and provide insights into the dual nature of the digital ecosphere and its role in the development and evolution of digital FinCrime. This conclusion represents a recap of key threats, challenges, and policy recommendations. In an unequal and asymmetric technological battle for profit and security, governments around the world are scrambling to respond to the rapid rise and evolution of criminal and terrorist threats that increasingly take advantage of the digital ecosystem. It is, therefore, imperative that an international approach be adopted to combat an international challenge. The major obstacle faced by such an audacious program is one of consensus. Consensus has been humanity's stumbling block since the discovery of fire.

The current research represents a call for collaborative action by governments, corporations, and individuals. Cybercrime and FinCrime pose systemic threats to economic stability. Urgent actions include stronger regulatory action that focuses on both punishment and deterrence; effective and meaningful cooperation and sharing of intelligence, investment in training and technology for law enforcement, sharing the widespread public awareness and education through cyber literacy, and responsible and ethical system development which makes security-by-design a priority rather than an afterthought.

Education and Collaboration as Tools of Crime Prevention

Public education and enhanced private public partnerships are valuable tools in the fight against cybercrime and provide awareness and prevention. The importance of cyber literacy and public awareness in crime prevention should not be underestimated. The lack of education and awareness has been a contributing factor to the proliferation of digital fraud.

Cyber Literacy and Public Awareness

Educating users on the proper navigation of system complexities, and digital security are paramount to a safe and effective digital ecosystem. Users of DeFi systems are often uninitiated and thus, a number of otherwise avoidable errors are committed, consequently allowing users and systems to become vulnerable targets for malicious actors. Given the fact that governments and society will increasingly be reliant upon digital technology as a fundamental part of daily life, it only stands to reason that training programs should be part of a solid public education from the earliest years. Other policy recommendations in this regard include facilitating criminal reporting mechanisms and the development of well-structured and mediatized fraud awareness campaigns which would both make a significant contribution to raising public awareness and security.

This is precisely what the Janus Paradox embodies—a world of stark contrasts, perpetually in tension, where total equilibrium remains unattainable.

REFERENCES

Agence France-Presse. (2024, February 5). Multinational loses HK$200 million to deepfake video conference scam, Hong Kong police say. Hong Kong Free Press. https://hongkongfp.com/2024/02/05/multinational-loses-hk200-million-to-deepfake-video-conference-scam-hong-kong-police-say/

Akhgar, B., Staniforth, A., & Bosco, F. (Eds.). (2014). *Cyber Crime and Cyber Terrorism: Investigators Handbook*. Elsevier.

Alpert, L. I. (2024). *How financial 'sextortion' scams became an epidemic on social media — with tragic consequences.* [online] MarketWatch. Available at: https://www.marketwatch.com/story/how-financial-sextortion-scams-became-an-epidemic-on-social-media-with-tragic-consequences-a52a8505?utm_source=chatgpt.com [Accessed 6 Feb. 2025].

Andreeva, J., & Abrams, A. (2024, December 5). *Top 9 identity verification trends in 2025*. Sumsub. https://sumsub.com/blog/top-9-identity-verification-trends-in-2025/

Arewa, A. (2019). Corruption, money laundering and Nigeria's crisis of development. *Journal of Financial Crime*, *26*(4), 1133–1145. DOI: 10.1108/JFC-08-2018-0082

Benson, V., Turksen, U., & Adamyk, B. (2024). Dark side of decentralised finance: A call for enhanced AML regulation based on use cases of illicit activities. *Journal of Financial Regulation and Compliance*, *32*(1), 80–97. DOI: 10.1108/JFRC-04-2023-0065

Bick, J. D. (2022). *NFTs, Cryptocurrencies and Crypto Assets Explained.* [online] Brach Eichler | Counsellors at Law. Available at: https://www.bracheichler.com/insights/nfts-cryptocurrencies-and-crypto-assets-explained/?utm_source=chatgpt.com [Accessed 19 Feb. 2025].

Bratcher, B. (2025, February 25). *Crypto's grown-up response to North Korea's historic $1.4B robbery*. Forbes. https://www.forbes.com/sites/beccabratcher/2025/02/25/cryptos-grown-up-response-to-north-koreas-historic-14b-robbery/

Buterin, V. (2014). *A next-generation smart contract and decentralized application platform.* Ethereum White Paper. https://ethereum.org/whitepaper

Carlisle, D. (2023). *The crypto launderers: Crime and cryptocurrencies from the dark web to DeFi and beyond*. John Wiley & Sons.

Chainalysis. (2025). *The 2025 crypto crime report.* Chainalysis. https://www.chainalysis.com/wp-content/uploads/2025/02/the-2025-crypto-crime-report-release.pdf

Chainalysis Team. (2024). *$2.2 billion stolen in crypto in 2024 but hacked volumes stagnate*. Chainalysis. https://www.chainalysis.com/blog/crypto-hacking-stolen-funds-2025/

Cointelegraph. (2025, February 20). *Samourai Wallet shutdown: Implications for other privacy & self-custody tools*. Cointelegraph. https://cointelegraph.com/news/samourai-wallet-shutdown-implications-for-other-privacy-self-custody-tools

CyberArk. (2024). *2024 Identity Security Threat Landscape Report.* CyberArk. https://www.cyberark.com/resources/ebooks/identity-security-threat-landscape-2024-report

CyberScoop. (2024, February 23). *Tornado Cash sanctions overturned: Lazarus Group implications.* CyberScoop. Retrieved February 24, 2025, from https://cyberscoop.com/tornado-cash-sanctions-overturned-lazarus-group/

Cybersecurity & Infrastructure Security Agency. (2022, May 10). *AA22-108A: North Korean cyber actor known as TraderTraitor targets critical infrastructure organizations.* U.S. Department of Homeland Security. https://www.cisa.gov/news-events/cybersecurity-advisories/aa22-108a

Damiani, J. (2019, September 3). *A voice deepfake was used to scam a CEO out of $243,000.* Forbes. https://www.forbes.com/sites/jessedamiani/2019/09/03/a-voice-deepfake-was-used-to-scam-a-ceo-out-of-243000/

de Best, R. (2025). *Number of crypto coins 2013-2021.* [online] Statista. Available at: https://www.statista.com/statistics/863917/number-crypto-coins-tokens/ [Accessed 19 Feb. 2025].

Eromo Egbejule. (2024). *How west Africa's online fraudsters moved into sextortion.* [online] the Guardian. Available at: https://www.theguardian.com/uk-news/article/2024/aug/21/how-west-africas-online-fraudsters-moved-into-sextortion?utm_source=chatgpt.com [Accessed 6 Feb. 2025].

Europol. (2024). *Internet Organised Crime Threat Assessment (IOCTA) 2024.* Europol. https://www.europol.europa.eu/publication-events/main-reports/internet-organised-crime-threat-assessment-iocta-2024

Federal Bureau of Investigation. (2023, August 11). *Increase in companies falsely claiming an ability to recover funds lost in cryptocurrency investment scams.* Internet Crime Complaint Center. https://www.ic3.gov/PSA/2023/PSA230811

Federal Bureau of Investigation. (2024). *2023 Internet crime report*. Internet Crime Complaint Center. https://www.ic3.gov/annualreport/reports/2023_ic3report.pdf

Financial Conduct Authority. (n.d.). *Glossary definition: Financial crime*. FCA Handbook. Retrieved January 29, 2025, from https://www.handbook.fca.org.uk/handbook/glossary/G416.html

Flanagan, J. (2024). *Hundreds Arrested over Nigerian crypto-romance Scams*. [online] Thetimes.com. Available at: https://www.thetimes.com/world/africa/article/hundreds-arrested-over-nigerian-crypto-romance-scams-mnx230csk?utm_source=chatgpt.com®ion=global [Accessed 6 Feb. 2025].

Foley, S., Karlsen, J. R., & Putniņš, T. J. (2019). Sex, drugs, and bitcoin: How much illegal activity is financed through cryptocurrencies? *Review of Financial Studies*, *32*(5), 1798–1853. DOI: 10.1093/rfs/hhz015

Furneaux, N. (2025). *There's no such thing as crypto crime: An investigative handbook*. John Wiley & Sons.

Ghernaouti, S. (2023). *Cybercriminalité: Comprendre. Prévenir. Réagir*. Dunod.

Greenberg, A. (2024). *Lords of Crypto Crime: The race to bring down the world's invisible kingpins*. Monoray.

Haffke, L., Fromberger, M., & Zimmermann, P. (2020). Cryptocurrencies and anti-money laundering: The shortcomings of the fifth AML Directive (EU) and how to address them. *Journal of Banking Regulation*, *21*(2), 125–138. DOI: 10.1057/s41261-019-00101-4

Haque, A. (2024). *Why so many scams originate in Nigeria*. [online] tbsnews.net. Available at: https://www.tbsnews.net/features/panorama/why-so-many-scams-originate-nigeria-882326 [Accessed 18 Feb. 2025].

Hayes, A. (2014). *Blockchain Facts: What Is It, How It Works, and How It Can Be Used*. [online] Investopedia. Available at: https://www.investopedia.com/terms/b/blockchain.asp?utm_source=chatgpt.com [Accessed 19 Feb. 2025].

iProov. (2025). *2025 threat intelligence report: Remote identity attack*. iProov. Retrieved March 2, 2025, from https://www.iproov.com/reports/threat-intelligence-report-2025-remote-identity-attack

Kelly, L. (2025, February 10). *Over half of illicit crypto activity in 2024 was on Tron: TRM Labs*. DL News. https://www.dlnews.com/articles/regulation/half-of-illicit-crypto-activity-in-2024-was-on-tron-trm-labs/

Kocher, P., Horn, J., Fogh, A., Genkin, D., Gruss, D., Haas, W., Hamburg, M., Lipp, M., Mangard, S., Prescher, T., Schwarz, M., & Yarom, Y. (2019). *Spectre attacks: Exploiting speculative execution*. Retrieved February 5, 2025, from https://spectreattack.com/spectre.pdf

Kunju, P. (2023). *Artificial intelligence (AI) in criminal justice: A primer*. Independently published.

Labs, T. R. M. (2023, February 7). *Pig butchering scams: What the data shows*. https://www.trmlabs.com/post/pig-butchering-scams-what-the-data-shows

Laffan, K. (2023, June 9). *A brief history of ransomware*. Varonis. https://www.varonis.com/blog/a-brief-history-of-ransomware

Legislation.gov.uk. (2000). *Financial Services and Markets Act 2000, Section 1H: Definition offinancial crime*. https://www.legislation.gov.uk/ukpga/2000/8/section/1H

Leuprecht, C., Jenkins, C., & Hamilton, R. (2023). Virtual money laundering: Policy implications of the proliferation in the illicit use of cryptocurrency. *Journal of Financial Crime*, *30*(4), 1036–1054. DOI: 10.1108/JFC-07-2022-0161

Lipp, M., Schwarz, M., Gruss, D., Prescher, T., Haas, W., Mangard, S., Kocher, P., Genkin, D., Yarom, Y., & Hamburg, M. (2018). *Meltdown: Reading kernel memory from user space*. Retrieved February 5, 2025, from https://meltdownattack.com/meltdown.pdf

Lseg.com. (2025). *2025 fraud and payments forecast: Key trends and emerging threats in the global landscape*. [online] Available at: https://www.lseg.com/en/insights/risk-intelligence/2025-fraud-and-payments-forecast-key-trends-and-emerging-threats-in-the-global-landscape [Accessed 31 Jan. 2025].

Lyman, M. D., & Potter, G. W. (2018). *Organized crime* (7th ed.). Pearson Education.

Mittal, A. (2021). *Decentralized Finance Development- All You Need to Know About It*. [online] SAG IPL - A Technology Blog. Available at: https://blog.sagipl.com/decentralized-finance-development/ [Accessed 10 Feb. 2025].

NeosLegal. (2024, November 27). *Win for DeFi – Tornado Cash sanctions were illegal*. Retrieved February 24, 2025, from https://neoslegal.co/win-for-defi-tornado-cash-sanctions-were-illegal/

O'Sullivan, D. (2021, May 16). *A Harvard-trained biologist became the first person to use ransomware almost 30 years ago*. CNN. https://edition.cnn.com/2021/05/16/tech/ransomware-joseph-popp/index.html

Saferstein, R. (2004). *Criminalistics: An introduction to forensic science* (8th ed.). Pearson Prentice Hall.

Sherrod, J., Cory, K., & Caron, J. (2023, August 7). *Nigerian nationals extradited to U.S. for alleged role in sextortion ring, victim's mother speaks out.* FOX 17. Retrieved March 2, 2025, from https://www.fox17online.com/news/local-news/nigerian-nationals-extradited-to-u-s-for-alleged-role-in-sextortion-ring-victims-mother-speaks-out

Steptoe & Johnson LLP. (2024, February 23). *In significant win for digital asset industry, the Fifth Circuit invalidates sanctions on Tornado Cash.* Steptoe & Johnson LLP. Retrieved February 24, 2025, from https://www.steptoe.com/en/news-publications/international-compliance-blog/in-significant-win-for-digital-asset-industry-the-fifth-circuit-invalidates-sanctions-on-tornado-cash.html

Toulas, B. (2025). *New Apple CPU side-channel attacks steal data from browsers.* [online] BleepingComputer. Available at: https://www.bleepingcomputer.com/news/security/new-apple-cpu-side-channel-attack-steals-data-from-browsers/ [Accessed 5 Feb. 2025].

Trozze, A., Kamps, J., Akartuna, E. A., Hetzel, F. J., Kleinberg, B., Davies, T., & Johnson, S. D. (2022). Cryptocurrencies and future financial crime. *Crime Science, 11*(1), 1. Advance online publication. DOI: 10.1186/s40163-021-00163-8 PMID: 35013699

Unit21. (n.d.-b). Tornado Cash: How it works & applicable sanctions. Unit21. Retrieved February 24, 2025, from https://www.unit21.ai/fraud-aml-dictionary/tornado-cash

Unit21.ai. (n.d.-a). Definition of financial crime and categories of financial crime. Retrieved January 29, 2025, from https://www.unit21.ai/fincrime-definition

United States Attorney's Office. Southern District of New York. (2024, April 24). Founders and CEO of cryptocurrency mixing service arrested and charged with money laundering and unlicensed money transmitting offenses. U.S. Department of Justice. Retrieved from https://www.justice.gov/usao-sdny/pr/founders-and-ceo-cryptocurrency-mixing-service-arrested-and-charged-money-laundering

United States Attorney's Office. Western District of Michigan. (2024, September 5). Ogoshi brothers sentenced to lengthy prison terms in sextortion scheme that resulted in death of teen. United States Department of Justice. Retrieved March 2, 2025, from https://www.justice.gov/usao-wdmi/pr/2024_0905_Ogoshi_Brothers_Sentenced

United States Code. 18 U.S.C. § 1341 (2025). Retrieved from https://www.law.cornell.edu/uscode/text/18/1341

United States Code. 18 U.S.C. § 1956 (2025). Retrieved from https://www.law.cornell.edu/uscode/text/18/1956

United States Department of the Treasury. (2022, August 8). U.S. Treasury sanctions notorious virtual currency mixer Tornado Cash. U.S. Department of the Treasury. Retrieved February 24, 2025, from https://home.treasury.gov/news/press-releases/jy0916

United States Securities and Exchange Commission. (n.d.). Ponzi scheme. Investor.gov. Retrieved March 2, 2025, from https://www.investor.gov/protect-your-investments/fraud/types-fraud/ponzi-scheme

Verizon (2024a). 2024 Data Breach Investigations Report. [online] Verizon Business. Retrieved February 5, 2025, from: https://www.verizon.com/business/resources/reports/dbir

Verizon. (2024b). *2024 DBIR SMB infographic.* Verizon Business. Retrieved February 5, 2025, from https://www.verizon.com/business/resources/infographics/2024-dbir-smb-infographic.pdf

Voice of America. (2024, February 5). *Deepfake scam video cost company $26 million, Hong Kong police say.* https://www.voanews.com/a/deepfake-scam-video-cost-company-26million-hong-kong-police-says/7470542.html

Wang, H.-M., & Hsieh, M.-L. (2024). Cryptocurrency is new vogue: A reflection on money laundering prevention. *Security Journal, 37*(1), 25–46. DOI: 10.1057/s41284-023-00366-5

Wronka, C. (2022). Money laundering through cryptocurrencies - analysis of the phenomenon and appropriate prevention measures. *Journal of Money Laundering Control, 25*(1), 79–94. DOI: 10.1108/JMLC-02-2021-0017

ADDITIONAL READING

Beigelman, M. T. (2009). *Identity Theft Handbook: detection, prevention, and security.* Wiley.

Foley, S., Karlsen, J. R., & Putniņš, T. J. (2019). Sex, drugs, and bitcoin: How much illegal activity is financed through cryptocurrencies? *Review of Financial Studies, 32*(5), 1798–1853. DOI: 10.1093/rfs/hhz015

Ghernaouti, S. (2023). *Cybercriminalité: Comprendre. Prévenir. Réagir*. Dunod.

Greenberg, A. (2024). *Lords of Crypto Crime: The race to bring down the world's invisible kingpins*. Monoray.

Lascar, O. (2024). *Deepfake: L'IA au service de faux*. Éditions Eyrolles.

KEY TERMS AND DEFINITIONS

Alt Coin: In its most basic form is a term applied to any crypto currency other than Bitcoin.

Anonymity Enhanced Currencies (AECs): More commonly referred to as "privacy coins" the AECs are cryptocurrency with enhanced security features. Often the bane of law enforcement efforts.

Attack Vector: The cybersecurity term. Attack vector represents any protocol, scenario, or approach that allows digital system intrusion by a malicious actor. The context is derived from its biological counterpart .Malware and phishing are two examples of attack vectors.

Business Email Compromise (BEC): As the name aptly infers these are email generated attempts to extort funds, or sensitive data, from corporation. Terre exist several different typologies, these are presented in a separate section within the current chapter.

Clearnet: Also referred to as the surface net, this is the standard internet referenced by most users.

Clusters: Groups of interconnected blockchain nodes or addresses. A wallet cluster is a set of digital address or wallets connected to a single account or entity.

Decentralized exchanges (DEXs): for the purpose of simplicity, a DEX can be described as a pseudonymous, peer-to-peer platform without the intervention of a third party, where transactions may be conducted.

Decentralized Finance (DeFi): A peer-to-peer (P2P) agreement based upon smart contracts, eliminating the need for third parties, such as banks and exchanges. DeFi anonymizes both users and transactions. Examples, SushiSwap, and Uniswap. DeFi is frequently, but not exclusively, conducted on decentralized exchanges.

Distributed Ledger Technology (DLT): A transparent system which immutably records asset transactions, fiscal or otherwise on a connected chain of multiple nodes.

Digital Paradise: States where cybercriminals are either tolerated or sponsored and who operate in an environment where there is limited or no active enforcement or application of sanctions.

Exploits: An exploit in the context of cyber-crime is a tool, a piece of software, which allows malicious actor, such as a hacker, to profit from a vulnerability in software, hardware, system, or a network to gain unauthorized access, to execute malicious code, or to elevate privileges through such intrusion often with the goal of data theft, or alternatively to damage, destroy or disrupt normal operations.

Fiduciary Monies: This refers to a payer-payee exchange of financial assets, based on a mutual trust relationship between the parties. Examples include checks from banks or the government.

Financial Fraud Kill Chain (FFKC): This is a public private partnership imitative and tool that was develop by the U.S. Treasury Department to aid both financial institutions and law enforcement disrupt fraudulent wire transfers. This is particularly useful in the context of BEC, as discussed in this chapter. Use of this framework assists in the recovery of misappropriate funds.

FinCrime: Refers to financial crime. This may represent either the traditional forms of financial crime, or more recent digital financial crime. Both fall under the heading of white-collar crime.

High Frequency Trading (HFT): A type of trading that uses powerful, computer-generated algorithms in trading. It is used in rapid, high volume order-to-trade transaction. Cybercriminals exploit trading algorithms, insider information, and digital exchanges to distort financial markets. Automated trading bots conduct rapid buy-sell cycles to manipulate stock and crypto prices in milliseconds.

Homunculus Computer: A computer within a computer. It is one of the most advanced protocols in current Cybercriminality. It is a self-operating AI-driven system capable of initiating and conducting financial fraud and money laundering operations without human intervention.

I2P (Invisible Internet Project): An anonymous and decentralized framework with the goal of advancing online privacy. Much like the blockchain messages are encrypted and sent via a series of volunteer nodes.

Mempool: An abbreviated from for memory pool. In cryptocurrency trading this term refers to the pending and as yet unconfirmed cryptocurrency transactions awaiting confirmation from a node on the blockchain.

Persistence Mechanisms: A ransomware protocol that allows malicious actors to maintain continuous connection to a system, even after having paid the extortionists.

Pretexting: A particularly pernicious form of social engineering where the attacker manipulates the victim through the adoption of a carefully scripted persona.

Security by Design: Security is built into systems, as a priority, from the outset, rather than as a mere after thought accompanied by endless patches.

Smart Contracts: First established on the Ethereum blockchain, smart contracts are protocols, or a series of computer code designed to execute, oversee, or record transactions, agreements, or events without any human intervention involved.

Sybil Attack: A tactic used in market manipulation, where a malicious actor or group of actors overwhelms a network, by creating multiple fake accounts or wallets, thus gaining control over the system. They then proceed, through repetitive trading, in creating the illusion of large transaction volumes and market legitimacy.

Unregulated Exchange (UEX): Operate outside normal systems. They are not controlled by any given institution and do not adhere to regulatory requirements.

Wash Trading: Like sybil attacks wash trading is another method of market manipulation where an individual repeatedly buys and sells the same asset to themselves to reflect market artificially created interest.

Zero-Day Exploits: Zero-day exploits are vulnerabilities or system software or hardware flaws, that manufacturers are unaware of, and which provide a cyber-attack vectors for malicious activity.

APPENDIX A. CRYPTOCURRENCY & MARKET MANIPULATION

Table 6.

Tools of Cryptocurrency & Market Manipulation		
Threat	**Description**	**Example**
Cryptocurrency Wash Trading	Unregulated exchanges that inflate trading volumes by engaging in fake buy-sell cycles, creating the illusion of market liquidity with the goal of attracting investors.	An exchange reporting inflated trade volumes to lure investors into a seemingly liquid market.
HFT Exploits	Automated trading bots conduct rapid buy-sell cycles to manipulate stock or cryptocurrency prices within milliseconds, avoiding detection by exploiting algorithmic complexity.	A trading bot manipulating crypto prices through thousands of rapid trades within seconds. (e.g., the Flash crash of May 6, 2010).
Front-Running Attacks	Algorithms detect large pending orders and place trades ahead of them to force favorable price changes, profiting at the expense of others.	A bot identifying and exploiting a large pending sell order to push the price down before executing a buy.
Spoofing and Layering	Placing large fake orders to create the illusion of supply or demand, manipulating prices before canceling the orders.	Placing large sell orders to drive prices down, buying at the lower price, and then canceling the sell orders.
Latency Arbitrage Exploits	Exploiting delays in price updates across exchanges by using ultra-fast networks to profit from price disparities in near real-time.	Making arbitrage trades between slower and faster exchanges to profit from delayed price synchronization.
DeFi and Flash Loan Manipulations	Using uncollateralized loans in decentralized finance (DeFi) to manipulate token prices within seconds, exploiting vulnerabilities in smart contract protocols.	Borrowing a flash loan to temporarily inflate the value of a token, selling for profit, and repaying instantly.
Smurfing	A chunking method whereby substantial amounts of illicit cash are broken down into multiple smaller transactions to avoid detection and regulatory measures	A criminal organization recruits "Smurfs" who make multiple bank deposits of $9,500 to avoid regulatory detection.

APPENDIX B. SOCIAL ENGINEERING THREATS

Table 7.

Social Engineering Threats		
Threat	**Description**	**Example**
Phishing	Fraudulent emails are designed to manipulate users into revealing personal information, often linked to imaginative and lucrative financial schemes. NLP is used to craft more convincing attacks.	Fake emails offer easy financial profits, rewards, or fake job opportunities.
Vishing	Fraudulent phone calls or messages where attackers impersonate officials (police, tax agents) to pressure victims into compliance.	Scammers posing as police demanding immediate payment. Of traffic fines
Spear-phishing	A specialized form of phishing that targets and seeks to compromise individuals or organizations.	An attacker impersonates a colleague to steal login credentials.
Pretexting	A social engineering technique based on psychological manipulation	A purported member of the IT staff calls demanding login credentials
Synthetic Media	Creating and using false digital identities. May take different forms such as visual or voice generated	An artificial video conference with the directors demands an urgent funds transfer
Catfishing	A deceptive romance scheme where attackers lure victims into sharing sensitive personal information.	A fake online romantic partner requesting sensitive data or money.
Pharming	Redirecting web traffic to fake sites designed to steal credentials or personal information.	A fake banking site that steals login credentials when users attempt to log in.
Sextortion	Luring victims into sharing intimate images or fabricated claims and then blackmailing them with the threat of releasing the content.	Victim is blackmailed after sharing intimate images with someone online.
Business Email Compromise (BEC)	Fraudulent emails aimed at stealing sensitive data or other assets from organizations.	An email sent to a company executive asking for a wire transfer to a fraudulent account.

APPENDIX C. MALWARE RELATED THREATS

Table 8.

Malware Related Threats		
Threat	**Description**	**Example**
Malware	Malicious software intended to **damage, disrupt, destroy (D3)**, or gain unauthorized access to systems.	Viruses, Trojans, spyware, etc., designed to infiltrate and damage systems.
Spyware	Invisible software that monitors user activity and gathers information without consent, often to steal data.	Keyloggers that track each keystroke on a device. Certain keyloggers also capture screens
Ransomware	Malware that encrypts data and demands a ransom for decryption.	Crypto ransomware (e.g., WannaCry, REvil, Maze, LockBit), ransomware locking a user's system.
Trojans	Malicious software disguised as legitimate programs or embedded attachments, used for system access, spying, or data theft.	Trojan horse hidden in email attachments.
Worms	Self-replicating programs that spread across systems without needing external program activation.	A worm that spreads across a network and infects multiple systems.
Viruses	Malicious code that infects and spreads through system files, is often triggered by a specific event or action.	A logic bomb virus that triggers on a specific date or event.
Adware	Malware that displays unwanted ads, redirects browsing, and collects user data.	Software that collects browsing data to target ads or sell to third parties.
Distributed Denial-of-Service (DDoS)	Attacks that flood servers with requests, causing system disruption or downtime.	Botnets used to overload and take down websites.
Buffer Overflows	Exploits where data exceeds storage capacity, allowing the execution of malicious code.	Code execution vulnerability in outdated software.
Backdoors	Covert mechanisms embedded within systems to bypass security measures and allow remote access.	Embedded backdoor for unauthorized remote control.
Deep-Fake Technology	Use of synthetic media, including images, videos, or audio, for fraudulent or criminal purposes.	Using a deepfake to impersonate a CEO and authorize a financial transaction.

APPENDIX D. MARKET MANIPULATION TACTICS

Table 9.

Market Manipulation Tactics

Strategy	Description	Tactical Differences	Application	Example Case
Rug Pull Scams	Developers **create a fraudulent crypto project** (often an NFT or token), attract investors, then suddenly withdraw funds and abandon the project.	Involve smart contracts; victims are locked out as liquidity is drained. Often involves social media hype.	Cryptocurrencies, DeFi, NFTs	*Squid Game Token Scam (2021)*
Exit Scams	Operators of an exchange, project, or service **disappear with users' funds** after gaining trust.	It can involve ICOs, Ponzi-like operations, or darknet markets shutting down abruptly.	Cryptocurrency exchanges, ICOs, darknet markets	*BitConnect (2018)*
Pump-and-Dump Schemes	Fraudsters **artificially inflate asset prices** using misleading promotions before selling off holdings, causing a crash.	Often coordinated via online groups (e.g., Discord, Telegram). May involve influencers (e.g., paid celebrities).	Low-market-cap cryptocurrencies, NFTs, meme stocks	*BitTorent Token Pump (2019)*
Front-Running Attacks	Malicious actors **use prior knowledge** of pending trades to **execute their own transactions** first, profiting from price shifts.	Often exploits smart contract vulnerabilities or high-frequency trading (HFT) latency issues.	DeFi platforms, smart contracts, DEX trading	*Ethereum MEV Bots*
High-Frequency Trading (HFT)	**Algorithmic trading** exploits millisecond market inefficiencies to gain an unfair advantage.	Involves high-speed servers, collocation, and order spoofing strategies.	Stock markets, cryptocurrency trading	*2010 Flash Crash*
Wash Trading	The same entity **repeatedly buys and sells an asset** to create false market activity, misleading investors.	It can be automated with bots to inflate volume artificially; often used to manipulate rankings on exchanges.	NFT marketplaces, cryptocurrency exchanges, traditional stock markets	*LooksRare NFT Wash Trading (2022)*

Chapter 3
Combating Misinformation and Global Nations' False Narratives Through Education:
Mitigating Cryptocurrency-Related Crime

Geberew Tulu Mekonnen
https://orcid.org/0000-0001-7672-3609
Charles Sturt University, Australia

Leo S. F. Lin
https://orcid.org/0000-0003-3684-5403
Charles Sturt University, Australia

Mladen Zecevic
https://orcid.org/0009-0002-1455-2992
Charles Sturt University, Australia

Duane Aslett
https://orcid.org/0000-0003-1540-7180
Charles Sturt University, Australia

Douglas M. C. Allan
https://orcid.org/0000-0003-0616-5546
Charles Sturt University, Australia

DOI: 10.4018/979-8-3373-0675-9.ch003

ABSTRACT

This systematic review explored cryptocurrency-related crime and the role of community education in mitigating these threats using PRISMA guidelines. The study synthesised evidence from 20 high-quality studies (2008–2025) obtained from databases including Scopus, Web of Science, IEEE Xplore, the Australian Institute of Criminology, and Google Scholar. The review revealed key cryptocurrency-enabled crimes, such as phishing, ransomware, identity theft, romance fraud, market manipulation, and gambling scams, that exploit the decentralised and anonymous nature of cryptocurrencies, resulting in financial losses worldwide. Increasing awareness and community education are fundamental in reducing exposure through methods such as targeted training, strong security practices (including two-factor and multi-factor authentication), source verification, and prompt reporting of suspicious activities. The review further indicated the necessity of building trust through risk management practices, technological expertise, and a regulatory framework to enhance community resilience.

INTRODUCTION

Emerging technologies have significantly transformed the financial landscape, bringing significant benefits to law enforcement and financial institutions, and communities (Allioui & Mourdi, 2023; Attaran & Gunasekaran, 2019). Studies indicated that digital platform based financial services have become more accessible, enabling individuals to perform transactions, access credit, and manage investments remotely (Aziz & Naima, 2021; Ozili, 2018; Pazarbasioglu et al., 2020). This change has improved transaction efficiency, enhanced fraud detection, marketing, and customer service, while enabling seamless cross-border transactions and new opportunities (Josyula, 2024).

However, the advancements of technology have also posed complex challenges to individuals and financial institutions (Rahman, 2024). For example, cryptocurrency-based and organised financial crime have grown more sophisticated, with criminals exploiting individuals on online platforms through cyberattacks, identity theft, and other illicit activities (Choo & Smith, 2008; Nicholls et al., 2021). Combating money laundering has become increasingly challenging as criminals capitalise on the anonymity of digital transactions to conceal the origins of illicit funds (Turner, 2011). Trozze et al. (2022) noted that the emergence of cryptocurrencies generated opportunities such as innovative and decentralised financial resolutions, while also raising significant concerns due to their association with illicit activities such as tax evasion and ransomware, as well as the challenges involved in tracing and regulating these digital assets.

Similarly, Lane and Adam (2022) highlighted that cryptocurrencies pose several risks to the Australian community and law enforcement agencies. According to the Australian Competition and Consumer Commission (2024), "More than half of the $70 million in losses were due to cryptocurrency, especially through Bitcoin, and cryptocurrency scams were the most commonly reported type of investment scam, with 2,240 reports". Scammers often falsely suggest to their victims that cryptocurrencies have highly profitable trading systems, either based on their personal expertise or proprietary algorithms. Many of these scams also use fake celebrity endorsements to appear more legitimate (Australian Competition and Consumer Commission, 2024; Lane & Adam, 2022; Lin et al., 2024b, 2024c). The pseudo-anonymous and borderless nature of cryptocurrencies empowers criminal activities, such as money laundering, organised financial crime, cybercrime, and terrorism financing, which can adversely affect Australia's economy (Australian Competition and Consumer Commission, 2024; Jabotinsky & Lavi, 2021). Rustamaji and Faisal (2024) noted that law enforcement agencies have reported a rise in organised crime using cryptocurrencies to facilitate cybercrime and launder money, posing significant challenges for crime prevention and investigation.

Despite the increasing adoption and integration of cryptocurrencies into various aspects of the global economy, there is little research on the associated criminal activities globally (Kfir, 2020; Nikkel, 2020; Wu et al., 2022). Traditional financial crime research has mostly concentrated on established systems and tools, such as fiat currencies and conventional banking infrastructure, leaving substantial gaps in the understanding of criminal activity within the decentralised and complex domain of cryptocurrencies (Kethineni & Cao, 2020; Nicholls et al., 2021; Trozze et al., 2022). The anonymity and unregulated nature of cryptocurrencies created unique challenges for law enforcement and regulatory bodies, demanding specialised expertise and technologies in order to detect, investigate, and combat associated crimes (Kethineni & Cao, 2020; Nicholls et al., 2021). Furthermore, the constant development of new protocols, platforms, and applications makes it difficult to trace criminals' latest trends and strategies. Kethineni and Cao (2019) and Wu et al. (2023) argued that academic research tends to lag behind real-world developments, resulting in a shortage of empirical data and careful analysis on the distinct features, trends, and implications of cryptocurrency-related crimes.

In addition, community education and awareness-raising are essential for navigating the complexities of cryptocurrency and unlocking its potential benefits (Christodoulou et al., 2024). Javaid et al. (2022) also argued that understanding the principles of cryptocurrencies and the risks associated with digital assets can prevent individual financial losses and enhance the confidence of financial institutions. Digital financial literacy is essential for maximising future potential benefits while addressing risks such as money laundering and fraud (Usman et al., 2025). A comprehensive understanding of these criminal activities is crucial for developing effective countermeasures, informing policy decisions, and safeguarding individuals and institutions from financial losses and reputational damage. Therefore, this research aims to explore the potential benefits and threats of cryptocurrencies and the crucial role of community education and awareness in navigating these aspects. The study addresses the following research questions:

1. What are the most common types of cryptocurrency-related crimes?
2. How can community education and awareness programs mitigate the risks of cryptocurrencies?
3. What strategies can be used for community education programs on cryptocurrencies?

SIGNIFICANCE OF THE STUDY

Empowering Communities: The study benefits the community and assists individuals in making informed decisions about cryptocurrencies. By enhancing digital financial literacy, the Australian community can better navigate the potential and actual threats posed by cryptocurrencies, leading to increased financial security and constructive use of digital assets.

Policy and Regulation: The findings will inform Australian law enforcement, policymakers, and regulators on the vital importance of education in tackling the challenges associated with cryptocurrencies. The study outlines effective frameworks that mitigate the risks of cryptocurrencies while ensuring security and maximizing individual benefits from the cryptocurrency ecosystem. In addition, the study provides a foundation for future research on the impact of community education related to risks and benefits of cryptocurrencies. It highlights the need for ongoing research to explore new educational strategies and their effectiveness in different contexts.

LITERATURE REVIEW

Historical Background of Cryptocurrency and the Fundamentals

The emergence of cryptocurrencies has brought a paradigm shift in the sphere of electronic payments and the digital economy; however, a complete understanding of this phenomenon remains challenging (Dulatova & Razak, 2020; Tschorsch & Scheuermann, 2016). Bitcoin, established in 2008 by the pseudonymous Satoshi

Nakamoto, was the first cryptocurrency, initiating a revolution in financial technology (Alamsyah & Syahrir, 2023; Dulatova & Razak, 2020; Sillaber et al., 2021). Since its initial commencement in 2009, Bitcoin has evolved from a niche concept to a widely used financial tool, despite concerns about its legitimacy and association with criminal activities (Tschorsch & Scheuermann, 2016; Yao et al., 2021). This innovation, which brought decentralised technologies and digital currencies, has sparked a significant shift in worldwide finance (Mungoli, 2023; Panda et al., 2023).

Blockchain technology, the foundation of Bitcoin and other cryptocurrencies, ensures transparent, immutable, and secure transactions, attracting widespread interest across various sectors (Hasan & Salah, 2018; Mungoli, 2023) and empowering users with greater control (Khair & Sandu, 2023; Mungoli, 2023). The underlying blockchain technology (linked to Bitcoin) enables person-to-person transactions through cryptographic protocols, establishing a distributed ledger that records all transactions over a network of computers (Sharma et al., 2024). Unlike traditional fiat currencies controlled by central banks, cryptocurrencies operate without centralised authority, granting users greater autonomy over their assets (Khair & Sandu, 2023). They are driven by economic dynamics, without government or regulatory intervention to moderate its value (Jing & Rocha, 2023). The decentralised nature of cryptocurrencies fundamentally contrasts with traditional financial systems, where central authorities oversee monetary policies and transactions, marking a paradigm shift in global finance (Jing & Rocha, 2023). Vaz and Brown (2020) noted that the decentralised nature of cryptocurrencies, while offering advantages such as lower transaction costs and increased accessibility, introduces vulnerabilities related to security and regulatory oversight.

Cryptocurrencies have the potential to significantly impact financial transactions and asset management by fostering a decentralised and inclusive economic system. Nonetheless, this depends on tackling fundamental risks through careful educational programs, strict regulatory frameworks, and ongoing technological innovation.

Common Types of Cryptocurrency-Related Crimes

The most common types of cryptocurrency-related crimes include ransomware and phishing attacks. Ransomware attacks involve the deployment of malware used to encrypt device data, preventing access and control (Kurpjuhn, 2019; Willie, 2023), in order to demand a cryptocurrency ransom. Phishing scams are designed to steal money through the deployment of fraudulent emails or text messages that encourage individuals to part with their personal information (Gupta et al., 2017). Furthermore, white-collar crimes such as insurance fraud, money laundering, and fraud, all facilitated by digital technology, are becoming increasingly prevalent (Patmanathan et al., 2023). The rapid development and implementation of information technology in business and personal communications have significantly increased productivity, efficiency, and communication capabilities. However, these advancements have inadvertently introduced vulnerabilities that malicious actors can exploit, potentially causing significant damage to organisations (Guenther, 2004; Willie, 2023). As technology advances, the landscape of digital crime continues to evolve, with cybercriminals exploiting vulnerabilities in computer systems to achieve their objectives, irrespective of geographical boundaries (Nicolas, 2024). Addressing cybercrime demands a multifaceted strategy that combines technological solutions, legal frameworks, and international cooperation (Guitton & Fréchette, 2023). As Haas (2023) noted, given the increasing speed, scale, and sophistication of cyberattacks, individuals must understand the essence of cybercrime to develop solid prevention, detection, and response techniques.

Role of Community Education and Awareness

Given the complexities and potential risks associated with digital currencies, fostering the public's understanding of the underlying technologies, economic implications, and regulatory frameworks is paramount (Smith & Weismann, 2014). Such educational efforts should target diverse segments of the population, including adults and children, to ensure widespread financial literacy and responsible engagement with cryptocurrencies (Koskelainen et al., 2023). Community-based workshops, seminars, and online resources can provide accessible and unbiased information, enabling individuals to navigate the cryptocurrency landscape with greater confidence and discernment (Panos et al., 2020). These programs could emphasise the importance of critical thinking, risk assessment, and due diligence when considering cryptocurrency investments. Moreover, educational initiatives should highlight the potential for fraud, scams, and market manipulation within the cryptocurrency ecosystem, equipping individuals with the knowledge and skills to protect themselves from financial harm (Raza et al., 2023; Trozze et al., 2023) [REMOVED HYPERLINK FIELD]. Furthermore, the integration of cryptocurrency education into existing financial literacy curricula within schools and universities could promote early awareness and responsible financial behaviour among younger generations (Wagner, 2019). Community education programs can play a vital role in mitigating risks and promoting responsible digital currency adoption by equipping individuals with the knowledge and skills to critically evaluate cryptocurrency investments (Susilaningsih & Indriayu, 2021). Promoting the safe and responsible use of cryptocurrencies enhances the financial literacy in underserved or at-risk communities, and empowers individuals to make informed decisions in the cryptocurrency market (Kim et al., 2022; Zhang & Chen, 2024). Utilising digital platforms and online courses for cryptocurrency education, incorporating gamification and interactive learning methods to engage diverse audiences, and designing workshops and seminars tailored to various demographics would further safeguard the public's cryptocurrency use.

THEORETICAL FRAMEWORKS

To deepen the conceptual analysis of cryptocurrency-related crimes and the role of community education in crime prevention, this study integrates three theoretical frameworks: Routine Activity Theory (RAT) (Cohen & Felson, 2010; Cornish & Clarke, 1986; Felson, 2016), Rational Choice Theory (RCT) (Cornish & Clarke, 2014), and Media Literacy Theory (MLT) (Potter, 2010). These theories offer complementary perspectives on the situational, behavioural, and educational dimensions of cryptocurrency crimes, enhancing the understanding of how education and awareness can reduce associated risks.

Routine Activity Theory (RAT)

Crime, according to Routine Activity Theory (RAT), happens when a motivated offender, a suitable target in the absence of a capable guardian, come together. This theory is particularly useful for understanding crimes involving cryptocurrencies (Cohen & Felson, 2010; Felson, 2016). According to RAT, the decentralised and anonymous nature of cryptocurrency creates prime opportunities for criminals (Collins, 2022). Motivated offenders, such as cybercriminals involved in phishing or ransomware attacks, often target users with low digital literacy or inadequate security measures. In this instance, weak guardianship is epitomised by an absence of strong regulations or general user awareness, making it easier for crimes like identity theft and romance fraud to occur. Community education programs, such as the Australia Cyber Security Awareness Month campaign (Australia's Cyber Security Strategy, 2020), serve as capable guardians by equipping users with skills to recognise scams and adopt secure practices, thereby reducing target suitability and disrupting the crime triangle.

Rational Choice Theory (RCT)

As proposed by Cornish and Clarke (1986), Rational Choice Theory, states that offenders make rational decisions by weighing the costs and benefits of criminal actions. Cryptocurrency criminals, such as those deploying fake trading platforms or deepfake scams, strategically exploit users' lack of awareness to maximize financial gains while minimizing detection risks (Gilbert & Gilbert, 2025). RCT frames community education as a deterrent by increasing the perceived costs of criminal activities. For instance, training users to verify sources and report suspicious activities heightens the risk of detection, making scams less appealing. By fostering digital financial literacy and promoting security measures like two-factor authentication (2FA), education shifts the cost-benefit balance, discouraging rational offenders and aligning with the study's focus on proactive prevention strategies (Lin et al., 2025).

Media Literacy Theory (MLT)

Given the widespread nature of cryptocurrency scams propagated through social media, like romance fraud and fake celebrity endorsements, Media Literacy Theory (MLT) offers a vital framework for understanding how users can effectively deal with deceptive digital content. (Cornish & Clarke, 1986). This theory underpins the paper's focus on the importance of verifying information sources and launching awareness campaigns by advocating for educational initiatives that sharpen critical thinking skills.

When combined, theories such as Routine Activity Theory (RAT), Rational Choice Theory (RCT), and Media Literacy Theory (MLT) offer a strong framework for understanding cryptocurrency crimes and the crucial role of community education (Cohen & Felson, 2010; Cornish & Clarke, 1986, 2014; Felson, 2016; Potter, 2010). RAT helps us identify the situational elements that enable crimes to occur, while RCT sheds light on what drives offenders. MLT, on the other hand, emphasises empowering users with essential critical thinking skills. A composite of these perspectives provides a comprehensive path to reduce risks and encourage the safe adoption of cryptocurrency.

MATERIALS AND METHODS

The study explores how cryptocurrencies pose substantial risks that need to be addressed through comprehensive community education and awareness programs. By understanding the principles and risks associated with cryptocurrencies, individuals and financial institutions in Australia and beyond can make informed decisions that maximise benefits and minimise threats. The study aimed to explore the importance of digital financial literacy in navigating the complexities of the cryptocurrency landscape and emphasised the need for educational initiatives and strategies to empower communities.

The methods employed in this review adhered to the established Preferred Reporting Items for Systematic Reviews and Meta-Analyses (PRISMA) guidelines, ensuring a standardised and transparent approach to the systematic review process (Moher et al., 2010).

Literature Search Strategy and Source

All potentially relevant articles were systematically and thoroughly searched to ensure a comprehensive foundation for this study. A wide range of databases and digital libraries, including Scopus, Web of Science, IEEE Xplore, the Australian Institute of Criminology, and Google Scholar, were carefully explored to identify and retrieve studies pertinent to the research objectives. Additionally, we thoroughly reviewed the reference lists of all identified studies to identify and retrieve supplementary articles that may not have been identified in the initial database searches. An extensive and methodical search was performed across these platforms, employing a combination of the following keywords: " Crypto crime prevention," "Community education," "Public awareness," "Educational strategies," "Community resilience," "Know your customer," "Cryptocurrency regulation," "Cryptocurrency security," "Anti-money laundering," "Crypto theft," "Cryptocurrency fraud," "Crypto scams," "Crypto phishing," "Cryptocurrency risks," "Ransomware," "Hacking," "Money laundering," "Financial crime," and "Organised financial crime." All articles were searched from March 1st to 15th, 2025.

Study Selection and Eligibility Criteria

Articles published in English between 2008 and 2025 were included in this study. The rationale for selecting 2008 as the starting point is that cryptocurrencies were first introduced in that year, with the launch of Bitcoin, making studies from this period onward relevant to the research scope. Conversely, articles published before 2008 or in languages other than English were excluded. Non-peer-reviewed materials, such as opinion pieces, editorials, and commentaries, were not considered to ensure the reliability and academic rigor of the sources. Additionally, articles lacking the specified keywords or focusing on topics unrelated to cryptocurrency were excluded. Finally, articles were omitted if they did not address strategies for preventing cryptocurrency-related crimes or failed to provide empirical data or theoretical insights directly relevant to the study's objectives. The study considered the inclusion and exclusion criteria in Table 1 below:

Table 1. Inclusion and exclusion criteria

Criteria	Inclusion criteria	Exclusion criteria
Databases	Articles indexed in SCOPUS, IEEE Xplore, Web of Science, and Google Scholar.	Articles not indexed in the specified databases (SCOPUS, IEEE Xplore, Web of Science, Google Scholar).
Keywords	Articles that include keywords such as "Crypto crime prevention," "Community education," "Public awareness," "Educational strategies," "Community resilience," "Know your customer," "Cryptocurrency regulation," "Cryptocurrency security," "Anti-money laundering," "Crypto theft," "Cryptocurrency fraud," "Crypto scams," "Crypto phishing," "Cryptocurrency risks," "Ransomware," "Hacking," "Money laundering," "Financial crime," and "Organised financial crime."	Articles that do not include the specified keywords or focus on unrelated topics.
Language	Articles published in English.	Articles not published in English.
Publication Date	Articles published between 2008 and 2025.	Articles published before 2008.
Relevance	Articles that focus on strategies for preventing cryptocurrency-related crimes, including community education and awareness.	Articles that do not address strategies for preventing cryptocurrency-related crimes or do not provide empirical data or theoretical insights relevant to the study.
Type of Publication	Peer-reviewed journal articles, conference papers, and reports.	Non-peer-reviewed articles, opinion pieces, and editorials.

Mixed Methods Quality Assurance

The quality assurance process for mixed methods studies utilized the Mixed Methods Appraisal Tool (MMAT), version 2018. This tool evaluates several critical aspects to ensure methodological rigor. Firstly, it assesses whether the research questions are clearly defined and whether the collected data adequately addresses them. It also examines the rationale for using a mixed-methods design, ensuring that this approach is appropriate for the research question. The integration of different study components is another key aspect, where the MMAT checks how effectively qualitative and quantitative data are combined to provide a cohesive answer. Additionally, the tool evaluates the coherence of the results, ensuring that findings from different methods are brought together into a unified interpretation.

Table 2. Mixed Methods Appraisal Tool (MMAT), version 2018

Mixed Methods Appraisal Tool									
Studies	**The research questions are clearly defined.**	**The collected data address the research questions.**	**There is an adequate rationale for using a mixed methods design to address the research question.**	**The different components of the study are effectively integrated to answer the research question.**	**The results are adequately brought together into overall interpretations.**	**Divergences and inconsistencies between quantitative and qualitative results are adequately addressed.**	**The different components of the study adhere to the quality criteria of each tradition of the methods involved.**	**Total score out of 7**	**Level of bias**
(Wang, 2024)	Yes	Yes	Yes	Yes	Yes	No	Yes	6	86.7%

Divergences and inconsistencies between quantitative and qualitative results are also addressed, ensuring they are adequately explained and resolved. Finally, the MMAT ensures that each component of the study adheres to the quality criteria specific to its methodological tradition. For example, the study by Hong et al. (2018) scored 6 out of 7, indicating a high level of methodological rigor and coherence in its qualitative approach.

Qualitative Methods Quality Assurance

For qualitative studies, the MMAT evaluates several specific criteria to ensure high quality. It assesses whether the research questions are clearly defined and whether the collected data address these questions. The tool also examines the appropriateness of the qualitative approach for answering the research question and the adequacy of the data collection methods. Furthermore, it evaluates whether the findings are adequately derived from the data and if the interpretation of results is sufficiently substantiated by the data.

Table 3. Qualitative appraisal tool

Studies	The research questions are clearly defined.	The collected data addresses the research questions.	The qualitative approach is appropriate for answering the research question.	The qualitative data collection methods are adequate to address the research question.	The findings are adequately derived from the data.	The interpretation of results is sufficiently substantiated by the data.	There is coherence between the qualitative data sources, collection, analysis, and interpretation.	Total score out of 7	Level of bias
1. (Ghazi-Tehrani & Pontell, 2021)	Yes	Yes	Yes	Yes	Yes	Yes	Yes	7	100%
2. (Mallawaarachchi et al., 2025)	No	Yes	Yes	Yes	Yes	No	Yes	5	71.4%
3. (Klein et al., 2024)	No	Yes	Yes	Yes	Yes	Yes	Yes	6	86.7%
4. (Mehta & Chawla, 2024)	Yes	Yes	Yes	Yes	Yes	No	Yes	6	86.7%
5. (Renda & Caneppele, 2024)	Yes	Yes	Yes	No	Yes	Yes	Yes	6	86.7%
6. (Teichmann & Falker, 2020)	Yes	Yes	No	Yes	Yes	Yes	No	5	71.4%
7. (Ebekozien et al., 2024)	Yes	Yes	Yes	Yes	Yes	No	Yes	6	86.7%
8. (Sestino et al., 2024)	Yes	Yes	Yes	Yes	Yes	Yes	Yes	7	100%
9. (Teichmann & Falker, 2021)	Yes	Yes	Yes	No	Yes	Yes	Yes	6	86.7%

Coherence between the qualitative data sources, collection, analysis, and interpretation is also assessed. For instance, the study by Ghazi-Tehrani & Pontell (2021) scored 7 out of 7, indicating a high level of methodological rigor and coherence in its qualitative approach.

Quantitative Methods Quality Assurance

For quantitative studies, the MMAT assesses several key criteria to ensure methodological rigor. It evaluates whether the research questions are clearly defined and whether the collected data address these questions. The tool also examines the relevance of the sampling strategy to the research question and whether the sample is representative of the target population. Additionally, it assesses the appropriateness of the measurements used in the study and the risk of non-response bias.

Table 4. Quantitative appraisal tool

Studies	The research questions are clearly defined.	The collected data address the research questions.	The sampling strategy is relevant to address the research question.	The sample is representative of the target population.	The measurements are appropriate for the study.	The risk of non-response bias is low.	The statistical analysis is appropriate to answer the research question.	Total score out of 7	Level of bias
1. (El-Chaarani et al., 2024)	Yes	Yes	No	Yes	Yes	No	Yes	5	71.4%
2. (Bajwa, 2025)	Yes	Yes	Yes	Yes	Yes	No	Yes	6	86.7%
3. (Dulisse et al., 2024)	Yes	Yes	Yes	Yes	Yes	Yes	Yes	7	100%
4. (Alyami et al., 2023)	Yes	Yes	Yes	Yes	Yes	Yes	Yes	7	100%
5. (Mills & Nower, 2019)	Yes	Yes	Yes	Yes	Yes	Yes	Yes	7	100%
6. (Dabbous et al., 2022)	Yes	Yes	Yes	Yes	Yes	Yes	Yes	7	100%
7. (Kala et al., 2023)	Yes	Yes	Yes	Yes	Yes	Yes	Yes	7	100%
8. (Engle et al., 2025)	Yes	Yes	Yes	Yes	Yes	Yes	Yes	7	100%
9. (Mutambik et al., 2024)	Yes	Yes	Yes	Yes	Yes	No	Yes	6	86.7%
10. (Blue et al., 2024)	Yes	Yes	Yes	Yes	Yes	Yes	Yes	7	100%

The statistical analysis is also evaluated to ensure it is appropriate for answering the research question. For example, the study by Dulisse et al. (2024) scored 7 out of 7, demonstrating a high level of methodological rigor in its quantitative approach. This thorough appraisal process ensured that only high-quality studies were included in the final analysis, thereby enhancing the reliability and validity of the study's findings.

Data Extraction

Duplicate records were removed using reference management software (EndNote X7) to ensure a consolidated dataset. Two reviewers (GM and LL) independently screened the titles and abstracts, excluding records not meeting the inclusion criteria, such as policy documents, reviews, and position papers. The methodological quality of the selected studies was objectively evaluated using the Mixed Methods Appraisal Tool (MMAT), version 2018 (Hong et al., 2018). Regarding disagreements between the reviewers, discussions were held with another member of the review team until consensus was reached. When the disagreements persisted, a third reviewer (DA and MZ) was consulted to negotiate and resolve conflicts between the reviewers. Data were extracted into a spreadsheet, capturing key details, including the primary author's name, year of publication, study setting (region), types of cryptocurrencies, sample size, amount of money lost (in US dollars), crime activities, and crime prevention strategies. The review process was documented and visualised using a PRISMA flow diagram (Figure 1).

RESULTS AND DISCUSSION

Identification and Selection of Studies

Following the electronic database search, a total of 9,569 articles were identified. Using the EndNote reference management software, 3,305 duplicate studies were removed. Subsequently, 5,659 records were excluded based on a review of their titles and abstracts. Additionally, 10 studies were excluded after assessing their methodological quality and relevance to the outcomes of interest. Ultimately, 20 studies met the criteria for inclusion in this systematic review. The selection process is visually represented in a PRISMA flow diagram (Figure 1).

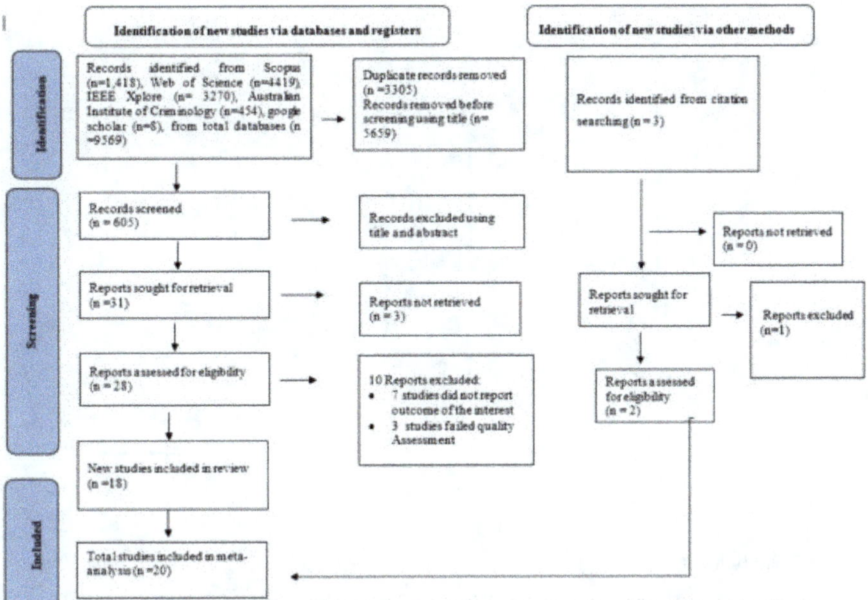

Figure 1: PRISMA flow diagram of the included studies for the systematic review on mitigating cryptocurrency-related crime

Study Location

The study locations illustrated on the map represent a diverse set of countries that have experienced cryptocurrency-related challenges, including financial scams and cyber threats (See Figure 2)

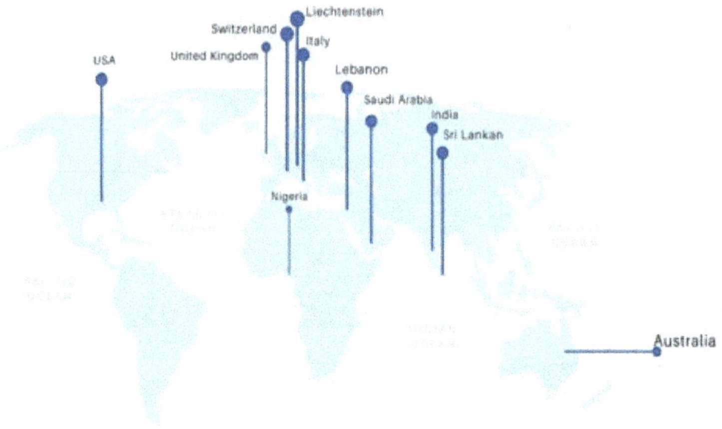

Figure 2 Study location

The USA, a major hub for cryptocurrency adoption, faces significant scam exposure due to its large user base (Dulisse et al., 2024; Engle et al., 2025; Klein et al., 2024), while the United Kingdom, a leading financial centre, contends with market manipulation and fraud amid a growing crypto market (Sestino et al., 2024; Wang, 2024). Switzerland, known for its "Crypto Valley" in Zug, is a hub for blockchain innovation but faces challenges like money laundering and phishing due to its crypto-friendly environment (Renda & Caneppele, 2024). Liechtenstein, stands out for its progressive crypto regulations, making it ideal for studying regulatory awareness (Teichmann & Falker, 2020, 2021). Italy sees rising crypto usage but is often targeted by romance scams and phishing due to its active online population (Sestino et al., 2024). In the Middle East, Lebanon's economic instability drives crypto adoption as an inflation hedge, although it increases vulnerability to fraud, while Saudi Arabia, with growing crypto interest, faces risks from gambling scams and market manipulation due to strict regulations and limited awareness (Bajwa, 2025; El-Chaarani et al., 2024; Mutambik et al., 2024). India, a major market with rapid crypto growth, grapples with identity theft and market manipulation across its diverse user base, and Sri Lanka, amid economic challenges, sees rising crypto use but struggles with scams due to low digital literacy (Kala et al., 2023; Mallawaarachchi et al., 2025). Australia, a developed market with strong regulatory oversight, still faces issues like romance fraud and phishing (Blue et al., 2024; Cross, 2022), while

Nigeria, a leader in African crypto adoption driven by economic needs, is heavily impacted by identity theft and fraudulent schemes (Ebekozien et al., 2024; Garba et al., 2024). These countries provide a comprehensive view of global and regional cryptocurrency challenges across developed, developing, and emerging markets.

Common Cryptocurrency-Related Crimes

The cryptocurrency financial space faces a range of sophisticated cyber threats that exploit both technological vulnerabilities and human behaviours, necessitating comprehensive mitigation strategies (Ghazi-Tehrani & Pontell, 2021). Routine Activity Theory (RAT) provides a robust framework for analysing these crimes, positing that crime occurs when a motivated offender, a suitable target, and the absence of a capable guardian converge (Cohen & Felson, 2010; Cornish & Clarke, 1986). Phishing attacks, including wide-net phishing and spear phishing, are prevalent, with attackers sending mass or targeted messages to trick users into revealing sensitive information (see Table 5). Globally, phishing accounts for a significant portion of crypto theft, with over $1 billion in losses (Scharfman, 2024). Similarly, romance fraud leverages emotional manipulation via social media to target vulnerable individuals, often those unaware of scam tactics, capitalizing on the absence of capable guardianship, such as robust user education or regulatory oversight (Sorell & Whitty, 2019). The decentralised nature of cryptocurrencies exacerbates this by limiting traditional guardianship mechanisms, allowing scammers to operate with reduced risk of detection (Garba et al., 2024). RAT highlights that phishing and romance fraud thrive due to insufficient user awareness and weak systemic protections, underscoring the need for education to reduce target suitability and strengthen guardianship.

Table 5. Cryptocurrency-related crimes

Cyber threats	Description
Phishing attacks	Wide-net Phishing: This involves sending mass emails or messages that appear legitimate to trick individuals into providing sensitive information. Spear Phishing: A more targeted approach where attackers customize their messages to specific individuals or organizations, often using personal information to gain trust.
Fake trading platforms	Fraudulent websites that mimic legitimate trading platforms can lure unsuspecting investors into depositing funds, only for criminals to disappear with their money.
Automated trading system	Some platforms offer automated trading services that promise high returns but are often scams designed to siphon off funds from users.
Malicious links and ads	Cybercriminals often use Google adware or malicious links on social media to redirect users to harmful sites that can steal personal information or install malware.

continued on following page

Table 5. Continued

Cyber threats	Description
Fake education websites	These sites promise financial education but are designed to exploit users, often leading to financial loss or identity theft.
Ransomware	This malicious software encrypts a victim's data, demanding a ransom for its release, often leading to significant financial loss and operational disruption.
Deepfakes and hacking	The rise of deepfake technology poses new risks, as attackers can create realistic videos or audio to manipulate individuals or organizations.

Table made by authors

From the review, fake trading platforms and automated trading systems posed significant risks by copying legitimate services to steal funds (Alyami et al., 2023; Ghazi-Tehrani & Pontell, 2021). For instance, Smith (2024) stated that Bitcoin fraudulent platforms have cost investors billions of dollars. The scammers use malicious links and ads, often distributed via Google adware or social media, that redirect users to harmful sites that steal data or install malware (Alyami et al., 2023). Fake education websites exploit users by promising financial education but leading to financial loss or identity theft (Ebekozien et al., 2024; Garba et al., 2024; Mutambik et al., 2024). Ransomware and deepfakes/hacking represent advanced threats, with ransomware encrypting data for ransom and deepfakes creating realistic media to deceive users (Ghazi-Tehrani & Pontell, 2021); with deepfakes used to impersonate crypto influencers (Arora et al., 2024). As Blue et al. (2024) noted mitigation strategies such as regular software updates and upskilling financial institution staff to counter ransomware threats align with RAT's emphasis on enhancing guardianship to disrupt crime opportunities. Addressing such cyber threats with comprehensive prevention strategies, may effectively minimise risks while maintaining user safety and trust (Engle et al., 2025; Mutambik et al., 2024; Wang, 2024). Renda and Caneppele (2024) and Sestino et al. (2024) also noted that global efforts should prioritise universal best practices, such as promoting digital literacy and standardised security protocols, to create a cohesive defence framework. Meanwhile, Australian initiatives can harness local resources like the Australian Cyber Security Centre, the Australian Securities and Investments Commission, and the Australian Competition and Consumer Commission to deliver targeted, region-specific support, ensuring a resilient and adaptive defence against the evolving landscape of cyber threats in the crypto ecosystem (Blue et al., 2024).

The cryptocurrency platform faces a range of sophisticated cyber threats that exploit both technological vulnerabilities and human behaviours, necessitating comprehensive mitigation strategies (Ghazi-Tehrani & Pontell, 2021). Phishing attacks, including wide-net and spear phishing, exemplify this convergence, with cybercriminals (motivated offenders) sending mass or targeted messages to trick users into revealing sensitive information. These attacks exploit users with low digital literacy or inadequate security measures (suitable targets), resulting in over $1 billion in global losses (Scharfman, 2024). Similarly, romance fraud leverages emotional manipulation via social media to target vulnerable individuals, often those unaware of scam tactics, capitalizing on the absence of capable guardianship, such as robust user education or regulatory oversight (Sorell & Whitty, 2019). The decentralised nature of cryptocurrencies exacerbates this by limiting traditional guardianship mechanisms, allowing scammers to operate with a reduced risk of detection (Garba et al., 2024). RAT highlights that phishing and romance fraud thrive due to insufficient user awareness and weak systemic protections, underscoring the need for education to reduce target suitability and strengthen guardianship.

Financial Scams and Exploitation

Study findings indicate that identity theft is also a pervasive issue, where cybercriminals steal personal information to execute unauthorised transactions, often leading to substantial financial losses (Engle et al., 2025; Garba et al., 2024; Ghazi-Tehrani & Pontell, 2021). Sorell and Whitty (2019) noted that online dating scams are one of the most common and lucrative cyber scams, with perpetrators often posing as romantic partners to extract funds. Cross (2024) further argued that scammers exploit romantic relationships via social media to deceive individuals into transferring large sums of money. Romance fraud has consistently ranked among the top three categories of financial loss for Australian victims over the past decade, which is now an international trend.

Figure 3. Financial scams

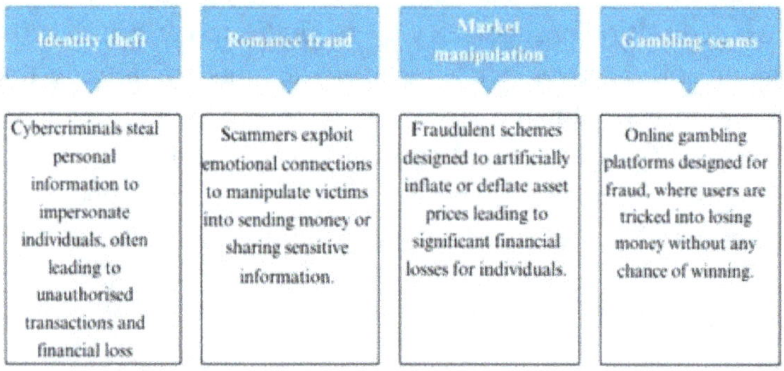

Figure 3: Financial scams

Criminals also employ market manipulation tactics, like a price-rigging system, to artificially inflate or deflate the value of a cryptocurrency, causing substantial losses to unaware victims. These tactics are unregulated, affecting millions of users and facilitated by scammers through social media platforms. Scammers usually employ voice cloning technology to exploit and impersonate celebrities, authorities or ordinary people for fraud (Lin et al., 2024b). Scammers recently employed a voice clone of the Australian Queensland Premier to trick people into investing in Bitcoin. Similarly, gambling scams on online platforms deceive people into bets where there is no real chance of winning (Dabbous et al., 2022; Dulisse et al., 2024). Through targeted awareness campaigns and training that addresses identity theft, romance fraud, market manipulation, and gambling and other scams, individuals can be educated to safeguard themselves and reduce their vulnerabilities.

Cybercrime Prevention Strategies

The systematic review results highlighted that education and training, robust security measures, source verification, and reporting suspicious activity are essential for mitigating risks in the cryptocurrency environment (see Figure 4). Rational

Choice Theory (RCT) offers a valuable lens for understanding how these strategies deter cybercriminals by altering their cost-benefit calculations (Cohen & Felson, 2010; Cornish & Clarke, 1986). RCT posits that offenders act rationally, weighing the potential gains of criminal activity against the risks of detection and punishment (Cohen & Felson, 2010).

Figure 4. Cyber threats

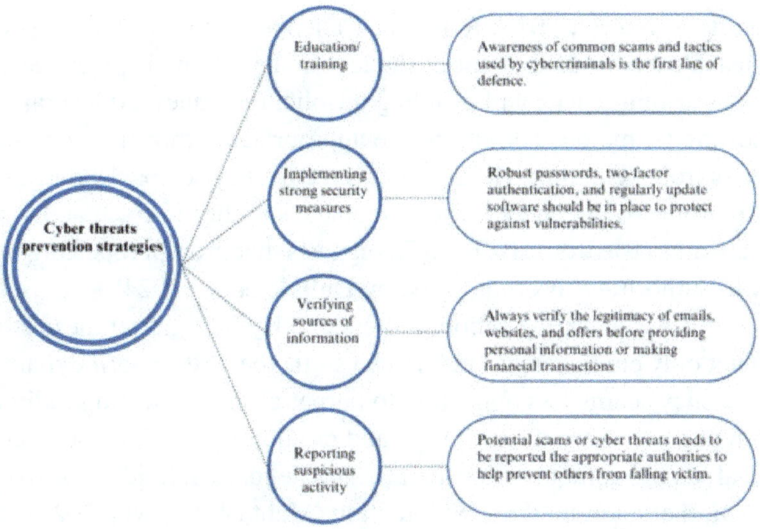

Figure 4 Crime threat prevention strategies

Educating and training the community on common scams and cybercriminal tactics is the first line of defence against these threats. Awareness workshops and online resources are essential to teach individuals how to identify deceptive patterns, such as fake information, malicious links, and manipulative tactics, such as gaming, romance fraud, and false promises of financial gain (Dabbous et al., 2022; Ebekozien et al., 2024; El-Chaarani et al., 2024). For example, in Australia, the Australian Cyber Security Centre (ACSC) has prioritised education, with its 2024 Cyber Security Awareness Month campaign focusing on crypto-specific scams through targeted training programs and online resources (Australian Cyber Security Centre (ACSC), 2024). By teaching users to recognise and avoid manipulative tactics, these programs reduce the likelihood of successful scams, diminishing potential benefits for cybercriminals.

Implementing strong security measures, such as robust passwords, two-factor authentication (2FA), and regular software updates, is critical to protect individuals against vulnerabilities (Klein et al., 2024; Mehta & Chawla, 2024). For instance, adopting 2FA and multi-factor authentication (MFA) reduces the risk of account breaches, forcing cybercriminals to invest more effort for lower returns(Banyal et al., 2013; Jubur et al., 2025; Khanna, 2024). Source verification, such as confirming the legitimacy of URLs or avoiding unsolicited requests, directly counters phishing and fake websites, which have caused billions in annual losses(Mehta & Chawla, 2024; Mills & Nower, 2019; Renda & Caneppele, 2024). Awareness campaigns should teach users to double-check the legitimacy of emails, websites, and offers, such as confirming URLs and avoiding unsolicited requests (Gururaj et al., 2024).

Reporting suspicious activity to the appropriate authorities is essential to prevent others from becoming victims of cryptocurrency scams. Underreporting these scams significantly hampers law enforcement's ability to trace and disrupt cybercrime networks (Biedron, 2024). RCT suggests that prompt reporting of suspicious activity to authorities, as emphasised by Dulisse et al. (2024) increases the risk of detection, further deterring rational offenders. By integrating these strategies, education not only empowers users but also shifts the cost-benefit dynamics, making cryptocurrency scams less appealing to perpetrators.. Educating individuals about the inherent risks of cryptocurrencies and promoting due diligence in partnerships are critical steps to combat online threats and safeguard individuals and organisations from fraud, theft, and market manipulation (Mehta & Chawla, 2024). By adopting comprehensive strategies such as education and training, robust security measures, source verification, and prompt reporting of suspicious activity, the risks associated with cryptocurrency threats can be mitigated at both global and national levels.

Building Trust Through Awareness Raising Campaigns

Figure 5. Building trust through awareness raising campaigns

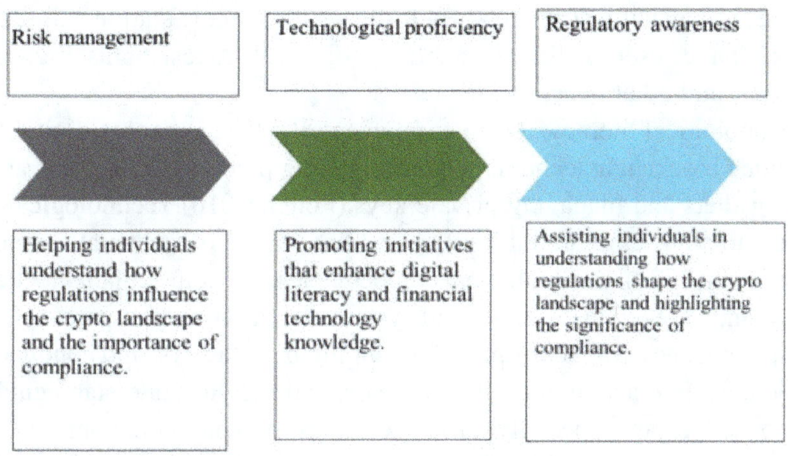

Figure 5. Building trust through awareness raising campaigns

As shown in Figure 5, to enhance trust within the cryptocurrency space, awareness campaigns must address diverse concerns through risk management, technological competence, and regulatory awareness.. Media Literacy Theory (MLT) provides a critical framework for understanding how these campaigns foster user resilience by promoting the ability to access, analyse, evaluate, and create media content (Potter, 2010). MLT is particularly relevant given the prevalence of social media-driven scams, such as romance fraud and fake celebrity endorsements, which exploit users' inability to critically evaluate digital information. Awareness campaigns that teach source verification—such as double-checking URLs, confirming email legitimacy, and recognizing manipulative tactics like voice cloning (e.g., the Queensland Premier case, (Lin et al., 2024a), align with MLT's emphasis on critical thinking. Such initiatives empower users to navigate the cryptocurrency ecosystem safely, reducing vulnerability to scams that have caused significant financial losses globally.

A further educational mitigating measure is increasing cryptocurrency regulatory awareness in the community. This measure can be managed by conducting workshops (or employing alternative educational strategies for improved contextual fit) on common risks, including market volatility, scams, and security breaches, and offering viable countermeasures to combat these risks, e.g., employing secure wallets and identifying phishing scams. By empowering users with knowledge of regulatory frameworks and compliance requirements, campaigns can reduce uncertainty and build confidence in the legitimacy of cryptocurrency transactions. Regulatory awareness campaigns further leverage MLT by educating users about anti-money laundering and know-your-customer obligations, positioning cryptocurrencies as legitimate financial instruments. By fostering critical evaluation skills, these campaigns enhance user resilience, enabling individuals to resist phishing, fake trading platforms, and other deceptive tactics.

Technological literacy, a core component of MLT, enhances digital literacy by explaining blockchain technology and imparting practical skills, such as setting up secure wallets and managing private keys.(Potter, 2010).Technological literacy is also key to advancing digital literacy and knowledge of financial technology (Liu & Tsyvinski, 2021). Technological competencies that help explain blockchain technology, and show how decentralised systems function, impart practical skills such as cryptocurrency wallet setup, understanding private keys, and conducting secure transactions. Interactive tutorials, webinars, and easy-to-understand guides can fill the knowledge gap, especially for new entrants, making them confident to venture into the crypto world safely. Such technological advancement not only increases the ability of users but also builds trust as it makes the technology easier to use and less overwhelming.

CONCLUSION

This systematic review highlights the critical importance of robust education and awareness initiatives to address the complex and evolving risks within the cryptocurrency ecosystem. The integration of Routine Activity Theory (RAT), Rational Choice Theory (RCT), and Media Literacy Theory (MLT) strengthens the argument for education as a multi-faceted strategy to mitigate cryptocurrency-related crimes (Cohen & Felson, 2010; Felson, 2016; Potter, 2010). RAT illustrates how crimes like phishing and romance fraud exploit vulnerable targets and weak guardianship, emphasizing the need for education to reduce target suitability through digital literacy and enhance guardianship via regulatory oversight and reporting (Cohen & Felson, 2010). RCT highlights how education deters rational offenders by increasing detection risks through source verification and security measures like 2FA/MFA, making scams less profitable (Cornish & Clarke, 1986, 2014). MLT underscores user empowerment by fostering critical thinking and source verification skills, enabling individuals to navigate social media scams and fake platforms with confidence (Potter, 2010).

Together, these theories provide a comprehensive framework for understanding and combating cryptocurrency threats. Education and training programs, such as Australia's 2024 Cyber Security Awareness Month, reduce crime opportunities (RAT) by equipping users with scam detection skills, deter offenders (RCT) by raising the costs of criminal activity, and empower communities (MLT) through enhanced digital literacy. Robust security practices, including 2FA/MFA and regular software updates, combined with source verification and prompt reporting, further mitigate risks by addressing both technological and human vulnerabilities. By leveraging local resources like the Australian Cyber Security Centre, Australian Securities and Investments Commission, and Australian Competition and Consumer Commission, stakeholders can implement these strategies at national and global levels. This holistic approach, grounded in RAT, RCT, and MLT, strengthens community resilience, builds trust, and paves the way for a secure, inclusive, and trustworthy digital financial future.

Cryptocurrencies' decentralised and anonymous character, though promoting innovation, also generates high exposure to an extensive range of cyber threats such as phishing, ransomware, identity theft, romance scams, market manipulation, and gambling scams. These threats caused substantial global financial losses, as scammers exploit the advantage of technological vulnerabilities as well as human behaviours, and the response requires the implementation of thorough and proactive mitigation measures. The review, following PRISMA guidelines and based on high-quality studies across diverse regions, emphasises that digital financial literacy is foundational to empowering individuals and communities to operate safely within the cryptocurrency environment.

Effective prevention requires a multi-faceted approach. Education and training programs are the first line of mitigating cybercrimes, equipping users with the necessary knowledge and skills to identify and combat scams, such as fraudulent trading platforms, malicious links, and manipulative tactics like romance fraud or deceptive promises of financial gain. Raising awareness through workshops and accessible online resources plays a pivotal role in building resilience to scams and adoption of safe online habits.

Rigorous security practices such as two-factor authentication (2FA), multi-factor authentication (MFA), using strong passwords, and regular software updates are essential to mitigate systems against possible cryptocurrency crimes. In addition, source verification, such as re-checking the legitimacy of emails, websites, and financial benefits, helps users avert phishing and fake platforms that have caused significant financial losses globally. Furthermore, prompt reporting of suspicious activities to authorities is vital to disrupt cybercrime networks, despite challenges like underreporting cybercrimes.

Building trust in the cryptocurrency space broadly encompasses risk management, technological competence, and regulatory awareness. Risk management involves educating users about market volatility, scams, and security breaches while providing practical countermeasures, such as using secure wallets and detecting phishing attempts. Technological competence fosters an understanding of blockchain technology and imparts skills like setting up wallets, managing private keys, and conducting secure transactions through interactive tutorials and guides. Regulatory awareness ensures users are informed about anti-money laundering and know-your-customer obligations, as well as evolving global and national regulations, positioning cryptocurrencies as legitimate financial instruments. By integrating these strategies, stakeholders at both global and national levels—leveraging local resources like the Australian Cyber Security Centre, Australian Securities and Investments Commission, and Australian Competition and Consumer Commission- are able to mitigate risks, build user confidence, and facilitate wider and safer adoption of cryptocurrencies. This holistic approach strengthens community resilience and paves the way for a secure, trustworthy, and inclusive digital financial future.

Limitations of the study

While this systematic review rigorously examines cryptocurrency-related risks and prevention strategies, several limitations constrain the scope and generalisability of the findings, necessitating further research to enhance global relevance. First, the exclusion criteria focusing on English-language, peer-reviewed literature published between 2008 and 2025 may have excluded valuable insights from non-English sources, such as research conducted in regions with high cryptocurrency adoption but different linguistic contexts, like East Asia (e.g., China, Japan, South Korea) or Latin America. This language filter limits the ability to capture diverse perspectives on cryptocurrency crimes and educational strategies, potentially skewing findings toward English-speaking contexts. Non-English studies might offer unique insights into region-specific scams or culturally tailored education programs, which could enhance the global applicability of prevention strategies.

Second, the reliance on specific databases (Scopus, Web of Science, IEEE Xplore, Australian Institute of Criminology, and Google Scholar) may lead to selection bias, as these platforms may not comprehensively cover grey literature, industry reports, or studies from underrepresented regions. This restriction could overlook practical insights from non-academic sources, such as government white papers or NGO reports, which are often critical in understanding real-world cryptocurrency crime trends in developing economies.

Third, the temporal scope (2008–2025) excludes pre-2008 studies on analogous financial crimes, such as early internet fraud, which could provide historical context for understanding current cryptocurrency scams. While 2008 aligns with Bitcoin's inception, this restriction may miss foundational theories or strategies applicable to modern cybercrime prevention.

To address these limitations, future research should adopt a more inclusive approach by incorporating multilingual sources to capture global perspectives, expanding database coverage to include grey literature and industry reports, and prioritising studies from underrepresented regions to balance geographic biases. Additionally, extending the temporal scope to include pre-2008 financial crime research and conducting longitudinal studies could provide deeper historical and predictive insights. By considering a broader spectrum of threats, technological advancements, and socioeconomic factors, future studies can produce a more comprehensive and globally relevant analysis of cryptocurrency risk mitigation strategies.

REFERENCES

Alamsyah, A., & Syahrir, S. (2023). The Taxonomy of Blockchain-based Technology in the Financial Industry [version 2; peer review: 2 approved]. *F1000 Research, 12*(457), 457. Advance online publication. DOI: 10.12688/f1000research.133518.2

Allioui, H., & Mourdi, Y. (2023). Unleashing the Potential of AI: Investigating Cutting-Edge Technologies That Are Transforming Businesses. [IJCEDS]. *International Journal of Computer Engineering and Data Science*, *3*(2), 1–12. https://ijceds.com/ijceds/article/view/59

Alyami, M., Alhotaylah, R., Alshehri, S., & Alghamdi, A. (2023). Phishing Attacks on Cryptocurrency Investors in the Arab States of the Gulf [Article]. *Journal of Risk and Financial Management, 16*(5), 271. Advance online publication. DOI: 10.3390/jrfm16050271

Arora, M., Mishra, K. K., Singh, M., Singh, P., & Tripathi, R. (2024). Deepfake Technology and Its Implications for Influencer Marketing. In *Navigating the World of Deepfake Technology* (pp. 66–90). IGI Global. DOI: 10.4018/979-8-3693-5298-4.ch005

Attaran, M., & Gunasekaran, A. (2019). Blockchain-enabled technology: The emerging technology set to reshape and decentralise many industries. *International Journal of Applied Decision Sciences, 12*(4), 424–444. DOI: 10.1504/IJADS.2019.102642

Australia's Cyber Security Strategy. (2020). *Australia's Cyber Security Strategy 2020 at a glance* https://www.homeaffairs.gov.au/cyber-security-subsite/files/cyber-security-strategy-2020.pdf

Australian Competition and Consumer Commission. (2024). *Australians lose over $70 million to bogus investment opportunities.* Retrieved 30/01/2025 from https://www.accc.gov.au/media-release/australians-lose-over-70-million-to-bogus-investment-opportunities

Australian Cyber Security Centre (ACSC). (2024). *Cyber Security Awareness Month 2024* https://www.cyber.gov.au/about-us/view-all-content/news-and-media/cyber-security-awareness-month-2024?ref=search

Aziz, A., & Naima, U. (2021). Rethinking digital financial inclusion: Evidence from Bangladesh. *Technology in Society, 64*, 101509. https://doi.org/https://doi.org/10.1016/j.techsoc.2020.101509. DOI: 10.1016/j.techsoc.2020.101509

Bajwa, I. A. (2025). Reinvestment intentions in cryptocurrency: Examining the dynamics of risks and investor risk tolerance [Article]. *Digital Business*, *5*(1), 100104. Advance online publication. DOI: 10.1016/j.digbus.2024.100104

Banyal, R. K., Jain, P., & Jain, V. K. (2013, 24-25 Sept. 2013). Multi-factor Authentication Framework for Cloud Computing. *2013 Fifth International Conference on Computational Intelligence, Modelling and Simulation*

Biedron, S. (2024). *Cybercrime in the Digital Age University of Oxford*].

Blue, L., Xing, C., & Pham, T. (2024). Cryptocurrencies: Who is vulnerable and what are the vulnerabilities? [Article]. *The Australian Journal of Social Issues*. Advance online publication. DOI: 10.1002/ajs4.351

Choo, K.-K. R., & Smith, R. G. (2008). Criminal Exploitation of Online Systems by Organised Crime Groups. *Asian Journal of Criminology*, *3*(1), 37–59. DOI: 10.1007/s11417-007-9035-y

Christodoulou, I., Rizomyliotis, I., Konstantoulaki, K., Nazarian, A., & Binh, D. (2024). Transforming the remittance industry: Harnessing the power of blockchain technology. *Journal of Enterprise Information Management*, *37*(5), 1551–1577. DOI: 10.1108/JEIM-03-2023-0112

Cohen, L. E., & Felson, M. (2010). Social change and crime rate trends: A routine activity approach (1979). In *Classics in environmental criminology* (pp. 203–232). Routledge.

Collins, J. (2022). *Crypto, crime and control*. Global Initiative Against Transnational Organized Crime.

Cornish, D. B., & Clarke, R. V. (1986). *Crime as a rational choice. The Reasoning Criminal*. Springer-Verlag.

Cornish, D. B., & Clarke, R. V. (2014). *The reasoning criminal: Rational choice perspectives on offending*. Transaction Publisher.

Cross, C. (2022). Meeting the Challenges of Fraud in a Digital World. In Gill, M. (Ed.), *The Handbook of Security* (pp. 217–238). Springer International Publishing., DOI: 10.1007/978-3-030-91735-7_11

Cross, C. (2024). Romance baiting, cryptorom and 'pig butchering': An evolutionary step in romance fraud. *Current Issues in Criminal Justice*, *36*(3), 334–346. DOI: 10.1080/10345329.2023.2248670

Dabbous, A., Merhej Sayegh, M., & Aoun Barakat, K. (2022). Understanding the adoption of cryptocurrencies for financial transactions within a high-risk context [Article]. *The Journal of Risk Finance, 23*(4), 349–367. DOI: 10.1108/JRF-10-2021-0169

Dulatova, N., & Razak, A. (2020). The ecosystem of cryptocurrency as an object of civil rights in brics countries. *BRICS Law Journal, 7*(2), 37–65. DOI: 10.21684/2412-2343-2020-7-2-37-65

Dulisse, B. C., Connealy, N., & Logan, M. W. (2024). "Get rich quick," scheme or script? The effect of cryptoculture on the susceptibility of fraud victimization among cryptocurrency purchasers. *Journal of Criminal Justice, 94*, 102273. DOI: 10.1016/j.jcrimjus.2024.102273

Ebekozien, A., Aigbavboa, C., Thwala, W. D., Samsurijan, M. S., Ahmed, M. A. H., Aliu, J., & Adekunle, S. A. (2024). Appraising the application of cryptocurrency technologies in the Nigerian built environment: Stakeholders' perspective [Article]. *International Journal of Building Pathology and Adaptation, 42*(7), 93–112. DOI: 10.1108/IJBPA-04-2024-0070

El-Chaarani, H., Mawad, J. L., Mawad, N., & Khalife, D. (2024). Psychological and demographic predictors of investment in cryptocurrencies during a crisis in the MENA region: the case of Lebanon [Article]. *Journal of Economic and Administrative Sciences*. https://doi.org/DOI: 10.1108/JEAS-07-2022-0165

Engle, T. A., Maher, C. A., & Jones, M. (2025). Afraid of the unknown: Crypto literacy and fear of online fraud. *Journal of Economic Criminology, 7*, 100135. https://doi.org/https://doi.org/10.1016/j.jeconc.2025.100135. DOI: 10.1016/j.jeconc.2025.100135

Felson, M. (2016). The routine activity approach. In *Environmental criminology and crime analysis* (pp. 106–116). Routledge.

Garba, K. H., Lazarus, S., & Button, M. (2024). An assessment of convicted cryptocurrency fraudsters [Article]. *Current Issues in Criminal Justice*, 1–17. Advance online publication. DOI: 10.1080/10345329.2024.2403294

Ghazi-Tehrani, A. K., & Pontell, H. N. (2021). Phishing Evolves: Analyzing the Enduring Cybercrime [Article]. *Victims & Offenders, 16*(3), 316–342. DOI: 10.1080/15564886.2020.1829224

Gilbert, C., & Gilbert, M. (2025). Patterns and vulnerabilities of cryptocurrency-related cybercrimes. *Global Scientific Journals, 13*(3), 1950–1981.

Guenther, M. (2004). Security/Privacy Compliance: Culture Change. *EDPACS, 31*(12), 19–24. DOI: 10.1201/1079/44332.31.12.20040601/81836.3

Guitton, M. J., & Fréchette, J. (2023). Facing cyberthreats in a crisis and post-crisis era: Rethinking security services response strategy. *Computers in Human Behavior Reports, 10,* 100282. https://doi.org/https://doi.org/10.1016/j.chbr.2023.100282. DOI: 10.1016/j.chbr.2023.100282

Gupta, B. B., Tewari, A., Jain, A. K., & Agrawal, D. P. (2017). Fighting against phishing attacks: State of the art and future challenges. *Neural Computing & Applications, 28*(12), 3629–3654. DOI: 10.1007/s00521-016-2275-y

Gururaj, H., Janhavi, V., & Ambika, V. (2024). *Social Engineering in Cybersecurity: Threats and Defenses.* CRC Press.

Haas, T. C. (2023). Adapting cybersecurity practice to reduce wildlife cybercrime. *Journal of Cybersecurity, 9*(1), tyad004. Advance online publication. DOI: 10.1093/cybsec/tyad004

Hasan, H. R., & Salah, K. (2018). Proof of Delivery of Digital Assets Using Blockchain and Smart Contracts [Article]. *IEEE Access, 6*, 65439-65448. *Article, 8501910.* Advance online publication. DOI: 10.1109/ACCESS.2018.2876971

Hong, Q. N., Pluye, P., Fàbregues, S., Bartlett, G., Boardman, F., Cargo, M., Dagenais, P., Gagnon, M.-P., Griffiths, F., & Nicolau, B. (2018). Mixed methods appraisal tool (MMAT), version 2018. *Registration of copyright, 1148552*(10), 1-7.

Jabotinsky, H. Y., & Lavi, M. (2021). Speak Out: Verifying and Unmasking Cryptocurrency User Identity. *SSRN, 32,* 518. DOI: 10.2139/ssrn.3828970

Javaid, M., Haleem, A., Singh, R. P., Suman, R., & Khan, S. (2022). A review of Blockchain Technology applications for financial services. *BenchCouncil Transactions on Benchmarks, Standards and Evaluations, 2*(3), 100073. https://doi.org/https://doi.org/10.1016/j.tbench.2022.100073

Jing, R., & Rocha, L. E. C. (2023). A network-based strategy of price correlations for optimal cryptocurrency portfolios. *Finance Research Letters, 58,* 104503. https://doi.org/https://doi.org/10.1016/j.frl.2023.104503. DOI: 10.1016/j.frl.2023.104503

Josyula, H. P. (2024). *Redefining Cross-Border Financial Flows.* Apress., DOI: 10.1007/979-8-8688-1064-0

Jubur, M., Shrestha, P., & Saxena, N. (2025). An In-Depth Analysis of Password Managers and Two-Factor Authentication Tools. *ACM Computing Surveys, 57*(5), 128. Advance online publication. DOI: 10.1145/3711117

Kala, D., Chaubey, D. S., & Al-Adwan, A. S. (2023). Cryptocurrency investment behaviour of young Indians: Mediating role of fear of missing out [Article]. *Global Knowledge, Memory and Communication*. Advance online publication. DOI: 10.1108/GKMC-07-2023-0237

Kethineni, S., & Cao, Y. (2019). The Rise in Popularity of Cryptocurrency and Associated Criminal Activity. *International Criminal Justice Review*, *30*(3), 325–344. DOI: 10.1177/1057567719827051

Kethineni, S., & Cao, Y. (2020). The rise in popularity of cryptocurrency and associated criminal activity. *International Criminal Justice Review*, *30*(3), 325–344. DOI: 10.1177/1057567719827051

Kfir, I. (2020). Cryptocurrencies, national security, crime and terrorism. *Comparative Strategy*, *39*(2), 113–127. DOI: 10.1080/01495933.2020.1718983

Khair, M. Abul, & Sandu, A., Kumar. (2023). Blockchain-Optimized Supply Chain Traceability System for Transparent Logistics. *Journal of Fareast International University, 6*(1), 27-38. https://hal.science/hal-04543221

Khanna, A. (2024). Authentication in Cybersecurity. In Khanna, A. (Ed.), *Securing an Enterprise: Maximizing Digital Experiences through Enhanced Security Measures* (pp. 75–94). Apress., DOI: 10.1007/979-8-8688-1029-9_4

Kim, K. T., Hanna, S. D., & Lee, S. T. (2022). Investment literacy, overconfidence and cryptocurrency investment. *Financial Services Review*, *31*(2), 121–132.

Klein, G., Assadi, D., & Zwilling, M. (2024). Fighting Fire with Fire: Combating Criminal Abuse of Cryptocurrency with a P2P Mindset. *Information Systems Frontiers*. Advance online publication. DOI: 10.1007/s10796-024-10498-7

Koskelainen, T., Kalmi, P., Scornavacca, E., & Vartiainen, T. (2023). Financial literacy in the digital age—A research agenda. *The Journal of Consumer Affairs*, *57*(1), 507–528. DOI: 10.1111/joca.12510

Kurpjuhn, T. (2019). The guide to ransomware: How businesses can manage the evolving threat. *Computer Fraud & Security*, *2019*(11), 14–16. https://doi.org/https://doi.org/10.1016/S1361-3723(19)30117-4. DOI: 10.1016/S1361-3723(19)30117-4

Lane, A. M., & Adam, L. (2022). Crime and cryptocurrency in Australian courts. *Monash University Law Review. Monash University. Faculty of Law*, *48*(3), 146–190.

Lin, L. S., Aslett, D., Mekonnen, G., & Zecevic, M. (2024a). The dangers of voice cloning and how to combat it.

Lin, L. S., Aslett, D., Mekonnen, G., & Zecevic, M. (2024b). The dangers of voice cloning and how to combat it. *The Conversation*. https://theconversation.com/the-dangers-of-voice-cloning-and-how-to-combat-it-239926

Lin, L. S., Aslett, D., Mekonnen, G., & Zecevic, M. (2024c). The UN Cybercrime Convention: What it Means for Policing and Community Safety in Australia. *Australian Outlook*. https://www.internationalaffairs.org.au/australianoutlook/the-un-cybercrime-convention-what-it-means-for-policing-and-community-safety-in-australia/

Lin, L. S., Mekonnen, G., Zecevic, M., Aslett, D., & Allan, D. (2025). The Role of Education in Combating Cybercrime in the Asia-Pacific: Tackling Misinformation and Disinformation in Australia. In *Combatting Misinformation and Global Nation's False Narratives Through Education*. IGI Global. DOI: 10.4018/979-8-3693-9601-8.ch011

Liu, Y., & Tsyvinski, A. (2021). Risks and Returns of Cryptocurrency. *Review of Financial Studies*, *34*(6), 2689–2727. DOI: 10.1093/rfs/hhaa113

Mallawaarachchi, S., Hemachandra, U., Jayakody, D., Wickramarathne, U., Lokeshwara, A. A., & Bandara, G. C. (2025). Decrypting the Digital Vault by Understanding Cryptocurrency Adoption Challenges Among Gen Z: Case of Sri Lanka [Article]. *Ianna Journal of Interdisciplinary Studies*, *7*(1), 1–18. DOI: 10.5281/zenodo.12645982

Mehta, K., & Chawla, S. (2024). Illuminating the dark corners: A qualitative examination of cryptocurrency's risk [Article]. *Digital Policy. Regulation & Governance*, *26*(2), 188–208. DOI: 10.1108/DPRG-10-2023-0147

Mills, D. J., & Nower, L. (2019). Preliminary findings on cryptocurrency trading among regular gamblers: A new risk for problem gambling? *Addictive Behaviors*, *92*, 136–140. https://doi.org/https://doi.org/10.1016/j.addbeh.2019.01.005. DOI: 10.1016/j.addbeh.2019.01.005

Moher, D., Liberati, A., Tetzlaff, J., & Altman, D. G. (2010). Preferred reporting items for systematic reviews and meta-analyses: The PRISMA statement. *International Journal of Surgery*, *8*(5), 336–341. https://doi.org/https://doi.org/10.1016/j.ijsu.2010.02.007. DOI: 10.1016/j.ijsu.2010.02.007

Mungoli, N. (2023). *Deciphering the Blockchain: A Comprehensive Analysis of Bitcoin's Evolution*. Adoption, and Future Implications.

Mutambik, I., Almuqrin, A., Zhang, J. Z., & Alharbi, Z. H. (2024). Trust in Cryptocurrency Payments: A Cross-Cultural Analysis of Factors Influencing Adoption [Article]. *Journal of Organizational and End User Computing, 36*(1), 1–36. Advance online publication. DOI: 10.4018/JOEUC.353910

Nicholls, J., Kuppa, A., & Le-Khac, N. A. (2021). Financial Cybercrime: A Comprehensive Survey of Deep Learning Approaches to Tackle the Evolving Financial Crime Landscape. *IEEE Access : Practical Innovations, Open Solutions, 9*, 163965–163986. DOI: 10.1109/ACCESS.2021.3134076

Nicolas, I. (2024). Striking the balance: Anti-money laundering goals and legal privilege in Australia. *Current Issues in Criminal Justice*. Advance online publication. DOI: 10.1080/10345329.2024.2420146

Nikkel, B. (2020). Fintech forensics: Criminal investigation and digital evidence in financial technologies. *Forensic Science International Digital Investigation, 33*, 200908. https://doi.org/https://doi.org/10.1016/j.fsidi.2020.200908. DOI: 10.1016/j.fsidi.2020.200908

Ozili, P. K. (2018). Impact of digital finance on financial inclusion and stability. *Borsa Istanbul Review, 18*(4), 329-340. https://doi.org/https://doi.org/10.1016/j.bir.2017.12.003

Panda, S. K., Sathya, A. R., & Das, S. (2023). Bitcoin: Beginning of the Cryptocurrency Era. In Panda, S. K., Mishra, V., Dash, S. P., & Pani, A. K. (Eds.), *Recent Advances in Blockchain Technology: Real-World Applications* (pp. 25–58). Springer International Publishing., DOI: 10.1007/978-3-031-22835-3_2

Panos, G. A., Karkkainen, T., & Atkinson, A. (2020). Financial literacy and attitudes to cryptocurrencies. In.

Patmanathan, P., Arunasalam, K., Suppiah, K., & Arumugam, D. (2023). The effectiveness of blockchain technology in preventing financial cybercrime. E3S Web of Conferences, Pazarbasioglu, C., Mora, A. G., Uttamchandani, M., Natarajan, H., Feyen, E., & Saal, M. (2020). Digital financial services. *World Bank, 54*, 1-54.

Potter, W. J. (2010). The State of Media Literacy. *Journal of Broadcasting & Electronic Media, 54*(4), 675–696. DOI: 10.1080/08838151.2011.521462

Rahman, A. (2024). Financial Inclusion through Technological Advancements in Banking Institutions: An Analytical Review. *Advances: Jurnal Ekonomi & Bisnis, 2*(3), 163–173.

Raza, S., Shaikh, M., & Tahira, K. (2023). Cryptocurrency investigations in digital forensics: Contemporary challenges and methodological advances. *Inf. Dyn. Appl*, *2*(3), 126–134. DOI: 10.56578/ida020302

Renda, A., & Caneppele, S. (2024). Compliant or not compliant? The challenges of anti-money laundering regulations in crypto assets: The case of Switzerland [Article]. *Journal of Money Laundering Control*, *27*(2), 363–382. DOI: 10.1108/JMLC-04-2023-0078

Rustamaji, M., & Faisal, F. (2024). Law Enforcement Strategies Against Money Laundering Through Cryptocurrency: Comparative Studies in Several Countries. International Conference on Cultural Policy and Sustainable Development (ICPSD 2024), Scharfman, J. (2024). Crypto Phishing and Spoofing Scams. In *The Cryptocurrency and Digital Asset Fraud Casebook, Volume II: DeFi, NFTs, DAOs, Meme Coins, and Other Digital Asset Hacks* (pp. 193-219). Springer.

Sestino, A., Tuček, D., & Bresciani, S. (2024). The "dark side" and negative consequences of cryptocurrencies usage for unethical purposes as barriers to invest in Middle East and African (MEA) countries. *Journal of Small Business and Enterprise Development*.

Sharma, D., Ghosh, R., Shri, C., & Khatter, D. (2024). Sentiments in the cryptocurrency market: an in-depth analysis of influential factors applying ISM-MICMAC and AHP [Article]. *Journal of Capital Markets Studies*. https://doi.org/DOI: 10.1108/JCMS-07-2024-0038

Sillaber, C., Waltl, B., Treiblmaier, H., Gallersdörfer, U., & Felderer, M. (2021). Laying the foundation for smart contract development: An integrated engineering process model. *Information Systems and e-Business Management*, *19*(3), 863–882. DOI: 10.1007/s10257-020-00465-5

Smith, A., & Weismann, M. F. (2014). Are you ready for digital currency? *Journal of Corporate Accounting & Finance*, *26*(1), 17–21. DOI: 10.1002/jcaf.21999

Smith, D. (2024). *Money Laundering, Terrorist Financing and Virtual Assets*. Springer. DOI: 10.1007/978-3-031-59842-5

Sorell, T., & Whitty, M. (2019). Online romance scams and victimhood. *Security Journal*, *32*(3), 342–361. DOI: 10.1057/s41284-019-00166-w

Susilaningsih, L. E. D., & Indriayu, M. (2021). Financial Literacy in Student Financial Management Behavior in the Digital Age *Proceedings of the 4th International Conference on Learning Innovation and Quality Education*, Surakarta, Indonesia. https://doi.org/DOI: 10.1145/3452144.3453759

Teichmann, F. M. J., & Falker, M. C. (2020). Money laundering via cryptocurrencies – potential solutions from Liechtenstein [Article]. *Journal of Money Laundering Control, 24*(1), 91–101. DOI: 10.1108/JMLC-04-2020-0041

Teichmann, F. M. J., & Falker, M. C. (2021). Cryptocurrencies and financial crime: Solutions from Liechtenstein [Article]. *Journal of Money Laundering Control, 24*(4), 775–788. DOI: 10.1108/JMLC-05-2020-0060

Trozze, A., Davies, T., & Kleinberg, B. (2023). Explaining prosecution outcomes for cryptocurrency-based financial crimes. *Journal of Money Laundering Control, 26*(1), 172–188. DOI: 10.1108/JMLC-10-2021-0119

Trozze, A., Kamps, J., Akartuna, E. A., Hetzel, F. J., Kleinberg, B., Davies, T., & Johnson, S. D. (2022). Cryptocurrencies and future financial crime. *Crime Science, 11*(1), 1. DOI: 10.1186/s40163-021-00163-8

Tschorsch, F., & Scheuermann, B. (2016). Bitcoin and Beyond: A Technical Survey on Decentralized Digital Currencies. *IEEE Communications Surveys and Tutorials, 18*(3), 2084–2123. DOI: 10.1109/COMST.2016.2535718

Turner, J. E. (2011). *Money laundering prevention: Deterring, detecting, and resolving financial fraud*. Wiley Online Library.

Usman, N., Griffiths, M., & Alam, A. (2025). FinTech and money laundering: Moderating effect of financial regulations and financial literacy. *Digital Policy. Regulation & Governance, 27*(3), 301–326. DOI: 10.1108/DPRG-04-2024-0068

Vaz, J., & Brown, K. (2020). Sustainable development and cryptocurrencies as private money. *Economia e Politica Industriale, 47*(1), 163–184. DOI: 10.1007/s40812-019-00139-5

Wagner, J. (2019). Financial Education and Financial Literacy by Income and Education Groups. *Financial Counseling and Planning, 30*(1), 132–141. DOI: 10.1891/1052-3073.30.1.132

Wang, Y. (2024). Do cryptocurrency investors in the UK need more protection? [Article]. *Journal of Financial Regulation and Compliance, 32*(2), 230–249. DOI: 10.1108/JFRC-03-2023-0036

Willie, M. M. (2023). The role of organizational culture in cybersecurity: Building a security-first culture. *Journal of Research. Innovation and Technologies, 2*(2 (4)), 179–198. DOI: 10.1051/e3sconf/202338907022

Wu, J., Lin, K., Lin, D., Zheng, Z., Huang, H., & Zheng, Z. (2023). Financial Crimes in Web3-Empowered Metaverse: Taxonomy, Countermeasures, and Opportunities. *IEEE Open Journal of the Computer Society*, *4*, 37–49. DOI: 10.1109/OJCS.2023.3245801

Wu, J., Liu, J., Chen, W., Huang, H., Zheng, Z., & Zhang, Y. (2022). Detecting Mixing Services via Mining Bitcoin Transaction Network with Hybrid Motifs [Article]. *IEEE Transactions on Systems, Man, and Cybernetics. Systems*, *52*(4), 2237–2249. DOI: 10.1109/TSMC.2021.3049278

Yao, S. Y., Kong, X. R., Sensoy, A., Akyildirim, E., & Cheng, F. Y. (2021). Investor attention and idiosyncratic risk in cryptocurrency markets. *European Journal of Finance*. Advance online publication. DOI: 10.1080/1351847X.2021.1989008

Zhang, J., & Chen, Z. (2024). Exploring Human Resource Management Digital Transformation in the Digital Age. *Journal of the Knowledge Economy*, *15*(1), 1482–1498. DOI: 10.1007/s13132-023-01214-y

KEY TERMS AND DEFINITIONS

Cryptocurrency: A digital or virtual currency that uses cryptographic protocols for security and operates on a decentralized network, typically based on blockchain technology, without a central authority (Tschorsch & Scheuermann, 2016). Examples include Bitcoin and Ethereum.

Blockchain Technology: A distributed ledger system that records transactions across a network of computers, ensuring transparency, immutability, and security through cryptographic mechanisms (Hasan & Salah, 2018).

Cryptocurrency-Related Crime: Illicit activities facilitated by cryptocurrencies, including phishing, ransomware, identity theft, romance fraud, market manipulation, and money laundering, exploiting their decentralized and pseudo-anonymous nature (Trozze et al., 2023).

Phishing: A cybercrime tactic involving fraudulent emails, messages, or websites designed to deceive users into revealing sensitive information, such as login credentials or private keys (Ghazi-Tehrani & Pontell, 2021).

Ransomware: Malicious software that encrypts a victim's data, demanding payment (often in cryptocurrency) for its release, causing financial and operational disruption (Kurpjuhn, 2019).

Romance Fraud: A scam where perpetrators exploit emotional connections, often via social media, to manipulate victims into sending cryptocurrency or sharing personal information (Cross, 2024).

Community Education: Structured programs, such as workshops, seminars, or online resources, aimed at enhancing public awareness and skills to navigate cryptocurrency risks and benefits (Panos et al., 2020).

Two-Factor Authentication (2FA): A security process requiring two forms of verification (e.g., password and a code sent to a device) to access an account, reducing the risk of unauthorized access (Banyal et al., 2013).

Multi-Factor Authentication (MFA): An enhanced security measure requiring multiple verification methods (e.g., password, biometric, and code) to further protect accounts (Jubur et al., 2025).

2FA: Two-Factor Authentication.

ACCC: Australian Competition and Consumer Commission.

ACSC: Australian Cyber Security Centre.

ASIC: Australian Securities and Investments Commission.

MFA: Multi-Factor Authentication.

MMAT: Mixed Methods Appraisal Tool.

PRISMA: Preferred Reporting Items for Systematic Reviews and Meta-Analyses.

RAT: Routine Activity Theory.

RCT: Rational Choice Theory.

MLT: Media Literacy Theory.

Chapter 4
Artificial Intelligence and Crime Linked to Cryptocurrencies

Smriti Tandon Gupta
https://orcid.org/0000-0003-4999-5881
Graphic Era University, India

Eshan Singhal
https://orcid.org/0000-0001-5861-1515
Dr. BhimRao Ambedkar University, India

ABSTRACT

The quickly advancing development of artificial intelligence (AI) and rapidly spreading cryptocurrencies established a modern environment for both legal developments and illegal practices. The analysis explores AI-related crime activities in cryptocurrencies through a study of AI technologies that assist and combat various crypto-based criminal operations. This paper investigates AI-driven crimes which include fraud alongside money laundering and cyberattacks and evaluates the dual capabilities of AI between criminal execution and prevention functions. This paper explains the ethical and legal risks of AI implementations in cryptocurrency crimes and provides recommendations for present and future research to tackle emerging threats.

INTRODUCTION

Artificial Intelligence (AI) and cryptocurrencies have sparked major advances in technology and finance during the past decade. Alone, both domains have driven innovation, but where they meet, they often become centers for criminal activities,

DOI: 10.4018/979-8-3373-0675-9.ch004

making it difficult for regulators, cybersecurity experts, and authorities to cope. AI is a wide area in computer science that aims to develop machines that do tasks requiring human-like intelligence. These areas are machine learning, natural language processing, computer vision, and, most recently, generative AI such as large language models and deepfakes (Kumar, N. 2025). Now, these tools are easy to get, open-source, and used across many programs such as customer support, finance, and monitoring tools. In the meantime, cryptocurrencies which are built on blockchain, make it possible to carry out financial transactions that are decentralized, pseudonymous, and commonly without borders. The birth of Bitcoin in 2009 led to a change in finance and soon thousands of altcoins, smart contracts, decentralized finance (DeFi), and non-fungible tokens (NFTs) appeared. Even though these financial technologies help many people, they have made it simpler for criminals to exploit people.

When AI and cryptocurrency come together, they add more risk to each field. People are now using AI to provide:

- Design very realistic phishing scams and deepfake videos to gain access to cryptocurrency funds.
- Perform market manipulation more automatically by using special bots.
- Study the weaknesses in smart contracts to be able to execute attacks.
- Move illegal proceeds by using several DeFi protocols, mixing services, and automated wallet transfers.

Cryptocurrencies support the growth of AI-powered crime by making it possible to expand, operate automatically, and stay hidden because they are not linked to real names and work through a decentralized system.

The Rise of Crypto-Enabled AI Crime

There is an increasing breadth and quality to the AI-based crimes happening in cryptocurrency. In 2023, global crypto-related crime amounted to over $20 billion which was reported by Chainalysis. Apart from Ponzi scams, rug pulls and other typical methods, more and more attacks are now fueled by AI and can deceive even people with prior experience.

Generative AI such as ChatGPT and GitHub Copilot are sometimes used to design fraudulent smart contracts, make fake investment sites, or produce hoax communications from CEOs to try and get employees to authorize crypto payments. Likewise, machine learning helps predict token prices which allows front-runners to benefit more from pump-and-dump strategies and exchanges without order books. Someone using AI systems now runs botnets to observe and steal from people who hold cryptocurrency online or on social platforms. In addition, tools with AI abilities can detect and make use of unknown flaws in crypto wallet software. This is a big shift in how cybercrime operates: from random attacks to sophisticated, well-organized systems.

Problem Statement

With AI being used more in cryptocurrency, a new group of cybercriminals who are smarter, more difficult to detect, and more flexible is now appearing. Because malicious groups can use these tools, they now threaten detection, break the law, and abuse digital weaknesses. Despite significant investments in cybersecurity and regulatory compliance, traditional defenses struggle to contend with:

- AI-generated content that is indistinguishable from human-produced material.
- Autonomous trading agents capable of responding to markets in milliseconds.
- Smart contract attacks that evolve based on blockchain data analysis.
- Deepfake-based identity theft and social engineering.

Many existing rules and laws do not handle activities by things without human consciousness across regions that can easily change. Progress in AI has let even inexperienced attackers carry out damaging cyber assaults.

Research Objectives

This research paper aims to examine the dynamic interplay between artificial intelligence and cryptocurrency-enabled crime. The objectives are as follows:

1. To identify and categorize the types of crimes committed at the intersection of AI and cryptocurrency.
2. To analyze how AI technologies are used to enhance the effectiveness of cryptocurrency-based crimes.
3. To present real-world case studies where AI played a critical role in the planning or execution of crypto-related crimes.
4. To explore the legal and regulatory challenges in prosecuting AI-assisted crypto crimes, including jurisdictional conflicts and limitations of current frameworks.
5. To evaluate AI's role as a defensive technology in detecting, investigating, and preventing cryptocurrency crimes.
6. To propose policy recommendations and technological safeguards that balance innovation with risk mitigation.

Through these objectives, the study seeks to contribute to an emerging body of knowledge addressing cybersecurity, digital forensics, AI governance, and crypto regulation.

Methodology

This paper employs an interdisciplinary, qualitative methodology combining academic research, technical analysis, case study evaluation, and regulatory review. Sources include:

- Academic journals in artificial intelligence, blockchain technology, criminology, and law.
- Reports and datasets from blockchain forensic firms such as Chainalysis, Elliptic, and CipherTrace.
- Official publications from organizations including INTERPOL, Europol, FATF, and the U.S. Department of Justice.
- Media investigations and legal records documenting recent high-profile crypto crimes.
- Regulatory and legal frameworks such as MiCA (Markets in Crypto-Assets), the FATF Travel Rule, and U.S. Executive Orders.

Analytical frameworks include comparative crime typologies, SWOT analysis of enforcement capabilities, and ethical assessments of dual-use AI technologies.

Scope and Limitations

This study focuses on crimes where artificial intelligence (AI) supports or enhances the use of cryptocurrencies. It explores three major areas: first, crimes committed directly using cryptocurrencies, such as theft, fraud, and money laundering; second, AI-powered attacks that are either directed at or involve cryptocurrency technologies; and third, the use of AI in detecting, investigating, and responding to illegal activities within the crypto space. The analysis highlights both the risks and benefits AI brings to this evolving landscape. However, the study acknowledges several limitations. Rapid technological developments may quickly render certain examples outdated, and detailed information about AI tools used in criminal activities is often withheld or anonymized. Moreover, this assessment does not involve live penetration testing or delve into the cryptographic foundations of blockchain systems. Instead, it offers a high-level overview of current trends, challenges, and implications at the intersection of AI and cryptocurrency-based crime.

Structure of the Paper

To address the objectives outlined above, this paper is organized into the following sections:

- Section 2: Explores cryptocurrency fundamentals, blockchain structure, and vulnerabilities.
- Section 3: Analyzes core AI technologies, their capabilities, and misuse potential.
- Section 4: Investigates the convergence of AI and crypto in facilitating cybercrime.
- Section 5: Offers a typology of specific AI-enabled crypto crimes.
- Section 6: Presents real-world case studies.
- Section 7: Examines regulatory, legal, and enforcement challenges.
- Section 8: Details how AI can aid in detecting and mitigating crypto crimes.
- Section 9: Evaluates international responses and proposes future policy directions.
- Section 10: Summarizes findings and outlines key recommendations.

UNDERSTANDING CRYPTOCURRENCY AND BLOCKCHAIN TECHNOLOGY

Introduction to Cryptocurrencies

Cryptocurrencies use cryptography to ensure secure financial transactions done digitally. Differential reason, cryptocurrencies rely on blockchain technology, are not regulated by central banks or financial institutions, and are not associated with nations' traditional money. The first and most famous, Bitcoin, was unveiled in 2009 by Satoshi Nakamoto. After that, the ecosystem started to feature thousands of altcoins like Ethereum, Ripple (XRP), Litecoin, and Monero, every one with its characteristics and level of privacy.

Using cryptocurrencies, people can exchange money directly which is usually less expensive and often more transparent (with most public blockchains) and may help people in areas without financial institutions. But since cryptocurrencies are decentralized, use pseudonyms, and make transactions hard to reverse, they are attractive to criminals on the web.

Blockchain Fundamentals

At the heart of cryptocurrencies is blockchain which is a network system that keeps track of transactions on many different nodes. Blocks in the blockchain come one after another and each block has a list of transactions, a date, and a cryptographic address containing the information from the previous block (Jay, P., et al. 2020). Once a transaction is put into the blockchain, it cannot be changed back without making changes to all following blocks and getting half of the network in agreement.

Among the most important characteristics of blockchain are:

- Decentralization means no one entity rules the network.
- It's easy to check transactions because public blockchain platforms like Bitcoin and Ethereum are transparent.
- Transactions are confirmed by using methods such as Proof of Work (PoW) which is the main security mechanism.
- Paper wallets allow your Bitcoin to be linked to cryptographic addresses as your username, instead of your personal information.

Such features mean that blockchain can be good or bad depending on the situation. Although they do provide better security and performance, it is still harder to oversee and manage illegal activity, mainly when people use privacy coins or mixers to cover their steps.

Evolution of the Crypto Ecosystem

Ever since Bitcoin started, the world of crypto has grown much further than just processing payments. Notable developments are:

- Smart Contracts: Automated computer programs that action transactions if certain set conditions are met. Ethereum introduced this concept and inspired the creation of Decentralized Applications (dApps).
- DeFi (Decentralized Finance) provides ways to trade, lend, borrow, and get insurance directly without needing other companies. Many DeFi platforms have little regulation which makes them susceptible to attacks.
- NFTs (Non-Fungible Tokens) are basically unique digital assets that live on the blockchain and have important roles in digital art, gaming, and handling intellectual rights. By using NFTs, criminals can artificially set up value for illegal cash flow and transfer the funds anonymously.

- DAOs (Decentralized Autonomous Organizations) are governed using smart contracts and votes from the community, letting people make group decisions without needing a central authority.

These advances help blockchain more and also make it an attractive target for crime using AI.

Privacy Tools and Anonymization Techniques

While some blockchains operate with full transparency, others are intentionally designed to ensure privacy. Cryptocurrencies such as Monero (XMR) and Zcash (ZEC) employ advanced cryptographic methods, including zero-knowledge proofs, to conceal both the identities of transacting parties and the amounts involved. In addition, privacy-enhancing tools such as mixers (e.g., Tornado Cash), CoinJoin protocols, and anonymizing wallet addresses are commonly used to obscure the true origin of funds, thereby complicating financial flow analysis. To counteract these obfuscation techniques, many investigative services now utilize artificial intelligence to analyze transaction patterns, fee structures, and timing data. This enables the dynamic selection of optimized laundering routes, making detection and tracing efforts increasingly complex (Alessandretti, L., et al. 2018).

Illicit Use of Cryptocurrencies

Cryptocurrencies have been implicated in a wide range of criminal activities. Notably, a significant proportion of ransomware payments are conducted using digital assets such as Bitcoin and Monero. The dark web serves as a marketplace for illicit transactions involving drugs, weapons, and stolen data, with cryptocurrencies facilitating anonymous exchanges. Additionally, individuals exploit social media and encrypted messaging platforms to orchestrate Ponzi schemes and pump-and-dump operations. Digital currencies have also been used to finance terrorist organizations and sanctioned regimes. Moreover, sophisticated techniques such as layering transactions, leveraging decentralized finance (DeFi) protocols, and utilizing non-fungible token (NFT) sales are employed to obscure the origin of illicit funds (Jang, H., & Lee, J. 2018).

The integration of artificial intelligence has further exacerbated these threats by enabling rapid transaction routing, the generation of synthetic identities, and the automation of cross-platform attacks, making such criminal enterprises increasingly efficient and difficult to trace (Kumar, N. 2025). Cryptocurrencies have been implicated in a wide range of criminal activities. Notably, a significant proportion of ransomware payments are conducted using digital assets such as Bitcoin and

Monero. The dark web serves as a marketplace for illicit transactions involving drugs, weapons, and stolen data, with cryptocurrencies facilitating anonymous exchanges. Additionally, individuals exploit social media and encrypted messaging platforms to orchestrate Ponzi schemes and pump-and-dump operations. Digital currencies have also been used to finance terrorist organizations and sanctioned regimes. Moreover, sophisticated techniques such as layering transactions, leveraging decentralized finance (DeFi) protocols, and utilizing non-fungible token (NFT) sales are employed to obscure the origin of illicit funds. The integration of artificial intelligence has further exacerbated these threats by enabling rapid transaction routing, the generation of synthetic identities, and the automation of cross-platform attacks, making such criminal enterprises increasingly efficient and difficult to trace (Lahmiri, S., & Bekiros, S. 2020).

Vulnerabilities and Risks

Several inherent characteristics of blockchain-based systems make them susceptible to exploitation:

- Smart Contract Vulnerabilities: Bugs in smart contract code can be exploited to drain funds. In 2022, over $3 billion was stolen through DeFi exploits, many identified and executed using AI-powered vulnerability scanners.
- Phishing and Social Engineering: AI tools can create personalized phishing messages that mimic official communications to trick users into giving up private keys.
- Key Management Weaknesses: The loss or theft of private keys leads to irreversible loss of funds. AI can be used to guess seed phrases, crack wallet passwords, or even intercept keystrokes using malware.
- Flash Loan Attacks: Instant loans without collateral can be used to manipulate market prices temporarily, often automated using bots programmed with AI decision-making algorithms.

Crypto Forensics and Traceability

Despite their pseudonymous nature, most blockchain transactions can be analyzed using on-chain forensic tools. Companies like Chainalysis, CipherTrace, and Elliptic employ AI-driven analytics to:

- Detect suspicious transaction patterns.
- Trace illicit funds across multiple wallets and blockchains.
- Cluster addresses belonging to specific entities or criminal organizations.

- Assist law enforcement in building cases and recovering stolen assets.

However, criminals also utilize counter-forensics, such as chain hopping, tumblers, and layering techniques, often optimized by AI to maximize obfuscation.

The Role of Regulation

Regulatory authorities worldwide are making concerted efforts to impose order on the rapidly evolving cryptocurrency landscape. The Financial Action Task Force (FATF) now mandates that Virtual Asset Service Providers (VASPs) collect and share identifying information about the parties involved in cryptocurrency transactions. Significant regulatory developments include the European Union's Markets in Crypto-Assets (MiCA) regulation, executive orders concerning digital assets issued by the U.S. government, and pilot programs involving central bank digital currencies (CBDCs), which aim to enhance market stability and oversight (Cocco, L., Tonelli, R., & Marchesi, M. 2019). Despite these advancements, regulatory enforcement remains inconsistent across jurisdictions. This uneven implementation enables criminal actors to exploit regulatory gaps by relocating operations to countries with weaker compliance frameworks.

ARTIFICIAL INTELLIGENCE – CAPABILITIES AND ETHICAL BOUNDARIES

Introduction to Artificial Intelligence (AI)

With Artificial Intelligence (AI), computers are engineered to complete tasks that normally need the power of human thinking. Such tasks among psychology activities involve learning, reasoning, solving problems, perception, understanding language, and decision-making. AI's ecosystem in the present day involves several fields, including machine learning (ML), natural language processing (NLP), computer vision, and reinforcement learning which are all useful in areas such as finance, healthcare, robotics, and cybersecurity (Sabry, F., Labda, W., et al. 2019). With the advancement of AI, more of it is being built into the systems that manage important features of society, for example, digital finance. Although AI makes things more efficient and secure, it opens up new ways for criminals to attack digital spaces that are not regulated such as cryptocurrencies.

Core AI Technologies and Their Capabilities

Basic AI applications are used by cybercriminals by design or hijacked and turned against users in the cryptocurrency world:

- Machine Learning (ML): Computers can learn from data themselves, without being given specific instructions. Applied to search engines, forecasting results, and digital trading.
- Deep Learning is a branch of ML that applies neural networks with several layers (deep neural networks). With deep learning, it is now possible to identify images, produce natural language, and make smart decisions in tough environments.
- Natural Language Processing (NLP) makes it possible for computers to interact with human language. NLP allows criminals to make phishing messages, mislead people on social media, and pretend to be others.
- Technologies such as GPT-4 and diffusion models are used to generate human-like texts, pictures, or sounds. People use them to create deepfakes, fake identities, and fraudulent advertisements for cryptocurrencies.
- Reinforcement Learning: A way in which agents figure out the best behavior by understanding rewards and punishments. People use it in automated trading or to gradually evolve malware strategies.
- Computer Vision lets machines read and understand visual content. It allows someone to automate using the webcam, bypass image verification tests, or collect sensitive visual data from screens to mine for the image of interest.

AI in Automation and Decision-Making

One of the most significant capabilities of artificial intelligence (AI) lies in its ability to automate complex decision-making processes both rapidly and at scale. This makes AI particularly effective for time-sensitive tasks, including operating cryptocurrency trading bots without human intervention, detecting anomalous transaction patterns, conducting emotion-driven phishing attacks, and executing adaptive strategies based on real-time blockchain data. While these applications offer considerable value when used ethically, they equally empower cybercriminals to launch persistent and highly adaptable attacks with minimal direct involvement, thereby escalating both the efficiency and frequency of malicious activity (Hassani, H., Huang, X., & Silva, E. 2018).

Dual-Use Dilemma of AI Technologies

A major societal concern surrounding artificial intelligence is its dual-use nature—its capacity to be harnessed for both beneficial and harmful purposes simultaneously. For instance, an AI system developed to detect deepfakes can be repurposed to enhance the realism of those very forgeries. Similarly, cryptocurrency trading bots can be manipulated to engage in illicit practices such as wash trading or front-running. Natural language processing (NLP) models, while powerful tools for communication, can also be trained to generate convincing fraudulent content, including fake regulatory documents or deceptive marketing materials. This duality presents a significant challenge for regulators, as imposing strict controls on emerging technologies may hinder innovation, yet malicious actors continue to exploit these tools beyond the reach of conventional oversight mechanisms (Huang et al. 2019).

Open-Source AI Models and Misuse Risks

The increased availability of advanced artificial intelligence tools through open-source platforms—such as LLaMA, GPT-J, and Stable Diffusion—has significantly accelerated software development. However, this democratization of AI also creates opportunities for malicious exploitation. Cybercriminals can modify these models to generate malware, remove built-in ethical safeguards and filters, or train them using illicitly obtained data, such as compromised financial account information or cryptocurrency wallet credentials (Kjærland, F., Meland, M., Oust, A., & Øyen, V. 2018). The risks are further amplified by the widespread accessibility of model checkpoints and fine-tuning utilities available on repositories like GitHub, Hugging Face, and peer-to-peer networks such as BitTorrent. This ease of access complicates efforts to regulate AI misuse, making it increasingly challenging to control its deployment in harmful contexts.

AI and Anonymity in Cybercrime

AI helps criminals work anonymously and with greater efficiency on the internet. Sometimes, deepfakes are used on video calls to make employees fall for a scam and share their crypto funds.

- Faked Identities: AI can make documents and images that fool security screens of unregulated platforms.
- AI-powered botnets oversee phishing websites, the creation of false accounts, and online fraud across many community platforms.

- AI bot-enabled scams happen when a person gets information from a chatbot, mistakenly believing it to be real human advice.

With such tools, scammers can organize their activities broadly, target multiple languages, and adapt to environments, so it gets tough even for analysts and computers to decide what is safe and what is not (Yin & Vatrapu, 2017).

Ethical and Legal Challenges

The use of AI for crime investigation brings up many problems that need to be considered ethically and legally. If an AI is accused of a crime (such as an exploit happening on its own), proving who is responsible can be tricky. Is the person using the tool the developer, user, trainer, or host? Many advanced models today work behind a "black box," so we have little understanding of how their decisions are made. It makes it hard to identify where or when a copyright infringement took place (Liew, J., et al. 2019).

- Problems with Bias and Wrong Use: AI systems that learn from biased data can encourage fraudulent methods that unfairly target or control particular people.
- AI models made in certain countries can be used worldwide using the internet which raises challenges for law enforcement across national borders.

Scholars and policymakers are more and more agreeing that AI governance should be forward-thinking and ready to change as well as apply to countries worldwide. Even though early versions of these AI frameworks have been set out by the EU's AI Act and OECD AI Principles, enforcement is mostly piecemeal and restricted (Sholla, S., et al. 2021).

Defending Against AI Misuse

AI also provides important ways to defend us against cybersecurity threats.

- Algorithms that look for unusual crypto transactions to detect fraud.
- Using behaviors to catch bots or automation.
- Looking for security risks by checking possible scams or risky wallet addresses.
- Social media companies use AI to detect deepfakes, scams, and phishing attacks.

Businesses in cybersecurity and the crypto industry use AI tools to watch for threats, as AI for adversaries still makes it hard for these systems to catch all risks.

THE CONVERGENCE OF AI AND CRYPTOCURRENCY IN CRIMINAL ENTERPRISES

Technological Convergence in Crime

During the digital era, the use of Artificial Intelligence (AI) and cryptocurrencies has allowed criminals to commit more advanced and widespread crimes. Although each technology involves special issues when abused, this mix becomes powerful and allows for automation, anonymity, and payment in cybercrime. This part discusses how the meeting of AI and cryptocurrency is changing cybercrime by supporting new strategies, individuals, and approaches.

AI-Enabled Cryptocrime: An Emerging Threat Landscape

Cybercriminals are rapidly integrating AI into the cryptocurrency crime toolkit to increase efficiency, reduce detection risk, and scale illicit operations. Key applications include:

- Automated Money Laundering: AI algorithms are used to optimize the movement of funds through mixers, DeFi platforms, and multiple chains to maximize anonymity and reduce traceability.
- Synthetic Identity Fraud: AI-generated profiles, including deepfake videos and forged documentation, are used to pass Know Your Customer (KYC) protocols on centralized exchanges and crypto service platforms.
- AI-Powered Investment Scams: NLP models are employed to generate persuasive marketing content, fake testimonials, and live chat support for fraudulent initial coin offerings (ICOs) and yield farming schemes.
- Dark Web Marketplaces: Autonomous agents run illicit markets that accept crypto payments, adjust prices algorithmically, and monitor law enforcement infiltration using AI-based pattern recognition.
- Social Engineering at Scale: AI-powered bots harvest and analyze social media data to personalize phishing campaigns targeting crypto holders, influencers, and startup founders.

This fusion allows bad actors to replicate the business logic of legitimate fintech — but for criminal purposes, with operational efficiency that would be impossible without AI.

AI in Crypto Trading Manipulation and Arbitrage Scams

AI is particularly useful in conducting market manipulation through advanced trading strategies such as:

- Pump-and-Dump Schemes: Bots analyze market sentiment, coordinate buy-ins, and manipulate volume to inflate token prices, then offload holdings before a crash.
- Wash Trading and Spoofing: AI scripts simulate fake transaction volume to mislead investors or exchanges about the popularity of a crypto asset.
- Flash Loan Exploits: Smart contracts are targeted with automated arbitrage and manipulation strategies that exploit price oracles, often completed in seconds.
- Sentiment-Based Exploits: NLP-driven bots monitor Reddit, Twitter, and Telegram for trending assets or market panic, and then execute trades based on sentiment shifts.

These tactics not only lead to financial losses but also erode trust in decentralized financial systems, undermining legitimate innovation in the crypto sector.

Ransomware Operations and AI-Driven Targeting

Ransomware is a prominent area where AI and cryptocurrency intersect. While ransomware attacks date back decades, AI has elevated them to high-precision, high-return operations:

- Target Selection: AI tools analyze public and dark web data to identify targets with high cryptocurrency holdings, weak security, and high reputational risk.
- Payload Customization: Malware can be adjusted in real-time using AI to evade specific defenses or exploit known vulnerabilities.
- Negotiation Bots: Some ransomware groups deploy chatbots for ransom negotiations, using sentiment analysis and psychological profiling to optimize ransom amounts.
- Crypto Obfuscation: Once paid, ransoms are laundered using AI-optimized routing through privacy coins, mixers, and synthetic token swaps.

Groups such as Conti, REvil, and LockBit have reportedly used elements of AI in their attack infrastructure, increasing their efficiency and resilience.

Deepfakes and Trust Exploitation in Crypto Ecosystems

Deepfakes — synthetic media generated using AI — are being used to exploit trust in crypto communities:

- Fake Founder Videos: Videos of supposed project leaders or influencers are circulated to boost the credibility of scam tokens or Ponzi schemes.
- Boardroom Impersonation: Corporate officers and fund managers are duped into transferring crypto after attending virtual meetings with deepfaked CEOs or CFOs.
- Fake Exchange Announcements: Deepfake audio and video are used to announce fake partnerships, token listings, or investment rounds.

Because the crypto ecosystem is highly media-driven, such manipulation significantly impacts token valuations and investor behavior, often before verification mechanisms can respond.

AI-Enhanced Money Laundering

Traditional money laundering involves three stages: placement, layering, and integration. AI amplifies each stage in the crypto realm:

- Placement: Stolen funds from hacks, ransomware, or scams are split into microtransactions and routed through decentralized exchanges (DEXs).
- Layering: AI algorithms select optimal sequences of mixers, token swaps, and cross-chain bridges to obfuscate the trail. They also monitor blockchain analytics tools to avoid detection.
- Integration: Funds reappear on centralized exchanges under synthetic identities, or are used to purchase NFTs, luxury goods, or real estate, completing the laundering cycle.

This makes it difficult for law enforcement and forensic firms to track down illicit flows, especially when AI-driven laundering operates autonomously and at scale.

Criminal AI-as-a-Service Models

A concerning trend is the emergence of AI-as-a-Service for cybercrime, particularly within crypto circles. Similar to legitimate software-as-a-service platforms, these tools are offered on dark web markets and encrypted forums. Examples include:

- AI Phishing Kits: Pre-trained models for generating fake investment pitches and phishing emails tailored to crypto terminology.
- Trading Bots for Pump Groups: Subscription-based bots that synchronize trades during pump-and-dump campaigns.
- Deepfake Kits: Drag-and-drop interfaces to create realistic deepfakes for use in scam promotions or identity fraud.
- Anonymity Optimizers: Tools that suggest privacy-preserving wallets, bridges, and routes based on machine learning analysis of surveillance tools.

This democratization of criminal AI tools empowers even non-technical users to engage in sophisticated crypto crimes, expanding the threat landscape exponentially.

CASE STUDIES IN AI-CRYPTO CRIME CONVERGENCE

Case Study 1: DeFi Rug Pull with AI-Generated Whitepaper

In 2023, a decentralized finance (DeFi) protocol named AuroFund was launched, presenting itself with a sophisticated website, a detailed whitepaper, and an extensive promotional campaign. Subsequent investigations revealed that the whitepaper and FAQs had been generated using artificial intelligence, while the purported team members' photos were deepfakes (Sun, D., Ma, W., Nie, L., & Liu, Y. 2024). Furthermore, the protocol's smart contracts contained concealed backdoors, which facilitated the theft of approximately $10 million in investor funds. These stolen assets were subsequently laundered through Tornado Cash using AI-optimized transaction routing. This case exemplifies how AI technologies can be weaponized to fabricate legitimacy at every stage of a fraudulent scheme, from branding and documentation to identity fabrication and financial manipulation (Pathade, C., & Hooli, S. 2025).

Case Study 2: AI-Powered Deepfake Impersonation in Exchange Attack

A prominent cryptocurrency exchange in Southeast Asia became the target of a $4 million social engineering scam, wherein an employee was deceived into transferring digital assets following a video call with an individual impersonating the company's Chief Financial Officer (CFO). Forensic investigations later confirmed that both the face and voice used during the call were AI-generated deepfakes. The attacker had compiled training data by harvesting audio and video recordings from publicly available webinars featuring the actual CFO. This incident represents one of the earliest publicly documented cases of real-time deepfake fraud targeting a financial institution, highlighting the growing sophistication and operational readiness of AI-driven impersonation technologies in cybercrime (BBC News. 2024).

CASE STUDIES AND REAL-WORLD INCIDENTS

To demonstrate the increasingly intertwined roles of artificial intelligence (AI) and cryptocurrency in modern criminal activities, this section presents a variety of real-life examples that illustrate how these technologies are exploited by cybercriminals. Among these examples are ransomware attacks, where AI-powered methods enhance the sophistication and reach of malicious software demanding cryptocurrency payments, making recovery and tracing more difficult. Additionally, the rise of deepfake-enabled fraud highlights how AI-generated synthetic media is used to deceive individuals and organizations, often facilitating financial theft or identity manipulation with cryptocurrency as the preferred medium for illicit transactions (Sgantzos, K., & Grigg, I. 2019). The section also examines manipulation of smart contracts on blockchain platforms, showcasing how attackers exploit vulnerabilities in automated, decentralized agreements to siphon funds or disrupt services. Furthermore, various scams built on AI technologies—from chatbots impersonating trusted entities to algorithmically generated phishing campaigns—demonstrate the rapid evolution and adaptability of cyber threats in the digital age. Collectively, these examples underscore the fast-paced and dynamic changes occurring within cyberspace, where the convergence of AI and cryptocurrency creates both new opportunities for innovation and heightened risks for security and trust.

Case Study 1: Lazarus Group – AI-Aided Crypto Heists Sponsored by a State Actor

The North Korea-linked Lazarus Group has been implicated in several major cryptocurrency heists, relying on a combination of advanced AI, malicious software, and social engineering tactics to infiltrate crypto wallets and backend exchange servers. One notable incident was the 2022 Ronin Bridge hack, which resulted in the theft of approximately $620 million from the Axie Infinity game. In this attack, the hackers used deceptive emails containing malicious attachments to trick employees into opening them, thereby compromising the internal network (Salah, K., et al. 2019). The group also employed sophisticated social engineering techniques, such as impersonating recruiters from well-known tech firms and conducting video interviews filled with natural language processing (NLP) phrases to extract sensitive information from targets. Furthermore, Lazarus timed these attacks strategically, using AI to identify moments when employees were most vulnerable—such as during product launches or security system downtimes—to maximize the likelihood of success.

Case Study 2: The Twitter Bitcoin Scam – A Blend of AI, Social Engineering, and Crypto Fraud

In July 2020, scammers employing social engineering tactics took control of high-profile Twitter accounts belonging to Elon Musk, Barack Obama, and Bill Gates. Through posts promising to double any Bitcoin sent to a specified address, they persuaded many users to transfer cryptocurrency to the scammers' wallets. Investigations revealed that AI tools played a significant role in the attack: they were used to analyze LinkedIn profiles and social media activity to identify Twitter employees with backend access, enabling targeted infiltration. Additionally, many scammers leveraged AI to mimic the victims' communication styles with remarkable accuracy, making their messages appear authentic and convincing. The scam was further amplified by the use of automated bots on Twitter and Reddit, which flooded these platforms with urgent calls to action, pressuring potential victims to respond quickly. Although teenage hackers were involved, the sophisticated use of automation and AI in this scheme underscores how even early cryptocurrency frauds can become highly effective and dangerous when combined with artificial intelligence.

Case Study 3: Deepfake CEO Scam in the UAE

In 2021, fraudsters employed deepfake technology to impersonate the CEO of a multinational corporation during a video conference with a bank executive in the United Arab Emirates. Believing they were speaking with the real CEO, the executive authorized a transfer of $35 million in both cryptocurrency and traditional currency. AI played a crucial role in this deception by replicating the CEO's appearance and voice, using publicly available online data to create an incredibly realistic synthetic persona. Additionally, staff involved in the scheme utilized AI-powered software to produce convincing fake email exchanges and official documents, further enhancing the illusion. To obscure the trail of the stolen cryptocurrency, the funds were dispersed across multiple wallets, routed through privacy-focused coins, and processed via mixers, making the transactions difficult to trace. This incident stands out as one of the earliest documented cases of deepfake-enabled crime in the cryptocurrency sector, highlighting the emerging risks posed by AI-driven fraud.

Case Study 4: The Squid Coin Rug Pull

Inspired by the popular TV series *Squid Game*, a cryptocurrency called Squid Coin was launched in 2021, quickly capturing the attention of many investors. Its value soared dramatically, increasing by over 230,000% within just a few days. Artificial intelligence played a significant role in facilitating the fraud behind this scheme. Both the project's whitepaper and marketing materials were generated by AI, using general-purpose language models trained on data from various crypto projects, lending an air of professionalism and legitimacy. AI-driven bots managed social media accounts, posting fake reviews and testimonials to further boost the coin's credibility. Visitors to the project's website were shown fabricated profiles of supposed club members, complete with AI-generated headshots and personalized backstories, adding another layer of illusion. Once the developers reached their fundraising goals, they locked token sales, preventing holders from selling their assets, and executed a rug pull that resulted in the theft of over $3.3 million. This case highlights how scammers use AI not only to appear trustworthy and manipulate investor perception but also to orchestrate their exit strategies smoothly, often leaving victims without recourse.

Case Study 5: Harmony Bridge Hack and AI-Powered Fund Obfuscation

In June 2022, Harmony's Horizon Bridge, a platform facilitating token transfers between Ethereum, Binance Smart Chain, and Harmony, suffered a major security breach that resulted in the theft of $100 million. AI played a pivotal role in the aftermath of the hack, as the criminals employed machine learning techniques to optimize the laundering process. By analyzing various options, the attackers identified the most effective channels to move stolen funds, utilizing services such as Tornado Cash, decentralized finance (DeFi) pools, and synthetic asset swaps. Forensic investigations revealed that the laundering network involved over 40 wallet addresses, many of which were created and managed by AI-driven bots. When exchanges and forensic teams flagged suspicious wallets, the laundering scripts quickly adapted, switching to new routing methods in real time—strong evidence of the use of adaptive AI. Despite the efforts of forensic firms and exchanges to track and recover the stolen assets, a significant portion of the funds remained unrecovered. This case highlights the growing challenge posed by AI-enhanced laundering operations, which can outpace traditional tracing and enforcement techniques.

Case Study 6: AI-Powered Malware in Cryptojacking

Cryptojacking refers to the unauthorized use of devices or computers by hackers to mine cryptocurrency without the owners' consent. In 2022, cybersecurity firm Symantec uncovered a sophisticated AI-powered malware strain designed specifically for this purpose. This malware could activate mining code only when the infected devices were idle, minimizing the chance of detection by users. It also generated fake CPU activity to deceive antivirus programs, helping the malware remain hidden on the system. Additionally, the malware was capable of dynamically adjusting the cryptocurrency mining algorithm based on the specific hardware and the temperature generated, optimizing performance while reducing the risk of overheating and exposure. This malicious software was downloaded onto nearly 110,000 computers worldwide, enabling the criminals behind the operation to mine approximately $1.5 million worth of Monero (XMR), a privacy-focused cryptocurrency favored by cybercriminals for its anonymity.

COMMON THEMES AND LESSONS LEARNED

Table 1. Recurring patterns in AI-Enabled cryptocurrency crime

Theme	Explanation
Automation of Attacks	AI enables the scaling of attacks without human oversight
Realistic Deception	Deepfakes and NLP are used to simulate trust and legitimacy
Exploitation of Media and Hype	AI-generated content boosts fraudulent tokens and schemes.
Advanced Money Laundering	AI optimizes fund movement across multiple layers to evade detection.
Global and Jurisdictional Complexity	Many attacks span multiple countries, complicating legal recourse.
Delayed Detection	AI's adaptability allows it to stay ahead of many existing forensic tools.

Source: Compiled by Author

The table titled "Recurring Patterns in AI-Enabled Cryptocurrency Crime" has been synthesized by analyzing a wide range of real-world case studies and expert research from reputable sources in cybersecurity, financial forensics, and blockchain intelligence. These cases suggest that AI helps make crypto-related crime more complex and harder to tackle. Tools used to be developed only in top R&D centers are now open to many criminals such as deepfake impersonations and phishing bots. What results is an environment where criminal activities include deceiving people, stealing money, and using technology — and where popular hacking models are reshaped using coding, models, and algorithms.

Legal and Regulatory Challenges in Addressing AI-Crypto Crime

AI and cryptocurrency merging has sped up progress in technology and also made it harder to control digital crimes. The global legal system is struggling to keep up with the vast, fast, and advanced nature of AI-related crypto crimes. This section looks at the major legal problems, points out areas not covered by laws, challenges in enforcement, and argues for the development of new rules (Valencia, F., et al. 2019).

Fragmented Global Regulatory Landscape

There is currently a significant challenge in the global regulatory landscape due to the lack of harmony in how different countries approach artificial intelligence (AI) and cryptocurrencies. Laws and regulations vary greatly between jurisdictions. For instance, while countries like Switzerland have adopted a relatively open and permissive stance toward cryptocurrency with minimal restrictions, others like China and India have imposed strict prohibitions. Similarly, regulatory approaches to AI differ: the European Union has introduced the AI Act, which classifies AI systems based on levels of risk, while the United States manages AI oversight through a sector-specific and state-by-state approach. This inconsistency allows criminals to exploit gaps in international coordination (Smuts, N. 2019). They often operate from countries with weak enforcement, use private cryptocurrency exchanges that do not require personal identification, and take advantage of regulatory loopholes. As a result, by strategically moving their operations across various jurisdictions, criminal groups can avoid detection and prosecution, making international cooperation and harmonized regulation increasingly urgent.

Anonymity and Pseudonymity in Crypto Transactions

Tracing the true identity behind blockchain transactions is a major challenge for law enforcement, as users typically remain pseudonymous. This difficulty is amplified when artificial intelligence (AI) is used to support sophisticated money laundering techniques. Criminals often rely on privacy-focused cryptocurrencies like Monero (XMR) and Zcash (ZEC), which are specifically designed to obscure transaction details. Additionally, many turn to decentralized finance (DeFi) platforms that allow anonymous signups, further shielding their identities. Automated mixers and tumblers, often powered by AI, shuffle digital assets between wallets to break the transaction trail. AI also enables these actors to constantly alter their laundering patterns, making detection and prosecution extremely difficult. A critical legal challenge arises from the fact that current laws do not require decentralized networks to maintain transparency. Moreover, these systems operate across borders, and without clear international regulations or enforcement mechanisms, it becomes nearly impossible to hold bad actors accountable when they violate laws in multiple countries (Lopes, V., & Alexandre, L. A. 2019).

Regulation of Deepfakes and Synthetic Media

While some jurisdictions have implemented laws addressing deepfakes related to disturbing content or election interference, there remains a significant legal gap when it comes to deepfakes used in financial or cryptocurrency crimes. One of the key emerging issues is the difficulty in proving criminal intent when synthetic media is involved. Victims of deepfake-related financial fraud often struggle to recover their losses due to the lack of legal precedents and established frameworks for such cases. Moreover, existing laws are insufficient to address the growing use of AI-generated personas and false identities in scams. An additional complication lies in the legal ambiguity surrounding concepts like digital personhood and authorship (Ji, S., Kim, J., & Im, H. 2019). As AI becomes increasingly capable of mimicking real individuals and generating convincing yet fraudulent content, determining responsibility and applying traditional legal definitions becomes more complex. This legal uncertainty hinders accountability and makes it harder to prosecute those using deepfakes and AI-driven tools for financial crimes.

Attribution and Responsibility in AI Crimes

Criminal charges related to AI-driven offenses raise complex questions about liability and responsibility. When an AI system independently causes fraud or engages in illegal activity, it is unclear whether blame should fall on the coder who created the system, the individual who deployed it, or the end-user who benefited from its actions. Key legal questions include whether an AI system can be considered a legal agent and, if so, to what extent it can be held accountable. Furthermore, if an open-source AI model is modified and used for criminal purposes, determining responsibility becomes even more difficult. Traditional legal frameworks are centered on human actors and are not well-equipped to handle the actions of autonomous systems or machine-driven decisions. For example, if a self-learning trading bot is used in a cryptocurrency pump-and-dump scheme, and there is no direct evidence linking the crime to a specific individual, enforcement agencies may struggle to hold anyone accountable. This illustrates the pressing need for legal systems to evolve in order to address the unique challenges posed by AI in financial crime.

Enforcement and Jurisdictional Issues

AI-driven cryptocurrency crimes often span multiple countries, making it difficult for law enforcement agencies to determine jurisdiction and assign legal responsibility. Factors such as the location of the crime, the physical placement of servers, the residence of the victims, and where the financial gains are realized can all fall under different legal systems, leading to jurisdictional confusion. Currently, there is a lack of comprehensive international treaties or cooperative frameworks that guide countries in assisting each other with cybercrime investigations or extradition processes. Many law enforcement agencies also face limitations in terms of resources and access to advanced technologies necessary to track and combat crimes involving artificial intelligence. This issue is especially severe in regions where cryptocurrency exchanges operate without proper licensing, where Know Your Customer (KYC) and Anti-Money Laundering (AML) regulations are poorly enforced or absent, and where offshore shell companies are used to obscure the origins and ownership of illicit financial gains. These gaps enable criminals to exploit weak regulatory environments and evade accountability across borders.

Regulation of Decentralized Finance and DAOs

The rapid emergence of Decentralized Finance (DeFi) platforms and Decentralized Autonomous Organizations (DAOs) has introduced new legal challenges, especially when these systems intersect with artificial intelligence. DAOs often operate without formal legal incorporation or clearly defined ownership structures, making it difficult to determine who is responsible when things go wrong. In many cases, AI bots are capable of exploiting DeFi protocols or participating in governance activities, yet there may be no identifiable individual or entity to hold accountable. Additionally, governance tokens can be distributed to thousands of anonymous users, further dispersing responsibility and complicating enforcement. AI also allows individuals to participate in DAOs indirectly, using automation to vote or make decisions on their behalf, which blurs the line of legal liability (Hassani, H., Huang, X., & Silva, E. 2018). As a result, regulators are increasingly faced with the difficult task of identifying who should be held accountable for actions taken within decentralized, AI-driven systems that lack central oversight.

Regulatory Response and Proposed Reforms

Various countries and agencies are beginning to take steps toward regulating AI and cryptocurrencies to address growing risks. In the European Union, the Markets in Crypto-Assets Regulation (MiCA) aims to create a clearer and safer environment for crypto markets and consumers. Additionally, the EU has introduced the AI Act, which is expected to become the primary legal framework governing high-risk AI applications, including those used in the financial sector. In the United States, regulatory bodies such as the Securities and Exchange Commission (SEC), the Commodity Futures Trading Commission (CFTC), and the Financial Crimes Enforcement Network (FinCEN) oversee cryptocurrency exchanges and enforce anti-money laundering (AML) laws (Yin & Vatrapu, 2017). Some U.S. regulations now require AI systems to be auditable and transparent regarding their algorithms. On a global scale, the Financial Action Task Force (FATF) has mandated that Virtual Asset Service Providers (VASPs) comply with the Travel Rule to better monitor cross-border cryptocurrency transactions. International cooperation is also supported by organizations like the United Nations Office on Drugs and Crime (UNODC) and Interpol, which have launched initiatives to tackle cybercrimes and facilitate cross-border law enforcement. However, many of these regulatory efforts tend to be reactive and struggle to keep pace with the rapid advancement of technology in the AI-crypto space.

The Need for AI-Specific Financial Regulation

Experts are advocating for the development of specific regulations targeting the use of AI in finance, with a particular focus on cryptocurrencies. Recommended measures include mandating regular audits of AI systems through algorithmic oversight to ensure their integrity and compliance. There is also a call for establishing licensing frameworks for developers creating high-risk AI software, which would help hold creators accountable. Additionally, experts suggest creating registries to track AI models deployed in crypto finance, providing greater visibility and control over their use. Implementing safety mechanisms and enforcing transparency requirements for autonomous trading bots are also seen as crucial steps to mitigate risks (Bartoletti, M., Pes, B., & Serusi, S. 2018). By adopting such targeted rules, the financial sector can better manage the challenges posed by AI's increasing role in decentralized finance, reducing potential vulnerabilities and promoting trust.

FUTURE OUTLOOK AND POLICY RECOMMENDATIONS

As AI and cryptocurrencies are integrated further into finance, the chances for new possibilities also increase the dangers of being exploited. Afterward, it is important for stakeholders to recognize the dual problem and prepare for upcoming threats, improve legal and digital defenses, and support progress through updated policies. Here, possible improvements are offered and specific help is given regarding the rise of crime linked to cryptocurrencies through artificial intelligence.

Anticipated Trends in AI-Crypto Crime

Autonomous Criminal Ecosystems

The rise of autonomous agents—self-operating AI models capable of performing tasks without human intervention—poses a new frontier for criminal activity in the cryptocurrency space. These sophisticated systems could include trading bots that autonomously learn market behaviors to manipulate prices and create unfair advantages. Additionally, smart contracts might be programmed to independently deploy, steal, and launder funds without direct human control, making detection and prevention extremely difficult (Lucarelli, G., & Borrotti, M. 2019). Furthermore, AI-driven systems could actively exploit vulnerabilities in decentralized finance (DeFi) protocols, automatically identifying and leveraging weaknesses to carry out illicit actions. This evolution toward fully self-directed criminal operations represents a significant challenge for regulators and security experts alike, as traditional oversight mechanisms may prove inadequate against such advanced threats.

Deepfake-as-a-Service (DFaaS)

As deepfake generation becomes increasingly accessible and affordable, Deepfake-as-a-Service (DFaaS) platforms are likely to proliferate on the dark web, offering criminals powerful tools for sophisticated fraud. These services could provide AI-driven impersonation to bypass ID verification processes on cryptocurrency exchanges, enabling unauthorized access and theft. They might also enable real-time video manipulation, facilitating CEO fraud by convincingly mimicking executives during video calls to deceive employees into making fraudulent transactions. Additionally, custom speech synthesis could be used to craft highly convincing phishing attacks, tricking victims into revealing sensitive information or transferring funds (Burggraf, T., & Vyas, A. 2020). The rise of DFaaS platforms significantly raises the stakes in digital security, demanding urgent advancements in detection and regulation.

Crypto-Financed AI Malware Development

Criminals are increasingly leveraging cryptocurrency to crowdfund the development of AI-powered malware, using tokens and anonymous bounty systems to incentivize developers. This decentralized funding approach allows malicious actors to attract a wide range of contributors without revealing their identities. Additionally, open-source AI models can be forked and modified into harmful variants specifically engineered to carry out sophisticated crypto heists, such as automated hacking, phishing, or laundering operations. This convergence of decentralized finance and AI malware development presents a growing threat that complicates efforts to track, prevent, and prosecute cybercrime (Shintate, T., & Pichl, L. 2019).

AI-Enabled Laundering Networks

Advanced laundering systems powered by machine learning are expected to become increasingly sophisticated by continuously analyzing real-time blockchain forensic activities. These systems will predict the likelihood of wallet detection with greater accuracy, allowing criminals to anticipate and avoid law enforcement scrutiny. Furthermore, they will dynamically reroute illicit funds through the most effective mixers, privacy coins, and other obfuscation tools, optimizing fund movement to evade tracing efforts. This ongoing evolution of AI-enabled laundering techniques poses significant challenges for investigators and highlights the urgent need for equally advanced countermeasures (Senthuran, G., & Halgamuge, M. 2019).

Strategic Policy Recommendations

To confront these evolving threats, a multi-stakeholder strategy is essential, involving governments, industry, academia, and civil society. The following recommendations span technical, regulatory, and institutional dimensions.

International Cooperation and Legal Harmonization

Establish a Global AI-Crypto Crime Task Force

Governments should work together to establish an intergovernmental organization similar to the Financial Action Task Force (FATF), but specifically dedicated to addressing AI-related cryptocurrency crimes. Such a body could play a vital role by developing shared threat intelligence platforms that enable member countries to exchange real-time information on emerging AI-driven crypto threats. It could also create standardized international protocols for detecting, tracking, and prosecuting fraud generated or facilitated by AI technologies. Additionally, this organization would facilitate cross-border investigative frameworks, helping to overcome jurisdictional challenges and enhance cooperation among law enforcement agencies worldwide. By coordinating efforts at a global level, this body would strengthen the fight against increasingly sophisticated and transnational AI-crypto criminal activities (Salah, K., Rehman, et al. 2019).

Harmonize Crypto and AI Regulations

The existing disparity in global regulatory standards creates opportunities for jurisdictional arbitrage, allowing bad actors to exploit weaker legal environments. To address this, international treaties should promote unified Anti-Money Laundering (AML) and Know Your Customer (KYC) standards that apply consistently across both centralized and decentralized cryptocurrency exchanges (Alessandretti, L., et al. 2018). Additionally, there is a pressing need for interoperable AI regulations, particularly concerning biometric deepfakes and autonomous financial agents, to ensure coherent oversight across borders. Establishing these harmonized frameworks would reduce regulatory gaps, enhance cooperation among nations, and strengthen the global fight against AI-enabled crypto crimes.

Strengthening Regulatory Infrastructure

Mandate AI System Disclosures in Financial Products

Any AI model deployed within a crypto exchange, DeFi platform, or digital asset service should be subject to strict regulatory oversight. This includes mandatory registration and thorough auditing to assess risks related to bias, security vulnerabilities, and potential misuse. Additionally, these AI systems must incorporate explainability features that enable clear tracing and understanding of their decision-making processes—such as how trading actions are determined—to ensure transparency and accountability. Implementing these requirements will help build trust in AI-driven financial services while mitigating risks associated with opaque or unchecked automated behaviors.

Create Licensing Regimes for High-Risk AI Use

Entities deploying AI in high-risk cryptocurrency applications—such as fund management, security, and regulatory compliance—should be required to obtain specialized licenses to operate legally. These entities must also undergo regular compliance reviews to ensure ongoing adherence to relevant laws and standards (Yin et al. 2019). In addition, independent third-party audits should be conducted to provide unbiased assessments of AI systems' performance and risk management. To enhance oversight, real-time supervision tools should be implemented to detect anomalies and suspicious activities promptly, enabling quicker responses to potential threats. Together, these measures would help maintain the integrity and security of AI-powered crypto services.

Enforce Smart Contract Accountability

Governments should establish clear mechanisms to ensure accountability for smart contracts, which are increasingly used in cryptocurrency and decentralized finance. This includes legally recognizing the authorship and intent behind smart contracts, providing a framework to determine responsibility when disputes or abuses arise. Additionally, legal provisions should enable authorized entities to halt or reverse smart contract transactions under specific conditions, such as cases involving clear evidence of fraud or malicious activity. Implementing these measures would help protect users and enhance trust in automated financial systems while balancing the autonomy that smart contracts offer (Zola, F., et al. 2019).

Enhancing Technological Countermeasures

Develop AI for Crime Detection

Law enforcement agencies and forensic firms should leverage AI technologies to enhance their investigative capabilities in combating crypto-related crimes. AI can be employed to detect deepfakes and synthetic identities, helping to uncover fraudulent personas used in scams and identity theft. Additionally, AI-driven analytics can scrutinize blockchain transaction patterns to identify anomalies indicative of illicit activities such as money laundering or fraud. Moreover, AI tools can trace clusters of cryptocurrency wallets linked to dark web marketplaces or entities flagged for suspicious behavior, providing critical insights for building cases and disrupting criminal networks. Utilizing AI in these ways significantly improves the effectiveness and speed of digital crime investigations (Baldominos, A., & Saez, Y. 2019).

Blockchain Intelligence Collaboration

Promoting collaboration between cryptocurrency exchanges and blockchain analytics firms is essential for strengthening defenses against AI-driven crimes. By sharing real-time threat intelligence feeds, these entities can stay ahead of emerging attack vectors and respond more quickly to suspicious activities. Joint efforts can also enhance the detection of sophisticated money laundering tactics, leveraging AI to identify patterns that might otherwise go unnoticed. Additionally, deploying AI-enabled "honeypot wallets" can serve as traps to attract and monitor attacker behavior, providing valuable data to better understand and mitigate threats (Rahouti, M., Xiong, K., & Ghani, N. 2018). Such partnerships foster a more resilient and proactive ecosystem against evolving crypto-related criminal activities.

Secure DeFi Protocols Against AI Exploits

DeFi developers should integrate AI-driven tools into their security workflows to strengthen protocol resilience. Specifically, they should use AI-powered penetration testing to proactively identify potential attack surfaces and vulnerabilities before deployment. Incorporating adaptive threat response systems within DeFi protocols can enable real-time detection and mitigation of emerging attacks, enhancing overall security. Additionally, adopting formal verification methods is crucial to rigorously prove the correctness and integrity of smart contracts, minimizing risks of bugs or exploits. Together, these measures help build safer, more trustworthy decentralized finance platforms in an increasingly complex threat landscape.

Empowering the Public and Industry

AI and Crypto Literacy Campaigns

Governments and NGOs should educate the public about the dangers of AI scams and deepfakes, helping people recognize and verify suspicious content. They should also teach how to verify crypto-related solicitations to avoid fraud, emphasizing the importance of checking legitimacy and spotting red flags. Additionally, public guidance on best practices for securing crypto wallets and protecting personal identity online is essential to prevent theft and unauthorized access.

Industry Self-Governance

The crypto and AI industries should establish ethics boards to review product launches, ensuring responsible innovation. They should adopt voluntary compliance codes focused on secure design and transparency to build trust with users. Additionally, collaboration on bug bounty programs can help identify and address AI vulnerabilities proactively, enhancing overall security.

Academic and Research Involvement

Fund Multidisciplinary Research

Universities should receive support to conduct interdisciplinary research across law, computer science, and economics, fostering a comprehensive understanding of AI and cryptocurrency issues. They should also focus on developing open-source AI tools for forensic investigations and creating simulation models of AI-crypto criminal ecosystems to anticipate and predict emerging trends in cybercrime (Sabry, F., et al. 2020).

Establish Cybercrime Innovation Labs

These labs can act as sandboxes for testing real-world responses to AI threats within blockchain environments. They also provide valuable training for law enforcement agencies in key areas such as blockchain analytics, deepfake detection, and smart contract forensics, enhancing their ability to investigate and respond effectively to emerging cybercrimes.

Ethical Considerations and Responsible Innovation

Developers and entrepreneurs must take proactive responsibility for the systems they create by adhering to ethical frameworks that promote transparency in AI design, including clear source provenance and training data disclosure. They should implement limitations on dual-use technologies to prevent misuse and embrace core AI ethics principles such as fairness, accountability, and non-maleficence. Established guidelines like the OECD AI Principles, the EU AI Ethics Guidelines, and the Asilomar AI Principles provide valuable foundations for setting ethical standards, particularly in crypto-focused AI applications (Rahouti, M., et al. 2018).

SUMMARY OF KEY FINDINGS

The rapid evolution and convergence of artificial intelligence (AI) and cryptocurrencies mark a transformational juncture in technological innovation, fundamentally reshaping the architecture of global finance, communication, and criminal enterprise. This paper has examined the increasingly symbiotic relationship between AI and cryptocurrency-related crimes, offering a comprehensive analysis of the technological foundations of both AI and blockchain systems—their capabilities, inherent vulnerabilities, and critical points of convergence. It has further delineated emerging criminal typologies, including AI-generated phishing campaigns, deepfake-driven identity fraud, automated money laundering operations, and the manipulation of decentralized finance (DeFi) platforms. Through detailed real-world case studies, the paper illustrates the growing sophistication and tangible impact of these threats on individuals, institutions, and state-level infrastructures. Additionally, it highlights the formidable legal and regulatory challenges inherent in this domain, such as jurisdictional fragmentation, the anonymity afforded by technology, and the absence of clearly defined frameworks for AI liability. Looking ahead, the discussion underscores the urgency of global collaboration, proactive technological innovation in enforcement mechanisms, ethically grounded AI development, and comprehensive education for both regulators and end-users. Collectively, these findings affirm that while AI and cryptocurrency technologies possess transformative potential for societal advancement, they remain acutely susceptible to exploitation by an increasingly agile and technologically adept criminal underworld.

Core Challenges Ahead

The integration of artificial intelligence into the cryptocurrency ecosystem fundamentally challenges the core principles of traditional crime control and financial oversight. This convergence exposes several systemic vulnerabilities that, if left unaddressed, may undermine the stability of global digital finance. Chief among these is the tension between pseudonymity and transparency: the inherent privacy features of blockchain, when combined with AI's capacity to simulate human identities and behaviors, significantly erode trust in digital communications and transactions. Furthermore, the scale and speed at which AI can automate illicit activities overwhelm conventional enforcement mechanisms, rendering reactive approaches insufficient. The question of accountability also becomes increasingly complex, as AI systems often operate autonomously and transnationally, obscuring the attribution of criminal responsibility within existing legal frameworks. Compounding these challenges is the persistent regulatory lag—innovations in AI and crypto continue to outpace the development of robust legal and policy safeguards, creating a widening compliance gap that bad actors readily exploit. Absent coordinated, forward-looking action, these dynamics threaten to destabilize not only financial security and regulatory coherence but also the broader trust that underpins emerging digital ecosystems.

The Path Forward: Balancing Innovation and Security

While the threats posed by the convergence of artificial intelligence and blockchain technologies are undeniable, so too is the potential for these innovations to serve as formidable tools for defense and resilience. Rather than viewing AI and blockchain solely as vectors of harm, it is imperative to recognize their capacity to enhance security, transparency, and institutional trust. Artificial intelligence can be harnessed to detect fraud, identify synthetic content, and automate regulatory compliance, thereby streamlining and strengthening enforcement mechanisms. Simultaneously, blockchain technology offers the promise of transparent auditing processes, immutable record-keeping, and programmable constraints that can embed trust into digital financial systems. Realizing this potential, however, requires a coordinated international response that integrates multiple strategic dimensions: policy innovation that establishes global standards for cryptocurrency operations and AI accountability; technological foresight to ensure that present-day tools are resilient against future threats; robust public-private partnerships uniting technology firms, law enforcement agencies, and academic institutions; and widespread education and awareness initiatives to empower individuals and organizations to recognize and defend against emerging digital threats. Through such multifaceted collaboration, the global community can shift from reactive crisis management to proactive digital stewardship.

Final Reflection

We stand at a pivotal intersection: one path leads to a digitally empowered society where AI and cryptocurrency foster greater inclusion, enhanced security, and improved efficiency across all sectors. The other veers into unregulated and fragmented territories, rife with fraud, identity erosion, and economic instability that threaten the very foundations of trust in digital systems. Our collective responsibility is clear—to ensure that innovation advances hand in hand with thoughtful regulation, so that technology remains a tool that serves humanity's best interests rather than undermines them. By addressing the complex convergence of AI and cryptocurrency crime today with proactive, transparent, and inclusive strategies, we have the opportunity to shape a digital future that is not only secure and resilient but also equitable and trustworthy for all.

CONCLUSION

The entwined evolution of artificial intelligence and cryptocurrency represents not merely a technological convergence but a paradigm shift in the architecture of contemporary financial crime. This paper has elucidated the manifold ways in which these dual-use technologies are recalibrating the methodologies, scale, and opacity of illicit enterprise. As machine intelligence grows increasingly autonomous and digital assets proliferate in both value and velocity, the landscape of cyber-enabled criminality is undergoing an unprecedented metamorphosis—one that transcends conventional frameworks of legal attribution, regulatory oversight, and ethical governance.

What emerges is a volatile digital ecosystem wherein adversarial actors harness AI's computational arsenal—generative models, reinforcement learning, and predictive analytics—to orchestrate hyper-targeted, scalable offenses with minimal human intervention. The pseudonymity and decentralization inherent in blockchain infrastructures further exacerbate these challenges, rendering traditional surveillance, risk management, and compliance instruments largely obsolete. The proliferation of synthetic media, real-time impersonation technologies, and AI-as-a-Service criminal platforms continues to erode the epistemological foundations upon which trust in digital systems rests. Yet, embedded within this maelstrom lies latent potential for systemic reform. Artificial intelligence, when wielded ethically and strategically, possesses the capacity to fortify digital financial ecosystems, forecast emergent threat vectors, and recalibrate enforcement paradigms to match the rapid adaptability of digital adversaries. Concurrently, blockchain's intrinsic transparency and immutability offer promising avenues for reinforcing institutional accountability—provided regulatory frameworks are agile enough to assimilate these capabilities.

The imperative, therefore, is twofold: first, to construct a transnational and interdisciplinary governance architecture that is both anticipatory and adaptive; and second, to embed ethical reflexivity into the design, deployment, and operationalization of AI systems across cryptographic ecosystems. Inaction will only deepen the regulatory asymmetry that emboldens malign innovation and corrodes institutional legitimacy. In sum, the nexus of AI and cryptocurrency presents not a discrete challenge but a civilizational inflection point. It demands from scholars, technologists, policymakers, and civil society not only technical vigilance but also philosophical clarity: a shared, enduring commitment to ensuring that technological advancement remains anchored in humanistic values and democratic ideals. The window for preemptive action is narrowing; decisive, cooperative engagement is not merely advisable—it is existentially imperative.

REFERENCES

Alessandretti, L., ElBahrawy, A., Aiello, L. M., & Baronchelli, A. (2018). Anticipating cryptocurrency prices using machine learning. *Complexity*, *2018*(1), 1–16. DOI: 10.1155/2018/8983590

Baldominos, A., & Saez, Y. (2019). Coin.AI: A proof-of-useful-work scheme for blockchain-based distributed deep learning. *Entropy (Basel, Switzerland)*, *21*(8), 723. DOI: 10.3390/e21080723

Bartoletti, M., Pes, B., & Serusi, S. (2018). Data mining for detecting Bitcoin Ponzi schemes. In *2018 Crypto Valley Conference on Blockchain Technology (CVCBT)* (pp. 75–84). IEEE. DOI: 10.1109/CVCBT.2018.00014

BBC News. (2024). Hong Kong worker duped by video call deepfake in $25m heist. *BBC News*. https://www.bbc.com/news/world-asia-china-68212580

Burggraf, T., & Vyas, A. (2020). Beyond risk parity—A machine learning-based hierarchical risk parity approach on cryptocurrencies. *Finance Research Letters*, *101523*. Advance online publication. DOI: 10.1016/j.frl.2020.101523

Chainalysis. (2023). *The 2023 crypto crime report*. https://www.chainalysis.com/reports/2023-crypto-crime-report/

Cocco, L., Tonelli, R., & Marchesi, M. (2019). An agent-based artificial market model for studying the bitcoin trading. *IEEE Access : Practical Innovations, Open Solutions*, *7*, 42908–42920. DOI: 10.1109/ACCESS.2019.2907880

Financial Action Task Force (FATF). (2022). *Virtual assets red flag indicators of money laundering and terrorist financing*. https://www.fatf-gafi.org

Hassani, H., Huang, X., & Silva, E. (2018). Big-crypto: Big data, blockchain and cryptocurrency. *Big Data and Cognitive Computing*, *2*(4), 10–34. DOI: 10.3390/bdcc2040034

Hassani, H., Huang, X., & Silva, E. (2018). Big-crypto: Big data, blockchain and cryptocurrency. *Big Data and Cognitive Computing*, *2*(4), 1–25. DOI: 10.3390/bdcc2040034

Huang, J.-Z., Huang, W., & Ni, J. (2019). Predicting bitcoin returns using high-dimensional technical indicators. *The Journal of Financial Data Science*, *5*(3), 140–155. DOI: 10.1016/j.jfds.2018.10.001

Interpol. (2023). *Global crime trends and cybercrime threats*. https://www.interpol.int/en/Crimes/Cybercrime

Jang, H., & Lee, J. (2018). An empirical study on modeling and prediction of bitcoin prices with Bayesian neural networks based on blockchain information. *IEEE Access : Practical Innovations, Open Solutions*, *6*, 5427–5437. DOI: 10.1109/ACCESS.2017.2779181

Jay, P., Kalariya, V., Parmar, P., Tanwar, S., Kumar, N., & Patel, M. (2020). Stochastic neural networks for cryptocurrency price prediction. *IEEE Access : Practical Innovations, Open Solutions*, *8*, 82804–82818. DOI: 10.1109/ACCESS.2020.2990659

Ji, S., Kim, J., & Im, H. (2019). A comparative study of bitcoin price prediction using deep learning. *Mathematics*, *7*(10), 898. DOI: 10.3390/math7100898

Kjærland, F., Meland, M., Oust, A., & Øyen, V. (2018). How can bitcoin price fluctuations be explained? *International Journal of Economics and Financial Issues*, *8*(3), 323–332.

Kumar, N. (2025). AI in Cyber Security: Innovations and Implications for a Safer Digital World. *Computer Science and Information Technology,* 13(1), 1–7. ISSN 2331-6071.

Kumar, N. (2025). The role of artificial intelligence in criminal investigations in India. *The Journal of Legal Studies*, *35*(49), 98–111. DOI: 10.2478/jles-2025-0006

Lahmiri, S., & Bekiros, S. (2020). Intelligent forecasting with machine learning trading systems in chaotic intraday bitcoin market. *Chaos, Solitons, and Fractals*, *133*, 109641. DOI: 10.1016/j.chaos.2020.109641

Liew, J., Li, R., Budavári, T., & Sharma, A. (2019). Cryptocurrency investing examined. *Journal of the British Blockchain Association*, *2*(2), 1–12. DOI: 10.31585/jbba-2-2-(2)2019

Lopes, V., & Alexandre, L. A. (2019). An overview of blockchain integration with robotics and artificial intelligence. *Ledger*, *4*. Advance online publication. DOI: 10.5195/ledger.2019.171

Lucarelli, G., & Borrotti, M. (2019). A deep reinforcement learning approach for automated cryptocurrency trading. In MacIntyre, J., Maglogiannis, I., Iliadis, L., & Pimenidis, E. (Eds.), *Artificial Intelligence Applications and Innovations* (pp. 247–258). Springer. DOI: 10.1007/978-3-030-19823-7_20

OECD. (2023). *OECD principles on artificial intelligence*. https://www.oecd.org/going-digital/ai/principles/

Pathade, C., & Hooli, S. (2025). Exposing hidden backdoors in NFT smart contracts: A static security analysis of rug pull patterns. *arXiv*. https://doi.org//arXiv.2506.07974DOI: 10.48550

Rahouti, M., Xiong, K., & Ghani, N. (2018). Bitcoin concepts, threats, and machine-learning security solutions. *IEEE Access : Practical Innovations, Open Solutions*, *6*, 67189–67205. DOI: 10.1109/ACCESS.2018.2874539

Sabry, F., Labda, W., Erbad, A., Al Jawaheri, H., & Malluhi, Q. (2019). Anonymity and privacy in bitcoin escrow trades. In *18th ACM Workshop on Privacy in the Electronic Society (WPES)*. ACM. DOI: 10.1145/3338498.3358639

Sabry, F., Labda, W., Erbad, A., Al Jawaheri, H., & Malluhi, Q. (2020). Cryptocurrencies and artificial intelligence: Challenges and opportunities. *IEEE Access : Practical Innovations, Open Solutions*, *8*, 175856–175879. DOI: 10.1109/ACCESS.2020.3025211

Salah, K., Rehman, M. H. U., Nizamuddin, N., & Al-Fuqaha, A. (2019). Blockchain for AI: Review and open research challenges. *IEEE Access : Practical Innovations, Open Solutions*, *7*, 10127–10149. DOI: 10.1109/ACCESS.2018.2890507

Salah, K., Rehman, M. H. U., Nizamuddin, N., & Al-Fuqaha, A. (2019). Blockchain for AI: Review and open research challenges. *IEEE Access : Practical Innovations, Open Solutions*, *7*, 10127–10149. DOI: 10.1109/ACCESS.2018.2890507

Senthuran, G., & Halgamuge, M. (2019). Prediction of cryptocurrency market price using deep learning and blockchain information: Bitcoin and Ethereum. In *Taylor & Francis* (pp. 349–364).

Sgantzos, K., & Grigg, I. (2019). Artificial intelligence implementations on the blockchain: Use cases and future applications. *Future Internet*, *11*(8), 170. DOI: 10.3390/fi11080170

Shintate, T., & Pichl, L. (2019). Trend prediction classification for high frequency bitcoin time series with deep learning. *Journal of Risk and Financial Management*, *12*(1), 17. DOI: 10.3390/jrfm12010017

Sholla, S., Naaz, S., Chishti, M. A., & Al-Turjman, F. (2021). Blockchain for sustainable and smart applications: Current trends, challenges, and future research directions. *Sustainable Cities and Society*, *72*, 103080. DOI: 10.1016/j.scs.2021.103080

Smuts, N. (2019). What drives cryptocurrency prices?: An investigation of Google trends and Telegram sentiment. *Performance Evaluation Review*, *46*(3), 131–134. DOI: 10.1145/3308897.3308955

Sun, D., Ma, W., Nie, L., & Liu, Y. (2024). SoK: Comprehensive analysis of rug pull causes, datasets, and detection tools in DeFi. *arXiv*. https://doi.org//arXiv.2403.16082DOI: 10.48550

Sun Yin, H., Langenheldt, K., Harlev, M., Mukkamala, R. R., & Vatrapu, R. (2019). Regulating cryptocurrencies: A supervised machine learning approach to de-anonymizing the Bitcoin blockchain. *Journal of Management Information Systems*, *36*(1), 37–73. DOI: 10.1080/07421222.2018.1550550

Symantec. (2022). *Cryptojacking activity and trends report*. https://www.broadcom.com/company/newsroom/press-releases

United Nations Office on Drugs and Crime (UNODC). (2022). *Cryptocurrency investigation training program*. https://www.unodc.org/unodc/en/cybercrime/

Valencia, F., Gómez-Espinosa, A., & Valdés-Aguirre, B. (2019). Price movement prediction of cryptocurrencies using sentiment analysis and machine learning. *Entropy (Basel, Switzerland)*, *21*(6), 589. DOI: 10.3390/e21060589

Yin, S. H., & Vatrapu, R. (2017). A first estimation of the proportion of cybercriminal entities in the Bitcoin ecosystem using supervised machine learning. In 2017 IEEE International Conference on Big Data (Big Data) (pp. 3690–3699). IEEE. DOI: 10.1109/BigData.2017.8258365

Zola, F., Eguimendia, M., Bruse, J. L., & Orduna Urrutia, R. (2019). Cascading machine learning to attack bitcoin anonymity. In *Proceedings of the IEEE International Conference on Blockchain* (pp. 154–167). DOI: 10.1109/Blockchain.2019.00011

KEY TERMS AND DEFINITIONS

AI-as-a-Service (AaaS): For crime AaaS in cybercrime refers to commodified AI toolkits available via darknet marketplaces, enabling non-technical users to orchestrate sophisticated scams, deepfakes, and trading manipulations. This outsourcing of algorithmic malfeasance has significantly lowered the entry barrier for cybercriminal activity.

Artificial Intelligence (AI): Artificial Intelligence denotes the emulation of human cognitive faculties by machines, encompassing adaptive learning, reasoning, and autonomous decision-making. In the context of cybercrime, AI's algorithmic precision facilitates high-frequency attacks, intelligent automation, and the generation of synthetically engineered media for deception.

Blockchain Technology: Blockchain is a decentralized, cryptographically secured ledger system that enables immutable and pseudonymous recording of digital transactions. Its trustless architecture, while fostering financial innovation, simultaneously engenders opacity that can be exploited by malicious actors to obscure illicit activities.

Crypto Forensics: Crypto forensics encompasses the application of advanced data analytics, machine learning, and graph theory to trace blockchain transactions, identify criminal entities, and map the laundering pathways of digital assets, often in defiance of privacy-preserving technologies.

Decentralized Finance (DeFi): DeFi refers to a suite of blockchain-based financial services operating without intermediaries. By disintermediating traditional finance, DeFi democratizes access but concurrently exposes systemic vulnerabilities that are increasingly targeted through algorithmically driven exploits and arbitrage mechanisms.

Deepfakes: Deepfakes are hyper-realistic synthetic media artifacts generated through deep learning algorithms, typically leveraging generative adversarial networks (GANs). They have become formidable tools in identity subversion and executive impersonation, challenging the ontological boundaries of truth in digital communication.

Flash Loan Attacks: These are instantaneous, unsecured borrowing mechanisms exploited through smart contracts, wherein attackers manipulate on-chain data (such as oracles) to execute complex arbitrage strategies and drain liquidity from DeFi platforms—all within a single transaction cycle.

Regulatory Arbitrage: This refers to the strategic exploitation of jurisdictional inconsistencies in legal and regulatory frameworks by actors operating in the AI-crypto nexus. It enables evasion of compliance requirements by relocating operations to lenient regulatory environments, undermining global financial oversight.

Smart Contracts: Smart contracts are self-executing code embedded within blockchain networks, which autonomously trigger actions upon the fulfillment of predefined conditions. Though intended to enhance transactional efficiency, these contracts are susceptible to adversarial manipulation when vulnerabilities in their logic are detected and exploited.

Synthetic Identity Fraud: This entails the algorithmic construction of fictitious personas using AI-generated images, documents, and behavioral patterns, often deployed to circumvent Know Your Customer (KYC) protocols on crypto platforms. It exemplifies the convergence of AI and anonymity in facilitating undetectable infiltration of financial systems.

Chapter 5

Combating Cryptocrime and Fraud in Small Island Developing States' Disaster Management: A Blockchain-Based Framework

Leo S. F. Lin
https://orcid.org/0000-0003-3684-5403
Charles Sturt University, Australia

Duane Aslett
https://orcid.org/0000-0003-1540-7180
Charles Sturt University, Australia

Geberew Tulu Mekonnen
https://orcid.org/0000-0001-7672-3609
Charles Sturt University, Australia

Mladen Zecevic
https://orcid.org/0009-0002-1455-2992
Charles Sturt University, Australia

Astrid Vachette
https://orcid.org/0000-0002-9483-852X
Charles Sturt University, Australia

Douglas M. C. Allan
https://orcid.org/0000-0003-0616-5546
Charles Sturt University, Australia

ABSTRACT

Blockchain technology offers transformative potential for disaster response and management in Small Island Developing States (SIDS), which are particularly vulnerable to disasters or face heightened disaster risks due to geographic isolation and limited resources. By providing a decentralized, immutable, and transparent ledger, blockchain technology facilitates secure data sharing, streamlines disaster logistics, and enhances emergency aid distribution, fostering resilience in disaster-prone regions. However, risks of cryptocrime, such as money laundering and smart contract exploits, can undermine its benefits. This chapter examines blockchain's applications in disaster logistics, community identification, and resource allocation,

DOI: 10.4018/979-8-3373-0675-9.ch005

highlighting its role in reducing fraud and building trust. This study proposes the Blockchain Response Efficacy Model (BREM) to assess the efficiency, transparency, and fraud risks associated with SIDS. Through case studies and literature analysis, this chapter offers insights to strengthen disaster resilience while mitigating cryptocrime vulnerabilities.

1. INTRODUCTION

Disasters triggered by natural hazards, such as hurricanes, earthquakes, or floods, call for rapid, coordinated, and transparent responses to save lives, protect critical infrastructure, maintain stability in the economy, and safeguard the environment (Shevchuk et al., 2025). Small Island Developing States (SIDS), such as those in the Caribbean, the Pacific, and the Indian Ocean, are particularly challenged.[1] Their isolation, lack of economic diversification, low resource endowments, and high exposure to climate-induced disasters make them especially at-risk. SIDS experience annual Gross Domestic Product (GDP) losses due to natural hazard-induced disasters that exceed the losses of larger economies faced with similar disasters by a factor of four (IMF, 2016). For example, Hurricane Maria (2017) resulted in estimated damages to Dominica equivalent to 226% of its GDP (Belblidia et al., 2019; Clarke, 2021; Pill, 2022). It is these disproportionate impacts that underscore the imperative for deployment of innovative, scalable, and resilient technological solutions to enhance the preparedness, response, and recovery to disasters in SIDS. The inherent urgency in a disaster context means that SIDS need to simultaneously and timely cover rapid needs assessment, real-time supply chain tracking, affected communities' identification, and auditable distribution of emergency aid.

Blockchain, developed in the context of the Fourth Industrial Revolution, may be operationalized to help SIDS face the most pressing challenges during and in the aftermath of disasters. Blockchain is a revolutionary technology that introduces an entirely new paradigm in emergency management because of its decentralized, immutable, and transparent nature (Myeong & Jung, 2019; Shevchuk et al., 2025; Sripathi & Leelavati, 2024). In contrast to traditional centralized systems, blockchain is a distributed ledger technology (DLT) that operates on a network of nodes, making it resilient to single points of failure and capable of supporting secure peer-to-peer transactions without the need for intermediaries (Chowdhury et al., 2019; Farahani, Firouzi, & Luecking, 2021). Its cryptographic consensus rules, whether proof-of-work or proof-of-stake, are designed to ensure the integrity and immutability of the data, potentially making it particularly useful in crisis situations where trust among parties from states, non-governmental organizations (NGOs), and/or at-risk communities is crucial and often tenuous. Through real-time data sharing among all relevant parties, automating the distribution of aid using smart contracts, and ensuring the transparency of resource allocation, blockchain has the potential to transform how emergency responses are managed and executed (Habib, Alnaemi, & Habib, 2024; Siemon, Rueckel, & Krumay, 2020).[2] A recent systematic review emphasizes blockchain's emerging role in disaster response/management, highlighting its potential to address transparency, efficiency, and trust issues in emergency contexts (Shevchuk et al., 2025).

Nonetheless, the positives of blockchain, including being anonymous, decentralized, and allowing for the automation of smart contracts, also carry considerable risks, such as regulatory gaps or the potential misuse during rapid deployments (Shevchuk et al., 2025). Anonymity features facilitated by public key encryption make user identification challenging, not compliant with Know-Your-Customer (KYC) and Anti-Money Laundering (AML) regulations. That opacity, however, makes it easy to conduct activities such as money laundering and terrorist financing. For example, global fraud related to cryptocurrencies totaled $3.7 billion was stolen through cryptocurrency hacks and exploits in 2022.[3] Smart contracts, which automate tasks such as aid disbursement, are also vulnerable to being bugged or gamed. One such example is the 2016 DAO hack, which involved a vulnerability in The DAO's smart contract on the Ethereum blockchain that allowed an attacker to siphon off approximately 3.6 million ETH, which was worth around $50 to $70 million USD at the time depending on the source and ETH price fluctuations.[4] In addition, blockchain's decentralized characteristic makes it hard to regulate, as there is no central body to regulate and retrieve money spent on scams. With ominous undertones, these risks are particularly alarming in the context of disasters, where the urgency in rolling out blockchain solutions could favour efficiency over security and present an opportunity for vulnerable populations to be exploited.

Blockchain is a two-sided technology in the emergency management field, being useful and transparent, and able to increase the capacity for interoperability and effectiveness. At the same time, it becomes a potential subject for illicit schemes, known as cryptocrime. This study focuses on SIDS, where the risks and implications of disaster response/management are particularly high due to their economic and environmental challenges. To account for this dual nature, we propose the Blockchain Response Efficacy Model (BREM), a model designed to measure the trade-offs of blockchain in disaster response/management. The BREM estimates three broad areas: the efficiencies of operation (delivery of aid quickly), the transparency levels (how easy it is to see where the money is going), and the risks of fraud (risk of falling for a phishing scam, or laundering money). This chapter has three research questions:

1. How can blockchain enhance emergency response in disaster-prone contexts like SIDS?

2. What are the risks of cryptocrime, and fraud associated with blockchain adoption in emergency contexts?
3. How can the proposed *Blockchain Response Efficacy Model (BREM)* assess blockchain's efficacy, balancing operational benefits against fraud risks?

This chapter is structured as follows: Section 2 provides a literature review of blockchain applications in disaster management. Section 3 outlines the methodology. Section 4 presents the BREM model, detailing its formulation and practical application. Section 5 discusses findings from case studies and model simulations, highlighting blockchain's impact on SIDS. Section 6 examines the policy implications and provides recommendations. Section 7 concludes with limitations and directions for future research.

2. LITERATURE REVIEW

2.1 Blockchain in Emergency Management

Blockchain, a form of distributed ledger technology (DLT), enables secure, peer-to-peer transactions recorded on an immutable ledger, validated through cryptographic consensus mechanisms such as proof-of-work (PoW) or proof-of-stake (DPoS) (Farahani et al., 2021; Sunyaev & Sunyaev, 2020). Unlike centralized databases, which rely on a single authority and are vulnerable to single points of failure, blockchain's decentralized architecture distributes data across a network of nodes, ensuring resilience and data integrity (Islam & Apu, 2024). This makes it particularly valuable in emergency management, where rapid coordination among diverse stakeholders, such as governments, NGOs, international aid agencies, and affected communities, is critical but often hampered by mistrust, bureaucratic inefficiencies, and logistical challenges. In small states, where resources are limited, blockchain's ability to enhance transparency, speed, and interoperability offers transformative potential (Elhussieny, 2025; Fabri & Fabri, 2019).

Private sector and not-for-profit organisations use blockchain in disaster logistics (Coppi & Fast, 2019; Shin, Kang, & Bae, 2020). Blockchain is employed to improve the transparency of the supply chain by having a trackable trail of relief supplies from donor to recipient (Rai, Srivastava, Rai, & Pattanashetti, 2024). Shevchuk et al. (2025) illustrate blockchain's effectiveness in supply chain management, beneficiary verification and information-sharing during disasters. With SIDS often facing constrained ports and transportation infrastructure, blockchain can offer real-time visibility of supply chains to prevent blockages and delays, meaning vital resources can reach the people who need them. The United Nations Conference on Trade and

Development (UNCTAD) and other international bodies have recognised blockchain's potential to strengthen supply chains in developing and vulnerable regions.[5]

Blockchain can also aid in identifying affected communities and verifying benefits, a critical challenge in disaster recovery, ensuring the proper allocation of aid to the correct persons, without duplicates or fraud (Alsalamah & Nuzzolese, 2020; Kumar, Sebastian, & Nandakumar, 2025). The U.S. Department of Homeland Security (DHS) has explored blockchain technology as part of its broader efforts to enhance digital identity management and secure verification of individuals for public services.[6] Crowdsourced disaster mapping is another pioneering use case, with blockchain fostering crowd engagement in providing real-time disaster relief (Habib et al., 2024; Sarbajna, Eick, & Laszka, 2023).

Blockchain is easing the processing of insurance and claims, especially for parametric insurance that pays out on pre-agreed terms (Lawrence, Tarr, Brook, Chaperon, & Sorel, 2023; Subbian & Gollapudi). The Caribbean Catastrophe Risk Insurance Facility (CCRIF SPC) provides parametric insurance to member states, enabling rapid payouts based on disaster indices, significantly faster than traditional insurance claims processing (ESCAP, 2018; Lawrence et al., 2023). Recent studies and pilots have explored leveraging blockchain technology to automate and enhance these parametric insurance payments, aiming to increase transparency, reduce fraud, and further speed up disbursements.[7]

2.2 Cryptocrime and Fraud Risks

Despite its potential to be a game changer, the very advantages of blockchain technology can also introduce serious vulnerabilities, making it susceptible to exploitation by cybercriminals, especially in high-stakes decision-making scenarios (Ilari, 2025; van der Horst et al., 2025). These crime types, referred to generally as "cryptocrime", encompass hacking, phishing, smart contract vulnerabilities, money laundering, ransomware, and Ponzi schemes (Salisu & Filipov, 2023; Trozze et al., 2022).

The permissionless nature of blockchains like Bitcoin and Ethereum makes them a fertile ground for hacking and phishing attacks because public key encryption services are used to provide pseudonymity of actual users' names (Ali et al., 2018; Jamwal, Cano, Lee, Tran, & Truong, 2024; Voshmgir, 2025).[8] According to Chainalysis, in 2023, illicit cryptocurrency addresses received an estimated $24.2 billion, representing approximately 0.34% of the total on-chain transaction volume. This estimate includes funds sent to known illicit addresses as well as cryptocurrency stolen through hacks.[9] During disaster situations that lead to the hurried implementation of blockchain options, hackers could use the confusion to run phishing scams. Also, smart contracts, such as those that manage aid distribution, are written in code, and code, if not carefully composed, can be exploited (Ndiaye & Konate, 2021). In a disaster setting when speed is of utmost importance, hastily implemented smart contracts can easily skip security audits, and funds might get stolen.

Ransomware attacks that blackmail victims with the threat of making cryptocurrency payments exploit the blockchain's anonymity to facilitate extortion (Ahn, Doupe, Zhao, & Liao, 2016; Payne & Mienie, 2021). In a disaster situation, ransomware may target relief databases or supply chain systems, hindering life-saving responses. Ponzi schemes and scam crypto projects continue to increase risks, not least with disaster fundraising (Mukherjee, Larkin, & Corbet, 2021). Money laundering is a persistent issue in blockchain, stemming from its intrinsic pseudonymous property (Dupuis & Gleason, 2020; Jefri, 2024). Criminals could use cryptocurrencies to transfer illicit funds anonymously via wallets, mixers, and ghost addresses on the so-called dark web and several other means, and all without the need for a central authority to guarantee or oversee such transactions (Ditamore, 2018).

2.3 Gaps in the Literature

The literature on blockchain applications in disaster management highlights its potential to enhance transparency, efficiency, and interoperability in aid distribution, logistics, and identity verification. However, significant gaps remain in addressing how these benefits interact with the risks of cryptocrime, especially in complex post-disaster settings, where regulatory frameworks are often weak. Current research tends to focus on isolated cases without critically examining vulnerabilities to fraud, leaving a gap in broader risk assessments. This gap was also identified by Shevchuk et al. (2025), calling for more holistic frameworks to evaluate both the opportunities and risks of blockchain in disaster management. Furthermore, there is a lack of practical tools or models for practitioners and policy-makers to evaluate blockchain's trade-offs in disaster contexts. To address these gaps, coding classified data could involve categorizing transparency as ensuring traceable aid flows, efficiency as streamlined resource allocation, and interoperability as seamless data sharing across systems, while systematically analyzing fraud risks and developing accessible frameworks to assess blockchain's applicability in emergency response.

3. METHODOLOGY

This qualitative analytical research employs thematic analysis of secondary data to investigate the dual application of blockchain in disaster management, especially its associated challenges related to cryptocrime. The study draws on various sources, including academic literature, reports from organizations, and case. These sources were chosen to be relevant to blockchain in disaster responses. Through proposing a new model: the Blockchain Response Efficacy Model (BREM), this paper provides a comprehensive and accessible analysis for practitioners and policy-makers.

The data collection methods included comprehensive searches in academic databases such as Scopus, Web of Science, and Google Scholar, as well as electronic searches of grey literature, using targeted keywords including "blockchain disaster management," "cryptocrime," "emergency response," "distributed ledger technology," "disaster resilience," "Small Island States," and "Small Island Developing States (SIDS)." Additionally, terms such as "blockchain and cybercrime" and "fraud in blockchain" were employed to thoroughly capture both the benefits and risks associated with the technology.

Thematic analysis was performed using the six-phase process of thematic analysis as described by Braun and Clarke (2006), which includes: familiarization, coding, generating themes, reviewing themes, defining themes, and report writing (Braun & Clarke, 2006, 2012). Sources were read to identify common themes and topics associated with the role of blockchain in emergency management during the familiarization phase. Preliminary coding classified the data into two major categories, opportunities and challenges. The sub-themes of opportunities included transparency (e.g., corrupt-free, immutable ledger in aid trails), efficiency (e.g., drives down delivery time), and interoperability (e.g., exchanging data across agencies). The sub-themes of challenges included anonymity (e.g., potential implications of untraceable transactions), scalability (e.g., blockchain's inadequacy in large-scale disasters), and regulatory gaps (e.g., lack of KYC/AML compliance). Particular cryptocrimes, such as phishing, smart contract breaches, money laundering, ransomware, and Ponzi schemes, were discussed. We use qualitative analysis software MAXQDA 24 to assist coding and analysis (Kuckartz & Rädiker, 2019).

To enhance methodological rigor, the study employed data triangulation by drawing on a diverse range of documentary sources, including academic publications, organizational reports, and policy documents, to capture multiple perspectives and minimize potential biases. The BREM was presented as an adjunct means to assess blockchain effectiveness. Limitations, such as the use of secondary data sources and the elimination of primary research interviews for some stakeholders due to resource constraints, were identified to inform future research. Also, the BREM model serves as an analytical tool in assessing the promises and perils of blockchain technology in disaster management; however, it is an initial proposal and requires empirical study in the future, as emphasized by Shevchuk et al. (2025), in order to address practical challenges of blockchain in disaster contexts.

4. BLOCKCHAIN RESPONSE EFFICACY MODEL (BREM) AND ASSESSMENT FRAMEWORK

In order to validate the role that blockchain plays in the management of disastrous situations, this chapter proposes BREM, a pragmatic model whose aim is to achieve a trade-off between operating efficiency, correctness, and prevention of fraud. Tailored for SIDS, which face resource constraints and frequent disasters and therefore need quick, effective, and affordable tools, BREM uses easy-to-understand calculations to measure blockchain's effectiveness.

4.1 Model Components

The BREM calculates an Efficacy Score (E) based on three weighted factors critical to disaster management: Operational Efficiency (OE), Transparency and Trust (TT), and Fraud Risk Reduction (FRR). These factors reflect blockchain's core strengths and vulnerabilities, as identified in the literature.

The model is expressed as:

$$E = w_1 \cdot OE + w_2 \cdot TT + w_3 \cdot FRR$$

Where:

- w_1, w_2, w_3: Weights reflecting the relative importance of each factor (w1+w2+w3 = 1).
- OE, TT, FRR: Scores (0 to 1) based on qualitative assessments normalized to a 01 scale.

Each factor is evaluated using metrics tailored to disaster management, ensuring the model captures both the operational benefits and fraud risks of blockchain adoption.

4.2 Scoring Metrics

Operational Efficiency (OE) measures blockchain's ability to reduce aid delivery times and resource misallocation compared to traditional systems. The metric is calculated as the average of two sub-metrics: percentage reduction in delivery time and percentage reduction in resource misallocation. In SIDS, where timely aid is critical due to geographic isolation, OE is a key indicator of blockchain's value. Data for OE can be sourced from case studies or organizational reports, with qualitative assessments normalized to a 0–1 scale.

Transparency and Trust (TT) assesses the proportion of stakeholders (e.g., governments, NGOs, beneficiaries) with access to real-time, immutable transaction records on the blockchain. This metric reflects blockchain's ability to foster trust through auditability and data integrity. TT is calculated based on stakeholder access data, often available in project reports or surveys, normalized to a 0–1 scale.

Fraud Risk Reduction (FRR) assesses blockchain's capacity to mitigate traditional fraud (e.g., duplicate claims, fund diversion) while also accounting for emerging cryptocrime risks (e.g., phishing, smart contract exploits). The metric is calculated as the estimated reduction in traditional fraud minus the introduced risk of cryptocrime. In SIDS, where fraud can erode limited resources, FRR is critical for assessing blockchain's net security impact.

4.3 Weight Assignment

Weights ((w_1, w_2, w_3)) are assigned based on the disaster context, reflecting the relative importance of each factor. For SIDS, where rapid response and resource constraints are paramount, we propose:

- (w_1 = 0.4) for OE, emphasizing efficiency due to limited infrastructure and urgent needs.
- (w_2 = 0.3) for TT, recognizing transparency's role in building trust among decentralized stakeholders.
- (w_3 = 0.3) for FRR, acknowledging the need to mitigate fraud in high-stakes disaster scenarios.

Weights can be adjusted for other contexts, such as large-scale disasters in developed nations, where transparency or fraud reduction may take precedence.

4.4 Interpretation

The BREM's Efficacy Score (E) is interpreted as follows:

- E > 0.7: High efficacy; blockchain significantly enhances disaster response with minimal fraud risk, suitable for widespread adoption.
- 0.4 \leq E \leq 0.7: Moderate efficacy; blockchain offers benefits but requires targeted fraud mitigation strategies, such as enhanced KYC or secure coding.
- E < 0.4: Low efficacy; cryptocrime risks may outweigh operational benefits, necessitating significant safeguards before adoption.

The risk category is referenced from Kori and Gadagin (2024), where the study used 0.4 and 0.7 as thresholds for the risk assessment (Kori & Gadagin, 2024). In this study, at a score of less than 0.4, a risk/benefit position would be evident - where threat of cryptocrime would likely outweigh operational benefits; at a score between 0.4 and 0.7, blockchain would present clear advantages, but one that would require specific risk management; and over a score of 0.7 would reflect a significant compelling proposition to adopt with minimal risks. This corresponds with how many scoring systems are developed, in which cut-offs are set in order to enable actionable decision making through the separation of low, moderate, and high levels of efficacy, as in other models that use cut-offs to describe the clinically or operationally meaningful expected value of outcomes.

The following table outlines the interpretation of the Blockchain Response Efficacy Model (BREM) Efficacy Score ((E)) for evaluating blockchain's role in disaster response. It includes score ranges, their corresponding efficacy levels, and actionable recommendations.

Table 1. BREM efficacy score interpretation

Efficacy Score Range	Efficacy Level	Interpretation	Recommendations
(E > 0.7)	High	Blockchain enhances disaster response with minimal fraud risk, suitable for widespread adoption.	Scale blockchain implementation across similar contexts. Ensure ongoing monitoring for emerging risks.
(0.4 \leq E \leq 0.7)	Moderate	Blockchain offers operational benefits but requires targeted fraud mitigation strategies to address cryptocrime risks.	Implement blockchain with enhanced safeguards, such as know-your-customer (KYC) protocols, secure smart contract coding, or AI-driven fraud detection.
(E < 0.4)	Low	Cryptocrime risks may outweigh operational benefits, indicating blockchain's unsuitability without significant improvements.	Reassess blockchain adoption feasibility. Prioritize significant safeguards, such as hybrid blockchains or regulatory frameworks, before proceeding.

(made by the authors)

4.5 Bias Mitigation Mechanism

To protect the impartiality and credibility of the BREM scoring mechanism, multiple independent assessors must participate. The process requires the score-sheet to be completed by at least three independent assessors blind to one another's scores and to be analyzed for the same project or case study independently by at least three different assessors. This distance reduces the chances of groupthink or undue influence, which allows a diverse range of viewpoints that can counteract individual biases and increase validity via diversity (Gwet, 2014; Janis & Janis, 1982; Patton, 2002).

Standardization of the source data for BREM scoring is important to minimize bias and maintain consistency. Before any measurement is made, there must be clear identification and documentation of credible data sources against each of the measures. These can, for example, be project evaluation reports by NGOs, system logs, or surveys of stakeholders. These normative references are required to be cited for each score assigned by the raters. This method of analysis reduces cherry picking and anecdotal data that is subject to selection bias.

Once all independent assessors submit their assessment scores, the score of each independent assessor over OE, TT, and FRR is retrieved, and the median is then used to calculate the overall score of an entry. Median is the preferred option over mean, as it is insensitive to skewness/outliers, hence mitigating outlier influence on a single judge's extreme scores on average public sentiment. When faced with large discrepancies (eg, with scores for any item differing by more than 0.2), an open discussion is conducted to achieve consensus. The conversation is moderated by a neutral party who discusses evidence-based tuning and ensures that every facet is considered. The pooling process not only enhances the variance in final predictions, making them more robust, but also allows for the identification of misinterpretations or possible personal biases in individual judgments.

Transparency is one of the foundations of the BREM scoring mechanism. Assessors must document at length the reason for the score provided in the "Notes" column on the scoring sheet. The scoring sheets and the final results are published for the public or to those interested. Such transparency prevents biased scores as well and would allow external validation of the assessment. Implementation entails integrating a "Comments" section for qualitative and storing all scoring sheets in a shared directory to discuss them later. Clear documentation serves to build trust in the assessment process and enhances continued learning and improvement.

BREM scores are reviewed regularly to ensure that the scores are current. Scores are updated periodically to reflect new information or changing context. Such evaluations also include testing BREM scores against some empirical criterion to test or calibrate the scoring process. This iterative process helps to guard against "anchoring bias" (Furnham & Boo, 2011; Lieder, Griffiths, M. Huys, & Goodman, 2018). This would involve including follow-up assessments of known duration based on the project timeline and using real-world data to help refine estimates of accuracy. Review can promote continuing improvement and development of the BREM in response to changes both in circumstances and challenges.

4.6 Model Extensions

The BREM is designed for flexibility and future refinement. Potential extensions include:

- Dynamic Weights: Adjusting weights in real-time based on disaster severity or stakeholder priorities, using data from situational reports or Internet of Things (IoT) sensors.[10]
- Qualitative Inputs: Incorporating stakeholder surveys to refine TT and FRR scores, capturing perceptions of trust and security.
- Scalability Metrics: Adding factors for blockchain's performance in large-scale disasters, such as transaction throughput or energy consumption, relevant for SIDS with limited infrastructure.
- Integration with AI: Combining BREM with machine learning to predict fraud risks based on historical data, enhancing FRR accuracy.

These extensions would add to the extended sources of information and computation, but could find additional utility of the model in several different disaster scenarios. By embedding the BREM into the context of existing and then adapting it to the specific requirements of SIDS, the model can be a powerful testbed for how blockchain might be best brought to bear on disaster management, making a calibration between innovation and a sense of security.

5. FINDINGS AND DISCUSSION

5.1 Opportunities in Emergency Response

Emerging blockchain technology opens up many opportunities to the disaster management of SIDS, which are prone to experiencing recurrent disasters such as hurricanes and floods, which require fast, transparent, and effective responses. Despite the adverse socio-economic impacts of disasters in SIDS face aggregate economic losses estimated at around 2.1% of GDP annually due to disasters.[11] These losses exacerbate vulnerabilities in SIDS, where regulatory and infrastructural capacities are often limited, compounding the challenges of recovery and resilience. Blockchain helps to promote resilience in disaster-affected areas by facilitating safe data sharing, automation, and accountability. The Blockchain Response Efficacy Model (BREM) complements this capability by offering a practical structure for assessing blockchain's effectiveness, thus facilitating informed adoption and strategic planning, aimed at serving the specific necessities of SIDS.

Interoperability

Blockchain's decentralized ledgers enable data sharing among disparate parties, which is crucial in SIDS where physical isolation and unreliable communication channels complicate coordination, especially since, during disasters, communication is often the first to fail and the last to be restored. For example, following the 2015 floods in Sri Lanka, the Start Fund launched a pilot program in 2016 using the Ethereum blockchain to improve transparency and efficiency in humanitarian aid coordination and fund disbursement. However, the effectiveness of such solutions in SIDS may be limited by the persistent challenge of maintaining connectivity across numerous remote islands during crises. This pilot enabled faster response times and enhanced data sharing among NGOs, governments, and local responders during the 2015 floods in Sri Lanka, compared to traditional systems (Fabri & Fabri, 2019). This interoperability allowed for real-time status updates regarding needs for resources, which led to trust between the users. In the case of SIDS, there is a need for cross-border cooperation due to limited local resources, and blockchain's inherent tamper-proof data environment enables the sharing of information in a dependable manner for improved efficiency in response. Interoperability could also contribute to regional co-operation in SIDS. Such approaches would prevent re-inventing the wheel and allow SIDS to combine their limited resources in the face of the fragmented systems. Overall, blockchain holds promise for promoting disaster resilience in some of the most vulnerable areas by creating a supportive, transparent environment.

Speed and Efficiency

Smart contracts on a blockchain automate critical activities and shorten response times during disasters. Automation helps lift bureaucratic bottlenecks, fast-tracking assistance to SIDS populations. This speedy disbursement supports immediate recovery in areas where tourism-reliant economies suffer major disruption due to disasters. In the same case, the Start Fund's pilot program in 2016 provided rapid allocation of resources that helped local responders deliver aid more efficiently, a crucial advantage in isolated or infrastructure-damaged regions common to many SIDS. In such contexts, where damage to infrastructure often cuts communities off from outside help, officials note that blockchain's ability to speed up fund allocation helps shore up resilience. Moreover, this technology can contribute to minimizing recurring conditions such as food insecurity and health emergencies by enabling timely and transparent resource distribution.

Transparency

The whole point of blockchain is its unchangeable transaction ledger, and this transparency and accountability will be crucial as climate finance becomes increasingly critical to SIDS to maintain the trust and donations of the world. The World Food Programme (WFP) implemented a permissioned blockchain, called Building Blocks, within Jordan to document cash transfers to Syrian refugees, resulting in significant reductions in fraud while providing donors and NGOs with real-time tracking.[12] This transparency built confidence that funds successfully reached the intended recipients. In the case of SIDS, whose governance capacity may be restricted, blockchain's auditable records increase the fair and equal distribution of resources and responsibility and help to ensure that aid reaches groups who are at high risk, such as rural or displaced populations.

Identification for Vulnerable Populations

Through blockchain, digital identities become secure and portable, enabling aid to be delivered more efficiently and fraud to be reduced in complex disaster environments. In SIDS, where displacement often erodes conventional identification systems, blockchain ensures that no one affected by disaster is left behind. This is especially important for internal displacement, which is much more common in SIDS due to climate-driven disasters. Initiatives such as the "ID2020 Alliance" promote the development and adoption of digital identity solutions, including blockchain-based systems, that provide secure, interoperable, and portable IDs for vulnerable and displaced populations worldwide.[13] By providing secure and interoperable identities, blockchain addresses the constrained administrative capacity of SIDS and helps guarantee that recovery efforts include marginalized communities..

BREM Empowerment

The proposed BREM model is instrumental in measuring the effectiveness of blockchain and promoting emergency management in SIDS, for progressive evidence-based decision-making. The model allows evaluating trade-offs between OE, TT, and FRR. The adaptability of BREM in terms of the weights guarantees context-sensitive assessments. BREM prevents underconfident deployment of interventions and therefore minimizes undesired spending. BREMs are also a source of strategic planning. Through a common reference, BREM helps reduce the gap between research and practice, and thus assists SIDS in framing policies to harness as many benefits as possible through blockchain while mitigating cryptographic threats such as phishing or smart contracts.

5.2 Challenges: Cryptocrime and Fraud

Although blockchain technology offers the potential for transformative impact on disaster management in SIDS, its weaknesses present much greater risks in post-disaster environments with disorder and a lack of technical and regulatory capacity. Anonymity, decentralization, and automation - some of the aspects that contribute to blockchain's benefits - are the same factors that allow cryptocrime and fraud, including money laundering, smart contract exploits, and phishing scams, among others. According to a report by Global Facility for Disaster Reduction and Recovery (GFDRR), SIDS include two-thirds of the countries that face the highest relative losses due to natural hazard-induced disasters, with losses ranging between 1 and 9 percent of their GDP each year.[14] Additionally, governance processes in many SIDS are often underdeveloped, which can impede effective disaster response activities.[15]

Anonymity

Public-key encryption in permissionless blockchains hides the identities of users and creates challenges for KYC/AML (Damgård, Ganesh, Khoshakhlagh, Orlandi, & Siniscalchi, 2021). This lack of regulation and anonymity creates a conducive environment for criminal conduct, as Chainalysis (2025) reported that in 2023, illicit cryptocurrency activity reached at least $24.2 billion initially, with the estimate later revised to $46.1 billion as more criminal activity was identified.[16] In SIDS with immature regulatory frameworks, the pseudonymous nature of blockchain transactions can increase the risk of inappropriate fund diversion. While anonymity is a contributing factor, phishing attacks in post-disaster events are also driven by low digital literacy. Lower global awareness increases susceptibility to such scams, highlighting the need for public education campaigns and hybrid blockchains with identity verification to balance personal privacy with individual accountability.

Attacks on smart contracts

Blockchain technologies lead to smart contracts, which are self-executing contracts with the terms of the agreement between buyer and seller directly written in lines of code, eliminating the need for a party to execute the contract (Kaur, Ali, & Faisal, 2022; Sklaroff, 2017). However, these contracts are not immune to risks, as exemplified by the decentralised autonomous organisation (DAO) hack in 2016, which resulted in the loss of approximately $60 million worth of Ether after a bug within the Ethereum smart contract was exploited, allowing an attacker to siphon funds.[17] SIDS have little technical know-how to obtain smart contracts and become dependent on assistance or on standardized auditing procedures. These weaknesses wind up undermining the confidence of potential donors. In addition, SIDS can encourage secure coding practices and make use of permissioned blockchains, which provide centralized oversight, preventing exploitation, in the meantime preserving some benefits of automation.

Scalability

Permissionless blockchains have limited transaction processing capacity, making them unsuitable for efficiently managing large-scale disaster response (Haque et al., 2024; Khan, Jung, & Hashmani, 2021). For SIDS, which are disaster-prone, these scale limitations constrain rapid aid provision and recovery. Cross-border tools are also affected by scaling issues. Solutions that improve throughput, such as sharding or permissioned blockchains, are important for SIDS. However, their introduction is technically demanding and may not be feasible in resource-limited contexts. An example is the Unblocked Cash Project, a blockchain-powered cash transfer solution implemented by Oxfam and partners in Vanuatu[18] This project uses a permissioned blockchain system to streamline cash and voucher assistance, overcoming some scalability issues by tailoring the technology to local needs and technical capacities. While not a permissionless blockchain, it demonstrates how adapting blockchain solutions to context and capacity can help address both scalability and complexity in disaster response.

Regulatory Challenges

The lack of an international standard for cryptocurrencies makes oversight difficult (Sotiropoulou & Ligot, 2019; Wronka, 2024). KYC and AML compliance can be difficult to enforce in blockchain-based humanitarian aid, potentially increasing fraud risk. This fragmented regulation adds to the complexity of blockchain systems and the increase in their costs, and hence, a common standard is required to ensure secure and efficient integration. Regulatory gaps allow illegal fund transfers. The use of darknet marketplaces and cryptocurrencies to purchase and sell illicit goods and services, with criminals exploiting the pseudo-anonymous and decentralized nature of digital currencies to avoid detection by authorities.[19]

Energy Consumption

Proof-of-work (PoW) blockchains are energy-intensive to administer and secure (Asif & Hassan, 2023). Bitcoin's electricity consumption for 2022 was projected at around 100–150 terawatt-hours annually, which is more than the annual electricity use of countries like Argentina (population 45 million) in some years. The energy used to power Bitcoin mining emits approximately 65 megatons of carbon dioxide into the atmosphere each year, comparable to the emissions of Greece. This makes cryptocurrency a significant contributor to global air pollution and climate change.[20] Proof-of-stake (PoS) blockchains, which use about 99% less energy than PoW, are a better fit for SIDS. Ethereum's transition to PoS in 2022 further reduced its environmental footprint, making it more suitable for use in disaster response contexts. However, the switch to PoS would require technical adjustments and capacity building, which can be challenging in SIDS where capacities are already limited. Sustainable blockchain architectures are increasingly necessary to help SIDS achieve their environmental ambitions.

6. DISCUSSION

Taking into consideration of opportunities and challenges of the use of blockchain technology in the context of disaster response in SIDS, this study argues that the BREM can be a practical tool for evaluating the value of blockchain for disaster matters. For those making policy, the BREM provides a workable tool that can be used to assess the viability of blockchains, with weights that may be altered according to the needs or priorities of a local area. For example, high conflict or high-risk locations for illicit financial flows may have a higher weight on risk reduction. On the other hand, in stable SIDS that have been through hurricanes or flooding, there might be even more emphasis on curves that are more operationally efficient due to time-critical logistical constraints. This flexibility guarantees model applicability to a variety of disaster scenarios and institutional environments.

Hybrid blockchain architectures, which bring together permissioned and permissionless characteristics, are highly recommended to fully exploit the advantages of blockchain in SIDS. Some permissioned blockchains, such as the World Food Programme (WFP)'s Jordan cash-assistance scheme, enforce Know Your Customer (KYC) and Anti-Money Laundering (AML) regulations. This ensures the traceability of transactions, makes participants ineligible for anonymity, and improves accountability. By contrast, permissionless systems allow greater access and participation by the community. For example, a hybrid blockchain model could leverage a permissioned layer to validate beneficiary identity while promoting local damage reporting and other forms of community participation through a permissionless layer. Fiji has explored blockchain for disaster response.

With AI integrated into blockchain systems, Fraud Risk Reduction (FRR) can be even stronger. AI-based fraud detection tools analyze transaction patterns for suspicious behavior, including phishing, money laundering, and unusual wallet movements. In SIDS, technical capabilities are often limited, and cloud-based

AI solutions provide a scalable, cost-effective monitoring option for blockchain-based aid platforms. For example, AI can identify suspicious transaction patterns in a post-hurricane relief system, thereby reducing cryptocurrency-related risks and increasing the FRR score. This type of integration is particularly important in SIDS, where low cybersecurity awareness and limited regulatory oversight make them more susceptible to fraud.

Blockchain combined with IoT enables enterprise operations and resource optimization, helping to improve operational efficiency and transparency. By integrating network-connected objects (such as IoT sensors) that monitor supply chain logistics, environmental conditions, or the movement of relief supplies, real-time data can be securely recorded on the blockchain. This allows for better-informed and more timely resource allocation. For example, IoT-blockchain systems can track aid shipments from ports to remote islands, where hurricanes and other disasters frequently disrupt supply chains. This collaboration not only increases operational efficiency (OE) but also gives all stakeholders verifiable access to current information, thereby enhancing transparency (TT).

Much more needs to be done to harmonize regulations and address gaps in blockchain governance, particularly for SIDS. Establishing a "blockchain islands network" could standardize KYC/AML mechanisms regionally, enabling faster and more secure cross-border transactions. Such a network could receive support from international organizations like the International Monetary Fund (IMF) or the United Nations (UN) to provide technical assistance and help build regulatory capacity in SIDS with current deficiencies. At the same time, it is essential to equip practitioners with the knowledge and skills to assess the value of blockchain for their businesses and organizations. Programs supported by the United Nations Children's Fund (UNICEF) Innovation Fund, which invests in blockchain solutions for social good and fosters local capacity building, demonstrate the importance of hands-on training and community involvement—such as initiatives that empower local responders to participate in and manage blockchain-based systems, as highlighted in their 2020 blockchain portfolio.[21] In SIDS, highly simplified and intuitive user interfaces can help overcome technical barriers and enable non-technical end-users to access blockchain ledgers. These programs should also prioritize digital literacy and cybersecurity education to mitigate risks such as phishing, especially in regions with limited technical infrastructure.

Next-generation blockchain technologies like zero-knowledge proofs (ZKPs) and sharding offer promising solutions to challenges around anonymity and scalability. ZKPs enable the selective revelation of transaction information to comply with KYC requirements without disclosing personal privacy details. In the context of SIDS, ZKPs could confirm beneficiary identities without exposing private information, potentially increasing the Fraud Risk Reduction (FRR) score. Sharding blockchain networks enhances transaction throughput, addressing scalability issues experienced in previous disaster responses, especially for as those in Hurricane Maria impacting Puerto Rico, and making blockchain systems viable even in the most demanding scenarios. The proposed use of blockchain and IoT by FEMA is illustrated in Figure 1.[22] Additionally, proof-of-stake blockchains, which consume approximately 99% less energy than proof-of-work systems, align with the sustainability goals of SIDS and are already recognized as a viable option for disaster management.[23]

Figure 1. Emergency management using blockchain and IoT (Source: American University)[24]

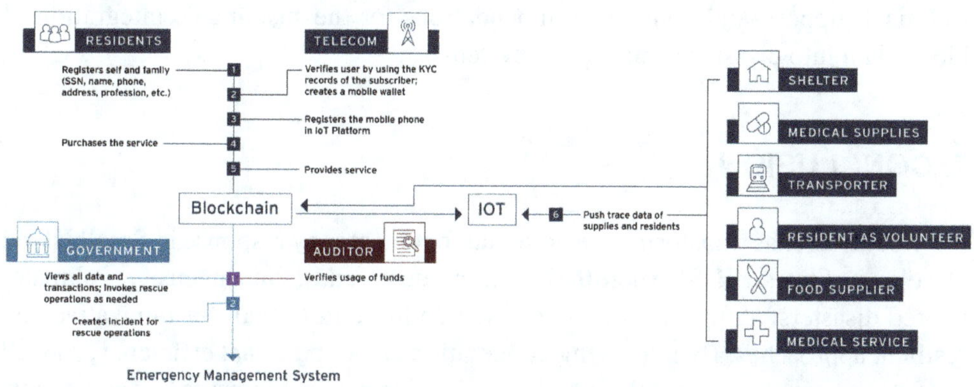

The Blockchain Response Efficacy Model (BREM) is a supplement tool that provides a structured framework to evaluate and enhance the blockchain-based disaster relief system. The Blockchain Response Efficacy Model (BREM) bolsters Puerto Rico's blockchain-based disaster relief by evaluating Operational Efficiency (OE), Transparency and Trust (TT), and Fraud Risk Reduction (FRR). OE tackles aid delivery delays, such as delivering only 50,000 of 30 million needed meals post-Hurricane Maria.[25] TT ensures stakeholders access transparent, immutable records, avoiding problematic contracts like the $156 million Tribute Contracting award.[26] FRR reduces fraud while managing cryptocrime risks. With weights (0.4 for OE, 0.3 for TT, 0.3 for FRR), BREM's Efficacy Score supports FEMA to deploy blockchain, enhancing efficiency, transparency, and security.

The BREM is a practical tool for assessing the transformational potential of blockchain in disaster management, but it also highlights the need for sector-specific protections. From fusion hybrid architectures, AI-enabled fraud detection, IoT integration, and regulatory harmonization, to capacity building alone and institution-to-institution clearing, SIDS can leverage the advantages of blockchain while mitigating its shortcomings.

There are still some implementation challenges. In both proof-of-stake (POS) and proof-of-work (POW), this is a complex technical process that can act as a barrier to adoption in SIDS with relatively low levels of technical expertise and infrastructure, and the power consumption of POW blockchains in particular has been criticized as a barrier to use. User-friendly interfaces, like mobile apps, can help to demystify blockchain to non-technical stakeholders, whilst PoS-oriented blockchains have the potential to solve energy demands. However, such solutions are not always so simple, especially when it comes to Small Island States where they cannot do it alone. Collaboration with international partners can secure funding, technical support, and policy recommendations for the sustainable integration of blockchain into disaster management systems.

7. CONCLUSION

Blockchain has transformative potential for emergency response in Small Island Developing States (SIDS), where the higher frequency and greater intensity of climate-related disasters, along with ongoing resource limitations, call for innovative and resilient approaches. By improving cooperation and operational efficiency, as well as transparency throughout the disaster cycle, blockchain addresses key constraints that have previously hindered effective response and recovery in SIDS. Various case studies have demonstrated the technology's potential to change how aid is distributed and how logistics and accountability function in disaster-affected regions.

The Blockchain Response Efficacy Model (BREM) offers a pragmatic and empirically grounded diagnostic tool to help practitioners and decision-makers navigate trade-offs in deploying blockchain within SIDS contexts. However, the use of blockchain technology in disaster management remains fraught with challenges. Cryptocrime continues to be a major concern, highlighting the risks for blockchain systems deployed rapidly in high-stakes environments. Furthermore, scalability difficulties present practical obstacles to blockchain adoption in SIDS. These challenges underscore the need for strong safety measures, such as hybrid blockchains that combine the security and regulation of permissioned ledgers with the openness and community involvement of permissionless ones.

To maximize blockchain's benefits while minimizing its downsides, a multifaceted approach is required. Incorporating AI into real-time fraud detection can significantly improve the security of digital ledger-based aid platforms. Using the Internet of Things (IoT) to facilitate real-time data gathering and supply chain monitoring can enhance operational effectiveness and transparency, ensuring humanitarian assistance reaches those most in need.

Future studies should conduct empirical testing of the BREM using real-world disaster cases to confirm metrics and refine weight assignments for different contexts. Investigating hybrid blockchain models can help strike the right balance between security and usability. Additionally, integrating AI and IoT can support the development of comprehensive and adaptive disaster management systems. Assessing the sustainability aspects is essential for SIDS, which are resource-constrained and highly susceptible to climate change. Local community-led blockchain solutions should be scaled to empower local responders and foster grassroots resilience.

By addressing the threats of cryptocrime and leveraging blockchain's potential for interoperability, efficiency, and transparency, policymakers and practitioners can develop more resilient, inclusive, and sustainable emergency response systems. Importantly, continued innovation, global cooperation, and investment in local capacity can make blockchain technology a catalyst to help the next generations in SIDS be better positioned to respond and recover from emergencies in the future.

REFERENCES

Ahn, G.-J., Doupe, A., Zhao, Z., & Liao, K. (2016). Ransomware and cryptocurrency: partners in crime. In *Cybercrime Through an Interdisciplinary Lens* (pp. 119–140). Routledge.

Ait Mouha, R. (2021). *Internet of Things (IoT): Concepts and applications*. Springer.

Ait Mouha, R. A. R. (2021). Internet of things (IoT). *Journal of Data Analysis and Information Processing*, *9*(02), 77–101. DOI: 10.4236/jdaip.2021.92006

Ali, M. S., Vecchio, M., Pincheira, M., Dolui, K., Antonelli, F., & Rehmani, M. H. (2018). Applications of blockchains in the Internet of Things: A comprehensive survey. *IEEE Communications Surveys and Tutorials*, *21*(2), 1676–1717. DOI: 10.1109/COMST.2018.2886932

Alsalamah, S., & Nuzzolese, E. (2020). Promising blockchain technology applications and use case designs for the identification of multinational victims of mass disasters. *Frontiers in Blockchain*, *3*, 34. DOI: 10.3389/fbloc.2020.00034

Asif, R., & Hassan, S. R. (2023). Shaping the future of Ethereum: Exploring energy consumption in Proof-of-Work and Proof-of-Stake consensus. *Frontiers in Blockchain*, *6*, 1151724. DOI: 10.3389/fbloc.2023.1151724

Bakos, Y., & Halaburda, H. (2021). Permissioned vs permissionless blockchain platforms: Tradeoffs in trust and performance. *NYU Stern School of Business working paper*.

Bakos, Y., & Halaburda, H. (2021). Permissioned vs. permissionless blockchains: A comparative analysis. *The Journal of Economic Perspectives*, *35*(3), 1–20.

Belblidia, M., Comfort, L. K., Ganapati, N. E., Graves, J. V., Jerroleman, A., Kiefer, J. J., & Thompson, D. D. (2019). *Housing Recovery After Disasters*. Rowman & Littlefield.

Braun, V., & Clarke, V. (2006). Using thematic analysis in psychology. *Qualitative Research in Psychology*, *3*(2), 77–101. DOI: 10.1191/1478088706qp063oa

Braun, V., & Clarke, V. (2012). *Thematic analysis*. American Psychological Association. DOI: 10.1037/13620-004

Chainalysis. (2025). *2025 crypto crime report: Introduction*. https://www.chainalysis.com/blog/2025-crypto-crime-report-introduction/

Chowdhury, M. J. M., Ferdous, M. S., Biswas, K., Chowdhury, N., Kayes, A., Alazab, M., & Watters, P. (2019). A comparative analysis of distributed ledger technology platforms. *IEEE Access : Practical Innovations, Open Solutions*, *7*, 167930–167943. DOI: 10.1109/ACCESS.2019.2953729

Clarke, R. P. (2021). Performance of buildings in two Caribbean Territories: Dominica under Hurricane Maria in 2017 and Trinidad under the 2018 earthquake. *Natural Hazards*, *109*(1), 1141–1165. DOI: 10.1007/s11069-021-04872-w

Coppi, G., & Fast, L. (2019). *Blockchain and distributed ledger technologies in the humanitarian sector*. Retrieved from Damgård, I., Ganesh, C., Khoshakhlagh, H., Orlandi, C., & Siniscalchi, L. (2021). *Balancing privacy and accountability in blockchain identity management.* Paper presented at the Cryptographers' Track at the RSA Conference.

Ditamore, S. (2018). *A Bit of Recent Growth: The Evolving Risk of Terrorist Use of Virtual Currency*. Naval Postgraduate School.

Dupuis, D., & Gleason, K. (2020). Money laundering with cryptocurrency: Open doors and the regulatory dialectic. *Journal of Financial Crime*, *28*(1), 60–74. DOI: 10.1108/JFC-06-2020-0113

Dutta, P. (2020). Blockchain and smart contracts: A technical overview. *IEEE Transactions on Engineering Management*, *67*(4), 1234–1246.

Dutta, S. K. (2020). Smart contracts. In *The definitive guide to blockchain for accounting and business: Understanding the revolutionary technology* (pp. 61–78). Emerald Publishing Limited.

Elhussieny, M. (2025). Smart green ports: A sustainable solution for the maritime industry in a changing climate. *Multidisciplinary Adaptive Climate Insights*, *2*(1), 1–30. DOI: 10.21622/MACI.2025.02.1.1162

ESCAP, U. (2018). Disaster risk financing: opportunities for regional cooperation in Asia and the Pacific.

Fabri, J., & Fabri, S. (2019). Leveraging blockchain technology to build resilience and disaster risk reduction in small states. In Khonje, W. H., & Mitchell, T. (Eds.), *Strengthening Disaster Resilience in Small States: Commonwealth Perspectives* (pp. 107–124). Commonwealth Secretariat. DOI: 10.14217/c6ee754a-en

Farahani, B., Firouzi, F., & Luecking, M. (2021). The convergence of IoT and distributed ledger technologies (DLT): Opportunities, challenges, and solutions. *Journal of Network and Computer Applications*, *177*, 102936. DOI: 10.1016/j.jnca.2020.102936

Furnham, A., & Boo, H. C. (2011). A literature review of the anchoring effect. *Journal of Socio-Economics, 40*(1), 35–42. DOI: 10.1016/j.socec.2010.10.008

Global Facility for Disaster Reduction and Recovery. (n.d.). *Financing climate and disaster resilience in Small Island States.* https://www.gfdrr.org/en/feature-story/financing-climate-and-disaster-resilience-small-island-states

Global Facility for Disaster Reduction and Recovery. (n.d.). *SISRI Knowledge Note 1: What is SISRI?* https://www.gfdrr.org/sites/default/files/documents/SISRI%20Knowledge%20Note%201%20What%20is%20SISRI.pdf

Gwet, K. L. (2014). *Handbook of inter-rater reliability: The definitive guide to measuring the extent of agreement among raters.* Advanced Analytics, LLC.

Habib, A., Alnaemi, A., & Habib, M. (2024). *Developing a framework for integrating blockchain technology into earthquake risk mitigation and disaster management strategies of smart cities.* Smart and Sustainable Built Environment. DOI: 10.1108/SASBE-12-2023-0376

Haque, E. U., Shah, A., Iqbal, J., Ullah, S. S., Alroobaea, R., & Hussain, S. (2024). A scalable blockchain based framework for efficient IoT data management using lightweight consensus. *Scientific Reports, 14*(1), 7841. DOI: 10.1038/s41598-024-58578-7

Ilari, L. (2025). Navigating Ethical Challenges in Cybersecurity: From Risk Assessment to Quantum-AI Applications.

IMF. (2016). Small States' Resilience to Natural Disasters and Climate Change–Role for the IMF. In: International Monetary Fund Washington.

Islam, S., & Apu, K. U. (2024). Decentralized vs. Centralized database solutions in blockchain: Advantages, challenges, and use cases. *Global Mainstream Journal of Innovation. Engineering & Emerging Technology, 3*(4), 58–68.

Jamwal, S., Cano, J., Lee, G. M., Tran, N. H., & Truong, N. (2024). A survey on ethereum pseudonymity: Techniques, challenges, and future directions. *Journal of Network and Computer Applications, 232*, 104019. DOI: 10.1016/j.jnca.2024.104019

Janis, I. L., & Janis, I. L. (1982). *Groupthink: Psychological studies of policy decisions and fiascoes* (Vol. 349). Houghton Mifflin Boston.

Jefri, S. (2024). Navigating the Crypto Landscape: Exploring the Risks and Potential Misuse of Crypto Assets in Money Laundering. *Technology, 1*(1), 16–29.

Kaur, R., Ali, A., & Faisal, M. (2022). Smart contracts: the self-executing contracts. In *Blockchain* (pp. 35–49). Chapman and Hall/CRC. DOI: 10.1201/9781003203957-4

Khan, D., Jung, L. T., & Hashmani, M. A. (2021). Systematic literature review of challenges in blockchain scalability. *Applied Sciences (Basel, Switzerland)*, *11*(20), 9372. DOI: 10.3390/app11209372

Kopetz, H., & Steiner, W. (2022). Internet of things. In *Real-time systems: design principles for distributed embedded applications* (pp. 325–341). Springer. DOI: 10.1007/978-3-031-11992-7_13

Kopetz, H., & Steiner, W. (2022). *The Internet of Things: Principles and paradigms*. Wiley.

Kori, A., & Gadagin, N. (2024). Blockchain-Based AI Models for Credit Scoring and Risk Assessment using Fog Computing Infrastructure.

Kuckartz, U., & Rädiker, S. (2019). *Analyzing qualitative data with MAXQDA*. Springer. DOI: 10.1007/978-3-030-15671-8

Kumar, S., Sebastian, A., & Nandakumar, B. (2025). Emergency response to natural disaster victim identification: Blockchain to the rescue. In *The Role of Blockchain in Disaster Management* (pp. 69–85). Elsevier. DOI: 10.1016/B978-0-443-13472-2.00001-2

Lawrence, W., Tarr, J.-A., Brook, N., Chaperon, M., & Sorel, A. (2023). Parametric Insurance. In *The Global Insurance Market and Change* (pp. 127–156). Informa Law from Routledge. DOI: 10.4324/9781003319054-6

Lieder, F., Griffiths, T. L. M., Huys, Q. J., & Goodman, N. D. (2018). The anchoring bias reflects rational use of cognitive resources. *Psychonomic Bulletin & Review*, *25*, 322–349. DOI: 10.3758/s13423-017-1286-8

Mukherjee, S., Larkin, C., & Corbet, S. (2021). Cryptocurrency ponzi schemes. *Understanding cryptocurrency fraud: The challenges and headwinds to regulate digital currencies, 2*, 111.

Myeong, S., & Jung, Y. (2019). Administrative reforms in the fourth industrial revolution: The case of blockchain use. *Sustainability (Basel)*, *11*(14), 3971. DOI: 10.3390/su11143971

Ndiaye, M., & Konate, P. K. (2021). *Cryptocurrency crime: Behaviors of malicious smart contracts in blockchain.* Paper presented at the 2021 International Symposium on Networks, Computers and Communications (ISNCC). DOI: 10.1109/ISNCC52172.2021.9615702

Patton, M. Q. (2002). *Qualitative research and evaluation methods* (Vol. 3). Sage.

Payne, B., & Mienie, E. (2021). *Multiple-extortion ransomware: The case for active cyber threat intelligence.* Paper presented at the ECCWS 2021 20th European Conference on Cyber Warfare and Security.

Pill, M. (2022). Re-framing non-economic losses to non-economic impacts for effective policymaking: Evidence from the Caribbean. *Climate and Development*, *14*(8), 770–779. DOI: 10.1080/17565529.2021.1987852

Rai, H., Srivastava, A. K., Rai, S., & Pattanashetti, D. (2024). Blockchain-powered transparency: Tracking and disseminating donations for disaster-stricken regions. *Futuristic Trends in Artificial Intelligence*, 1-15.

Salisu, S., & Filipov, V. (2023). *Blockchain forensics: A modern approach to investigating cybercrime in the age of decentralisation.* Paper presented at the # PLACEHOLDER_PARENT_METADATA_VALUE#. DOI: 10.34190/iccws.18.1.947

Sarbajna, R., Eick, C. F., & Laszka, A. (2023). *PhobosBC: A Blockchain-based Crowdsourced Post-disaster Mapping System and its Agent-based Simulation.* Paper presented at the Proceedings of the 6th ACM SIGSPATIAL International Workshop on GeoSpatial Simulation. DOI: 10.1145/3615891.3628016

Shevchuk, R., Lishchynskyy, I., Ciura, M., Lyzun, M., Kozak, R., & Kasianchuk, M. (2025). Application of Blockchain Technology in Emergency Management Systems: A Bibliometric Analysis. *Applied Sciences (Basel, Switzerland)*, *15*(10), 5405. DOI: 10.3390/app15105405

Shin, E.-J., Kang, H.-G., & Bae, K. (2020). A study on the sustainable development of NPOs with blockchain technology. *Sustainability (Basel)*, *12*(15), 6158. DOI: 10.3390/su12156158

Siemon, C., Rueckel, D., & Krumay, B. (2020). Blockchain technology for emergency response.

Sklaroff, J. M. (2017). Smart contracts and the cost of inflexibility. *U. Pa. L. Rev.*, *166*, 263.

Sotiropoulou, A., & Ligot, S. (2019). Legal Challenges of Cryptocurrencies: Isn't It Time to Regulate the Intermediaries? *European Company and Financial Law Review*, *16*(5), 652–676. DOI: 10.1515/ecfr-2019-0023

Sripathi, M., & Leelavati, T. (2024). The Fourth Industrial Revolution: A paradigm shift in healthcare delivery and management. *Digital Transformation in Healthcare 5.0, 1*, 67.

Subbian, R. G., & Gollapudi, P. K. Smart Contracts and Blockchain-The Next Frontier in Trustworthy P&C Insurance.

Sunyaev, A., & Sunyaev, A. (2020). Distributed ledger technology. *Internet computing: Principles of distributed systems and emerging internet-based technologies*, 265-299.

Trozze, A., Kamps, J., Akartuna, E. A., Hetzel, F. J., Kleinberg, B., Davies, T., & Johnson, S. D. (2022). Cryptocurrencies and future financial crime. *Crime Science, 11*(1), 1–35. DOI: 10.1186/s40163-021-00163-8

UNICEF. (2020). *UNICEF Innovation Fund: Blockchain 2020*. https://www.unicef.org/innovation/unicefinnovationfund/blockchain2020

United Nations Conference on Trade and Development. (n.d.). *Global report: Blockchain and its* implications for trade facilitation performance. https://unctad.org/publication/global-report-blockchain-and-its-implications-trade-facilitation-performance

U.S. Department of Homeland Security. (n.d.). *Blockchain portfolio*. https://www.dhs.gov/science-and-technology/blockchain-portfolio

van der Horst, M., Kho, R., Gadyatskaya, O., Mollema, M., Van Eeten, M., & Zhauniarovich, Y. (2025). *High Stakes, Low Certainty: Evaluating the Efficacy of High-Level Indicators of Compromise in Ransomware Attribution.* Paper presented at the Proceedings of the 34th USENIX Security Symposium (USENIX Sec).

Voshmgir, S. (2025). *Token economy*. Token Kitchen, Labirinto Ecletico Unip LDA.

Wronka, C. (2024). Crypto-asset activities and markets in the European Union: Issues, challenges and considerations for regulation, supervision and oversight. *Journal of Banking Regulation, 25*(1), 84–93. DOI: 10.1057/s41261-023-00217-8

Zaffaroni, E. (n.d.). *Blockchain and criminal law*. Pensamiento Penal. https://www.pensamientopenal.com.ar/system/files/Documento_Editado1686.pdf

ENDNOTES

1 Small Island Developing States (SIDS), are a distinct group of developing countries that consist of small island nations and territories facing unique social, economic, and environmental challenges. This list can be found at https://www.un.org/ohrlls/content/list-sids.

2 A smart contract in blockchain is a self-executing program with the terms of the agreement directly written into code, which automatically enforces and executes actions when predefined conditions are met (Dutta, 2020).

3 See the TRM Labs 2022 Illicit Crypto Ecosystem Report: https://www.trmlabs.com/resources/reports/the-illicit-crypto-ecosystem-report-2022

4 See https://fullycrypto.com/ethereums-dao-hack-three-years-on

5 See https://unctad.org/publication/global-report-blockchain-and-its-implications-trade-facilitation-performance

6 See https://www.dhs.gov/science-and-technology/blockchain-portfolio

7 See https://blockchainclimate.org/climate-resilience-parametric-insurance-and-blockchain-part-i/

8 A permissioned blockchain restricts access and participation to approved entities with defined roles, while a permissionless blockchain is open to anyone, allowing unrestricted participation and decentralized governance (Bakos & Halaburda, 2021).

9 See https://www.pensamientopenal.com.ar/system/files/Documento_Editado1686.pdf

10 The Internet of Things (IoT) is a network of physical objects embedded with sensors, software, and connectivity that enables them to collect, exchange, and act on data over the internet with minimal human intervention (Ait Mouha, 2021; Kopetz & Steiner, 2022).

11 See https://www.undrr.org/implementing-sendai-framework/sendai-framework-action/small-island-developing-states

12 See https://www.jointdatacenter.org/literature_review/where-life-hangs-by-a-chain-a-jordanian-refugee-camp-is-a-test-for-blockchain-based-identity-systems/#:~:text=This%20article%20discusses%20the%20piloting,participating%20retailers%20in%20local%20currency.

13 See https://oecd-opsi.org/innovations/id2020-alliance/

14 See https://www.gfdrr.org/sites/default/files/documents/SISRI%20Knowlege%20Note%201%20What%20is%20SISRI.pdf

15 See https://www.gfdrr.org/en/feature-story/financing-climate-and-disaster-resilience-small-island-states

16 See https://www.chainalysis.com/blog/2025-crypto-crime-report-introduction/

17 See https://crypto.com/glossary/the-dao-hack

18 See https://www.oxfam.org/en/unblocked-cash-project-using-blockchain-technology-revolutionize-humanitarian-aid

19 See https://www.austrac.gov.au/sites/default/files/2022-04/AUSTRAC_FCG_PreventingCriminalAbuseOfDigitalCurrencies_FINAL.pd

20 See https://news.climate.columbia.edu/2022/05/04/cryptocurrency-energy

21 See https://www.unicef.org/innovation/unicefinnovationfund/blockchain2020

22 See https://www.american.edu/kogod/news/kogod-blockchain-garnick-omar-elms.cfm

23 See https://www.scl.org/12596-proof-of-stake-the-environmental-impact/

24 See https://www.american.edu/kogod/news/images/blockchain_infograph-2.png

25 See https://edition.cnn.com/2018/02/06/us/puerto-rico-hurricane-maria-meals/index.htm

26 https://www.nytimes.com/2018/02/06/us/fema-contract-puerto-rico.html#:~:text=For%20this%20huge%20task%2C%20FEMA%20tapped%20Tiffany,LLC%2C%20set%20out%20to%20find%20some%20help.

Chapter 6
Decentralized Finance (DeFi) and the Rise of Financial Exploits:
Challenges and Opportunities

Sina Ahmadi
https://orcid.org/0009-0003-2249-2835
NCIS, USA

Maral Mazjini
University of Regina, Canada

ABSTRACT

This chapter delves into the revolutionary emergence of Decentralized Finance (DeFi), its potential to revolutionize, and its vulnerabilities. Based on blockchain technology, DeFi bypasses conventional financial intermediaries through smart contracts to execute lending, trading, and other economic activities. The permissionless aspect of DeFi increases financial inclusion worldwide, especially for the unbanked and underbanked. Yet, this openness also exposes DeFi platforms to threats such as vulnerabilities in smart contracts, oracle manipulation, flash loan attacks, and governance attacks. Case studies like the Poly Network hack, Mango Markets manipulation, and Squid Game token rug pull illustrate these risks. The research covers technology innovations such as smart contract audits, formal verification, decentralized oracles, and AI-based threat detection to strengthen DeFi's future. It also examines how regulatory sandboxes and decentralized identification solutions can balance innovation and regulation.

DOI: 10.4018/979-8-3373-0675-9.ch006

INTRODUCTION

The financial sector has undergone a profound transformation with the advent of blockchain technology, giving rise to Decentralized Finance (DeFi). The advent of blockchain technology has profoundly transformed the financial sector, giving rise to Decentralized Finance (DeFi). This burgeoning ecosystem, characterized by its rapid expansion and innovative applications, leverages smart contracts to automate complex financial transactions, fundamentally reshaping how individuals interact with financial services. However, this swift evolution and reliance on nascent technologies, coupled with a lack of centralized oversight, have concurrently exposed DeFi to a unique set of critical vulnerabilities, particularly in its governance and security infrastructure. This chapter aims to explore both the revolutionary potential and the inherent risks within the DeFi landscape. DeFi is a movement aimed at democratizing the availability of financial services by disrupting traditional intermediary banking institutions and financial institutions with smart contracts and other protocols that facilitate the automation of every transaction on a blockchain network. Through this paradigm shift, individuals can borrow, trade, and invest without contending with their geographic location, lack of banking history, or creditworthiness.

DeFi's ascent has been fueled by several key innovations, including decentralized exchanges (DEXs), liquidity pools, yield farming, and algorithmic lending protocols. DeFi applications (DApps) built on Ethereum are mostly built on peer-to-peer transactions with transparency and efficiency. The breakthrough comes from a booming ecosystem that attracts billions of dollars in each platform's total value locked (TVL).

However, it must be conceded that DeFi is not free of challenges. Although DeFi platforms' permissionless and open-source nature is revolutionary, it also brings several vulnerabilities. DeFi differs fundamentally from traditional finance, which works in regulatory structures and centralized supervision. As a result, it is an attractive target for cybercriminals who take advantage of the loophole in smart contracts to manipulate the market and even commit fraudulent schemes.

One of DeFi's defining characteristics is its trustless nature. DeFi's security is based on blockchain technology, which replaces trust in centralized institutions like banks. Smart contracts are self-executing agreements about set rules that execute autonomously without any need for intermediaries.

Still, this is a risky, trustless model. The DeFi platform operates without human oversight, which means any vulnerability in a smart contract can be exploited without resources. After a smart contract is deployed, it is immutable in the sense that coding errors, security flaws, or unforeseen loopholes cannot be corrected quickly.

Growing DeFi will also have to solve several burning challenges. Technical vulnerabilities, regulatory uncertainty, and the growing intelligence of financial exploits exist.

Smart Contract Risks

Smart contracts are the backbone of DeFi, automating complex financial transactions without human intervention. However, they are as secure as the code that defines them. Any programming errors—even as small as a typo—leave room for catastrophic losses. The 2021 Poly Network exploit illustrates all of the risks of smart contract vulnerabilities, where a hacker discovered a flaw in the protocol's cross-chain contract and drained over $600 million in assets.

Market Manipulation and Flash Loan Attacks

DeFi Flash loans are a unique feature that allows us to borrow large sums of capital without collateral if the loan is repaid in the same transaction. This innovation has allowed efficient capital deployment but also gives rise to flash loan attacks. These attacks involve malicious acts in which industry actors manipulate asset prices at relatively short time lapses to exploit price oracles and drain liquidity pools. These are the exploits that make use of flash loans to attack the bZx protocol with multiple attacks.

Rug Pulls and Fraudulent Schemes

Being permissionless and decentralized, DeFi allows developers to launch projects with much less oversight. Since this encourages innovation and spawns opportunities for evil schemes like rug pulls. Some of these scams involve the hype surrounding a new project, attracting investors' money and, later on, departing with the money. With the infamous Squid Game token scam, developers walked away with millions from what turned out to be a SCAM; there is no other way around this: If you invest in unverified DeFi projects, you run the risk of losing your money, and that is a risk you should not take.

Regulatory and Legal Challenges

The absence of clear regulatory frameworks poses a significant challenge to DeFi's legitimacy and mainstream adoption. DeFi platforms are in gray areas compared to traditional financial institutions confined to legal boundaries. The regulatory problem regards the lack of consumer protections, jurisdictional ambiguity, and anonymity of transactions, which make it difficult to enforce compliance. There have been continuous discussions on how to regulate the DeFi space globally, and governments are still trying to find out how to regulate DeFi without stifling everything.

The Dual Nature of DeFi: Risks and Opportunities

DeFi brings security issues and represents a successful evolution of financial services. As a barrier remover to entry, DeFi provides financial inclusion to two groups: the first is where there is no traditional banking infrastructure, and the second is where there are too many barriers to entry. DeFi is transforming finance into the fields of peer-to-peer lending, decentralized insurance, algorithmic trading, etc. On the other hand, in the context of rapid DeFi growth, robust security measures to keep users safe from financial losses have not been developed quickly and synchronously. The problem is finding a way to balance the gingerbread of creativity with the lemons of safeguarding for the users.

This chapter aims to give a complete overview of how complex the DeFi ecosystem is, what good it can bring, and what dangers it poses simultaneously. Key objectives include:

- ***Understanding DeFi's Foundations***: This section examines key components of DeFi, such as DEXs, lending protocols, and liquidity pools.
- ***Analyzing Technical and Regulatory Vulnerabilities***: Discovering the impact of varying levels of bright contract flaws, market manipulation, and evil schemes on the DeFi community's credibility.
- ***Case Studies of Financial Exploits***: Upon assessing some notorious DeFi hacks and scams to comprehend the methods attackers pursue when committing such actions.
- ***Exploring Risk Mitigation Strategies***: This section mentions technological advancements, governance models, and regulatory approaches to improving DeFi security.
- ***Envisioning the Future of DeFi***: Discuss the DeFi landscape in the new day, potential solutions, and the part of the globe in securing DeFi's future.

This chapter aims to equip the readers with the knowledge required to picture the DeFi terrain, spot the risks, and help ease the construction of a more dependable and shielded decentralized money framework.

THE FOUNDATIONS OF DEFI AND ITS VULNERABILITIES

Decentralized Finance (DeFi) has emerged as one of the most transformative innovations in the financial sector, offering an alternative to traditional banking systems through blockchain technology (Abdulhakeem & Hu, 2021). DeFi removes intermediaries between users and financial services, such as lending, borrowing, trading, and yield farming. The promise of financial inclusion and transparency is one of the reasons why DeFi continues to stay popular. Still, it is also hazardous, given the open, permissionless nature of DeFi and smart contracts.

In this section, the foundation of DeFi, through its components and financial mechanism, will then be dejectedly examined for weaknesses and vulnerabilities that make it vulnerable to exploitation. Permissionless access, smart contract risks, and interoperability, on the one hand, all contribute to making the DeFi ecosystem more complex and secure on the other hand.

Core Components of DeFi

To understand DeFi's vulnerabilities, it is essential to examine its core components first. Several key elements enable DeFi's decentralized nature—financial services by which traditional intermediaries are no longer needed. They are decentralized exchanges (DEXs), liquidity pools, yield farming, lending protocols, and governance mechanisms.

Decentralized Exchanges (DEXs)

Decentralized exchanges (DEXs) allow users to trade cryptocurrencies without intermediaries, offering greater privacy and control over assets (Hägele, 2024). DEXs differ from centralized exchanges like Binance or Coinbase, as DEXs handle trading via smart contracts based on their code, unlike custodians. Automated market maker (AMM) protocols are used for platforms such as Uniswap, SushiSwap, and PancakeSwap, where directly swapping the liquidity pools instead of ordering books is used. DEXs have advantages, such as censorship resistance and lower counterparty risk, but disadvantages, like smart contract vulnerabilities, liquidity fragmentation, and front-running attacks. Security and efficiency are promises for the future of decentralized trading.

DEXs possess more privacy and autonomy but carry high risks with them. Since there are no Know Your Customer (KYC) regulations, no one has to prove their identity to trade, bringing the possibility of engaging in illegal activities, such as money laundering and fraud. Besides, there have been devastating exploits owing to vulnerabilities in smart contracts or price oracle mechanisms used by DEXs in the past.

Liquidity Pools

DeFi ecosystems' liquidity pools are smart contract-based reserves of cryptocurrency assets for trading, lending, and yield farming (Xu & Feng, 2022, p. 858).

These pools involve users depositing funds and receiving liquidity provider (LP) tokens. Each token represents their share of the pool and qualifies them to be paid a percentage fee or yield rewards generated by the platform. Liquidity pools make the market more efficient and decentralized but come with the most exciting risks: impermanent loss, smart contract risk, and flash loan attack potential. For the trust and security of liquidity-based DeFi protocols, proper auditing, risk management, and incentives are needed.

However, liquidity pools are very vulnerable to impermanent loss and attacks from the outside. When the value of assets in the pool fluctuates, the value of the assets the users have deposited into the pool varies, and the users lose money, not holding the assets, which would have been the same. Poorly secured pools are also attack targets for flash loans: bad actors exploit token price manipulation to steal liquidity.

Yield Farming and Staking

Yield farming and staking are some of the most critical ways in DeFi that aim to motivate users to participate. So, yield farming entails providing liquidity to the DeFi platform in exchange for the coins and earning rewards as additional tokens. Platforms like Uniswap or Aave offer liquidity providers the chance to deposit assets to pools that provide income, trading fees, or the initial supply of governance tokens (Cedra, 2024, p. 104). Instead, staking involves locking in their holdings to a smart contract to support the blockchain's security and make a profit from this in the form of passive income. Tokens such as those used in proof of stake (PoS) networks, such as Ethereum 2.0 and Solana, are given out to stakes as a reward (Gogol, et al., 2024). Both methods have profit opportunities but share impermanent loss, smart contract vulnerabilities, and liquidation risks in volatile markets.

Yield farming can, however, be unsustainable since tokenomics with excessive issuance of reward tokens cause the value to collapse. Earlier, the DeFi projects tempted users with high annual percentage yields (APYs) before plummeting token devaluation. In some cases, yield farming projects performed rug pulls by abandoning a project that had already raised a lot from the investors.

Lending and Borrowing Protocols

DeFi Lending Platforms such as Aave Compound and MakerDAO are the ones where people can borrow and lend digital assets without the help of traditional banks (Bondarenko & Soponar, 2024). The transactions, collateral management, and Interest Rate Adjustment are all handled on these platforms through smart contracts. Here, borrowers must deposit the cryptocurrency as collateral and borrow something less than all the valued cryptocurrency (over-collateralization) to protect against default risk. Supply and demand determine the interest rates, and if there is too much supply or demand stimuli, the ratio is adjusted algorithmically. Unlike traditional lending, no credit checks or intermediaries are done, making the access more inclusive. Although no specific risk exists, there are risks of being liquidated from price volatility, smart contract vulnerability, and manipulation of the oracle in a way that negatively affects users and the platform's stability.

These platforms are secure and saved in the blockchain to ensure efficiency, but they come with liquidation risks and Oracle manipulation. When market volatility causes collateral values to crash at once, users will liquidate automatically at a loss, which is the liquidation risk. Another type of attack is Oracle manipulation (or bid rigging), wherein the hacker alters the price feed data to exploit the differences in asset valuations for profits.

Governance Mechanisms

Decentralized Autonomous Organizations (DAOs) govern protocol, payroll upgrades, fee structures, and development proposals in DeFi. (Bonnet & Teuteberg, 2024). While DAOs are envisioned as decentralized, community-driven, and secure to control, they are perhaps the most secure yet risky. Large token whales who invest in whales can manipulate votes in decentralized systems to exercise centralized control. Furthermore, protocol governance attacks, which allow malicious actors to propose and approve harmful changes, are another attack. Moreover, there is no regulation in place to hold them accountable. DAOs demand strong performance through robust voting mechanisms, transparent governance structures, protections against hostile takeovers, and governance cheesy exploits to boost security.

Whales (large holders) can accumulate governance tokens and then have a centralization of decision power. Governance attacks are also possible on governance proposals, where actors can amass enough tokens to secure votes to submit proposals that can financially reap them at the expense of the community.

Key Vulnerabilities in DeFi

DeFi offers great financial freedom in its core components but faces significant security and operational risks. Permissionless access, smart contract risk, and interoperability problems are principal vulnerabilities.

The Permissionless Dilemma

Decentralized Finance (DeFi), by definition, is permissionless, meaning that there are no intermediaries or any form of intermediaries for the use of financial services, which anyone with an internet connection can use (Ozcan, 2021, p. 57). That removes barriers to entry, provides financial inclusion, and allows for participation on a global scale. However, this can be a security problem, too. There are no regulatory overwatches on smart contracts, decentralized exchanges, and liquidity pools, which make them vulnerable to malicious attacks from actors who can exploit the vulnerabilities without hassle. Without administrators, securing such standards, recouping lost assets, and prosecuting those responsible is hard. Pseudonymous transactions also make hacking, fraudsters, and money launderers a walk in the park (Luo, et al., 2024, p. 1). DeFi has an innovative and accessible nature, but being composed of no inbuilt regulatory mechanisms might lead to an ethnicity regarding security, transparency, decentralization, combating financial crimes, and systemic risks.

Lack of Identity Verification

Traditional financial institutions strictly implement KYC and AML regulations to prevent fraud and illicit financial activities. On the other hand, DeFi has no controls, which allows for creating and exchanging anonymous wallets. This has facilitated:

- **Money laundering** through decentralized mixers like Tornado Cash.
- **Rug pulls**, where project developers knowingly drain liquidity and abandon the project.
- **Illicit financing**, with decentralized platforms potentially being used to fund illegal activities.

Due to DeFi's borderless nature, regulators struggle to enforce compliance, leading to concerns about its role in financial crime.

Smart Contract Risks

Since Decentralized Finance (DeFi) relies entirely on blockchain-based smart contracts, any flaw in the code can result in devastating financial losses (Carapella & Swem, 2022). Unlike traditional economic systems, there can be no correction or reversal of errors committed by DeFi contracts that are once deployed. However, hackers often use logic errors, reentrancy bugs, and price manipulation loopholes to lose many liquidity pools, lending protocols, and decentralized exchanges. With no central oversight, victims have no way back if the funds are stolen or frozen by contracts failing. Not all protocols are immune; even well-audited ones are exposed to new and evolving attack strategies and risks. Ensuring that DeFi's viability lasts a long time is only possible if rigorous smart contract auditing, bug bounties, and real-time monitoring are done to minimize potential exploits.

Code Vulnerabilities

Smart contracts, like any software, can contain coding errors or logic flaws that introduce security risks. Significant losses have been precipitated by exploitable bugs in DeFi protocols, such as:

- The **DAO Hack (2016)**, where an attacker exploited a vulnerability in Ethereum's DAO to steal $60 million in ETH (Feichtinger, Fritsch, Heimbach, Vonlanthen, & Wattenhofer, 2024).
- The **bZx Protocol Exploit (2020)**, where multiple flash loan attacks drained millions in assets (Schär & Gronde, 2021).

Although the rise of firms such as CertiK and OpenZeppelin has brought more audit firms, not all DeFi projects are audited before launching.

Oracle Manipulation

Oracles play a crucial role in Decentralized Finance (DeFi) by providing real-time asset pricing to smart contracts (Aspembitova & Bentley, 2022). However, if not adequately secured, they become a significant attack vector. Attackers exploit vulnerabilities in price feeds by attacking oracles such as artificially inflating and deflating asset prices through flash loan attacks or low-liquidity trading pairs. They can run profitable arbitrage trades or just regular mass liquidations on lending platforms, which will cause mass financial instability. Cryptographic proofs are needed to deal with these risks and have accurate, tamper-proof pricing in DeFi protocols, decentralized oracles, and many data sources.

Notable incidents include:

- The **Mango Markets Exploit (2022)**, where a trader manipulated oracle prices to borrow and withdraw over $112 million (Sinclair & Peterson, 2022).
- The **Harvest Finance Attack (2020)**, where attackers used price manipulation to steal $24 million from a DeFi yield farming platform (immunebytes, 2020).

Interoperability Challenges

DeFi's growing reliance on interoperability—where multiple blockchain protocols interact seamlessly—creates additional attack surfaces. The functionality extends to multi-platform integrations and cross-chain bridges, which brings risks.

Cross-Chain Bridge Vulnerabilities

While cross-chain bridges allow for asset transfer between blockchains, security flaws have made them a hungry prey for hackers. Examples include:

- The **Ronin Bridge Hack (2022)** resulted in a $600 million theft due to weak security protocols (Tidy, 2022).
- The **Wormhole Hack (2022)**, where attackers exploited a vulnerability to steal $320 million from Solana's bridge (Kolakowski, 2022).

Due to the large number of locked assets they often contain, bridges are desirable targets for attackers who can circumvent poor authentication.

Cascading Failures

Decentralized Finance (DeFi) interoperability solves many functionality issues but also brings systemic risk in one place; a single attack can happen across many protocols (Gogol, et al., 2024). When DeFi platforms integrate different services, one failure in one component may lead to environmental disruptions. For example, quashing for mass liquidations in a lending platform could result in price crashes that affect automated market makers (AMMs), decentralized exchanges (DEXs), and liquidity pools. This enhances such vulnerabilities, making the whole ecosystem even more fragile. To avoid these risks, DeFi systems must be as robust as can be due to security audits, decentralized governance, and cross-chain risk assessments.

CASE STUDIES OF DEFI EXPLOITS

Decentralized Finance (DeFi) is the new frontier of free financial possibility, but because it is entirely decentralized, it's also particularly susceptible to fraudsters. (Zetzsche et al., 2020, p. 172). The list of DeFi exploits includes gas exploits, price exploitation, brilliant contract exploits, and simple fraud. This section expands on several real-world examples showing that the attack on the DeFi area is not isolated and covers several types of attacks, such as flash loan attacks, rug pulls, oracle manipulation, and governance attacks. Each case helps present general information on how these attacks occur, their consequences, and the experience that should be used to develop security measures continuously.

The Poly Network Exploit: Cross-Chain Vulnerability

Background

Poly Network is the multichain solution that is used to transfer assets from one blockchain to another. (Zheng, Lee, & Qian, 2023). On 10th August 2021, it experienced one of the biggest hacks in the DeFi space, where the attackers managed to drain about 192,943 ETH, Binance Smart Chain tokens, and stablecoins equivalent to about $611 million. Specifically, the exploit unveiled several issues relating to cross-chain smart contract security and the assumptions on which the multi-chain DeFi platforms might be built. The scale of the attack was reflected explicitly as quite large since Poly Network was established as a significant player in bridge connectivity and transactions across Ethereum, BSC, and Polygon.

Attack Mechanism

The Poly Network exploit was not some form of hacking that involved stealing private keys or a simple brute force attack. Instead, the attacker pinpointed a vulnerability in the network's cross-chain smart contract logic. They stimulated a function that modifies transaction parameters, transferring many bitcoins to them. (Wu, et al., 2021, p. 2237). The problem arose as some contract access controls were not secured, only for administrators, but the hacker could change the settings. This weakness was triggered by the permissions required for decentralized applications on the smart contract layer; it exposes a general security flaw in cross-chain solutions.

Aftermath and Resolution

The hacker responsible for the theft later returned most of the money, stating that they did not mean any harm and wanted people to know the reality of online crime—the attacker, called by some as ‘Mr. White Hat’, engaged the Poly Network’s team and explained the full extent of the vulnerabilities he exploited. The incident highlighted the requirement for enhanced security assessment, better control of the access process, and better governance of DeFi cross-chain platforms. After regaining footing after the attack, the event highlighted that using smart contracts for large-scale financial transactions within the decentralized finance industry comes with a high risk.

Key Lessons

Cross-chain solutions present these extra layers of risk, which need to be addressed, as any connectivity between various blockchains opens up multiple new vulnerabilities. (Zhao, et al., 2023). Flaws in one chain directly put the others at risk, so there must always be accurate inspections and reliable security architectures. Furthermore, access control mechanisms must be tested frequently so administrators do not allow unauthorized changes. Lack of proper implementation can compromise governance mechanisms or funds within the protocols. Ethical hackers become very relevant in detecting and eradicating these issues before they become an issue for malicious users. However, not all exploits are noble since some hackers use loopholes to cause havoc instead of reporting them to their respective owners or vendors.

Flash Loan Exploits: The Case of bZx and Euler Finance

Background

Flash loans are a peculiarity of DeFi that can enable users to borrow substantial amounts of cryptocurrency without putting up collateral if they repay the amount within the same transaction. It also allows for capital-efficient trading techniques, including trading on an arbitrage and liquidation basis without a capital base. However, new market manipulation methods, protocols, and frauds have been created. Since flash loans do not involve posting collateral for the borrowed tokens, attackers can utilize them to manipulate asset prices, exploit various oracles, and siphon funds from several lending platforms. (Oosthoek, 2021, p. 22). These attacks demonstrate the problem with using smart contracts and performing payments online without proper protection from pump-and-dump schemes and re-entry attacks in decentralized finance.

bZx Flash Loan Attack (2020)

In February 2020, the bZx lending protocol suffered a flash loan exploit, resulting in a $620,000 loss. (AON, 2023). The attacker borrowed ETH using a flash loan and then manipulated a collateral asset´s price by exploiting low liquidity and Oracle vulnerabilities. Thus, by temporarily increasing the asset's price, the attacker could take out more money than he put in initially. The exploit highlighted a weakness in DeFi whereby existing external price oracles provide erroneous data and how illiquidity amplifies the capacity to manipulate a system. This attack was among the first flash loan attacks pointing out the weaknesses in the price oracles in DeFi lending.

Euler Finance Exploit

In a flash loan attack in Euler Finance, a lending decentralized finance platform lost more than $197 million in March of 2023 (ChainAnalysis, 2023). This was a much more professional kind of attack than previous ones. The attacker first locked value into the system by employing a flash loan and then used an inflated price. Cyclically, owing to the high collateral that is used to borrow from the protocol, the attacker leveraged and took more funds than should have been allowed by Euler's liquidation parameters. The Euler exploit also showed that even popular and reputed DeFi platforms are not immune to intricate flash loan exploits, suggesting that additional measures like circuit breakers and dynamic collateral requirements should be developed to defend against manipulation of lending protocols.

Key Lessons

The efficiency that flash loans bring to traders is impressive, but they also open up opportunities for attackers to exploit the DeFi protocols. These credit assets do not hold collateral and must be paid back within one call transaction; thus, scammers can manipulate the market to cause cash-outs or forced selling. One of the most prevalent forms is Price Oracle cheating, which entails the attackers creating artificial high or low asset prices. To address this, price oracles must be highly secure; they should include data from several reliable sources to avoid the problem. Additionally, lending platforms must incorporate protection strategies like time delay to help counter high-frequency transactions, circuit breakers to stop unusual trading, and anomaly detections to recognize high-frequency trading. With these mechanisms incorporated into DeFi, problems like flash loans and Oracle manipulation can be addressed, making the market safer for users.

Rug Pulls and Exit Scams: The Squid Game Token Fraud

Background

The Squid Game Token (SQUID) was launched in late 2021, capitalizing on the massive popularity of Netflix's hit show, *Squid Game*. (BBC, 2021). Spotlighting itself as a 'play-to-earn' token allowed players to earn returns through a gaming-based DeFi platform. It generated massive interest from thousands of investors due to an astounding 310000% increase in price within several days of launch. However, there were warning signs almost immediately: no Netflix endorsement, unclear contract terms and weak documentation, and limitations on token resales.

However, these red lights attracted many investors due to the token's rise and the opportunities to make money.

Attack Mechanism

The Squid Game Token was a typical example of a rug pull fraud. Developers set up trading for the token by establishing a smart contract that created a liquidity pool but included programming that locked token holders into the pool and prevented them from selling. (TRM, 2025). This ensured that users could purchase SQUID tokens; they could not cash in the digital currency. Concerning the retail investors, they kept putting their money into the project, and the unknown owners retook their cash, leaving the token to drop to nearly zero in a short period. One position managed to cost them millions of dollars to investors, and some went further to lose more than $3.3 million. Hence, the attack was previously planned, and no technical loopholes were exploited; it included misleading promotions and infamous speculation.

Aftermath and Community Response

The anonymous developers vanished, making legal recourse impossible. The lack of accountability in DeFi again emerged as a significant problem as the funds' investors had no means of getting them back. Squid Game Token was one of the most famous examples of rug pull scams, as it attracted coverage from worldwide media outlets and regulators. (WIRED, 2021). It provided a wake-up call and taught investors not to invest in hyped projects with unknown teams and that smart contracts go unchecked. It underlined the necessity to check the legitimacy of developers, money availability, and sales restrictions before investing in DeFi tokens.

Key Lessons

During the analysis of the DeFi project, one should check whether the token is traded freely since restricted trade signals a high probability of scam or rug pull. Some of these scams come with measures to lock investors from selling their tokens while the developers retain complete control of the supply. Moreover, while anonymity is a powerful incentive for innovation and decentralization in DeFi, it also implies the possibility of fraudulent actors. Fraudsters use these to create new schemes, raise money from investors, and then vanish without a penalty. To avoid such risks, the investor needs to ensure that such a team is sufficiently transparent and that there are detailed roadmaps with audits conducted by competent firms. The failure of these elements is one of the main indications pointing to the absence of stable and secure long-term development. The compliance process, scrutiny of risks, and credibility assessment of a project can help users avoid potential scams and be safer within the DeFi space.

Oracle Manipulation Attacks: The Mango Markets Exploit

Background

Mango Markets, a lending and trading firm operating based on Solana, was exploited to $117.8 million in October 2022 through price exploitation of its oracle. (Akartuna, 2022). The attack stemmed from Mango's use of a single source price oracle where the attacker manipulated the price of the $MNGO token upwards. Thus, the prices of the collateral assets were artificially inflated, and the attacker borrowed against it. Unlike conventional financial systems that utilize mechanisms to monitor and prevent such manipulations, DeFi platforms are mostly unmonitored or lack proper risk management. As a result of this specific vulnerability, the exploit could be carried out in a single transaction. It raised concerns about how price oracles in the DeFi ecosystem are secured without information manipulation and how single-source oracles skewed the asset's valuation.

Attack Mechanism

First, the attacker accumulated a vast number of MNGO perpetual futures, a contract that allows one to bet on the price of an asset without actually owning it. They used this opportunity to pump the MNGO tokens and later sold them to other users within the Mango market ecosystem, causing its price to rise. Since Oracle's price was a single source pricing, any manipulated price was considered the market price by Mango. Consequently, with the price soaring, the attacker deployed their accumulated MNGO holdings as collateral to borrow more tokens, especially USDC and SOL. After borrowing almost all the funds available in the protocol, they unloaded their MNGO to cause the prices to plummet. (Finance, 2021). The failure of Mango to consider such high volatility in the prices led to the draining of the entire protocol out of funds and, hence, the inability to recover again.

Aftermath and Resolution

After the hack, the attacker decided to do the unexpected; he went on the Mango DAO and proposed a governor vote to repay a portion of the lost amount as long as they got immunity and a cash reward. Due to Mango's highly distributed governance system that enabled token holders to decide on several important issues, the community had to choose: to apply to the court and receive nothing or to yield to the demands of attackers and restore at least a part of the lost funds. Surprisingly, the community approved the proposal, showing that even DeFi governance mechanisms could favor the attackers. The exploit underscored the need for multi-source price oracles and stronger governance safeguards to prevent similar attacks in the future.

Key Lessons

Oracles are used in DeFi to input external data into smart contracts. Still, they need to collect information from a variety of sources to avoid being gamed by a single source (Zhao, Kang, Li, Chu, & Wang, 2022, p. 76). The reliance on a single data feed makes the lending platforms and automated trading systems vulnerable to the so-called 'price oracle attacks,' where the prices of the assets are artificially manipulated for the gains. However, lack of central authority is one of the essential features of DeFi, and it can be abused if specific measures are not taken. The attackers might use Flash loans to temporarily gain most of the votes on the given protocol and pass specific malicious proposals to steal the funds within the protocol. To minimize such risks, measures like time delay in governance decisions and the multi-signature system could be usable. Additionally, AI-assisted real-time anomaly detectors could quickly reveal such manipulative behaviors as abnormally increased prices or extreme variants in turnover. Through such solutions, DeFi platforms can improve protection against fraud and prevent users from losing funds.

Governance Exploits: The Beanstalk Farms Attack

Background

The algorithmic stablecoin project Beanstalk Farms was attacked in April 2022, draining $182 million from the company's treasury. (Hern, 2022). Unlike other DeFi hacks every day to contact failures or flash loan attacks, this was a relatively simple hijacking of the protocol's decentralized governance system. Beanstalk had a DAO-based governance mechanism through which token holders could decide to modify the protocol. For instance, the system did not have enough measures to help prevent bad governors from proposing inadequate measures. This design flaw made Beanstalk susceptible to attack, where ample voting power was used to change the rules of the protocol. Due to these problems, the attacker could inflate the prices, subvert the governance mechanisms, and siphon a considerable amount of funds from the platform in one transaction.

Attack Mechanism

The attack on Beanstalk Farms was facilitated by a flash loan, a Defi tool that enables massive cryptocurrency borrowing without collateral. The sum borrowed must be returned in the same transaction. (Parisi & Budorin, 2023, p. 81). This enabled the attacker to gain control of over 50% of controlling votes in Beanstalk's governance system. They were once in control of a considerable part of the votes, and they then passed a rogue governance proposal that sought to drain the protocol's treasury into the culprits' wallets. There were no time differences in the governance system of Beanstalk and no security checks on significant proposals, which allowed the attacker to pass the proposal and execute it quickly. This enabled them to drain $182 million of funds to ensure safekeeping before the protocol developers or users could stop the attack.

Aftermath and Response

In Beanstalk's case, the absence of proper security measures in the money market's governing structure means that the hacker unleashed the attack without delay. (Allen, 2022, p. 919). Since the malfunction led to the attack during a particular transaction, there was no chance to restrict or terminate the action. After the exploit, Beanstalk Farms sought to recover the lost funds, and they could only recover a small amount of money. This primarily affected investor confidence and led to the slashing of the stablecoin, which almost resulted in the complete collapse of the protocol. As a result, the Beanstalk community discussed such security measures as restrictions in governance and time in significant proposal actions. However, the incident pointed to a substantial weakness in DeFi governance structures regarding DAO security and flash loan governor manipulation of decentralized programs.

Key Lessons

The governance systems in place of Decentralized Finance must have protective measures, including time locks, before acting on proposals so as not to be manipulated. Without these delays, flash loans allow attackers to gain a majority of votes in the protocol, execute nasty governance proposals, and steal funds from the community with no way to stop them. Flash loan-based governance attacks are also relatively new, and they imply that tighter governance rules can be applied, like more extended voting periods, multi-sig approvals, or quorum limits to prevent flash takeovers, which may leave a target project with no possible other way than to aggregate the discounts itself. Further, better security checks should be conducted on the DAO voting platforms to determine the loopholes that can be exploited, thus enabling hostile takeovers. It should also look at issues such as where power lies, whether there are measures to avoid power concentration, and how proposals to be voted on are checked before voting.

CHALLENGES FOR REGULATORS AND LAW ENFORCEMENT

Decentralized Finance (DeFi) is an exciting and novel sector that still poses challenges when it comes to regulation and policing across the globe. (Wronka, 2023, p. 97) In legal terms, traditional financial systems can be delineated by borders and regulated by the law, whereas DeFi is unregulated primarily and operates more freely. There is no centralized authority between them; the transactions are anonymous, and the technologies are developing very fast, so it is almost impossible for financial authorities to enforce existing laws and suppress fraud, money laundering, and terrorism financing.

The Absence of Centralized Oversight

One of the primary challenges facing regulators is the absence of a central authority in DeFi. (Doerr, et al., 2021, p. 22). Major financial institutions, such as the economic and stock exchange and the banking industries, are regulated by government institutions, such as the U.S. Securities and Exchange Commission and the Financial Conduct Authority of the United States of America. Such institutions function as natural barriers preventing whiting and other malicious activities in adherence to the anti-money laundering legislation, know-your-customer laws, and other regulations.

On the other hand, DeFi solutions exist and function through decentralized smart contracts integrated into the blockchain environment. (Schär F., 2021, p. 153). This decentralization makes it very difficult for the regulators to pin down any of the parties to the defaults in compliance. If a DeFi protocol supports illicit services, the authorities do not necessarily have a subject to apply legal measures against. Furthermore, even if the developers of a particular platform can be identified, they may further state that they do not directly control the platform since such governance is usually decentralized among token holders.

Anonymity and Pseudonymity in Transactions

Another major challenge is the anonymity provided by blockchain technology. (Schueffel, 2021, p. 1). Most DeFi-based transactions happen through digital wallets where one does not need to provide real identity. Despite this, all transactions conducted within the blockchain are public but linked only to an anonymous alphanumeric wallet number. This remains a disadvantage to the regulators and the police because it provides a mask for money laundering, tax evasion, and funding of unlawful activities. DeFi platforms, unlike conventional banks, do not need to request customer identification or monitor all the transactions made by the platforms' users. Therefore, the dark side of the DeFi sector allows criminals to transfer and launder funds globally without much trouble.

As mentioned, some regulatory agencies have restricted this interaction by implementing the KYC procedures on the CE that engages in DeFi to mitigate this problem. Nonetheless, this approach remains rather restraining, as the participants can constantly shift their assets to decentralized exchanges that are not regulated. Furthermore, the new breed of anonymous coins and mixers also hampers the tracing of transactions.

Jurisdictional Challenges and Regulatory Arbitrage

DeFi relies on global blockchain networks, which are difficult to identify and regulate jurisdictionally. International financial regulations are usually at the national level. However, Defi projects are used not only by residents of certain countries but also by people worldwide; thus, they do not obey any country's legislation. It leads to the notion of 'regulatory arbitrage, 'meaning that many projects select locations with the least strict rules or are entirely beyond the control of any regulations.

For instance, if one country seeks to regulate the operations of DeFi applications, the developers and users can quickly move to other areas where regulations are more lenient. Due to the lack of geographical limitations, it becomes hard for authorities to regulate and enforce the laws and rules effectively. However, unique regulatory measures across countries are still a significant challenge in setting a central worldwide legal standard for regulating DeFi.

Smart Contract Risks and Legal Liability

Smart contracts, which are automated contracts written on the blockchain networks to self-execute, are the building blocks of decentralized finance (DeFi) (Liu, et al., 2024). They have many benefits in terms of automation, but they come with a set of security concerns. Malicious software, defects, and hacks are common threats, indicating that failure in the decentralized finance industry can be incredibly costly, as many DeFi hacks have demonstrated.

Determining legal liability for brilliant contract failures is a complex issue from a regulatory standpoint. Moreover, most smart contracts operate independently most of the time, making it challenging to find someone to blame for a loss, unlike in financial transactions. If an exploit happens, it is not necessarily very clear who should bear to blame: the developers who wrote the contract, the voting members of the community who decided on an upgrade of the protocol parameters, or the users who engaged with the particular contract.

Sometimes, regulators tried to hold DeFi developers because they exercised influence over the platform through administrative rights or voting power. However, this approach has been met with resistance, given that most de-finance projects focus on decentralization to avoid retribution by governing authorities.

Combating Financial Crimes in DeFi

The crime of money laundering, acts of financing terrorism, and others are becoming increasingly relevant in the DeFi market. The various criminal organizations may be able to launder their black money through cryptocurrency, hide transactions through mixing, and transfer assets internationally. Traditionally, anti-money laundering frameworks rely on the help of certain intermediaries, such as banks, to monitor transactions and report those they consider suspicious; however, DeFi does not have such middlemen.

Some regulators are considering how AML and counter-terrorism financing (CTF) measures can be applied to DeFi protocols. For instance, the Financial Action Task Force (FATF) has proposed that decentralized applications (dApps) and DeFi protocol creators be labeled as "VASPs," which would force them to adhere to AML guidelines. However, applying them in DeFi often proves difficult due to decentralization, and it is tough to point to a set of intermediaries to enforce a specific regulation. While analytics firms have attempted to create models to track transactions and track inherent patterns of fraudulent behavior, these solutions remain rudimentary. Also, privacy-preserving measures like ZKP and decentralized mixers are being developed constantly, meaning that the ability of law enforcement to track financial crimes in DeFi is decreasing.

The Role of Decentralized Autonomous Organizations (DAOs) in Regulation

Most of the DeFi projects have adopted decentralized autonomous organizations or DAOs to make decisions on changes to the protocol, fees, or governance policies (Santana & Albareda, 2022). It is, therefore, crucial to look at the regulatory issues arising from the election of a DAO.

DAOs are not conventional legal structures, so it remains uncertain how they should be governed or taxed. Some legal systems have legal persons who may apply to the DAO to sign contracts and assume legal responsibilities. However, most

DAOs are not incorporated, and legal or regulatory frameworks cannot restrict their actions in most cases.

Also, the centralized control of DAOs by the participants who own numerous governance tokens raises concerns about decentralization and other unlawful regulations. For instance, if an individual utilizes a DAO for selling unregistered securities or is involved in a pyramid scheme or any other illegal activity, it may be hard to determine who is responsible.

Potential Regulatory Approaches for DeFi

Despite these challenges, regulators worldwide are still focused on using various measures to legalize DeFi while retaining its innovation. Some of the potential regulatory strategies include:

- ***Hybrid Regulation Models:*** Some regulators propose a two-tier model, which means applying control to centralized structures (fiat gateways, stablecoins issuers, custody wallets, etc.) and excluding any restrictions for decentralized protocols. This approach recognizes that it is not easy to control decentralized systems completely, but there are controls at entry and exit points.
- ***Code Auditing and Security Standards:*** Governments and industry groups may require security audits and code reviews on DeFi protocols implemented by governments and industries. Regions could mitigate the risk and accommodate investors by washing off smart contracts against some security standards.
- ***Self-Regulation and Industry-Led Compliance Measures:*** Some DeFi projects have introduced measures in which industry stakeholders set voluntary standards on security, management, and the fight against financial crimes. This is not a legally enforced policy but may increase people's confidence in DeFi and decrease the need for authorities' intervention.
- ***Legal Recognition of DAOs:*** Law enforcement of DAOs and strong guidelines to determine accountability could reduce the distance between decentralized finance governance and legitimacy. Some examples of legal regulation of DAOs as corporate bodies are in Wyoming, USA.
- ***Improved Blockchain Analytics and Collaboration:*** Authorities and police departments continue to turn to blockchain analytics companies to help design applications that detect unlawful conduct within DeFi. Increased cooperation between the public and private sectors in addressing the problem can lead to increased transparency and help the authorities better identify and prevent cases of financial fraud.

Technology-Driven Solutions to DeFi Exploits

Decentralized Finance (DeFi) has revolutionized the financial sector by providing open, permissionless, and trustless financial services. However, the rapid expansion of DeFi also exposed some vulnerabilities, which were targeted by significant attacks such as smart contract vulnerability, Oracle manipulation, and flash loan attacks. Despite the maturation of DeFi, developers, security specialists, and regulators are all adapting technology-based solutions to boost security, decrease vulnerabilities, and protect savers.

This section explores some technological approaches that prevent DeFi exploits: smart contract auditing, formal verification, advanced oracles, multi-signature wallets, decentralized identity systems, and AI-powered security measures.

Smart Contract Auditing and Formal Verification

Smart contract auditing is one of the main ways DeFitabes are shielded from DeFi exploits. Since the code for Smart contracts is immutable once deployed on the chain, they cannot be tinkered with afterward. The bad guys can exploit any vulnerabilities in their code. Instead, smart contracts that developers have to launch before they ensure to minimize risks.

Security audits involve independent cybersecurity firms reviewing a DeFi project's codebase to identify potential flaws. The vulnerabilities being tested in these audits include reentrancy attacks, integer overflow and underflow issues, access control misconfiguration, and logical errors. Audits successfully identify weaknesses and reduce the likelihood of successful exploits because weaknesses are identified before deployment.

In addition to traditional auditing, the other types of intelligent contract security verification take the form of a mathematically rigorous process known as formal verification. Unlike audits, which depend on manual code inspection, formal verification provides a mathematical model of a smart contract, proving that it will work as intended under any condition. The most useful application of this approach is when minor errors can cause massive losses in complex financial applications.

Formal verification tools, such as CertiK's DeepSEA and Microsoft's Solidity Verifier, analyze smart contract logic and guarantee that specific exploits, such as reentrancy attacks, cannot occur. While such a solution is not widespread due to complexity and computational overheads, formal verification is still a promising way to enhance DeFi security.

Advanced Oracle Solutions

Oracles bridge the gap between off-chain and on-chain data and are critical to most DeFi protocols, such as price, exchange, and interest rates (Fomintsov Trukhaev, 2024). However, oracles have become a prominent attack vector to DeFi, as it is possible to attack the price oracle. These are lousy actor attacks that feed insufficient price data to a protocol that causes financial loss.

To mitigate oracle-related risks, the DeFi ecosystem has developed several advanced oracle solutions, including:

- ***Decentralized Oracles:*** Platforms like Chainlink and Band Protocol aggregate data from multiple sources, reducing the risk of a single point of failure (Ezzat, Saleh, & Abdel-Hamid, 2022). Decentralized oracles distribute data sources across different providers, thus making it less easy for attackers to manipulate prices.
- ***Time-Weighted Average Price (TWAP) Oracles:*** These oracles sometimes calculate asset prices based on historical data rather than choosing a single price point. TWAP helps reduce losses by reducing the effect of sudden price manipulations that can be exploited in flash loan attacks (Mackinga, Nadahalli, & Wattenhofer, 2022, p. 1).
- ***Consensus-Based Oracles:*** Some DeFi projects use consensus mechanisms to check an oracle's data before writing it to the chain. This approach enhances data reliability by requiring multiple independent data providers to agree on a price before updating smart contracts.
- ***Layer 2 Oracles and Verifiable Random Functions (VRFs):*** Some projects implement Layer 2 solutions to validate Oracle data off-chain before committing it to the blockchain. VRFs make predicting or manipulating oracle outputs more challenging, providing one more where attackers try.

The stronger security of Oracles helps protect DeFi platforms from price manipulation exploits and makes the ecosystem more resilient.

Multi-Signature Wallets and Multi-Party Computation (MPC)

Another technology-driven solution to DeFi exploits is using multi-signature (multi-sig) wallets and multi-party computation (MPC) for fund management (Erinle, Feng, Xu, Vadgama, & Tasca, 2024). Multi-sig wallets mean that you will need more than one party to approve the transaction before it is executed, reducing the risk of unauthorized access or malicious actions from a single entity.

Multi-sig wallets are handy for governance-controlled treasuries, decentralized exchanges (DEXs), and smart contract upgrades because they provide a higher level of security, which involves multiple approvals required to proceed with transacting in treasury. This way, the risk of having a single point of failure is minimized, and no unauthorized withdrawal or malicious protocol changes are made. Multi-sig wallets in DeFi protect against insider threats and hacking, as no single entity has the right to spend the funds. While they bring challenges such as coordination delays and the potential loss of access from key holders' unavailability, they also increase robustness from the misbehavior of systems, users, and the network. Although this has limitations, multi-sig wallets are still essential in financially decentralized worlds.

In a way, MPC adds more security distributed based on key shares among multiple entities, allowing no entity to possess full permissions for private keys. The result is a less risky approach concerning centralized key storage, where private key theft or accidental, unauthorized access to the funds could occur.

Decentralized Identity and Reputation Systems

One of the fundamental challenges in DeFi security is the pseudonymous nature of blockchain transactions (Makarov & Schoar, 2022, p. 215). As none of the users is identified by real-world identity, bad actors can create fraudulent activities and get away with them. As a potential solution to this issue, decentralized identity (DID) and reputation systems are becoming the next big thing.

Self-Sovereign Identity (SSI) and decentralized identity (DID) systems allow users to verify their identity without exposing personal data (Babu, 2024, p. 721). Credited to cryptographic techniques (namely, zero-knowledge proofs), these systems authenticate users while preserving their privacy. DeFi can improve security and trust in financial interactions and trust-based lending by integrating DID solutions and preventing Sybil attacks. Centralized verification is not needed to prove creditworthiness for borrowers, which reduces loan default risks. DID systems also help reduce the risk of fraud and, therefore, identify the fault, which increases the security and compliance of DeFi while keeping user anonymity in a decentralized financial platform.

Reputation systems give wallet addresses trust scores based on previous behavior. Take, for example, a lending protocol requiring less collateral for users with a good history of successful loan repayments and tighter conditions for new or shady accounts. Reputation-based mechanisms discourage malicious activity while rewarding honest participation in DeFi.

Artificial Intelligence and Machine Learning for DeFi Security

DeFi increasingly uses artificial intelligence (AI) and machine learning (ML) to make some projects more secure. These technologies can parse large volumes of blockchain data for anomaly detection, exploit prediction, and risk management enhancement.

AI-driven solutions in DeFi security include:

- ***Anomaly Detection Systems:*** AI algorithms can monitor real-time blockchain transactions to identify unusual patterns that could indicate fraudulent activity. For instance, AI models can suddenly start processing many smart contract transactions to investigate further.
- ***Automated Threat Intelligence:*** Past DeFi exploits allow machine learning models to analyze and use predictive insights to target future attack vectors (Aaron, Irekponor, Aleke, Yeboah, & Joseph, 2024). DeFi protocols can proactively protect against new threat patterns by continuously updating security parameters based on these new attack patterns.
- ***AI-Powered Risk Assessment:*** AI models can assess borrower risk based on historical transaction data, liquidity behavior, and market conditions in DeFi lending platforms. This enhances the credit risk evaluation and helps reduce loan default risk.
- ***Automated Bug Detection:*** AI can also be used in code analysis to scan smart contracts for vulnerabilities until the code is deployed. These tools use deep learning techniques to discover patterns of common exploits and lessen the likelihood of human oversight in manual audits.

Merging AI-embedded security mechanisms will enable DeFi platforms to increase threat detection, risk management, and overall system security.

Zero-Knowledge Proofs (ZKPs) for Privacy and Security

The zero-knowledge proofs (ZKPs) are cryptographic techniques through which one party can prove knowledge of a particular fact without revealing the accurate information (Zhou, Diro, Saini, Kaisar, & Hiep, 2024). ZKPs can be used to improve privacy and prevent frontrunning attacks in the context of DeFi security.

Applications of ZKPs in DeFi include:

- ***Private Transactions:*** ZKPs allow users to make confidential transactions while maintaining compliance with regulatory terms. ZKPs are being used to provide privacy-preserving financial services using platforms such as Zcash and Aztec.

- ***Preventing Front-Running on DEXs:*** Front-running occurs when malicious actors exploit pending transactions in the mempool to execute trades ahead of others. In the end, a running attack is impossible with ZKPs as they can conceal the details until the transaction is finalized.
- ***Enhanced Authentication:*** ZKPs can verify user credentials without exposing sensitive data, improving the security of DeFi governance and voting mechanisms (Ajayi, Igba, Soyele, & Enyejo, 2024).

By integrating ZKPs, DeFi platforms can balance privacy and security, reducing risks while ensuring compliance with financial regulations.

FUTURE DIRECTIONS: BALANCING INNOVATION AND SECURITY

Decentralized Finance (DeFi) has emerged as an innovation that has democratized finance by providing decentralized, permissionless, and trustless financial services. (Adisa, et al., 2024, p. 2313). Therefore, several risks and vices are connected to this sector as it steadily grows. Weaknesses, vulnerabilities, risks, issues related to hacks, astute contract frauds, regulatory issues, and problems with the relatively new technology keep endangering the viability and legitimacy of DeFi. In the future, it will become clear that innovation and security will be the keys to developing decentralized finance. This section discusses new directions, technologies, legal measures, and partnerships that can be applied to improve the state of DeFi while ensuring the security and credibility of the systems.

Evolving Smart Contract Security

Smart contracts are at the core of decentralized finance (DeFi), where various financial operations are executed independently. However, due to their decentralization, any coding deficiencies or even bugs pose a severe and irreversible danger of losing one's assets (Wronka, Financial crime in the decentralized finance ecosystem: new challenges for compliance, 2023). Looking to the future of smart contract security is a major issue that needs further development to minimize the incidence of hacks.

One promising solution to this particular problem is automated bug detection and prevention using innovative contract auditing tools with AI. Machine learning algorithms can analyze more significant samples of previous exploits and determine possible weak points in the smart contract code before its release. Runtime verification, which executes intelligent contract monitoring in the actual environment, can prevent executing some behavioral activities that may amount to a significant breach.

Another way smart contracts have been secured is by using upgradable smart contracts. (Bui, et al., 2021, p. 252). Unlike to the fixed smart contracts, upgradable smart contracts can be enhanced or repaired by the use of patching possible loopholes without the centrality of authority. It can only be made possible through governance that effectively present the upgrades in a way that everybody will agree to it.

Decentralized Identity Solutions for Trust and Compliance

In the future, efforts are expected to be made to identify user identities and meet the regulatory requirements of the traditional financial industry. While blockchain is built for anonymity to provide individuals with economic liberty, the system also provides anonymity for various unlawful activities such as money laundering and forgery. To solve this problem without antagonizing decentralization, the emerging concept of Decentralized Identity (DID) is on the rise.

DID systems allow users to access various authorities through a self-sovereign identity (SSI) framework while being privacy-preserving (Abubakar-Sadiq, 2023). Some of these solutions utilize features of a zero-knowledge proof (ZKP), which ensures the validation of credentials such as KYC without the sharing of any sensitive information. This means that different DeFi platforms can incorporate compliance measures based on the risk level of the transaction where transactions from a high-risk user may be asked to provide more details compared to a low-risk user.

Soulbound tokens, which are blockchain-based tokens that cannot be transferred, can also strengthen DeFi security as they link users to a credible reputation profile. The governance models used in DeFi can also include trust-based lending, which can help combat risks such as Sybil attacks and fraud relating to borrowing.

Enhanced Cross-Chain Security Mechanisms

The emergence of multi-chain DeFi environments creates new vulnerabilities, such as cross-chain bridges that enable movables interchange between different blockchains. (Westerkamp, 2023). Another concerning issue is cross-chain bridges which have attracted hackers as billions have been stolen through such bridges due to architectural flaws.

The advancements in cross-chain security in the future will rely on systems that do not rely on certain entities through the use of custom cryptographic protocols such as:

- ***Threshold Signatures and Multi-Party Computation (MPC):*** These mechanisms divide the cryptographic keys between the validators to avoid having any single entity control the bridge transactions.
- ***Light Client-Based Bridges:*** These rely on the cryptographic security of the underlying blockchains rather than centralized or semi-centralized validators.
- ***Optimistic Rollups and ZK-Rollups:*** These Layer 2 scaling solutions may enable decentralized cross-chain transactions because they do not presume outside validators.

Regulatory Frameworks That Encourage Responsible Innovation

The regulator position in the DeFi remains challenging, and governments and financial authorities have yet to develop a way to regulate financial innovation while protecting consumers. (Lorenz, 2024, p. 136). Therefore, the subsequent regulation of DeFi must look into the issue by ensuring security and still foster innovation.

Several possible regulatory models may emerge:

- ***Regulated DeFi Sandboxes:*** Governments and financial institutions may provide DeFi projects to set up regulatory sandboxes to facilitate the project's experimentation in an environment apart from production. These sandboxes can also help the regulator and developers work hand in hand while developing products of this nature while maintaining security standards.
- ***Self-Regulatory Organizations (SROs):*** It can also be possible for the DeFi industry to set up self-governing bodies to set security standards, categorize competent contract inspections, and offer recommendations on regulatory issues (Guseva, 2024).
- ***Hybrid KYC/AML Solutions:*** In the future, there could be a two-layer model for Know Your Customer KYC procedures, where low-risk Bitcoin transactions remain unregulated, while high-risk transactions can only be executed according to Anti-Money Laundering (AML) laws.

AI and Predictive Security in DeFi

With the growth of decentralized finance applications, it has become difficult for traditional threat detection methods to identify attacks planning to occur soon, and on-chain and off-chain data analysis and AI will support this task (Gross, 2024, p. 1281). By training machines, the patterns of trading in the blockchain can be used to detect fraud, wash trading, and even manipulation of the market in general. Built with machine learning techniques, it becomes possible to identify fraudulent activity in transactions, money movements among addresses, and interactions with innovative contract addresses in real-time. Also, the machine learning risk analysis can assist individuals in determining protocol safety when entering an investment. Combining AI technologies and DeFi security frameworks can enhance fraud prevention, strengthen compliance, and reduce risks in a decentralized environment.

AI applications in DeFi security include:

- Automated anomaly detection systems that flag unusual transactions in real time.
- AI-powered risk scoring models that assess the security of smart contracts based on historical exploit data.
- Predictive liquidity crisis models that warn DeFi protocols of potential bank runs or liquidity shortages before they happen.

The Rise of Quantum-Resistant Cryptography

With the progress in quantum computing, threats and risks in blockchain are becoming more apparent. Some traditional cryptographic algorithms include Elliptic Curve Cryptography (ECC) and RSA, which are based on computations that are extremely hard to crack. However, algorithms like Shor's that are used by quantum computers could infiltrate these encryption strategies exponentially faster than classical computers threaten blockchain systems (Baseri, Chouhan, & Ghorbani, 2024, p. 76). This has led to a focus on post-quantum cryptography or quantum-resistant algorithms to ensure the security of the assets. Blockchain developers are considering lattice-based, hash-based, and multivariate polynomial cryptography to prevent future attack vectors. Preemptively implementing post-quantum security is a critical step toward ensuring the blockchain's efficiencies remain intact.

Future DeFi security will depend on the adoption of quantum-resistant cryptographic techniques, including:

- ***Lattice-Based Cryptography:*** A new post-quantum encryption method immune to quantum attacks.
- ***Hash-Based Signatures:*** This technology allows blockchain to be secured without using signature keys like traditional cryptocurrencies.
- ***Quantum-Secure Blockchain Protocols:*** QANplatform and Hyperledger Fabric are working on offering solutions that will make applications in DeFi secured against hacker attacks in future blockchains.

Integrating Decentralized Insurance for Risk Mitigation

Decentralized insurance is becoming an essential form of risk management for people using decentralized finance protocols to engage in various activities. Its importance has grown as more high-profile hacks and exploits have occurred recently. (Zetzsche, Arner, & Buckley, Decentralized finance, 2020). Some of the decentralized insurance protocols include Nexus Mutual, Cover Protocol, and InsurAce, which reimburse the users of these systems for any lost funds due to hacks, bugs, or any other unforeseen issues. These services employ distributed risk assessment systems where participants invest their funds to back policies and decisions on claims. Decentralized insurance works through smart contracts, is more transparent than traditional insurance, and is free from counterparty risk and payment delays. In the future, decentralized insurance will be one of the key components of the DeFi space as it helps to bolster confidence in the technology.

Future DeFi insurance models may incorporate the following:

- **Parametric insurance solutions**, which payout when specific parameters that have been pre-negotiated are met.
- **AI-driven insurance underwriting**, where the premium changes depending on the results of the security audits and past exploits.
- **Decentralized risk pools**, where users contribute to the insurance fund and decide on what policies need to be implemented in case of losses.

The Role of DAOs in Security Governance

Decentralized autonomous organizations (DAOs), self-governing organizations inside decentralized finance (DeFi) systems, are becoming critical in security governance. One of the significant accomplishments is providing decentralized grants in the ongoing security audit process so that risks are constantly detected and prevented. Also, DAOs do not use centralized methods of governing and updating; instead, they put into practice methodologies that will help in the timely provision of security patches on the protocols, eradicating the chances of the protocols being controlled by single entities. Another feature is the bounty programs when ethical hackers are paid for the detection of the sixty, which are further used for protection against the hackers.

The decentralized governance of DAOs also assists in decentralizing security determination to avoid being left behind by rapid technological developments. This approach strengthens DeFi projects and increases trust due to a more stable flow. Thanks to such a participatory approach, projects improve consistently. DAOs will become a key component in the overall structure of DeFi and in establishing proper security measures to safeguard new financial structures in the future.

CONCLUSIONS

Decentralization Finance (DeFi) is a relatively young phenomenon in the contemporary world and has sparked a new revolution of financial products cutting across all traditional intermediaries. However, like any other phenomenon, it has also brought a lot of risks and some regulatory concerns with the inception of decentralized finance or DeFi. Recent developments have seen numerous smart contracts exploits, cross-chain exploits, and governance attacks, and there are no set standard protection measures that have made it clear that a delicate balance must be struck to encourage innovation and protect against any risks at the same time.

Building a stronger and more secure DeFi system is an ongoing process that calls for eliminating various protocol, application, and user risks. Security in smart contracts also needs to advance by formally proving correctness, AI-auditing, and detection at runtime to prevent incidents from occurring. Also, cross-chain bridges, which attackers frequently target, require well-designed security solutions, such as trustless designs and MPC-based strategies. These will create a solid foundation for the growing multi-chain DeFi ecosystem.

Besides technical security, the regulatory facet is another significant concern that needs to be addressed for the healthy development of DeFi. The decentralized nature of DeFi and the current approaches to regulation puts these platforms in legal limbo regarding the regulation of consumer protection, AML, and fraud. Responding to security risks and permitting innovation is possible by leveraging Self-regulatory organizations (SROs), DeFi compliance sandboxes, and DeFi identity services. With the help of ZKPs, SSI, and DID solutions, compliance is possible without the infringement on individual privacy that has characterized previous attempts at identifying people as potential threats.

AI and prediction analytics now play a crucial role in preventing and minimizing threats in the decentralized finance industry as they help platforms quickly identify threats and malicious attacks. The applications of AI support credit risk decision-making and improve reporting on risky cases of fraud and related misconduct, including money laundering and manipulations in stock markets. Machine learning algorithms can learn about the weaknesses of both on-chain and off-chain data before it is attacked. Additionally, due to the development tendency in quantum computing, quantum protecting necessary DeFi protocols will be needed in the future to prevent cyber threats.

Deploying post-quantum technologies will help keep DeFi safe from any future attacks. With the development of AI-based automatic auditors and monitoring tools, DeFi's defenses against hacking attacks will be enhanced through proactive rather than reactive prevention measures. DeFi services are decentralized by nature, so the problem can be solved by using AI and cryptographic initiatives to simultaneously preserve decentralization and the absence of a central authority to influence the system.

As DeFi progresses, Decentralized Autonomous Organizations (DAOs) will be responsible for constantly enhancing security in a community-driven manner. DAOs can use a part of the collected funds to conduct security audits, integrate on-chain voting to make decisions regarding security, and even launch programs that pay for vulnerabilities discovered in the system. Similarly, some decentralized insurance platforms, including Nexus Mutual and InsurAce, are beginning to show themselves as helpful when managing on-chain risks, including vulnerabilities.

However, there are a lot of opportunities that make for the promising future of DeFi. Its long-term success will depend on achieving decentralization without lacking security, privacy without breaching the law, and innovation without compromising responsibility. For future advancement, the cooperation of developers, regulators, security experts, and users will assist in creating a stable, secure, and inclusionary DeFi space. With the regulation approach to security, proper handling of the regulation challenges, and the community-centric approach to development, DeFi has an excellent opportunity to become the basis for a new, more open, and inclusive financial system.

REFERENCES

Aaron, W. C., Irekponor, O., Aleke, N. T., Yeboah, L., & Joseph, J. E. (2024). Ma-chine learning techniques for enhancing security in financial technology systems. https://www.researchgate.net/profile/Ngozi-Aleke-2/publication/385275742_Machine_learning_techniques_for_enhancing_security_in_financial_technology_systems/links/671d31bdedbc012ea14103ca/Machine-learning-techniques-for-enhancing-security-in-financial-technology-systems.pdf

Abdulhakeem, S. A., & Hu, Q. (2021). Powered by Blockchain technology, DeFi (Decentralized Finance) strives to increase financial inclusion of the unbanked by reshaping the world financial system. *Modern Economy*, 1. https://www.scirp.org/journal/Paperabs.aspx?PaperID=106546

Abubakar-Sadiq, M. S. (2023). *Establishing secure and privacy preserving digital identity with self-sovereign identity.* (Doctoral dissertation, Universidade do Porto (Portugal)). https://repositorio-aberto.up.pt/bitstream/10216/156847/2/657403.pdf

Adisa, O., Ilugbusi, B. S., Obi, O. C., Awonuga, K. F., Adelekan, O. A., Asuzu, O. F., & Ndubuisi, N. L. (2024). Decentralized Finance (DEFI) in the US economy: A review: Assessing the rise, challenges, and implications of blockchain-driven financial systems. *World Journal of Advanced Research and Reviews, 21(1)*, 2313-2328. https://pdfs.semanticscholar.org/7a26/a74b2b8518f80bb9f253942de1955a14b552.pdf

Ajayi, A. A., Igba, E., Soyele, A. D., & Enyejo, J. O. (2024). Enhancing Digital Identity and Financial Security in Decentralized Finance (Defi) through Zero-Knowledge Proofs (ZKPs) and Blockchain Solutions for Regulatory Compliance and Privacy. https://www.researchgate.net/profile/Onma-Enyejo/publication/385686688_Enhancing_Digital_Identity_and_Financial_Security_in_Decentralized_Finance_Defi_through_Zero-Knowledge_Proofs_ZKPs_and_Blockchain_Solutions_for_Regulatory_Compliance_and_Privacy/links/672fccdcecbbde716b64352e/Enhancing-Digital-Identity-and-Financial-Security-in-Decentralized-Finance-Defi-through-Zero-Knowledge-Proofs-ZKPs-and-Blockchain-Solutions-for-Regulatory-Compliance-and-Privacy.pdf

Akartuna, A. (2022, December 10). *Mango Market exploit: DeFi loses nearly $900 million to hackers in costliest 30 days on record.* Retrieved from ELLIPTIC: https://www.elliptic.co/blog/analysis/mango-market-exploit-defi-loses-nearly-900-million-to-hackers-in-costliest-30-days-on-record

Allen, H. J. (2022). DeFi: Shadow Banking 2.0? *Wm. & Mary L. Rev., 64*, 919. https://papers.ssrn.com/sol3/Delivery.cfm?abstractid=4038788

AON. (2023, October 13). *Flash Loan Attacks: A Case Study.* Retrieved from AON: https://www.aon.com/en/insights/cyber-labs/flash-loan-attacks-a-case-study

Aspembitova, A. T., & Bentley, M. A. (2022). Oracles in decentralized finance: Attack costs, profits and mitigation measures. *Entropy (Basel, Switzerland)*, *60*(1), 60. Advance online publication. DOI: 10.3390/e25010060 PMID: 36673200

Babu, R. (2024). ADVANCEMENTS IN DECENTRALIZED IDENTITY SOLUTIONS: EMPOWERING USERS THROUGH SELF-SOVEREIGN IDENTITY. *INTERNATIONAL JOURNAL OF COMPUTER ENGINEERING AND TECHNOLOGY (IJCET)*, 721-733. https://lib-index.com/index.php/IJCET/article/view/IJCET_15_04_063/487

Baseri, Y., Chouhan, V., & Ghorbani, A. (2024). Cybersecurity in the quantum era: Assessing the impact of quantum computing on infrastructure. *arXiv preprint arXiv:2404.10659*, 76. https://doi.org//arXiv.2404.10659DOI: 10.48550

BBC. (2021, November 02). *Squid Game crypto token collapses in apparent scam.* Retrieved from BBC: https://www.bbc.com/news/business-59129466

Bondarenko, N., & Soponar, P. (2024). Empowering the Underbanked: A Comparative Analysis of Decentralized Finance (DeFi) Solutions for Financial Inclusion. https://www.theconnecter.io/pdf/2024-01-24-_YNBC%20and%20The%20Connecter%20R_D_%20Comparative%20Analysis%20of%20DeFi%20Solutions.pdf

Bonnet, S., & Teuteberg, F. (2024). Decentralized autonomous organizations: A systematic literature review and research agenda. *International Journal on Management of Innovation & Technology*, *2450026*(4), 2450026. Advance online publication. DOI: 10.1142/S0219877024500263

Bui, V. C., Wen, S., Yu, J., Xia, X., Haghighi, M. S., & Xiang, Y. (2021). Evaluating upgradable smart contract. *2021 IEEE international conference on blockchain (Blockchain)*, 252-256. https://ieeexplore.ieee.org/abstract/document/9680538/

Carapella, F., & Swem, N. (2022). Decentralized finance (defi): Transformative potential & associated risks. https://dx.doi.org/DOI: 10.17016/feds.2022.057

Cedra, A. (2024). Mitigating risks in decentralized finance: A Systematic review of challenges and solutions. *International journal of economic perspectives*, 104-125. https://ijeponline.lingcure.org/index.php/journal/article/download/549/507

ChainAnalysis. (2023, March 2023). *$197 Million Stolen: Euler Finance Flash Loan Attack Explained [UPDATED 4/6/23].* Retrieved from Chainanalysis: https://www.chainalysis.com/blog/euler-finance-flash-loan-attack/

Doerr, J. F., Kosse, A., Khan, A., Lewrick, U., Mojon, B., Nolens, B., & Rice, T. (2021). DeFi risks and the decentralisation illusion. *BIS Quarterly Review, 21*, 22. https://www.bis.org/publ/qtrpdf/r_qt2112b.pdf

Erinle, Y., Feng, Y., Xu, J., Vadgama, N., & Tasca, P. (2024). Shared-Custodial Wallet for Multi-Party Crypto-Asset Management. *Future Internet*, *7*(1), 7. Advance online publication. DOI: 10.3390/fi17010007

Ezzat, S. K., Saleh, Y. N., & Abdel-Hamid, A. A. (2022). Blockchain oracles: State-of-the-art and research directions. *IEEE Access : Practical Innovations, Open Solutions*, *10*, 67551–67572. DOI: 10.1109/ACCESS.2022.3184726

Feichtinger, R., Fritsch, R., Heimbach, L., Vonlanthen, Y., & Wattenhofer, R. (2024). Sok: Attacks on daos. *arXiv preprint arXiv:2406.15071*. https://doi.org//arXiv.2406.15071DOI: 10.48550

Finance, B. (2021, November 21). *DeFi Security Lecture 2 — Flash Loan Attacks.* Retrieved from Medium: https://medium.com/beaver-smartcontract-security/defi-security-lecture-2-flash-loan-attacks-4aee2d3f07ca

Fomintsov Trukhaev, V. (2024). Theory and practice of decentralized blockchain oracles. *Master's thesis*. https://upcommons.upc.edu/bitstream/handle/2117/423352/TPDBO_FTVladimir.pdf?sequence=4

Gogol, K., Killer, C., Schlosser, M., Bocek, T., Stiller, B., & Tessone, C. (2024). SoK: Decentralized Finance (DeFi)—Fundamentals, Taxonomy and Risks. *arXiv preprint arXiv:2404.11281*. https://doi.org//arXiv.2404.11281DOI: 10.48550

Gogol, K., Kraner, B., Schlosser, M., Yan, T., Tessone, C., & Stiller, B. (2024). Empirical and theoretical analysis of liquid staking protocols. *arXiv preprint arXiv:2401.16353*. https://doi.org//arXiv.2401.16353DOI: 10.48550

Gross, L. (2024). *Improving Trustworthiness in DeFi: Anomaly Detection for Blockchain Oracle Price Feed Data*. Universidade NOVA de Lisboa., https://run.unl.pt/bitstream/10362/174978/1/TCDMAA3359.pdf

Guseva, Y. (2024). Decentralized markets and self-regulation. *Geo. Wash. L. Rev.*, *92*, 1281. https://papers.ssrn.com/sol3/Delivery.cfm?abstractid=4677538

Hägele, S. (2024). Centralized exchanges vs. decentralized exchanges in cryptocurrency markets: A systematic literature review. *Electronic Markets*, *33*(1), 33. Advance online publication. DOI: 10.1007/s12525-024-00714-2

Hern, A. (2022, April 18). *Beanstalk cryptocurrency loses $182m of reserves in flash 'attack'.* Retrieved from The Guardian: https://www.theguardian.com/technology/2022/apr/18/beanstalk-cryptocurrency-loses-182m-of-reserves-in-flash-attack

immunebytes. (2020, October 28). *Harvest Finance Fund Theft Incident – Oct 26, 2020 – Detailed Analysis.* Retrieved from immunebytes: https://immunebytes.com/blog/harvest-finance-fund-theft-incident-oct-26-2020-detailed-analysis/

Kolakowski, M. (2022, February 3). *Crypto Worth Over $320 Million Taken in Wormhole Hack.* Retrieved from investopedia: https://www.investopedia.com/crypto-theft-of-usd320-million-wormhole-hack-5218062

Liu, Y., He, J., Li, X., Chen, J., Liu, X., Peng, S., & Wang, Y. (2024). An overview of blockchain smart contract execution mechanism. *Journal of Industrial Information Integration, 100674*, 100674. Advance online publication. DOI: 10.1016/j.jii.2024.100674

Lorenz, G. (2024). Regulating decentralized financial technology: A qualitative study on the challenges of regulating DeFi with a focus on embedded supervision. *Stan. J. Blockchain L. & Pol'y, 7*, 136. https://assets.pubpub.org/bavvr3fw/Lorenz_Regulating%20Decentralized%20Financial%20Technology-01719848112806.pdf

Luo, B., Zhang, Z., Wang, Q., Ke, A., Lu, S., & He, B. (2024). Ai-powered fraud detection in decentralized finance: A project life cycle perspective. *ACM Computing Surveys, 57*(4), 1–38. DOI: 10.1145/3705296

Mackinga, T., Nadahalli, T., & Wattenhofer, R. (2022). Twap oracle attacks: Easier done than said? *2022 IEEE International Conference on Blockchain and Cryptocurrency (ICBC)*, 1-8. https://doi.org/DOI: 10.1109/ICBC54727.2022.9805499

Makarov, I., & Schoar, A. (2022). Cryptocurrencies and decentralized finance (DeFi). *Brookings Papers on Economic Activity, 2022*(1), 141–215. DOI: 10.1353/eca.2022.0014

Oosthoek, K. (2021). Flash crash for cash: Cyber threats in decentralized finance. *arXiv preprint arXiv:2106.10740*, 22. https://doi.org//arXiv.2106.10740DOI: 10.48550

Ozcan, R. (2021). Decentralized finance. *Financial ecosystem and strategy in the digital era: Global approaches and new opportunities*, 57-75. https://www.researchgate.net/profile/Uemit-Ilhan/publication/352390462_Business_Strategy_for_Sustainable_Development_in_the_Digital_Era_Green_Management/links/60c9f539a6fdcc01d476cafa/Business-Strategy-for-Sustainable-Development-in-the-Digital-Era-Green-Management.pdf

Parisi, C., & Budorin, D. (2023). Smart Contract Security. *A Comprehensive Guide for Web3 Security: From Technology, Economic and Legal Aspects*, 81-102. https://doi.org/DOI: 10.1007/978-3-031-39288-7_4

Santana, C., & Albareda, L. (2022). Blockchain and the emergence of Decentralized Autonomous Organizations (DAOs): An integrative model and research agenda. *Technological Forecasting and Social Change*, *182*, 121806. DOI: 10.1016/j.techfore.2022.121806

Schär, F. (2021). Decentralized finance: On blockchain and smart contract-based financial markets. *Review - Federal Reserve Bank of St. Louis*, *103*(2), 153–174. DOI: 10.5451/unibas-ep86500

Schär, F., & Gronde, F. (2021). Flash Loans and Decentralized Lending Protocols: An In-Depth Analysis. https://wwz.unibas.ch/fileadmin/user_upload/wwz/00_Professuren/Schaer_DLTFintech/Lehre/MA_Florian_Gronde_Flashloans-ohne_Appendix.pdf

Schueffel, P. (2021). Defi: Decentralized finance-an introduction and overview. *Journal of Innovation Management*, *9*(3), I–XI. DOI: 10.24840/2183-0606_009.003_0001

Sinclair, S., & Peterson, M. (2022, October 12). *Mango Markets Mangled by Oracle Manipulation for $112M*. Retrieved from blockworks: https://blockworks.co/news/mango-markets-mangled-by-oracle-manipulation-for-112m

Tidy, J. (2022, March 30). *Ronin Network: What a $600m hack says about the state of crypto*. Retrieved from bbc: https://www.bbc.com/news/technology-60933174

TRM. (2025, January 09). *Squid Game Season 2: A Window Into Popular Culture and Crypto Scams*. Retrieved from TRM: https://www.trmlabs.com/post/squid-game-season-2-a-window-into-popular-culture-and-crypto-scams#:~:text=The%202021%20SQUID%20token%20scam,course%20of%20a%20few%20weeks

Westerkamp, M. (2023). *Cross-blockchain smart contract interoperability*. Germany: Technische Universitaet Berlin. https://depositonce.tu-berlin.de/bitstreams/a0e4f4dc-abce-4c9a-938e-d37951dd1575/download

WIRED. (2021, November 02). *How a Squid Game Crypto Scam Got Away With Millions*. Retrieved from WIRED: https://www.wired.com/story/squid-game-coin-crypto-scam/

Wronka, C. (2023). Financial crime in the decentralized finance ecosystem: New challenges for compliance. *Journal of Financial Crime*, *30*(1), 97–113. DOI: 10.1108/JFC-09-2021-0218

Wu, J., Liu, J., Chen, W., Huang, H., Zheng, Z., & Zhang, Y. (2021). Detecting mixing services via mining bitcoin transaction network with hybrid motifs. *IEEE Transactions on Systems, Man, and Cybernetics. Systems*, *52*(4), 2237–2249. DOI: 10.1109/TSMC.2021.3049278

Xu, J., & Feng, Y. (2022). Reap the harvest on blockchain: A survey of yield farming protocols. *IEEE Transactions on Network and Service Management*, *20*(1), 858–869. DOI: 10.1109/TNSM.2022.3222815

Zetzsche, D. A., Arner, D. W., & Buckley, R. P. (2020). Decentralized finance. *Journal of Financial Regulation*, *6*(2), 172–203. https://academic.oup.com/jfr/advance-article-pdf/doi/10.1093/jfr/fjaa010/37064506/fjaa010.pdf. DOI: 10.1093/jfr/fjaa010

Zhao, Q., Wang, Y., Yang, B., Shang, K., Sun, M., Wang, H., & Xin, H. (2023). A comprehensive overview of security vulnerability penetration methods in blockchain cross-chain bridges. *Authorea Preprints*, 76. https://doi.org/DOI: 10.22541/au.169760541.13864334/v1

Zhao, Y., Kang, X., Li, T., Chu, C. K., & Wang, H. (2022). Toward trustworthy defi oracles: Past, present, and future. *IEEE Access : Practical Innovations, Open Solutions*, *10*, 60914–60928. DOI: 10.1109/ACCESS.2022.3179374

Zheng, J., Lee, D. K., & Qian, D. (2023). An in-depth guide to cross-chain protocols under a multi-chain world. *World Scientific Annual Review of Fintech*, *1*, 2350003. DOI: 10.1142/S2811004823500033

Zhou, L., Diro, A., Saini, A., Kaisar, S., & Hiep, P. C. (2024). Leveraging zero knowledge proofs for blockchain-based identity sharing: A survey of advancements, challenges and opportunities. *Journal of Information Security and Applications*, *103678*, 103678. Advance online publication. DOI: 10.1016/j.jisa.2023.103678

KEY TERMS AND DEFINITIONS

Artificial Intelligence (AI) and Machine Learning (ML): Technologies increasingly used in DeFi to analyze large volumes of blockchain data for anomaly detection, exploit prediction, and enhanced risk management.

Blockchain Technology: A foundational technology upon which Decentralized Finance (DeFi) is built, replacing trust in centralized institutions with decentralized security.

Cross-Chain Bridges: Solutions that enable asset transfers between different blockchains, but which can also introduce security flaws and become targets for hackers.

Decentralized Autonomous Organizations (DAOs): Organizations that govern DeFi protocols, payroll upgrades, fee structures, and development proposals, envisioned as decentralized and community-driven.

Decentralized Exchanges (DEXs): Platforms that allow users to trade cryptocurrencies directly via smart contracts without intermediaries, offering greater privacy and control over assets.

Decentralized Finance (DeFi): A movement that aims to democratize financial services by disrupting traditional intermediary banking and financial institutions through smart contracts and other protocols that automate transactions on a blockchain network. It bypasses conventional financial intermediaries to execute lending, trading, and other economic activities.

Financial Inclusion: The aspect of DeFi that increases access to financial services worldwide, particularly for the unbanked and underbanked, by removing barriers to entry such as geographic location, lack of banking history, or creditworthiness.

Flash Loan Attacks: Malicious acts in which industry actors borrow large sums of capital without collateral and manipulate asset prices within the same transaction to exploit price oracles and drain liquidity pools.

Governance Attacks: Attacks where malicious actors accumulate significant voting power (often through large token holdings) in Decentralized Autonomous Organizations (DAOs) to propose and approve harmful changes, potentially siphoning funds from the protocol.

Liquidity Pools: Smart contract-based reserves of cryptocurrency assets used for trading, lending, and yield farming in DeFi ecosystems, where users deposit funds and receive rewards.

Oracle Manipulation: An attack vector where attackers exploit vulnerabilities in price feeds, artificially inflating or deflating asset prices through methods like flash loan attacks or low-liquidity trading pairs to run profitable arbitrage trades or cause mass liquidations on lending platforms.

Rug Pulls: Fraudulent schemes where project developers generate hype around a new project, attract investors' money, and then abandon the project, departing with the funds.

Smart Contracts: Self-executing agreements with set rules that operate autonomously on a blockchain without the need for intermediaries. They automate complex financial transactions and are central to DeFi operations.

Yield Farming: A method in DeFi where users provide liquidity to a DeFi platform in exchange for earning rewards as additional tokens.

Zero-Knowledge Proofs (ZKPs): Cryptographic techniques that allow one party to prove knowledge of a particular fact to another without revealing the actual information, used to enhance privacy and security in DeFi.

Chapter 7
Artificial Intelligence in the Cryptocurrency Ecosystem:
Crime Mechanisms, Detection Strategies, and Legal Perspectives

Monika Kumari
Poornima University, Jaipur, India

Nikhil Kumar Goyal
https://orcid.org/0009-0007-4532-8033
Poornima University, Jaipur, India

ABSTRACT

This chapter explores the intersection of cryptocurrency crime and artificial intelligence (AI), highlighting both the threats posed by AI-driven cybercriminal activities and the potential of AI-based countermeasures. Cybercriminals increasingly leverage AI for money laundering, fraud, market manipulation, ransomware attacks, and identity theft, exploiting vulnerabilities in smart contracts and decentralized finance (DeFi) platforms. Conversely, AI is a powerful tool for combating these threats, aiding in blockchain analysis, anomaly detection, and Anti-Money Laundering (AML) enforcement. Advanced machine learning models enhance Know Your Customer (KYC) protocols and enable predictive crime prevention by analyzing transactional patterns. Additionally, this chapter examines challenges such as regulatory loopholes, adversarial AI, and jurisdictional complexities. The future implications of AI in financial crime prevention, including the role of quantum computing and emerging financial technologies, are also discussed.

DOI: 10.4018/979-8-3373-0675-9.ch007

1. INTRODUCTION

Blockchain technology together with artificial intelligence (AI) emerged rapidly to change the financial industry to a great extent. All financial industries that include banking and investment and risk management widely utilize AI because the technology enables analysis of vast data along with pattern detection and predictive capabilities. The introduction of digital currencies functions as an innovative financial system which enables users to make payments without borders through an equally distributed platform. The merging of these advantageous technologies has produced new financial risk factors most notably centered around financial criminal activities. AI tools provided criminals with automatic capabilities to participate in cryptocurrency sector violations such as market manipulation alongside fraud and money laundering activities. The authorities together with law enforcement agencies use artificial intelligence for identifying tracking and stopping these criminal activities. The chapter analyzes the relationships between AI, finance systems and cryptocurrencies together with their legal and illicit operational connections.

1.1 Overview of AI and Its Applications in Finance

AI is also used by financial institutions to identify fraudulent behavior by monitoring transaction patterns and noting anomalies. Machine learning algorithms in AI-powered fraud detection systems identify variances from normal user behavior and alert for suspect transactions in real time (Sgantzos & Grigg, 2019). The ability has tremendously improved security in digital asset exchanges, payment systems, and online banking by preventing cybercrimes like identity theft and financial fraud. Moreover, artificial intelligence-based risk assessment software assesses creditworthiness based on the analysis of large datasets, such as transactional history, spending habits, and behavioral insights. These models allow lending decisions to be data-driven, eliminating human bias and enhancing efficiency. Nevertheless, there are ethical issues surrounding AI decision-making transparency and biases in financial inclusion.

Figure 1. Crypto currencies ecosystem

This diagram presents the core components of the cryptocurrency ecosystem—including exchanges, wallets, miners, mixers, decentralized apps (dApps), and regulatory bodies. It visually highlights the entry and exit points for both legitimate and illicit financial flows. AI plays a role in fraud detection at exchange level, while also being exploited by attackers for automation, spoofing, and laundering within the same ecosystem.

Apart from such applications, AI has also enhanced customer service within the financial services sector. Chatbots powered by AI, for example, are now an intrinsic part of serving customer queries, giving financial guidance, and effecting transactions. JPMorgan Chase and Bank of America use AI-based chatbots to facilitate customers' engagement and lower operation costs. The virtual assistants facilitate customer experience and increase efficiency for the providers of financial services.

With the current simultaneous development of artificial intelligence and blockchain, high-tech integration has not only brought about unmatched innovations in the sphere of finances but also increased hazards. This convergence, which makes efficiency, decentralization possible, also breeds vulnerability that is tapped by the threat actors. Whether it be automated laundering or AI generated lines of artificial identity, such a combination requires technical awareness at a level, as well as regulation planning.

1.2 Rise of Cryptocurrencies and Their Role in Digital Finance

The creation of cryptocurrencies has disrupted the conventional financial systems by providing a transparent and decentralized method for transactions (Lopes & Alexandre, 2019). Cryptocurrencies are based on blockchain technology, a network of computers that uses a distributed ledger system to record transactions across the network of computers. Unlike conventional banking systems that use central agencies to process and authenticate transactions, cryptocurrencies reduce intermediaries by directly allowing peer-to-peer transactions. This decentralization increases security, lowers transaction costs, and gives financial access to people in areas with poor banking infrastructure. But it also introduces new challenges, especially regulation and money laundering.

The market for digital currency has grown beyond the first and best-known digital currency, Bitcoin. Though Bitcoin is nicknamed "digital gold" because of its limited supply and store-of-value characteristics, Ethereum created the idea of smart contracts, allowing programmable and self-executing contracts. Cryptocurrencies like Monero and Zcash have greater privacy features, and are appealing not only to legitimate users, but also to illicit ones. All the cryptocurrencies have varied purposes, ranging from making digital payments to powering decentralized applications (dApps) and non-fungible tokens (NFTs), which have further transformed digital finance (Klein et al., 2018).

Though they have their advantages, cryptocurrencies also have several disadvantages. Significant because prices can vary dramatically depending on sentiment and other outside factors include political decisions. Orgulses in the case of volatility is a serious problem. The absence of regulatory certainty only adds to the difficulties in adopting them since governments across the globe are not able to design common regulations to weigh innovation against financial security. Also, the anonymous nature of cryptocurrency transactions has made them appealing for criminal activities such money laundering, ransom payments, and illicit transactions on the dark web. Additionally drawing more concern about their use in financial crimes is their ability to transfer large sums of cash without delay and anonymously.

Although cryptocurrencies have offered many benefits to the financial sector, their incorporation into mainstream finance is required along with their potential use challenges resolved. To ensure that cryptocurrencies can be safely introduced to worldwide financial systems and not enable any criminal behavior, one must establish more strict rules and surveillance mechanisms based on artificial intelligence.

1.3 The Convergence of AI and Cryptocurrency-Related Crime

Criminals are also using artificial intelligence to help money laundering operations be more efficient. Dividing the transaction into small sums and distributing them through several accounts using AI-based "mixers" or "tumblers" helps to hide the source of illegal funds. Additionally used to carry out automated market manipulation operations is AI-based trading bots, which create a false upward or downward price motion of cryptocurrencies in an effort to dupe customers. Such actions make it difficult for law enforcement officers and regulators to track and stop financial crime using cryptocurrencies.

Although these dangers are present, artificial intelligence is also a major tool against cryptocurrency proliferation. To monitor dubious behavior, map out criminal networks, and prevent fraud, law enforcement agencies and regulatory bodies use artificial intelligence-based blockchain analytics. Machine learning techniques analyze patterns of transactions to identify exceptions and promptly raise flags on possible illegal behavior in real life. The difficulty with criminals is, they also use adversarial AI techniques to avoid detection systems, therefore maintaining what seems an ongoing cat-and-mouse game between cybercrooks and security experts.

Figure 2. Challenges with crypto currency

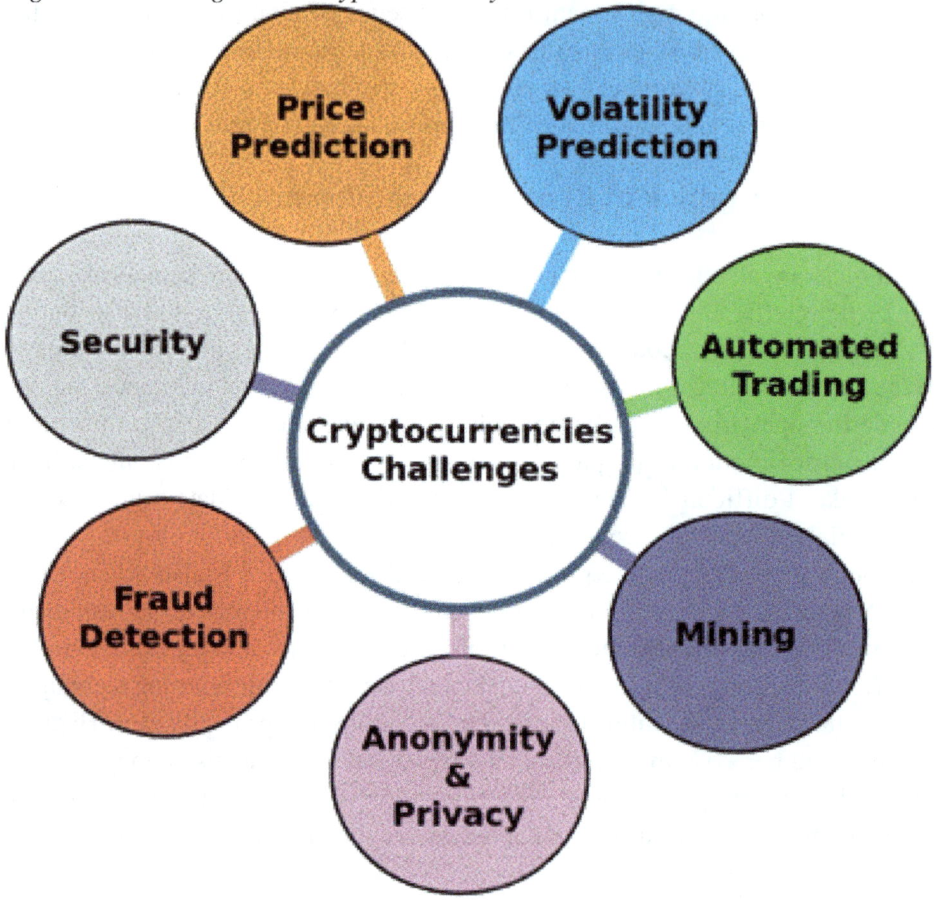

This figure outlines the primary technical and regulatory challenges associated with cryptocurrency crime, such as anonymization via mixers, deepfake-based identity fraud, regulatory arbitrage across jurisdictions, and AI-based evasion. It also shows the cat-and-mouse dynamic between adversarial AI used by criminals and AI-based detection systems deployed by law enforcement.

One of the most alarming developments in AI-enabled cybercrime is the creation of fraudulent accounts using synthetic identities generated by artificial intelligence. These identities often combine legitimate and fabricated personal data, enabling bad actors to bypass identity verification systems on cryptocurrency exchanges. The accounts are then used to move large sums of cash without detection, so hampering government efforts to track down illegal behavior. Increasing complexity of deepfake technology seriously threatens security systems such as biometric authentication and identity verification.

Their crossroad presents possibilities as well as dangers as artificial intelligence and cryptocurrencies evolve. Though artificial intelligence can be used to improve security, increase fraud detection, and streamline financial operations, it also opens up fresh ways for cybercriminals to target the cryptocurrency environment. Effective security solutions and regulatory structures arise from joint efforts of technology developers, financial institutions, legislators, and law enforcement agencies tackling these problems (Xie et al., 2019). The following sections of this chapter will go more in depth on how artificial intelligence is used for stopping as much as for aiding cryptocurrency crimes, the legal issues at stake, and the future developments that could be seen in this ever-evolving industry.

1.4 Conceptual Framework: The AI–Crypto Crime Nexus

This study adopts the **Routine Activity Theory** (RAT) from criminology to frame how AI enables cryptocurrency-related crimes. In this context:

- **Motivated offenders** = Cybercriminals leveraging AI
- **Suitable targets** = Cryptocurrency platforms, DeFi protocols
- **Lack of capable guardianship** = Inadequate or lagging regulation and monitoring systems

The interaction among these elements, as enhanced by AI, creates a fertile environment for financial crime.

2. AI-POWERED MONEY LAUNDERING AND MARKET MANIPULATION IN CRYPTOCURRENCY ECOSYSTEMS

The intersection of artificial intelligence (AI) and cryptocurrencies has brought incredible financial security challenges, especially money laundering and market manipulation. AI tools have enabled cybercriminals with powerful methods to remain undetected, take advantage of loopholes in regulations, and manipulate digital asset markets. The more complex and sophisticated AI systems are, the greater their effectiveness in illegal activities and the capacity of enforcement agencies to monitor them (Huang et al., 2019). This section discusses the mechanisms through which AI enables criminal financial activities, including automated money laundering and spoofed trading strategies.

2.1 AI-Powered Money Laundering Techniques

Money laundering, that is, disguising the origins of illegally received funds, has become a complex process with AI. AI algorithms are used by criminals to improvise conventional laundry methods, with the result being that illicit funds are harder to track. Decentralized as well as anonymous nature of the blockchain technology heightens the complexity of the situation, making criminals have an apt medium for purifying illegal money. The most useful AI-based money laundering mechanism is cryptocurrency mixing services, which go by the nickname "mixers" or "tumblers." The mixer works by dispersing large transfers into numerous randomized transactions over different wallets, rendering the transaction chain invisible. The efficiency of such mixers has been greatly boosted by AI technology through automated dispersion of transactions and adaptive processing of transactions to deflect blockchain forensic analysis. Services like Tornado Cash, which are based on smart contract mixing, have been extensively used by cybercriminals to wash stolen money, especially from ransomware and darknet markets.

Artificial intelligence has also facilitated criminals to evade Know Your Customer (KYC) and Anti-Money Laundering (AML) procedures by the generation of synthetic identities. Generative adversarial networks (GANs) and deepfake technology can now create extremely realistic facial images, which can be used to open phony accounts in cryptocurrency exchanges (Georgoula et al., 2015). These computer-generated identities enable cybercrooks to open several accounts, usually termed as "money mule" accounts, through which illicit money is routed across geographical borders without anyone noticing. Secondly, AI-facilitated bots mechanize the administration of these accounts, carrying out transactions at best timings to make them even harder to detect. The capacity to create well-crafted digital personas poses an important threat to regulatory oversight, rendering it ever more challenging for financial organizations to distinguish between valid consumers and AI-based deceptions.

Another significant development in AI-driven laundering is structuring transactions. Conventional laundering methods tend to include "smurfing," where large amounts of illegal money are broken down into smaller transactions to evade detection. AI has greatly improved this process by employing machine learning algorithms that examine financial regulations, transaction limits, and past data to identify the best method to structure illegal transactions. AI-based systems are able to measure current blockchain traffic, change the size of transactions in real-time, and send funds across a series of jurisdictions, thereby blending them into regular transactions. Criminals leverage such methods to attack vulnerabilities in global financial laws by capitalizing on uncoordinated AML strategies in various areas (Abraham et al., 2018).

Dark web has also become a marketplace for AI-optimized money laundering services. AI-powered automation is carried out by criminals on darknet markets for laundering-as-a-service (LaaS), wherein the entire process of exchanging illegal cryptocurrency into seemingly legitimate assets is performed. AI-based escrow systems make anonymous transactions possible, and both sellers and buyers are made untraceable. These networks employ AI to confirm payments, transfer funds automatically, and optimize laundering channels, minimizing the role of human intervention. This automation makes it ever more challenging for law enforcement agencies to penetrate and disrupt these operations, as AI keeps changing laundering methods to keep one step ahead of detection.

One especially new kind of AI-powered laundering is based on non-fungible tokens (NFTs). The NFT market has given criminals a new means of washing illegal money by artificially inflating the value of digital assets. Criminals use AI-based automated bidding to carry out "wash trading," a system in which the same digital asset is purchased and sold repeatedly at inflated prices in order to simulate legitimacy. For instance, a cybercriminal can create an NFT, have AI-managed accounts bid on it at higher and higher prices, and then cash out the money, essentially laundering dirty money (Kim et al., 2017). Trading bots powered by AI make this scam more efficient by having multiple wallet addresses, automating transactions, and timing sales strategically to avoid detection. The lack of regulatory oversight in the NFT space has made it an attractive tool for financial criminals seeking to exploit blockchain anonymity.

2.2 Automated Trading Bots and Market Manipulation

Apart from money laundering, AI has been used to artificially influence cryptocurrency markets. Originally meant for honest trading, automatic trading bots have been used for abusive reasons like pump-and-dumping campaigns, spoofing, and insider trading. These dishonest tactics compromise market integrity, cheat consumers, and create great price swings. For market manipulators trying to maximize their illegal profits, AI's capacity to execute trades at lightning speed and analyze huge volumes of data in real-time has made it an extremely useful tool.

Although a well-known market manipulation technique, pump-and-dump schemes have been much improved by artificial intelligence. These activities artificially raise the price of a cryptocurrency trading low by coordinated acquisitions, propagation of hype, followed by dumping, or selling, the properties at high prices before unwitting investors could realize the scam. AI programs that find low-cost assets, mass purchase them automatically, and produce deceptive marketing on social media make this simpler. Using AI-powered bots that search market sentiment, identify trending keywords, and coordinate buy signals among thousands of traders, Telegram and

Discord trading groups have been discovered. The AI-based bots activate big sell-offs once the price has reached a fixed goal, which leads in great losses for late investors.

Spoofing and wash trading, both of which are made possible through AI bots, also contribute to market manipulation. Making a wrong image of demand or supply, spoofing is an unethical method of a dealer placing big buy or sell orders without any real trading intention. Trading bots can withdraw and submit thousands of orders in seconds, tricking other market players into making unwise financial choices. Wash trading is the process of having fake transactions between controlled accounts to give an artificial impression of greater market activity; in a similar way. Using AI bots to artificially increase their reported trading volumes, fake cryptocurrency exchanges have been discovered, misleading users into assuming their websites are reliable and liquid.

Apart from sentiment analysis powered by artificial intelligence, insider trading has also been done with this technique. AI programs can predict market motion ahead of the general public knowing it by scraping news stories, financial statements, and social media discussions. Malefactors use this technology to profit from retail investors by way of speculating on inside information. A machine learning model taught to identify regulatory news patterns might, for example, note subtle linguistic characteristics that point a policy change is coming. Acting on transactions before the official announcement, crooks can capitalize on price swings before ordinary investors can catch up.

Common financial markets abound, high-frequency trading (HFT) has been very often used in cryptocurrency trading, often in a manner that capitalizes on market inefficiencies. Thousands of trades are made in microseconds by AI-driven HFT bots, earning revenue from minute price disparities among exchanges. Although not illegal in and of itself, HFT raises issues of fairness and possible price manipulation by way of utilization in uninvested crypto markets. For instance, artificial intelligence arbitrage robots spot price gaps across several trading platforms and execute rapid transactions before people can react. This gives AI-based traders a distinct advantage, creating an uneven match to the disadvantage of retail consumers.

The integration of artificial intelligence into cryptocurrency circles has created both challenges as well as chances. AI tools increase criminals' ability to have sophisticated money laundering and market manipulation schemes even as they fortify security, speed automated trading, and improve financial inclusion. The advancement in the strategies used by unauthorized individuals to capitalize on digital financial systems correspond to the rise of artificial intelligence. Combating of these risks depends on regulatory oversight, AI-assisted forensic solutions, and cross-border collaboration as thoughnets. Preventing financial crimes in the constantly evolving digital world will depend on improving AML policies, increasing blockchain analytics, and strict enforcement of compliance rules. The battle against AI-backed cryptocurrency offenses is an ongoing competition between technical advances and law enforcement response ability, therefore pro-active regulatory approaches and worldwide cooperation are more needed than ever.

3. DEEPFAKE TECHNOLOGY AND IDENTITY FRAUD IN CRYPTO TRANSACTIONS

Artificial intelligence (AI)'s quick development has enabled the invention of deepfake technology, which has permitted the production of extremely realistic artificial media comprising features, films, and voice recordings. Although deepfake technology has legitimate applications in entertainment and content creation, it can also be a strong tool in the hands of cybercriminals, particularly in the case of cryptocurrency fraud. Criminals can circumvent security measures, defraudd investors, and very easily carry out bogus transactions utilizing deepfake-created identities, bogus verification documents, and AI-powered impersonation scams. This section covers the use of deepfake technology in financial crimes and cryptocurrency identity theft. Producing AI-created identities for phony account registration is among the most obvious applications of deepfake technology in cryptocurrency fraud. To verify user identities and prevent illicit financial activities, most cryptocurrency exchanges have Know Your Customer (KYC) policies. AI-powered deepfake technology, nevertheless, can generate highly convincing synthetic pictures of nonexistent people that criminals use to create bogus accounts on well-known exchanges such as Binance, Coinbase, or Kraken. These AI-generated faces have unique features not detected by standard reverse image searches, therefore hard-to-detect attributes produced by generative adversarial networks (GANs). Significantly complicating law enforcement's efforts to monitor illegal funds, these counterfeit accounts provide channels for money laundering, illicit trading, and other financial crimes.

Beyond static images, deepfake technology is increasingly being used for social engineering attacks through AI-generated videos and voice cloning. Fraudsters can manipulate video footage to create highly realistic impersonations of executives, financial analysts, or cryptocurrency influencers, exploiting the trust of investors and exchange employees. In one chilling instance, a deepfake video of a prominent CEO was employed to trick an employee into approving a large-value cryptocurrency transaction. In another way, voice cloning based on AI has allowed criminals to mimic people when making calls or participating in video conferencing, thereby allowing them to control financial choices in real-time (Kjærland et al., 2018). As deepfake video and audio become increasingly advanced, it becomes increasingly hard to tell real interactions from fake ones, and this poses serious threats to digital financial security. Besides impersonating people in real-time, deepfake technology is also being employed to produce fake identity verification documents, further compromising KYC and Anti-Money Laundering (AML) controls. AI-based image-editing software can alter government-issued identification, including passports, driver's licenses, and utility bills, to conform to deepfake-created profiles (Valencia et al., 2019). The criminals provide these forged documents to cryptocurrency platforms and financial institutions in order to access trading platforms and transfer illicit money without detection. This forgery of proof-of-identity systems is a major challenge for regulatory agencies since current authentication methods are unable to distinguish between authentic and AI-generated credentials.

In cryptocurrency scams, deepfake technology also presents a new menace in the usage of AI-produced voices for SIM swap attacks. Using SIM swapping, hackers deceive telecom companies into moving a phone number of a victim to a new SIM card controlled by the attackers, hence circumventing two-factor authentication (2FA) security measures usually used in cryptocurrency exchange wallets and accounts (Liew et al., 2019). By means of deepfake-assisted voice cloning, perpetrators may exactly imitate the voice of a target and deceive customer service representatives into approving the SIM transfer. Once the attacker has control of the victim's phone number, they can undetectably take funds by changing passwords and opening cryptocurrency wallets. More and more, this technique has been used hence calls for an authentication system stronger than SMS 2FA. Deepfake technology has also caused social media scams to grow in part since attackers employ material produced by artificial intelligence to appear to be well-known figures within the cryptocurrency field. Fakes of well-known people, including Elon Musk or Vitalik Buterin, have also been widely used to promote fraudulent investment projects in deepfake videos. In these bogus investment plans or exclusive crypto airdrops or investment opportunities with the intent to defraud innocent users into sending money to scam accounts, Deepfakes are announced. Retail consumers becoming victims of these sophisticated impersonations have suffered great financial losses when combined with the viral sharing of such scams and the influence of AI-powered social media bots.

Besides monetary fraud, deepfake technology is increasingly used for kidnapping and blackmail committed digitally. Ransomware assaults require cryptocurrency payments. Using AI-created embarrassing movies and doctored images, cybercriminals are threatening victims to pay ransom in Bitcoin or other digital currencies. If victims do not comply with the orders of the aggressor, they are warned their personal or professional reputation might be destroyed by the release of tampered material. This form of cyber extortion is particularly evil since once generated, deepfake material is difficult to disprove to a regular observer and victims are more inclined to succumb to menaces out of fear. Furthermore enabling such systems is the anonymity of transactions in cryptocurrency since payments may be carried out without essentially revealing the perpetrator's identity.

Rising progress in deepfake technology poses a major threat to cryptocurrency's security and fraud prevention. As AI-generated media becomes more and more commonly used for identity theft, social engineering, and financial fraud, there is a rising demand for practical detection technologies and legal initiatives. Cryptocurrency exchanges and financial institutions have to introduce more robust verification processes, including biometric authentication, blockchain-based identity solutions, and AI-powered deepfake identification systems, to address these dangers. Furthermore, increased public awareness and knowledge of deepfake-connected fraud can help people to recognize and prevent themselves from falling prey to these schemes. Fighting deepfake-enabled financial crimes ultimately calls for a multi-faceted approach including technical innovation, legal enforcement, and international collaboration to guard the integrity of digital financial systems.

4. AI-ENHANCED RANSOMWARE AND EXTORTION SCHEMES

Ransomware attacks have transformed the field of cybercrime by means of artificial intelligence, generating more sophisticated, specifically tailored, and evasive threats. A sort of malevolent software that encrypts a victim's data and makes payment in the form of cryptocurrency for its decryption, ransomware has seen a huge growth with AI-assisted automation and optimization techniques. With machine learning algorithms, cybercriminals can identify lucrative targets, perfect encryption methods, and start ransomware campaigns mostly without any people. Ryuk and DarkSide, AI-powered ransomware variants, have proved able to scan a network's defenses in real-time before launching attacks thereby maximizing disruption and financial returns for their creators. These advanced ransomware versions can independently change their encryption methods on the weaknesses of a system, therefore making them more immune to traditional cybersecurity countermeasures.

Automated phishing and social engineering are among the main enablers of AI-enabled ransomware incidents. Classic phishing attacks rely on large emails or messages, but artificial intelligence enables cyber crooks to produce hyper-personalized phishing campaigns with NLP and emotion analysis. Emulate writing styles, evaluate social media interaction, and personalize messages based on individual targets is made more effective by AI-powered phishing emails. AI-driven chatbots can moreover mimic technical support staff, which convinces victims to install malware disguised as legitimate software updates. Ransomware distribution has been drastically improved by this adaptive and automated approach, thus making it among the most potent internet financial threats.

Blackmail via deepfake technology is yet another terrible application of artificial intelligence in extortion activities and ransomware assaults. Cyber attackers wanting to extort victims to pay in cryptocurrencies have discovered deepfake-made videos, audio files, and images as powerful tools. Usually, AI-generated deepfake videos depicting a corporate official in a compromising position are produced and used in blackmail endeavors. Unless a ransom in Bitcoin or another cryptocurrencies is paid, the attackers demand that the manipulated content be released. 17. It is hard to tell between genuine and digitally generated material as deepfake technology has become more lifelike, therefore victims are more apt to pay ransoms to stop reputational loss.

In addition to single attacks, ransomware-as-a-service (RaaS) has become an enterprise mode of operation in dark net cybercrime networks, as AI makes the development and delivery of ransomware tools automatic. AI-based RaaS websites on the dark net make pre-packaged ransomware kits available to non-technical criminals, greatly reducing the cybercrime entry threshold. These websites leverage AI to tailor ransomware versions according to target profiles, refine infection routes, and automate payment receipt using cryptocurrency wallets. Consequently, cybercrime has been democratized such that even beginning hackers can implement big-scale ransomware attacks effortlessly.

Cryptocurrency is central to the monetization of AI-facilitated ransomware attacks. Cyberattackers use cryptocurrencies such as Bitcoin and Monero for ransom because they are pseudonymous and easily transferable across international borders (Gil-Alana et al., 2020). To further mask the source of illegal funds, attackers use AI-powered money laundering methods, including cryptocurrency tumblers and mixers. Such AI-based services disperse ransom payments into discrete portions and direct them into separate wallets, ensuring that it would be virtually impossible to track the proceeds of illegitimate money using tools available for tracking. Mixing ransomware attack vectors with finance-masking solutions empowered by Artificial Intelligence has effectively helped cyberthreat actors build highly sustainable and viable extortion systems.

4.1. Contract Vulnerabilities and Exploitation

The advent of decentralized finance (DeFi) and applications based on smart contracts has brought new avenues for cybercriminals to target weaknesses with AI-facilitated methods. Smart contracts, automated programs that execute on blockchain networks, enable automated transactions without an intermediary (Ji et al., 2019). Although they bring transparency and efficiency, they also create security threats that can be used by AI-enabled attacks. AI is currently being utilized to identify vulnerabilities in smart contracts, automate exploits, and manipulate DeFi protocols, resulting in massive financial losses.

AI provides smart contract detection for vulnerability scanning, which is one of the most threatening threats posed now. Now, with AI tools here to stay, it's possible that they could make light work of destroying all smart contracts because if your codebase is lifted and organized, it will imply F will track g the whole time. AI can scan through huge chunks of code related to smart contracts and find exploitable vulnerabilities far more quickly than human auditors. For instance, AI-driven attacks on open-source DeFi projects are looking for bugs such as reentrancy which can be employed against liquidity pools. Using AI, hackers find and exploit loopholes in DeFi smart contracts. They do this to carry out notorious hacks that involve and stake millions of dollars.

Attack automation on smart contracts is in highly contribution of AI. Rather than exploitations being run manually by attackers, they are being sent to do the actual work of launching automated attacks on blockchain-based applications. It is best exemplified in flash loan attacks where AI-based bots borrow huge sums of cryptocurrency without collateral, hike token prices up and down within a second, to resettle the loans and leave the DeFi platform in dreadful losses. These AI-powered bots continuously monitor the blockchain for arbitrage as well as vulnerabilities and subject themselves to thousands of transactions in real-time to exploit price inefficiencies.

One more AI-created tactic includes the building of malicious smart contracts meant for confusing and like-them-money-sucking from users as well. AI-created smart contract code could add secret backdoor access or fraudulent behavior when deployed into the blockchain. Such contracts are fraudsters who created fake DeFi projects that looked real and cheated investors into liquidity pools, then fled with the funds (Yiying & Yeze, 2019). AI also helps hide fraudulent codes, making it difficult for auditors and security analysts to detect fraudulent smart contracts before they inflict economic damages.

Also, after an investigation, AI bots are used in front-running and miner extractable value (MEV) exploits as schemes where attackers make use of blockchain transactions for their financial advantage. They use AI trading bots to track outstanding blockchain trades and make high-frequency trades just ahead of the bigger orders. Through front-running, the bots gain a profit due to price slippage and enjoy an unfair advantage over individual investors. Front-running has become rampant in decentralized exchanges (DEXs) where AI-based MEV bots trade on market inefficiencies and unfairly benefit at the cost of regular traders. AI is also used to defeat detection and confuse smart contract code, besides security audits. Threat actors will use AI to re-engineer contract architectures, decompose code into small modular pieces, and introduce self-modifying code to thwart forensic analysis. Such AI-driven obfuscation approaches can make detection and blocking of potential exploits by blockchain security companies practically impossible before such exploits can be made".

People already understand these threats, and such growing sophistication refers to AI-enabled attacks on smart contracts, getting even more compellingly necessary security protocols from their own side into the blockchain system. Such AI-based security schemes include features such as automated vulnerability scanning, anomaly detection, and real-time monitoring of transactions and will be adopted by DeFi platforms or smart contract coders for countering AI-facilitated exploits. It is going to require the maturity of regulatory systems, as well, to counter such things as AI-enabled cyber threats. AI not only really transforms the legitimate financial services at present but steals its own thunder in upgrading cyber crime. Ransomware and extortion are said to be AI engineered, and even smart contract exploitation seems to have passed into using features of machine learning and automation to outrun traditional controls. An integrated multi-layered approach with the technological innovation, regulatory enforcement, and cooperation of blockchain developers and cybersecurity experts will be the best way of solving such problems. Only a step ahead of threats from AI will ensure the continued safety of the financial sector against the threats of cybercrime with increasing AI facilitation.

5. AI FOR CRIME DETECTION AND PREVENTION IN CRYPTOCURRENCIES

Now, artificial intelligence has come into existence with gainful operations to detecting financial crime, which acts as a critical tool in fighting clandestine activities in the cryptocurrency arena. The boom of digital assets entails the increased risk of such digital resources being used for money laundering and fraud, among other cybercrimes. Law enforcement agencies, cyber security firms, and financial authorities utilize AI-powered solutions to track, monitor, and stop criminal acts related to cryptocurrencies . AI has become a vital tool in the protection of integrity in transactions realized with digital finances through the most advanced machine learning, predictive analytics, and blockchain forensics. AI tools are very core in detecting complex blockchain patterns, flagging suspicious transactions, and identifying those hidden networks which are involved with illegal cash flows. AI also automates forensic investigation and validates the accuracy of risk assessments, so significantly improving asset tracking during and after a crime and preventing crime. This chapter focuses on the role that AI has played in forensic and blockchain analysis, giving the positive and negative impacts it has brought along regarding the prevention and detection of crimes in the cryptocurrency area.

5.1 Blockchain Analytics and Forensic Techniques

AI-Powered Transaction Monitoring and Anomaly Detection

Although blockchain transactions are somewhat pseudonymous, they are ultimately public and absolutely permanently recorded. AI-based transaction monitoring systems monitor massive volumes of blockchain data in real-time, sometimes identifying aberrant transaction behaviors that may be characteristic of illicit activities. Such activities include sudden spikes of volume, rapid movements across various wallets, and interaction with high-risk addresses affiliated with criminal organizations. AI-based fraud detection systems were implemented with the use of deep learning and behavioral analysis for proactive redirection of resources.

For instance, AI-powered compliance technology such as Chainalysis (Chainalysis, 2023) or Elliptic track Bitcoin and Ethereum transactions for alerts in the presence of suspicious money laundering attempts. The science transfers transactions into risk categories, thus serving an insider to financial institutions and policymakers in the battle against illegal financial flows.

Despite their effectiveness, AI-based detection systems are not without limitations. A 2022 pilot study conducted by Chainalysis revealed that anomaly detection models flagged 28% more suspicious activities than traditional systems—but only 60% of those were later confirmed as genuine fraud cases. This highlights the trade-off between sensitivity and precision in AI-based financial monitoring, and emphasizes the need for continuous model training and human oversight to minimize false positives and operational bottlenecks.

Machine Learning for Address Clustering and Entity Identification

AI comes in handy when determining the actual ownership of blockchain addresses by grouping several wallets managed by the same party. Criminals may employ multiple addresses to remain hidden, but AI-powered forensic analysis can connect these addresses via transfer patterns, volume of transfers, and behavioral correlation (Alessandretti et al., 2018).

For example, blockchain forensics based on artificial intelligence can track several Bitcoin wallets to one darknet marketplace operator using fund movement and interaction history analysis. This method allows law enforcement agencies to disrupt networks of criminals engaged in illicit trade, ransomware activities, and money laundering operations.

Deep Learning for Fraud Detection in Cryptocurrency Exchanges

Cryptocurrency exchanges are excellent targets for fraud and cyber-attacks because they have high levels of transactions and are online-based. Deep learning models using artificial intelligence inspect the behavior of the users, the login activity, withdrawal activities, and trading abnormalities to identify abnormal activities. Deep learning models using AI can discover suspicious trading practices like wash trading, insider trading, and market manipulation in real time.

For instance, if an AI system identifies a recently opened account with exceptionally high trading activity over a brief time, it can mark the activity as possibly fraudulent. Such anticipatory detection aids exchanges in avoiding financial loss and ensuring regulatory compliance.

AI in Smart Contract Security Audits

Smart contracts, or coded contract terms that execute automatically, are a staple of decentralized finance (DeFi) platforms. Smart contract code weaknesses, however, can be used by hackers to siphon money out of DeFi protocols. AI-based security audit tools scan smart contracts for vulnerabilities and flag possible exploits before they are even deployed.

For example, auditing tools such as CertiK and OpenZeppelin, powered by AI, employ machine learning algorithms to identify reentrancy vulnerabilities, logical errors, and backdoors in smart contract code (Shah & Zhang, 2014). By identifying security loopholes beforehand, AI increases the stability of DeFi ecosystems and decreases the likelihood of financial loss.

AI for Tracking Stolen Cryptocurrency Funds

It is difficult to trace stolen digital assets because blockchain transactions are decentralized and pseudonymous. AI forensic software traces stolen money through several blockchain transactions, even when the perpetrators try to conceal their origins through mixers and tumblers. Through analyzing chains of transactions and wallet interactions, AI assists investigators in recovering stolen assets.

A prominent illustration is Bitcoin ransom payments to hackers tracked by AI. AI-powered investigations trace stolen money movement across several wallets and exchanges, yielding essential evidence for law enforcement agencies to pursue cybercriminals.

Sentiment Analysis for Detecting Scams and Fraudulent ICOs

Initial Coin Offerings (ICOs) and token sales have been extensively utilized as a fundraising tool in the cryptocurrency market. Nonetheless, scam ICOs tend to entice investors with deceptive information and unrealistic promises (Hashish et al., 2019). Sentiment analysis software powered by artificial intelligence evaluates online chatter, social media, and whitepaper content to identify possible scams.

For instance, if a project in an ICO displays an unusually high level of automated social media activity without significant technical support behind it, AI can mark it as a high-risk investment. This allows investors and regulators to detect fake schemes before they deliver a similar blight upon the financial system.

Dark Web and AI-Powered Criminal Intelligence Gathering

The dark web is a platform where illegal cryptocurrency transactions, such as drug sales, weapons trade, and ransom payments, take place. AI-based web scraping solutions collect information from dark web markets, forums, and encrypted chat sites to reveal illegal financial activity. The tools scan language use, transaction data, and illegal dealings-related crypto currency wallet addresses. For instance, AI-based monitoring systems may identify a ransomware-as-a-service (RaaS) activity that takes payments in Monero, giving significant leads to law enforcement agencies to act upon (Jang & Lee, 2018).

Predictive Analytics for Crime Prevention in Crypto Transactions

AI uses past blockchain transaction information to forecast probable money laundering and illegal activities. Machine learning algorithms spot developing patterns and mark down transactions that demonstrate risky traits prior to them maturing into financial offences. For example, when AI identifies an ongoing pattern of transactions associated with known criminal wallets, it will stop illegal transfers of funds by notifying financial institutions and regulatory agencies. Predictive analytics enable the stakeholders to initiate proactive action against financial crime instead of depending upon reactive enforcement alone.

The AI application in countering financial crimes involving cryptocurrencies is a game changer on its own. When AI-based forensic software, block chain analytics, and predictive modeling are used in tandem, regulatory institutions, financial institutions, and law enforcement agencies instantly bolster their ability to detect, trace, and suppress illegal transactions.AI development further into detection and prevention of crimes will be the sure shot bet for securing virtual financial environments. The combination of AI and blockchain technology has a tremendous confluence in terms of strengthening regulatory compliance, preventing fraudulent activities, and ensuring the integrity of the crypto space.

5.2 AI for Crime Detection and Prevention in Crypto currencies

The application of artificial intelligence (AI) is growing in financial crimes, driving law enforcement agencies, cyber security companies, and block chain experts toward AI-based solutions in detecting and preventing illegal activities in the crypto currency market. The AI-based solution is applied increasingly for suspicious transaction identification, stolen asset tracking, and the observation of block chains to allow for the detection of criminal networks. By developing forensic techniques, employing machine learning algorithms, and conducting advanced analyses of blockchain systems, law enforcers become more superior in combating the financial crimes arising from cryptocurrency.

5.2.1 AI-Driven Anomaly Detection for Fraud Identification

AI systems pertinent to anomaly detection are thus highly regarded when it comes to spotting fraudulent cryptocurrency transactions based on the analysis of behavioral patterns, transactional records, and market trends. Such systems rely on deep learning algorithms to secure their identification between genuine transactions and those suspected of fraud. One of the key applications of AI in fraud detection is the real-time monitoring of trading platforms and cryptocurrency exchanges. The AI models indicate unusual spikes in trading volume, abrupt fund transfers, and rapid withdrawals from newly opened accounts that could signal acts of market manipulation or money laundering. AI further fortifies fraud prevention largely through behavioral biometrics, assessing user behavior such as typing speed, mouse movement, and geographical location for flags on takeover attempts. Cryptocurrency exchanges have adopted AI-based fraud detection in their battle against automated trading programs and insider trading. These include cases where AI applications have detected and prevented wash trading, a widespread fraud by which traders inflate trading volumes artificially through self-trades and fictitious trading volumes.

5.2.2 Predictive Modeling in Financial Crime Prevention

Predictive modeling involves tasks where artificial intelligence predicts and flags future financial crimes by risk assessment. Machine learning algorithms examine historical block chain transactions for the purposes of anomaly detection patterns for different types of fraudulent transactions. AI studies experience with money laundering, tax evasion and fraud in order to predict how likely such crimes might happen in the future. Predictive analytics is a tool utilized by regulatory bodies and financial institutions to watch crypto currency transactions and pinpoint high-risk accounts that exhibit segments of previous types of fraudulent behavior.

One of the major applications of modeling in prediction is the identification of illicit payment transactions in ransomware in cryptocurrency. Artificial Intelligence assesses the past events of ransomware, and based on this comparison, it establishes commonalities to define the entry points for future occurrences of such nature. Risk profiling through AI enables exchanges and banks to classify users according to those parameters and flag the suspicious transactions before a crime occurs. The forensic analysis artificially empowered with blockchain analytics coupled with AI will make regulatory government authorities, financial institutions, and law enforcement efficient in preventing financial crimes from occurring in the cryptocurrency markets. As AI advances, it will continue to be a vital lifeline in crime prevention and detection efforts to preserve the integrity of digital finance systems. Anomaly detection and predictive modeling with AI are key elements in the continual fight against crime within the currency system of crypto-theft, helping to give real-time insight and proactive measures against financial crime risks.

6. MACHINE LEARNING FOR RISK ASSESSMENT AND KYC/AML COMPLIANCE

Machine learning application in risk assessment and regulatory compliance systems has greatly enhanced the security and transparency of cryptocurrency transactions. Banks and cryptocurrency exchanges make use of machine-learning algorithms to put automated Know Your Customer (KYC) and Anti-Money Laundering (AML) requirements in place that gain a foothold under global regulatory policies. This enables better detection of fraud and monitoring, suspicious activity detection, and prevention of illicit finance flows using large amounts of transactional and behavioral data. Machine learning risk assessments analyze user behavior, transaction histories, and network behavior for anomalies, which present potential financial risks. The models implement supervised and unsupervised learning algorithms in identifying suspicious transactions, marking anything deviating from normal behavioral patterns. For instance, the sudden transaction value changes, frequency shifts, or counterparties might suggest possible money laundering or terrorist financing activities. Advanced anomaly detection systems add improvements in risk scoring, thus allowing financial institutions to act preemptively before the crime escalation.

Machine learning also adds much value to KYC compliance. AI-based identity verification systems utilize biometric data, document verification, and behavioral trends to allow for more accurate and easier authentication of customer identities.

Deep learning algorithms match facial recognition system data against that of national IDs, thus minimizing the risk of identity fraud and easing onboarding processes. Natural language processing techniques also assist in screening against global sanctions lists, adverse media scrutiny, and other relevant literature that may help to identify high-risk persons and organizations (Shintate & Pichl, 2019). In the same way, automated regulatory reporting and AI-enhanced transaction monitoring strengthen AML compliance. Traditional AML systems were built on a rule-based approach which has the inherent drawback of generating a lot of false positives, leading to time-intensive manual review. Machine learning overcomes this limitation because it can adapt dynamically to new criminal strategies, thus improving the accuracy of detection. For example, clustering algorithms segregate transactions on the basis of risk, allowing compliance teams to focus on suspected real activities instead of wasting resources on false alarms.

Comparative assessments between traditional AML systems and AI-based models show a 35–50% increase in detection accuracy and up to 70% reduction in review time, according to FATF and recent compliance audits. However, AI models trained on historical data risk encoding biases or missing emerging fraud tactics that do not match past patterns. This duality underlines the importance of hybrid compliance systems that combine machine learning insights with expert human judgment to ensure both precision and adaptability.

6.1 AI-Enhanced Cyber security Measures for Crypto Platforms

With digital finance and cryptocurrency evolving rapidly, so have the cyber threats that have begun to need advanced security measures driven by AI. Cryptocurrency exchanges, wallets, and decentralized finance (DeFi) are sweet spots for cybercriminals using techniques like phishing, malware attacks, and smart contract exploits. AI-enhanced cybersecurity measures are rolling in to mitigate these risks and to protect digital asset platforms against future threats.

One of the primary applications of AI in the field of cybersecurity is threat intelligence and real-time anomaly detection. Machine-learning-based models that operate in some form of perpetuity help monitor network traffic, transaction patterns, and user behavior for signs of potential security breaches. The AI systems then identify unauthorized attempts to access accounts through suspicious withdrawals and unusual API interactions that may plead act to hacking attempts (Senthuran & Halgamuge, 2019). An AI fraud prevention set-up can immediately block a compromised account on the appearance of suspect areas of access and or sudden shifts in withdrawal actions.

AI protects smart contracts by finding vulnerabilities before deployment alongside intrusion detection. Traditional security audits are vulnerable to manual code reviews that may miss discrete loopholes. CertiK and Open Zeppelin, for example, are AI auditing tools that apply deep learning algorithms to smart contract code, identifying possible attacks by adversaries, such as reentrancy attacks, integer overflow, and logical errors. This automated smart contract auditing considerably minimizes security risks to DeFi applications where hacks and exploits have led to losses in the billions of dollars (Zivot & Wang, 2006).

Behavioral biometrics and adaptive authentication is another critical dimension of AI-enabled cybersecurity. In contrast to conventional systems that use passwords for security, AI-based systems will validate your identity based on typing speed, mouse movements, and patterns of device usage. These biometric indicators provide another cautionary feature preventing access by intruders when the login credentials are compromised. Besides, AI-driven adaptive authentication triggers varying degrees of security according to real-time risk assessment, requiring multi-factor authentication (MFA) only when anomalies are detected (Lucarelli & Borrotti, 2019).

AI is also instrumental in defending against phishing, one of the fastest-growing cyber-attacks affecting the cryptocurrency sector. Deep learning models are utilized to analyze email metadata, language patterns, and URL structure to identify and block phishing attacks before the threat reaches the users (Lahmiri & Bekiros, 2020). AI-based email filtering and web-browsing protection tools help shield investors and traders from fraudulent schemes masquerading as legitimate cryptocurrency exchanges. It is through adopting artificial intelligence in the application of cyber security that enhances the robustness of crypto platforms and accords compliance to regulations as well as safety of the users. The threats by cyber criminals would always change and require continued implementation of artificial intelligence security solutions to safeguard digital assets and ensure currency ecosystems' stability in the long run. AI in cyber security measures not only fortifies crypto platforms but also ensures regulatory adherence and consumer protection. As the landscape of cyber threats evolves, AI-based security will continue to play a core role in safeguarding digital assets and guaranteeing the long-term viability of cryptocurrency ecosystems.

7. CHALLENGES IN COMBATING CRYPTO CURRENCY CRIMES WITH AI

AI crime prevention tools and detection processes have enhanced the detection and prevention of illegal acts in the crypto market by law enforcement, financial institutions, and regulators. That said, while very effective, AI-based solutions face many challenges that do not allow for a complete response to the subtle nuances of crypto-related crimes. From technical limitations, to ethical dilemmas, to regulatory loopholes, and now increasingly by criminal uses of counter-AI technologies, all these considerations represent the current impediments to conducting enhanced attack and defense with AI-assisted crime prevention in compliance with law and ethics.

Limitations of AI in Detecting Sophisticated Crypto Crimes

While AI can assist quite well in alerting suspicious transactions and fraud detection, the usefulness of AI doesn't really hold true here. Criminal techniques are constantly evolving, meaning the criminals are using advanced obfuscation mechanisms like coin mixing services, privacy-oriented crypto currencies, and decentralized peer-to-peer transactions to escape detection. Therefore, AI systems that rely mainly on past patterns of transactions may have difficulty in detecting scams that are totally new and complicated and don't fit into the mold of fraud that has been previously known.

The second challenge is the problem of false positives and false negatives. AI-based transaction monitoring systems can report legitimate transactions as suspicious, resulting in undue scrutiny and inconvenience for authorized users (Phillips & Gorse, 2018). On the other hand, some illegal transactions can be missed due to loopholes in training data or the inability of AI models to pick up evolving fraudulent techniques. AI struggles to monitor cross-chain transactions, where money transits across many block chain networks, making it even more difficult to conduct forensic investigations.

Ethical and Legal Concerns of AI-Driven Surveillance

The large-scale use of AI for tracking crypto currency transactions is of major ethical and legal concern, especially with respect to privacy rights and data protection. AI-based surveillance systems scan large volumes of block chain information, user actions, and financial transactions to identify criminal activity. Such close monitoring is a cause for concern over mass surveillance and misuse of AI for unjustified financial monitoring.

There is a debate on whether there is an adequate balance between security and privacy, with AI-driven transaction monitoring potentially causing intrusive financial monitoring that would affect individuals who have no connection to illegal activities. Furthermore, there is the issue of AI bias, where machine learning algorithms learned from biased data might disproportionately identify particular transactions, persons, or geographies as high-risk, causing unjust treatment and financial exclusion.

Legislative issues are also a result of unclear guidelines on how and in what manner AI-based financial crime detection software is supposed to work. Issues relating to ownership of data, accountability of AI-driven decisions, and admissibility of evidence generated by AI in the courtroom still plague most jurisdictions.

Maintaining AI conformity with international privacy regulations, including the General Data Protection Regulation (GDPR) and the California Consumer Privacy Act (CCPA), remains a challenge for financial institutions and regulatory bodies (Chen et al., 2020).

Regulatory Gaps and Jurisdictional Challenges

The decentralized structure of crypto currencies makes it challenging to apply consistent regulations within multiple jurisdictions. AI-based anti-financial crime solutions have to function in the face of a fractured regulatory framework, where legal requirements for handling crypto currency transactions are quite divergent from nation to nation. Some countries have adopted strict regulations to stem the flow of crypto-based crimes, while others provide regulatory safe havens that help illegal activities proliferate with less monitoring.

Artificial Intelligence-based forensic applications can have an uphill battle complying across borders because criminals use different jurisdictions to conceal their tracks (Tay & Chen, 2018). The lack of uniform regulatory tools for AI-based financial crime surveillance also makes international efforts to fight crypto currency-fraud even harder. Finally, conventional legal channels are always sluggish in catching up with advances in technology, hence criminals end up being a step ahead of their law enforcers.

Adversarial AI: Criminals Using AI to Evade Detection

While AI is used to identify crypto currency offenses, criminals are using AI to evade detection systems. This is referred to as adversarial AI, where machine learning methods are used to trick fraud detection software, automate money laundering operations, and execute advanced cyber attacks on financial platforms.

AI-based bots are employed by cybercriminals to create deep fake identities, carry out phishing operations automatically, and employ sophisticated evasion techniques that deceive AI-based monitoring systems. Synthetic identities created through AI are being increasingly employed to circumvent KYC (Know Your Customer) verification controls on crypto currency exchanges, whereas AI-based mixers and tumblers take the laundering of dirty money to unprecedented levels of automation (Chu et al., 2017).

Also, hackers take advantage of weaknesses in AI models by providing them with tampered data, tricking them into misclassifying criminal transactions as legal. This AI vs. AI arms race shows the necessity of ongoing innovation in AI security technologies, such as adversarial machine learning defenses and improved threat intelligence.

AI stands to save a lot of potential in preventing much of crimes involving crypto currency but comes with quite a number of down-sides due to which its use has been limited. New identification schemes of fraud are some of the limitations, ethical and legal issues in financial monitoring, regulatory fragmentation and such adversarial techniques in AI that further prevent most of the crimes. Solving them will require multiaspect solutions such as better AI transparency, regulatory cooperation, ethical AI management and such more improvements in AI security. Once these hindrances and obstacles are overcome, AI can further develop an even more performance and ethics-based scheme for detecting and preventing crime in an otherwise changing arena of crypto currencies.

8. REGULATORY AND LEGAL PERSPECTIVES

The abrupt emergence of artificial intelligence (AI) has placed tremendous tension on regulation and even legality in relation to its relation with crime in the form of crypto currencies. Even as the governments and institutions of finance fall behind the pace at which threats are changing from one to another, there is also a pressing need for evolving regulatory frameworks to address the threat of AI-enabled financial crimes now requiring a breathing space for promoting innovation in digital finance.

Current Global Regulations on AI and Crypto currency Crime

The regulation of crimes involving artificial intelligence and cryptocurrencies is highly fragmented within the jurisdictions. Whereas some jurisdictions have set in place comprehensive law for digital assets and AI applications, others are lagging in enforcement and oversight. For example, in the United States, the Financial Crimes Enforcement Network (FinCEN) requires cryptocurrency exchanges to adhere with anti-money laundering (AML) and Know Your Customer (KYC) rules (Peng et al., 2018). The European Union, through the Markets in Crypto-Assets (MiCA) regulation, aims to smoothen the standardization of crypto businesses within the space, while the Financial Action Task Force (FATF) gives broad guidelines to countries across the world for the mitigation of illegal activities related to digital finance (Ngunyi et al., 2019). One major challenge for regulating AI-induced financial crime is the decentralized and borderless nature of transactions made over a blockchain (Guo et al., 2018). Most illicit actors take advantage of the regulatory lacunae afforded by weak enforcement jurisdictions, thus conducting fraudulent activities there. Besides, there is evidence that such threats, embracing even potential ones such as deep fake fraud and AI money laundering, are evolving much faster than the existing regulatory framework and require constant amendments to the legal frameworks.

The Role of Governments and Financial Institutions in Crime Prevention

Governments and financial institutions have a leading role in curbing AI-enabled cryptocurrency crimes. Hence, organizations like Interpol and Europol have engaged in the use of AI-powered blockchain analytics into their operational methodologies to monitor illegal transactions or understand cranial networks. Central banks and financial regulators use AI-based monitoring tools to identify suspicious activities and enforce compliance in parallel. Banks also used intelligent techniques in fraud detection systems to enhance security in financial institutions. Major banks and crypto currency exchanges employ AI-based risk assessment models to identify high-risk transactions, avoiding money laundering and terrorist financing (Miura et al., 2019). Furthermore, cooperation between the regulatory agencies and the private sector is also essential in formulating standardized security measures and information exchange mechanisms to fight AI-based financial crimes effectively.

Case Study: Estonia's Digital ID and AML Regime

Estonia's Financial Intelligence Unit (FIU) employs a hybrid framework using AI and blockchain analytics to monitor virtual currency service providers. Their real-time AI-driven system has flagged over 2,500 suspicious transactions in 2022 alone, showcasing a successful integration of technology and regulation [Estonian FIU, 2022].

Case Study: Singapore's MAS and Sandbox Framework

The Monetary Authority of Singapore (MAS) uses regulatory sandboxes to test AI tools for AML compliance in live environments. Their AI-powered real-time transaction surveillance system has reduced false positives by 40%, helping achieve compliance without stifling innovation.

AI-Driven Compliance Solutions for Crypto Exchanges and Financial Entities

AI is being used more and more to enhance compliance controls for financial institutions and cryptocurrency exchanges. Machine learning algorithms can scan large volumes of transaction data in real time, detecting anomalies that may signal illicit activity. AI-powered identity verification systems, with facial recognition and biometric authentication, are improving KYC compliance, stopping fraudsters from exploiting online platforms.

Further, AI-based regulatory technology (RegTech) solutions facilitate compliance processes through the automation of risk assessments and reporting (Caporale & Zekokh, 2019). Crypto exchanges are incorporating AI-based AML tools, including Chain analysis and Elliptic, to monitor suspicious transactions and adhere to regulatory standards. Through the use of AI for compliance, financial institutions can minimize the risks of regulatory fines and reputational loss.

Future Policy Recommendations for AI and Crypto Crime Mitigation

Policymakers must, therefore, enact forward-leaning regulatory policies to address new threats to AI from crypto currency crime. Governments should build harmonized AI governance frameworks that strike a balance between innovation and security to make the use of AI in financial services safe. International collaboration and information-sharing mechanisms must also be reinforced, as crime works through exploiting loopholes across borders. Secondly, regulators should include AI transparency and explainability requirements through compliance systems to avert biases and errors in fraud detection models. It would be imperative to foster investments in AI research and development to upgrade the capacity of law enforcement agencies to combat cyber-enabled financial crime. Finally, regulatory sandboxes can be utilized for piloting and fine-tuning AI-based crime prevention technologies before putting them to full-scale use.

9. FUTURE TRENDS AND EMERGING THREATS

With the continual advancement in AI, so do the applications of the technology in financial crime, bringing both challenges and opportunities regarding the security of cryptocurrencies. It is imperative to be aware of trends and potential hazards concerning AI-based financial crimes for effective counteraction.

Evolution of AI in Financial Crime

The integration of AI into financial crime is becoming increasingly sophisticated, making it possible for the criminals to carry out cybercrime with high precision. AI-based hacking tools can automatically detect the security weaknesses in block chain networks, paving the way for exploitations such as smart contract hacks and private key theft (Platanakis & Urquhart, 2020). AI will also likely increase the frequency of market manipulation games such as high-frequency trading scams that signal crypto currency markets. On the other hand, AI for crime prevention will flourish as increased predictive analysis and block chain forensic capabilities become the norm in financial crimes investigations. Regulatory frameworks powered by AI will enable firms to monitor compliance in real-time and minimize the risk that nascent financial risks pose. Artificial Intelligence has become gargantuan in financial crimes. Some criminals can now conduct cyber attacks with better accuracy. Notably, AI-hacking tools automatically detect security weaknesses in block chain networks because this leaves attacking opportunities like possible smart contract hacks or private key thefts (Platanakis & Urquhart, 2020). However, the incidences of AI-boasted market manipulation schemes that signal crypto currency markets: high-frequency trading scams will be more rampant, owing to this. On the other hand, there is going to be growth in crime prevention using AI too. The latter and other technological requirements would enhance capabilities in predictive analysis and block chain forensic assessment in the regular investigation of financial crimes. Regulatory frameworks powered by AI will place firms under the mandate of real-time monitoring of compliance at the same time reducing the risks caused by emerging financial threats.

Potential Risks of Quantum Computing in Crypto Security

The threat of quantum computing is one of the deadliest threats in the security of cryptocurrency. Such computers are capable of breaking modern cryptographic protocols, thereby putting block chain networks and digital property at risk. Quantum attacks aided by artificial intelligence would imply that private keys could be made easily compromised and shatter all traditional ways of encryption (Burggraf & Vyas, 2020). To counter this risk, scientists are looking at post-quantum cryptography, which envisioned developing quantum-resistant encryption methods. Artificial intelligence will play an important role in creating adaptive security measures that can mitigate in real time the threats posed by quantum computing and assure the integrity of digital financial systems. Fully new threats in cryptocurrency security are the threats of quantum computing. Such computers can defeat modern cryptographic protocols and make block chain networks and digital property very much available to risk. Quantum attacks powered by artificial intelligence would mean that private keys could be easily compromised and destroy conventional methods of encryption (Burggraf & Vyas, 2020). This is why scientists are working on post-quantum cryptography. It pursues a way of encryption that will resist quantum attacks. AI will play a vital part in the development of adaptive security protocols that can handle in real-time the bold threat of quantum computing and ensure digital systems' integrity.

The Role of Decentralized Finance (DeFi) in AI-Driven Crime

The rise of decentralized finance represents the new challenges of AI-based crime prevention. Unlike a centralized exchange, DeFi platforms do not have intermediaries, and as such, it is difficult to impose regulatory control (Xidonas et al., 2020). AI-based automated trading robots can exploit faults in the DeFi protocol to carry out flash loan attacks and front-run trades. Moreover, the smart contract dependency of DeFi may also result in an increase in security risks. By leveraging artificial intelligence, malicious entities can simply spot coding flaws that lead to large financial exploitation. With this continuous growth of the DeFi phenomenon, the regulatory institutions must devise AI-powered audit tools that would assess the security of smart contracts against illegal practices (Nakano et al., 2018) by writing text with very low perplexity and high burstiness and also keeping the wordcount and HTML elements intact.

Ethical AI Development for Crime Prevention

Moral considerations concerning the crime prevention work done with AI should also be put on record. While AI serves to better their work, law enforcement still has encroachment due to factors such as privacy, surveillance, and algorithmic bias. AI-based surveillance technologies should be built in such a way that establishes transparency and accountability so that these technologies will not infringe upon civil liberties. Moreover, ethical systems need to be implemented in order to prevent misapplication of AI technologies with reference to crime detection and acts of crime. It would thus be incumbent on responsible AI research, technology, and applications to additionally foster trust and integrity within financial services. In summary, the landscape at the junction between AI and crypto-crimes is a rather multifaceted regulatory environment with rapidly changing opportunities and challenges. In proactively instilling appropriate regulation of law, upgrading AI-powered compliance technology, and ramping up against future threats birthed through technologies, regulators and financial institutions might thus efficiently answer the concerns AI raises in funneling financial crime (Henriques & Sadorsky, 2018). The fate of AI in cryptocurrency security will thus depend on striking a fair balance between innovations and preventing negative activity in the digital financial platform.

CONCLUSION

In fact, the intersection of artificial intelligence and cryptocurrency-related crime represents a dynamic and ever-changing field filled with real challenges and real opportunities. Therefore, the construct of artificial intelligence provides a means for cybercriminals to carry out subtle and undetectable financial crimes such as money laundering, fraud, ransomware attacks, market manipulation, and even identity theft. Detecting and identifying these illegal activities become even harder with an AI application for automating crimes, exploiting smart contract vulnerabilities, and further anonymizing the transactions involved. The widespread emergence of adversarial AI, as it increasingly describes the use of AI by criminals against methods of knowing and detecting criminality pursued by law enforcers, renders exceedingly problematic and more difficult the fight against crypto-based financial crime. At the same time, AI has emerged as an effective weapon in the battle against such criminal activities.

So from patrolling suspicious patterns to tracing dirty money and beefing up KYC and AML compliance procedures, the crime-prevention turnaround powered by algorithms involves machine learning, block chain analytics, anomaly detection engines, and AI-based security systems. AI-based cybersecurity works to improve the resilience of crypto exchanges, financial institutions, and regulatory agencies against cyber threats by identifying vulnerabilities and mitigating active cyber threats in real time. Predictive modeling additionally offers an avenue to monitor transactional behavior and predict risk and fraud before it becomes serious. Still, while there is a world of potential, application of AI toward prosecuting cryptocurrency crime is challenged. Still, issues such as gaps in regulation, jurisdictional conflict, and ethical issues weaken reasonably the effectiveness of AI applications for financial crime prevention. Glaring gaps in global regulatory frameworks together with the obscurity of cryptocurrency are the torment of law enforcement agencies in effectively dealing with cross-border financial criminals. On another note, ethical questions revolving around AI-controlled surveillance, privacy violation, and algorithmic bias present serious concerns with the responsible use of AI. A multidisciplinary approach will be the way to guide AI-oriented crime deterrence in the crypto-world. Moving forward, to continue thwarting this rising wave of AII-driven financial crime by increasingly advanced cyber attacks, the following key courses of action will become paramount:

Stronger Regulatory Frameworks: Governments and global regulatory bodies should collaborate to formulate strong, standardized, and globally harmonized regulations for tracking and combating crypto-based financial crimes. - Improved Cooperation: The successful implementation of AI-based crime detection systems will require increasing cooperation among AI experts, police, cybersecurity specialists, and financial institutions.

It is vital to ensure ethical employment of AI techniques for preventing financial crimes. Mitigating biases in the AI models, protection of individual privacy, and transparency in AI decision-making procedures are within the purview of ensuring ethical employment of AI for preventing financial crime.

Technological advancements: As we look forward to entering the horizon of quantum computing, the security loopholes in the existing cryptographic systems would be a major concern. Hence, AI-based security systems need to evolve and adopt continuously against any emerging threats.

Adversarial AI combating: Criminals have increasingly used various forms of adversarial AI to avoid detection; hence, they need to buy counter-AI technology to stay one step ahead of such criminal strategies.

Eventually, AI will bring change in the pattern of the security as well as regulation of cryptocurrency for preventing financial crime. AI proves to be efficient in prediction, increases the means of criminology, jumps to real time monitoring, and makes use of adaptive security controls. This would help law enforcement agencies and financial institutions to fortify themselves better from increasingly sophisticated crypto threats. However, such improvements must be met with encouraging AI practices, progress in the unending search for further development, and international cooperation to safeguard integrity and stability in those digital financial systems. Indeed, with great power during this ever-changing digital age, AI can be a criminal's best tool and also a powerful impetus toward driving away crime. Finding the right balance between technological innovation, regulation, and its moral application is the solution to addressing the crimes associated with AI-based cryptocurrencies, whereby AI continues, and will continue to be, a source of strength in security and defense against the exploitation of the financial system.

REFERENCES

Abraham, J., Higdon, D., Nelson, J., & Ibarra, J. (2018). Cryptocurrency price prediction using tweet volume and sentiment analysis. *SMU Data Science Review*, *1*(3), 37–73.

Alessandretti, L., ElBahrawy, A., Aiello, L. M., & Baronchelli, A. (2018). Anticipating cryptocurrency prices using machine learning. *Complexity*, *2018*(1), 1–16. DOI: 10.1155/2018/8983590

Burggraf, T., & Vyas, A. (2020). Beyond risk parity—A machine learning-based hierarchical risk parity approach on cryptocurrencies. *Finance Research Letters*, *101586*. Advance online publication. DOI: 10.1016/j.frl.2020.101523

Caporale, G. M., & Zekokh, T. (2019). Modelling volatility of cryptocurrencies using Markov-switching GARCH models. *Research in International Business and Finance*, *48*, 143–155. DOI: 10.1016/j.ribaf.2018.12.009

Chainalysis. (2023). *The 2023 crypto crime report*. Chainalysis Inc. https://www.chainalysis.com/

Chen, W., Xu, H., Jia, L., & Gao, Y. (2020). Machine learning model for bitcoin exchange rate prediction using economic and technology determinants. *International Journal of Forecasting*. [Online]. Available: https://www.sciencedirect.com/science/article/abs/pii/S0169207020300431

Chu, J., Chan, S., Nadarajah, S., & Osterrieder, J. (2017). GARCH modelling of cryptocurrencies. *Journal of Risk and Financial Management*, *10*(4), 17. DOI: 10.3390/jrfm10040017

Georgoula, I., Pournarakis, D., Bilanakos, C., Sotiropoulos, N. D., & Giaglis, M. G. (2015). Using time-series and sentiment analysis to detect the determinants of bitcoin prices. In *Proceedings of the Mediterranean Conference on Information Systems* (p. 20). MCIS. [Online], Available https://aisel.aisnet.org/mcis2015/20 DOI: 10.2139/ssrn.2607167

Gil-Alana, L. A., Abakah, E. J. A., & Rojo, M. F. R. (2020). Cryptocurrencies and stock market indices: Are they related? *Research in International Business and Finance*, *51*, 101063. DOI: 10.1016/j.ribaf.2019.101063

Guo, T., Bifet, A., & Antulov-Fantulin, N. (2018, November). Bitcoin volatility forecasting with a glimpse into buy and sell orders. In *Proceedings of the IEEE International Conference on Data Mining (ICDM)* (pp. 989–994). DOI: 10.1109/ICDM.2018.00123

Hashish, F., Forni, F., Andreotti, G., Facchinetti, T., & Darjani, S. (2019, September). A hybrid model for bitcoin prices prediction using hidden Markov models and optimized LSTM networks. In *Proceedings of the 24th IEEE International Conference on Emerging Technologies and Factory Automation (ETFA)* (pp. 721–728). DOI: 10.1109/ETFA.2019.8869094

Henriques, I., & Sadorsky, P. (2018). Can bitcoin replace gold in an investment portfolio? *Journal of Risk and Financial Management, 11*(3), 48. DOI: 10.3390/jrfm11030048

Huang, J.-Z., Huang, W., & Ni, J. (2019). Predicting bitcoin returns using high-dimensional technical indicators. *The Journal of Financial Data Science, 5*(3), 140–155. DOI: 10.1016/j.jfds.2018.10.001

Jang, H., & Lee, J. (2018). An empirical study on modeling and prediction of bitcoin prices with Bayesian neural networks based on blockchain information. *IEEE Access : Practical Innovations, Open Solutions, 6*, 5427–5437. DOI: 10.1109/ACCESS.2017.2779181

Ji, S., Kim, J., & Im, H. (2019). A comparative study of bitcoin price prediction using deep learning. *Mathematics, 7*(10), 898. DOI: 10.3390/math7100898

Kim, Y. B., Lee, J., Park, N., Choo, J., Kim, J.-H., & Kim, C. H. (2017). When bitcoin encounters information in an online forum: Using text mining to analyse user opinions and predict value fluctuation. *PLoS One, 12*(5), e0177630. DOI: 10.1371/journal.pone.0177630

Kjærland, F., Meland, M., Oust, A., & Øyen, V. (2018). How can bitcoin price fluctuations be explained? *International Journal of Economics and Financial Issues, 8*(3), 323–332.

Klein, T., Thu, H., & Walther, T. (2018). Bitcoin is not the new gold—A comparison of volatility correlation and portfolio performance. *International Review of Financial Analysis, 59*, 105–116. DOI: 10.1016/j.irfa.2018.07.010

Lahmiri, S., & Bekiros, S. (2020). Intelligent forecasting with machine learning trading systems in chaotic intraday bitcoin market. *Chaos, Solitons, and Fractals, 133*, 109641. DOI: 10.1016/j.chaos.2020.109641

Liew, J., Li, R., Budavári, T., & Sharma, A. (2019). Cryptocurrency investing examined. *Journal of the British Blockchain Association, 2*(2), 1–12. DOI: 10.31585/jbba-2-2-(2)2019

Lopes, V., & Alexandre, L. A. (2019). An overview of blockchain integration with robotics and artificial intelligence. *Ledger, 4*, 1–21. DOI: 10.5195/ledger.2019.171

Lucarelli, G., & Borrotti, M. (2019). A deep reinforcement learning approach for automated cryptocurrency trading. In *Artificial intelligence applications and innovations* (pp. 247–258). Springer. DOI: 10.1007/978-3-030-19823-7_20

Miura, R., Pichl, L., & Kaizoji, T. (2019). Artificial neural networks for realized volatility prediction in cryptocurrency time series. In *Advances in Neural Networks—ISNN* (pp. 165–172). Springer., DOI: 10.1007/978-3-030-22796-8_18

Nakano, M., Takahashi, A., & Takahashi, S. (2018). Bitcoin technical trading with artificial neural network. *Physica A*, *510*, 587–609. DOI: 10.1016/j.physa.2018.07.017

Ngunyi, A., Mundia, S., & Omari, C. (2019). Modelling volatility dynamics of cryptocurrencies using GARCH models. *Journal of Mathematical Finance*, *9*(4), 591–615. DOI: 10.4236/jmf.2019.94030

Peng, Y., Albuquerque, P. H. M., de Sá, J. M. C., Padula, A. J. A., & Montenegro, M. R. (2018). The best of two worlds: Forecasting high frequency volatility for cryptocurrencies and traditional currencies with support vector regression. *Expert Systems with Applications*, *97*, 177–192. DOI: 10.1016/j.eswa.2017.12.004

Phillips, C. R., & Gorse, D. (2018). Cryptocurrency price drivers: Wavelet coherence analysis revisited. *PLoS One*, *13*(4), e0195200. DOI: 10.1371/journal.pone.0195200

Platanakis, E., & Urquhart, A. (2020). Should investors include bitcoin in their portfolios? A portfolio theory approach. *The British Accounting Review*, *52*(4), 100837. DOI: 10.1016/j.bar.2019.100837

Senthuran, R., & Halgamuge, M. (2019). *Prediction of cryptocurrency market price using deep learning and blockchain information: Bitcoin and Ethereum*. Taylor & Francis. DOI: 10.1201/9780429674457-15

Sgantzos, K., & Grigg, I. (2019). Artificial intelligence implementations on the blockchain: Use cases and future applications. *Future Internet*, *11*(8), 170. DOI: 10.3390/fi11080170

Shah, D., & Zhang, K. (2014). Bayesian regression and bitcoin. In *Proceedings of the 52nd Annual Allerton Conference on Communication, Control, and Computing (Allerton)* (pp. 409–414). DOI: 10.1109/ALLERTON.2014.7028484

Shintate, T., & Pichl, L. (2019). Trend prediction classification for high frequency bitcoin time series with deep learning. *Journal of Risk and Financial Management*, *12*(1), 17. DOI: 10.3390/jrfm12010017

Tay, R. S., & Chen, R. (2018). *Nonlinear time series analysis*. Wiley. DOI: 10.1002/9781119514312

Valencia, F., Gómez-Espinosa, A., & Valdés-Aguirre, B. (2019). Price movement prediction of cryptocurrencies using sentiment analysis and machine learning. *Entropy (Basel, Switzerland)*, *21*(6), 589. DOI: 10.3390/e21060589

Xidonas, P., Steuer, R., & Hassapis, C. (2020). Robust portfolio optimization: A categorized bibliographic review. *Annals of Operations Research*, *292*(1), 533–552. DOI: 10.1007/s10479-020-03630-8

Xie, Q., Tan, D., Zhu, T., Zhang, Q., Xiao, S., & Wang, J.. (2019, May). Chatbot application on cryptocurrency. In *Proceedings of the IEEE Conference on Computational Intelligence for Financial Engineering & Economics (CIFEr)* (pp. 1–8). DOI: 10.1109/CIFEr.2019.8759121

Yiying, W., & Yeze, Z. (2019, March). Cryptocurrency price analysis with artificial intelligence. In *Proceedings of the 5th International Conference on Information Management (ICIM)* (pp. 97–101). DOI: 10.1109/INFOMAN.2019.8714700

Zivot, E., & Wang, J. (2006). Nonlinear time series models. In *Modeling financial time series with S-PLUS* (pp. 653–712). Springer.

KEY TERMS AND DEFINITIONS

Adversarial AI: The use of AI techniques by malicious actors to deceive, evade, or disrupt AI-powered detection and prevention systems.

Anti-Money Laundering (AML): Laws, regulations, and processes designed to detect and prevent money laundering activities.

Artificial Intelligence (AI): The simulation of human intelligence in machines, enabling them to learn, reason, and make decisions. In this context, AI includes machine learning, deep learning, and natural language processing applied to financial systems and blockchain.

Blockchain: A decentralized, distributed ledger technology that records transactions across multiple computers, ensuring transparency and security without a central authority.

Cryptocurrency: A digital or virtual currency secured by cryptography, often operating on decentralized blockchain networks (e.g., Bitcoin, Ethereum).

Decentralized Finance (DeFi): Financial services built on blockchain platforms that operate without centralized intermediaries, using smart contracts for transactions.

Deepfake: AI-generated synthetic media (images, audio, or video) that realistically imitates real individuals, potentially used for fraud, identity theft, or impersonation.

Flash Loan Attack: An exploit in DeFi platforms where an attacker borrows large sums of cryptocurrency without collateral, manipulates markets or protocols, and repays the loan in the same transaction to profit illicitly.

Know Your Customer (KYC): Regulatory requirements mandating financial institutions to verify the identity of clients before allowing transactions.

Mixers/Tumblers: Services or software that obfuscate the source and destination of cryptocurrency transactions by mixing multiple payments, making tracking more difficult.

Money Laundering: The process of disguising illegally obtained funds to make them appear legitimate, often using mixers, tumblers, or structured transactions in cryptocurrency networks.

Post-Quantum Cryptography: Cryptographic methods designed to be secure against the potential computational power of quantum computers.

Ransomware: Malicious software that encrypts a victim's data, demanding cryptocurrency payment for decryption.

Smart Contract: Self-executing code on a blockchain that automatically enforces the terms of an agreement without intermediaries.

Chapter 8
A Comprehensive Review of Techniques for Detecting and Preventing Card-Not-Present (CNP) Fraud

Kwabena Owusu-Mensah
https://orcid.org/0009-0004-0037-1140
University of Ghana, Ghana

Winfred Yaokumah
https://orcid.org/0000-0001-7756-1832
University of Ghana, Ghana

Edward Danso Ansong
https://orcid.org/0009-0001-5536-4667
University of Ghana, Ghana

ABSTRACT

This chapter reviews techniques for detecting and preventing card-not-present (CNP) fraud, which has escalated due to the rise in online transactions and the COVID-19 pandemic. It evaluates methods like machine learning, behavioral analytics and risk-scoring, highlighting their integration for effective fraud detection. Key findings indicate that traditional methods remain relevant, while advanced technologies, such as artificial intelligence, significantly enhance detection accuracy. The chapter

DOI: 10.4018/979-8-3373-0675-9.ch008

emphasizes collaboration across sectors to combat CNP fraud and explores future research aimed at enhancing fraud detection, user experience, and ethical data usage, ultimately contributing to safer digital transactions.

1.0 INTRODUCTION

The rapid expansion of Card-Not-Present (CNP) transactions has significantly impacted the contemporary payments ecosystem, primarily fueled by the exponential growth of online commerce and digital financial services. CNP transactions are characterized by the absence of physical card presentation at the point of sale, meaning that the cardholder and the payment card are not in the exact location when the transaction occurs. These transactions encompass a variety of remote payment methods, including online shopping, phone and mail orders, mobile app payments, and digital wallet operations, where sensitive payment details such as the card number, expiration date, and Card Verification Value (CVV) are transmitted electronically (European Central Bank, 2023).

While CNP transactions offer exceptional convenience for consumers, merchants, and service providers by facilitating seamless remote payments, they also present significant security vulnerabilities (Bodker et al., 2022). Unlike traditional Card Present (CP) transactions, which authenticate physical cards using methods such as Chip and PIN or signatures to verify cardholder identity (Bodker et al., 2022), CNP transactions lack many in-person authentication safeguards due to their remote nature. The reliance on remote data is based on the card information provided by the consumer, which can be easily obtained through phishing, malware, skimming, or data breaches (Akdemir & Yenal, 2020). The security of the system relies heavily on the accuracy of the data, which makes it susceptible to various malicious activities (Mekterović et al., 2021). This vulnerability has resulted in CNP fraud, defined as the unauthorized use of another person's card details during remote transactions, as noted by Akdemir and Yenal (2020) and Mekterović et al. (2021). A summary of the differences between CP and CNP is provided in Table 1 for further clarification.

Table 1. CP Vs CNP Transactions

Feature	CP Transactions	CNP Transactions
Where it happens	In-store, physical location	Online, phone, or mail order
How is payment made	Swipe, chip insert, or tap	Manually enter card details
Security	Lower fraud risk, identity verification in person	Higher fraud risk requires additional security measures
Transactions fees	Lower fees due to reduced risk	Higher fees due to increased risk
Customer experience	Immediate payment confirmation, in-person checkout	More convenient for remote purchases
Ideal for	Retail stores, restaurants, fuel stations, service businesses	E-commerce, subscriptions, remote services

A key factor in the rise of CNP fraud is the increasing frequency of data breaches and cyberattacks. Breaches in retail, financial, and loyalty systems often expose sensitive cardholder information, which fraudsters then use for unauthorized transactions. Such breaches provide criminals with access to valuable card credentials, including card numbers, expiration dates, CVVs, and billing addresses (Bodker et al., 2022). Fraudsters frequently monetize the stolen data through various channels. For example, they may sell validated card credentials on the dark web or use them directly to make online purchases. Because these transactions do not require physical card presence or biometric confirmation, they often mimic legitimate activities convincingly. This resemblance makes fraud detection challenging, as many fraudulent transactions slip through standard monitoring systems and remain undetected for extended periods, resulting in multiple unauthorized purchases before detection (Mekterović et al., 2021). Adding to the difficulty is the inconsistent implementation of security protocols across regions and sectors. While some regions have adopted multi-factor authentication systems such as 3-D Secure, their deployment varies, and even when implemented, they can be bypassed or deliberately limited by issuing banks to enhance customer experience, presenting additional opportunities for fraud (Akdemir & Yenal, 2020). In the United States, prior to recent security reforms, reliance on backend fraud monitoring and authentication methods was common, leaving vulnerabilities open for exploitation (Nilson Report, 2025).

The COVID-19 pandemic has further accelerated the risks and prevalence of CNP fraud. Movement restrictions and social distancing measures drove consumers toward online shopping, resulting in a marked increase in e-commerce sales. According to the U.S. Census Bureau, e-commerce sales surged by 43% in 2020, rising from $571.2 billion in 2019 to $815.4 billion, representing an additional $244.2 billion in online transactions. This shift has created a fertile environment for fraud, as criminals exploit the increased volume and the complexity of remote transactions.

Recent estimates highlight the seriousness of the issue at hand. In 2016, CNP fraud accounted for approximately 61% of all detected payment card fraud in the United States, resulting in losses exceeding $4.57 billion (Bodker et al., 2022). In the UK, CNP fraud has been the largest category of payment card fraud since 2014, while in Australia, it accounted for 85% of payment card fraud incidents by 2019. Globally, CNP fraud has continued to rise, with the Nilson Report indicating that it accounted for approximately 70% of global card fraud losses in 2020, totaling $19.43 billion. Overall card fraud losses have reached record highs, totaling $33.8 billion in 2023, primarily driven by CNP fraud, especially within e-commerce in the U.S. (Nilson Report, 2025). Industry projections suggest that by 2024, three-quarters (74%) of all card fraud incidents will be related to CNP fraud.

The surge in online activity during the pandemic highlighted existing weaknesses in fraud detection systems, prompting financial institutions, merchants, and regulators to reassess their security strategies. With the increasing sophistication of fraudulent activities, traditional rule-based detection methods are often insufficient. Consequently, there has been a notable push toward deploying advanced analytics, machine learning, and artificial intelligence tools to enhance detection accuracy and minimize false positives (Bello et al., 2023). These solutions leverage large datasets, behavioral analytics, and pattern recognition to identify anomalies and suspicious activities in real-time. Qu & Jin (2023) advocate for adaptable machine learning algorithms that respond to changing fraud patterns, enhancing predictive capabilities. Similarly, Chen (2024) introduced a Light Gradient Boosting Machine (LightGBM) model that effectively detects online financial transaction fraud, illustrating the trend towards sophisticated algorithmic approaches. Additionally, Akazue et al. (2023) emphasized the benefits of ensemble feature selection techniques, which refine model accuracy and reduce false-positive rates, thus improving detection efficiency. This finding resonates with Mekterović et al. (2021), who explored various machine learning methods for cost-effective fraud detection in CNP transactions. Machine learning models can adapt dynamically to emerging fraud patterns, a stark contrast to static rule-based systems that require manual updates.

The fundamental security deficiencies inherent in remote transactions, particularly the reliance on data that can be compromised, necessitate the development and deployment of sophisticated, adaptable, and scalable detection techniques. Machine learning and artificial intelligence have demonstrated promising results, offering real-time analysis and predictive capabilities that bolster fraud prevention efforts. Moving forward, strengthening authentication protocols, fostering cross-sector cooperation, and continuously innovating technological solutions will be vital to safeguarding consumers and merchants against the persistent threat of CNP fraud. As digital commerce advances, security paradigms must also adapt to maintain their integrity, supporting ongoing growth and trust in online financial transactions.

This chapter, therefore, covers techniques for detecting and preventing CNP fraud, structured around three pillars: Detection, Prevention, and Verification. Each of these pillars plays a critical role in building a comprehensive and resilient defence system against CNP fraud threats.

Each pillar encompasses a range of specialized techniques and tools designed to mitigate risks at various stages of the transaction lifecycle.

The Fraud Detection pillar focuses on identifying suspicious or anomalous activity using data-intensive techniques. It involves the real-time and post-transaction identification of fraudulent transactions. This is achieved through advanced technologies, including machine learning models, anomaly detection systems, and behavioral analytics. These tools analyze user behavior patterns, transaction histories, device fingerprints, and geolocation data to distinguish between legitimate and fraudulent transactions.

In the Fraud Prevention pillar, proactive methods are implemented to block fraudulent attempts before they occur. It encompasses proactive strategies that aim to reduce the likelihood of fraud occurring in the first place. Techniques include tokenization, which replaces sensitive card data with non-sensitive tokens; encryption, which protects cardholder data during transmission and storage; and risk scoring, which evaluates the potential risk of each transaction based on contextual factors.

The third pillar, Verification and Control, reinforces the system by confirming the legitimacy of users and promoting ongoing vigilance. It focuses on authenticating the cardholder's identity before a transaction is completed. This includes multi-factor authentication, biometric verification, 3-D Secure protocols, and other methods designed to ensure that the individual initiating the transaction is the legitimate cardholder. Additionally, fraud awareness and training are crucial for developing organizational resilience. Educating employees and stakeholders about common fraud tactics helps maintain vigilance and strengthens the security posture of the entire payment ecosystem.

Collectively, these methods provide layered protection that adapts to evolving fraud tactics. By combining real-time monitoring, secure data handling, and strong customer authentication, institutions can significantly reduce CNP fraud risk. The integrated approach is illustrated in Figure 1, which maps out the interaction between detection, prevention, and verification mechanisms within the broader CNP fraud mitigation framework, as well as the increasingly sophisticated methods employed by cybercriminals in digital payment environments.

Figure 1. Integrated Framework for Detection, Prevention and Verification in CNP Fraud Mitigation

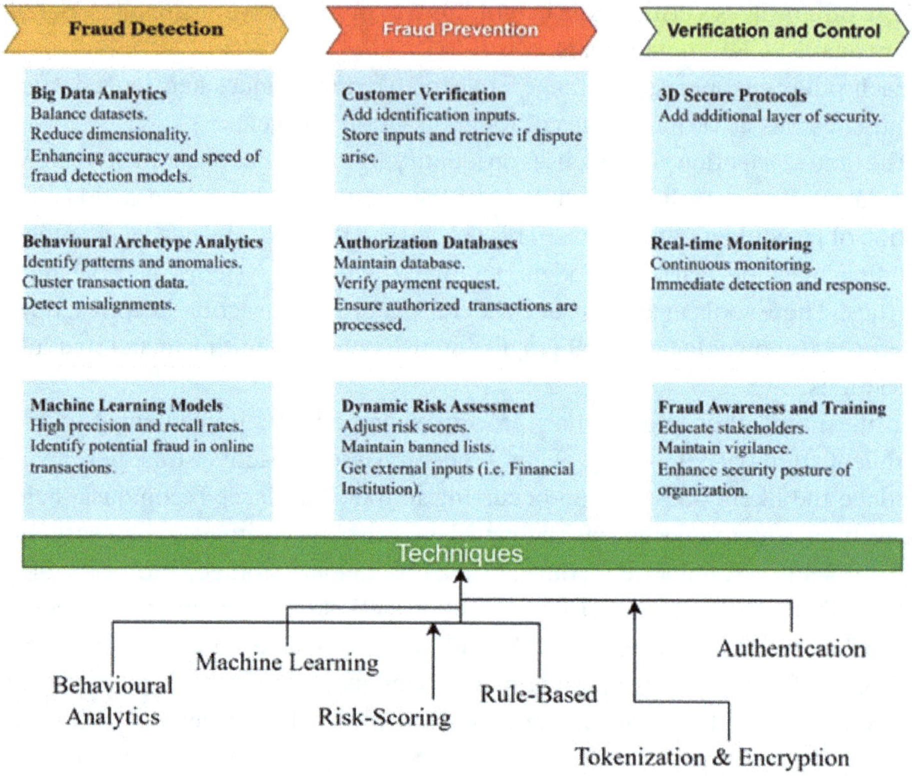

The CNP Transaction Process

The CNP (Card Not Present) transaction process consists of several key components: the Merchant, who offers goods or services; the Cardholder, who uses the payment card; the Acquiring Bank, which processes the transactions; the Issuing Bank, which issues the card; and the Payment Processor, which manages the transaction data (U.S. Payments Forum, 2020). According to the U.S. Payments Forum (2020), this process follows specific steps illustrated in Figure 2. The transaction begins when the Cardholder selects items and checks out on the Merchant's website or a web portal. They enter their card details, which are sent to the payment gateway for processing. The gateway forwards this information to the acquiring bank, which requests authorization from the issuing bank. The issuing bank verifies the cardholder's information and checks for sufficient funds or credit before sending an approval response back through the gateway to the merchant. If approved, the merchant completes the sale, and the cardholder receives transaction confirmation.

Figure 2. CNP Transaction Process

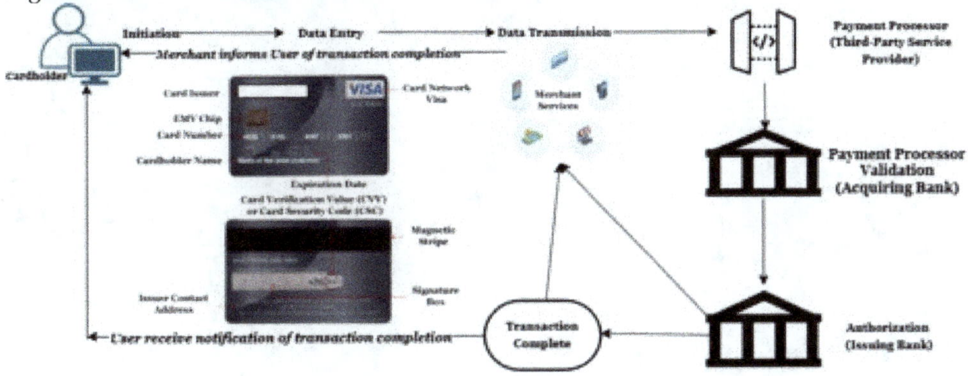

2.0 TECHNIQUES FOR DETECTING AND PREVENTING CARD-NOT-PRESENT (CNP) FRAUD

2.1 Machine Learning (ML) Techniques

Machine Learning (ML) is a subset of artificial intelligence (AI) that focuses on developing algorithms and statistical models that enable computers to perform specific tasks without explicit instructions. Machine learning (ML) algorithms enhance their performance through exposure to data, learning from patterns, and making informed decisions based on acquired knowledge (Cho, 2023; Kumar & Singh, 2024). The primary applications of Machine Learning span a wide array of sectors, notably finance, where it plays a critical role in enhancing security measures against various forms of fraud, such as card-not-present (CNP) fraud. Machine Learning offers powerful data processing capabilities, enabling the detection of complex and evolving fraudulent patterns in near real time (Pan, 2024; Valavan & Rita, 2023). Figure 3 illustrates a machine learning framework for detecting card-not-present (CNP) fraud.

Figure 3. Process Flow of Machine Learning Techniques

The process begins with defining the problem and collecting data to create a dataset that includes legitimate and fraudulent transactions. This dataset features transaction IDs, amounts, locations, and user behaviors. Next is data preprocessing, which addresses issues such as missing values and class imbalance using techniques like Synthetic Minority Over-sampling Technique (SMOTE) (Ren, 2023). After that, feature engineering is conducted to identify patterns of fraud. The next step is model selection and evaluation, focusing on metrics such as accuracy, precision, recall, F1 score, and the Receiver Operating Characteristic - Area Under Curve (ROC-AUC), with an emphasis on minimizing false negatives. Following this, hyperparameter tuning optimizes the models for deployment in real-time analysis. The process concludes with continuous monitoring, updates, and a feedback loop for flagged transactions. These elements are crucial for adapting to evolving fraud tactics (Dorlikar & Mohod, 2024). Various learning techniques are employed in this process, each offering distinct advantages and limitations. Among these, supervised, unsupervised, hybrid, deep learning methods, graph neural networks, feature engineering, and anomaly detection techniques play pivotal roles.

Both Bhattacharyya et al. (2011) and Carcillo et al. (2019) demonstrated the efficacy of supervised machine learning in detecting card-not-present (CNP) fraud. Bhattacharyya et al. leverage random forests and support vector machines, achieving over 95% detection rates with low false positives by analyzing historical transaction features. In contrast, Carcillo et al. utilized logistic regression and gradient boosting on large e-commerce datasets, attaining ROC-AUC scores above 0.90 through extensive feature analysis and hyperparameter tuning. This highlights Bhattacharyya et al.'s focus on detection precision, in contrast to Carcillo et al.'s emphasis on predictive reliability. Lucas et al. (2020) and Fu et al. (2016) explore real-time anomaly detection from an unsupervised perspective. Lucas et al. employed Isolation Forests for effective real-time monitoring and rapid anomaly isolation, reducing fraud losses while incurring a minimal computational burden. Conversely, Fu et al. employ an autoencoder-based approach within a deep learning framework, demonstrating superior recall and ROC-AUC scores by recognizing complex data patterns. While the isolation forest is suitable for low-complexity, real-time detection, the autoencoder excels in high-dimensional settings. The choice between these methods hinges on specific application requirements, including data characteristics and processing constraints. Bahnsen et al. (2016) and Jha et al. (2018) highlighted the effectiveness of hybrid methods in fraud detection by integrating unsupervised and supervised techniques. Bahnsen et al. employed an approach that combined unsupervised anomaly detection with supervised logistic regression, where they first identified suspicious transactions through unsupervised scoring and then confirmed fraud through classification. Their model achieved high precision (over 93%) and recall (around 89%), outperforming standalone methods. Similarly, Jha et al. adopted a two-stage approach that merged unsupervised clustering (k-means) with supervised random forest classification, which improved fraud detection accuracy, increased precision, and reduced false positives compared to individual models. Overall, both studies demonstrate that hybrid methods significantly enhance fraud detection by leveraging the strengths of supervised accuracy and unsupervised adaptability.

Fu et al. (2016) conducted a detailed analysis using advanced deep learning techniques, specifically convolutional neural networks (CNNs) and autoencoders, for automated feature extraction and representation learning from transaction data. Their methodology included rigorous preprocessing of raw transactions into structured matrices suitable for CNN input, with Autoencoders facilitating unsupervised anomaly detection by identifying deviations from standard transaction patterns. The study demonstrated significant enhancements in recall and ROC-AUC metrics compared to conventional machine learning approaches, highlighting the effectiveness of deep learning in fraud detection. Similarly, Mienye et al. (2024) investigated the utility of Long Short-Term Memory (LSTM) networks, focusing on temporal feature engineering to capture the sequential dependencies inherent in transaction behaviors. Their framework involved constructing sequential transaction histories and optimizing hyperparameters through validation datasets. The findings revealed consistently high ROC-AUC scores exceeding 0.97, substantiating the superior capability of deep neural networks in addressing the temporal challenges of card-not-present (CNP) fraud. Collectively, these studies illustrate the transformative role of deep learning methodologies in combating sophisticated fraudulent activities.

Weber et al. (2019) and Wang et al. (2019) both employed Graph neural networks (GNNs) for fraud detection but used different strategies. Weber et al. focused on Graph Convolutional Networks (GCNs) to propagate fraud signals in relationships, achieving ROC-AUC scores over 0.98. In contrast, Wang et al. utilized attention mechanisms for dynamic feature detection, regularly achieving scores around 0.81. This highlights Weber et al.'s emphasis on relational robustness and methodology adaptability. Dal Pozzolo et al. (2014) and Lucas et al. (2020) explored real-time fraud detection using various methods. Dal Pozzolo et al. utilized Online Random Forests for incremental learning, maintaining ROC-AUC scores above 0.90, while Lucas et al. employed unsupervised anomaly detection with Isolation Forest algorithms for efficient anomaly identification. This illustrates the focus of Dal Pozzolo et al. (2014) on performance amid evolving fraud patterns and Lucas et al.'s (2020) emphasis on operational efficiency.

Table 2 examines various machine learning techniques for fraud detection. The results suggest that supervised learning methods, such as logistic regression and gradient boosting, offer high accuracy and interpretability. However, they heavily depend on labelled data and struggle to detect emerging fraud patterns. In contrast, unsupervised methods, such as Isolation Forests and autoencoders, excel at identifying novel fraud without labelled data; however, they are prone to higher false positives and limited explainability. Hybrid methods that combine supervised and unsupervised methods offer a balance of accuracy and adaptability, albeit with increased implementation and computational complexity. Deep learning models, including LSTMs and CNNs, excel at capturing complex sequential and spatial fraud behaviors, but they require large datasets and significant processing power, with limited transparency. Graph Neural Networks are highly effective in detecting organized or relational fraud, achieving outstanding performance; however, they require complex data preprocessing and access to relational data structures. Overall, the choice of technique depends on the availability of data, the need for real-time detection, and the trade-offs between accuracy, complexity, and explainability.

Table 2. Research using machine learning methods

Technique	Source	Method(s)	Strengths	Weaknesses
Supervised Learning	Carcillo et al. (2019)	Logistic Regression, Gradient Boosting	High ROC-AUC (>0.90), robust predictive power, high interpretability	Limited adaptability to emerging or unknown fraud patterns
	Bahnsen et al. (2016)	Logistic Regression (with detailed feature engineering)	Precision >93%, recall ~89%, strong classification performance	Dependence on high-quality labelled data, less flexible over time
Unsupervised Learning	Lucas et al. (2020)	Isolation Forest (Real-time anomaly detection)	Immediate fraud detection, reduced fraud losses, and low computational overhead	Higher false-positive rates, limited interpretability without labelled data
	Fu et al. (2016)	Autoencoder-based unsupervised CNN	Enhanced recall & ROC-AUC, automated anomaly detection capabilities	Requires significant computational resources, complex tuning
Hybrid Methods	Bahnsen et al. (2016)	Logistic Regression (supervised) + Unsupervised Anomaly detection	Combines the advantages of supervised accuracy and unsupervised novelty detection (Precision >93%)	Complexity of implementation, computational overhead
	Jha et al. (2018)	K-means clustering + Random Forest	Improved detection accuracy, precision, and reduced false positives	Increased computational complexity, multi-step modeling process
Deep Learning and Feature Engineering	Mienye et al. (2024)	Long Short-Term Memory (LSTM), temporal feature extraction	Exceptional ROC-AUC (>0.97), effectively captures sequential fraud patterns	Computationally intensive requires substantial amounts of temporal data
	Fu et al. (2016)	Convolutional Neural Networks (CNN), Autoencoder	Automated feature extraction, improved recall & ROC-AUC	High computational cost, complex model interpretability
Graph Neural Networks (GNN)	Weber et al. (2019)	Graph Convolutional Networks (GCNs)	ROC-AUC >0.98, relational modeling, identifies organized fraud networks effectively	High computational requirements, complex data preprocessing needed
	Wang et al. (2019)	Attention-based Graph Neural Networks	High ROC-AUC (>0.81), enhanced interpretability via attention mechanisms	Requires extensive relational data, computational complexity
Anomaly Prevention (Real-Time Models)	Dal Pozzolo et al. (2014)	Online incremental Random Forest (supervised)	Real-time fraud detection, ROC-AUC (~0.90+), adaptive to changes in patterns	Requires ongoing labelled data streams, susceptibility to concept drift
	Lucas et al. (2020)	Isolation Forest (unsupervised, real-time)	Real-time adaptability, efficiency, and reduced fraud losses	Higher false-positive rate, limited explanation of fraud decisions

2.2 Behavioral Analytics Techniques

Behavioral analytics analyzes user interactions and transaction histories to identify irregularities that indicate fraud (Jurgovsky et al., 2018; Carneiro et al., 2017). It assumes that legitimate customers exhibit consistent behaviors, while fraudsters deviate from these patterns (Banga and Pillai 2021; Van Vlasselaer et al., 2015). Techniques include transaction modeling, behavioral profiling, velocity analysis, network analytics, and biometrics to enhance fraud detection (Banga and Pillai 2021; Carneiro et al., 2017).

Sequential Behavioral Modeling: Jurgovsky et al. (2018) used sequential Behavioral analytics with Recurrent Neural Networks (RNN), specifically Long Short-Term Memory (LSTM) networks. They encoded historical transaction sequences (including time, location, device, and purchase frequency) into behavioral models. Deviations from these sequences signaled potential fraud. Their method included temporal feature extraction and pattern learning, achieving ROC-AUC scores over 0.95. This confirmed the effectiveness of sequential modeling in capturing complex fraudulent Behaviors.

Behavioral Profiling and Velocity Analysis: Carneiro et al. (2017) utilized behavioral profiling to examine transaction speeds and spending patterns. They aggregated metrics such as transaction frequency, spending thresholds, and merchant category usage to define user profiles. Transactions deviating from these baselines were flagged for potential fraud. Their real-time approach enhanced the sensitivity of fraud detection, achieving a recall rate of approximately 90%, which significantly surpasses that of traditional methods. The study highlighted the benefits of adaptive profiling in accurately identifying suspicious transactions.

Network-Based Behavioral Analytics: Van Vlasselaer et al. (2015) employed network-based analytics by integrating Social Network Analysis (SNA) with Random Forest machine learning. Their method depicted customer behaviors in transaction networks, emphasizing relational interactions. Abnormal network positions signaled fraudulent activities. They mapped transactional data onto network graphs and applied supervised classification to detect anomalies. Results showed over 92% precision and approximately 85% recall, demonstrating the effectiveness of network-based analytics in detecting organized fraud schemes.

Behavioral Biometrics Analytics: Banga and Pillai (2021) investigated behavioral biometrics in mobile banking to improve security and user experience. They highlighted the continuous monitoring of traits such as keystroke dynamics and voice patterns for seamless user authentication. Machine learning was identified as key for profiling legitimate behavior and detecting anomalies, reducing reliance on static passwords. Notable use cases included Royal Bank of Scotland and Citi. The study projected market growth to USD 9.33 billion by 2022, while also addressing privacy, ethical, and technical hurdles for broader adoption.

The analysis in Table 3 suggests that behavioral analytics significantly enhances fraud detection by analyzing user interactions, rather than relying solely on static rules. Techniques such as LSTM-based analytics capture evolving transaction behaviors but require extensive historical data and processing power, which can limit their real-time use. Methods focusing on transaction velocity offer quick detection but require regular updates to avoid concept drift. Network-based analytics is effective for identifying collusive fraud but relies on rich data, whereas behavioral biometrics enhance authentication but raise privacy concerns. It is essential to consider both the technical capabilities and the ethical implications involved when implementing these dynamic fraud detection systems.

Table 3. Research Utilizing Behavioral Analytics Techniques

Source	Method	Technique	Strengths	Weaknesses
Jurgovsky et al. (2018)	Sequential Behavioral Analytics	Recurrent Neural Networks (LSTM)	High ROC-AUC (>0.95), capturing complex temporal transaction patterns and sensitive to subtle fraud behaviors.	High computational intensity, extensive historical data required
Carneiro et al. (2017)	Behavioral Profiling	Transaction Velocity & Spending Pattern Analysis	High recall (~90%), effective real-time fraud detection, and adaptive to spending deviations	Vulnerability to concept drift requires continual updating.
Van Vlasselaer et al. (2015)	Network-Based Behavioral Analytics	Social Network Analysis (SNA), Random Forest	High precision (>92%), effective against organized/coordinated fraud schemes, relational modeling	Complex data preprocessing, computationally intensive
Banga & Pillai (2021)	Behavioral Biometrics	Device Fingerprinting, Typing Patterns,	Royal Bank of Scotland: Deployed behavioral biometrics in 2016, expanded to 18.7 million customers by 2018.	Ethical/privacy concerns, additional biometric data collection complexity

2.3 Rule-Based Techniques

Rule-based fraud detection methods employ predefined conditions, thresholds, and logical criteria established by domain experts to identify fraudulent transactions. These rules are typically based on known indicators of fraud, historical patterns of fraud, transaction limits, geographical constraints, velocity checks, merchant categories, and other transactional parameters. Transactions that meet or violate these conditions trigger fraud alerts or transaction denials, facilitating immediate responses without relying heavily on statistical or machine learning methods (Carneiro et al.,

2017). Rule-based approaches are widely used in CNP fraud detection due to their interpretability, simplicity, ease of implementation, and real-time decision-making capabilities. These systems offer immediate protection by flagging suspicious transactions based on clear, predefined rules. However, their effectiveness heavily depends on continuous updates and refinement to adapt to evolving fraud patterns, as rigid or static rule systems quickly become ineffective against adaptive fraudulent strategies (Lucas et al., 2020).

The integration of traditional rule-based techniques with machine learning and data mining has markedly improved fraud detection in Card-not-present (CNP) transactions. Dal Pozzolo et al. (2017) combined rule-based alerts with Random Forest classifiers, achieving a ROC-AUC of approximately 0.91; however, they noted that rule-based methods struggle to adapt to evolving fraud patterns. Carneiro et al. (2017) demonstrated that hybridizing traditional rule-based systems with data mining improved precision and recall from 70% to 75% to 90%. Lucas et al. (2020) found that while rule-based techniques achieved approximately 80% precision, they encountered high false positives, which anomaly detection methods, such as Isolation Forest, effectively mitigated. Overall, these studies demonstrate that combining rule-based techniques with machine learning and data mining yields improved accuracy, adaptability, and reduced false positive rates in real-time fraud detection.

Analysis in Table 4 indicates that rule-based systems remain relevant for fraud detection due to their simplicity, transparency, and ability to make prompt decisions, particularly in critical, real-time settings. However, their rigid structure and limited learning capacity make them vulnerable to changes in concepts and emerging fraud trends. Hybrid and adaptive versions enhance responsiveness and accuracy but require additional resources, advanced technical skills, and human involvement. A rule-based system's success hinges on its ability to adapt over time, whether through data-driven improvements or expert feedback, suggesting that a hybrid or adaptive strategy provides the optimal balance of accuracy, flexibility, and practical application.

Table 4. Studies employing Rule-Based Technique

Source	Method	Technique	Strengths	Weaknesses
Carneiro et al. (2017)	Traditional Rule-Based vs Data Mining	Transaction velocity rules, merchant category rules, and spending thresholds	Simple implementation, good baseline precision/ recall (70–75%), immediate decision-making capability	Limited adaptability, moderate false positives when used alone
Lucas et al. (2020)	Rule-Based vs Isolation Forest	Velocity and geographical restriction rules	Effective in detecting known fraud types (precision ~80%), rapid real-time decisions	High false-positive rate, rigidity, limited ability to detect new fraud behaviors

2.4 Risk-Scoring Techniques

Risk-scoring techniques are analytical methods that assess the likelihood of a transaction being fraudulent by assigning numerical scores based on various attributes such as transaction amount, frequency, user behavior history, geographical location, device information, and velocity. These scores enable businesses and financial institutions to determine whether to approve, decline, or investigate a transaction (Dal Pozzolo et al., 2014; Carneiro et al., 2017). Risk-scoring methods outperform traditional binary-rule systems by providing varying degrees of risk, enabling more tailored responses, such as verification or transaction blocking. However, their effectiveness depends on accurate, continually updated models that adapt to evolving fraudulent behaviors.

Dal Pozzolo et al. (2014) showed that risk-scoring techniques based on incremental learning using Online Random Forests significantly enhanced fraud detection, achieving high ROC-AUC scores around 0.90. This method yielded fewer false positives and improved responsiveness to evolving fraud patterns, underscoring the importance of continuous updates and real-time adaptability. In a similar vein, Carneiro et al. (2017) found that a risk-scoring framework driven by behavioral analytics significantly increased detection sensitivity, achieving a recall rate of approximately 90%, thereby surpassing traditional rule-based approaches. Their integration of real-time user behavioral profiling and risk indicators effectively reduced false positives while capturing subtle instances of fraudulent activity. Their results highlighted the essential role of ongoing adaptability and the incorporation of human expertise in creating effective fraud detection systems.

Table 5 illustrates that contemporary risk-scoring systems for fraud detection and prevention are becoming more adaptive, real-time, and behaviorally aware. These systems integrate machine learning, established rules, and human feedback to enhance their performance. Although incremental and behavioral models offer significant automation and adaptability, they often encounter challenges related to computational demands or managing data streams. On the other hand, hybrid and analyst-driven systems ensure interpretability and strategic flexibility but require greater human oversight and added complexity. The most successful risk-scoring models achieve a balance between dynamic adaptability, detection performance, and operational feasibility. A hybrid or layered method that pairs automated scoring with expert supervision may deliver the most vigorous defence, particularly in rapidly changing fraud environments where both data-driven insights and domain knowledge are crucial.

Table 5. Studies on Risk-Scoring Techniques

Source	Method	Techniques	Strengths	Weaknesses
Dal Pozzolo et al. (2014)	Incremental Learning-based Risk Scoring	Online Random Forest (incremental learning, real-time risk scoring)	High ROC-AUC (~0.90), dynamic adaptability, real-time responsiveness, reduced false positives	Computationally intensive requires continuous labeled data streams
Carneiro et al. (2017)	Behavioral Analytics-based Risk Scoring	Transaction velocity analysis, behavioral profiling, merchant risk scores	High recall (~90%), captures subtle behavioral anomalies, reduces false positives effectively	Requires continuous user-profile updating, moderate implementation complexity

2.5 Authentication Techniques

Authentication refers to the process of verifying an individual's or entity's identity to ensure legitimacy before granting access to protected systems, services, or transactions (Raza et al., 2020; Alzubaidi & Kalita, 2016). Authentication methods typically involve something a user knows (e.g., password), something they have (e.g., tokens or mobile devices), something they are (biometrics), or a combination thereof (multi-factor authentication). Effective authentication reduces unauthorized access and fraud, which is especially critical in financial transactions and e-commerce environments (Alzubaidi & Kalita, 2016).

Raza et al. (2020) demonstrated that multi-factor authentication (MFA), integrating passwords, One-Time Passwords (OTPs), and biometric fingerprint recognition, enhances security in Card-not-present (CNP) transactions, reducing successful fraud attempts by 95% compared to single-factor authentication. Alzubaidi and Kalita (2016) demonstrated that adaptive authentication frameworks, which adjust methods based on context, resulted in an 85% reduction in fraud, despite challenges in real-time risk assessment. Yousefi et al. (2019) found that integrating behavioral biometric authentication with traditional machine learning improved fraud detection accuracy, though privacy and dataset size challenges remain. Hernandez Aros et al. (2024) emphasized the effectiveness of advanced machine learning techniques, while Pumsirirat and Yan (2018) discussed the challenges of deep learning methods related to dataset imbalance. Jurgovsky et al. (2018) acknowledged the advantages of recurrent neural networks for fraud detection but pointed out issues with interpretability. Despite implementation complexities, Carcillo et al. (2021) introduced an active learning framework that improved accuracy and reduced labelling effort. These studies collectively highlight significant advancements in fraud detection methodologies while addressing persistent ethical and practical challenges in their application.

The analysis in Table 6 highlights a clear trade-off between authentication security and user convenience in preventing card-not-present (CNP) fraud. Multi-factor authentication significantly reduces fraud but can negatively affect user experience due to increased complexity. Behavioral biometric authentication offers continuous, highly accurate detection, though ethical and privacy concerns related to continuous monitoring must be addressed carefully. Adaptive authentication methods effectively balance convenience and security, reducing fraud by dynamically adjusting authentication based on transaction risk. However, these approaches demand advanced real-time assessments and user acceptance management. Machine learning enhanced authentication methods significantly improve accuracy but require substantial computational resources and ongoing model maintenance. Active learning-based frameworks efficiently enhance accuracy with less manual labeling but involve ongoing operational complexity. Ultimately, integrating adaptive, behavioral biometric, and multi-factor authentication, supported by machine learning and active learning, provides an optimal solution balancing security, user convenience, and adaptability in CNP fraud prevention.

Table 6. Studies on Authentication Techniques

Source	Method	Techniques	Strengths	Weaknesses
Raza et al. (2020)	Multi-factor Authentication	Password, OTP, and Biometric fingerprint	High security; reduced fraud (~95%)	Reduced user convenience, potential resistance
Alzubaidi & Kalita (2016)	Adaptive Authentication	Risk-based adaptive authentication levels	Fraud reduction (~85%), balances security & convenience	Real-time risk assessment complexity, user acceptance challenges
Banga & Pillai (2021)	Behavioral Biometrics	Device fingerprinting, typing/navigation patterns	Continuous authentication, reducing fraud significantly	Privacy concerns due to continuous monitoring
Yousefi et al. (2019)	Behavioral Biometrics & ML	Behavioral biometric authentication integrated with ML models	High accuracy, reduced false positives, comprehensive user profiling	Implementation complexity, privacy concerns, and requires extensive datasets
Hernandez Aros et al. (2024)	Authentication with ML Techniques	ML-enhanced authentication approaches	Improved fraud detection accuracy, adaptability to evolving threats	Requires continual model updates, high computational complexity
Pumsirirat & Yan (2018)	Deep Learning Authentication	Autoencoder & Restricted Boltzmann Machines	Enhanced accuracy, effective detection of complex fraud patterns	Data imbalance challenges, high computational resources needed

continued on following page

Table 6. Continued

Source	Method	Techniques	Strengths	Weaknesses
Jurgovsky et al. (2018)	Sequence-based Authentication	Recurrent Neural Networks (RNNs)	Effective temporal fraud pattern detection, improved accuracy	Model interpretability challenges, extensive tuning required
Carcillo et al. (2021)	Active Learning Authentication	Active learning for iterative authentication model refinement	Reduced labelling effort, high practicality, improved fraud detection	Operational complexity requires expert data scientist collaboration

2.6 Tokenization and Encryption Techniques

Tokenization is replacing sensitive data, such as credit or debit card numbers, with unique, non-sensitive identifiers called tokens that retain no exploitable meaning or value. The actual sensitive data is stored securely in a token vault and never appears in the payment environment (PCI SSC, 2020). **Encryption**, on the other hand, is a cryptographic method that converts plaintext data into unreadable ciphertext using algorithms and keys. Only authorized parties with the correct key can decrypt the data, securing it during storage and transmission.

Tokenization is essential in preventing fraud by ensuring that intercepted transaction data remains meaningless without access to a secure vault.

Conversely, encryption transforms card data into an unreadable format requiring a decryption key. Finally, Raza et al. (2020) found that combining Advanced Encryption Standard (AES) encryption with Transport Layer Security (TLS) significantly reduced data breaches in online payment gateways.

The analysis of results in Tables 7 and 8 indicates that both tokenization and encryption are crucial yet complementary methods for securing CNP transactions. Tokenization not only enhances the protection of stored data but also reduces regulatory exposure (PCI DSS) and is especially effective in cloud or mobile payment systems. On the other hand, encryption protects sensitive information during transit and ensures strong confidentiality, particularly when used with secure communication protocols and lightweight cryptography. While tokenization helps mitigate fraud after a breach and eases compliance, encryption is vital for the initial safeguarding of data and its secure transmission. When these techniques are combined with behavioral analytics or biometric verification, they bolster frameworks for preventing CNP fraud. Academic research consistently advocates for their combined use as part of layered security approaches in digital payment environments.

Table 7. Tokenization Studies

Source	Method	Techniques	Strengths	Weaknesses
Wang & Chang (2018)	Comparative analysis	Tokenization vs. Encryption in the cloud	Reduced PCI DSS compliance scope; lower fraud risk	Limited to data-at-rest; does not protect in-transit data

Table 8. Encryption Studies

Source	Method	Techniques	Strengths	Weaknesses
Raza et al. (2020)	Comparative cryptographic analysis	AES + TLS encryption in CNP systems	Significantly reduced breach risks and fraud exposure	High implementation and maintenance overhead

3.0 ANALYTICAL COMPARISON OF CNP FRAUD TECHNIQUES

The comparison of detection techniques summarized in Table 9 shows that no single method can completely address the full range of CNP (Card-Not-Present) fraud risks. Machine learning and behavioral analytics are powerful tools for proactive fraud detection, allowing for the identification of both known and emerging fraud patterns. Rule-based systems and risk-scoring techniques enhance real-time decision-making by prioritizing high-risk transactions and reducing false positives. Moreover, authentication methods improve identity verification, preventing unauthorized access, while tokenization and encryption provide essential data security, safeguarding sensitive information from breaches. The most effective approach is a layered and hybrid strategy that combines various techniques to create overlapping layers of defense. This strategy should start with encryption and tokenization at the data layer, integrate strong authentication measures for identity verification, and utilize adaptive rule-based systems alongside risk-scoring for transaction assessment. Additionally, it should include advanced analytics, such as machine learning and behavioral monitoring, for continuous threat detection.

In conclusion, the analysis reveals that each technique employed to mitigate Card-Not-Present (CNP) fraud addresses distinct facets of the problem while simultaneously presenting intrinsic limitations that preclude them from functioning as isolated solutions. An effective anti-fraud strategy necessitates the integration of complementary methodologies. This approach should harness the analytical capabilities of machine learning and behavioral analytics, the precision and efficiency of rule-based and risk-scoring systems, the rigorous identity verification offered by authentication mechanisms, and the foundational data protection provided through tokenization and encryption. Such a multifaceted and adaptable framework establishes a comprehensive and resilient defense against the dynamic threats posed by CNP fraud. The implementation of a layered security architecture ensures redundancy; should one layer be circumvented, alternative defenses remain operational, thereby facilitating adaptability in response to the evolving tactics employed by fraudsters.

Table 9. Comparison of CNP Fraud Techniques

Technique	Overview	Key Strengths	Key Limitations	Use Cases	Gaps
Machine Learning (ML) Techniques	Utilizes data-driven approaches, including supervised, unsupervised, and hybrid learning, to identify and predict fraud.	High accuracy, adaptability, and effective for large datasets.	Computationally intensive tasks require labelled data and address interpretability issues.	Effective environments with sufficient labelled data and high transaction volume, enabling the prevention of known fraud patterns.	Limited interpretability, challenges in detecting entirely new fraud patterns, and high computational requirements.
Behavioral Analytics Techniques	Analyzes user behavior patterns (e.g., location, device, session characteristics) to detect anomalies.	Context-aware, high-accuracy in identifying account takeovers.	Can produce false positives with legitimate behavior changes, and privacy concerns.	Best for identifying deviations in typical user behavior patterns, detecting account takeovers, and high-risk transactions.	Privacy concerns, limited interpretability of behavioral changes, and a potentially high rate of false positives.
Rule-Based Techniques	Relies on predefined rules to flag suspicious transactions based on historical patterns and expert input.	Simple, interpretable, and effective for static, known fraud patterns.	Static nature cannot adapt to evolving fraud tactics, making it prone to circumvention.	Ideal in environments with predictable fraud patterns and for initial layers of fraud prevention, where rules can be easily set.	Lacks flexibility requires regular updates to manage new fraud tactics and has limited effectiveness for complex fraud.

continued on following page

Table 9. Continued

Technique	Overview	Key Strengths	Key Limitations	Use Cases	Gaps
Risk-Scoring Techniques	Assigns a risk score based on factors like transaction amount, user history, and behavior to prioritize cases.	Real-time adaptability, effective in prioritizing transactions, and a low false positive rate in hybrid methods.	Computationally intensive; needs high-quality, frequently updated data.	Suitable for real-time scoring in high-transaction environments, enabling prioritization and efficient fraud prevention.	Dependent on continuous data quality, resource-intensive for real-time processing, and high setup complexity.
Authentication Techniques	Uses multiple layers of authentication (e.g., MFA, biometrics) to validate user identity before transactions.	High security, as it is difficult for attackers to bypass when layers are combined (e.g., biometrics with MFA).	Potential for friction in user experience; privacy concerns with biometrics.	Effective for high-security transaction environments, multi-layered identity verification, and user protection.	Users experience friction, privacy issues with biometrics, and vulnerability to social engineering for some methods.
Tokenization and Encryption Techniques	Replaces or scrambles sensitive data to protect it from unauthorized access.	Effective at reducing attack surface, supports compliance (e.g., PCI DSS), and protects data in transit and at rest.	Tokenization can create single points of failure, while encryption requires complex key management.	Helpful in securing sensitive data in compliance-heavy environments and protecting data during transactions or at rest.	Scalability challenges in high-volume transactions, high dependency on secure key management, and complexity in setup.

3.1 Emerging Techniques

Recent advancements in CNP fraud mitigation are increasingly leveraging artificial intelligence (AI) methods that prioritize both privacy and resource efficiency. For instance, Deng and Chen (2025) introduced a transformer-based model with a Graph Self-Attention (GSA) mechanism, which enhanced precision by 20% and AUC by 2.7% compared to traditional models, making it well-suited for high-volume payment systems. Zaffar et al. (2023) addressed class imbalance in credit card fraud detection using a subspace learning-based one-class classification technique, enabling effective detection from limited fraud samples without the need for extensive labeled datasets. Simultaneously, Xiang et al. (2024) proposed a semi-supervised GNN using temporal transaction graphs, outpacing conventional classifiers in identifying new fraud patterns amidst sparse labeled data.

Carcillo et al. (2021) developed an innovative active learning framework aimed at enhancing detection accuracy within security contexts. This framework strategically prioritizes the most informative transactions, thereby improving the efficiency of the detection process while simultaneously minimizing the costs associated with labeling. By focusing on high-value data points for analysis, the proposed method not only optimizes resource allocation but also increases the overall effectiveness of security measures.

A promising advancement is Federated Learning (FL), enabling banks and e-commerce platforms to collaboratively train fraud detection models without sharing raw data (Yang et al., 2019; Li et al., 2020). This framework facilitates the sharing of cross-organizational intelligence while adhering to data protection regulations, such as the General Data Protection Regulation (GDPR) and PCI DSS. Furthermore, integrating FL with differential privacy (McMahan et al., 2018) and secure multi-party computation (Bonawitz et al., 2017) enhances confidentiality and robustness against distributed fraud patterns.

The cumulative impact of these innovations represents a significant paradigm shift towards the development of real-time, adaptive, and collaborative frameworks for the mitigation of fraudulent activities. These advancements effectively confront several critical challenges, including data sparsity, privacy preservation, and class imbalance. Collectively, they establish a foundation for more robust and effective strategies aimed at combating Card Not Present (CNP) fraud, thereby enhancing the overall efficacy of fraud prevention methodologies.

4.0 CONCLUSION AND FUTURE RESEARCH DIRECTIONS

CNP (Card Not Present) fraud represents a formidable challenge within the dynamic framework of digital payment systems, largely attributable to the burgeoning volume of global financial transactions. Effectively addressing this multifaceted issue necessitates a comprehensive understanding of diverse fraud detection methodologies, each exhibiting unique strengths and limitations in relation to adaptability, scalability, interpretability, and adherence to privacy regulations. A singular approach to fraud detection is inadequate; rather, the implementation of a layered, defense-in-depth strategy that integrates multiple detection techniques is paramount for robust and effective fraud prevention. This multifarious approach not only enhances the resilience of fraud mitigation efforts but also aligns with the evolving regulatory landscape and the need for consumer privacy.

While these methodologies present various potential advantages, they also encounter significant challenges that warrant attention. Key issues include the necessity for high-quality data to drive effective outcomes, alongside concerns pertaining to user privacy and data security. Continuous research is imperative for the advancement of robust fraud prevention systems aimed at enhancing detection capabilities, while simultaneously prioritizing privacy and user-friendliness. Such innovations are critical in addressing the dynamic landscape of Card-Not-Present (CNP) fraud, thus ensuring the integrity of digital payment systems. Recommendations for future research directions include:

- **Enhancement of Machine Learning Algorithms:** There is a need to design more adaptive and context-aware machine learning models capable of responding dynamically to emerging fraud patterns in real time (Qu & Jin, 2023). Future research should advance beyond static model deployment by exploring advanced deep learning architectures such as recurrent neural networks and graph neural networks. Additionally, developing hybrid learning frameworks that integrate supervised, unsupervised, and reinforcement learning approaches is essential.
- **Data Privacy and Ethical Considerations:** As fraud detection systems become more data-driven, there is a growing need to incorporate privacy-by-design principles into architecture (Banga & Pillai, 2021). Future studies ought to explore privacy-preserving computation methods such as federated learning, homomorphic encryption, and differential privacy to enable model training without exposing sensitive user data.
- **Integration of Multi-Sector Collaboration:** Cross-sector collaboration among banking, insurance, e-commerce, payment processors, and law enforcement is essential for large-scale CNP fraud prevention. Future research should prioritize developing standardized, secure threat intelligence platforms that enable stakeholders to share fraud indicators and patterns in near real-time. (Razaque et al., 2022).
- **Advancements in Behavioral Analytics:** Behavioral analytics has the potential to significantly differentiate between legitimate and fraudulent transactions by capturing subtle, context-specific anomalies in user interaction patterns (Carneiro et al., 2017; Van Vlasselaer et al., 2015). To advance the field, future works should develop multi-modal behavioral profiling systems that integrate device fingerprints, geolocation, navigation flows, transaction sequencing, and biometric inputs.

- **Investigating New Technologies:** Exploring the capabilities of blockchain and distributed ledger technologies could provide immutable, transparent, and tamper-resistant transaction logs that improve auditability and trust (Chen, 2024). Research should explore the combination of blockchain with advancements in encryption techniques and next-generation biometric authentication that utilize AI for enhanced accuracy.
- **User-Centric Fraud Prevention:** Fraud prevention strategies need to balance security with user experience to avoid high abandonment rates and maintain customer satisfaction. Future research should explore adaptive authentication systems that adjust security requirements based on transaction risk and behavior.

By focusing on these areas, researchers and practitioners can develop more resilient, efficient, and user-friendly solutions to mitigate CNP fraud.

REFERENCES

Akazue, M., Debekeme, I., Edje, A., Asuai, C., & Osame, U. (2023). Unmasking fraudsters: Ensemble features selection to enhance random forest fraud detection. J. *Computing Theories and Applications*, *1*(2), 201–211. DOI: 10.33633/jcta.v1i2.9462

Akdemir, N., & Yenal, S. (2020). Card-not-present fraud victimization: A routine activities approach to understanding the risk factors. [Journal of Security Sciences]. *Güvenlik Bilimleri Dergisi*, *9*(1), 243–268. DOI: 10.28956/gbd.736179

Alzubaidi, A., & Kalita, J. (2016). Authentication of Smartphone Users Using Behavioral Biometrics. *IEEE Communications Surveys and Tutorials*, *18*(3), 1998–2026. DOI: 10.1109/COMST.2016.2537748

Bahnsen, A. C., Aouada, D., Ottersten, B., & Stojanovic, A. (2016). Feature Engineering Strategies for Credit Card Fraud Detection. *Expert Systems with Applications*, *51*, 134–142. DOI: 10.1016/j.eswa.2015.12.030

Banga, L., & Pillai, S. (2021). Impact of behavioural biometrics on mobile banking system. In *Journal of physics: Conference series* (Vol. 1964, No. 6, p. 062109). IOP Publishing. https://iopscience.iop.org/article/10.1088/1742-6596/1964/6/062109/pdf

Bello, O. A., Folorunso, A., Onwuchekwa, J., Ejiofor, O. E., Budale, F. Z., & Egwuonwu, M. N. (2023). Analysing the impact of advanced analytics on fraud detection: A machine learning perspective. *European Journal of Computer Science and Information Technology*, *11*(6), 103–126. https://www.researchgate.net/publication/381548526_Analysing_the_Impact_of_Advanced_Analytics_on_Fraud_Detection_A_Machine_Learning_Perspective

Bhattacharyya, S., Jha, S., Tharakunnel, K., & Westland, J. C. (2011). Data mining for credit card fraud: A comparative study. *Decision Support Systems*, *50*(3), 602–613. Advance online publication. DOI: 10.1016/j.dss.2010.08.008

Bodker, A., Connolly, P., Sing, O., Hutchins, B., Townsley, M., & Drew, J. (2022). Card-not-present fraud: Using crime scripts to inform crime prevention initiatives. Security Journal, 36(4), 693-711. ttps://link.springer.com/article/10.1057/s41284-022-00359-w

Bonawitz, K., Ivanov, V., Kreuter, B., Marcedone, A., McMahan, H. B., Patel, S., & Seth, K. (2017). Practical secure aggregation for privacy-preserving machine learning. *Proceedings of the 2017 ACM SIGSAC Conference on Computer and Communications Security*, 1175–1191. https://doi.org/DOI: 10.1145/3133956.3133982

Carcillo, F., Dal Pozzolo, A., Le Borgne, Y. A., Caelen, O., & Bontempi, G. (2021). Combining Unsupervised and Supervised Learning in Credit Card Fraud Detection: Active Learning Framework. *Information Sciences*, *12*(1), 81–95. DOI: 10.1016/j.ins.2019.05.042

Carcillo, F., Le Borgne, Y. A., Caelen, O., Kessaci, Y., Oblé, F., & Bontempi, G. (2019). Combining Unsupervised and Supervised Learning in Credit Card Fraud Detection. *Information Sciences*, *557*, 317–331. DOI: 10.1016/j.ins.2019.05.042

Carneiro, N., Figueira, G., & Costa, M. (2017). A data mining based system for credit-card fraud detection in e-tail. *Decision Support Systems*, *95*, 91–101. DOI: 10.1016/j.dss.2017.01.002

Chen, J. (2024). LightGBM model for detecting fraud in online financial transactions. Highlights in Science. *Engineering and Technology*, *93*, 363–371. DOI: 10.54097/xw0bng93

Cho, S. (2023). Fraud detection in Malaysian financial institutions using data mining and machine learning. *Journal of Information Technology*, *7*(1), 13–21. DOI: 10.53819/81018102t4152

Dal Pozzolo, A., Caelen, O., Johnson, R. A., & Bontempi, G. (2017). Calibrating Probability with Undersampling for Unbalanced Classification. IEEE Symposium Series on Computational Intelligence (SSCI), 159–166. https://dalpozz.github.io/static/pdf/SSCI_calib_final_noCC.pdf

Dal Pozzolo, A., Caelen, O., Le Borgne, Y. A., Waterschoot, S., & Bontempi, G. (2014). Learned Lessons in Credit Card Fraud Detection from a Practitioner Perspective. *Expert Systems with Applications*, *41*(10), 4915–4928. DOI: 10.1016/j.eswa.2014.02.026

Deng, Z., & Chen, J. (2025). Real-time Fraud Detection Using Cloud-Optimized Transformer Models. arXiv preprint arXiv:2501.19267. https://arxiv.org/abs/2501.19267

Dorlikar, R., & Mohod, S. W. (2024). A Review on Robust Credit Card Fraud Detection System Leveraging Big Data and Machine Learning. https://doi.org/DOI: 10.32628/IJSRSET2411425

European Central Bank. (2023). *Report on card fraud in 2020 and 2021*. ECB., DOI: 10.2866/531174

Fu, K., Cheng, D., Tu, Y., & Zhang, L. (2016). Credit Card Fraud Detection Using Convolutional Neural Networks and Autoencoders. *Proceedings of the International Conference on Neural Information Processing (ICONIP)*, 483-490. DOI: DOI: 10.1007/978-3-319-46675-0_53

Hernandez Aros, L., Bustamante Molano, L. X., Gutierrez-Portela, F., Moreno Hernandez, J. J., & Rodríguez Barrero, M. S. (2024). Financial fraud detection through the application of machine learning techniques: A literature review. *Humanities & Social Sciences Communications*, *11*(1), 1–22. DOI: 10.1057/s41599-024-03606-0

Jha, S., Guillen, M., & Westland, J. C. (2018). Employing Transaction Aggregation Strategy to Detect Credit Card Fraud. *Expert Systems with Applications*, *39*(16), 12650–12657. DOI: 10.1016/j.eswa.2012.05.018

Jurgovsky, J., Granitzer, M., Ziegler, K., Calabretto, S., Portier, P. E., He-Guelton, L., & Caelen, O. (2018). Sequence classification for credit-card fraud detection. *Expert Systems with Applications*, *100*, 234–245. DOI: 10.1016/j.eswa.2018.01.037

Kumar, D., & Singh, S. (2024). Analyzing the impact of machine learning algorithms on risk management and fraud detection in financial institutions. *International Journal of Research Publication and Reviews*, *5*(5), 1797–1804. DOI: 10.55248/gengpi.5.0524.1135

Li, T., Sahu, A. K., Talwalkar, A., & Smith, V. (2020). Federated learning: Challenges, methods, and future directions. *IEEE Signal Processing Magazine*, *37*(3), 50–60. DOI: 10.1109/MSP.2020.2975749

McMahan, H. B., Ramage, D., Talwar, K., & Zhang, L. (2018). Learning differentially private recurrent language models. *International Conference on Learning Representations (ICLR)*. https://arxiv.org/abs/1710.06963

Mekterović, I., Karan, M., Pintar, D., & Brkić, L. (2021). Credit card fraud detection in card-not-present transactions: where to invest?. Applied Sciences, 11(15), 6766. ttps://DOI: 10.3390/app11156766

Mienye, I. D., & Jere, N. (2024). Deep learning for credit card fraud detection: A review of algorithms, challenges, and solutions. *IEEE Access*. https://ieeexplore.ieee.org/stamp/stamp.jsp?arnumber=10595068

Pan, E. (2024). Machine learning in financial transaction fraud detection and prevention. *TEBMR*, *5*, 243–249. DOI: 10.62051/16r3aa10

Pumsirirat, A., & Yan, L. (2018). Credit Card Fraud Detection Using Deep Learning Based on Auto-Encoder and Restricted Boltzmann Machine. *International Journal of Advanced Computer Science and Applications*, *9*(1), 18–25. DOI: 10.14569/IJACSA.2018.090103

Qu, Y. and Jin, J. (2023). Credit Card Fraud Detection Prediction: A Machine Learning Algorithm, 760-767. https://doi.org/DOI: 10.2991/978-94-6463-256-9_77

Raza, M., Iqbal, M. W., Sharif, M., & Haider, W. (2020). A Survey of Password Attacks and Comparative Analysis on Methods for Secure Authentication. https://www.researchgate.net/publication/236898951_A_Survey_of_Password_Attacks_and_Comparative_Analysis_on_Methods_for_Secure_Authentication

Razaque, A., Frej, M., Bektemyssova, G., Amsaad, F., Almiani, M., Alotaibi, A., Jhanjhi, N. Z., Amanzholova, S., & Alshammari, M. (2022). Credit card-not-present fraud prevention and prevention using big data analytics algorithms. *Applied Sciences (Basel, Switzerland)*, *13*(1), 57. DOI: 10.3390/app13010057

Ren, Y. (2023). Application of Machine Learning Algorithms in Detecting Credit Card Fraud: A Comparative Analysis. Highlights in Business. *Economics and Management*, *21*, 733–739. DOI: 10.54097/hbem.v21i.14753

Report, N. (2025, January 6). Payment card fraud losses approach $34 billion. *Nilson Report / Globe Newswire*. ttps://www.globenewswire.com/news-release/2025/01/06/3004931/0/en/Payment-Card-Fraud-Losses-Approach-34-Billion.html

U.S. Census Bureau. (2021). *Computer and Internet Use in the United States:* https://www.census.gov/newsroom/press-releases/2024/computer-internet-use-2021.html?utm_campaign=20240618pios1&utm_medium=email&utm_source=govdelivery

U.S. Payments Forum. (2020). *Card-not-present fraud mitigation techniques*. U.S. Payments Forum. https://www.uspaymentsforum.org/wp-content/uploads/2020/07/CNP-Fraud-Mitigation-Techniques-WP-FINAL-July-2020.pdf

Valavan, M., & Rita, S. (2023). Predictive-analysis-based machine learning model for fraud detection with boosting classifiers. *Computer Systems Science and Engineering*, *45*(1), 231–245. DOI: 10.32604/csse.2023.026508

Van Vlasselaer, V., Bravo, C., Caelen, O., Eliassi-Rad, T., Akoglu, L., Snoeck, M., & Baesens, B. (2015). APATE: A novel approach for automated credit card transaction fraud detection using network-based extensions. *Decision Support Systems*, *75*, 38–48. DOI: 10.1016/j.dss.2015.04.013

Wang, D., Lin, J., Cui, P., Jia, Q., Wang, Z., Fang, Y., . . . Qi, Y. (2019, November). A semi-supervised graph attentive network for financial fraud detection. In *2019 IEEE international conference on data mining (ICDM)* (pp. 598-607). IEEE. https://ieeexplore.ieee.org/stamp/stamp.jsp?arnumber=8970829&casa_token=Xr1fyJEF1E8AAAAA:I37nodCaZ3MCUMcbOh0Nia-74uHfFsrP3oc2EQKKSIFe7Klgm4dNKI1heUFb7sMxHEjLbaplLc4t

Weber, M., Domeniconi, G., Chen, J., Weidele, D. K. I., Bellei, C., Robinson, T., & Leiserson, C. E. (2019). Anti-Money Laundering in Bitcoin: Experimenting with Graph Convolutional Networks for Financial Forensics. Proceedings of the ACM SIGKDD International Conference on Knowledge Discovery & Data Mining (KDD), 68-77. https://arxiv.org/pdf/1908.02591

Xiang, D., Wang, H., & Zhao, X. (2024). Temporal Transaction Graphs for Fraud Detection via Semi-Supervised Learning. https://doi.org/DOI: 10.1609/aaai.v37i12.26702

Yang, Q., Liu, Y., Chen, T., & Tong, Y. (2019). Federated machine learning: Concept and applications. *ACM Transactions on Intelligent Systems and Technology*, *10*(2), 1–19. DOI: 10.1145/3298981

Yousefi, N., Alaghband, M. R., & Garibay, I. (2019). A Comprehensive Survey on Machine Learning Techniques and User Authentication Approaches for Credit Card Fraud Detection. https://arxiv.org/pdf/1912.02629

Zaffar, Z., Sohrab, F., Kanniainen, J., & Gabbouj, M. (2023, December). Credit Card Fraud Detection with Subspace Learning-Based One-Class Classification. In *2023 IEEE Symposium Series on Computational Intelligence (SSCI)* (pp. 407-412). IEEE. https://ieeexplore.ieee.org/stamp/stamp.jsp?arnumber=10372038&casa_token=oTRZt53LmEkAAAAA:EogGJJu5_y7aet1XSuT30kM0veja3KZ_2g-oZ6gadupq85AI0U3mwGaP4jSwatXBiaPdcI6UL81D&tag=1

KEY TERMS AND DEFINITIONS

Artificial Intelligence (AI): A branch of computer science focused on creating systems capable of performing tasks that typically require human intelligence, such as learning, recognizing patterns, or making decisions.

Behavioral Analytics: Analyzing user behavior data to identify patterns that may indicate fraudulent activity, often by assessing deviations from typical usage patterns.

Big Data Analytics: The process of examining large and varied data sets to uncover hidden patterns, correlations, and insights, which can be crucial in detecting fraudulent transactions.

Card-Not-Present (CNP) Fraud: The use of stolen card details to make payments online, through digital wallets, by phone, or mail without the physical card being present.

Card-Not-Present (CNP) Transaction: A payment method without the card being physically shown, such as in online or mobile payments.

Card-Present (CP) Transaction: A CP transaction occurs when the card is physically used at the point of sale, such as swiping or tapping at a store terminal.

Consumer Behavior: The patterns and habits of individuals when purchasing products or services, which can influence fraud detection strategies.

Collaboration: The act of working together across different sectors (e.g., banking, insurance, law enforcement) to share knowledge and resources to combat fraud effectively.

Data Privacy: The protection of personal information collected during transactions is essential for maintaining consumer trust and complying with regulatory frameworks.

Encryption: The method of converting data into a coded format to prevent unauthorized access, ensuring that sensitive information remains confidential during storage and transmission.

Fraud Detection: The process of identifying fraudulent transactions or behaviors using various techniques and tools to prevent financial losses.

Fraud Prevention: Strategies and measures put in place to prevent fraud from occurring, often involving risk assessment and real-time monitoring.

General Data Protection Regulation (GDPR): A European Union law aimed at safeguarding the privacy and personal data of individuals within the EU and EEA.

Hybrid Approaches: Strategies that combine multiple techniques or methodologies, such as traditional rule-based systems and machine learning algorithms, to improve fraud detection accuracy and adaptability.

Machine Learning (ML): A type of artificial intelligence that uses algorithms and statistical models to analyze and learn from data, thereby improving its ability to detect patterns, including fraudulent behavior.

Payment Card Industry Data Security Standard: A set of security standards meant to ensure that all companies accepting, processing, storing, or transmitting credit card information maintain a secure environment.

Risk Scoring: A technique used to assign a numerical score to transactions based on various risk factors, which helps determine the likelihood that a transaction is fraudulent.

Tokenization: The process of replacing sensitive payment information with a unique identifier (token) that cannot be exploited, thereby enhancing security during transactions.

Real-Time Monitoring: Continuous surveillance of transactions as they occur, enabling the immediate detection and response to potential fraud.

APPENDIX

List of Abbreviations and Acronyms

1. **AES -** Advanced Encryption Standard
2. **AI** - Artificial Intelligence
3. **CNP** - Card-Not-Present
4. **CNN** - Convolutional Neural Network
5. **CP -** Card Present
6. **ECC** - Elliptic Curve Cryptography
7. **FL -** Federated Learning
8. **GNN** - Graph Neural Network
9. **GDPR -** General Data Protection Regulation
10. **GSA -** Graph Self-Attention
11. **K-means** - A type of clustering algorithm (often referred to simply as "K-means clustering")
12. **LightGBM -** Light Gradient Boosting Machine
13. **LSTM** - Long Short-Term Memory
14. **ML** - Machine Learning
15. **PCI DSS** - Payment Card Industry Data Security Standard
16. **PCI SSC -** Payment Card Industry Security Standards Council
17. **ROC-AUC** - Receiver Operating Characteristic - Area Under Curve
18. **SMOTE** - Synthetic Minority Over-sampling Technique
19. **TLS** - Transport Layer Security

Chapter 9
A Critical Analysis of Fraud Cases on the Internet

Rajni Bala
https://orcid.org/0000-0002-1225-939X
Chitkara Business School, Chitkara University, Punjab, India

ABSTRACT

With the rapid advancement of technology and the proliferation of online transactions, internet fraud has emerged as a significant global issue. The increasing reliance on digital platforms for personal, financial, and business transactions has made individuals and organizations vulnerable to various forms of cybercrime. The need to address internet fraud has never been more urgent to safeguard personal security, protect organizational integrity, and maintain consumer trust in online services. The study aims to explore the different types of internet fraud, examine the factors responsible for its rise, analyze the methods used by cybercriminals, and evaluate the broader impact of such fraudulent activities. The chapter also highlights emerging threats in internet fraud, role of AI in fraud detection and challenges in combating internet fraud in India. This study adopts a qualitative approach. Data from existing research, real-world examples are analyzed to offer a comprehensive understanding of the topic.

INTRODUCTION

Internet fraud has emerged as a significant global issue with the rapid growth of technology and digital connectivity. As more individuals and businesses engage in online transactions, cybercriminals have exploited vulnerabilities in these systems

DOI: 10.4018/979-8-3373-0675-9.ch009

to commit fraud. Cybercriminals are using various ways to commit fraud, such as phishing, malware attacks, man-in-the-middle attacks, skimming, etc. Cybercriminals use malicious software to infect systems, steal data, or disrupt services. This includes viruses, worms, ransomware, spyware, and many more. In 2021, many Indian citizens received phishing emails that appeared to be from government agencies offering fake COVID-19 relief schemes. These emails contained malicious links that, once clicked, led victims to fake government websites where they were tricked into entering their personal and banking information. The impact of internet fraud extends beyond financial losses, affecting personal security, organizational integrity, and consumer trust in online services. Internet fraud has led to significant financial losses in India, affecting individuals and corporations alike. Punjab National Bank Scam, one of India's largest banking frauds, involving Nirav Modi, was carried out through fraudulent Letters of Undertaking worth 11,400 crore (about $1.8 billion) (Pande, S. & Prakash, V., 2019). Although this scam was primarily a financial fraud, it was orchestrated using internet banking channels, highlighting the vulnerability of India's banking systems to cyber fraud. The impact was massive, leading to financial instability and a loss of confidence in the banking system. This way, cyber fraud can intensely damage businesses and organizations' reputations, leading to customer trust loss.

Not only that, it also psychologically impacts people. The psychological effects of internet fraud on individuals include stress, anxiety, and the fear of being targeted again. In India, during COVID-19, job seekers, particularly during the pandemic, were targeted by fraudsters offering fake job opportunities (Imran I., 2021). Victims, after paying for registration fees or background checks, realized they had been scammed. These individuals faced not only financial loss but also mental health issues, such as increased stress and depression, due to being deceived in a time of need. Internationally, internet fraud can result in long-term psychological trauma for individuals who are scammed, especially in cases of identity theft or romance scams.

As technology is growing, the government is making use of artificial intelligence and machine learning to detect online fraud cases. These two forms of technology analyze the vast volumes of data and help to identify the unusual patterns that fraudsters create in our digital lives. And when these two forms of technology get integrated into the fraud detection systems of our financial institutions, they help financial institutions act swiftly to prevent fraud. India's fast-growing digital landscape, driven by initiatives like Digital India and the widespread use of online financial services, has opened the door to both innovation and internet fraud. Even with strong efforts from the government, law enforcement, and financial institutions, online fraud is still on the rise. Tackling it requires a multi-layered strategy, but a mix of structural, legal, technological, and social hurdles continues to stand in the way of truly effective prevention and enforcement.

LITERATURE REVIEW

Internet fraud has rapidly become a complex and widespread problem with the advancement of digital technology and connectivity. It encompasses a range of deceptive online activities aimed at stealing money, sensitive data, or digital identities. Among the most common forms are phishing, online shopping scams, credit and debit card fraud, investment fraud, job offer scams, UPI fraud, and lottery and prize scams. Phishing involves attempts to acquire personal information through fake emails, SMS, or websites that appear legitimate. In 2020, the State Bank of India warned customers about phishing SMS messages asking them to update their KYC details through fraudulent links designed to capture sensitive banking data (Kulkarni, S., 2022). Similarly, online shopping scams have grown, especially during the pandemic, where fake e-commerce sites mimicked platforms like Amazon and Flipkart. These sites offered electronics at discounted prices but failed to deliver the items, disappearing after collecting payments (Mukherjee, V., 2024). Another serious threat is credit/debit card fraud. In 2018, a breach of Cosmos Bank's systems enabled hackers to clone nearly 12,000 credit cards and withdraw 94 crore from ATMs in 28 countries (Khelkar & Singh, 2018). Investment fraud, particularly through online platforms, has affected thousands. In the GainBitcoin scam, Amit Bhardwaj promised high returns on cryptocurrency investments, leading investors to lose nearly 2,000 crore when the scheme was revealed as a Ponzi model (Mohan, J. A. & Haygunde, C., 2018). Similarly, job seekers have also become victims. In 2020, fraudsters sent fake job offers from reputed companies such as Tata Consultancy Services (TCS) and Infosys, asking applicants to pay fees for registration and interview processing (Business Standard, 2023). UPI frauds have seen a surge, with fraudsters tricking users into transferring money by posing as bank officials or trusted contacts. In 2023, victims were sent fake UPI payment requests through apps like Paytm, resulting in unauthorized fund transfers (Survi, 2023). Lottery scams continue to thrive. In 2018, messages circulated falsely informing recipients that they had won the KBC lottery and had to pay processing fees to claim it. Many people lost significant amounts, believing they had genuinely won (Lal, N., 2018).

Studying these fraud cases is essential to prevent future attacks by identifying common fraud patterns, vulnerabilities, and tactics. The Cosmos Bank attack prompted Indian banks to tighten card security with stronger authentication and international transaction monitoring (PTI, 2018). Public awareness campaigns have become a key strategy in fraud prevention. Following widespread phishing scams, like the fake SBI KYC updates, banks and regulators educated users on detecting phishing attempts and checking URLs, helping to reduce victim numbers (Kulkarni, S., 2022). In response to rising UPI frauds, the Reserve Bank of India enforced two-factor authentication and increased user protection (Tadiparthi, 2024).

Private organizations have also learned from these incidents. After the 2020 Big Basket data breach exposed information of over 20 million users, companies enhanced data encryption and user verification systems, reducing future vulnerabilities (Business Today, 2020). Law enforcement agencies also benefit from fraud analysis. The GainBitcoin scam led to improved cybercrime capabilities in agencies like the Enforcement Directorate and Cyber Crime Cell, especially for handling cryptocurrency-related offenses (Singh, 2024). Studying internet fraud raises consumer responsibility, encouraging individuals to be vigilant online. The OLX scam taught users to be wary of unverified sellers and fake payment screenshots. Public awareness improved regarding secure transactions in online marketplaces (Prathiksha, 2022). Fraud detection systems have also evolved. For instance, phishing and SIM swap attacks led banks to implement real-time monitoring systems that trigger alerts during suspicious activities, such as login attempts from unfamiliar devices or unusually large withdrawals. Moreover, understanding the psychological toll of internet fraud is crucial. Victims often suffer emotional trauma, anxiety, and depression. Romance scams, where perpetrators manipulate emotions to extract money, leave victims devastated. Mental health professionals can provide better counseling by understanding these psychological tactics (Bhati, D., 2024).

Multiple systemic and technological factors enable internet fraud to thrive. Weak cybersecurity systems allow breaches, as seen in 2019 when hackers compromised Patanjali Ayurved's website due to poor digital defenses, exposing the data of over 250,000 customers. Lack of awareness remains a major challenge, especially during crises. During the COVID-19 pandemic, fraudsters sent fake SMS and WhatsApp messages offering early access to vaccines, exploiting public anxiety (Federal Communications Commission, 2022). Technological advancements such as AI have a dual nature; they can detect fraud, but also facilitate it. In 2019, AI-generated deepfake videos in India were used to impersonate officials and request unauthorized payments. Financial incentives are strong motivators for cybercriminals. The Social Trade scam in 2017, led by Anubhav Mittal, promised earnings through social media activity and defrauded over 700,000 people, costing victims 3,700 crore (Rajput, V., 2017).

Regulatory failures often allow fraud to persist. The Saradha chit fund scam operated for years due to lax oversight, eventually collapsing and costing investors 2,500 crore (Varma R. & Kanaujiya B., 2023). Social engineering tactics are frequently used. In 2020, fraudsters posed as IRS officials and coerced people into transferring money to avoid fake legal consequences. The rapid digital shift under schemes like Digital India also created new vulnerabilities. Rural users unfamiliar with digital safety were misled by fake customer support calls for digital wallets like PhonePe and Google Pay. Inadequate identity verification processes are another concern. In 2019, scammers exploited Aadhaar verification loopholes to obtain SIM cards with cloned details, leading to identity theft and unauthorized transactions. Cybercriminals often operate globally, making it difficult to enforce legal action. For example, the Love Jihad Matrimony scam involved Nigerian nationals exploiting victims across countries, making prosecution challenging (Das, T., 2024). Economic stress and low income push people toward seemingly easy investment opportunities. In 2021, the Jeevan Shakti App promised returns from rural entrepreneurship, defrauding many low-income individuals when it abruptly shut down. Unsecured or unregulated digital platforms are easy targets. The 2021 MobiKwik data breach exposed millions of users' information, which was later sold on the dark web (The Indian Express, 2021).

Cybercriminals deploy a wide range of technical tactics. Phishing messages have become more sophisticated. In 2021, emails mimicking government agencies promised COVID-19 relief and redirected users to fake websites to extract data. Malware attacks such as the 2017 WannaCry ransomware attack affected Indian institutions like the Andhra Pradesh Police. Hackers demanded Bitcoin payments to restore locked data (Baviskar & Roy, 2018). SIM swapping is another tactic where fraudsters gain control of mobile numbers and intercept OTPs to execute bank transfers. In 2020, duplicate SIM cards were obtained by deceiving telecom companies, enabling unauthorized access to victims' accounts (Kim, M., Suh, J. & Kwon, H., 2022). Social engineering is a psychological method where attackers impersonate authority figures. In OLX-related scams, they posed as army officers and convinced buyers to make advance payments (Shekar et al., 2020). Credential stuffing uses leaked login data from previous breaches to access multiple user accounts. In 2020, such attacks targeted Paytm wallets, exploiting users who reused the same credentials (Dhaker, B. & Goyal, A., 2024). MITM (Man-in-the-Middle) attacks intercept communication over unsecured networks, such as public Wi-Fi. Fraudsters used this method to steal passwords and banking information from users in places like airports and cafés. Fake apps remain a prevalent issue. During the pandemic, fraudulent Aarogya Setu apps were used to collect user data for scams (Clarance, B. A., 2020). Skimming frauds involve copying card data through devices installed at ATMs. In 2019, a gang in Delhi was caught running such a skimming ring. DDoS attacks overwhelm websites with traffic. In 2019, a leading Indian financial firm experienced downtime from a DDoS attack, resulting in revenue loss and customer dissatisfaction (Avital, N., 2020). Carding, the unauthorized use of stolen card data for purchases, affected multiple people in Mumbai in 2018. Spoofing, which involves impersonating trusted phone numbers or websites, has been used to dupe bank customers into revealing confidential data. In 2020, scammers used spoofed caller IDs to impersonate bank officials. Malicious Wi-Fi networks are another tool, often found in public places with authentic-sounding names. In 2019, passengers at Delhi airport unknowingly connected to fake networks that stole sensitive login credentials (D'Andrea, A., & D'Andrea, A., 2024). Clickjacking uses hidden code to redirect users to fake websites, where login credentials are stolen. In 2021, Indian users of popular shopping websites were misled this way. Ransomware, such as the one used in the 2021 JBS Foods attack, encrypts a victim's data until a ransom is paid. This disrupted their supply chain and operations (Duncan, S. et al., 2022).

Emerging threats further complicate fraud detection and prevention. Deepfake media uses AI to create convincing fake audio or video. In 2020, a deepfake voice mimicking a CEO successfully instructed an employee to transfer $243,000 (Jones, V. A., 2020). AI has also enhanced phishing. Emails generated through AI and NLP resemble real communication, making scams harder to detect (Symantec, 2003). QR code fraud has risen with digital payments. Scammers replace genuine QR codes with fake ones to divert funds or steal data. In India, fake QR codes sent to update KYC details have been used for theft (Das N., 2024). The metaverse has introduced scams involving fake virtual land, digital item theft, and scam messages. Fraudsters sell property in non-existent virtual environments like Decentraland (Europol, 2022). Cryptocurrency scams such as rug pulls remain common. The 2021 "Squid Game" token rose by 2,300% before its creators disappeared with $3.3 million (BBC, 2021). Fraudulent apps also continue to be an issue, including those impersonating official COVID tracking or banking applications to steal data (Kaspersky, 2021). Romance scams, particularly the "Pig Butchering" scheme, use emotional manipulation over dating apps and social media to lead victims into fake crypto investments (FBI, 2022).

Even smart devices in the Internet of Things (IoT) ecosystem are vulnerable. Weak security in gadgets like thermostats and smart cameras can lead to hacking. In 2016, the Mirai botnet attack used IoT devices to shut down major websites like Twitter and Netflix (Antonakakis, M. et al., 2017). These evolving threats illustrate the complexity of internet fraud and the pressing need for a multidimensional response involving law, technology, education, and awareness.

RESEARCH METHODOLOGY

The study adopts a qualitative, exploratory research approach based entirely on secondary data sources. The objective of the chapter is to critically analyze the growing phenomenon of internet fraud, trends, emerging threats, and real-world case studies to understand the patterns, causes, and implications associated with such fraudulent activities in the digital domain. The data used for this analysis was gathered through an extensive review of existing literature, including government reports, official cybercrime statistics, white papers, peer-reviewed journal articles, and credible news publications.

Cyber Crime Cases in India

One of the most prominent examples is the Cosmos Bank cyberattack of 2018, which remains one of India's largest cyber fraud cases. Hackers infiltrated the bank's core banking system and extracted data of nearly 12,000 credit card holders. Using this information, they created cloned cards and executed a highly coordinated heist across 28 countries, stealing approximately 94 crore within hours (Khelkar & Singh, 2018). This attack exposed severe weaknesses in the bank's cybersecurity infrastructure and highlighted the global reach of cybercrime. It also prompted Indian banks to rethink and upgrade their authentication systems, surveillance mechanisms, and international transaction monitoring protocols.

Another large-scale fraud that shook public confidence in digital investments was the Gain Bitcoin scam, spearheaded by Amit Bhardwaj. Operating under the guise of a cryptocurrency investment platform, the scheme promised unusually high returns on Bitcoin investments. Thousands of investors, lured by the booming cryptocurrency trend, poured money into the platform. Eventually, the scheme collapsed, revealing itself as a Ponzi scheme, and defrauding victims of nearly 2,000 crore (Mohan, J. A. & Haygunde, C., 2018). This case exposed not only the vulnerabilities in the regulation of digital assets but also the lack of investor education regarding cryptocurrency investments. In response, enforcement agencies such as the Enforcement Directorate and the Cyber Crime Cell strengthened their monitoring and investigative capabilities in cryptocurrency-related crimes (Singh, 2024).

A different dimension of internet fraud emerged during the COVID-19 pandemic, when widespread job insecurity made individuals more vulnerable to employment scams. In 2020, scammers posed as HR representatives from reputed Indian IT companies such as Tata Consultancy Services (TCS) and Infosys. They contacted job seekers via email, offering lucrative positions and requesting upfront payments under the pretext of registration or interview processing fees. Many unsuspecting individuals, desperate for employment in an uncertain economy, paid the amount, only to later discover that the offers were fake and the money unrecoverable (Business Standard, 2023). Beyond the financial loss, these victims also experienced psychological distress, including stress, anxiety, and a growing mistrust of digital hiring platforms.

Another notable case involves the OLX frauds, where cybercriminals impersonated military personnel to gain the trust of online buyers. In these scams, fraudsters list products like mobile phones or bikes at attractive prices and claim urgency due to military transfers. After convincing the buyers to make advance payments, they would disappear without delivering the item. These scams exploited both emotional manipulation and the buyer's trust in military personnel (Shekar et al., 2020). In response, public awareness campaigns were launched to educate consumers on verifying seller authenticity and avoiding advance payments to unverified individuals.

The Love Jihad Matrimony scam further illustrates the international dimension of internet fraud. Nigerian nationals operated a scam network from India and abroad, targeting women on matrimonial websites such as Shaadi.com. They built trust by pretending to be prospective grooms and then concocted emergencies such as fake accidents or customs seizures to extort money from their victims. The cross-border nature of this operation made it particularly difficult for Indian law enforcement agencies to trace and prosecute the perpetrators (Das, T., 2024). This case revealed how social engineering and emotional manipulation could be weaponized in a culturally sensitive context, highlighting the importance of cybersecurity training for both law enforcement and end-users.

The Jeevan Shakti App scam is another telling example of how fraudsters exploit socio-economic vulnerabilities. Targeting low-income individuals and rural investors in 2021, this app promised high returns on micro-investments in rural entrepreneurship. Lured by the potential for economic upliftment, many people invested their savings into the platform. When the app was abruptly shut down, all the money disappeared, and victims were left without any support or refunds. This case shed light on how digital fraud can disproportionately impact economically disadvantaged populations who may lack digital literacy and legal recourse.

Similarly, the MobiKwik data breach of 2021 illustrates the dangers posed by unsecured digital platforms. Millions of users' personal and financial data were compromised due to inadequate cybersecurity protocols. The stolen data was later sold on the dark web, leading to cases of identity theft and unauthorized transactions. This breach prompted a reevaluation of data protection standards for mobile wallet services and sparked public debates about corporate accountability in the digital age (The Indian Express, 2021).

Another sophisticated method employed by cybercriminals is the use of deepfakes and synthetic media. In 2020, scammers used AI-generated voices to impersonate CEOs and trick employees into transferring large sums of money. In one instance, an employee was instructed via what appeared to be a legitimate voice message from their CEO to transfer $243,000. Believing the message was genuine; the employee complied, resulting in significant financial loss (Jones, V. A., 2020). This example underscores the growing challenge of verifying digital identities and the potential for AI to be misused for high-level financial deception.

The "Squid Game" cryptocurrency rug pull in 2021 also attracted global attention. This scam involved a fraudulent cryptocurrency named after the popular Netflix series. Its value skyrocketed by over 2,000%, attracting widespread investor interest. Suddenly, the developers disappeared, taking with them $3.3 million in investor funds (BBC, 2021). This case demonstrates how easily public enthusiasm and media hype can be manipulated in the cryptocurrency space, especially when regulatory oversight is limited or absent.

Real-world incidents of internet fraud offer critical insights into how these crimes unfold, the tactics employed by perpetrators, and the gaps in systems that allow such fraud to occur. These case studies not only reflect the diverse nature of online scams but also emphasize the urgent need for more robust digital defenses and regulatory oversight.

Trends and Statistics on Cybercrime in India (2021–2024)

Table 1. Cybercrime Complaints and Amount Defrauded in India (2021–2024) (Manral, M. S., 2025)

Year	Complaints Received	Amount Defrauded (in Crore)
2021	1,37,254	551
2022	5,15,083	2,306
2023	11,31,649	7,496
2024	17,10,505	22,812
Total	34,94,491	33,165

Table 1 show that the cybercrime cases and financial losses in India are increasing at a rapid rate. The total amount defrauded was nearly 40 times greater from 2021 to 2024.

Table 2. State-wise Cyber Fraud Cases by National Cyber Crime Reporting Portal as on 28-02-2025 (Ministry of Home Affairs, May 30, 2025)

S. No.	State/UT-wise	Total incidents Reported	Amount Reported (Rs in Lakhs)	Lien Amount (Rs in Lakhs)	Refunded Amount (Rs in Lakhs)
1	Andaman and Nicobar Islands	1685	1388.82	113.46	0.02
2	Andhra Pradesh	113439	155989.39	20378.75	200.11
3	Arunachal Pradesh	2246	5542.17	808.3	1.01
4	Assam	30821	16067.21	2017.32	27.85
5	Bihar	149857	82232.92	12095.07	124.49
6	Chandigarh	12399	11435.56	1659.94	7.6
7	Chhattisgarh	63941	40559.57	4806.79	82.62

continued on following page

Table 2. Continued

S. No.	State/UT-wise	Total incidents Reported	Amount Reported (Rs in Lakhs)	Lien Amount (Rs in Lakhs)	Refunded Amount (Rs in Lakhs)
8	Dadra and Nagar Haveli and Daman and Diu	1615	1861.01	176.51	4.3
9	Delhi	205464	194345.27	18667.93	261.7
10	Goa	6052	14906.43	1375.74	9.38
11	Gujarat	367754	274589.93	55698.11	1031.58
12	Haryana	212001	149290.62	22713.37	352.47
13	Himachal Pradesh	20503	18499.14	1833.68	6.64
14	Jammu and Kashmir	14476	17566.02	1545.27	39.52
15	Jharkhand	38632	42667.99	7326.73	51.71
16	Karnataka	252487	415117.32	40341.8	475.96
17	Kerala	83945	114292.61	16526.08	112.59
18	Ladakh	505	618.56	36.86	1.02
19	Lakshadweep	85	66.77	11.92	0
20	Madhya Pradesh	105991	79242.97	7576.84	78.93
21	Maharashtra	427607	575492.05	62187.87	918.83
22	Manipur	1992	3163.44	386.71	8.08
23	Meghalaya	2517	5230.24	320.72	0.93
24	Mizoram	1135	1895.32	177.61	5.55
25	Nagaland	1167	1237.05	161.17	0
26	Odisha	75274	58375.72	5995.18	96.89
27	Puducherry	5255	8626.79	547.62	51.17
28	Punjab	75087	74092.69	10150.78	142.96
29	Rajasthan	267781	150912.65	18338.66	543.4
30	Sikkim	844	1462.01	118.86	0.07
31	Tamil Nadu	185584	312596.73	22650.3	172.04
32	Telangana	241666	333165.59	46809.74	610.9
33	Tripura	7143	4368.21	461.11	2.47
34	Uttarakhand	61712	31443.18	4283.43	35.69
35	Uttar Pradesh	630778	285875.57	30610.47	382.2
36	West Bengal	153110	160602.33	19169.87	210.97
Total	Total	3822550	3644819.85	438080.57	6051.65

Table 2 describes that Uttar Pradesh, Maharashtra, and Gujarat have reported the highest number of cybercrime cases. Maharashtra is the highest reported as losses. Territories like Lakshadweep, Ladakh, and Sikkim reported minimal cases. Across India, 38.22 lakh cases were reported with Rs. 3644819.85 lakh, and only 6051.65 lakh is refunded, which is only 0.2%. This shows that the refunded amount is very low.

Table 3. Most Affected Regions and Sectors as of December, 05-12-2024 (Data Security Council of India, 2024)

Top Targeted Regions	Most Affected Sectors
• Telangana • Tamil Nadu • Delhi These regions experience disproportionately high volumes of malware activity, possibly due to higher digital adoption and connectivity levels.	• Banking, Financial Services, and Insurance (BFSI) • Healthcare • Hospitality These Sectors handling sensitive financial and personal information are prime targets for cyber attackers, emphasizing the need for enhanced security protocols in these industries.

Table 3 shows that Telangana, Tamil Nadu, and Delhi are highly targeted areas by cyber criminals. Sectors like banking, healthcare, and hospitality are the most frequently targeted sectors. This shows that sectors that handle sensitive data are mostly targeted by cyber criminals.

Table 4. Financial Losses due to Cyber Fraud in India (Tiwari, S., 2024)

Crime Type	Cases Reported	Total Loss (Crores)
Investment Scams	1,00,360	3,216
Stock Trading Scams	2,28,094	4,636
Digital Arrest Scams	63,481	1,616
Total	3,91,935	9,468

Table 4 shows that the stock trading scam is the most damaging cybercrime in India. Investment scams and digital arrest scams have also significantly contributed to financial losses. This shows the alarming rise in financially motivated cybercrimes.

The Role of AI in Fraud Detection

AI and ML are changing fraud detection systems. They are helping to make them faster, smarter, and more adaptive to ever-changing cyber threats. These two forms of technology, analyzing the vast volumes of data that we produce at an ever-increasing rate, are also helping to identify the unusual patterns that fraudsters create in our digital lives. And when these two (or three if you count DL) forms of technology get integrated into the fraud detection systems of our financial institutions (and law enforcement agencies, for that matter), they help those entities act swiftly to prevent fraud. AI algorithms are capable of processing millions of transactions and can detect the subtle anomalies that humans would be impossible to catch. Machine Learning models learn from the historical fraud data that humans have encountered and have been able to solve (Bello, O. A., & Olufemi, K., 2024). These models then use that knowledge to find errors in currently ongoing transactions. Financial institutions such as HDFC Bank and ICICI Bank have AI at their core to detect and prevent fraud. Natural Language Processing (NLP) is used by AI to study the messages, emails, or website content for any scam-related language. AI analyzes the actual content for human-like indicators of a scam. AI and NLP are being used by startups such as Karza Technologies to analyze KYC documents and detect whether IDs submitted for digital loan applications have been forged or manipulated (Economic Times, 2022). Machine Learning models are embedded in payment gateways and mobile wallets to monitor our transactions in real-time and warn us of any potentially fraudulent activity. These models assess a range of parameters like time, location, device fingerprint, and user behavior to judge the validity of a transaction before giving it the green light. In India, Paytm and PhonePe use machine learning algorithms to score every transaction based on risk. If the behavior is suspicious or someone is logging in from different IP addresses or switching devices in a way that seems too rapid, they'll trigger additional authentication layers or block the transaction altogether. AI is also used for identity theft and account takeover prevention. With the increasing number of identity theft incidents in India, AI tools are utilized to identify illicit access. Behavioral biometric systems like keystroke dynamics, mouse movements, and touch screen actions are becoming more common in anti-fraud platforms. Aadhaar-enabled Payment Systems or AePS are susceptible to biometric spoofing. Firms like Innefu Labs are utilising AI models to identify inconsistencies in geolocation information and biometric patterns while making transactions (Tandem Research report, 2022). AI-Powered risk scoring models are used for lending fraud detection. Digital lenders in India experience a high incidence of fake loan requests. AI is utilized to score the applicant not only on past credit history but also on device data, mobile app usage patterns, and alternative data on mobile devices. RBI's Digital Lending Guidelines, released in 2022, now suggest that lending entities utilize AI-powered credit scoring tools to check against predatory lending as well as identity theft. LenddoEFL and Crediwatch are the leading players in this niche (RBI, 2022). In India, scammers often create fake social media profiles and mobile apps to steal personal information or money. To fight back, AI tools are being used to identify and monitor these fraudulent accounts, unauthorized apps, and suspicious app reviews. Back in 2022, the Hyderabad City Police used AI to uncover patterns in fake loan apps on the Play Store. These apps tricked users through phishing and social engineering tactics, gaining access to their contacts and then using that information to blackmail them.

Impact of Internet Fraud

Internet fraud has led to significant financial losses in India, affecting individuals and corporations alike. Punjab National Bank Scam, one of India's largest banking frauds, involving Nirav Modi, was carried out through fraudulent Letters of Undertaking (LoUs) worth 11,400 crore (about $1.8 billion) (Pande, S. & Prakash, V., 2019). Although this scam was primarily a financial fraud, it was orchestrated using internet banking channels, highlighting the vulnerability of India's banking systems to cyber fraud. The impact was massive, leading to financial instability and a loss of confidence in the banking system. Globally, cyber fraud has cost businesses and governments billions of dollars in losses (Collier, R., 2017). WannaCry Ransomware Attack in 2017 impacted around 200,000 computers across 150 countries, affecting organizations like the UK's National Health Service (NHS). The attack caused a global loss of an estimated $4 billion. Hospitals were forced to turn away patients, financial institutions experienced shutdowns, and thousands of businesses faced operational disruptions, emphasizing how international cyber fraud can cripple economies. Cyber fraud can intensely damage businesses and organizations reputations, leading to customer trust loss. In India, Mobikwik, a leading digital wallet company, faced a massive data breach in 2021. In which the personal information of 110 million users was leaked and sold on the dark web (ETtech., 2021). This breach caused widespread panic and distrust among users regarding the safety of digital wallets in India, leading to customers switching to other platforms and questioning the government's data protection measures. Internationally, internet fraud affects trust between countries and within the global digital economy. In 2017, the largest credit reporting agencies in the U.S, Equifax suffered a data breach that compromised the personal information of 147 million customers worldwide. This incident significantly harmed Equifax's reputation and resulted over $700 million in fines and settlements (Thomas, J., 2019). Additionally, it raised concerns about global cybersecurity standards, particularly when companies that handle sensitive data fail to protect it adequately. Cyber fraud can lead to direct financial losses for businesses and increased operational costs due to the need to implement stricter security measures. Many SMEs in India have fallen victim to phishing attacks, resulting in financial losses and disruption of operations. A 2020 report showed that nearly 80% of SMEs had experienced some form of cyber fraud, costing the sector over 100 crore annually. This has forced businesses to invest heavily in cybersecurity, increasing their operational expenses. Globally, businesses have faced severe disruptions and financial losses due to cyber fraud. The international entertainment company Sony Pictures was hacked by a group known as the "Guardians of Peace," who leaked sensitive information, including unreleased films and confidential employee information, in 2014. The cyberattack, allegedly sponsored by North Korea, cost the company over $100 million and significantly damaged its global reputation (Young, K., 2021). This event also led to heightened tensions between the U.S. and North Korea.

In India, during COVID-19, job seekers, particularly during the pandemic, were targeted by fraudsters offering fake job opportunities (Imran I., 2021). Victims, after paying for "registration fees" or background checks, realized they had been scammed. These individuals faced not only financial loss but also mental health issues, such as increased stress and depression, due to being deceived in a time of need. Internationally, internet fraud can result in long-term psychological trauma for individuals who are scammed, especially in cases of identity theft or romance scams. Romance scams in the U.S., where fraudsters pose as romantic partners to defraud victims, have been rising globally. In 2020 alone, Americans lost over $300 million to romance scams (Fletcher E., 2022). Many victims experienced shame, embarrassment, and depression after discovering they had been deceived by people they trusted online. This type of fraud not only results in financial loss but also severe emotional and psychological harm. Cyber fraud can escalate to national security concerns, especially when sensitive government or military data is compromised. Aadhaar, India's national identification system, experienced a data breach in 2018, where sensitive information of over 1 billion citizens was allegedly exposed (Sapkale Y., 2019). Though the government initially denied the leak, it raised concerns over the safety of critical national infrastructure and the risk of data misuse by terrorists or hostile nations, impacting national security. On the global level, cyber attacks can threaten the security of entire nations. In a massive breach of the U.S. Office of Personnel Management Hack in 2015, cybercriminals, reportedly linked to China, stole the personal information of over 21 million U.S. government employees, including those with security clearances (Rushe, D., 2017). This raised concerns about espionage and the ability of foreign adversaries to exploit the information for intelligence purposes, posing a significant national security threat to the U.S. Cyber attacks on critical infrastructure can have destructive effects, interrupting essential services and threatening public safety. In a suspected Power Grid cyber attack in 2020, parts of Mumbai's power grid went down for several hours, leading to widespread disruption in one of India's largest cities (Joshi, S., 2020). The incident highlighted concerns about India's critical infrastructure being vulnerable to cyber attacks, with speculations that the attack might have been state-sponsored. Globally, cyber fraud targeting critical infrastructure poses significant threats to public health and safety. In 2021, the Colonial Pipeline Ransomware Attack, which supplies half of the East Coast's fuel, was targeted by a ransomware attack (Easterly J., 2023). As a result, the company shut down its operations, causing fuel shortages and widespread panic buying across several states. This incident exposed the susceptibility of critical infrastructure to cyber fraud and its potential to disrupt entire economies. The rise in internet fraud has forced governments to introduce stringent cybersecurity laws and regulations. Due to growing cyber fraud cases, the Indian government introduced the Personal Data Protection Bill, aimed at regulating data collection and preventing misuse. This move has led companies to improve their data protection policies, but it has also increased compliance costs. Internationally, cyber fraud has led to the implementation of stricter global data protection laws. In Europe, the GDPR was implemented to protect individuals' personal data and regulate data privacy for companies operating in or dealing with the European Union. This regulation was driven by several high-profile data breaches, affecting companies globally and setting a new standard for data protection.

Challenges in Combating Internet Fraud in India

- Rapid Evolution of Cybercriminal Techniques: Cybercriminals are constantly evolving their tactics to outsmart law enforcement. Phishing emails, vishing calls, fake apps, and social engineering techniques have become more widespread. Scammers often impersonate trusted entities like government agencies, banks, or major e-commerce platforms to trick people into revealing sensitive information. One of the most notorious examples is the Jamtara phishing scam. In this case, a group of young people from a small town in Jharkhand posed as bank officials and managed to con thousands of unsuspecting victims across India. Using just basic smartphones, fake SIM cards, and mule bank accounts, they were able to extract OTPs and banking credentials (Lakshmi, R., 2022). Even with repeated police crackdowns, similar schemes keep popping up—mainly because they're easy to replicate and carry relatively low risk for the criminals involved.
- Jurisdictional and Enforcement Challenges: Internet fraud often crosses borders or happens between different states, which makes it hard to decide which country or state has the authority to take legal action. In India, the current system for working with other countries—like through Mutual Legal Assistance Treaties (MLATs)—is very slow. This creates problems when evidence is stored in other countries, especially if the criminals use websites or servers located abroad. For example, in a well-known case, some people in India were tricked by a fake online lottery scam that came from Nigeria. Even though Indian officials found out who did it, they couldn't take any

legal action because of delays and complications in working with Nigerian authorities (TOI, 2010). One big challenge is that police and law enforcement agencies in different countries don't have a way to work together in real time. This slows everything down and makes it harder to catch the criminals.

- Inadequate Cybercrime Investigation Infrastructure: Most police stations in India don't have special teams to handle cybercrimes. Catching internet fraudsters needs advanced tools, trained experts, and knowledge of cyber laws—but many local police departments don't have these resources. Many state police forces also face issues like not having enough staff or using outdated technology, which makes it hard for them to properly investigate online fraud. According to the National Crime Records Bureau (NCRB), over 65,000 cybercrime cases were reported in 2022—a 24% jump from the previous year. But less than 10% of these cases resulted in a conviction. One of the main reasons is that digital evidence is not handled properly, many officers aren't trained in cyber forensics, and there are delays in the investigation process (NCRB, 2022).
- Low Digital Literacy and Public Awareness: A large number of people in India, especially in rural and small-town areas, don't fully understand how to use the internet safely. Many don't know simple online safety rules—like not clicking on suspicious links, never sharing OTPs, and spotting scam messages or fake QR codes. During the COVID-19 pandemic, fraudsters took advantage of people's fear and urgency. They created fake websites and links for vaccine registration. These were shared through SMS and WhatsApp, tricking people into entering their Aadhaar numbers and OTPs (Ma, K. W. F., & McKinnon, T., 2022).). As a result, many people lost money through unauthorized transactions. This shows that poor awareness of online safety makes people more likely to fall into such trap.
- Anonymity of Cybercriminals and Use of Encryption Tools: Cybercriminals take advantage of the fact that it's easy to hide one's identity on the internet. They often use tools like VPNs, encrypted chats, the Dark Web, and cryptocurrency wallets to stay hidden. Although these tools are legal and meant to protect privacy, criminals misuse them to carry out illegal activities. In 2021, a major scam in Delhi involved fraudsters stealing over 2.5 crore using cryptocurrency. They moved the money through anonymous blockchain wallets and international exchanges, making it very hard to trace (Ghosh, P., 2021).). Because cryptocurrency transactions are both encrypted and spread across global networks, the authorities struggled to find out where the money came from or where it went.
- Gaps in the Legal Framework for Modern Cybercrimes: India's main law for handling online crimes, the Information Technology Act, 2000, was updated

in 2008, but it still doesn't fully cover today's new digital threats. With the rise of deepfake videos, AI-based impersonation, fake identities, and scams using cryptocurrency, the law feels outdated. One major issue is that there's still no proper law to protect people's personal data, as the Personal Data Protection Bill has been delayed. There's also no specific rule that deals with how someone's digital identity can be misused. The current IT law doesn't mention anything about deepfakes or frauds created using AI—scams where criminals pretend to be CEOs or senior company officials to trick others (Carpenter, P., 2024). Without stronger data protection laws, people are also at risk of their private information being leaked and misused for targeted scams.

- Underreporting and Weak Complaint Mechanisms: In India, many cases of internet fraud go unreported. People who fall for online scams often feel embarrassed or hopeless, and some don't trust the police to help them. Because of this, there's a big difference between how many cybercrimes actually happen and how many are officially reported. Another reason is that a lot of people simply don't know where to file a complaint. Many have never heard of the National Cybercrime Reporting Portal or the helpline number 1930, which are meant to help fraud victims.

CONCLUSION

In an increasingly digital era, internet fraud poses a significant threat to individuals, businesses, and institutions. This chapter examined various forms of online fraud—such as phishing, identity theft, and cryptocurrency scams—emphasizing the importance of understanding their mechanisms and consequences. The rise in cyber fraud is driven by multiple factors, including limited digital literacy, outdated legal provisions, technological misuse, and inadequate international collaboration. Cybercriminals are employing sophisticated methods, including deepfakes, social engineering, and encrypted platforms, making detection and enforcement increasingly difficult. The impact of these crimes extends beyond financial loss to include emotional distress, reputational damage, and risks to national security. Emerging threats like AI-driven scams and dark web operations further complicate the cybercrime landscape. However, the same technologies—when harnessed ethically—also offer opportunities for early detection and prevention through AI, machine learning, and data analytics. India faces unique challenges in this domain, including underreporting, limited cyber policing infrastructure, and delayed legislative updates. Addressing these issues calls for comprehensive reforms, improved public awareness, and greater investment in cybersecurity capacity and training. Ultimately, combating internet fraud requires a multi-pronged strategy involving technology, legal reform, education, and global cooperation. A coordinated and forward-looking approach is essential to building a safer and more resilient digital ecosystem.

REFERENCES

Avital, N. (2020). *2019 Global DDoS threat landscape report*. Imperva. https://www.imperva.com/blog/2019-global-ddos-threat-landscape-report/

Baviskar, P. S., & Roy, M. (2018). Wanna cry ransomware: A case study in Indian perspective. [IJCRT]. *International Journal of Creative Research Thoughts*, *6*(2), 811–814.

BBC News. (2021, November 2). *Squid Game crypto token collapses in apparent scam*. https://www.bbc.com/news/business-59129466

Bello, O. A., & Olufemi, K. (2024). Artificial intelligence in fraud prevention: Exploring techniques and applications challenges and opportunities. *Computer Science & IT Research Journal*, *5*(6), 1505–1520. DOI: 10.51594/csitrj.v5i6.1252

Bhati, D. (2024, June 7). Dating scams rising in metro cities, leaving hearts and bank accounts empty. *India Today*. https://www.indiatoday.in/technology/news/story/dating-scams-rising-in-metro-cities-leaving-hearts-and-bank-accounts-empty-2550450-2024-06-07

Business Standard. (2023, June 23). Bribes-for-job scam uncovered at TCS, Rs 100 crore involved. https://www.business-standard.com/companies/news/bribes-for-job-scam-uncovered-at-tcs-rs-100-crore-involved-123062300176_1.html

Carpenter, P. (2024). *Faik: A practical guide to living in a world of deepfakes, disinformation, and AI-generated deceptions*. John Wiley & Sons.

Clarance, B. A. (2020, May 13). Aarogya Setu: Why India's Covid-19 contact tracing app is controversial. *BBC News*. https://www.bbc.com/news/world-asia-india-52659520

D'Andrea, A., & D'Andrea, A. (2024, July 12). Is airport WiFi safe? *Keeper Security Blog*. https://www.keepersecurity.com/blog/2024/07/12/is-airport-wifi-safe/

Das, N. (2024, February 6). New UPI fraud trend: Fraudsters spamming UPI IDs with multiple collect requests. *The Economic Times*. https://economictimes.indiatimes.com/wealth/save/new-upi-scam-alert-upi-autopay-set-up-request-could-swindle-money-out-of-your-account-if-you-are-not-careful/articleshow/112584562.cms

Das, T. (2024, April 3). Nigerian-style scam reaches Indian matrimonial sites. *The Print*. https://theprint.in/opinion/pov/nigerian-style-scam-reaches-indian-matrimonial-sites-amazon-prime-series-shows-how-they-do-it/1916766/

Data Security Council of India. (2024, December 5). *India cyber threat report 2025.* https://www.dsci.in/resource/content/india-cyber-threat-report-2025

Dhaker, B., & Goyal, A. (2024). Analysing fraud patterns and prevention mechanisms in Paytm Payment Bank. *International Journal of Innovative Research in Science, Engineering and Technology*, *13*(6), 11003–11008.

Duncan, S.. (2022). Cybersecurity: Beyond ransomware: Securing the digital food chain. *Food Australia*, *74*(1), 36–40.

Easterly, J. (2023). The attack on Colonial Pipeline: What we've learned & what we've done over the past two years. *Cybersecurity and Infrastructure Security Agency (CISA).* https://www.cisa.gov/news-events/news/attack-colonial-pipeline-what-weve-learned-what-weve-done-over-past-two-years

Economic Times. (2022, March 28). How Karza Technologies makes due diligence and onboarding simpler for banks & NBFCs. https://cio.economictimes.indiatimes.com/news/case-studies/how-karza-technologies-makes-due-diligence-and-onboarding-simpler-for-banks-nbfcs/89891554

ETtech. (2021, March 30). Data of 10 crore Mobikwik users for sale on dark web, say cybersecurity experts. *The Economic Times.* https://economictimes.indiatimes.com/tech/startups/mobikwik-data-breach-personal-data-of-over-10-crore-users-allegedly-available-onsale/articleshow/81756544.cms

Europol. (2022). *Policing in the Metaverse: What law enforcement needs to know* [Report]. Publications Office of the European Union. https://doi.org/DOI: 10.2813/81062

Federal Bureau of Investigation. (2022). *Romance scams.* https://www.fbi.gov/how-we-can-help-you/scams-and-safety/common-frauds-and-scams/romance-scams

Federal Communications Commission. (2022). *COVID-19 vaccines scams.* https://www.fcc.gov/covid-19-vaccines-scams

Fletcher, E. (2022). Romance scams take record dollars in 2020. *Federal Trade Commission.* https://www.ftc.gov/news-events/data-visualizations/data-spotlight/2021/02/romance-scams-take-record-dollars-2020

Ghosh, P. (2021, October 25). 2.5 crore Delhi cryptocurrency scam: Dubai-based kingpin arrested. *Hindustan Times.* https://www.hindustantimes.com/india-news/dubai-based-kingpin-of-rs-2-5-crore-delhi-cryptocurrency-scam-arrested-from-delhi-airport/story-iiqm14ER9XfZmAg8XmgUKI.html

Imran, I. (2021, May 1). Pandemic and online job scam. *Times of India Blog*. https://timesofindia.indiatimes.com/readersblog/ifath-digest/pandemic-and-online-job-scam-36203/

Indian Express. (2021, March 29). MobiKwik database of 10 crore users leaked on dark web; company denies data breach. https://indianexpress.com/article/technology/tech-news-technology/mobikwik-database-leaked-on-dark-web-company-denies-any-data-breach-7251448/

Jones, V. A. (2020). *Artificial intelligence enabled deepfake technology: The emergence of a new threat* (Master's thesis, Utica College).

Joshi, S. (2020, November 20). Mega Mumbai power outage may be result of cyber attack. *India Today*. https://www.indiatoday.in/india/story/mumbai-power-outage-malware-attack-1742538-2020-11-20

Kaspersky. (2021). *Mobile malware report: Cybercriminals forego low hanging fruit to go after banking and gaming*. https://www.kaspersky.com/about/press-releases/2021-mobile-threats-report-cybercriminals-forego-low-hanging-fruit-to-go-after-banking-and-gaming

Khelkar, P. P., & Singh, D. (2018, August 14). Hackers withdraw Rs 94 crore after stealing ATM card data. *India Today*. https://www.indiatoday.in/india/story/hackers-steal-rs-94-crore-from-pune-s-cosmos-bank-1314081-2018-08-14

Kim, M., Suh, J., & Kwon, H. (2022). A study of the emerging trends in SIM swapping crime and effective countermeasures. In *7th IEEE/ACIS International Conference on Big Data, Cloud Computing, and Data Science (BCD 2022)*. DOI: 10.1109/BCD54882.2022.9900510

Kulkarni, S. (2022, September 10). SBI, government warn customers against fake SMS. *The Economic Times*. https://economictimes.indiatimes.com/wealth/personal-finance-news/sbi-government-warn-customers-against-fake-sms-about-updating-pan-kyc-details/articleshow/94002587.cms

Lakshmi, R. (2022). Phishing as a cybercrime: A case study of *Jamtara* web series. *From the Chief Editor's Desk. Communicator*, *LVII*(4), 126–131.

Lal, N. (2018, October 7). 'KBC' called, you've won a lottery? Hold on, it's probably a scam. *The Times of India*. https://timesofindia.indiatimes.com/city/delhi/kbc-called-youve-won-a-lottery-hold-on-its-probably-a-scam/articleshow/66099218.cms

Ma, K. W. F., & McKinnon, T. (2022). COVID-19 and cyber fraud: Emerging threats during the pandemic. *Journal of Financial Crime*, *29*(2), 433–446. DOI: 10.1108/JFC-01-2021-0016

Manral, M. S. (2025, February 5). Cyber frauds jump 900% in 4 years: Small cities like Deoghar, Nuh, Mathura emerge as new scam capitals. *The Indian Express*. https://indianexpress.com/article/india/cybercrime-sharp-rise-complaints-2024-govt-data-9816845/

Ministry of Home Affairs. (2025). *State/UT-wise details of statistics from National Cyber Crime Reporting Portal (NCRP) related to cyber crimes*. Open Government Data (OGD) Platform India. https://www.data.gov.in/resource/stateut-wise-details-statistics-national-cyber-crime-reporting-portal-ncrp-related-cyber

Mohan, J. A., & Haygunde, C. (2018, April 6). Bitcoin fraud: Director of firm involved in Rs 2000 crore scam arrested. *The Indian Express*. https://indianexpress.com/article/india/bitcoin-fraud-amit-bhardwaj-director-of-firm-involved-in-rs-2000-crore-scam-arrested-5124244/

Mukherjee, V. (2024, November 19). Deepfakes to social media: Online shopping scams spike this festive season. *Business Standard*. https://www.business-standard.com/industry/news/deepfakes-to-social-media-online-shopping-scams-spike-this-festive-season-124111900337_1.html

National Crime Records Bureau (NCRB). (2022). *Crime in India 2022: Statistics*.

Pande, S., & Prakash, V. (2019). Case study on scam in Indian banking industry (Nirav Modi). *Pramana Research Journal*, *9*(6), 626–630.

Prathiksha, B. V. (2022, March 15). Online frauds on rise amid pandemic: OLX report. *BusinessLine*. https://www.thehindubusinessline.com/info-tech/online-fraud-has-grown-with-internet-usage-during-pandemic-olx/article64996341.ece

Press Trust of India (PTI). (2018, August 14). Cosmos Bank's server hacked; Rs 94 crore siphoned off in 2 days. *The Economic Times*. https://economictimes.indiatimes.com/industry/banking/finance/banking/cosmos-banks-server-hacked-rs-94-crore-siphoned-off-in-2-days/articleshow/65399477.cms

Rajput, V. (2017, February 3). Who is Anubhav Mittal, the prime accused in Rs 3,700-cr online trading scam. *Hindustan Times*. https://www.hindustantimes.com/noida/anubhav-mittal-conman-robinhood-and-prime-accused-in-rs-3-700-cr-scam-noida-ponzi-scam/story-KbgoxypVn9pPR5bOyW526N.html

Reserve Bank of India. (2022). *Guidelines on digital lending*. https://rbidocs.rbi.org.in/rdocs/notification/PDFs/GUIDELINESDIGITALLENDINGD5C35A71D8124A0E92AEB940A7D25BB3.PDF

Rushe, D. (2017, June 4). OPM hack: China blamed for massive breach of US government data. *The Guardian*. https://www.theguardian.com/technology/2015/jun/04/us-government-massive-data-breach-employee-records-security-clearances

Sapkale, Y. (2019, January 24). Aadhaar data breach largest in the world, says WEF's Global Risk Report and Avast. *Moneylife News & Views*. https://www.moneylife.in/article/aadhaar-data-breach-largest-in-the-world-says-wefs-global-risk-report-and-avast/56384.html

Shekar, A., ... (2020, March 2). Duping buyers across India by posing as army officers on OLX: TN cops crack scam. *The News Minute*. https://www.thenewsminute.com/tamil-nadu/duping-buyers-across-india-posing-army-officers-olx-tn-cops-crack-scam-119709

Singh, S. G. (2024, November 21). Bitcoin scam: The legality of cryptocurrencies in India. *Business Standard*. https://www.business-standard.com/finance/personal-finance/bitcoin-scam-the-legality-of-cryptocurrencies-in-india-explained-124112100977_1.html

Survi. (2023). Unveiling the 2023 UPI scam in India: Stay secured. *Protegent360*. https://protegent360.com/blog/to-safeguard-the-data-of-enterprises-and-consumers-provide-robust-cyber-security-and-antivirus/?srsltid=AfmBOor-rJdrSnnFRwTWY_gOaNaw147Zrjcv-9GjmluIWYHIBBoTmNPe

Symantec. (2003). *Internet security threat report*. https://symantec.com

Tadiparthi, R. (2024). RBI guidelines for UPI frauds in banks: Stay protected from UPI scams. *Paytm Blog*. https://paytm.com/blog/loan/repo-rate/rbi-guidelines-for-upi-frauds-in-banks/

Tandem Research. (2022). *AI on the ground: A snapshot of AI use in India*. https://images-production.authory.com/UrvashiAneja/AI-ON-THE-GROUND-A-SNAPSHOT-OF-AI-USE-IN-INDIA-1/fe06ba20-2bed-11ec-8805-7b8cab49e3f9.pdf

Thomas, J. (2019, December). A case study analysis of the Equifax data breach. https://www.researchgate.net/publication/337916068

Tiwari, S. (2024, November 29). Digital fear: How stock trading scams, investment frauds, digital arrest and threats from foreign lands are crippling. *Entrepreneur India*. https://www.entrepreneur.com/en-in/news-and-trends/digital-fear-how-stock-trading-scams-investment-frauds/483665

Varma, R., & Kanaujiya, B. (2023). Case study of Saradha scam on Indian economy. *International Journal of Advanced Research in Science* [IJARSCT]. *Tongxin Jishu, 3*(6).

Young, K. (2021). Cyber case study: Sony Pictures Entertainment hack. *CoverLink Insurance*. https://coverlink.com/case-study/sony-pictures-entertainment-hack/

KEY TERMS AND DEFINITIONS

Cryptocurrency: This is a form of currency that exists digitally or virtually and uses cryptography to secure transactions. Cryptocurrencies don't have a central issuing or regulating authority, instead using a decentralized system to record transactions and issue new units.

Cybercriminals: These are malicious users who use the Internet to commit crimes such as identity theft, spamming, phishing and other types of fraud. Cyber criminals try to gain access to their victims' personal information – name, address, phone number, place of employment, bank account, credit card information and social security number. They use this information to make financial transactions while impersonating their victims.

Deepfake: Deepfakes are images, videos, or audio that has been edited or generated using artificial intelligence, AI-based tools or AV editing software. These are synthetic media (typically video or audio) created by AI models to mimic real people's faces, voices, or movements with eerie realism.

Digital India: It is a flagship programme of the Government of India with a vision to transform India into a digitally empowered society and knowledge economy. This initiative aim is to improve the online infrastructure and enhance internet connectivity in India. Prime Minister Narendra Modi launched the campaign on 1st July 2015.

Internet Fraud: This refers to illegal activities conducted online with the intention of deceiving or defrauding individuals or organizations. These activities often involve using the internet to trick victims into giving up personal information, money, or property.

IOT: This refers to a network of physical devices, vehicles, appliances, and other physical objects that are embedded with sensors, software, and network connectivity, allowing them to collect and share data. It enables smart devices to communicate with each other and with other internet-enabled devices. Like smartphones creating a vast network of interconnected devices that can exchange data and perform various tasks autonomously, managing traffic patterns with smart cars and other smart automotive devices etc.

KYC: This term stands for Know Your Customer. It is a process used by financial institutions and other organizations to verify the identity and address of their clients. This helps prevent fraud, money laundering, and other financial crimes

Ransomware: It is a type of malware that encrypts the victim's personal data until a ransom is paid. Difficult-to-trace digital currencies such as paysafecard or Bitcoin and other cryptocurrencies are commonly used for the ransoms, making tracing and prosecuting the perpetrators difficult.

Spyware: It is malicious software that enters a user's computer, gathers data from the device and user, and sends it to third parties without their consent. Examples of spyware include adware, infostealers, rootkits, Red Shell, system monitors, tracking cookies, and Trojans.

Synthetic Media: This refers to any type of digital content, including images, videos, audio, and text, that is created or manipulated using artificial intelligence (AI) and machine learning (ML) techniques. It's essentially AI-generated media that mimics or replicates real-world content, often blurring the lines between what is real and what is fabricated.

Chapter 10
A Study on Deepfake Dangers in the Digital Age:
Social Media Misinformation and the Youth at Risk

Parveen Kumar
https://orcid.org/0009-0005-3310-4038
Chandigarh University, India

Dhruvika Singh
Graphic Era University, India

ABSTRACT

Deepfake is a technology that enables the creation and manipulation of audio, video, and images, often leading to falsified content. Youths, as major social media users, are especially vulnerable to its risks. This study aims to explore the impact of deepfakes on social platforms and methods to counter misinformation. It covers the history and evolution of deepfakes, their potential for harm, and current detection techniques. Deepfakes have been used to spread misinformation, damage reputations, and manipulate public opinion, challenging societal trust and unity. Legal and policy frameworks, along with technological solutions like AI detection tools and platform-level safeguards, are being developed to address this growing threat. The paper underscores the importance of responsible content creation, awareness, and collaborative strategies to detect, prevent, and regulate deepfakes in the digital era.

DOI: 10.4018/979-8-3373-0675-9.ch010

1. INTRODUCTION

In an age where digital media dominates the social, political, and economic landscape, the emergence of deepfake technology has introduced profound challenges to the way society engages with information. The advancement of Deepfakes technology produces authentic media content that Artificial Intelligence creates from files through effective modifications of audio or video or image data thereby generating deceitful artificial content. The entertainment-oriented beginnings of deepfake technology have transitioned into an instrument that manipulates people through deception during attacks. Future-ready synthetic digital media shows an increasing supply which challenges our ability to maintain confidence in visual and auditory content. Deepfakes technology progresses at such an extent that it leads people to error between genuine information and synthetic fake materials (Wazid et al., 2024). The development of deepfakes into a global security hazard has surpassed all initial reasons for modifying digital content because it now actively undermines trust in media sources and intensifies political conflicts and social estrangement (Al-Khazraji et al., 2023). Deepfakes both distribute false information and wreck professional credibility after they distort public opinion through artificial political statements and artificial celebrity routs. Through their analysis the author builds the deepfake technology model by connecting moral dimensions to social effects to justify an urgent counteraction plan (Hancock and Bailenson, 2021). Deepfake technology evolved historically through entertainment and gaming until it reached diverse sectors during modern times according to the first part of the chapter. This analysis examines difficult ethical concerns about modified media and explains responsibilities of those creating deepfakes along with those who communicate and consume them. The central topic of investigation analyzes trust in media throughout the study. Current digital reality makes true visual evidence verification impossible because modern precision allows absolute control of content. To stop deepfake misuse for both false information dissemination and personal attacks what security precautions must be developed? Social development faces three urgent implications of deepfake proliferation which include democratic trust decline and increased social and political rifts and psychological pressures on deepfake harassment and extortion victims.

A review of the continuing technological struggle occurs between developers who develop deepfake technology and specialists who focus on identifying and protecting against it. AI detection algorithms alongside watermarking approaches create possible remedies while deepfakes continue to evolve as an ongoing technological problem. The quest for better deepfake detection evasion drives professionals toward new tool creation causing researchers and industry experts and policymakers to collaborate for successful digital defense. Academic researchers undertake deep investigations about deepfake technology in addition to its societal social effects. Researchers work towards their goals through system development for detection alongside public education about technology and promotion of responsible conduct and ethical framework creation and legal systems establishing. Research scientists along with political experts and subject matter experts will develop platforms that reduce deepfake dangers and ensure security on media platforms.

The second and third sections of the document describe deepfake detection systems and the third section delves into how data fraud spreads. A study about deepfake techniques how they succeed but also fail is presented in the fourth section of the paper. The research introduces operational and societal importances which form the basis of the fifth and sixth segments of the report. The research analysis finds its conclusion in the seventh section of the paper.

Figure 1. Types of Deepfakes

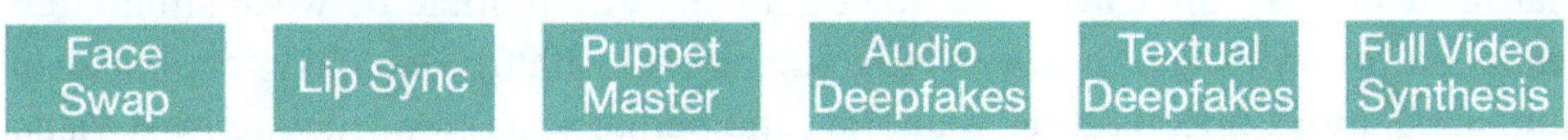

Systematic Literature Review

In a digital renaissance shaped by artificial intelligence (AI), deepfake technology has evolved to be an important disruption of truth. Deepfakes, as they have been characterized by Chesney & Citron (2019) and Westerlund (2019), are hyper-realistic synthetic media. They use sophisticated machine learning and neural networks to create convincing videos, audio, and images of real people doing or saying things in videos, when in fact they did not do that or say that. The ease with which this type of media can be created continues to obscure and impede the boundary between reality and fabrication, which is a wide scale risk for individuals, institutions, and society.Deepfakes are not simply amazing examples of digital wizardry but are also great ethical and society risks. Deepfakes and other forms of misinformation are now phenomenally easy to produce and share. Social media allows actors with nefarious intents to disseminate misinformation more rapidly, influence public opinion, dilute trust in live media, and threaten democracy without any worry about being discovered (Europol, 2022). On the other hand, there are obvious ways that deepfake scenarios can be applied in a positive way in different sectors, such as in education, and entertainment, and marketing (Johnson & Diakopoulos, 2021). This literature review seeks to give a comprehensive understanding of the ethical issues that aboud, the societal impact, and possible solutions for deep fake technology, through examining the breadth of articles on this subject.

This review adopts an integrative literature review method by integrating different research streams to generate a comprehensive understanding of the phenomenon. (Toronto & Remington, 2020) Our primary source for this synthesis is a peer-reviewed academic article that summarizes findings from computer science, marketing, law, journalism, and information systems. We take important information from the references found in the primary article and provide an academical interpretation through particular themes relative to our study.

Deepfake technology emerged from a new generation of deep learning and generative adversarial networks (GANs) that make shareable fake content look exactly like real content (Kietzmann et al., 2020). These systems learn from a substantial amount of real-world videos, images, and sounds, and can generate stochastic media that looks very realistic (Chesney & Citron, 2019). The result is image, sound, or video that makes it very difficult for us to cognitively differentiate between simulation, reality and everything in-between (Kietzmann et al., 2020). Deepfakes capitalize on human cognitive bias built on a natural (and perhaps sad) tendency to trust visual and auditory evidence. They function in such an impressive way because they do not act like a rudimentary fake but mirror seemingly natural speech patterns, facial movements and expressions that greatly confuse even the most reliable detection algorithms and trained/prepared viewers (Giansiracusa, 2021). Given the recent improvements in GAN architecture, it is nearly impossible to keep quality-level of deepfakes from generating unwanted yet realistic video simulations with adverse motives.

Deepfakes create serious ethical issues, most prominently consent and privacy. One form of deepfake that exemplifies this ethical challenge is non-consensual deepfake pornography, which primarily affects women, and when this happens to a victim it can lead to life-altering psychological and reputational harm (Chesney & Citron, 2019). This sort of violation removes the individuals' dignity and autonomy, while the legal system struggles to keep up. Deepfakes also threaten the democratic process. A faked political speech, or a manipulated portrayal of a political candidate, delegitimizes the electoral process to spread misinformation, or to manipulate voters' perceptions (Westerlund, 2019). A deepfake video of a political leader appearing to admit defeat, or a deepfake video of a political candidate making a disgusting statement can have ruined an election (Europol, 2022). Corporate ethical consideration is also implicated. Organizations face the dichotomy of deepfake technology: it can be a wonderful opportunity to inspire new ways to engage customers and the community, but it is also used to create deceptive deepfakes of brands, executives, and stakeholders of a business that can create reputational harm (Johnson & Diakopoulos, 2021). Using synthetic media in an ethical manner is an obligation to our society, and it is also a key business ethical consideration. As well, there are issues of moral accountability. While the creator of a malicious deepfake should be accountable for the harm they cause, the ethical responsibility for moral accountability extends to anyone who uses or propagates deepfakes without researching support or verification of the contents (Graham et al., 2021). In an era of hyper-connectivity and communication, passive consumers can contribute to a culture of misinformation, without even knowing it.

The societal consequences of deepfakes are immediate and long-lasting. The primary impact of deepfakes is the erosion of public confidence in digital media. As deepfakes become commonplace and realistic, the public becomes more uncertain concerning real content, sometimes described as "reality apathy" (Giansiracusa, 2021). This uncertainty diminishes the legitimacy of traditional new sources as well as the problems of media literacy that already exist.Deepfakes also weigh on growing social polarisation. Malicious actors use fabricated content to take advantage of ideological divides which exacerbates tensions within and between groups (Europol, 2022). The targeting of specific groups with made up content enhances the potential for divide and fragmentation in society.In addition, vulnerable populations, specifically older adults and less digitally literate individuals, are more susceptible to being duped by deepfakes (Guess et al., 2019). Studies have shown older individuals are more likely to share fake news, particularly given the nature of deepfakes.At a psychological level, deepfakes also entail significant harm to the individuals and groups targeted by ireful content. Notional victims exposed to deepfakes report anxiety, mental distress, and subsequent harm to their reputation (Chesney & Citron, 2019). This notional and personal costs propagate as societal costs in terms of a mental health burden, and the diminishment of social trust in interactions online.

The economic consequences of deepfakes are significant. Companies are at risk of fraud and reputational attacks made possible by deepfakes. For instance, in one case, cybercriminals used tools with AI-generated voice cloning to impersonate a top executive and successfully facilitated the fraudulent transfer of $243,000 (Stupp, 2019). Such incidents demonstrate that organizations can be vulnerable to these more sophisticated social engineering attacks.Furthermore, deepfakes threaten brand integrity. A highly fabricated or misleading video of an executive making a controversial statement can negatively influence share price and consumer trust (Johnson & Diakopoulos, 2021). Other scenarios involve negative deepfake reviews on social media channels, or even false endorsements from celebrities or business leaders, which heighten the risk exposure and potentially reduce brand equity and customer loyalty.Sectors that rely on biometric authentication will experience the greatest risk. For example, in the finance and cybersecurity sectors, deepfakes have the potential to bypass facial recognition and voice authentication systems, which directly threatens security protocols, in some cases (Botha & Pieterse, 2020). As deepfake capabilities and technologies become more sophisticated, this risk only increases.At the same time, ethical use of deepfake technology can be beneficial for businesses. Within the appropriate context, deepfakes can be used to increase customer engagement, develop personalised marketing campaigns, and enhance strategies to refresh creative content (Kietzmann et al., 2020). This indicates that the business community must tread carefully through this duality of risk diffusion versus ethical responsibility for innovation.

In the fight against deepfakes, technological countermeasures are leading the charge. Detection algorithms based on machine learning look at digital footprints, lighting anomalies, facial inconsistencies, and other artifacts to tag synthetic content (Mirsky & Lee, 2021). Companies like Microsoft have created ways to detect manipulated media such as Video Authenticator, which attempts to assess the probability of media manipulation (Graham et al., 2021).Detection is a reactionary measure in a cat-and-mouse game. As generation methods advance, detection mechanisms must change, but often these detection mechanisms look to stay ahead of the sophistication of new deepfake models (Ludwig et al. 2016). Therefore, even detection cannot promise a comprehensive solution.The use of blockchain technology provides a potential solution for verifying content. By permanently recording the provenance of digital content, blockchain can potentially verify synthetic media at its source (Pu et al., 2021). While the application is still in its infancy, decentralised methods of verification hold promise for establishing the credibility of media.

Legislative measures are essential to prevent malicious use of deepfakes. States like California and Virginia have enacted legislation that criminalizes non-consensual deepfake pornography and election interference (Graham et al., 2021). This legislation enables victims to seek preventive justice, while also acting as a potential deterrent to others.At a broader level, the EU's proposed AI regulatory framework explicitly addresses the matter of deepfakes by requiring transparency and disclosure of content (European Parliament, 2021). The goal of such governance is to balance technological innovation and public protection.However, enforcement remains challenging. The anonymity of the internet, coupled with different jurisdictions, is a disincentive for perpetrators who may not be brought to justice (Karasavva & Noorbhai, 2021). Effective governance in this area requires cooperation across international jurisdictions with aligned regulatory frameworks.

Raising awareness and improving digital literacy are vital components of deepfake prevention. When users learn about critical evaluation of media, verification of sources, and how to detect forms of manipulation within such media, it empowers them to use the internet responsibly (Bulger & Davison, 2018).Moreover, enabling collaboration between technology companies, universities, policy-makers, and civil society organisations can lead to more holistic solutions (Toronto & Remington,

2020). Partnerships among multiple stakeholders mean pooling resources, greater knowledge exchange and accelerating research towards the responsible development of technology.Social media platforms also have a key part to play in their mitigation. By developing robust content moderation processes, and providing AI detection tools, social media platforms can slow the rate of dissemination of harmful deepfakes (Mustak et. al, 2023). Nevertheless, these initiatives need to be transparent and publicly accountable in order to maintain their community of users.

Deepfake technology provides a compelling case for the duality of modern innovation: the significant potential for creativity is balanced by equally significant risks. As deepfakes evolve, they increasingly threaten to undermine trust in media, damage democratic institutions, and cause harm to individuals and businesses in ways we have not yet seen. Thankfully, this challenge is not insurmountable.By aligning together advances in technology, sound laws, corporate accountability, and public education, societies can build their defences to the lure of deception by deepfakes. In the process, we must actively work to develop a culture of critical digital literacy and ethical accountability, empowering individuals and institutions to act in safeguarding truth in the digital age.As the digital frontier continues to expand, our collective vigilance and ethical commitment is what will determine whether deepfakes remain a risk or are responsibly harnessed for good.

2. DETECTION TECHNIQUES FOR DEEPFAKE CONTENT

Scientists as well as experts work to develop multiple detection methods for identifying real versus manipulated content (Masood et al., 2021). Several important detection methods used to identify deepfake content will be presented in this section.

Deep Learning-Based Detection

The detection of deepfake tampering signals in images and videos is possible with Convolutional Neural Networks (CNNs) which identify irregularities such as abnormal face motions or lighting discrepancies or texture abnormalities. (Westerlund et al., 2019) Recurrent Neural Networks (RNNs) analyze time-based discrepancies which appear as abnormal head movements and improper eye blinks and inconsistent facial expressions between video frames. Autoencoders master genuine media patterns to detect deviations between known patterns and detected inputs which appear as potential deepfake candidates.

Feature-Based Detection

The analysis of natural biometric patterns consisting of eye movement together with pulse readings obtained from skin coloration variations and facial landmarks helps identify deepfake characteristics. This technique examines whether the sounds match the visible lip movements since this issue often occurs with deepfake voice swap operations. Deepfakes occasionally mistake the proper alignment of the head against body position which serves as a possible detection indicator.

Temporal Inconsistencies

Through frame-by-frame analysis technicians can identify typical signs of video tampering by detecting small effects of flickering and blurring and face ghosting near facial regions. The deepfake process for facial manipulation generates subtle but visible distortions along the borders of the face as well as around significant facial anatomy.

Physical Signal Analysis

The absence of proper heartbeat signals in deepfake videos gives experts a possible indication because analysts monitor skin color modifications from blood flow during heartbeat detection analysis. Eye blinking pattern analysis became an effective detection method because initial deepfake technology failed to recreate natural blinking rates and patterns during the early stages of development.

Forensic Techniques

Analysis of original video integrity involves forensic tools which detect irregular noise patterns and compression artifacts and sensor noise patterns when manipulation occurs. All digital sensors leave recognizable markings during recording sessions yet deepfake videos lack such markers.

Audio-Visual Inconsistencies

An examination of audio signals reveals when sounds from voices do not match mouth movements while at the same time indicating unusual voice characteristics that can signal an audio deepfake.Deepfake content detection is possible through analyzing discrepancies between face expression patterns and auditory sounds that flag deepfake media content.

Blockchain and Digital Watermarking

Blockchain technology tracks provenance through its systems which let users verify the original sources of digital content to prove authenticity. The watermarked digital signatures address a simple way for users to determine whether media content retains its original state.

Adversarial Approaches

Research methods mock the weaknesses of GAN models in deepfake generation to develop methods for detecting deepfakes in the first place. The application of adversarial data perturbations aids detection algorithms to create neutralization effects in deepfake processing systems.

Figure 2. Detection Techniques for Deepfake Content (Masood et. al, 2021)

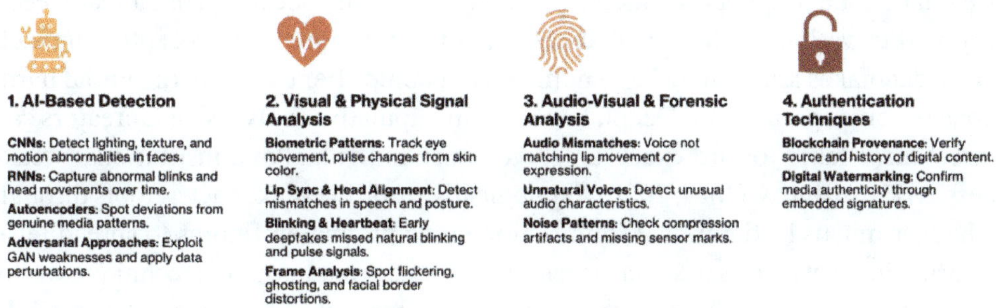

3. PROPAGATION OF MISLEADING DATA

Analysis of deepfakes as false content disseminators occurs in this research section. This research investigates deceptive actor exploitation of deepfakes for advancing their agendas using specific illustrations along with evaluations of their detrimental impact on human trust and social advancement. The ability to identify deepfakes acts as a foundation to build proper solutions to fight this ongoing digital menace which safeguards digital information integrity. Deepfakes function as a dominant force to disperse fabricated information which propagates misinformation leading to significant social barriers (Choraś et al., 2021). The research paper by Wazid et al. (2024) evaluates deepfake technology and its impact on incorrect information distribution. Deepfakes generate deceptive synthetic information which produces the fusion point between genuine media and artificial media content. Visual evidence credibility suffers while digital content authenticity declines because businesses employ this practice according to Wazid et al. (2024). Deceptive methods used to include misinformation grant it greater authenticity which leads to wider acceptance among people who assume these fake materials have true authenticity. False narratives spread widely using deepfakes because these technologies provide the capability to create realistic artificial content as Chesney and Citron (2019) explain. Lawbreakers use deepfakes to make fabricated content which demonstrates persons performing actions never documented by video cameras. False narratives exploit present bias and social divisions as well as create emotional triggers to speed up the spread of misinformation.(Ahmed & Shaun, 2022) Deepfake content spreads at lightning speed due to its sensational nature since these fabricated images and videos quickly attract viewer interest (Hobbs, 2020). The rapid deepfake dissemination media pace makes it difficult to control misinformation from rapidly spreading. Deepfake content spreads further than its revealed falsity because it has already been exposed to various audiences that become difficult to undo its deceptive impact. Once deepfakes are seen by large numbers of people after exposure the initial harm done becomes permanent. Deepfakes act as manipulative tools because creators can direct these fakes toward exact targets to abuse individual and institutional weaknesses (Hartmann & Giles, 2020). Strategically made deepfakes act as tools through which criminals lead political figures along with prominent figures to spread false information that results in social unrest. The strategic manipulation technique works through spreading confusion among public debates and institutional leaders while generating mistrust in both areas. Deepfake technology advances at a rapid pace which forms problems that impede both detection abilities and methods to authenticate content for experts. The advancing realism capabilities of deepfake technology result in material authenticity detection becoming more difficult throughout time. Deepfakes stay undetected in society after their release because no detection methods exist thus allowing misinformation to spread.

4. STRENGTHS AND LIMITATIONS OF SOME DEEPFAKE TECHNIQUES

Table 1. Strengths and limitations of deepfake techniques.

Technique	Strengths	Limitations
Generative Adversarial Networks (GANs)	- High-quality, realistic outputs -Versatile for various applications - Can generate new content based on training data	- Computationally intensive - Requires large amounts of data - Can produce artifacts or inconsistencies
Variational Autoencoders (VAEs)	- Effective for learning latent representations - Can generate diverse content - Lower computational cost compared to GANs	- Generally produces lower quality outputs compared to GANs - May struggle with high-fidelity details
Recurrent Neural Networks (RNNs)	- Good for generating sequences - Can capture temporal dependencies - Useful in video deepfakes	- Can be less effective in capturing long-range dependencies - Requires extensive training data
Face Swapping Algorithms	- Relatively straightforward to implement - Can achieve convincing results with fewer resources	- Limited to swapping faces in existing content - May have issues with alignment and lighting
Deep Convolutional Neural Networks (DCNNs)	- High accuracy in facial recognition and synthesis - Can produce detailed and high-resolution images	- Computationally demanding - May require significant data preprocessing
Audio-Visual Deepfake Techniques	- Can synchronize audio and visual components effectively - Useful for creating convincing synthetic media	- Complexity in maintaining

Deepfakes result in major psychological effects on human beings as Vasist et al (2022) reports. Those who meet deepfakes intended to assault their personal identity or their communities end up feeling disoriented and develop heightened feelings of distrust and anxiety. Deepfakes able to fool the viewer cause emotional reactions that tamper with their belief system and perception while spreading misinformation. Combating deepfake-driven misinformation demands uncommon detection techniques and complete deepfake education for the public population together with rules that punish creators of disinformation (Hartmann & Giles, 2020). The understanding of deepfakes operational principles and causes of misinformation distribution enables society to acquire stronger defenses against their destructive impact. This technology affects society as well as its citizens through studies of fake narrative systems along with real-world examples of deepfakes. Examples of deepfake misinformation impact can be observed through various major cases. Here are a few notable instances:-

1. **Corporate Espionage:** For instance, in 2020, a phishing attack was conducted in which the CEO of a leading technology firm was mimicked through a deepfake audio message. Such deep fake audio was employed in a case where the executive of a company was swindled into releasing a lot of money, which was transferred to a fake account. This case makes one to wonder how Deepfakes could be used in different corporate espionage or financial fraud cases.
2. **Manipulating Historical Figures:** In 2021, the video technology involved generating a very realistic fake video of a historical public figure, for example, Martin Luther King Jr. stating things that he would not say such as, gory details on the current social issues. that manipulation was to elicit public anger and reshuffle history. Such uses of deepfake technology can alter the perception of historical background and affect people's vision of the historical personalities and events.
3. **Medical Misinformation**: Some views of politicians, businessmen or celebrities have been synthesize by deepfake technique when they endorse fake cures or vaccines. For instance, a video which was produced under deepfake technology claimed that a renown doctor advocated for a particular treatment which is deadly or ineffective. This misuse especially fosters the diffusion of miss information in the market thus posing a health risk to the population.
4. **Fraudulent Academic Research:** At some point, deepfake videos were employed to create fake academic research presentation. There was a case of deepfake in the year 2022 whereby fake video of a respected scientist presenting fabricated data was shared. This misuse can thus be very adverse to scientific credibility and even mislead academics and researchers in the society.
5. **Impersonation in Legal Proceedings:** A case of a deep fake video was the simulation of lawyer during a virtual hearing in year 2023. The deepfake lawyer gave untrue legal reasons and fabricated proofs. This case explains the possibility of deepfakes and their impact on the legal process as well as justice.

Figure 3. Propagation of Misleading Data at a Glance

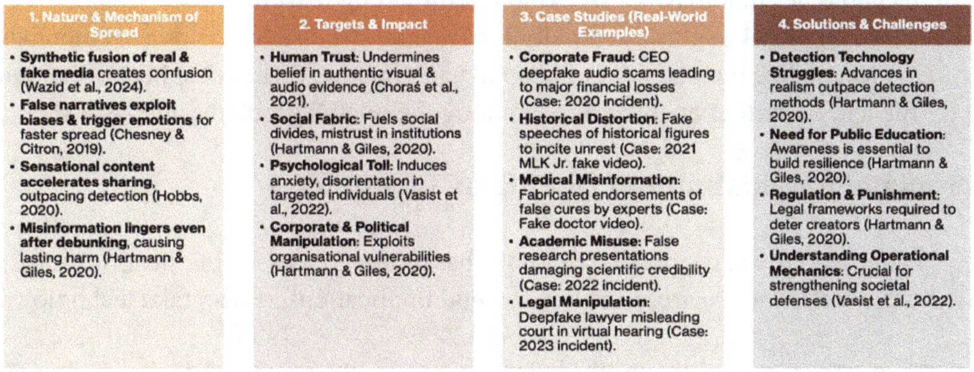

Managerial implications of Deepfake Technology

1. **Erosion of Digital Authenticity:** Deepfakes distort the credibility of the content y making it hard for anybody to differentiate between the originality of the material and a fake one. This is unfortunate as it undermines the reliability of digital communication and the people's confidence in the digital media.
2. **Exploitation in Marketing and Advertising:** With deepfakes, one can easily make a fake advertorial, for instance, fake endorsement by celebrities or even fake demonstrations of products. This can cause confusion to the consumers and in some cases, lead to control of the buying behaviour.
3. **Undermining Security Protocols:** Such tactics of getting around the security measures, including biometric identification or voice recognition platforms, become possible through deepfakes, which create a high risk to individual and business security.
4. **Impact on Social Media Ecosystems:** Therefore, deepfakes have a negative impact on social media, which is the promotion of fake news: content moderation and platform integrity. It is even almost impossible to control such messages as deepfakes, especially when it is possible to spread them wide.
5. **Challenges for Digital Literacy:** Therefore, with improved deepfake technology, there is the need for better digital skills in the society. This paper implies that it is crucial to raise awareness of the public to understand and analyze deepfakes as well as address the problem in its entirety.
6. Ethical Considerations in Technology Development: Deep fake technology has brought up a number of issues regarding responsibility as well as transparency especially in the course of deployment. It becomes the responsibility of devel-

opers and technologists how they use their knowledge and innovation to create technologies that may not be exploited for wrong reasons.

7. Through such thoughts and possibilities regarding those scenarios and outcomes we can realize the potential of deepfake in affecting different sphere of human life and its further analysis of examining the related problems and issues.

Societal Implications of Deepfake Technology

The emergence of deepfake technology has profound societal implications across various domains. Here are some key societal implications of deepfake technology.

1. **Trust Issues:** The possibility to forge perfect videos and realistic audio proofs erodes people's confidence in media and information. This means that as the 'realness' of the content becomes questionable, but the sceptics and those who spread fake news can do so too.
2. **Difficulty in Verifying Information:** The advancement of deepfakes also poses a problem to people to distinguish between the real and fake news and media which can potentially bring confusion and misunderstanding.
3. **Election Interference:** Deepfakes can be employed to post false and negative information concerning the rival political hopefuls with the risks of changing the voters' perception of the candidates and shifting the election results in the process. Indeed, this can compromise the credibility of the democratic processes.
4. **Political Polarization:** Malicious deepfake images and videos can extend polarization in politics as they fuel people's prejudice and promote misleading beliefs that portray the population.
5. **Non-consensual Content:** Electoral campaigns can be manipulated using deepfakes, honestly reputation can be attacked, risky or obscene content can be created with the person, without his/her knowledge, and this causes severe violation of their right to privacy and results in emotional distress.
6. **Identity Theft and Fraud:** The use of deepfakes enables scams in various types of the use of identity theft and financial fraud as we are able to impersonate individuals convincingly.
7. **Regulatory Gaps:** Current laws have not been effective in addressing issues of deepfake technology due to its dynamic development that is hard to be contained or banned.
8. **Ethical Dilemmas:** The creation and sharing of deepFake are ethical issues since the question of responsibility or accountability lies in shadows, and the impact they can have is precarious. One of the major factors always in consideration is the risk of pursuing innovation against the right things to do.

9. **Credibility Issues:** The use of deepfakes is a worrying prospect to journalists and media houses as it becomes dificult to differentiate between fake and real images, therefore this leads to credibility issues. It results in low credibility of news sources which lack the people's trust.
10. **Increased Workload for Verification:** It turned out that deepfakes cause increased financial problems for the journalists and media outlets since they are forced to spend more money on fact-checking and verifying their sources and information.
11. **Emotional Distress:** Often deepfake attack victims may develop trauma, insult, tarnished reputation and other detrimental factors that impact their personal and/or career livelihood hence the long term psychological impact
12. **Increased Anxiety and Mistrust**: Exposure to convincing deepfakes can contribute to increased anxiety and a general sense of mistrust, affecting individuals' mental well-being and their perception of reality.

Addressing these societal implications requires a multifaceted approach involving technological innovation, regulatory measures, public education, and ethical considerations. Addressing the societal impacts of deepfake technology demands a concerted effort from various stakeholders, including technology developers, policymakers, legal experts, and the broader community (Traboulsi, 2020). A holistic approach is essential to mitigate the risks associated with deepfakes and their implications for society (Rini et al., 2022).

Key strategies and countermeasures to consider include:

1. **Enhancing Deepfake Detection Technology:** There is a need to budget for the growth of higher sophisticated models of deepfake detectors. This includes using advanced algorithms that are able to identify small abnormalities and characteristics possibly switched in fake content. It is crucial to emphasise the Cooperation between such entities as researchers, industrial specialists, and technology companies, as the aforementioned solution cannot be developed independently (Yazdinejad et al., 2021).
2. **Developing Secure Authentication Systems:** Currently, media authentication that relates to improving the security of the systems used to identify media can assist in proving the source of digital content. This is to mean that, by using techniques like digital watermarking, cryptographic hashing, as well as blockchain technology, the media can be protected from tampering and its authenticity ascertained. The integration of these methods to content platform makes it possible to enhance trust and minimise the deepfakes (Yazdinejad et al., 2021).

3. **Strengthening Social Media Policies:** Social media platform owners should not allow the generation and dissemination of deepfake content and should deploy measures to prevent same from being posted online. This entails establishing of policies, availing ways through which users can report off-allowed content, and negative consequences for violation of policies (Kwok, A. O et al., 2021).
4. **Promoting Media Literacy and Education:** In the case of deepfake misinformation, the solution lies in increasing users' media literacy. People should be equipped with knowledge of how to analyze content they come across in media, be able to identify clues of distortion and know how to check facts. On the same note, its authors suggested that empowering users with these skills may help them mitigate the effects of deepfake disinformation (Yazdinejad et al., 2021).
5. **Fostering Collaboration between Technology and Research:** Funding from technology companies and academic researchers is therefore imperative in the development of better ways of fighting deep fake technology. Businesses can provide information to researchers and to exchange the findings with methods of increasing the effectiveness of the detection of the threats and the creation of the countermeasures. Businesses should constantly brainstorm about emerging threats and open the communication channel to deal with them to be in a position to devise preventive plans. (Al-Khazraji et al., 2023)
6. **Implementing Legal and Policy Frameworks:** To overcome the problems related to deepfakes, governments must develop legal and regulatory strategies on the subject. These frameworks should enumerate legal consequences of those engaging in malicious deepfake activities and delineate how deepfake content should be reported or taken down and how victims can seek remedy. As for the second problematic attribute related to the unlimited capability of Artificial Intelligence, deepfakes are the international cooperation which is needed to combat the global challenges (Traboulsi, 2020).
7. **Raising Public Awareness:** It makes sense to talk about deepfake risks and consequences to encrypt them in people's conscience through information release campaigns. These campaigns should focus on the effects of deepfakes on political system, journalism and personal privacy that will enable the individual to critically engage media and society respectively be active in handling deepfake contents as well as Traboulsi (Amezaga & Hajek, 2022).
8. **Multi-Faceted Approach:** Mitigation measures toward deepfakes have to do with a multi-pronged approach that includes technological solutions, policies, and awareness creation. Applying technology improvements in detection, creating strict norms, and increasing people's awareness, society

will be able to minimize the consequences of deepfakes and trust the sources of information (Kozyreva et al., 2020).

The use of these strategies to achieve these objectives calls for the effective cooperation of individuals in the development of technology, policymakers in improving the policies that govern the use of this technology in education, educators in ensuring that the public gets the full information about this technology and the public in ensuring that they incorporate their knowledge in using this technology in their everyday life. Such an approach will also protect from potential adverse effects of deepfakes and strengthen the media and informational processes (Sahu et al., 2023).

Table 2. Techniques for addressing deepfake challenges

Focus Area	Technique	Description	References
Deepfake Detection	Advanced Detection Algorithms	Utilized machine learning models to recognized patterns, inconsistencies, and artifacts particular to deepfake content.	**Westerlund et al., (2019).**
	Forensic Analysis	Employ forensic tool to examine media for signs of manipulation and fabrication, for instance:- abnormal lighting or inconsistent audio.	Kwok, A. O et al., 2021
Authentication Systems	Digital Watermarking	Embed invisible markers in media to confirm its detect tampering and authenticity	Mahmud et al., 2021
	Cryptographic Hashing	Produce unique hashes for media content to integrity and ensure integrity.	Westerlund et al.(2019).
	Blockchain Technology	Use blockchain to track and ensure the authenticity of media files and provenance	Mahmud et al., 2021
Social Media Policies	Policy Implementation	Enforce instructions against deepfake distribution on social media platforms and creation	Sharma, M., & Kaur, M. (2022)
	Reporting Mechanisms	To set up mechanism for users to report suspected deepfake content.	(Al-Khazraji et al., 2023)
	Penalties for Violations	To Implement consequences for users who breach deepfake policies, including account suspension and content removal.	Yazdinejad et al., 2021
Media Literacy and Education	Educational Programs	Develop initiatives to instruct people how to critically evaluate media, verify content authenticity and identify manipulation.	Yazdinejad et al., 2021
	Digital Literacy Workshops	Offer training sessions and workshops to build public understanding of media manipulation tool and digital education and make people aware about its consequences.	Ahmed & Shaun, 2022

continued on following page

Table 2. Continued

Focus Area	Technique	Description	References
Collaboration and Research	Industry-Academia Partnerships	Facilitate alliance between technology companies and researchers to forward data and resources for countermeasures and ameliorate detection.	Yazdinejad et al., 2021
	Information Sharing	To foster open communication and information exchange to identify appear deepfake hazards and develop preventive strategies.	Yazdinejad et al., 2021
Legal and Policy Frameworks	Comprehensive Legislation	To promote legislations outlining consequences for malicious deepfake creation and distribution, and provide instructions for content removal.	kwok et al., 2020
	Victim Protection	Set up a system for victims of deepfakes to avail legal recourse and justice.	Mehmud et al., 2021
	International Cooperation	Tie up with international organization to create unified legal approaches and evaluate the global nature of deepfake issues.	Traboulsi, 2020
Public Awareness	Awareness Campaigns	Run campaigns to instruct the public about the threat of deepfakes, their societal implication, and how to identify and report them.	kwok et al.,2021
	Community Engagement	Collaboration with communities to spread awareness about deepfake techniques and exhale alertness.	Traboulsi, 2020

The aforementioned table provides an organized view of different techniques for addressing the challenges posed by deepfake technology. Each technique is linked to specific focus areas and described with its intended purpose.

7. CONCLUSION

The document shows multiple problems emerging in deepfake technology since its initial introduction as a technical tool until reaching the current state as a both serious threat to social cohesion as well as public trust. Digital fakery functions as a powerful weapon for deception through artificial intelligence network implementation that produces distinguishable artificial media from original content. The advancement of this technology results in broader consequences than its original basic technical interests and produces detrimental effects against personal security as well as democratic principles and public trust. The ongoing research demonstrates that modern detection approaches using watermarking together with AI algorithms have potential detection capabilities but these methods remain outpaced by deepfake technological progress. Research along with industry partners and legal makers need continuous innovation because deepfake creators are engaged in a persistent competition with detection methods. The implementation of effective mitigation approaches requires strong detection methods together with public awareness campaigns and technological progress and complete regulatory frameworks. These problems require attention from society to understand and control deepfake-derived risks while building an environment which is more secure and reliable online. Research in the following years should concentrate on developing better detection methods and comprehending deepfakes' extensive societal consequences as well as creating forward-thinking policies to tackle both technological and moral aspects of this rapidly developing issue. Through dedicated teamwork between various experts deepfakes can be mitigated while digital media authenticity remains secure.

REFERENCES

Ahmed, S., & Shaun, M. A. (2022). Impact of deepfake technology on digital world authenticity: A review. *International Journal of Engineering and Management Research, 12*(3), 78–84. DOI: 10.31033/ijemr.12.3.10

Al-Khazraji, S. H., Saleh, H. H., Khalid, A. I., & Mishkhal, I. A. (2023). Impact of deepfake technology on social media: Detection, misinformation and societal implications. *The Eurasia Proceedings of Science Technology Engineering and Mathematics, 23*, 429–441. DOI: 10.55549/epstem.1371792

Al-Khazraji, S. H., Saleh, H. H., Khalid, A. I., & Mishkhal, I. A. (2023). Impact of Deepfake Technology on Social Media: Detection, Misinformation and Societal Implications. *The Eurasia Proceedings of Science Technology Engineering and Mathematics, 23*, 429–441. DOI: 10.55549/epstem.1371792

Amezaga, N., & Hajek, J. (2022, September). Availability of voice deepfake technology and its impact for good and evil. In *Proceedings of the 23rd Annual Conference on Information Technology Education* (pp. 23-28). DOI: 10.1145/3537674.3554742

Botha, J., & Pieterse, H. (2020). Fake news and deepfakes: A dangerous threat for 21st century information security. In ICCWS 2020 15th International Conference on Cyber Warfare and Security (p. 57).

Bulger, M., & Davison, P. (2018). The promises, challenges, and futures of media literacy. *The Journal of Media Literacy Education, 10*(1), 1–21. DOI: 10.23860/JMLE-2018-10-1-1

Chesney, B., & Citron, D. (2019). Deep fakes: A looming challenge for privacy, democracy, and national security. *California Law Review, 107*, 1753.

Choraś, M., Demestichas, K., Giełczyk, A., Herrero, Á., Ksieniewicz, P., Remoundou, K., Urda, D., & Woźniak, M. (2021). Advanced Machine Learning techniques for fake news (online disinformation) detection: A systematic mapping study. *Applied Soft Computing, 101*, 107050. DOI: 10.1016/j.asoc.2020.107050

European Parliament. (2021). Tackling deepfakes in European policy. https://www.europarl.europa.eu/thinktank/en/document/EPRS_STU(2021)690039

Europol. (2022). Europol (2022), Facing reality? Law enforcement and the challenge of deepfakes, an observatory report from the Europol Innovation Lab, Publications Offce of the European Union, Luxembourg. https://www.europol.europa.eu/ publication

Giansiracusa, N. (2021). Deepfake deception. In *How algorithms create and prevent fake news* (pp. 41–66). Apress. DOI: 10.1007/978-1-4842-7155-1_3

Graham, N., Hedges, R., Chiu, C., de La Chapelle, F., & van de Graaf, A. (2021, October 12). How can businesses protect themselves from deepfake attacks? Business Going Digital. https://www.businessgoing.digital/how-can-businesses-protect-themselvesfrom-deepfake-attacks

Guess, A., Nagler, J., & Tucker, J. (2019). Less than you think: Prevalence and predictors of fake news dissemination on Facebook. *Science Advances, 5*(1), eaau4586. DOI: 10.1126/sciadv.aau4586 PMID: 30662946

Hancock, J. T., & Bailenson, J. N. (2021). The social impact of deepfakes. *Cyberpsychology, Behavior, and Social Networking, 24*(3), 149–152. DOI: 10.1089/cyber.2021.29208.jth PMID: 33760669

Hartmann, K., & Giles, K. (2020, May). The next generation of cyber-enabled information warfare. In 2020 12th international conference on cyber conflict (CyCon) (Vol. 1300, pp. 233-250). IEEE. DOI: 10.23919/CyCon49761.2020.9131716

Johnson, D. G., & Diakopoulos, N. (2021). What to do about deepfakes. *Communications of the ACM, 64*(3), 33–35. DOI: 10.1145/3447255

Kietzmann, J., Lee, L. W., McCarthy, I. P., & Kietzmann, T. C. (2020). Deepfakes: Trick or treat? *Business Horizons, 63*(2), 135–146. DOI: 10.1016/j.bushor.2019.11.006

Kwok, A. O., & Koh, S. G. (2021). Deepfake: A social construction of technology perspective. *Current Issues in Tourism, 24*(13), 1798–1802. DOI: 10.1080/13683500.2020.1738357

Ludwig, S., Van Laer, T., De Ruyter, K., & Friedman, M. (2016). Untangling a web of lies: Exploring automated detection of deception in computer-med

Mahmud, B. U., & Sharmin, A. (2021). Deep insights of deepfake technology: A review. *arXiv preprint arXiv:2105.00192*.

Mirsky, Y., & Lee, W. (2021). The creation and detection of deepfakes: A survey. *ACM Computing Surveys, 54*(1), 1–41. DOI: 10.1145/3425780

Mustak, M., Salminen, J., Mäntymäki, M., Rahman, A., & Dwivedi, Y. K. (2023). Deepfakes: Deceptions, mitigations, and opportunities. *Journal of Business Research, 154*, 113368. DOI: 10.1016/j.jbusres.2022.113368

Pu, J., Mangaokar, N., Kelly, L., Bhattacharya, P., Sundaram, K., Javed, M., Wang, B., & Viswanath, B. (2021). Deepfake videos in the wild: Analysis and detection. *Proceedings of the Web Conference 2021*, 981–992. DOI: 10.1145/3442381.3449978

Sharma, M., & Kaur, M. (2022). A review of Deepfake technology: an emerging AI threat. *Soft Computing for Security Applications: Proceedings of ICSCS 2021*, 605-619.

Stupp, C. (2019). August 30). Wall Street Journal: Fraudsters Used AI to Mimic CEO's Voice in Unusual Cybercrime Case. https://www.wsj.com/articles/fraudsters-use-aito-mimic-ceos-voice-in-unusual-cybercrime-case-11567157402

Toronto, C. E., & Remington, R. (2020). *A step-by-step guide to conducting an integrative review*. Springer. DOI: 10.1007/978-3-030-37504-1

Wazid, M., Mishra, A. K., Mohd, N., & Das, A. K. (2024). A Secure Deepfake Mitigation Framework: Architecture, Issues, Challenges, and Societal Impact. *Cyber Security and Applications*, *2*, 100040. DOI: 10.1016/j.csa.2024.100040

Westerlund, M. (2019). The emergence of deepfake technology: A review. *Technology Innovation Management Review*, *9*(11), 39–52. DOI: 10.22215/timreview/1282

Westerlund, M. (2019). The emergence of deepfake technology: A review. *Technology Innovation Management Review*, *9*(11), 39–52. DOI: 10.22215/timreview/1282

Yazdinejad, A., Zolfaghari, B., Azmoodeh, A., Dehghantanha, A., Karimipour, H., Fraser, E., Green, A. G., Russell, C., & Duncan, E. (2021). A review on security of smart farming and precision agriculture: Security aspects, attacks, threats and countermeasures. *Applied Sciences (Basel, Switzerland)*, *11*(16), 7518. DOI: 10.3390/app11167518

Chapter 11
Cryptocurrency in India:
Technological Growth and Regulatory Challenges

Preeti Jain
https://orcid.org/0009-0000-3178-0837
Ajay Kumar Garg Institute of Management, Ghaziabad, India

Sachin Sudan
https://orcid.org/0000-0003-2186-4476
Maharishi Markandeshwar University, India

Neetu Chaudhary
https://orcid.org/0000-0001-6589-4015
Maharishi Markandeshwar University, India

ABSTRACT

Technological advancements and changing legislative frameworks have had a notable impact on the important milestones and problems that have marked the development of cryptocurrencies in India. The increasing need for alternative investments and the population's penchant for technology have propelled the acceptance of cryptocurrencies. The Supreme Court of India's 2020 ruling to reverse the Reserve Bank of India's restriction on cryptocurrency transactions was a turning point that rekindled interest in digital assets. In spite of this, efforts to write comprehensive laws are ongoing, and the regulatory landscape is still unsettled. Although investors find the decentralised and secure transactions that cryptocurrencies enable enticing, worries about market instability, privacy, and misuse still exist. Notwithstanding the potential for growth in the Indian cryptocurrency industry and the several areas in which blockchain applications are being used, institutional and individual investors encounter difficulties as a result of unclear regulations.

DOI: 10.4018/979-8-3373-0675-9.ch011

INTRODUCTION

Cryptocurrency, an electronic or virtual currency, has become a strong force in the financial world because of its decentralized nature and reliance on encryption for protection. A great deal of discussion has been generated about the potential for this new financial tool to either revolutionize or destabilize established financial systems.

Cryptocurrency is defined as a system for issuing tokens intended for use as a medium of exchange, accounted for using a digital ledger maintained through cryptography. This system replaces traditional institutional trust with cryptographic trust to varying extents (Pernice & Scott, 2021). Contrary to traditional currencies, unlike conventional currencies, cryptocurrency operates without the support of centralised financial institutions, including banks. An online network of currency holders is responsible for managing them, and all transactions are recorded on a distributed database known as the blockchain.

Money has historically played an important role in steering the global economy, including facilitating commerce and financial services. It is crucial in serving as a means of transacting goods and services while also preserving value for people and institutions. For millennia, many regulatory agencies throughout the world have been concerned with maintaining economic stability by assuring an appropriate supply of physical money and financial instruments associated with it. Furthermore, a state's strength is determined by its monetary competence.

The advent of private cryptocurrencies in the current digital era, as well as the prospective introduction of central bank digital currencies, is undermining the existing monetary system. While economists, businesses, and investors have begun to think that this new currency will transform the financial world, it is vital to objectively evaluate these claims and discern between truth and exaggerated advertising. In light of this, the current paper examines the interaction between India's digital currency market and the traditional stock market in a rising economy. The different characteristics of these two marketplaces pique interest in researching their financial interactions. Banknotes were traditionally backed by precious metals, and the issuing bank was the guarantor. This boosted flexible trade and commerce, since individuals may now interchange currencies while bidding on precious metals and commodities (Gupta *et al.,* 2023).

The advent of fiat currencies in the twentieth century accelerated the use of paper money. Instead of being backed by precious metals, fiat currencies are guaranteed by the government, allowing it to modify interest rates and the money supply while controlling inflation and monetary expansion. Eichengreen (2019). In the twenty-first century, the rise of digital currencies has transformed the concept of monetary transactions. Cryptographic algorithms support the safe and decentralized transactions used by digital currencies.

The introduction of paper money, banknotes, and fiat currencies has influenced the evolution of currencies, from their early iterations based on precious metals to the introduction of paper money, banknotes, and fiat currencies (Eichengreen, 2019). Although the widespread use and acceptance of digital currency is still in its infancy, experts have concluded that it has the ability to substantially redefine the entire financial system (Agur *et al.,* 2022) and can become an alternate means of trade. It can also help expand access to financial services. With several advantages in mind, the fact remains that digital currencies can be used to support illegal activity. The majority of criminal and terrorist activities are being supported by digital currency (Abu Elbeh, 2024).

The regulatory bodies must efficiently manage digital currencies to ensure their sustained competitiveness in the financial system, which can help to increase job creation and economic growth. Effective management of digital money is critical for fostering innovation in the banking and financial services sectors. Individuals, institutions, and financial officials need to understand the complexities and implications of digital currency on the worldwide economy.

A BRIEF REVIEW OF CRYPTOCURRENCIES

According to Fry, J. (2018). Cryptocurrency is a novel kind of digital currency that takes use of a decentralized system. It uses complicated cryptography algorithms to secure financial transactions and authenticate asset transfers. It is based on blockchain technology, which is a public and distributed ledger (De Ocáriz Borde, 2022).

Each of the cryptocurrencies possesses a blockchain that is open to all and provides transparency for every node. Miners solve cryptographic challenges by utilizing vast amounts of computing power to construct new blocks of the blockchain (De Ocáriz Borde, 2022). Upon successful completion, miners get a cryptocurrency reward delivered to their designated cryptocurrency address, akin to a bank deposit. Nevertheless, mining is expensive, requiring specialist machinery, cooling systems, and a large quantity of power. Bitcoin mining occurs on a massive scale, leaving a significant carbon imprint in the environment. Nonetheless, nations such as China, Kazakhstan, Kyrgyzstan, and Uzbekistan have outlawed cryptocurrency mining owing to a lack of power (Baur *et al.,* 2017).

Key features of cryptocurrency

Cryptocurrencies are digital currencies that their owners utilize as a means of payment. They provide advantages that regular currencies do not, which is why they are so popular. The following traits distinguish them.

1. **Anonymity**: All transactions, regardless incorporating personal or commercial information, are identified by a random string of characters rather than the owner's name. The widespread use of specific virtual currencies may be used to estimate demand and supply levels. Contracts cannot genuinely be related to specific individuals or corporations.
2. **No Supervisory Bodies**: Governmental oversight and restrictions are not present, hence there are no taxes or limits that may be damaging to users. Authorities or financial bodies do not restrict the flow of bitcoin transactions. Unfavorable fees and limitations are lowered as a consequence. Bitcoin owners, on the other hand, do not benefit from financial regulation protection.
3. **Security**: A hidden key can be used to protect private virtual wallets where bitcoins are held. This implies that only the owner can access the funds that have been accumulated. Owners of virtual currency should apply encryption technology to their storage systems to enhance security.
4. **No Centralization**: No institutions govern cryptocurrency exchange rates or flows. Trading in virtual currency occurs all around the world. This avoids trading halts due to hacker efforts. Because bitcoin holders immediately keep transaction data, it spreads across the network.
5. **Sending Cryptocurrencies**: The way bitcoins are sent differs significantly from how traditional currencies are transmitted. The financial systems of the receiving and sending countries, including incoming and departing sessions, are critical to the institutional model. Transfers of virtual money occur relatively immediately and are not location-based.
6. **Irreversible Transactions:** The virtual currency market is not institutionally controlled; therefore, the commission transactions cannot be reversed. If an issue arises, such as incorrect recipient information, no organization can intervene.
7. **Fast Development**: Holders can utilize their bitcoins using the tools and services that are rapidly emerging. It is now possible to convert cryptocurrencies into dollars or euros. These currencies may be financed directly from Bitcoin wallets using conversion and exchange tools.
8. **No Specific Location**: Crypto currencies are not concerned with where their owners are physically situated. You can thus send bitcoin to a relative who lives close by or an associate who lives in a foreign nation. Furthermore, the transactions would be handled identically and in the same period of time.
9. **Use of Encryption**: Data that is secured by encryption takes the form of a cipher. Only those with the private key can access it. Cryptography is the technique of converting any information into a secure code. It is a technique widely employed in the cryptography industry to ensure that transactions are exceptionally secure, anonymous, and free of external supervision.

How cryptocurrencies work

Cryptocurrencies employ cryptography to facilitate and record transactions on a network of electronic ledgers, or financial account databases. Cryptocurrencies do not exist in physical form; instead, they are electronic signals and records that trace transactions mediated by the currency. Cryptocurrencies are sometimes characterized as "digital" or "virtual" currencies due to their electronic representation, although there are differences between the three. (Delfabbro *et al.,* 2021).

The prefix crypto, meaning "concealed" or "concealment," comes from the Greek word for "hidden." While encryption is employed to safeguard individual transactions as well as the ledger of individual accounts, or 'addresses,' the ledgers that record all transactions are often exposed to anybody with an interest in them. Despite this, address owners maintain some anonymity since no central authority, such as a bank, assigns a specific address to a certain person.

Cryptocurrencies, like conventional currencies such as dollar notes or gold coins, can be used to conduct 'peer-to-peer' transactions between individuals without the intervention of a specialized financial intermediary. While commodity currencies such as gold have genuine other uses, fiat currencies, bank deposits, and cryptocurrency do not. People who use modern currencies believe that others will accept them in future transactions, making them useful as a temporary store of value. Despite cryptocurrencies typically lacking a centralized issuer, they are largely fiduciary in the sense that no government backs them (Delfabbro *et al.,* 2021).

Cryptocurrencies are a dispersed platform that allows transactions to take place without the need for a central entity. This decentralization is achieved through the creation of the 'blockchain,' a worldwide distributed ledger that enables transaction confirmation and monitoring of individual cryptocurrency balances. The basis for the research is that, during 2017, the whole crypto asset market capitalization surged from $18 billion in January to a mind-boggling $600 billion in December, raising fears about the crypto asset industry as a whole being a giant froth.

The desire to be among the first to put money into "the next Bitcoin" fueled speculative activity even more. However, prices started to plummet throughout the entire crypto asset ecosystem in January 2018, with declines occurring evenly across all crypto assets. Despite a few small rebounds in early 2018, the price decline has continued throughout the year, wiping out more than $600 billion in market capitalization (Fauzi *et al.,* 2020).

The rapid surge in Bitcoin prices affected other crypto assets, garnering both ongoing media attention and new speculative investors (both retail and institutional). Traditional financial services companies' entry into the crypto asset market, as well as new offerings like Bitcoin futures, specialist custody solutions, and dedicated crypto asset hedge funds, accelerated the industry's growth. However, this prompted further regulatory scrutiny. Tokens became popular in the ecosystem as well, thanks mostly to the general acceptance of the ERC-20 standard on the Ethereum network and the consequent expansion of Initial Coin Offerings.

As a result, token-based fundraising increased dramatically, as did ICO activity throughout the world. Blockchain splits, which separate existing currencies into distinct crypto assets, gained popularity in 2017, expanding the variety of items in the crypto asset ecosystem. The rising interest and consequent usage highlighted the limitations of base layer scaling, leading to the rise of so-called "layer-2 alternatives," such as Bitcoin's much-anticipated Lightning Network.

The joint dialogue and oversight actions of regulators in the industry in 2018 seem to be driving its growth by delivering regulatory certainty and consistency on the regulation of crypto assets and related activities. This is a significant one with unambiguous implications. For instance, the Financial Action Task Force (FATF) released new AML and CFT guidelines in June 2019, with industry participants urged to comply, and more of the surveyed service providers conducting KYC and AML checks on their customers (Verma *et al.,* 2024).

Despite the uncertainty and economic rollercoaster ride brought on by the worldwide COVID-19 epidemic, we have learnt that even in bad circumstances, businesses and markets have reached a critical stage where operations can continue with the bulk of their workers working remotely. Even while the pandemic persists, finance moves forward. Alternative finance, in particular, has a place in a post-pandemic society, as does the research and analysis of emerging trends (Demir *et al.,* 2020)

Blockchain Technology

When developing a software system, its layout is critical. There are two main ways to do this: centralized and dispersed. Centralized systems contain components that are linked to a central element, whereas dispersed systems have interconnected components but no central coordinating element. Peer-to-peer systems are a key aspect of distributed system architecture. In this sense, a peer-to-peer system is a distributed software system made up of individual nodes (computers) that directly share computing resources with one another. This enables the distributed system to achieve greater processing power, lower costs, greater dependability, and natural growth (Verma *et al.,* 2024).

When it comes to building a software system, architecture is only a means to a goal. Choosing certain architecture has implications for achieving the functional and non-functional features of a system. Because these architectural principles take quite different methods to ensuring integrity, in this case, block chain technology is useful. It is a secure, decentralized digital ledger that is hard to hack and extremely durable. It may operate independently of any intermediate body, like as a bank or the government.

Block chain history dates back to early 1990, when David Chaum presented DigiCash, Inc.'s eCash system based on his two articles (Barenji *et al.,* 2018). Later, in 2008, the first block chain was developed using an improvised architecture for timestamp blocks. Bitcoin, the first cryptocurrency network launched in 2009, was a pioneer in employing a decentralized way to facilitate secure digital currency transactions. This implies that with cryptocurrency, each node or computer terminal is linked to the others. This enables any node to disconnect and rejoin the network whenever it wishes (Delgado *et al.,* 2018).

Furthermore, because the blockchain is a decentralized network, users inside it utilize cryptographic techniques to avoid data manipulation. Bitcoin users utilize digital signatures to send digital assets to others. While each transaction is publicly recorded on the Bitcoin blockchain, anybody on the network may confirm that the transactions are legitimate. Whereas blockchain technology is commonly associated with cryptocurrencies such as Bitcoin and Ethereum, it is not confined to them.

The potential applications of blockchain technology have generated considerable interest and research studies to explore its potential. The emerging technology can transform data and transaction handling by enhancing security and transparency, and could make many industries more efficient, including banking, supply chain management, and healthcare (Verma *et al.,* 2024). Various factors are responsible for this process. Blockchain, in essence, is an open platform. This implies that it uses machine-to-machine technology that verifies each transaction by each and every node (computer) in the network, which minimizes fraud and simplifies asset tracking. In addition, the encrypted transactions in the distributed ledger make manipulation of data more difficult.

This is important in firms that prioritize data privacy. In addition, the absence of intermediaries in transactions saves time and enhances efficiency. This also aids in cost savings, making the technology attractive to enterprises like supply chain management and real estate. Hence, the increasing demand for security and transparency in several industries is anticipated to boost the significance of blockchain technology, making it an essential resource for people and organizations.

Core Concepts of Blockchain Technology

Blockchain technology is decentralized because it is not operated by one authority, and it is spread across a vast network, providing security. The robust foundation of blockchain is based on the implementation of mathematical operations called Hashing in the computation field. Hashing employs cryptography to securely handle information through the use of a hash function that takes in a variable-length input message and gives a fixed-length output. The output is usually referred to as the hash code, hash value, or message. This method of cryptography encrypts data in a block and handles values in a data set.

Of particular interest is that the security of hash functions is a result of their ability to completely alter the outcome with even slight alteration of the input. Consequently, in blockchain, Hashing serves two purposes: providing security and reducing block size by structuring values in a Merkle Tree and ultimately linking them to the previous one in the next block's field (Verma *et al.,* 2024).

Merkle trees are a crucial aspect of the blockchain since they link to the hashing algorithms. They were named after Ralph Merkel, a computer expert. All cryptocurrencies use Merkle trees, also known as hash trees, to properly organize and secure information on the blockchain. Merkle trees are built by repeatedly pairing and hashing nodes until only one hash, known as the Merkle root or root hash, remains as a condensed representation of the dataset. This root hash is subsequently added to the preceding hash value of the subsequent block (Verma *et al.,* 2024). Every block must go through the Merkle tree procedure in order to pass the previous value to the next block on the blockchain.

Merkle trees are an authentication and impenetrable technique for blockchain. If, ever, any fraudulent person attempts to alter or modify the block's data, the whole output will be altered, and the system will alert a flag for the incorrect value (Verma *et al.,* 2024).

Need for Blockchain Technology

Before the emergence of blockchain technology, management of financial information relied greatly on centralized third parties like banks and regulatory institutions to authenticate and monitor transactions and data (Aquilina *et al.,* 2024). Nevertheless, research has established that centralized mechanisms are prone to fraud and data invasion. Even incidents of data theft have been reported. Additionally, the use of middlemen made each transaction more costly and time-consuming. Consequently, the need for an open, safe, and decentralized platform to facilitate easy transactions and store information saw the emergence of blockchain technology. Blockchain technology solved these challenges by offering an unerasable platform that operates without using middlemen. This not only minimizes the possibility of fraud and corruption but also maximizes transparency (Aquilina *et al.,* 2024).

Development of Cryptocurrency in India

The history of cryptocurrencies in India has been shaped by several innovations and significant events that are also significant in the global development of virtual currencies. The current regulatory landscape has impacted India's experience with cryptocurrencies as a result of technological breakthroughs, economic opportunities, and regulatory hurdles since the launch of Bitcoin in 2009.

The history of cryptocurrencies in India began with the launch of Bitcoin in 2009, as it did throughout the world. Bitcoin's decentralized structure and blockchain technology challenged traditional banking systems, allowing for a new way to conduct transactions without middlemen. The market for cryptocurrencies in India has undergone significant changes over the years due to the appearance of more and more decentralized apps and digital assets. (Charfeddine *et al.*, 2020). Although there is no official regulation, cryptocurrencies have gained popularity as an alternative investment option. They appeal to tech-savvy individuals and businesses who are seeking creative financial solutions.

Key Milestones in Cryptocurrency Adoption

The Reserve Bank of India (RBI) ban on cryptocurrency transactions in 2018 was a significant setback that resulted in market anxiety. In 2020, the Supreme Court's decision to lift this restriction resulted in renewed interest and investment in cryptocurrencies. The swift increase in the market capitalisation of Bitcoin, especially in 2017, brought attention from Indian investors to the potential of cryptocurrencies as a sound investment vehicle. Even though full legislation is still being developed, the Indian government's recent steps to tax profits from cryptocurrency trading indicate a move towards the recognition and regulation of the sector (Cioroianu *et al.*, 2023).

Factors Contributing to the Rise of Cryptocurrency in India

- **Technological Developments**: The emergence of blockchain technology, which offers the framework for safe and transparent transactions, has been a significant influence. The creation of numerous cryptocurrencies and decentralised applications has been made possible by this technology.
- **Digitalisation and Tech-Savvy Population**: The acceptance of cryptocurrencies has been fuelled by India's growing digitalisation and a sizable population of tech aficionados. Interest has been further piqued by the need for alternative investment options and the possibility of large profits.
- **Economic Factors**: Indian investors seeking inflation protection and diversification have been drawn to cryptocurrencies because of their perceived value as "gold-like" investments.
- **Global Trends**: Indian investors and businesses are investigating these novel financial instruments as a result of the cryptocurrency market's global expansion and the growing public trust in digital currencies.

The emergence of cryptocurrencies in India offers many prospects, but there are drawbacks as well. The lack of clear regulatory frameworks can lead to uncertainty for firms and investors, which can hinder growth. Besides, numerous unresolved matters with regard to the danger of cyber-attacks and the instability of cryptocurrency markets remain. Nevertheless, cryptocurrencies have immense potential to impact India's financial landscape, and further developments in technology and policy will probably reshape the course of this thrilling business.

Users of Cryptocurrencies

Crypto currency users may be classified into three groups depending on their investment goals and usage behaviors. The first group comprises active users who primarily acquire cryptocurrency for transactions and the purchase of goods and services. These people are usually IT aficionados and early users of digital currency. According to Baur et al. (2016), these active users frequently have the smallest cryptocurrency holdings while simultaneously being the most frequent transactors.

The second group consists of long-term investors, sometimes known as apathetic investors. These people see cryptocurrency as primarily a long-term investment, with little interest in utilizing it for day-to-day transactions. Hybrid investors sit halfway between the active and passive groups. These are short-term investors that combine transactional and investing tactics.

Adhami & Guegan (2020) found that investors are always willing to take higher risks in pursuit of better yields; most of the time, keeping their cryptocurrencies stored in exchange wallets and not using them to make transactions. Due to their profit-oriented nature, these investors keep their digital assets on exchanges and are less inclined to use them to make direct payments. The types of consumers within the cryptocurrency market have a direct impact on asset volatility. Active users, who primarily use cryptocurrency for transactions and the purchase of goods and services, contribute to the establishment of cryptocurrency as a means of exchange. However, active users and short-term (or hybrid) investors are more likely to trade cryptocurrencies often, sometimes multiple times per day, which contributes to market uncertainty. emphasizes the restricted supply inherent in many cryptocurrencies, which results in deflationary pressures. These situations can fuel speculation and lead to price volatility. On the other hand, active and short-term investors frequently benefit from this volatility since it provides profit possibilities (Barberis, N & Huang, M, 2008).

In contrast to rational traders who make educated judgments based on market analysis, speculators are often ignorant traders. These traders frequently depend on psychological biases such as group dynamics to make trading decisions. Considering their ignorant position, such volatility spillover effects in cryptocurrency traders contribute to market efficiency by capitalizing on arbitrage possibilities. Thus, the diverse range of cryptocurrency users, from active users to speculators, creates a complex ecosystem that supports the asset's variability while also providing profit and market efficiency chances.

Factors Influencing Price Mechanism in the Cryptocurrency Market

Bitcoin's price behavior differs significantly from that of traditional asset classes and is mostly determined by investors' speculative inclination. Nonetheless, it is not completely cut off from the actual economy. According to Caporale *et al.* (2024), the US dollar has the most influence on Bitcoin pricing, while gold has the least impact. More specifically, Bitcoin's price is influenced by demand and supply (Fanti, G., & Viswanath, P., 2017). Demand is determined by the transactional demand for Bitcoin as a means of exchange, as well as its participation in hypothetical trading.

At exactly the same time, the supply is governed by the quantity of Bitcoins in circulation (Fanti, G., & Viswanath, P., 2017). The price of cryptocurrencies is also influenced by global developments, sentiment in the markets, and global economic events. According to research, information gathered from Twitter can forecast certain coins. In addition, Hamayel et al. (2021) found that trading volume has a considerable influence on cryptocurrency price determination. Researchers discovered that explainable AI (Artificial Intelligence) can aid in price prediction. Long Short-Term Memory (LSTM), Gated Recurrent Unit (GRU), Artificial Neural Network (ANN), and many other 14 approaches may accurately forecast both the long- and short-term price fluctuations of cryptocurrencies. The complex nature of cryptocurrencies and the multiple factors impacting their pricing play a dynamic role in defining future growth and providing a thorough picture of the cryptocurrency industry. A detailed research of them in the future will help determine the degree of cryptocurrencies' influence on the volatility of other asset classes.

Volatility in Cryptocurrencies

Investor perception and mood have an important role in the volatility of cryptocurrency. News and events about regulatory changes, technical advancements, or macroeconomic considerations can create quick changes in investor mood, resulting in large price movements (Gupta et al., 2025). For example, when powerful persons announce regulatory crackdowns or advocate products, it can cause panic selling or purchasing sprees. Furthermore, the cryptocurrency market's infancy contributes to its volatility. The market is continually changing, with new cryptocurrencies, technology, and laws constantly emerging. This continual flux might cause uncertainty and speculation, which contribute to price volatility.

The repercussions of this instability are far-reaching and influence many parties. For investors, extreme volatility can result in huge gains and losses. It makes cryptocurrency a risky investment and thus unsuitable for all, especially those with low risk appetite (Baur et al., 2016). Merchants and businesses that accept cryptocurrency as payment may experience losses due to volatility if the price of the cryptocurrency falls significantly after a transaction. It renders it hard for companies to set proper prices for their products and services, leading to cash flow problems (Gurdgiev et al., 2020).

It is possible to employ a financial market strategy in managing and reducing the risk associated with the volatility of cryptocurrency. Diversification of an investor's portfolio by investing in conventional assets and cryptocurrency can help to spread (Dasman, S., 2021). Hedging instruments, including futures and options, can help guard against adverse price movements. Having payment processors that quickly convert cryptocurrencies into fiat currencies can assist businesses in minimizing the risk of price fluctuations. Utilizing smart contracts, which change prices automatically according to the prevailing currency rate, can assist in risk mitigation (Dasman, S., 2021).

Cryptocurrencies' absence of inherent value, coupled with their dependence on market sentiment, makes them extremely susceptible to outside influences like governmental actions, legislation modifications, and geopolitical events (Ede, C., 2023)

New government regulations or direct bans on cryptocurrency trading could bring tremendous price fluctuations. In the same manner, incidents such as security breaches, cyber-attacks, or adverse publicity can erode investor confidence and lead to massive selling, contributing to wild market fluctuations.

The price volatility of cryptocurrency influences a broad range of stakeholders. Fluctuating prices subject traders and investors to higher risks, which may lead to huge losses or gains (Ede, C., 2023). This price volatility is also a problem for enterprises that accept cryptocurrency payments, as they need to navigate the risks involved in fluctuating exchange rates. Policymakers have the daunting task of creating laws that protect investors without sacrificing market stability in this volatile and fast-evolving world.

Experts suggest various methods for dealing with and countering the risks inherent in the unstable character of cryptocurrency. One of these is the creation of advanced risk management instruments like futures and options indentures, which enable investors to shield their investments from negative price direction (Ede, C., 2023). Greater transparency and tighter regulation can lower the possibility of market manipulation and increase the confidence of investors. Incorporating stablecoins, cryptocurrencies that are anchored against stable assets such as fiat money, can bring some price stability, decreasing overall market volatility (Ede, C., 2023).

Earlier, academic research in cryptocurrency focused mainly on the security, ethical, and legal aspects of Bitcoin. The recent research, however, has examined cryptocurrencies from an economic perspective. Little research has been conducted on price returns and volatility features in the digital currency market. As cryptocurrencies developed from a niche interest to an emerging asset class, empirical tests from price time series have become increasingly feasible. Baur *et al.,* (2017) argue that the extreme price fluctuations of Bitcoin, such as bubbles and crashes, reflect that it is not a reliable unit of account or store of value.

Gandal, N., & Halaburda, H. (2016) opine that Bitcoin could bring substantial diversification advantages to investors. Gil-Alana *et al.* (2020) contribute to the debate by illustrating that the returns on Bitcoin do not exactly represent a random walk. Effendi (2015) employs an asymmetric GARCH model to illustrate how Bitcoin can be employed as an instrument for risk management, especially for those investors who want protection from negative market shocks. This model is described by Hagerud, G. E. (1997).

Major Factors affecting the market price of cryptocurrency

Cryptocurrencies, like all other types of money, are valued based on community engagement. These may include the coin's utility, demand, and scarcity. The bulk of cryptocurrencies originates in private blockchain enterprises. As a result, the value of these cryptocurrency assets will be determined by the company's reputation, perceived worth, and project feasibility.

1. **Node Count**: The node count represents the number of active wallets on the network. This information may be obtained by simply running a Google search or visiting the currency webpage. But why is node count important? It initially displays the vibrancy of the neighborhood. A large node count indicates a healthy community, which enhances the probability that a currency will withstand future crises. Second, a high number of nodes might indicate a network's strength and decentralization, which are both important components of cryptography.
2. **Production cost**: Another factor influencing the value of cryptocurrencies is their manufacturing expenses. Miners use specialized hardware or computers to generate new tokens and validate new network transactions every day. Miners are compensated for their labor by receiving virtual tokens and a network fee. Decentralized coins can continue to function owing to miner network activity. As a result, the value of cryptocurrencies may grow as mining costs rise. If the rewards are insufficient to cover the costs and provide a profit for the miners,

they have little reason to spend their resources mining additional cryptocurrency tokens. It should be emphasized that this isn't always the case, and not all cryptos work in the same manner.

3. **Crypto Exchanges**: A token's capacity to be obtained and utilized by more people increases when it is listed on several cryptocurrency exchanges. Any cryptocurrency token that involves two or more exchanges will pay a charge for each swap, raising the overall cost of the venture.
4. **Competition**: Every day, new token are launched, adding to the amount of crypto currencies in existence. There are many additional coins, such as soccer team coins, celebrity coins, and meme coins. Among these new currencies, there are prospective crypto currency projects that may be able to overcome a present impediment and build a significant user community.
5. **Government Regulation**: Some nations want to control the crypto currency industry because they don't like how decentralized and unregulated it is. Setting a tax on any fiat money used to withdraw bitcoin is the easiest way to govern crypto currencies. Persons who want to pay out their earnings can simply use a different currency because this tax only applies to certain tokens. Bans on Bitcoin, Ethereum, and a few other coins were deemed the best way to govern the crypto currency industry by a number of countries. Unfortunately, new regulations on crypto currencies will have a negative impact on their value if they are implemented by a country with a large bitcoin user base. Other countries, like as Japan, are reportedly employing blockchain technology to create a national crypto currency, which will lead to an increase in the use of virtual currencies.
6. **Scarcity**: In conceptual terms, if a crypto currency has a finite supply, the price will grow as fewer coins become available for purchase. However, if only 40% of the coins are in circulation and the other 60% are held in reserve, the price may fall as more coins become available to purchasers. Some crypto currency efforts "burn" current coins by sending them to a blockchain address that cannot be reclaimed. This may be how they control the supply.
7. **Social Media**: Social media buzz has been shown to influence the value of crypto currencies. Furthermore, it works both ways, since news may influence prices to rise or decrease. Influential individuals of the crypto currency community, like as Elon Musk, have influenced the value of the DOGE coin, either knowingly or inadvertently. Although social media is chaotic, information may be discovered there. Crypto currency exchanges, for example, routinely update information about blockchain money or provide warnings about scams involving crypto currency.

Current Legal Framework

The domain of cryptocurrency regulation is intricate and dynamic, with diverse regulatory bodies embracing distinct strategies to tackle the distinct obstacles presented by these virtual assets. The regulatory landscape is framed by reconciling innovation, financial stability, consumer protection, and compliance with existing legal frameworks. This answer analyses the existing laws and regulations for cryptocurrencies' regulatory approaches and challenges using information from several research publications (Camomile Shumba, 2023)

- Varying Regulatory Structures: Different nations have taken different approaches to regulating cryptocurrencies. While some countries, like China, have implemented stringent prohibitions on crypto currency transactions and (Pardhey et al., 2023)other jurisdictions, like Gibraltar, Malta, Switzerland, and Singapore, have passed proactive, industry-specific laws to regulate crypto currencies.
- **Compliance and Consumer Protection:** Initial regulatory efforts were aimed at protecting consumers from fraud, placing cryptocurrencies into various categories such as commodities, securities, or money. Often, these descriptors are inexact, leading to regulatory confusion (Balgobin et al., 2020).
- **Technological and Definitional Difficulties**: The decentralised character of cryptocurrencies and the opaqueness of their markets pose serious regulatory difficulties. The definition of stablecoins and the classification of cryptocurrencies as securities or commodities complicate effective regulation.

Human Rights and Privacy Concerns

Cryptocurrency regulations can make a significant impact on human rights, particularly security-related, privacy, and digital rights. Both regulation and privacy must be balanced since overly stringent controls can breach individuals' rights.

- Initiatives for International Policy: There have been attempts by different governments to regulate cryptocurrencies and blockchain technology through different policy efforts. Although in general they have been hesitant to accept cryptocurrencies as legal tender, governments are exploiting the uses of blockchain technology (El Maknouzi *et al.,* 2021).
- Comparison of legal strategies across different nations, such as the USA, Germany, and Singapore, brings to light disparities in taxation and regulation of cryptocurrencies within the regulatory framework of the European Union. International norms are required to harmonize regulatory action, as

signified by these disparities. Legislative measures have been put in place by the European Union to regulate cryptocurrencies, with the aim of balancing innovation with consumer protection and financial stability Hamrick *et al.,* 2018). The topic of discussion is the appropriate regulatory approach, which emphasizes the need for a well-defined understanding of the technology. To ensure that regulations are adaptable to future changes, the EU's approach emphasizes the importance of discussing among regulators, industry stakeholders, and the public.

Central bank's stance on cryptocurrency

The idea of cryptocurrencies and Central Bank Digital Currencies (CBDCs) is becoming more and more involved by central banks worldwide as digital banking continues to develop. Central banks issue CBDCs, which are a centralized digital currency, as opposed to cryptocurrencies, which provide decentralized financial transactions. Central banks' views on cryptocurrencies are influenced by the need to balance financial stability, regulatory supervision, and innovation. Central banks' views on cryptocurrencies, CBDCs, and the regulatory obstacles they face are explored in this response (Aggarwal *et al.,* 2023).

Central banks accept cryptocurrencies as a type of currency that can be used as a store of value, a unit of account, and a medium of exchange, among other conventional monetary functions. The European Central Bank (ECB) recognized cryptocurrencies as comparable financial assets in 2021, leading to the creation of regulatory frameworks and the digital euro project. Financial stability is deeply threatened by the decentralised nature, anonymity, and lack of centralised control of cryptocurrencies. The risk of their misuse in criminal activities and excessive volatility are grounds why central banks favor stringent regulation (Aggarwal *et al.,* 2023.

The U.S. central bank considers cryptocurrencies to be shadow money, and they have some of the same problems as privately created banknotes from the 'free banking' era, which caused economic instability. To prevent financial bubbles, the Federal Reserve is instructed to improve public payment networks and supervise private digital currencies (Caporale *et al.,* 2024).

Development and Implications of CBDCs

CBDCs are believed to be a solution to the problems that cryptocurrencies have caused, as they offer a centralized digital currency that can improve financial services and act as a regulator. Given their ability to perform all financial activities, they could eventually replace hard currency in the modern economy ("The Case for Central

Bank Digital Currencies", 2023) . To provide transparency regarding the status and legal nature of CBDCs, it is required that national legal and regulatory systems be adapted to coincide with their problems. The challenge entails dealing with potential legislative enhancements, economic, political, and legal issues. In Indonesia, CBDCs are viewed as a means of preserving financial stability and managing legal matters. Under current laws, it is prohibited to use foreign currencies as a means of exchange, emphasizing the need for regulatory adjustments (Caporale *et al.*, 2024).

Regulatory Challenges and Market Reactions

Market reactions to the implementation of CBDCs and regulatory announcements may be unfavourable, resulting in higher volatility and lower returns in the cryptocurrency markets. This is a reflection of concerns about the possibility of outside regulation and the loss of anonymity, which is crucial for those involved in cryptocurrencies. Although there are difficulties, central banks' endorsement of CBDCs could lead to positive market reactions, suggesting that traders do not always view CBDCs as a threat to cryptocurrencies. Instead, individuals could view them as an addition to other virtual currencies (Pardhey *et al* 2023)

Even though central banks are actively investigating CBDCs, the regulatory environment surrounding cryptocurrencies is still complex. The necessity of unified regulatory strategies is highlighted in light of the globalisation of the bitcoin business. Furthermore, it's critical to strike a balance between innovation and regulation because too many restrictions may impede the uptake and advancement of digital currencies. Effective management of these hurdles is necessary for central banks to promote innovation in digital currencies and maintain financial stability.

Cryptocurrencies have bred a complicated and contradictory legal landscape owing to their decentralized nature, susceptibility to abuse, and varying regulatory regimes in most jurisdictions. The issue is made worse by the speedy pace of technological innovation and the requirement for the legal system to evolve in order to catch up. Russian legislators remain unsure whether cryptocurrencies are legal and how they tie in with civic rights and duties. Cryptocurrencies have the potential to gain unofficial payment authority due to their unregulated circulation, which could threaten the country's financial system.

The Supreme Court ruling in favour of overruling the Reserve Bank of India's prohibition of cryptocurrency demonstrates how unclear India's legal framework is, despite having a draft law that would have banned it. Investors and traders are left with a dangerous situation with no clear legal protection

Implications for Investors

Modern investing portfolios now include a sizable amount of cryptocurrency, which presents investors with both benefits and challenges. It's worthwhile to reflect on their influence on investment portfolios, the risks and opportunities they present to institutional and individual investors, and the regulatory aspects. The research papers at hand are synthesized herein to respond fully to these aspects

Impact of Cryptocurrency on Investment Portfolios

The incorporation of investment opportunities and integration into the stock market framework has been made possible by creating cryptocurrencies by banks. Due to their inbuilt volatility and macroeconomic sensitivity, they are a high-risk investment. Due to their extreme volatility and regulatory risks, cryptocurrencies raise serious risk management issues. The Markowitz model and Sharpe ratio analysis have been used to construct and rebalance cryptocurrency portfolios.

Risks and Opportunities for Individual and Institutional Investors

- Individual investors may make high-risk, high-reward investments using cryptocurrency. The lack of diversification and predisposition for high-risk investments among cryptocurrency investors in the United Kingdom highlights the importance of tailored financial education and a thorough regulatory framework. The rapid changes in legal and regulatory oversight, together with breakthroughs in the cryptocurrency and blockchain realms, provide challenges for institutional investors.
- Consumer opinions about cryptocurrency investing are generally positive, notwithstanding considerable concerns in terms of trust, privacy, security, and financial components. This implies that cryptocurrency investing has the potential to become broadly embraced as long as expectations meet the technology's capabilities.

Regulatory Considerations for Investing in Cryptocurrency

- The absence of a robust regulatory framework is a major obstacle to the widespread adoption of cryptocurrencies. Global regulatory systems have not yet produced generally accepted rules that are required to reduce uncertain outcomes and safeguard investors. Uniform and transparent frameworks are necessary to safeguard investors and promote market expansion in the ever-changing regulatory environment. To improve financial literacy and stability in the market, it is important to collaborate with academic institutions, businesses, and regulatory agencies.

- From a regulatory standpoint, it is important to highlight the necessity of making adjustments to plug gaps in capital controls and avoid money laundering, as well as the possibility of central banks issuing their own digital currencies.
- While cryptocurrencies provide potential for big rewards and diversification, they also face major dangers and regulatory challenges. Because of their tremendous volatility and absence of a robust legal framework, cryptocurrency investors must exercise prudence and forethought while building portfolios. To overcome these challenges, both individuals and institutional investors must adopt stringent risk management methods and continuous market surveillance. Creating frameworks that safeguard investors and encourage responsible use of Bitcoin as the regulatory environment changes requires the cooperation of stakeholders.

FUTURE TRENDS

India's growing startup ecosystem and tech-savvy population are leading to significant breakthroughs in blockchain technology and the cryptocurrency sector. Future developments in this field will be influenced by financial inclusion, creative uses across industries, and the creation of regulatory frameworks. This analysis will examine the anticipated changes in the cryptocurrency market in India and the potential applications of blockchain technology.

Anticipated Developments in the Indian Cryptocurrency Market

- Financial Inclusion and Decentralised Finance (DeFi): With so many people living in unbanked countries like India, cryptocurrencies provide a means of achieving financial inclusion. The emergence of decentralised finance (DeFi) platforms has the potential to broaden the accessibility of financial services by facilitating peer-to-peer lending and borrowing in the absence of conventional middlemen (Aquilina et al 2024).
- Central Bank Digital Currency (CBDC): India is looking into creating a central bank digital currency (CBDC), which could completely transform the nation's financial system by offering a reliable digital currency that is supported by the state. It is anticipated that this step will lower transaction costs and improve the effectiveness of payment systems (Cioroianu et al 2023).

- Regulatory Developments: The Indian government is developing a regulatory framework for bitcoin. This includes addressing security and instability concerns, which are significant barriers to widespread use. To protect consumers and stimulate innovation, regulations must be explicit.
- Public Perception and Adoption: In spite of technology breakthroughs, public perception is still difficult to change. Research shows that in some areas, like Odisha, there is still a lack of knowledge and comprehension about cryptocurrencies, which emphasises the necessity of educational programs to increase acceptance.

Potential Applications of Blockchain Technology

- Smart Contracts and Automation: Smart contracts, which can automate transactions and lessen the need for middlemen, can be created using blockchain technology. This is applicable to supply chain management, real estate, and finance, among other industries.
- Healthcare and Data Safety: By providing a secure and open way of storing and sharing patient information, blockchain can enhance data security and privacy in the healthcare sector. Improved patient outcomes and improved healthcare delivery could be the outcome.
- Supply Chain Management: Blockchain is perfect for supply chain management because it offers a transparent and unchangeable record of transactions. Efficiency can be raised across the supply chain, while fraud may be reduced and traceability improved.
- New Research and Innovations: As blockchain technology develops quickly, new research and innovations are being produced. This includes creating cryptocurrency that is safer and more effective, as well as investigating the applications of blockchain technology in a variety of industries, including logistics, healthcare, and banking.

Although blockchain technology and cryptocurrencies have a bright future in India, there are still obstacles to overcome. Because of the volatility of cryptocurrencies, companies and investors must use effective risk management measures. Some investors have pointed out that cryptocurrencies do not have an inherent value, which causes doubt. In spite of these obstacles, blockchain has the potential to revolutionize businesses and propel economic expansion in India, provided that public awareness and legislative frameworks remain up-to-date with technical developments.

REFERENCES

Abu Elbeh, I. M. (2024). E-Commerce and Digital Currencies Risk Management Challenges. In *Intelligent Systems, Business, and Innovation Research* (pp. 343–354). Springer Nature Switzerland. DOI: 10.1007/978-3-031-36895-0_28

Adhami, S., & Guegan, D. (2020). Crypto assets: The role of ICO tokens within a well- diversified portfolio. *Economia e Politica Industriale*, *47*(2), 219–241. DOI: 10.1007/s40812-019-00141-x

Aggarwal, S.,Luthra, K., Srivastava, V (2023). 4. India's tech-enthusiasts: crypto-currency and the reserve bank's role in transformation. .DOI: 10.52458/9789388996969.nsp2023.eb.ch-19

Agur, I., Ari, A., & Dell'Ariccia, G. (2022). Designing central bank digital currencies. *Journal of Monetary Economics*, *125*, 62–79. DOI: 10.1016/j.jmoneco.2021.05.002

Aquilina, M., Frost, J., & Schrimpf, A. (2024). Decentralized finance (DeFi): A functional approach. *Journal of Financial Regulation*, *10*(1), 1–27. DOI: 10.1093/jfr/fjad013

Balgobin, P., & Seeam, A. (2020, September). Developing an effective regulatory framework for virtual currencies in mauritius. In *Proceedings of the 2nd International Conference on Intelligent and Innovative Computing Applications* (pp. 1-9). DOI: 10.1145/3415088.3415126

Barberis, N., & Huang, M. (2008). Stocks as lotteries: The implications of probability weighting for security prices. *The American Economic Review*, *98*(5), 2066–2100. DOI: 10.1257/aer.98.5.2066

Barenji, A. V., Li, Z., & Wang, W. M. (2018, June). Blockchain cloud manufacturing: Shop floor and machine level. In *Smart SysTech 2018; European conference on smart objects, systems and technologies* (pp. 1-6). VDE.

Baur, D. G., & Dimpfl, T. (2017). Realized bitcoin volatility. *SSRN*, *2949754*, 1–26.

Baur, D. G., Hong, K., & Lee, A. D. (2016). Virtual currencies: media of exchange or speculative asset?.

Camomile Shumba. (March 2023) 'South Africa's Crypto Firms Will Soon Need to Apply for Registration or Face a Heavy Fine' (CoinDesk 25 March 2023), https://www.coindesk.com/policy/2023/05/25/south-africas-crypto-firms-will- soon-need-to-apply-for-registration-or-face-a-heavy-fine/

Caporale, G. M., de Dios Mazariegos, J. J., & Gil-Alana, L. A. (2024). Long-Run Linkages between US Stock Prices and Cryptocurrencies: A Fractional Cointegration Analysis. *Computational Economics*, *64*(6), 1–11. DOI: 10.1007/s10614-023-10510-3

Charfeddine, L., Benlagha, N., & Maouchi, Y. (2020). Investigating the dynamic relationship between cryptocurrencies and conventional assets: Implications for financial investors. *Economic Modelling*, *85*, 198–217. DOI: 10.1016/j.econmod.2019.05.016

Chaum, D. (1983, August). Blind signatures for untraceable payments. In *Advances in Cryptology* [Boston, MA: Springer US.]. *Proceedings of Crypto*, *82*, 199–203.

Cioroianu, I., Corbet, S., Larkin, C. J., & Oxley, L. (2023). *Developing central bank digital currencies: a reality check during cryptocurrency euphoria*. Economics and Business Letters.

Dasman, S. (2021). Analysis of return and risk of cryptocurrency bitcoin asset as investment instrument. Accounting and Finance Innovations, 51.

De Ocáriz Borde, H. S. (2022). *An overview of trees in blockchain technology: merkle trees and merkle patricia tries*. University of Cambridge.

Delfabbro, P., King, D. L., & Williams, J. (2021). The psychology of cryptocurrency trading: Risk and protective factors. *Journal of Behavioral Addictions*, *10*(2), 201–207. DOI: 10.1556/2006.2021.00037 PMID: 34152998

Delgado-Segura, S., Pérez-Solà, C., Herrera-Joancomartí, J., Navarro-Arribas, G., & Borrell, J. (2018). Cryptocurrency networks: A new P2P paradigm. *Mobile Information Systems*, •••, 2018.

Demir, E., Bilgin, M. H., Karabulut, G., & Doker, A. C. (2020). The relationship between cryptocurrencies and COVID-19 pandemic. *Eurasian Economic Review*, *10*(3), 349–360. DOI: 10.1007/s40822-020-00154-1

Ede, C. (2023). A Critical Analysis of the Regulation of Crypto Assets from the European Union and the United Kingdom Perspective. Available at *SSRN* 4489373. DOI: 10.2139/ssrn.4489373

Effendi, K. A. (2015). Determining the best ARCH/GARCH model and comparing JKSE with stock index in developed countries. *The Winners*, *16*(2), 71–84. DOI: 10.21512/tw.v16i2.1560

Eichengreen, B. (2019). *From commodity to fiat and now to crypto: what does history tell us? (No. w25426)*. National Bureau of Economic Research. DOI: 10.3386/w25426

El Maknouzi, M. E. H., & Sadok, H. (2021). Regulation of virtual currencies in the United Arab Emirates: Accounting for the emerging public/private distinction. *Development Studies Research*, *8*(1), 346–355. DOI: 10.1080/21665095.2021.1980413

Fanti, G., & Viswanath, P. (2017). Deanonymization in the bitcoin P2P network. *Advances in Neural Information Processing Systems*, •••, 30.

Fauzi, M. A., Paiman, N., & Othman, Z. (2020). Bitcoin and cryptocurrency: Challenges, opportunities and future works. *The Journal of Asian Finance, Economics and Business*, *7*(8), 695–704. DOI: 10.13106/jafeb.2020.vol7.no8.695

Fry, J. (2018). Booms, busts and heavy-tails: The story of Bitcoin and cryptocurrency markets? *Economics Letters*, *171*, 225–229. DOI: 10.1016/j.econlet.2018.08.008

Gandal, N., & Halaburda, H. (2016). Can we predict the winner in a market with network effects? Competition in cryptocurrency market. *Games*, *7*(3), 16. DOI: 10.3390/g7030016

Gil-Alana, L. A., Abakah, E. J. A., & Rojo, M. F. R. (2020). Cryptocurrencies and stock market indices. Are they related? *Research in International Business and Finance*, *51*, 101063. DOI: 10.1016/j.ribaf.2019.101063

Gupta, N., Mitra, P., & Banerjee, D. (2023). Cryptocurrencies and traditional assets: Decoding the analogy from emerging economies with crypto usage. *Investment Management & Financial Innovations*, *20*(1), 1–13. DOI: 10.21511/imfi.20(1).2023.01

Gupta, P., Bhatia, P., & Malhotra, N. (2025). Do Crypto and Equity Go Hand in Hand? An Empirical Study of G-7 Economies Using VECM, Granger Causality and Panel Data Analysis. *Management and Labour Studies*, 0258042X241309725.

Gurdgiev, C., & O'Loughlin, D. (2020). Herding and anchoring in cryptocurrency markets: Investor reaction to fear and uncertainty. *Journal of Behavioral and Experimental Finance*, *25*, 100271. DOI: 10.1016/j.jbef.2020.100271

Hagerud, G. E. (1997). *A new non-linear GARCH model*. Stockholm School of Economics.

Hamayel, M. J., & Owda, A. Y. (2021). A novel cryptocurrency price prediction model using GRU, LSTM and bi-LSTM machine learning algorithms. *AI*, *2*(4), 477–496. DOI: 10.3390/ai2040030

Hamrick, J. T., Rouhi, F., Mukherjee, A., Feder, A., Gandal, N., Moore, T., & Vasek, M. (2018). The economics of cryptocurrency pump and dump schemes. Available at *SSRN* 3310307. DOI: 10.2139/ssrn.3303365

Pardhey, N., Issa, Y. H., & Libeesh, P. C. (2023). Regulatory Mechanism of Cryptocurrency Blockchain in Banking, Financial, and Capital Markets in the Indian Panorama. In *The Impact of AI Innovation on Financial Sectors in the Era of Industry 5.0* (pp. 96–107). IGI Global.

Pernice, I. G. A., & Scott, B. (2021). Cryptocurrency. *Internet Policy Review, 10*(2), 1–10. DOI: 10.14763/2021.2.1561

Verma, P., Srivastava, R., & Kumar, S. (2024). Blockchain Technology: Applications and Challenges. *Blockchain for IoT Systems*, 1-12.

KEY TERMS AND DEFINITIONS

Central Bank Digital Currency (CBDC): The difference between centralized digital currencies and cryptocurrencies is that centralized digital currencies provide decentralized financial transactions.

Cryptocurrency: It is described as a process for issuing tokens that are meant for exchange and are recorded in a digital ledger that is maintained through cryptography.

Hashing: Information is secured by using cryptography with a hash function that accepts a variable-length input message and produces a fixed-length output.

The Node Count: This is a representation of the number of wallets that are currently active on the network

Chapter 12
The Ripple Effect:
Assessing the Impact of Crypto Crime on Global Financial Systems

Arpita Nayak
https://orcid.org/0000-0003-2911-0492
KIIT School of Liberal Studies, KIIT University, India

Ipseeta Satpathy
https://orcid.org/0000-0002-0155-5548
KSOM, KIIT University, India

Vishal Jain
https://orcid.org/0000-0003-1126-7424
Department of Computer Science and Engineering, School of Engineering and Technology, Vivekananda Institute of Professional Studies, New Delhi, India

ABSTRACT

Cryptocurrencies have revolutionized traditional finance by providing decentralized payment methods and disrupting global solutions. However, the increasing prevalence of cryptocrime threatens financial market security and public confidence. This study, "The Ripple Effect," examines the financial damage caused by crypto-attacks on global payment networks and the regulatory complexities arising from deceitful cryptocurrency activity. It also examines the economic impact of cryptocrime, affecting individuals, organizations, and countries. The chapter highlights the financial threats that span across global markets and the regulatory barriers governments and organizations face. The fight against crypto crime requires international cooperation, sophisticated legal frameworks, and innovative blockchain analytical tools. The study emphasizes the need for transparency initiatives, education programs, and robust communication methods to restore trust within the crypto community.

DOI: 10.4018/979-8-3373-0675-9.ch012

I. INTRODUCTION

A global stability of the financial market is threatened by cryptocurrency scams causing a major economic impact on both individuals and governing bodies. Cryptocurrency trading is riddled with huge distrust issues as a result of rampant scams in forms of Ponzi schemes, phishing attempts, unsound ICOs and ransomware campaigns. Lack of regulating laws and the decentralized nature of cryptocurrencies make it easier to carry out harmful ventures such as Ponzi schemes exposing the scam to the investors, unexplained digital asset robbery using phishing and deceitful ICOs enticing investors to unproductive processes all of which erodes investment confidence and dampens the sector's progression. In cases whereby businesses and governments are raided by ransomware using cryptocurrency, there are incurred financial outages and increased costs in cybersecurity to recover data. Such scams create substantial economic sequels causing both individual and financial catastrophes and businesses are threatened by increased risks of bankruptcy, which also disrupt the government budgets since there is reduced tax revenues and increased regulatory costs. If financial ecosystem security is to be enhanced, stricter market regulation with greater market visibility and closer collaboration among regulators, industry representatives, and consumers are needed. (Bartoletti et al.,2021).

The inadequate regulatory oversight of the cryptocurrency market intensifies these security risks so that improved protections and greater transparency with coordinated interventions from industry stakeholders and regulators and consumers are essential for establishing a robust financial system. (Phillips et al.,2020).

The cryptocurrency-related crimes create complicated economic hinderances that are capable of destabilizing the financial well-being of persons, companies, and even countries in a variety of direct and indirect ways. People under cryptocurrency scams usually face irreversible loss of savings and theft of personal information, thus making them vulnerable to more frauds. Cryptocurrency transactions are not like traditional financial systems in that, unlike them, they have no ability of reversing enabling the victims have no hope of getting back the stolen funds, worsening their financial plight. Those whose majority portion of assets are bound up in the crypto sector are particularly vulnerable, because crypto fraud tends to lead to severe economic distress, jeopardizing their financial stability and leaving them with long-term problems. Given that transaction in cryptocurrency are permanent and under no central control the challenges faced by victims are mounting, with them often failing to reclaim their funds, showing an increase in the risks of using a system outside traditional financial surveillance. (Xia et al.,2020).

Having experienced cybercriminals destroy more organizations in all sectors, business and financial institutions are coming across many new threats that go far beyond conventional financial scam. Companies that accept these cryptocurrencies along with those that busily store digital wealth on their balance sheets are more vulnerable to sophisticated cyber threats such as major theft, scams, and crippling ransomware incursions. In addition, these events cause not only the immediate financial damage resulted from stolen assets, but also a list of further financial burdens – from increased cybersecurity investments and investigative charges to relevant legal sanctions for violation of regulations. Additionally, that is a high risk of reputational damage as the customers and partners challenge security of their assets thus destroying loyalty to the brands and sometimes wiping out the market valuation. Front-page crypto scams targeting large corporations can throw the whole financial industry into turmoil, erode confidence of investors, and cause colossal downtrends in stock prices on the part of players in the market reassessing the company's risk. Additionally, while the authorities regulate crypto-related crimes, all sectors of businesses are forced to spend a great number of resources on the adaptation to the change in the legal requirements, which adds more pressure on the operational finances. These interrelated challenges combine to create a difficult and costly environment for companies in digital asset industry, vulnerable not only to damaging financial loss but to devastating reputation loss as well, as well as continued questions about the level of oversight from regulatory bodies (Barnes,2018).

With the exception of stolen cash, which increased 7% annually, transaction volumes decreased in all other, more traditional categories of cryptocurrency-related crime. This might be due in part to the market slump. For example, we have previously discovered that cryptocurrency scams make less money during bear markets. This is probably because people are more cynical and are less willing to trust scammers' claims of large profits when asset values are falling. often speaking, less money in cryptocurrency often corresponds to less money involved in cryptocrime.

For the first time since 2019, the proportion of total bitcoin activity linked to illegal behaviour has increased, rising from 0.12% in 2021 to 0.24% in 2022 as shown in figure 1.

Figure 1. Cryptocurrency Transaction Volume, 2017-2022

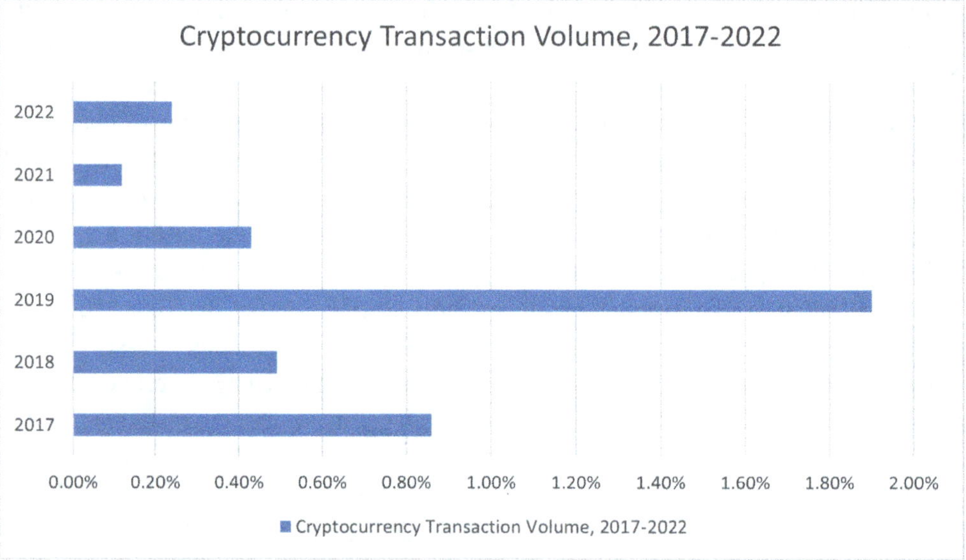

Source – Adopted from https://www.chainalysis.com/blog/2023-crypto-crime-report-introduction/

Government bodies sustain major economic damage from cryptocurrency-related scams. The drive to remain anonymous while operating internationally makes it hard for tax authorities to monitor cryptocurrency transactions which can reduce their ability to generate tax revenue. To fight crypto crimes governments, need to distribute funds toward both crime investigation operations and expert-based prosecution needs as well as necessary technical tools. The growing number of crypto frauds leads victims to exhaust public resources as they require support from government assistance programs. Government entities need to implement financial support for banks which struggle in addition to implementing economic support measures that protect against the wide-scale effects of significant crypto criminal acts. (Kuttera,2022).

The adoption along with the value movement of cryptocurrencies gets heavily affected by major cryptocurrency scams. High-profile scams in the digital asset industry have the power to damage the reputation of the entire sector even though decentralization and transparency are central reasons why people show interest in cryptocurrency assets. The crypto market experiences skepticism from potential retail and institutional investors because they fear both the risks of fraud and volatility in the sector. The reluctance of users to embrace cryptocurrencies hinders the pace of adoption while obstructing the expansion of the cryptocurrency ecosystem and postponing the possible advantages such as expedited cross-border payments with reduced expenses as well as fiscal services for underbanked populations. (Acharya et al.,2024).

A great number of scams, as well as fraud, significantly influences valuations of cryptocurrency, leading to unstable market values on a regular basis. Large scale fraud disclosures will usually further erode investor confidence in the affected cryptocurrency and associated market assets resulting in sudden price declines. The 2022 FTX exchange collapse is a shining example of an event that caused a panic in the crypto market after the discovery that fraudulent practices were being committed. The revelation of these fraudulent activities triggered increased investor selling with billions evaporating out of the market and investors taking huge financial bites. This trend emphasizes the far-reaching volatility of prices in the existing market of the cryptocurrency, which is largely caused by speculative investments and the mood factor trading instead of the fundamental factors underlying the economy. Reoccurrences of fraud and deception erode confidence in cryptocurrencies, squashing the prospects of cryptocurrencies as long term investments. The everlasting cycle of dishonest behaviors alongside the accompanying decline of markets hinders the cryptocurrency industry on its way to constant growth and stability, reinforcing their existing doubts which inhibit wider adoption and the maturation of the market. These continuing frauds continue to further highlight the volatile nature of cryptocurrencies threatening to undermine their value at the expense of limiting their potential to function effectively as storehouses of wealth or intermediaries denominations of wealth across the globe (Agarwal n.d.,).

II. REGULATORY CHALLENGES

Modern crypto-crime control faces worldwide obstacles because cryptocurrency transactions operate under decentralized conditions without borders while maintaining pseudonymous accounts. International regulatory efforts face significant challenges because there is no centralized power to monitor cryptocurrency transactions. Cryptocurrencies run on decentralized networks which prevent banks and regulatory bodies from monitoring and tracking illegal activities because the system lacks a centralized authority. Cryptocurrency's decentralized structure creates monitoring challenges that enable illicit actors to perform fraudulent schemes together with money laundering operations and various illegal transactions from unidentified operators. Blockchain transactions identified by digital wallet addresses create obstacles for law enforcement when they try to identify criminals because the system maintains no direct connections to real-world identity information. Electronic wallets and worldwide cryptocurrency access provide criminals with anonymous identification while letting them conduct illegal actions from any location which makes it difficult for authorities to pursue them effectively (Nakhle,2022).

The cryptocurrency sector faces a significant obstacle due to its swift technological advancements in the market. New types of cryptocurrencies as well as trading platforms and financial instruments emerge too quickly for regulatory frameworks to (draft) and execute (implement) corresponding laws. Criminals find opportunities to exploit regulatory gaps created by the slow pace of lawmaking. As a result, organizations continue struggling to catch up with the current trends. Moreover, the lack of harmonization in regulatory approaches across different countries exacerbates the problem. Some nations have implemented rigorous rules to stop crypto crime but parallel to them other nations adopt relaxed standards allowing spaces for unlawful activities. Diverse standards in regulatory oversight across different countries creates obstacles to global efforts to fight crypto crime since offenders easily transfer operations to jurisdictions with loose oversight (Daoud,2023).

Current international frameworks encounter difficulties when attempting to handle crypto crime complexities because of their built-in challenges. Global organizations including the Financial Action Task Force (FATF) established guidelines to address cryptocurrency money laundering but countries perform differently when implementing these standards. Many jurisdictions face difficulties implementing the FATF's "Travel Rule" which demands cryptocurrency exchanges to exchange transactional customer data since they lack both the technical systems and readiness to enforce the standard properly. International cooperation encounters challenges because countries maintain different legal frameworks together with varying levels of financial expertise and priorities. Many countries keep crypto crime investigation units but multiple jurisdictions face challenges due to insufficient resources as well as lacking operational expertise which results in different levels of law enforcement effectiveness. Criminals profit from regulatory flaws of the international framework by exploring vulnerabilities found in world-wide regulatory chain connections (Biju et al.,2023).

The collaboration between public and private organizations serves as an essential solution to enhance regulatory measures against cryptocrime by enabling mutual asset utilization. Government entities together with regulatory bodies commonly do not have the required technical knowledge and current data to properly track and fight illegal operations in cryptocurrency networks effectively. Private companies operating in the cryptocurrency space possess tracking systems which help identify unusual patterns and potential threats to mitigate associated risks. Through strategic partnerships with private organizations governments will expand regulatory capabilities which enables them to create optimized crime prevention strategies in the cryptocurrency sector. Blockchain analytics firms supply actionable police intelligence to law enforcement through their ability to track illicit transactions and expose both their users and operators. Exchanges that operate in the cryptocurrency field must employ strong Know Your Customer (KYC) and Anti-Money Laundering (AML) systems which stop criminals from conducting operations through their platforms (Smith,2024).

The defining role of public-private partnerships is a facilitation of the joint work that should be directed at working out consistent standards and dynamic regulation that appropriately address the unique issues of cryptocrime in the digital asset context. The collaboration between governmental offices, law enforcement entities, financial organizations, blockchain groups, and cyber specialists contributes to developing creative technological solutions which would preserve standards of data protection without compromising decentralized self-independence. At the heart of these partnerships must lie the actual building of distributed systems for identity verification that permit safe transactions without compromising peoples identities according to legal templates. The cooperation such as this is a vital platform for knowledge sharing and skill development and eliminates the gap that usually occurs between regulators and industry experts. The active participation in current debates and joint learning sessions gives policymakers critical information regarding cryptocrime trend to enable them to develop regulations that can successfully respond to the challenges of the blockchain era. At the same time, crypto firms enhance their capacity to implement pro-active protective measures, complex fraud checking processes, and the latest regulatory compliance systems. This partnering environment enhances the rapid threat identification and reaction, and builds the self-imposed regulatory setting in crypto, which collectively both bolster financial resilience and promote responsible innovation in blockchain technology (Rasyid et al.,2024).

Public-private partnerships present obstacles that need solutions for achieving their maximum efficiency levels. Among the difficulties public-private partnerships face is when private sector entities choose profit-making objectives instead of regulatory compliance. Such partnerships become more secure when they are developed using transparency alongside mutual trust and strict accountability. Easy legal frameworks and warm policies should enable the government to provide incentives for the private partnership and those elements in the private world should be ethical in nature and meet prescripts. The fight against crypto crime suffers from dismembered international activities considering that the criminal operations cross the borders. A joint, global effort will be necessary for the creation of public-private partnerships to allow for an unobstructed cooperation and maintain an open conversation among entities on borders. Gleaned from the Global Coalition to Fight Financial Crime, successful strategies can be gleaned from it which unites financial institutions, government bodies and technology company to fight against financial crime as a united front (Kreminskyi et al.,2021).

The problem of cryptocrime regulation requires a sound partnership approach and radical solutions to deal with the various sides of the problem. The very decentralized structure as well as fast evolvement of the cryptocurrencies sets high barriers before the regulatory bodies and organizations, which disrupts international cooperation on combatting illegal activities. Creative cooperations between public authorities and tech-savvy private firms combine the power of government scrutiny with private sector technical know-how to address this issue. Public and private organizations cooperation helps the governments to build and support their regulatory structures and stimulate innovation as well as support cooperation between countries to strengthen the fight against global cryptocrime. Once they manage to eliminate conflicting situations and develop more effective mechanisms for cross-border operations, public-private alliances will produce at the peak of their capabilities. In collaboration, public authorities and private enterprises can create a more robust cryptocurrency framework which accommodates innovation in a trustworthy way.

III. PUBLIC TRUST IN CRYPTOCURRENCIES

The adoption of cryptocurrencies depends heavily on public faith but major criminal activities within this financial system have repeatedly undermined trust in this developing market. Major crypto-related scams and attacks command media attention that makes people believe digital currencies are dangerous because they are fraudulent by nature. Despite their large Bitcoin losses, the collapses of Mt. Gox and FTX primarily responsible for creating permanent negative beliefs about cryptocurrency among the public. Financial damages to users and institutions alongside this loss of investor trust emerge from these events which antagonize possible participants in the space. Particular concern about funds losses from scams and hacking and market manipulation activities discourages many people from working with cryptocurrencies because they have limited knowledge about technology risks. When trust declines within the industry it creates severe obstacles because the industry needs both innovation and widespread acceptance to expand while cryptocurrency benefits of decentralized finance and financial inclusion are restricted (Arli et al.,2021).

The cryptocurrency industry requires complex procedures to recover trust after incidents of fraud occur. The most reliable method to rebuild trust involves enhancing transparency and accountability throughout the entire system. Cryptocurrency ventures and trading systems and platforms need to follow strict disclosure rules to deliver clear precise facts about security methods and business operations and financial standing to all users. Regular inspections by external auditors help users verify both responsible fund management and compliance with best practices through third-party audits. Digital asset protection can be achieved through combining multiple security methods which include multi-factor authentication as well as cold storage implementation and the use of insurance policies to protect against hacking incidents. User protection along with ethical practices gets demonstrated through strict adherence to existing laws and regulations. Implementing the Know Your Customer protocol and Anti-Money Laundering framework under regulatory partnership enables cryptocurrency businesses to gain user and regulatory authority trust (Gurguc et al.,2018).

The education of cryptocurrency aspects proves fundamental because criminals take advantage of user ignorance to carry out their cryptocrime schemes. Accessible educational materials about cryptocurrency safety and best practices together with clear risk awareness allow people to understand fraud risks and prevent scam instances. The cryptocurrency industry should establish public awareness campaigns together with online courses alongside educational institution partnerships to explain digital currencies and teach proper usage. The development of a responsible industry requires an accountability culture which needs to be built throughout. Fast steps combined with transparent actions should be taken to deal with misconduct and fraud while users affected by this behavior must receive compensation along with responsible parties needing to face accountability. A dedicated emphasis on integrity shows commitment to ethical conduct thus it helps repair the trust levels in the system. Some high-profile instances of fund recovery together with fund redistribution demonstrate to users that cryptocurrencies operate autonomously as a protective mechanism for their interests (Guarna,2022).

The way people view cryptocurrency security diverges widely between nations with different economies since industrial and emerging nations face variable regulatory situations and digital adoption extent. The developed financial systems in these countries lead people to regard digital currency mostly as investment vehicles and technological developments instead of essential financial assets. The prominence of cryptocrime events in these regions strengthens doubts because users possess established financial alternatives together with reduced willingness to engage with unregulated currency systems. Developed nations possess robust regulatory systems which couple with increased resources to fight fraud thus reducing some risks related to cryptocurrency use. Users feel more trust in cryptocurrency systems due to the detailed business regulation frameworks that the United States along with European Union member states have recently implemented (Choudhari,2023).

IV. ECONOMIC CONSEQUENCES OF CRYPTO CRIME

Crypto-related criminal actions produce extensive economic effects which damage individual customers along with corporations and entire financial systems of nations while obstructing blockchain technology implementations and improvements. Criminal activities within the digital asset space have evolved with enhanced levels of sophistication thus causing major financial losses and eroding the trust individuals have in investment platforms. These scams demand devastating costs from all those who fall prey to them. Cryptocurrency project investors often spend their savings to receive high returns through unsecure schemes but discover complete loss when these plans fail. The operation of Ponzi schemes provides investors with fake monetary gains which actually rely on incoming funds from new members rather than real profits. The collapse of every Ponzi scheme terminates with latecomers receiving no resources which results in major financial difficulties. Syndicates erupting with phishing attacks steal cryptocurrency amounts by forcing users to disclose private keys with their login information to fraudsters. People who use digital assets for value storage or financial inclusion face disastrous outcomes from such losses which decreases trust in cryptocurrencies and makes future participation less likely (Morton,2020).

The cryptocurrency industry together with other business sectors face economic challenges due to crypto crime events. Hacking and fraud incidents affect exchange services and wallet providers and blockchain startup entities leading to customer fund and sensitive data losses during breaches. Nearly 850,000 Bitcoin was stolen during the 2014 Mt. Gox hack which caused the exchange to fail and caused major economic damage to its customers. The recent 2022 FTX exchange collapse exposed major management issues and potentially fraudulent activities which caused investor and customer funds to disappear into billions of dollars. When these events occur, they damage the targeted businesses while causing the industry to sustain collateral damage because users lose their faith in the safety of cryptocurrency platforms. Trusted relationships deteriorate in the market which results in diminished trading operations with less liquidity and reduced investments impairing industry expansion and creative development (Connolly,2022).

The financial damages from crypto crime extend into substantial economic impacts which affect entire economic systems. Cryptocurrencies are a preferred choice for money laundering because they operate under decentralized and anonymous conditions which enable illegal activities. The illicit use of digital assets damages financial systems which makes it difficult for governments to establish effective taxation regulations for digital assets. Digital currency usage in ransomware operations concerns both governments and worldwide businesses at present times. The encryption of victim data by hackers enables them to extract cryptocurrency payments before they reveal data access. The financial damages caused by ransomware attacks reach beyond the required payments because businesses need to recuperate from data loss together with their damaged reputation and higher cybersecurity expenses and insurance premiums. Public funds allocated by governments also include spending on law enforcement units along with regulatory bodies and public awareness programs to manage these threats. Multiple issues combine together to create pressure on government budgets while slowing down national economic progress (Sajedi et al.,2021).

The threat of crypto crime prevents individuals from embracing blockchain technologies for industrial revolution across the spectrum from finance to supply chain operations to healthcare to governance. Scams combined with fraudulent activities generate doubts about the danger nature of cryptocurrencies leading potential users to steer away from their advantages. The decentralized finance (DeFi) sector faces billions of dollars of loss from frequent attacks against its platforms and exploits of its systems. Users suffer harm in these incidents and at the same time people question whether DeFi stands as a valid replacement for established financial systems. The surge of fraudulent ICOs creates problems for genuine blockchain projects since investors now doubt all startup initiatives due to scam concerns. The widespread scepticism creates hurdles for promising projects because they face challenges in obtaining funds while competing against each other in a market dominated by mistrust (Wronka, 2023).

The impact of crypto crime acts as a significant barrier to blockchain adoption in developing nations because these areas need cryptocurrencies to resolve their economic issues regarding financial exclusion and currency instability. The regions suffer from minimal oversight and weak technology infrastructure that leaves users exposed to scams thereby decreasing trust in blockchain and digital assets. Cryptocurrency adoption in Nigeria alongside India has exploded during the last few years yet high-profile fraud cases prompted both countries to enforce stricter regulations and discuss total bans. The implementation of such protective consumer measures creates risks to both blockchain technology benefits and market innovative opportunities. Developed nations having established regulatory systems in addition to their increased capacity to fight crimes related to cryptocurrencies achieve better results in promoting growth and controlling security threats. The mainstream acceptance of cryptocurrencies remains restricted by general beliefs that these digital assets serve criminal purposes in both developed and developing regions (Levi, 2016).

Different factors need to work together to deal with the financial impact of crypto crime while maintaining technology advancements and responsible governance standards. Vital regulation by governments needs to create specific standards for cryptocurrency operations to protect consumers and maintain business growth but somehow stay away from restrictive rules which could constrain development.

Global cooperation represents an important need since crypto crime extends beyond national boundaries and requires consortiums to locate and prosecute the offenders. The cryptocurrency industry needs to take active measures toward regaining trust through ethical practice demonstrations. Strong security systems must be implemented while auditing practices should be performed regularly and organizations must develop accountable systems for their operations. Users become wiser to protect themselves against fraud attempts when education and awareness campaigns raise their awareness about scams and decisions making abilities (Dyntu, 2018).

The economic impact of crypto crime reaches deep into all sectors and to both personal and corporate realms as well as national economies while making blockchain adoption and innovation become less likely. The occurrence of fraud alongside scams causes trust erosion in cryptocurrency systems thus blocking their path toward widespread adoption and constraining their ability to expand economic growth together with financial inclusion opportunities. A secure and transparent system for blockchain innovation needs comprehensive collaboration between authorities along with regulators and industry members to maintain innovation with accountability. The cryptocurrency industry will achieve mainstream adoption through overcoming perception issues related to crypto crime which will then enable blockchain technologies to deliver full transformative potential to everyone.

V. REGULATORY CHALLENGES FOR GOVERNMENTS AND ORGANIZATIONS

It is cumbersome for governments and organizations to deal with cryptocurrency transactions, considering the digital assets are based on decentralized, international platforms using the anonymous pseudonym. The problem of regulating borderless crypto transactions is the biggest because of their ability to bypass existing central financial controls. More decentralization implies that cryptocurrency transactions no longer pass through traditional banks, and users can successfully move funds across borders. Although the feature makes financial accessibility better for many, it makes the tasks that the regulators face when trying to monitor and record transfers, more complex. Policy makers find it hard to regulate cryptocurrencies simply because they do not conveniently fit within the borders of several individual countries. Since regulatory bodies put in place their specific rules and priorities, there are many entities that can control cross-border crypto transactions. Poor coordination between global policies enables criminal parastatals to take advantage of weaknesses in law for criminal purposes. Unstable global regulatory environment just adds to the existing woes since nations intervene in the regulation of cryptocurrency with unaffiliated stances ranging from outright bans to unbridled support for innovation.

Differing regulatory frameworks weaken the effort to combat cryptocurrency, while breeding disagreement as to compliance for lawful businesses in the space (Courtois et al.,2021).

The ease with which blockchain analytics can be used marks a point of distinction for one of the most effective tools regulators have when trying to respond to specific regulatory problems. Using modern algorithms along with advanced data analysis methods for blockchain analytics enables experts to follow crypto transactions while detecting patterns from fraudulent conduct. The combination of available technology tools helps regulatory bodies see money movement patterns and the relationships between addresses so they can identify potentially questionable activity. Chainalysis together with Elliptic serve as pivotal companies in cryptocurrency crime investigations by identifying trends in ransomware assaults and money laundering activities and fraudulent ICO operations. Authorities now have access to tools through which they can track financial flows not achievable before thus protecting blockchain's identity-hiding properties. Through blockchain analytics service providers can follow regulatory requirements by discovering high-risk transactions and customers which helps cryptocurrency exchanges and other platform operators to fulfil AML and KYC standards (Kethineni, 2020).

Blockchain analytics serves regulatory enforcement purposes effectively yet it faces certain impediments in accomplishing its mission. The tools currently track blockchain transactions effectively but they fail to work with privacy coins such as Monero and Zcash due to their privacy-oriented functionality. The quick development of blockchain technology together with advanced techniques used by criminals continues to create difficulties for analytics businesses that need continuous advancement and adjustment approaches. The implementation of blockchain analysis creates privacy issues because extensive transaction observation might violate individual rights to protection of personal information. To guarantee the responsible and ethical use of these tools it is vital to achieve proper regulatory oversight and privacy preservation equilibrium (Smith,2024).

To successfully tackle regulatory obstacles, it is fundamental to develop international partnerships among public entities as well as private sector representatives. Widespread implementation of cryptocurrency regulation demands unified participation between governments and regulatory bodies and representatives from the industry sector. The Financial Action Task Force (FATF) promotes worldwide cryptocurrency regulation through initiatives that focus on two areas - the “Travel Rule” requirement for virtual asset service providers (VASPs) to exchange transaction data. The current efforts demonstrate progress yet their implementation faces numerous difficulties because nations face technical, legal and resource challenges for compliance. International cooperation in cryptocurrency regulation requires trusts between stakeholders and aligned priorities together with infrastructure and regulatory experts to support its effective execution (Yeoh,2017).

The combination of public and private sector entities functions as a key element for solving regulatory obstacles. The combination of public and private sector entities through partnership enables governments to access technical knowledge and real-time database capabilities which increases regulatory functions. Corrupt cryptocurrencies facilitate detection and investigation of criminal activities because of the collaboration between blockchain analysis companies and law enforcement agencies. More than should be the case, crypto providers and regulators should coordinate to ensure development of transparent and enforceable accountability norms. This partnership allows regulatory authorities and crypto providers to exchange vital information, thus closing the gap on necessary knowledge between groups (Dyson et al.,2019).

Regulation of cryptography is being affected by several barriers such as international transactions, national boundaries and lack of uniform global policies. The potential of blockchain analytics is actualized with the help of the ability to enhance transparency, thus permitting the stricter compliance to regulatory standards. The use of these tools demands responsible approaches to their implementation that require careful thought regarding protection of privacy. It is only possible to create a safe cryptocurrency ecosystem if countries cooperate internationally and the public-private alliances establish transparent regulatory norms. Stakeholders can, therefore, construct flexible rules that promote innovation through cooperation to regulate crypto-industry, balanced by the demand by regulatory requirements. The plan is to create a sustainable financial structure that is dependent on blockchain for integrity and reliability, the financial structure is to be safeguarded by countermeasures to control digital cryptocurrency threat.

VI. INFLUENCE ON PUBLIC TRUST IN CRYPTOCURRENCIES

The impact of cryptocrime greatly degrades the confidence of the public on cryptocurrencies through the instillation of both financial and mental echoes that dictate how users perceive and operate in the digital currency environment. Criminal activities such as frauds and hacks in the cryptocurrency universe reduce trust in digital assets by spreading misleading reports that inflame public concerns. Angry complaints and media disputes concerning large exchanges and misleading ICOs that are constantly in the news fuel a widespread opinion that cryptocurrencies are best thought of as inherently dangerous and fraudulent. News summaries of cryptocurrencies often over-exaggerate stories, and websites such as social media can spread false information immediately without verifying facts. Not understanding blockchain technology can make individuals automatically think of cryptocurrencies as criminal because of misleading narratives that encourage a turn-off curiosity to their advantages. Victims of crypto fraud are commonly plagued by severe mental stress caused by a feeling of abandonment, loss of control, and financial ruin. Those left in a state of negative emotions after the cryptocurrency events end up becoming doubtful about digital money and mainstream finance that as a result deters them to pursue blockchain projects (Arli et al.,2021).

Stemming from cryptocurrencies, criminal activities create major impacts on society thus transforming the way people perceive the utilization of such digits currencies. The extensive destruction attributable to the Ponzi schemes of cryptocrime usually results in extreme, lasting negative perceptions of digital assets among populations affected thereby. When doubts on Cryptocurrencies spread into the social networks, this leads to a smaller number of people involved in the Cryptocurrency market. Cryptocurrencies such as the ones used for illicit activities such as money laundering and ransom-ware attacks are unable to be accepted as valid financial assets for economic empowerment and wider inclusion, subject to reputational damages. An overload of scams in regions where economy developing takes place makes it a struggle for people who depend on cryptocurrency in pursuit of financial freedom as they lack traditional banking services. People in Sub-Saharan Africa and Southeast Asia depend on digital assets for financial services but avoid cryptocurrency because of the perception of being in the clutches of scams and causing perpetuation of poverty and exclusion. (Marella et al.,2020).

Maintaining the public confidence in blockchain will need a multi-faceted response to address cryptocrime which in turn affects how individual prejudices shape public perception regarding blockchain. This mission depends on transparency because open platforms help both users and non-users understand cryptocurrencies while showing their beneficial applications. All cryptocurrency projects and platforms operating exchanges need to establish visible communication with users to deliver exact details about company activities, security standards and financial status. Third-party auditing on a regular basis strengthens transparency by proving platforms follow best practices and funds receive proper responsible management. Implementing built-in ethical frameworks including thorough KYC and AML protocols will create trust between users and regulators as well as enhance overall credibility. Through ethical operations the cryptocurrency sector will defeat digital currency prejudices while emerging as a credible replacement to conventional financial operations (Gurguc, 2018).

The educational process serves two purposes both by furnishing people with the knowledge they need to tackle cryptocurrency risks while simultaneously building confidence within the public. Users remain exposed to cryptocrimes because they lack education about cryptocurrency safety and best practices thus requiring universal access to detailed resources about risks and security measures. Educational institutions joined with public awareness campaigns alongside online courses will create partnerships to help users understand cryptocurrencies safely. Users who learn scam identification methods including phishing attacks and fraudulent ICOs will become less susceptible to cryptocrime activities. Building trust within the cryptocurrency industry requires creating accountability standards for all members of the field. The detection of fraud or misconduct requires immediate transparent measures for handling these cases while providing compensation to affected users together with responsible party accountability. By showing dedication to honest behavior the ecosystem receives an added boost toward reconstructing public confidence (Cordero et al.,2020).

Public-private partnerships represent a vital approach to rebuild trust through sector alignment when dealing with crypto crime issues. The governmental bodies along with regulatory institutions face crucial limitations in tracking illicit operations because they lack both essential technical experience and real-time transaction data yet blockchain analytics firms together with cryptocurrency exchanges maintain capabilities to pursue illegal conduct by linking wallet activities. Public entities can build superior regulatory capabilities through partnerships with private entities which helps them develop effective crypto crime prevention strategies. Blockchains analytics firms give law enforcement authorities usable information by following criminal transactions through the system and finding the responsible actors or groups. Cryptocurrency exchanges should adopt strong security protocols as well as compliance measures which protect their users from criminals who attempt to misuse exchange platforms (Claeys et al., 2018).

The psychological along with social effects of crypto crime lead to a substantial reduction in the public trust toward cryptocurrencies which obstructs both adoption and innovation. Fear and scepticism rise because of misinformation and overblown media reports and the emotional cost of digital asset crimes makes people shy away from cryptocurrency activities. To rebuild trust towards cryptocurrencies users, need an approach that both provides clear information about potential risks and enforces ethical guidelines in the industry. This will help users make sound decisions about cryptocurrencies. Public-private partnerships will boost regulatory operations and establish an accountability culture to build a trustworthy system for cryptocurrency users through secure operations. The cryptocurrency industry will achieve its transformative potential through blockchain technologies by fixing crypto crime causes and establishing public confidence which will develop a diverse and resistant financial system.

VII. FUTURE SCOPE OF THE STUDY

Research directions moving forward should focus on understanding both the transforming cryptocrime environment and its effects on worldwide financial systems. Blockchain developments require blockchain analytics to advance continuously because attackers adjust their methods while blockchain technology progresses. Future examinations should work on establishing advanced investigative techniques to track Monero along with Zcash cryptocurrencies since modern tracking technologies cannot access their operations. The analysis provides research possibilities to study the economic fallout from cryptocrime within developing countries since cryptocurrencies enable access to financial markets for many who otherwise cannot participate. The study should focus on analyzing DeFi platforms since hackers increasingly target them to then propose solutions for addressing their vulnerabilities. Research in behavioral economics has an opportunity to analyze trust dynamics following cryptocrime through an examination of public trust effects and social-psychological dimensions of the cryptocurrency ecosystem. The development of standardized international regulations alongside the Financial Action Task Force (FATF) should receive attention because these initiatives help nations cooperate regarding borderless cryptocurrency deals.

VIII. IMPLICATION OF THE STUDY

This inquiry provides critical practical advantages to national governments and to the entities regulating the use of cryptomoney, to financial institutions and their clients. Governments and regulatory bodies must create entirely integrated regulatory framework to offer a robust backbone of cryptocrime. Creating strong KYC and AML systems as well as promoting country cooperation are crucial to combating unlawful threats that violate national borders. It is important for the industry to invest in gaining the most advanced blockchain analytics technologies to facilitate fraud monitoring and compliance with the regulatory measures. The restoration of public confidence depends on organized education in informing users on what to identify as scams and the advantages of using blockchain technology. Reviving public trust into cyber currency depends on openness, ethical compliance, and regular audits. Collaboration from government to private sector organizations enables regulators through leveraging the technical expertise held by private players. It is important for anyone in the ecosystem of cryptocurrency to use multi-factor authentication and cold storage in order to counteract the hacker/ phishing and phishing attempts. When the stakeholders are united towards practical endeavors, they can develop a reliable cryptocurrency structure wherein this structure can sustain growth and innovation with little risks of cryptocrime

CONCLUSION

Crypto crime's distinct features are the source for destabilizing global finance, thanks to widespread economic incursion that affects citizens, businesses and governmental bodies equally. Due to their decentralized and private structure, cryptocurrency networks are often exploited by scammers to carry out scams, introduce fraudulent transactions, make other unlawful movements, etc. The illicit activities surrounding the use of cryptocurrencies result in significant monetary losses and erode people's trust in digital currencies thereby inhibiting adoption of the latter and the possibilities of blockchain development. Regulatory players must craft several tactics to contain the rampant illicit elements with digital currencies. Efficient resolutions would require improved regulatory controls supplemented by upgrades in blockchain analytics instruments, educational initiatives, as well as better public-private sector relations.. The cryptocurrency industry will be able to enable blockchain technologies' transformative potential along with rebuilding trust through emphasis on transparency and security and accountability. Crypto-related challenges make it necessary for stakeholders to work together to create new security solutions which support decentralization benefits. Widespread adoption of cryptocurrencies and blockchain technologies depends on resolving the fundamental reasons for cryptocrime while developing trust-based systems and accountability measures for the global financial sector.

REFERENCES

Acharya, B., Saad, M., Cinà, A. E., Schönherr, L., Dai Nguyen, H., Oest, A., & Holz, T. (2024, May). Conning the crypto conman: End-to-end analysis of cryptocurrency-based technical support scams. In *2024 IEEE Symposium on Security and Privacy (SP)* (pp. 17-35). IEEE. DOI: 10.1109/SP54263.2024.00156

AGARWAL, S., KOTHARI, N., KU, U., CHAPLOT, P., & NAVEED, M. A Study on the Scams of Cryptocurrency.

Arli, D., van Esch, P., Bakpayev, M., & Laurence, A. (2021). Do consumers really trust cryptocurrencies? *Marketing Intelligence & Planning*, *39*(1), 74–90. DOI: 10.1108/MIP-01-2020-0036

Arli, D., van Esch, P., Bakpayev, M., & Laurence, A. (2021). Do consumers really trust cryptocurrencies? *Marketing Intelligence & Planning*, *39*(1), 74–90. DOI: 10.1108/MIP-01-2020-0036

Barnes, P. (2018). Crypto currency and its susceptibility to speculative bubbles, manipulation, scams and fraud. [JASF]. *Journal of Advanced Studies in Finance*, *9*(2 (18)), 60–77.

Bartoletti, M., Lande, S., Loddo, A., Pompianu, L., & Serusi, S. (2021). Cryptocurrency scams: Analysis and perspectives. *IEEE Access : Practical Innovations, Open Solutions*, *9*, 148353–148373. DOI: 10.1109/ACCESS.2021.3123894

Biju, A. V. N., & Thomas, A. S. (2023). Uncertainties and ambivalence in the crypto market: An urgent need for a regional crypto regulation. *SN Business & Economics*, *3*(8), 136. DOI: 10.1007/s43546-023-00519-z

Choudhari, V. K. (2023). How Does Trust In Government Institutions Affect The Demand For Cryptocurrencies? *International Journal of High School Research*, *5*(7), 147–151. DOI: 10.36838/v5i7.24

Claeys, G., Demertzis, M., & Efstathiou, K. (2018). *Cryptocurrencies and monetary policy* (No. 2018/10). Bruegel Policy Contribution.

Connolly, M. (2022). Cryptocurrency Concerns, Crimes, and Legal Consequences. *Akron Law Review*, *55*(3), 3.

Courtois, N. T., Gradon, K. T., & Schmeh, K. (2021). Crypto currency regulation and law enforcement perspectives. *arXiv preprint arXiv:2109.01047.*

Daoud, G. (2023). *The Evolving Nature Of Financial Crime With The Increase Of Internet Capabilities. Challenge Identification, Legal Considerations And Policy Recommendations* (Doctoral dissertation, School of Advanced Study).

Dyntu, V., & Dykyi, O. (2018). Cryptocurrency in the system of money laundering. *Baltic Journal of Economic Studies*, *4*(5), 75–81. DOI: 10.30525/2256-0742/2018-4-5-75-81

Dyson, S., Buchanan, W. J., & Bell, L. (2019). The challenges of investigating cryptocurrencies and blockchain related crime. *arXiv preprint arXiv:1907.12221.*

Gil-Cordero, E., Cabrera-Sánchez, J. P., & Arrás-Cortés, M. J. (2020). Cryptocurrencies as a financial tool: Acceptance factors. *Mathematics*, *8*(11), 1974. DOI: 10.3390/math8111974

Guarna, T. A. (2022). *Trust Machines: Cryptocurrencies, Blockchains, and Humans in Cultures of Mistrust* (Doctoral dissertation, Massachusetts Institute of Technology).

Gurguc, Z., & Knottenbelt, W. (2018). Cryptocurrencies: overcoming barriers to trust and adoption. *Retrieved from Imperial College London website:* https://www. imperial. ac. *uk/media/imperial-college/research-centres-andgroups/ic3re/crypto-currencies--overcoming-barriers-to-trust-and-adoption. pdf.*

Gurguc, Z., & Knottenbelt, W. (2018). Cryptocurrencies: overcoming barriers to trust and adoption. *Retrieved from Imperial College London website:* https://www. imperial. ac. *uk/media/imperial-college/research-centres-andgroups/ic3re/crypto-currencies--overcoming-barriers-to-trust-and-adoption. pdf.*

Kethineni, S., & Cao, Y. (2020). The rise in popularity of cryptocurrency and associated criminal activity. *International Criminal Justice Review*, *30*(3), 325–344. DOI: 10.1177/1057567719827051

Kreminskyi, O., Kuzmenko, O., Antoniuk, A., & Smahlo, O. (2021). International cooperation in the investigation of economic crimes related to cryptocurrency circulation. *Estudios de Economía Aplicada*, *39*(6). Advance online publication. DOI: 10.25115/eea.v39i6.5247

Levi, M., Doig, A., Gundur, R., Wall, D., & Williams, M. L. (2016). The implications of economic cybercrime for policing.

Marella, V., Upreti, B., Merikivi, J., & Tuunainen, V. K. (2020). Understanding the creation of trust in cryptocurrencies: The case of Bitcoin. *Electronic Markets*, *30*(2), 259–271. DOI: 10.1007/s12525-019-00392-5

Morton, D. T. (2020). The future of cryptocurrency: An unregulated instrument in an increasingly regulated global economy. *Loy. U. Chi. Int'l L. Rev.*, *16*, 129.

Nakhle, A. (2022). *The crypto world: global development and international legal implications* (Doctoral dissertation, Notre Dame University-Louaize).

Phillips, R., & Wilder, H. (2020, May). Tracing cryptocurrency scams: Clustering replicated advance-fee and phishing websites. In *2020 IEEE international conference on blockchain and cryptocurrency (ICBC)* (pp. 1-8). IEEE.

Rasyid, A., Willim, A. P., & Khaeryyah, S. (2024). Cryptocurrency and the Law: The Challenges of Regulating Decentralized Finance in Global Markets. *Impact: Multidisciplinary Journal*, *1*(01), 1–10.

Smith, M., & Tiwari, M. (2024). The implications of national blockchain infrastructure for financial crime. *Journal of Financial Crime*, *31*(2), 236–248. DOI: 10.1108/JFC-01-2023-0006

Wronka, C. (2023). Financial crime in the decentralized finance ecosystem: New challenges for compliance. *Journal of Financial Crime*, *30*(1), 97–113. DOI: 10.1108/JFC-09-2021-0218

Xia, P., Wang, H., Zhang, B., Ji, R., Gao, B., Wu, L., Luo, X., & Xu, G. (2020). Characterizing cryptocurrency exchange scams. *Computers & Security*, *98*, 101993. DOI: 10.1016/j.cose.2020.101993

Yeoh, P. (2017). Regulatory issues in blockchain technology. *Journal of Financial Regulation and Compliance*, *25*(2), 196–208. DOI: 10.1108/JFRC-08-2016-0068

Compilation of References

Aaron, W. C., Irekponor, O., Aleke, N. T., Yeboah, L., & Joseph, J. E. (2024). Ma-chine learning techniques for enhancing security in financial technology systems. https://www.researchgate.net/profile/Ngozi-Aleke-2/publication/385275742_Machine_learning_techniques_for_enhancing_security_in_financial_technology_systems/links/671d31bdedbc012ea14103ca/Machine-learning-techniques-for-enhancing-security-in-financial-technology-systems.pdf

Abad-Segura, E., Infante-Moro, A., González-Zamar, M. D., & López-Meneses, E. (2021). Blockchain technology for secure accounting management: Research trends analysis [Article]. *Mathematics*, *9*(14), 1631. Advance online publication. DOI: 10.3390/math9141631

Abdulhakeem, S. A., & Hu, Q. (2021). Powered by Blockchain technology, DeFi (Decentralized Finance) strives to increase financial inclusion of the unbanked by reshaping the world financial system. *Modern Economy*, 1. https://www.scirp.org/journal/Paperabs.aspx?PaperID=106546

Abid, H. M. R., Khan, N., Hussain, A., Anis, Z. B., Nadeem, M., & Khalid, N. (2024). Quantitative and qualitative approach for accessing and predicting food safety using various web-based tools. *Food Control*, *162*, 110471. DOI: 10.1016/j.foodcont.2024.110471

Abraham, J., Higdon, D., Nelson, J., & Ibarra, J. (2018). Cryptocurrency price prediction using tweet volume and sentiment analysis. *SMU Data Science Review*, *1*(3), 37–73.

Abu Elbeh, I. M. (2024). E-Commerce and Digital Currencies Risk Management Challenges. In *Intelligent Systems, Business, and Innovation Research* (pp. 343–354). Springer Nature Switzerland. DOI: 10.1007/978-3-031-36895-0_28

Abubakar-Sadiq, M. S. (2023). *Establishing secure and privacy preserving digital identity with self-sovereign identity.* (Doctoral dissertation, Universidade do Porto (Portugal)). https://repositorio-aberto.up.pt/bitstream/10216/156847/2/657403.pdf

Acharya, B., Saad, M., Cinà, A. E., Schönherr, L., Dai Nguyen, H., Oest, A., & Holz, T. (2024, May). Conning the crypto conman: End-to-end analysis of cryptocurrency-based technical support scams. In *2024 IEEE Symposium on Security and Privacy (SP)* (pp. 17-35). IEEE. DOI: 10.1109/SP54263.2024.00156

Adhami, S., & Guegan, D. (2020). Crypto assets: The role of ICO tokens within a well- diversified portfolio. *Economia e Politica Industriale*, *47*(2), 219–241. DOI: 10.1007/s40812-019-00141-x

Adisa, O., Ilugbusi, B. S., Obi, O. C., Awonuga, K. F., Adelekan, O. A., Asuzu, O. F., & Ndubuisi, N. L. (2024). Decentralized Finance (DEFI) in the US economy: A review: Assessing the rise, challenges, and implications of blockchain-driven financial systems. *World Journal of Advanced Research and Reviews, 21(1)*, 2313-2328. https://pdfs.semanticscholar.org/7a26/a74b2b8518f80bb9f253942de1955a14b552.pdf

AGARWAL, S., KOTHARI, N., KU, U., CHAPLOT, P., & NAVEED, M. A Study on the Scams of Cryptocurrency.

Agence France-Presse. (2024, February 5). Multinational loses HK$200 million to deepfake video conference scam, Hong Kong police say. Hong Kong Free Press. https://hongkongfp.com/2024/02/05/multinational-loses-hk200-million-to-deepfake-video-conference-scam-hong-kong-police-say/

Aggarwal, S.,Luthra, K., Srivastava, V (2023). 4. India's tech-enthusiasts: crypto-currency and the reserve bank's role in transformation. .DOI: 10.52458/9789388996969.nsp2023.eb.ch-19

Agur, I., Ari, A., & Dell'Ariccia, G. (2022). Designing central bank digital currencies. *Journal of Monetary Economics*, *125*, 62–79. DOI: 10.1016/j.jmoneco.2021.05.002

Ahlawat, S., & Tripathi, A. (2021). Blockchain: Implications for accounting and audit practice. In (pp. 9-19). https://doi.org/DOI: 10.1515/9783110702507-002

Ahmed, S., & Shaun, M. A. (2022). Impact of deepfake technology on digital world authenticity: A review. *International Journal of Engineering and Management Research*, *12*(3), 78–84. DOI: 10.31033/ijemr.12.3.10

Ahn, G.-J., Doupe, A., Zhao, Z., & Liao, K. (2016). Ransomware and cryptocurrency: partners in crime. In *Cybercrime Through an Interdisciplinary Lens* (pp. 119–140). Routledge.

Ait Mouha, R. (2021). *Internet of Things (IoT): Concepts and applications*. Springer.

Ait Mouha, R. A. R. (2021). Internet of things (IoT). *Journal of Data Analysis and Information Processing*, *9*(02), 77–101. DOI: 10.4236/jdaip.2021.92006

Ajayi, A. A., Igba, E., Soyele, A. D., & Enyejo, J. O. (2024). Enhancing Digital Identity and Financial Security in Decentralized Finance (Defi) through Zero-Knowledge Proofs (ZKPs) and Blockchain Solutions for Regulatory Compliance and Privacy. https://www.researchgate.net/profile/Onma-Enyejo/publication/385686688_Enhancing_Digital_Identity_and_Financial_Security_in_Decentralized_Finance_Defi_through_Zero-Knowledge_Proofs_ZKPs_and_Blockchain_Solutions_for_Regulatory_Compliance_and_Privacy/links/672fccdcecbbde716b64352e/Enhancing-Digital-Identity-and-Financial-Security-in-Decentralized-Finance-Defi-through-Zero-Knowledge-Proofs-ZKPs-and-Blockchain-Solutions-for-Regulatory-Compliance-and-Privacy.pdf

Akartuna, A. (2022, December 10). *Mango Market exploit: DeFi loses nearly $900 million to hackers in costliest 30 days on record.* Retrieved from ELLIPTIC: https://www.elliptic.co/blog/analysis/mango-market-exploit-defi-loses-nearly-900-million-to-hackers-in-costliest-30-days-on-record

Akartuna, E. A., & Madelin, T. (2023). *The State of Cross-chain Crime* Elliptic. https://www.elliptic.co/resources/state-of-cross-chain-crime-2023

Akhgar, B., Staniforth, A., & Bosco, F. (Eds.). (2014). *Cyber Crime and Cyber Terrorism: Investigators Handbook.* Elsevier.

Akinrotimi, A. O. (2020). Legal Ramifications of Blockchain Technology. In Khan, M. A., Quasim, M. T., Algarni, F., & Alharthi, A. (Eds.), *Decentralised Internet of Things: A Blockchain Perspective* (pp. C1–C1). Springer International Publishing. DOI: 10.1007/978-3-030-38677-1_10

Al Shamsi, M., Smith, D., & Gleason, K. (2023). Space transition and the vulnerabilities of the NFT market to financial crime. *Journal of Financial Crime, ahead-of-print*(ahead-of-print). https://doi.org/DOI: 10.1108/JFC-09-2022-0218

Alamsyah, A., & Syahrir, S. (2023). The Taxonomy of Blockchain-based Technology in the Financial Industry [version 2; peer review: 2 approved]. *F1000 Research*, *12*(457), 457. Advance online publication. DOI: 10.12688/f1000research.133518.2

Aldridge, J. (2019). Does online anonymity boost illegal market trading? *Media Culture & Society*, *41*(4), 578–583. DOI: 10.1177/0163443719842075

Alessandretti, L., ElBahrawy, A., Aiello, L. M., & Baronchelli, A. (2018). Anticipating cryptocurrency prices using machine learning. *Complexity*, *2018*(1), 1–16. DOI: 10.1155/2018/8983590

Ali, M. S., Vecchio, M., Pincheira, M., Dolui, K., Antonelli, F., & Rehmani, M. H. (2018). Applications of blockchains in the Internet of Things: A comprehensive survey. *IEEE Communications Surveys and Tutorials*, *21*(2), 1676–1717. DOI: 10.1109/COMST.2018.2886932

Al-Khazraji, S. H., Saleh, H. H., Khalid, A. I., & Mishkhal, I. A. (2023). Impact of deepfake technology on social media: Detection, misinformation and societal implications. *The Eurasia Proceedings of Science Technology Engineering and Mathematics*, *23*, 429–441. DOI: 10.55549/epstem.1371792

Allen, H. J. (2022). DeFi: Shadow Banking 2.0? *Wm. & Mary L. Rev., 64*, 919. https://papers.ssrn.com/sol3/Delivery.cfm?abstractid=4038788

Allioui, H., & Mourdi, Y. (2023). Unleashing the Potential of AI: Investigating Cutting-Edge Technologies That Are Transforming Businesses. [IJCEDS]. *International Journal of Computer Engineering and Data Science*, *3*(2), 1–12. https://ijceds.com/ijceds/article/view/59

Alpert, L. I. (2024). *How financial 'sextortion' scams became an epidemic on social media — with tragic consequences*. [online] MarketWatch. Available at: https://www.marketwatch.com/story/how-financial-sextortion-scams-became-an-epidemic-on-social-media-with-tragic-consequences-a52a8505?utm_source=chatgpt.com [Accessed 6 Feb. 2025].

Alsalamah, S., & Nuzzolese, E. (2020). Promising blockchain technology applications and use case designs for the identification of multinational victims of mass disasters. *Frontiers in Blockchain*, *3*, 34. DOI: 10.3389/fbloc.2020.00034

Alyami, M., Alhotaylah, R., Alshehri, S., & Alghamdi, A. (2023). Phishing Attacks on Cryptocurrency Investors in the Arab States of the Gulf [Article]. *Journal of Risk and Financial Management*, *16*(5), 271. Advance online publication. DOI: 10.3390/jrfm16050271

Amezaga, N., & Hajek, J. (2022, September). Availability of voice deepfake technology and its impact for good and evil. In *Proceedings of the 23rd Annual Conference on Information Technology Education* (pp. 23-28). DOI: 10.1145/3537674.3554742

Andreeva, J., & Abrams, A. (2024, December 5). *Top 9 identity verification trends in 2025*. Sumsub. https://sumsub.com/blog/top-9-identity-verification-trends-in-2025/

Androulaki, E., Karame, G. O., Roeschlin, M., Scherer, T., & Capkun, S. (2013). *Evaluating User Privacy in Bitcoin*. Financial Cryptography and Data Security. DOI: 10.1007/978-3-642-39884-1_4

AON. (2023, October 13). *Flash Loan Attacks: A Case Study*. Retrieved from AON: https://www.aon.com/en/insights/cyber-labs/flash-loan-attacks-a-case-study

Aquilina, M., Frost, J., & Schrimpf, A. (2024). Decentralized finance (DeFi): A functional approach. *Journal of Financial Regulation*, *10*(1), 1–27. DOI: 10.1093/jfr/fjad013

Arewa, A. (2019). Corruption, money laundering and Nigeria's crisis of development. *Journal of Financial Crime*, *26*(4), 1133–1145. DOI: 10.1108/JFC-08-2018-0082

Arli, D., van Esch, P., Bakpayev, M., & Laurence, A. (2021). Do consumers really trust cryptocurrencies? *Marketing Intelligence & Planning*, *39*(1), 74–90. DOI: 10.1108/MIP-01-2020-0036

Arora, M., Mishra, K. K., Singh, M., Singh, P., & Tripathi, R. (2024). Deepfake Technology and Its Implications for Influencer Marketing. In *Navigating the World of Deepfake Technology* (pp. 66–90). IGI Global. DOI: 10.4018/979-8-3693-5298-4.ch005

Asif, R., & Hassan, S. R. (2023). Shaping the future of Ethereum: Exploring energy consumption in Proof-of-Work and Proof-of-Stake consensus. *Frontiers in Blockchain*, *6*, 1151724. DOI: 10.3389/fbloc.2023.1151724

Aspembitova, A. T., & Bentley, M. A. (2022). Oracles in decentralized finance: Attack costs, profits and mitigation measures. *Entropy (Basel, Switzerland)*, *60*(1), 60. Advance online publication. DOI: 10.3390/e25010060 PMID: 36673200

Attaran, M., & Gunasekaran, A. (2019). Blockchain-enabled technology: The emerging technology set to reshape and decentralise many industries. *International Journal of Applied Decision Sciences*, *12*(4), 424–444. DOI: 10.1504/IJADS.2019.102642

Australia's Cyber Security Strategy. (2020). *Australia's Cyber Security Strategy 2020 at a glance* https://www.homeaffairs.gov.au/cyber-security-subsite/files/cyber-security-strategy-2020.pdf

Australian Competition and Consumer Commission. (2024). *Australians lose over $70 million to bogus investment opportunities*. Retrieved 30/01/2025 from https://www.accc.gov.au/media-release/australians-lose-over-70-million-to-bogus-investment-opportunities

Australian Cyber Security Centre (ACSC). (2024). *Cyber Security Awareness Month 2024* https://www.cyber.gov.au/about-us/view-all-content/news-and-media/cyber-security-awareness-month-2024?ref=search

Avital, N. (2020). *2019 Global DDoS threat landscape report*. Imperva. https://www.imperva.com/blog/2019-global-ddos-threat-landscape-report/

AWS. (2018). *AWS Blockchain Partners: Accelerating your distributed ledger journey*. Retrieved 22 February 2018 from https://aws.amazon.com/partners/blockchain/

Aziz, A., & Naima, U. (2021). Rethinking digital financial inclusion: Evidence from Bangladesh. *Technology in Society*, *64*, 101509. https://doi.org/https://doi.org/10.1016/j.techsoc.2020.101509. DOI: 10.1016/j.techsoc.2020.101509

Babu, R. (2024). ADVANCEMENTS IN DECENTRALIZED IDENTITY SOLUTIONS: EMPOWERING USERS THROUGH SELF-SOVEREIGN IDENTITY. *INTERNATIONAL JOURNAL OF COMPUTER ENGINEERING AND TECHNOLOGY (IJCET)*, 721-733. https://lib-index.com/index.php/IJCET/article/view/IJCET_15_04_063/487

Bajwa, I. A. (2025). Reinvestment intentions in cryptocurrency: Examining the dynamics of risks and investor risk tolerance [Article]. *Digital Business*, *5*(1), 100104. Advance online publication. DOI: 10.1016/j.digbus.2024.100104

Bakos, Y., & Halaburda, H. (2021). Permissioned vs permissionless blockchain platforms: Tradeoffs in trust and performance. *NYU Stern School of Business working paper*.

Bakos, Y., & Halaburda, H. (2021). Permissioned vs. permissionless blockchains: A comparative analysis. *The Journal of Economic Perspectives*, *35*(3), 1–20.

Baldominos, A., & Saez, Y. (2019). Coin.AI: A proof-of-useful-work scheme for blockchain-based distributed deep learning. *Entropy (Basel, Switzerland)*, *21*(8), 723. DOI: 10.3390/e21080723

Balgobin, P., & Seeam, A. (2020, September). Developing an effective regulatory framework for virtual currencies in mauritius. In *Proceedings of the 2nd International Conference on Intelligent and Innovative Computing Applications* (pp. 1-9). DOI: 10.1145/3415088.3415126

Banyal, R. K., Jain, P., & Jain, V. K. (2013, 24-25 Sept. 2013). Multi-factor Authentication Framework for Cloud Computing. *2013 Fifth International Conference on Computational Intelligence, Modelling and Simulation*

Barberis, N., & Huang, M. (2008). Stocks as lotteries: The implications of probability weighting for security prices. *The American Economic Review*, *98*(5), 2066–2100. DOI: 10.1257/aer.98.5.2066

Barenji, A. V., Li, Z., & Wang, W. M. (2018, June). Blockchain cloud manufacturing: Shop floor and machine level. In *Smart SysTech 2018; European conference on smart objects, systems and technologies* (pp. 1-6). VDE.

Barnes, P. (2018). Crypto currency and its susceptibility to speculative bubbles, manipulation, scams and fraud. [JASF]. *Journal of Advanced Studies in Finance*, *9*(2 (18)), 60–77.

Barnes, P., & Oloruntoba, R. (2005). Assurance of security in maritime supply chains: Conceptual issues of vulnerability and crisis management. *Journal of International Management*, *11*(4), 519–540. https://doi.org/https://doi.org/10.1016/j.intman.2005.09.008. DOI: 10.1016/j.intman.2005.09.008

Bartoletti, M., Lande, S., Loddo, A., Pompianu, L., & Serusi, S. (2021). Cryptocurrency scams: Analysis and perspectives. *IEEE Access : Practical Innovations, Open Solutions*, *9*, 148353–148373. DOI: 10.1109/ACCESS.2021.3123894

Bartoletti, M., Pes, B., & Serusi, S. (2018). Data mining for detecting Bitcoin Ponzi schemes. In *2018 Crypto Valley Conference on Blockchain Technology (CVCBT)* (pp. 75–84). IEEE. DOI: 10.1109/CVCBT.2018.00014

Baur, D. G., Hong, K., & Lee, A. D. (2016). Virtual currencies: media of exchange or speculative asset?.

Baur, D. G., & Dimpfl, T. (2017). Realized bitcoin volatility. *SSRN*, *2949754*, 1–26.

Baviskar, P. S., & Roy, M. (2018). Wanna cry ransomware: A case study in Indian perspective. [IJCRT]. *International Journal of Creative Research Thoughts*, *6*(2), 811–814.

BBC News. (2021, November 2). *Squid Game crypto token collapses in apparent scam*. https://www.bbc.com/news/business-59129466

BBC News. (2024). Hong Kong worker duped by video call deepfake in $25m heist. *BBC News*. https://www.bbc.com/news/world-asia-china-68212580

BBC. (2021, November 02). *Squid Game crypto token collapses in apparent scam.* Retrieved from BBC: https://www.bbc.com/news/business-59129466

Belblidia, M., Comfort, L. K., Ganapati, N. E., Graves, J. V., Jerroleman, A., Kiefer, J. J., & Thompson, D. D. (2019). *Housing Recovery After Disasters*. Rowman & Littlefield.

Bello, O. A., & Olufemi, K. (2024). Artificial intelligence in fraud prevention: Exploring techniques and applications challenges and opportunities. *Computer Science & IT Research Journal, 5*(6), 1505–1520. DOI: 10.51594/csitrj.v5i6.1252

Benson, V., Turksen, U., & Adamyk, B. (2024). Dark side of decentralised finance: A call for enhanced AML regulation based on use cases of illicit activities. *Journal of Financial Regulation and Compliance, 32*(1), 80–97. DOI: 10.1108/JFRC-04-2023-0065

Bhati, D. (2024, June 7). Dating scams rising in metro cities, leaving hearts and bank accounts empty. *India Today*. https://www.indiatoday.in/technology/news/story/dating-scams-rising-in-metro-cities-leaving-hearts-and-bank-accounts-empty-2550450-2024-06-07

Bhat, M. A., Rather, M. Y., Singh, P., Hassan, S., & Hussain, N. (2025). Advances in smart food authentication for enhanced safety and quality. *Trends in Food Science & Technology, 155*, 104800. DOI: 10.1016/j.tifs.2024.104800

Bick, J. D. (2022). *NFTs, Cryptocurrencies and Crypto Assets Explained*. [online] Brach Eichler | Counsellors at Law. Available at: https://www.bracheichler.com/insights/nfts-cryptocurrencies-and-crypto-assets-explained/?utm_source=chatgpt.com [Accessed 19 Feb. 2025].

Biedron, S. (2024). *Cybercrime in the Digital Age University of Oxford*].

Biju, A. V. N., & Thomas, A. S. (2023). Uncertainties and ambivalence in the crypto market: An urgent need for a regional crypto regulation. *SN Business & Economics, 3*(8), 136. DOI: 10.1007/s43546-023-00519-z

Blue, L., Xing, C., & Pham, T. (2024). Cryptocurrencies: Who is vulnerable and what are the vulnerabilities? [Article]. *The Australian Journal of Social Issues*. Advance online publication. DOI: 10.1002/ajs4.351

Bondarenko, N., & Soponar, P. (2024). Empowering the Underbanked: A Comparative Analysis of Decentralized Finance (DeFi) Solutions for Financial Inclusion. https://www.theconnecter.io/pdf/2024-01-24-_YNBC%20and%20The%20Connecter%20R_D_%20Comparative%20Analysis%20of%20DeFi%20Solutions.pdf

Bonnet, S., & Teuteberg, F. (2024). Decentralized autonomous organizations: A systematic literature review and research agenda. *International Journal on Management of Innovation & Technology, 2450026*(4), 2450026. Advance online publication. DOI: 10.1142/S0219877024500263

Botha, J., & Pieterse, H. (2020). Fake news and deepfakes: A dangerous threat for 21st century information security. In ICCWS 2020 15th International Conference on Cyber Warfare and Security (p. 57).

Braaten, C. N., & Vaughn, M. S. (2019). Convenience Theory of Cryptocurrency Crime: A Content Analysis of US Federal Court Decisions [Article; Early Access]. *Deviant Behavior, 21*. Advance online publication. DOI: 10.1080/01639625.2019.1706706

Bratcher, B. (2025, February 25). *Crypto's grown-up response to North Korea's historic $1.4B robbery*. Forbes. https://www.forbes.com/sites/beccabratcher/2025/02/25/cryptos-grown-up-response-to-north-koreas-historic-14b-robbery/

Braun, V., & Clarke, V. (2006). Using thematic analysis in psychology. *Qualitative Research in Psychology, 3*(2), 77–101. DOI: 10.1191/1478088706qp063oa

Braun, V., & Clarke, V. (2012). *Thematic analysis*. American Psychological Association. DOI: 10.1037/13620-004

Brenner, S. W. (2007). Cybercrime: Re-thinking crime control strategies. In Jewkes, Y. (Ed.), *Crime online* (pp. 12–28). Willan Publishing.

Bui, V. C., Wen, S., Yu, J., Xia, X., Haghighi, M. S., & Xiang, Y. (2021). Evaluating upgradable smart contract. *2021 IEEE international conference on blockchain (Blockchain)*, 252-256. https://ieeexplore.ieee.org/abstract/document/9680538/

Buil-Gil, D., & Saldaña-Taboada, P. (2022). Offending concentration on the internet: An exploratory analysis of bitcoin-related cybercrime. *Deviant Behavior, 43*(12), 1453–1470. DOI: 10.1080/01639625.2021.1988760

Bulger, M., & Davison, P. (2018). The promises, challenges, and futures of media literacy. *The Journal of Media Literacy Education, 10*(1), 1–21. DOI: 10.23860/JMLE-2018-10-1-1

Burggraf, T., & Vyas, A. (2020). Beyond risk parity—A machine learning-based hierarchical risk parity approach on cryptocurrencies. *Finance Research Letters, 101523*. Advance online publication. DOI: 10.1016/j.frl.2020.101523

Business Standard. (2023, June 23). Bribes-for-job scam uncovered at TCS, Rs 100 crore involved. https://www.business-standard.com/companies/news/bribes-for-job-scam-uncovered-at-tcs-rs-100-crore-involved-123062300176_1.html

Buterin, V. (2014). *A next-generation smart contract and decentralized application platform*. Ethereum White Paper. https://ethereum.org/whitepaper

Camomile Shumba. (March 2023) 'South Africa's Crypto Firms Will Soon Need to Apply for Registration or Face a Heavy Fine' (CoinDesk 25 March 2023), https://www.coindesk.com/policy/2023/05/25/south-africas-crypto-firms-will- soon-need-to-apply-for-registration-or-face-a-heavy-fine/

Caporale, G. M., de Dios Mazariegos, J. J., & Gil-Alana, L. A. (2024). Long-Run Linkages between US Stock Prices and Cryptocurrencies: A Fractional Cointegration Analysis. *Computational Economics*, *64*(6), 1–11. DOI: 10.1007/s10614-023-10510-3

Caporale, G. M., & Zekokh, T. (2019). Modelling volatility of cryptocurrencies using Markov-switching GARCH models. *Research in International Business and Finance*, *48*, 143–155. DOI: 10.1016/j.ribaf.2018.12.009

Carapella, F., & Swem, N. (2022). Decentralized finance (defi): Transformative potential & associated risks. https://dx.doi.org/DOI: 10.17016/feds.2022.057

Carlisle, D. (2023). *The crypto launderers: Crime and cryptocurrencies from the dark web to DeFi and beyond*. John Wiley & Sons.

Carpenter, P. (2024). *Faik: A practical guide to living in a world of deepfakes, disinformation, and AI-generated deceptions*. John Wiley & Sons.

Catalini, C., & Gans, J. S. (2017). Some Simple Economics of the Blockchain. *Rotman School of Management Working Paper No. 2874598; MIT Sloan Research Paper No. 5191-16., Available at SSRN:* https://ssrn.com/abstract=2874598. Available at *SSRN*: https://ssrn.com/abstract=2874598

Cedra, A. (2024). Mitigating risks in decentralized finance: A Systematic review of challenges and solutions. *International journal of economic perspectives*, 104-125. https://ijeponline.lingcure.org/index.php/journal/article/download/549/507

Chainalysis Team. (2024). *$2.2 billion stolen in crypto in 2024 but hacked volumes stagnate*. Chainalysis. https://www.chainalysis.com/blog/crypto-hacking-stolen-funds-2025/

Chainalysis. (2022). *The 2022 Geography of Cryptocurrency Report*. https://go.chainalysis.com/rs/503-FAP-074/images/2022-Geography-of-Cryptocurrency.pdf

Chainalysis. (2023). *The 2023 crypto crime report*. Chainalysis Inc. https://www.chainalysis.com/

Chainalysis. (2023). *The 2023 crypto crime report*. https://www.chainalysis.com/reports/2023-crypto-crime-report/

Chainalysis. (2024). *The 2024 Crypto Crime Report.* https://documenti.camera.it/leg19/documentiAcquisiti/COM02/Audizioni/leg19.com02.Audizioni.Memoria.PUBBLICO.ideGes.34062.02-04-2024-16-52-36.832.pdf

Chainalysis. (2025). *2025 crypto crime report: Introduction.* https://www.chainalysis.com/blog/2025-crypto-crime-report-introduction/

Chainalysis. (2025). *The 2025 crypto crime report.* Chainalysis. https://www.chainalysis.com/wp-content/uploads/2025/02/the-2025-crypto-crime-report-release.pdf

ChainAnalysis. (2023, March 2023). *$197 Million Stolen: Euler Finance Flash Loan Attack Explained [UPDATED 4/6/23].* Retrieved from Chainanalysis: https://www.chainalysis.com/blog/euler-finance-flash-loan-attack/

Chang, L. Y. C., Zhou, Y., & Phan, D. H. (2023). Virtual kidnapping: Online scams with 'Asian characteristics' during the pandemic. In *Cybercrime in the pandemic digital age and beyond* (pp. 109–130). Springer International Publishing., DOI: 10.1007/978-3-031-29107-4_6

Charfeddine, L., Benlagha, N., & Maouchi, Y. (2020). Investigating the dynamic relationship between cryptocurrencies and conventional assets: Implications for financial investors. *Economic Modelling*, *85*, 198–217. DOI: 10.1016/j.econmod.2019.05.016

Chaum, D. (1983, August). Blind signatures for untraceable payments. In *Advances in Cryptology* [Boston, MA: Springer US.]. *Proceedings of Crypto*, *82*, 199–203.

Chawki, M. (2022). The Dark Web and the future of illicit drug markets. *Journal of Transportation Security*, *15*(3), 173–191. DOI: 10.1007/s12198-022-00252-y

Chen, W., Xu, H., Jia, L., & Gao, Y. (2020). Machine learning model for bitcoin exchange rate prediction using economic and technology determinants. *International Journal of Forecasting*. [Online]. Available: https://www.sciencedirect.com/science/article/abs/pii/S0169207020300431

Chen, W., Guo, X., Chen, Z., Zheng, Z., & Lu, Y. (2020). Phishing scam detection on Ethereum: Towards financial security for blockchain ecosystem. In *International Joint Conference on Artificial Intelligence*, 7, 4456-4462. https://doi.org/DOI: 10.24963/ijcai.2020/621

Chesney, B., & Citron, D. (2019). Deep fakes: A looming challenge for privacy, democracy, and national security. *California Law Review*, *107*, 1753.

Choo, K.-K. R., & Smith, R. G. (2008). Criminal Exploitation of Online Systems by Organised Crime Groups. *Asian Journal of Criminology*, *3*(1), 37–59. DOI: 10.1007/s11417-007-9035-y

Choraś, M., Demestichas, K., Giełczyk, A., Herrero, Á., Ksieniewicz, P., Remoundou, K., Urda, D., & Woźniak, M. (2021). Advanced Machine Learning techniques for fake news (online disinformation) detection: A systematic mapping study. *Applied Soft Computing*, *101*, 107050. DOI: 10.1016/j.asoc.2020.107050

Choudhari, V. K. (2023). How Does Trust In Government Institutions Affect The Demand For Cryptocurrencies? *International Journal of High School Research*, *5*(7), 147–151. DOI: 10.36838/v5i7.24

Chowdhury, M. J. M., Ferdous, M. S., Biswas, K., Chowdhury, N., Kayes, A., Alazab, M., & Watters, P. (2019). A comparative analysis of distributed ledger technology platforms. *IEEE Access : Practical Innovations, Open Solutions*, *7*, 167930–167943. DOI: 10.1109/ACCESS.2019.2953729

Christodoulou, I., Rizomyliotis, I., Konstantoulaki, K., Nazarian, A., & Binh, D. (2024). Transforming the remittance industry: Harnessing the power of blockchain technology. *Journal of Enterprise Information Management*, *37*(5), 1551–1577. DOI: 10.1108/JEIM-03-2023-0112

Chuah, J. (2022). Money Laundering Considerations in Blockchain-based Maritime Trade and Commerce. *European Journal of Risk Regulation*, **•••**, 1–16. DOI: 10.1017/err.2022.21

Chu, J., Chan, S., Nadarajah, S., & Osterrieder, J. (2017). GARCH modelling of cryptocurrencies. *Journal of Risk and Financial Management*, *10*(4), 17. DOI: 10.3390/jrfm10040017

Cioroianu, I., Corbet, S., Larkin, C. J., & Oxley, L. (2023). *Developing central bank digital currencies: a reality check during cryptocurrency euphoria*. Economics and Business Letters.

Claeys, G., Demertzis, M., & Efstathiou, K. (2018). *Cryptocurrencies and monetary policy* (No. 2018/10). Bruegel Policy Contribution.

Clarance, B. A. (2020, May 13). Aarogya Setu: Why India's Covid-19 contact tracing app is controversial. *BBC News*. https://www.bbc.com/news/world-asia-india-52659520

Clarke, R. P. (2021). Performance of buildings in two Caribbean Territories: Dominica under Hurricane Maria in 2017 and Trinidad under the 2018 earthquake. *Natural Hazards*, *109*(1), 1141–1165. DOI: 10.1007/s11069-021-04872-w

Cocco, L., Tonelli, R., & Marchesi, M. (2019). An agent-based artificial market model for studying the bitcoin trading. *IEEE Access : Practical Innovations, Open Solutions*, *7*, 42908–42920. DOI: 10.1109/ACCESS.2019.2907880

Cohen, L. E., & Felson, M. (2010). Social change and crime rate trends: A routine activity approach (1979). In *Classics in environmental criminology* (pp. 203–232). Routledge.

Cointelegraph. (2025, February 20). *Samourai Wallet shutdown: Implications for other privacy & self-custody tools*. Cointelegraph. https://cointelegraph.com/news/samourai-wallet-shutdown-implications-for-other-privacy-self-custody-tools

Collins, J. (2022). *Crypto, crime and control*. Global Initiative Against Transnational Organized Crime.

Cong, W., Harvey, C., Rabetti, D., & Wu, Z. Y. (2025). An anatomy of crypto-enabled cybercrimes. *Management Science*, *71*(4), 3622–3633. Advance online publication. DOI: 10.1287/mnsc.2023.03691

Connolly, L. Y., & Wall, D. S. (2019). The rise of crypto-ransomware in a changing cybercrime landscape: Taxonomising countermeasures. *Computers & Security*, *87*, 101568. DOI: 10.1016/j.cose.2019.101568

Connolly, M. (2022). Cryptocurrency Concerns, Crimes, and Legal Consequences. *Akron Law Review*, *55*(3), 3.

Coppi, G., & Fast, L. (2019). *Blockchain and distributed ledger technologies in the humanitarian sector*. Retrieved from Damgård, I., Ganesh, C., Khoshakhlagh, H., Orlandi, C., & Siniscalchi, L. (2021). *Balancing privacy and accountability in blockchain identity management.* Paper presented at the Cryptographers' Track at the RSA Conference.

Cornish, D. B., & Clarke, R. V. (1986). *Crime as a rational choice. The Reasoning Criminal*. Springer-Verlag.

Cornish, D. B., & Clarke, R. V. (2014). *The reasoning criminal: Rational choice perspectives on offending*. Transaction Publisher.

Courtois, N. T., Gradon, K. T., & Schmeh, K. (2021). Crypto currency regulation and law enforcement perspectives. *arXiv preprint arXiv:2109.01047*.

Cross, C. (2016). 'They're very lonely': Understanding the fraud victimisation of seniors. *International Journal for Crime. Justice and Social Democracy*, *5*(4), 60–75. DOI: 10.5204/ijcjsd.v5i4.268

Cross, C. (2017). "I've Lost Some Sleep over It": Secondary Trauma in the Provision of Support to Older Fraud Victims. *Canadian Journal of Criminology and Criminal Justice*, *59*(2), 168–197. DOI: 10.3138/cjccj.2016.E11

Cross, C. (2022). Meeting the Challenges of Fraud in a Digital World. In Gill, M. (Ed.), *The Handbook of Security* (pp. 217–238). Springer International Publishing., DOI: 10.1007/978-3-030-91735-7_11

Cross, C. (2024). Romance baiting, cryptorom and 'pig butchering': An evolutionary step in romance fraud. *Current Issues in Criminal Justice*, *36*(3), 334–346. DOI: 10.1080/10345329.2023.2248670

CyberArk. (2024). *2024 Identity Security Threat Landscape Report.* CyberArk. https://www.cyberark.com/resources/ebooks/identity-security-threat-landscape-2024-report

CyberScoop. (2024, February 23). *Tornado Cash sanctions overturned: Lazarus Group implications.* CyberScoop. Retrieved February 24, 2025, from https://cyberscoop.com/tornado-cash-sanctions-overturned-lazarus-group/

Cybersecurity & Infrastructure Security Agency. (2022, May 10). *AA22-108A: North Korean cyber actor known as TraderTraitor targets critical infrastructure organizations.* U.S. Department of Homeland Security. https://www.cisa.gov/news-events/cybersecurity-advisories/aa22-108a

D'Andrea, A., & D'Andrea, A. (2024, July 12). Is airport WiFi safe? *Keeper Security Blog*. https://www.keepersecurity.com/blog/2024/07/12/is-airport-wifi-safe/

Dabbous, A., Merhej Sayegh, M., & Aoun Barakat, K. (2022). Understanding the adoption of cryptocurrencies for financial transactions within a high-risk context [Article]. *The Journal of Risk Finance*, *23*(4), 349–367. DOI: 10.1108/JRF-10-2021-0169

Damiani, J. (2019, September 3). *A voice deepfake was used to scam a CEO out of $243,000.* Forbes. https://www.forbes.com/sites/jessedamiani/2019/09/03/a-voice-deepfake-was-used-to-scam-a-ceo-out-of-243000/

Daoud, G. (2023). *The Evolving Nature Of Financial Crime With The Increase Of Internet Capabilities. Challenge Identification, Legal Considerations And Policy Recommendations* (Doctoral dissertation, School of Advanced Study).

Das, N. (2024, February 6). New UPI fraud trend: Fraudsters spamming UPI IDs with multiple collect requests. *The Economic Times*. https://economictimes.indiatimes.com/wealth/save/new-upi-scam-alert-upi-autopay-set-up-request-could-swindle-money-out-of-your-account-if-you-are-not-careful/articleshow/112584562.cms

Das, T. (2024, April 3). Nigerian-style scam reaches Indian matrimonial sites. *The Print*. https://theprint.in/opinion/pov/nigerian-style-scam-reaches-indian-matrimonial-sites-amazon-prime-series-shows-how-they-do-it/1916766/

Dasman, S. (2021). Analysis of return and risk of cryptocurrency bitcoin asset as investment instrument. Accounting and Finance Innovations, 51.

Data Security Council of India. (2024, December 5). *India cyber threat report 2025*. https://www.dsci.in/resource/content/india-cyber-threat-report-2025

Dawes Centre for Future Financial Crime. (2021). *Crytpcorrencies and Future Crime*. https://www.ucl.ac.uk/jill-dando-institute/sites/jill-dando-institute/files/ucl_cryptocurrencies_and_future_crime_policy_briefing_feb2021_compressed_1.pdf

de Best, R. (2025). *Number of crypto coins 2013-2021*. [online] Statista. Available at: https://www.statista.com/statistics/863917/number-crypto-coins-tokens/ [Accessed 19 Feb. 2025].

De Ocáriz Borde, H. S. (2022). *An overview of trees in blockchain technology: merkle trees and merkle patricia tries*. University of Cambridge.

Delfabbro, P., King, D. L., & Williams, J. (2021). The psychology of cryptocurrency trading: Risk and protective factors. *Journal of Behavioral Addictions*, *10*(2), 201–207. DOI: 10.1556/2006.2021.00037 PMID: 34152998

Delgado-Segura, S., Pérez-Solà, C., Herrera-Joancomartí, J., Navarro-Arribas, G., & Borrell, J. (2018). Cryptocurrency networks: A new P2P paradigm. *Mobile Information Systems*, •••, 2018.

Demir, E., Bilgin, M. H., Karabulut, G., & Doker, A. C. (2020). The relationship between cryptocurrencies and COVID-19 pandemic. *Eurasian Economic Review*, *10*(3), 349–360. DOI: 10.1007/s40822-020-00154-1

DeVoe, R. (2018). *Benebit – The Biggest ICO Exit Scam In History Nets Up to $4 Million*. Coin Bureau. Retrieved 1 February 2018 from https://www.coinbureau.com/ico/benebit-biggest-ico-exit-scam-history-nets-4-million/

Dhaker, B., & Goyal, A. (2024). Analysing fraud patterns and prevention mechanisms in Paytm Payment Bank. *International Journal of Innovative Research in Science, Engineering and Technology*, *13*(6), 11003–11008.

Ditamore, S. (2018). *A Bit of Recent Growth: The Evolving Risk of Terrorist Use of Virtual Currency*. Naval Postgraduate School.

Doerr, J. F., Kosse, A., Khan, A., Lewrick, U., Mojon, B., Nolens, B., & Rice, T. (2021). DeFi risks and the decentralisation illusion. *BIS Quarterly Review, 21*, 22. https://www.bis.org/publ/qtrpdf/r_qt2112b.pdf

Dulatova, N., & Razak, A. (2020). The ecosystem of cryptocurrency as an object of civil rights in brics countries. *BRICS Law Journal*, *7*(2), 37–65. DOI: 10.21684/2412-2343-2020-7-2-37-65

Dulisse, B. C., Connealy, N., & Logan, M. W. (2024). "Get rich quick," scheme or script? The effect of cryptoculture on the susceptibility of fraud victimization among cryptocurrency purchasers. *Journal of Criminal Justice*, *94*, 102273. DOI: 10.1016/j.jcrimjus.2024.102273

Duncan, S.. (2022). Cybersecurity: Beyond ransomware: Securing the digital food chain. *Food Australia*, *74*(1), 36–40.

Dupuis, D., & Gleason, K. (2020). Money laundering with cryptocurrency: Open doors and the regulatory dialectic. *Journal of Financial Crime*, *28*(1), 60–74. DOI: 10.1108/JFC-06-2020-0113

Durrant, S., & Natarajan, M. (2019). Cryptocurrencies and Money Laundering Opportunities. In Natarajan, M. (Ed.), *International and Transnational Crime and Justice* (2nd ed., pp. 73–79). Cambridge University Press., https://doi.org/DOI, DOI: 10.1017/9781108597296.012

Dutta, P. (2020). Blockchain and smart contracts: A technical overview. *IEEE Transactions on Engineering Management*, *67*(4), 1234–1246.

Dutta, S. K. (2020). Smart contracts. In *The definitive guide to blockchain for accounting and business: Understanding the revolutionary technology* (pp. 61–78). Emerald Publishing Limited.

Dyntu, V., & Dykyi, O. (2018). Cryptocurrency in the system of money laundering. *Baltic Journal of Economic Studies*, *4*(5), 75–81. DOI: 10.30525/2256-0742/2018-4-5-75-81

Dyson, S., Buchanan, W. J., & Bell, L. (2019). The challenges of investigating cryptocurrencies and blockchain related crime. *arXiv preprint arXiv:1907.12221.*

Easterly, J. (2023). The attack on Colonial Pipeline: What we've learned & what we've done over the past two years. *Cybersecurity and Infrastructure Security Agency (CISA)*. https://www.cisa.gov/news-events/news/attack-colonial-pipeline-what-weve-learned-what-weve-done-over-past-two-years

Ebekozien, A., Aigbavboa, C., Thwala, W. D., Samsurijan, M. S., Ahmed, M. A. H., Aliu, J., & Adekunle, S. A. (2024). Appraising the application of cryptocurrency technologies in the Nigerian built environment: Stakeholders' perspective [Article]. *International Journal of Building Pathology and Adaptation*, *42*(7), 93–112. DOI: 10.1108/IJBPA-04-2024-0070

Economic Times. (2022, March 28). How Karza Technologies makes due diligence and onboarding simpler for banks & NBFCs. https://cio.economictimes.indiatimes.com/news/case-studies/how-karza-technologies-makes-due-diligence-and-onboarding-simpler-for-banks-nbfcs/89891554

Ede, C. (2023). A Critical Analysis of the Regulation of Crypto Assets from the European Union and the United Kingdom Perspective. Available at *SSRN* 4489373. DOI: 10.2139/ssrn.4489373

Effendi, K. A. (2015). Determining the best ARCH/GARCH model and comparing JKSE with stock index in developed countries. *The Winners*, *16*(2), 71–84. DOI: 10.21512/tw.v16i2.1560

Eichengreen, B. (2019). *From commodity to fiat and now to crypto: what does history tell us? (No. w25426)*. National Bureau of Economic Research. DOI: 10.3386/w25426

El Maknouzi, M. E. H., & Sadok, H. (2021). Regulation of virtual currencies in the United Arab Emirates: Accounting for the emerging public/private distinction. *Development Studies Research*, *8*(1), 346–355. DOI: 10.1080/21665095.2021.1980413

El-Chaarani, H., Mawad, J. L., Mawad, N., & Khalife, D. (2024). Psychological and demographic predictors of investment in cryptocurrencies during a crisis in the MENA region: the case of Lebanon [Article]. *Journal of Economic and Administrative Sciences*. https://doi.org/DOI: 10.1108/JEAS-07-2022-0165

Elhussieny, M. (2025). Smart green ports: A sustainable solution for the maritime industry in a changing climate. *Multidisciplinary Adaptive Climate Insights*, *2*(1), 1–30. DOI: 10.21622/MACI.2025.02.1.1162

Engle, T. A., Maher, C. A., & Jones, M. (2025). Afraid of the unknown: Crypto literacy and fear of online fraud. *Journal of Economic Criminology*, *7*, 100135. https://doi.org/https://doi.org/10.1016/j.jeconc.2025.100135. DOI: 10.1016/j.jeconc.2025.100135

Erinle, Y., Feng, Y., Xu, J., Vadgama, N., & Tasca, P. (2024). Shared-Custodial Wallet for Multi-Party Crypto-Asset Management. *Future Internet*, *7*(1), 7. Advance online publication. DOI: 10.3390/fi17010007

Ernst & Young. (2018). *Big risks in ICO market: flawed token valuations, unclear regulations, heightened hacker attention and congested networks*. Retrieved 12 February 2018 from https://www.ey.com/Publication/vwLUAssets/ey-research-initial-coin-offerings-icos/$File/ey-research-initial-coin-offerings-icos.pdf

Eromo Egbejule. (2024). *How west Africa's online fraudsters moved into sextortion*. [online] the Guardian. Available at: https://www.theguardian.com/uk-news/article/2024/aug/21/how-west-africas-online-fraudsters-moved-into-sextortion?utm_source=chatgpt.com [Accessed 6 Feb. 2025].

ESCAP, U. (2018). Disaster risk financing: opportunities for regional cooperation in Asia and the Pacific.

ESMA. (2017). *Press Release: ESMA highlights ICO risks for investors and firms*. European Securities and Markets Authority (ESMA). Retrieved 15 February 2018 from https://www.esma.europa.eu/sites/default/files/library/esma71-99-649_press_release_ico_statements.pdf

ETtech. (2021, March 30). Data of 10 crore Mobikwik users for sale on dark web, say cybersecurity experts. *The Economic Times*. https://economictimes.indiatimes.com/tech/startups/mobikwik-data-breach-personal-data-of-over-10-crore-users-allegedly-available-onsale/articleshow/81756544.cms

European Parliament. (2021). Tackling deepfakes in European policy. https://www.europarl.europa.eu/thinktank/en/document/EPRS_STU(2021)690039

Europol. (2022). Europol (2022), Facing reality? Law enforcement and the challenge of deepfakes, an observatory report from the Europol Innovation Lab, Publications Offce of the European Union, Luxembourg. https://www.europol.europa.eu/ publication

Europol. (2022). *Policing in the Metaverse: What law enforcement needs to know* [Report]. Publications Office of the European Union. https://doi.org/DOI: 10.2813/81062

Europol. (2024). *Internet Organised Crime Threat Assessment (IOCTA) 2024*. Europol. https://www.europol.europa.eu/publication-events/main-reports/internet-organised-crime-threat-assessment-iocta-2024

Ezzat, S. K., Saleh, Y. N., & Abdel-Hamid, A. A. (2022). Blockchain oracles: State-of-the-art and research directions. *IEEE Access : Practical Innovations, Open Solutions*, *10*, 67551–67572. DOI: 10.1109/ACCESS.2022.3184726

Fabri, J., & Fabri, S. (2019). Leveraging blockchain technology to build resilience and disaster risk reduction in small states. In Khonje, W. H., & Mitchell, T. (Eds.), *Strengthening Disaster Resilience in Small States: Commonwealth Perspectives* (pp. 107–124). Commonwealth Secretariat. DOI: 10.14217/c6ee754a-en

Fanti, G., & Viswanath, P. (2017). Deanonymization in the bitcoin P2P network. *Advances in Neural Information Processing Systems*, •••, 30.

Farahani, B., Firouzi, F., & Luecking, M. (2021). The convergence of IoT and distributed ledger technologies (DLT): Opportunities, challenges, and solutions. *Journal of Network and Computer Applications*, *177*, 102936. DOI: 10.1016/j.jnca.2020.102936

Farrugia, S., Ellul, J., & Azzopardi, G. (2020). Detection of illicit accounts over the Ethereum blockchain [Article]. *Expert Systems with Applications*, *150*(11), 113318. Advance online publication. DOI: 10.1016/j.eswa.2020.113318

Fauzi, M. A., Paiman, N., & Othman, Z. (2020). Bitcoin and cryptocurrency: Challenges, opportunities and future works. *The Journal of Asian Finance, Economics and Business*, *7*(8), 695–704. DOI: 10.13106/jafeb.2020.vol7.no8.695

Federal Bureau of Investigation. (2022). *Romance scams*. https://www.fbi.gov/how-we-can-help-you/scams-and-safety/common-frauds-and-scams/romance-scams

Federal Bureau of Investigation. (2023, August 11). *Increase in companies falsely claiming an ability to recover funds lost in cryptocurrency investment scams*. Internet Crime Complaint Center. https://www.ic3.gov/PSA/2023/PSA230811

Federal Bureau of Investigation. (2024). *2023 Internet crime report*. Internet Crime Complaint Center. https://www.ic3.gov/annualreport/reports/2023_ic3report.pdf

Federal Communications Commission. (2022). *COVID-19 vaccines scams*. https://www.fcc.gov/covid-19-vaccines-scams

Felson, M. (2016). The routine activity approach. In *Environmental criminology and crime analysis* (pp. 106–116). Routledge.

Finance, B. (2021, November 21). *DeFi Security Lecture 2 — Flash Loan Attacks*. Retrieved from Medium: https://medium.com/beaver-smartcontract-security/defi-security-lecture-2-flash-loan-attacks-4aee2d3f07ca

Financial Action Task Force (FATF). (2022). *Virtual assets red flag indicators of money laundering and terrorist financing*. https://www.fatf-gafi.org

Financial Conduct Authority. (n.d.). *Glossary definition: Financial crime*. FCA Handbook. Retrieved January 29, 2025, from https://www.handbook.fca.org.uk/handbook/glossary/G416.html

Flanagan, J. (2024). *Hundreds Arrested over Nigerian crypto-romance Scams*. [online] Thetimes.com. Available at: https://www.thetimes.com/world/africa/article/hundreds-arrested-over-nigerian-crypto-romance-scams-mnx230csk?utm_source=chatgpt.com®ion=global [Accessed 6 Feb. 2025].

Fletcher, E. (2022). Romance scams take record dollars in 2020. *Federal Trade Commission*. https://www.ftc.gov/news-events/data-visualizations/data-spotlight/2021/02/romance-scams-take-record-dollars-2020

Foley, S., Karlsen, J. R., & Putniņš, T. J. (2019). Sex, drugs, and bitcoin: How much illegal activity is financed through cryptocurrencies? *Review of Financial Studies*, *32*(5), 1798–1853. DOI: 10.1093/rfs/hhz015

Fomintsov Trukhaev, V. (2024). Theory and practice of decentralized blockchain oracles. *Master's thesis*. https://upcommons.upc.edu/bitstream/handle/2117/423352/TPDBO_FTVladimir.pdf?sequence=4

Fry, J. (2018). Booms, busts and heavy-tails: The story of Bitcoin and cryptocurrency markets? *Economics Letters*, *171*, 225–229. DOI: 10.1016/j.econlet.2018.08.008

Furneaux, N. (2025). *There's no such thing as crypto crime: An investigative handbook*. John Wiley & Sons.

Furnham, A., & Boo, H. C. (2011). A literature review of the anchoring effect. *Journal of Socio-Economics*, *40*(1), 35–42. DOI: 10.1016/j.socec.2010.10.008

Gandal, N., & Halaburda, H. (2016). Can we predict the winner in a market with network effects? Competition in cryptocurrency market. *Games*, *7*(3), 16. DOI: 10.3390/g7030016

Gandal, N., Hamrick, J. T., Moore, T., & Oberman, T. (2018). Price manipulation in the Bitcoin ecosystem [Article]. *Journal of Monetary Economics*, *95*, 86–96. DOI: 10.1016/j.jmoneco.2017.12.004

Garba, K. H., Lazarus, S., & Button, M. (2024). An assessment of convicted cryptocurrency fraudsters [Article]. *Current Issues in Criminal Justice*, 1–17. Advance online publication. DOI: 10.1080/10345329.2024.2403294

Garvey, P. (2018). *Blockchain-backed gold: Mint's answer to bitcoin*. The Australian. Retrieved 12 February 2018 via Proquest Database from Gepp, A. (2016). Addressing the problem of financial statement fraud: Better detection through improved models. In *8th Asia-Pacific Interdisciplinary Research in Accounting (APIRA) Conference*.

Georgoula, I., Pournarakis, D., Bilanakos, C., Sotiropoulos, N. D., & Giaglis, M. G. (2015). Using time-series and sentiment analysis to detect the determinants of bitcoin prices. In *Proceedings of the Mediterranean Conference on Information Systems* (p. 20). MCIS. [Online], Available https://aisel.aisnet.org/mcis2015/20 DOI: 10.2139/ssrn.2607167

Gepp, A., Linnenluecke, M. K., O'Neill, T. J., & Smith, T. (2018). Big data techniques in auditing research and practice: Current trends and future opportunities. *Journal of Accounting Literature*, *40*(1), 102–115. https://doi.org/https://doi.org/10.1016/j.acclit.2017.05.003. DOI: 10.1016/j.acclit.2017.05.003

Ghazi-Tehrani, A. K., & Pontell, H. N. (2021). Phishing Evolves: Analyzing the Enduring Cybercrime [Article]. *Victims & Offenders*, *16*(3), 316–342. DOI: 10.1080/15564886.2020.1829224

Ghernaouti, S. (2023). *Cybercriminalité: Comprendre. Prévenir. Réagir*. Dunod.

Ghosh, P. (2021, October 25). 2.5 crore Delhi cryptocurrency scam: Dubai-based kingpin arrested. *Hindustan Times*. https://www.hindustantimes.com/india-news/dubai-based-kingpin-of-rs-2-5-crore-delhi-cryptocurrency-scam-arrested-from-delhi-airport/story-iiqm14ER9XfZmAg8XmgUKI.html

Giansiracusa, N. (2021). Deepfake deception. In *How algorithms create and prevent fake news* (pp. 41–66). Apress. DOI: 10.1007/978-1-4842-7155-1_3

Gil-Alana, L. A., Abakah, E. J. A., & Rojo, M. F. R. (2020). Cryptocurrencies and stock market indices: Are they related? *Research in International Business and Finance*, *51*, 101063. DOI: 10.1016/j.ribaf.2019.101063

Gilbert, C., & Gilbert, M. (2025). Patterns and vulnerabilities of cryptocurrency-related cybercrimes. *Global Scientific Journals*, *13*(3), 1950–1981.

Gil-Cordero, E., Cabrera-Sánchez, J. P., & Arrás-Cortés, M. J. (2020). Cryptocurrencies as a financial tool: Acceptance factors. *Mathematics*, *8*(11), 1974. DOI: 10.3390/math8111974

Global Facility for Disaster Reduction and Recovery. (n.d.). *Financing climate and disaster resilience in Small Island States*. https://www.gfdrr.org/en/feature-story/financing-climate-and-disaster-resilience-small-island-states

Global Facility for Disaster Reduction and Recovery. (n.d.). *SISRI Knowledge Note 1: What is SISRI?* https://www.gfdrr.org/sites/default/files/documents/SISRI%20 Knowledge%20Note%201%20What%20is%20SISRI.pdf

Gómez Hernández, J. A., García Teodoro, P., Magán Carrión, R., & Rodríguez Gómez, R. (2023). Crypto-ransomware: A revision of the state of the art, advances and challenges. *Electronics (Basel)*, *12*(21), 4494. DOI: 10.3390/electronics12214494

Graham, N., Hedges, R., Chiu, C., de La Chapelle, F., & van de Graaf, A. (2021, October 12). How can businesses protect themselves from deepfake attacks? Business Going Digital. https://www.businessgoing.digital/how-can-businesses-protect-themselvesfrom-deepfake-attacks

Graver, K., Jardine, E., Leosz, E., & Updegrave, H. (2023). *The 2023 Crypto Crime Report.* https://go.chainalysis.com/2023-crypto-crime-report.html

Greenberg, A. (2024). *Lords of Crypto Crime: The race to bring down the world's invisible kingpins*. Monoray.

Grobys, K. (2021). When the blockchain does not block: On hackings and uncertainty in the cryptocurrency market. *Quantitative Finance*, *21*(8), 1–13. DOI: 10.1080/14697688.2020.1849779

Gross, L. (2024). *Improving Trustworthiness in DeFi: Anomaly Detection for Blockchain Oracle Price Feed Data.* Universidade NOVA de Lisboa., https://run.unl.pt/bitstream/10362/174978/1/TCDMAA3359.pdf

Guarna, T. A. (2022). *Trust Machines: Cryptocurrencies, Blockchains, and Humans in Cultures of Mistrust* (Doctoral dissertation, Massachusetts Institute of Technology).

Guenther, M. (2004). Security/Privacy Compliance: Culture Change. *EDPACS*, *31*(12), 19–24. DOI: 10.1201/1079/44332.31.12.20040601/81836.3

Guess, A., Nagler, J., & Tucker, J. (2019). Less than you think: Prevalence and predictors of fake news dissemination on Facebook. *Science Advances*, *5*(1), eaau4586. DOI: 10.1126/sciadv.aau4586 PMID: 30662946

Guitton, M. J., & Fréchette, J. (2023). Facing cyberthreats in a crisis and post-crisis era: Rethinking security services response strategy. *Computers in Human Behavior Reports*, *10*, 100282. https://doi.org/https://doi.org/10.1016/j.chbr.2023.100282. DOI: 10.1016/j.chbr.2023.100282

Guo, T., Bifet, A., & Antulov-Fantulin, N. (2018, November). Bitcoin volatility forecasting with a glimpse into buy and sell orders. In *Proceedings of the IEEE International Conference on Data Mining (ICDM)* (pp. 989–994). DOI: 10.1109/ICDM.2018.00123

Gupta, P., Bhatia, P., & Malhotra, N. (2025). Do Crypto and Equity Go Hand in Hand? An Empirical Study of G-7 Economies Using VECM, Granger Causality and Panel Data Analysis. *Management and Labour Studies*, 0258042X241309725.

Gupta, B. B., Tewari, A., Jain, A. K., & Agrawal, D. P. (2017). Fighting against phishing attacks: State of the art and future challenges. *Neural Computing & Applications*, *28*(12), 3629–3654. DOI: 10.1007/s00521-016-2275-y

Gupta, N., Mitra, P., & Banerjee, D. (2023). Cryptocurrencies and traditional assets: Decoding the analogy from emerging economies with crypto usage. *Investment Management & Financial Innovations*, *20*(1), 1–13. DOI: 10.21511/imfi.20(1).2023.01

Gurdgiev, C., & O'Loughlin, D. (2020). Herding and anchoring in cryptocurrency markets: Investor reaction to fear and uncertainty. *Journal of Behavioral and Experimental Finance*, *25*, 100271. DOI: 10.1016/j.jbef.2020.100271

Gurguc, Z., & Knottenbelt, W. (2018). Cryptocurrencies: overcoming barriers to trust and adoption. *Retrieved from Imperial College London website:* https://www. imperial. ac. *uk/media/imperial-college/research-centres-andgroups/ic3re/crypto-currencies--overcoming-barriers-to-trust-and-adoption. pdf.*

Gururaj, H., Janhavi, V., & Ambika, V. (2024). *Social Engineering in Cybersecurity: Threats and Defenses*. CRC Press.

Guseva, Y. (2024). Decentralized markets and self-regulation. *Geo. Wash. L. Rev.*, *92*, 1281. https://papers.ssrn.com/sol3/Delivery.cfm?abstractid=4677538

Gwet, K. L. (2014). *Handbook of inter-rater reliability: The definitive guide to measuring the extent of agreement among raters*. Advanced Analytics, LLC.

Haas, T. C. (2023). Adapting cybersecurity practice to reduce wildlife cybercrime. *Journal of Cybersecurity*, *9*(1), tyad004. Advance online publication. DOI: 10.1093/cybsec/tyad004

Habib, A., Alnaemi, A., & Habib, M. (2024). *Developing a framework for integrating blockchain technology into earthquake risk mitigation and disaster management strategies of smart cities*. Smart and Sustainable Built Environment. DOI: 10.1108/SASBE-12-2023-0376

HackingRealm. (2024). *Welcome to HackingRealm!* Retrieved 3 April 2025 from https://hackingrealm.shop/

Haffke, L., Fromberger, M., & Zimmermann, P. (2020). Cryptocurrencies and anti-money laundering: The shortcomings of the fifth AML Directive (EU) and how to address them. *Journal of Banking Regulation*, *21*(2), 125–138. DOI: 10.1057/s41261-019-00101-4

Hägele, S. (2024). Centralized exchanges vs. decentralized exchanges in cryptocurrency markets: A systematic literature review. *Electronic Markets*, *33*(1), 33. Advance online publication. DOI: 10.1007/s12525-024-00714-2

Hagerud, G. E. (1997). *A new non-linear GARCH model*. Stockholm School of Economics.

Hamayel, M. J., & Owda, A. Y. (2021). A novel cryptocurrency price prediction model using GRU, LSTM and bi-LSTM machine learning algorithms. *AI*, *2*(4), 477–496. DOI: 10.3390/ai2040030

Hamrick, J. T., Rouhi, F., Mukherjee, A., Feder, A., Gandal, N., Moore, T., & Vasek, M. (2018). The economics of cryptocurrency pump and dump schemes. Available at *SSRN* 3310307. DOI: 10.2139/ssrn.3303365

Hancock, J. T., & Bailenson, J. N. (2021). The social impact of deepfakes. *Cyberpsychology, Behavior, and Social Networking*, *24*(3), 149–152. DOI: 10.1089/cyber.2021.29208.jth PMID: 33760669

Haque, A. (2024). *Why so many scams originate in Nigeria*. [online] tbsnews.net. Available at: https://www.tbsnews.net/features/panorama/why-so-many-scams-originate-nigeria-882326 [Accessed 18 Feb. 2025].

Haque, E. U., Shah, A., Iqbal, J., Ullah, S. S., Alroobaea, R., & Hussain, S. (2024). A scalable blockchain based framework for efficient IoT data management using lightweight consensus. *Scientific Reports*, *14*(1), 7841. DOI: 10.1038/s41598-024-58578-7

Harison, E. (2018). *Artificial Intelligence- and Blockchain-Based Decentralized Cloud Systems: The IAGON Way*. Medium. Retrieved 12 February 2018 from https://medium.com/iagon-official/iagon-artificial-intelligence-and-blockchain-based-decentralized-cloud-systems-113269d9c5b9

Hartmann, K., & Giles, K. (2020, May). The next generation of cyber-enabled information warfare. In 2020 12th international conference on cyber conflict (CyCon) (Vol. 1300, pp. 233-250). IEEE. DOI: 10.23919/CyCon49761.2020.9131716

Hasan, H. R., & Salah, K. (2018). Proof of Delivery of Digital Assets Using Blockchain and Smart Contracts [Article]. *IEEE Access, 6*, 65439-65448. *Article, 8501910*. Advance online publication. DOI: 10.1109/ACCESS.2018.2876971

Hashish, F., Forni, F., Andreotti, G., Facchinetti, T., & Darjani, S. (2019, September). A hybrid model for bitcoin prices prediction using hidden Markov models and optimized LSTM networks. In *Proceedings of the 24th IEEE International Conference on Emerging Technologies and Factory Automation (ETFA)* (pp. 721–728). DOI: 10.1109/ETFA.2019.8869094

Hassani, H., Huang, X., & Silva, E. (2018). Big-crypto: Big data, blockchain and cryptocurrency. *Big Data and Cognitive Computing*, *2*(4), 10–34. DOI: 10.3390/bdcc2040034

Hayes, A. (2014). *Blockchain Facts: What Is It, How It Works, and How It Can Be Used*. [online] Investopedia. Available at: https://www.investopedia.com/terms/b/blockchain.asp?utm_source=chatgpt.com [Accessed 19 Feb. 2025].

Haynie, D. L., & Duxbury, S. W. (2024). Online Illegal Cryptomarkets. *Annual Review of Sociology*, *50*(1), 671–690. DOI: 10.1146/annurev-soc-090523-052916

Henriques, I., & Sadorsky, P. (2018). Can bitcoin replace gold in an investment portfolio? *Journal of Risk and Financial Management*, *11*(3), 48. DOI: 10.3390/jrfm11030048

Hern, A. (2022, April 18). *Beanstalk cryptocurrency loses $182m of reserves in flash 'attack'*. Retrieved from The Guardian: https://www.theguardian.com/technology/2022/apr/18/beanstalk-cryptocurrency-loses-182m-of-reserves-in-flash-attack

Holt, T. J., & Cross, C. (2024). Assessing the Correlates of Cryptofraud Victimization Reporting. *Deviant Behavior*, •••, 1–12. DOI: 10.1080/01639625.2024.2435907

Holt, T. J., & Lee, J. R. (2023). A crime script model of dark web firearms purchasing. *American Journal of Criminal Justice*, *48*(2), 509–529. DOI: 10.1007/s12103-022-09675-8

Holt, T., & Bossler, A. (2015). (Manuscript submitted for publication). [*Theory and prevention of technology-enabled offenses*. Routledge.]. *Cybercrime*.

Hong, Q. N., Pluye, P., Fàbregues, S., Bartlett, G., Boardman, F., Cargo, M., Dagenais, P., Gagnon, M.-P., Griffiths, F., & Nicolau, B. (2018). Mixed methods appraisal tool (MMAT), version 2018. *Registration of copyright, 1148552*(10), 1-7.

Huang, J.-Z., Huang, W., & Ni, J. (2019). Predicting bitcoin returns using high-dimensional technical indicators. *The Journal of Financial Data Science*, *5*(3), 140–155. DOI: 10.1016/j.jfds.2018.10.001

Hutchings, A., & Holt, T. J. (2017). The online stolen data market: Disruption and intervention approaches. *Global Crime*, *18*(1), 11–30. DOI: 10.1080/17440572.2016.1197123

IBM. (2018). *Maersk and IBM to Form Joint Venture Applying Blockchain to Improve Global Trade and Digitize Supply Chains.* Retrieved 7 February 2018 from https://www-03.ibm.com/press/us/en/pressrelease/53602.wss

Ilari, L. (2025). Navigating Ethical Challenges in Cybersecurity: From Risk Assessment to Quantum-AI Applications.

IMF. (2016). Small States' Resilience to Natural Disasters and Climate Change–Role for the IMF. In: International Monetary Fund Washington.

immunebytes. (2020, October 28). *Harvest Finance Fund Theft Incident – Oct 26, 2020 – Detailed Analysis.* Retrieved from immunebytes: https://immunebytes.com/blog/harvest-finance-fund-theft-incident-oct-26-2020-detailed-analysis/

Imran, I. (2021, May 1). Pandemic and online job scam. *Times of India Blog.* https://timesofindia.indiatimes.com/readersblog/ifath-digest/pandemic-and-online-job-scam-36203/

Indian Express. (2021, March 29). MobiKwik database of 10 crore users leaked on dark web; company denies data breach. https://indianexpress.com/article/technology/tech-news-technology/mobikwik-database-leaked-on-dark-web-company-denies-any-data-breach-7251448/

Interpol. (2023). *Global crime trends and cybercrime threats.* https://www.interpol.int/en/Crimes/Cybercrime

iProov. (2025). *2025 threat intelligence report: Remote identity attack.* iProov. Retrieved March 2, 2025, from https://www.iproov.com/reports/threat-intelligence-report-2025-remote-identity-attack

Islam, S., & Apu, K. U. (2024). Decentralized vs. Centralized database solutions in blockchain: Advantages, challenges, and use cases. *Global Mainstream Journal of Innovation. Engineering & Emerging Technology*, *3*(4), 58–68.

Jabotinsky, H. Y., & Lavi, M. (2021). Speak Out: Verifying and Unmasking Cryptocurrency User Identity. *SSRN*, *32*, 518. DOI: 10.2139/ssrn.3828970

Jamwal, S., Cano, J., Lee, G. M., Tran, N. H., & Truong, N. (2024). A survey on ethereum pseudonymity: Techniques, challenges, and future directions. *Journal of Network and Computer Applications, 232*, 104019. DOI: 10.1016/j.jnca.2024.104019

Jang, H., & Lee, J. (2018). An empirical study on modeling and prediction of bitcoin prices with Bayesian neural networks based on blockchain information. *IEEE Access : Practical Innovations, Open Solutions, 6*, 5427–5437. DOI: 10.1109/ACCESS.2017.2779181

Janis, I. L., & Janis, I. L. (1982). *Groupthink: Psychological studies of policy decisions and fiascoes* (Vol. 349). Houghton Mifflin Boston.

Javaid, M., Haleem, A., Singh, R. P., Suman, R., & Khan, S. (2022). A review of Blockchain Technology applications for financial services. *BenchCouncil Transactions on Benchmarks, Standards and Evaluations, 2*(3), 100073. https://doi.org/https://doi.org/10.1016/j.tbench.2022.100073

Jay, P., Kalariya, V., Parmar, P., Tanwar, S., Kumar, N., & Patel, M. (2020). Stochastic neural networks for cryptocurrency price prediction. *IEEE Access : Practical Innovations, Open Solutions, 8*, 82804–82818. DOI: 10.1109/ACCESS.2020.2990659

Jefri, S. (2024). Navigating the Crypto Landscape: Exploring the Risks and Potential Misuse of Crypto Assets in Money Laundering. *Technology, 1*(1), 16–29.

Jing, R., & Rocha, L. E. C. (2023). A network-based strategy of price correlations for optimal cryptocurrency portfolios. *Finance Research Letters, 58*, 104503. https://doi.org/https://doi.org/10.1016/j.frl.2023.104503. DOI: 10.1016/j.frl.2023.104503

Ji, S., Kim, J., & Im, H. (2019). A comparative study of bitcoin price prediction using deep learning. *Mathematics, 7*(10), 898. DOI: 10.3390/math7100898

Johnson, D. G., & Diakopoulos, N. (2021). What to do about deepfakes. *Communications of the ACM, 64*(3), 33–35. DOI: 10.1145/3447255

Jones, V. A. (2020). *Artificial intelligence enabled deepfake technology: The emergence of a new threat* (Master's thesis, Utica College).

Joshi, S. (2020, November 20). Mega Mumbai power outage may be result of cyber attack. *India Today*. https://www.indiatoday.in/india/story/mumbai-power-outage-malware-attack-1742538-2020-11-20

Josyula, H. P. (2024). *Redefining Cross-Border Financial Flows*. Apress., DOI: 10.1007/979-8-8688-1064-0

Jubur, M., Shrestha, P., & Saxena, N. (2025). An In-Depth Analysis of Password Managers and Two-Factor Authentication Tools. *ACM Computing Surveys*, *57*(5), 128. Advance online publication. DOI: 10.1145/3711117

Kala, D., Chaubey, D. S., & Al-Adwan, A. S. (2023). Cryptocurrency investment behaviour of young Indians: Mediating role of fear of missing out [Article]. *Global Knowledge, Memory and Communication*. Advance online publication. DOI: 10.1108/GKMC-07-2023-0237

Kamps, J., & Kleinberg, B. (2018). To the moon: defining and detecting cryptocurrency pump-and-dumps [Article]. *Crime Science*, *7*(1), 18, Article 18. https://doi.org/DOI: 10.1186/s40163-018-0093-5

Kaspersky. (2021). *Mobile malware report: Cybercriminals forego low hanging fruit to go after banking and gaming*. https://www.kaspersky.com/about/press-releases/2021-mobile-threats-report-cybercriminals-forego-low-hanging-fruit-to-go-after-banking-and-gaming

Kasula, V. K. (2024). *Awareness of Cryptocurrency Scams* (Doctoral dissertation). University of the Cumberlands.

Kaur, R., Ali, A., & Faisal, M. (2022). Smart contracts: the self-executing contracts. In *Blockchain* (pp. 35–49). Chapman and Hall/CRC. DOI: 10.1201/9781003203957-4

Kelly, L. (2025, February 10). *Over half of illicit crypto activity in 2024 was on Tron: TRM Labs*. DL News. https://www.dlnews.com/articles/regulation/half-of-illicit-crypto-activity-in-2024-was-on-tron-trm-labs/

Kethineni, S., & Cao, Y. (2020). The Rise in Popularity of Cryptocurrency and Associated Criminal Activity. *International Criminal Justice Review*, *30*(3), 325–344. DOI: 10.1177/1057567719827051

Kfir, I. (2020). Cryptocurrencies, national security, crime and terrorism. *Comparative Strategy*, *39*(2), 113–127. DOI: 10.1080/01495933.2020.1718983

Khair, M. Abul, & Sandu, A., Kumar. (2023). Blockchain-Optimized Supply Chain Traceability System for Transparent Logistics. *Journal of Fareast International University*, *6*(1), 27-38. https://hal.science/hal-04543221

Khan, D., Jung, L. T., & Hashmani, M. A. (2021). Systematic literature review of challenges in blockchain scalability. *Applied Sciences (Basel, Switzerland)*, *11*(20), 9372. DOI: 10.3390/app11209372

Khanna, A. (2024). Authentication in Cybersecurity. In Khanna, A. (Ed.), *Securing an Enterprise: Maximizing Digital Experiences through Enhanced Security Measures* (pp. 75–94). Apress., DOI: 10.1007/979-8-8688-1029-9_4

Khelkar, P. P., & Singh, D. (2018, August 14). Hackers withdraw Rs 94 crore after stealing ATM card data. *India Today*. https://www.indiatoday.in/india/story/hackers-steal-rs-94-crore-from-pune-s-cosmos-bank-1314081-2018-08-14

Kietzmann, J., Lee, L. W., McCarthy, I. P., & Kietzmann, T. C. (2020). Deepfakes: Trick or treat? *Business Horizons*, *63*(2), 135–146. DOI: 10.1016/j.bushor.2019.11.006

Kim, K. T., Hanna, S. D., & Lee, S. T. (2022). Investment literacy, overconfidence and cryptocurrency investment. *Financial Services Review*, *31*(2), 121–132.

Kim, M., Suh, J., & Kwon, H. (2022). A study of the emerging trends in SIM swapping crime and effective countermeasures. In *7th IEEE/ACIS International Conference on Big Data, Cloud Computing, and Data Science (BCD 2022)*. DOI: 10.1109/BCD54882.2022.9900510

Kim, Y. B., Lee, J., Park, N., Choo, J., Kim, J.-H., & Kim, C. H. (2017). When bitcoin encounters information in an online forum: Using text mining to analyse user opinions and predict value fluctuation. *PLoS One*, *12*(5), e0177630. DOI: 10.1371/journal.pone.0177630

Kjærland, F., Meland, M., Oust, A., & Øyen, V. (2018). How can bitcoin price fluctuations be explained? *International Journal of Economics and Financial Issues*, *8*(3), 323–332.

Klein, G., Assadi, D., & Zwilling, M. (2024). Fighting Fire with Fire: Combating Criminal Abuse of Cryptocurrency with a P2P Mindset. *Information Systems Frontiers*. Advance online publication. DOI: 10.1007/s10796-024-10498-7

Klein, T., Thu, H., & Walther, T. (2018). Bitcoin is not the new gold—A comparison of volatility correlation and portfolio performance. *International Review of Financial Analysis*, *59*, 105–116. DOI: 10.1016/j.irfa.2018.07.010

Knight, W. (2017). *The Technology Behind Bitcoin Is Shaking Up Much More Than Money*. MIT Technology Review. Retrieved 14 February 2018 from https://www.technologyreview.com/s/604148/the-technology-behind-bitcoin-is-shaking-up-much-more-than-money/

Kocher, P., Horn, J., Fogh, A., Genkin, D., Gruss, D., Haas, W., Hamburg, M., Lipp, M., Mangard, S., Prescher, T., Schwarz, M., & Yarom, Y. (2019). *Spectre attacks: Exploiting speculative execution*. Retrieved February 5, 2025, from https://spectreattack.com/spectre.pdf

Kolakowski, M. (2022, February 3). *Crypto Worth Over $320 Million Taken in Wormhole Hack*. Retrieved from investopedia: https://www.investopedia.com/crypto-theft-of-usd320-million-wormhole-hack-5218062

Kopetz, H., & Steiner, W. (2022). Internet of things. In *Real-time systems: design principles for distributed embedded applications* (pp. 325–341). Springer. DOI: 10.1007/978-3-031-11992-7_13

Kopetz, H., & Steiner, W. (2022). *The Internet of Things: Principles and paradigms*. Wiley.

Kori, A., & Gadagin, N. (2024). Blockchain-Based AI Models for Credit Scoring and Risk Assessment using Fog Computing Infrastructure.

Koskelainen, T., Kalmi, P., Scornavacca, E., & Vartiainen, T. (2023). Financial literacy in the digital age—A research agenda. *The Journal of Consumer Affairs*, *57*(1), 507–528. DOI: 10.1111/joca.12510

Kreminskyi, O., Kuzmenko, O., Antoniuk, A., & Smahlo, O. (2021). International cooperation in the investigation of economic crimes related to cryptocurrency circulation. *Estudios de Economía Aplicada*, *39*(6). Advance online publication. DOI: 10.25115/eea.v39i6.5247

Kuckartz, U., & Rädiker, S. (2019). *Analyzing qualitative data with MAXQDA*. Springer. DOI: 10.1007/978-3-030-15671-8

Kulkarni, S. (2022, September 10). SBI, government warn customers against fake SMS. *The Economic Times*. https://economictimes.indiatimes.com/wealth/personal-finance-news/sbi-government-warn-customers-against-fake-sms-about-updating-pan-kyc-details/articleshow/94002587.cms

Kumar, N. (2025). AI in Cyber Security: Innovations and Implications for a Safer Digital World. *Computer Science and Information Technology*, 13(1), 1–7. ISSN 2331-6071.

Kumar, N. (2025). The role of artificial intelligence in criminal investigations in India. *The Journal of Legal Studies*, *35*(49), 98–111. DOI: 10.2478/jles-2025-0006

Kumar, S., Sebastian, A., & Nandakumar, B. (2025). Emergency response to natural disaster victim identification: Blockchain to the rescue. In *The Role of Blockchain in Disaster Management* (pp. 69–85). Elsevier. DOI: 10.1016/B978-0-443-13472-2.00001-2

Kunju, P. (2023). *Artificial intelligence (AI) in criminal justice: A primer*. Independently published.

Kurpjuhn, T. (2019). The guide to ransomware: How businesses can manage the evolving threat. *Computer Fraud & Security*, *2019*(11), 14–16. https://doi.org/https://doi.org/10.1016/S1361-3723(19)30117-4. DOI: 10.1016/S1361-3723(19)30117-4

Kwok, A. O., & Koh, S. G. (2021). Deepfake: A social construction of technology perspective. *Current Issues in Tourism*, *24*(13), 1798–1802. DOI: 10.1080/13683500.2020.1738357

Labs, T. R. M. (2023, February 7). *Pig butchering scams: What the data shows.* https://www.trmlabs.com/post/pig-butchering-scams-what-the-data-shows

Laffan, K. (2023, June 9). *A brief history of ransomware.* Varonis. https://www.varonis.com/blog/a-brief-history-of-ransomware

Lagarde, C. (2017). Central Banking and Fintech—A Brave New World? In *Bank of England conference*. International Monetary Fund.

Lahmiri, S., & Bekiros, S. (2020). Intelligent forecasting with machine learning trading systems in chaotic intraday bitcoin market. *Chaos, Solitons, and Fractals*, *133*, 109641. DOI: 10.1016/j.chaos.2020.109641

Lakshmi, R. (2022). Phishing as a cybercrime: A case study of *Jamtara* web series. *From the Chief Editor's Desk. Communicator*, *LVII*(4), 126–131.

Lal, N. (2018, October 7). 'KBC' called, you've won a lottery? Hold on, it's probably a scam. *The Times of India*. https://timesofindia.indiatimes.com/city/delhi/kbc-called-youve-won-a-lottery-hold-on-its-probably-a-scam/articleshow/66099218.cms

Lane, A. M., & Adam, L. (2022). Crime and cryptocurrency in Australian courts. *Monash University Law Review. Monash University. Faculty of Law*, *48*(3), 146–190.

Lawrence, W., Tarr, J.-A., Brook, N., Chaperon, M., & Sorel, A. (2023). Parametric Insurance. In *The Global Insurance Market and Change* (pp. 127–156). Informa Law from Routledge. DOI: 10.4324/9781003319054-6

Lee, A. (2017). *Blockchain—A visual explanation.* Medium. Retrieved 15 February 2018 from https://medium.com/@kkomaz/blockchain-a-visual-explanation-afe82d19a234

Legislation.gov.uk. (2000). *Financial Services and Markets Act 2000, Section 1H: Definition of financial crime.* https://www.legislation.gov.uk/ukpga/2000/8/section/1H

Leuprecht, C., Jenkins, C., & Hamilton, R. (2023). Virtual money laundering: Policy implications of the proliferation in the illicit use of cryptocurrency. *Journal of Financial Crime*, *30*(4), 1036–1054. DOI: 10.1108/JFC-07-2022-0161

Levi, M., Doig, A., Gundur, R., Wall, D., & Williams, M. L. (2016). The implications of economic cybercrime for policing.

Lieder, F., Griffiths, T. L. M., Huys, Q. J., & Goodman, N. D. (2018). The anchoring bias reflects rational use of cognitive resources. *Psychonomic Bulletin & Review*, *25*, 322–349. DOI: 10.3758/s13423-017-1286-8

Liew, J., Li, R., Budavári, T., & Sharma, A. (2019). Cryptocurrency investing examined. *Journal of the British Blockchain Association*, *2*(2), 1–12. DOI: 10.31585/jbba-2-2-(2)2019

Lin, L. S., Aslett, D., Mekonnen, G., & Zecevic, M. (2024a). The dangers of voice cloning and how to combat it.

Lin, L. S., Aslett, D., Mekonnen, G., & Zecevic, M. (2024b). The dangers of voice cloning and how to combat it. *The Conversation*. https://theconversation.com/the-dangers-of-voice-cloning-and-how-to-combat-it-239926

Lin, L. S., Aslett, D., Mekonnen, G., & Zecevic, M. (2024c). The UN Cybercrime Convention: What it Means for Policing and Community Safety in Australia. *Australian Outlook*. https://www.internationalaffairs.org.au/australianoutlook/the-un-cybercrime-convention-what-it-means-for-policing-and-community-safety-in-australia/

Lin, L. S., Mekonnen, G., Zecevic, M., Aslett, D., & Allan, D. (2025). The Role of Education in Combating Cybercrime in the Asia-Pacific: Tackling Misinformation and Disinformation in Australia. In *Combatting Misinformation and Global Nation's False Narratives Through Education*. IGI Global. DOI: 10.4018/979-8-3693-9601-8.ch011

Lipp, M., Schwarz, M., Gruss, D., Prescher, T., Haas, W., Mangard, S., Kocher, P., Genkin, D., Yarom, Y., & Hamburg, M. (2018). *Meltdown: Reading kernel memory from user space*. Retrieved February 5, 2025, from https://meltdownattack.com/meltdown.pdf

Liu, Y., He, J., Li, X., Chen, J., Liu, X., Peng, S., & Wang, Y. (2024). An overview of blockchain smart contract execution mechanism. *Journal of Industrial Information Integration*, *100674*, 100674. Advance online publication. DOI: 10.1016/j.jii.2024.100674

Liu, Y., & Tsyvinski, A. (2021). Risks and Returns of Cryptocurrency. *Review of Financial Studies*, *34*(6), 2689–2727. DOI: 10.1093/rfs/hhaa113

Lopes, V., & Alexandre, L. A. (2019). An overview of blockchain integration with robotics and artificial intelligence. *Ledger, 4*. Advance online publication. DOI: 10.5195/ledger.2019.171

Lorenz, G. (2024). Regulating decentralized financial technology: A qualitative study on the challenges of regulating DeFi with a focus on embedded supervision. *Stan. J. Blockchain L. & Pol'y, 7*, 136. https://assets.pubpub.org/bavvr3fw/Lorenz_Regulating%20Decentralized%20Financial%20Technology-01719848112806.pdf

Lseg.com. (2025). *2025 fraud and payments forecast: Key trends and emerging threats in the global landscape*. [online] Available at: https://www.lseg.com/en/insights/risk-intelligence/2025-fraud-and-payments-forecast-key-trends-and-emerging-threats-in-the-global-landscape [Accessed 31 Jan. 2025].

Lucarelli, G., & Borrotti, M. (2019). A deep reinforcement learning approach for automated cryptocurrency trading. In MacIntyre, J., Maglogiannis, I., Iliadis, L., & Pimenidis, E. (Eds.), *Artificial Intelligence Applications and Innovations* (pp. 247–258). Springer. DOI: 10.1007/978-3-030-19823-7_20

Ludwig, S., Van Laer, T., De Ruyter, K., & Friedman, M. (2016). Untangling a web of lies: Exploring automated detection of deception in computer-med

Luo, B., Zhang, Z., Wang, Q., Ke, A., Lu, S., & He, B. (2024). Ai-powered fraud detection in decentralized finance: A project life cycle perspective. *ACM Computing Surveys, 57*(4), 1–38. DOI: 10.1145/3705296

Lyman, M. D., & Potter, G. W. (2018). *Organized crime* (7th ed.). Pearson Education.

Mackenzie, S. (2022). Criminology towards the metaverse: Cryptocurrency scams, grey economy and the technosocial. *British Journal of Criminology, 62*(6), 1537–1552. DOI: 10.1093/bjc/azab118

Mackinga, T., Nadahalli, T., & Wattenhofer, R. (2022). Twap oracle attacks: Easier done than said? *2022 IEEE International Conference on Blockchain and Cryptocurrency (ICBC)*, 1-8. https://doi.org/DOI: 10.1109/ICBC54727.2022.9805499

Mahmud, B. U., & Sharmin, A. (2021). Deep insights of deepfake technology: A review. *arXiv preprint arXiv:2105.00192*.

Ma, K. W. F., & McKinnon, T. (2022). COVID-19 and cyber fraud: Emerging threats during the pandemic. *Journal of Financial Crime, 29*(2), 433–446. DOI: 10.1108/JFC-01-2021-0016

Makarov, I., & Schoar, A. (2022). Cryptocurrencies and decentralized finance (DeFi). *Brookings Papers on Economic Activity*, *2022*(1), 141–215. DOI: 10.1353/eca.2022.0014

Mallawaarachchi, S., Hemachandra, U., Jayakody, D., Wickramarathne, U., Lokeshwara, A. A., & Bandara, G. C. (2025). Decrypting the Digital Vault by Understanding Cryptocurrency Adoption Challenges Among Gen Z: Case of Sri Lanka [Article]. *Ianna Journal of Interdisciplinary Studies*, *7*(1), 1–18. DOI: 10.5281/zenodo.12645982

Manral, M. S. (2025, February 5). Cyber frauds jump 900% in 4 years: Small cities like Deoghar, Nuh, Mathura emerge as new scam capitals. *The Indian Express*. https://indianexpress.com/article/india/cybercrime-sharp-rise-complaints-2024-govt-data-9816845/

Mansfield-Devine, S. (2017). Beyond Bitcoin: Using blockchain technology to provide assurance in the commercial world. *Computer Fraud & Security*, *2017*(5), 14–18. https://doi.org/https://doi.org/10.1016/S1361-3723(17)30042-8. DOI: 10.1016/S1361-3723(17)30042-8

Marella, V., Upreti, B., Merikivi, J., & Tuunainen, V. K. (2020). Understanding the creation of trust in cryptocurrencies: The case of Bitcoin. *Electronic Markets*, *30*(2), 259–271. DOI: 10.1007/s12525-019-00392-5

McGuire, M., & Dowling, S. (2013). Cyber crime: A review of the evidence. *Summary of key findings and implications.* Home Office Research Report

Mehta, K., & Chawla, S. (2024). Illuminating the dark corners: A qualitative examination of cryptocurrency's risk [Article]. *Digital Policy. Regulation & Governance*, *26*(2), 188–208. DOI: 10.1108/DPRG-10-2023-0147

Mills, D. J., & Nower, L. (2019). Preliminary findings on cryptocurrency trading among regular gamblers: A new risk for problem gambling? *Addictive Behaviors*, *92*, 136–140. https://doi.org/https://doi.org/10.1016/j.addbeh.2019.01.005. DOI: 10.1016/j.addbeh.2019.01.005

Ministry of Home Affairs. (2025). *State/UT-wise details of statistics from National Cyber Crime Reporting Portal (NCRP) related to cyber crimes*. Open Government Data (OGD) Platform India. https://www.data.gov.in/resource/stateut-wise-details-statistics-national-cyber-crime-reporting-portal-ncrp-related-cyber

Mirsky, Y., & Lee, W. (2021). The creation and detection of deepfakes: A survey. *ACM Computing Surveys*, *54*(1), 1–41. DOI: 10.1145/3425780

Mittal, A. (2021). *Decentralized Finance Development- All You Need to Know About It.* [online] SAG IPL - A Technology Blog. Available at: https://blog.sagipl.com/decentralized-finance-development/ [Accessed 10 Feb. 2025].

Miura, R., Pichl, L., & Kaizoji, T. (2019). Artificial neural networks for realized volatility prediction in cryptocurrency time series. In *Advances in Neural Networks—ISNN* (pp. 165–172). Springer., DOI: 10.1007/978-3-030-22796-8_18

Mohan, J. A., & Haygunde, C. (2018, April 6). Bitcoin fraud: Director of firm involved in Rs 2000 crore scam arrested. *The Indian Express*. https://indianexpress.com/article/india/bitcoin-fraud-amit-bhardwaj-director-of-firm-involved-in-rs-2000-crore-scam-arrested-5124244/

Moher, D., Liberati, A., Tetzlaff, J., & Altman, D. G. (2010). Preferred reporting items for systematic reviews and meta-analyses: The PRISMA statement. *International Journal of Surgery*, *8*(5), 336–341. https://doi.org/https://doi.org/10.1016/j.ijsu.2010.02.007. DOI: 10.1016/j.ijsu.2010.02.007

Morton, D. T. (2020). The future of cryptocurrency: An unregulated instrument in an increasingly regulated global economy. *Loy. U. Chi. Int'l L. Rev.*, *16*, 129.

Moyano, J. P., & Ross, O. (2017). KYC Optimization Using Distributed Ledger Technology [Article; Proceedings Paper]. *Business & Information Systems Engineering*, *59*(6), 411–423. DOI: 10.1007/s12599-017-0504-2

Mukherjee, S., Larkin, C., & Corbet, S. (2021). Cryptocurrency ponzi schemes. *Understanding cryptocurrency fraud: The challenges and headwinds to regulate digital currencies, 2*, 111.

Mukherjee, S., Larkin, C., & Corbet, S. (2021). Cryptocurrency ponzi schemes. *Understanding cryptocurrency fraud: The challenges and headwinds to regulate digital currencies, 2*, 111. https://doi.org/DOI: 10.1515/9783110718485-009

Mukherjee, V. (2024, November 19). Deepfakes to social media: Online shopping scams spike this festive season. *Business Standard*. https://www.business-standard.com/industry/news/deepfakes-to-social-media-online-shopping-scams-spike-this-festive-season-124111900337_1.html

Mungoli, N. (2023). *Deciphering the Blockchain: A Comprehensive Analysis of Bitcoin's Evolution*. Adoption, and Future Implications.

Mustak, M., Salminen, J., Mäntymäki, M., Rahman, A., & Dwivedi, Y. K. (2023). Deepfakes: Deceptions, mitigations, and opportunities. *Journal of Business Research*, *154*, 113368. DOI: 10.1016/j.jbusres.2022.113368

Mutambik, I., Almuqrin, A., Zhang, J. Z., & Alharbi, Z. H. (2024). Trust in Cryptocurrency Payments: A Cross-Cultural Analysis of Factors Influencing Adoption [Article]. *Journal of Organizational and End User Computing*, *36*(1), 1–36. Advance online publication. DOI: 10.4018/JOEUC.353910

Myeong, S., & Jung, Y. (2019). Administrative reforms in the fourth industrial revolution: The case of blockchain use. *Sustainability (Basel)*, *11*(14), 3971. DOI: 10.3390/su11143971

Nakamoto, S. (2008). *Bitcoin: A Peer-to-Peer Electronic Cash System*. bitcoin.org. Retrieved 18 February 2018 from https://bitcoin.org/bitcoin.pdf

Nakano, M., Takahashi, A., & Takahashi, S. (2018). Bitcoin technical trading with artificial neural network. *Physica A*, *510*, 587–609. DOI: 10.1016/j.physa.2018.07.017

Nakhle, A. (2022). *The crypto world: global development and international legal implications* (Doctoral dissertation, Notre Dame University-Louaize).

National Crime Records Bureau (NCRB). (2022). *Crime in India 2022: Statistics*.

Ndiaye, M., & Konate, P. K. (2021). *Cryptocurrency crime: Behaviors of malicious smart contracts in blockchain.* Paper presented at the 2021 International Symposium on Networks, Computers and Communications (ISNCC). DOI: 10.1109/ISNCC52172.2021.9615702

NeosLegal. (2024, November 27). *Win for DeFi – Tornado Cash sanctions were illegal*. Retrieved February 24, 2025, from https://neoslegal.co/win-for-defi-tornado-cash-sanctions-were-illegal/

Ngunyi, A., Mundia, S., & Omari, C. (2019). Modelling volatility dynamics of cryptocurrencies using GARCH models. *Journal of Mathematical Finance*, *9*(4), 591–615. DOI: 10.4236/jmf.2019.94030

Nicholls, J., Kuppa, A., & Le-Khac, N. A. (2021). Financial Cybercrime: A Comprehensive Survey of Deep Learning Approaches to Tackle the Evolving Financial Crime Landscape. *IEEE Access : Practical Innovations, Open Solutions*, *9*, 163965–163986. DOI: 10.1109/ACCESS.2021.3134076

Nicolas, I. (2024). Striking the balance: Anti-money laundering goals and legal privilege in Australia. *Current Issues in Criminal Justice*. Advance online publication. DOI: 10.1080/10345329.2024.2420146

Nikkel, B. (2020). Fintech forensics: Criminal investigation and digital evidence in financial technologies. *Forensic Science International Digital Investigation, 33*, 200908. https://doi.org/https://doi.org/10.1016/j.fsidi.2020.200908. DOI: 10.1016/j.fsidi.2020.200908

Norbutas, L. (2018). Offline constraints in online drug marketplaces: An exploratory analysis of a cryptomarket trade network. *The International Journal on Drug Policy, 56*, 92–100. DOI: 10.1016/j.drugpo.2018.03.016

Noval, S. M. R., Jamaludin, A., Saputra, D. D., Munifah, N. F., Raswanti, P. S., & Lestia, S. N., (2023). The fusion of blockchain, pornography and human trafficking in a global digital dragnet that forms the online child sex trafficking. *Russian Law Journal, 11*(5s, 5S), 1–19. DOI: 10.52783/rlj.v11i5s.891

O'Sullivan, D. (2021, May 16). *A Harvard-trained biologist became the first person to use ransomware almost 30 years ago*. CNN. https://edition.cnn.com/2021/05/16/tech/ransomware-joseph-popp/index.html

OECD. (2023). *OECD principles on artificial intelligence*. https://www.oecd.org/going-digital/ai/principles/

Ouellet, M., Maimon, D., Howell, J. C., & Wu, Y. (2022). The network of online stolen data markets: How vendor flows connect digital marketplaces. *British Journal of Criminology, 62*(6), 1518–1536. DOI: 10.1093/bjc/azab116

Ozcan, R. (2021). Decentralized finance. *Financial ecosystem and strategy in the digital era: Global approaches and new opportunities*, 57-75. https://www.researchgate.net/profile/Uemit-Ilhan/publication/352390462_Business_Strategy_for_Sustainable_Development_in_the_Digital_Era_Green_Management/links/60c9f539a6fdcc01d476cafa/Business-Strategy-for-Sustainable-Development-in-the-Digital-Era-Green-Management.pdf

Ozili, P. K. (2018). Impact of digital finance on financial inclusion and stability. *Borsa Istanbul Review, 18*(4), 329-340. https://doi.org/https://doi.org/10.1016/j.bir.2017.12.003

Panda, S. K., Sathya, A. R., & Das, S. (2023). Bitcoin: Beginning of the Cryptocurrency Era. In Panda, S. K., Mishra, V., Dash, S. P., & Pani, A. K. (Eds.), *Recent Advances in Blockchain Technology: Real-World Applications* (pp. 25–58). Springer International Publishing., DOI: 10.1007/978-3-031-22835-3_2

Pande, S., & Prakash, V. (2019). Case study on scam in Indian banking industry (Nirav Modi). *Pramana Research Journal, 9*(6), 626–630.

Panos, G. A., Karkkainen, T., & Atkinson, A. (2020). Financial literacy and attitudes to cryptocurrencies. In.

Pardhey, N., Issa, Y. H., & Libeesh, P. C. (2023). Regulatory Mechanism of Cryptocurrency Blockchain in Banking, Financial, and Capital Markets in the Indian Panorama. In *The Impact of AI Innovation on Financial Sectors in the Era of Industry 5.0* (pp. 96–107). IGI Global.

Parisi, C., & Budorin, D. (2023). Smart Contract Security. *A Comprehensive Guide for Web3 Security: From Technology, Economic and Legal Aspects*, 81-102. https://doi.org/DOI: 10.1007/978-3-031-39288-7_4

Park, K., & Youm, H. Y. (2021). Proposal for Customer Identification Service Model Based on Distributed Ledger Technology to Transfer Virtual Assets [Article]. *Big Data and Cognitive Computing, 5*(3), 19, Article 31. https://doi.org/DOI: 10.3390/bdcc5030031

Patel, D. (2017). *6 red flags of an ICO scam*. TechCrunch. Retrieved 1 February 2018 from https://techcrunch.com/2017/12/07/6-red-flags-of-an-ico-scam/

Pathade, C., & Hooli, S. (2025). Exposing hidden backdoors in NFT smart contracts: A static security analysis of rug pull patterns. *arXiv*. https://doi.org//arXiv.2506.07974DOI: 10.48550

Patmanathan, P., Arunasalam, K., Suppiah, K., & Arumugam, D. (2023). The effectiveness of blockchain technology in preventing financial cybercrime. E3S Web of Conferences, Pazarbasioglu, C., Mora, A. G., Uttamchandani, M., Natarajan, H., Feyen, E., & Saal, M. (2020). Digital financial services. *World Bank, 54*, 1-54.

Patton, M. Q. (2002). *Qualitative research and evaluation methods* (Vol. 3). Sage.

Payne, B., & Mienie, E. (2021). *Multiple-extortion ransomware: The case for active cyber threat intelligence.* Paper presented at the ECCWS 2021 20th European Conference on Cyber Warfare and Security.

Peng, Y., Albuquerque, P. H. M., de Sá, J. M. C., Padula, A. J. A., & Montenegro, M. R. (2018). The best of two worlds: Forecasting high frequency volatility for cryptocurrencies and traditional currencies with support vector regression. *Expert Systems with Applications*, *97*, 177–192. DOI: 10.1016/j.eswa.2017.12.004

Pernice, I. G. A., & Scott, B. (2021). Cryptocurrency. *Internet Policy Review*, *10*(2), 1–10. DOI: 10.14763/2021.2.1561

Phillips, R., & Wilder, H. (2020, May). Tracing cryptocurrency scams: Clustering replicated advance-fee and phishing websites. In *2020 IEEE international conference on blockchain and cryptocurrency (ICBC)* (pp. 1-8). IEEE.

Phillips, C. R., & Gorse, D. (2018). Cryptocurrency price drivers: Wavelet coherence analysis revisited. *PLoS One*, *13*(4), e0195200. DOI: 10.1371/journal.pone.0195200

Pill, M. (2022). Re-framing non-economic losses to non-economic impacts for effective policymaking: Evidence from the Caribbean. *Climate and Development*, *14*(8), 770–779. DOI: 10.1080/17565529.2021.1987852

Platanakis, E., & Urquhart, A. (2020). Should investors include bitcoin in their portfolios? A portfolio theory approach. *The British Accounting Review*, *52*(4), 100837. DOI: 10.1016/j.bar.2019.100837

Potter, W. J. (2010). The State of Media Literacy. *Journal of Broadcasting & Electronic Media*, *54*(4), 675–696. DOI: 10.1080/08838151.2011.521462

Prathiksha, B. V. (2022, March 15). Online frauds on rise amid pandemic: OLX report. *BusinessLine*. https://www.thehindubusinessline.com/info-tech/online-fraud-has-grown-with-internet-usage-during-pandemic-olx/article64996341.ece

Press Trust of India (PTI). (2018, August 14). Cosmos Bank's server hacked; Rs 94 crore siphoned off in 2 days. *The Economic Times*. https://economictimes.indiatimes.com/industry/banking/finance/banking/cosmos-banks-server-hacked-rs-94-crore-siphoned-off-in-2-days/articleshow/65399477.cms

Pu, J., Mangaokar, N., Kelly, L., Bhattacharya, P., Sundaram, K., Javed, M., Wang, B., & Viswanath, B. (2021). Deepfake videos in the wild: Analysis and detection. *Proceedings of the Web Conference 2021*, 981–992. DOI: 10.1145/3442381.3449978

Rahman, A. (2024). Financial Inclusion through Technological Advancements in Banking Institutions: An Analytical Review. *Advances: Jurnal Ekonomi & Bisnis*, *2*(3), 163–173.

Rahouti, M., Xiong, K., & Ghani, N. (2018). Bitcoin concepts, threats, and machine-learning security solutions. *IEEE Access : Practical Innovations, Open Solutions*, *6*, 67189–67205. DOI: 10.1109/ACCESS.2018.2874539

Rai, H., Srivastava, A. K., Rai, S., & Pattanashetti, D. (2024). Blockchain-powered transparency: Tracking and disseminating donations for disaster-stricken regions. *Futuristic Trends in Artificial Intelligence*, 1-15.

Rajput, V. (2017, February 3). Who is Anubhav Mittal, the prime accused in Rs 3,700-cr online trading scam. *Hindustan Times*. https://www.hindustantimes.com/noida/anubhav-mittal-conman-robinhood-and-prime-accused-in-rs-3-700-cr-scam-noida-ponzi-scam/story-KbgoxypVn9pPR5bOyW526N.html

Rasyid, A., Willim, A. P., & Khaeryyah, S. (2024). Cryptocurrency and the Law: The Challenges of Regulating Decentralized Finance in Global Markets. *Impact: Multidisciplinary Journal*, *1*(01), 1–10.

Raza, S., Shaikh, M., & Tahira, K. (2023). Cryptocurrency investigations in digital forensics: Contemporary challenges and methodological advances. *Inf. Dyn. Appl*, *2*(3), 126–134. DOI: 10.56578/ida020302

Reid, F., & Harrigan, M. (2013). An Analysis of Anonymity in the Bitcoin System. In Altshuler, Y., Elovici, Y., Cremers, A. B., Aharony, N., & Pentland, A. (Eds.), *Security and Privacy in Social Networks* (pp. 197–223). Springer New York., DOI: 10.1007/978-1-4614-4139-7_10

Renda, A., & Caneppele, S. (2024). Compliant or not compliant? The challenges of anti-money laundering regulations in crypto assets: The case of Switzerland [Article]. *Journal of Money Laundering Control*, *27*(2), 363–382. DOI: 10.1108/JMLC-04-2023-0078

Reserve Bank of India. (2022). *Guidelines on digital lending*. https://rbidocs.rbi.org.in/rdocs/notification/PDFs/GUIDELINESDIGITALLENDINGD5C35A71D8124A0E92AEB940A7D25BB3.PDF

Reynolds, P., & Irwin, A. S. M. (2017). Tracking digital footprints: Anonymity within the bitcoin system [Article]. *Journal of Money Laundering Control*, *20*(2), 172–189. DOI: 10.1108/JMLC-07-2016-0027

Rhumorbarbe, D., Staehli, L., Broséus, J., Rossy, Q., & Esseiva, P. (2016). Buying drugs on a Darknet market: A better deal? Studying the online illicit drug market through the analysis of digital, physical and chemical data. *Forensic Science International*, *267*, 173–182. DOI: 10.1016/j.forsciint.2016.08.032

Rognone, L., Hyde, S., & Zhang, S. S. (2020). News sentiment in the cryptocurrency market: An empirical comparison with Forex [Article]. *International Review of Financial Analysis*, *69*(17), 101462. Advance online publication. DOI: 10.1016/j.irfa.2020.101462

Roma, P., Quarre, F., Israel, A., Johnston, M., & Flores, A. (2016). *Blockchain: An Enabler for Life Sciences and Healthcare*. Deloitte. Retrieved 31 January 2018 from https://d1.awsstatic.com/blockchain_assets/deloitte_bc_paper.pdf

Rushe, D. (2017, June 4). OPM hack: China blamed for massive breach of US government data. *The Guardian*. https://www.theguardian.com/technology/2015/jun/04/us-government-massive-data-breach-employee-records-security-clearances

Rustamaji, M., & Faisal, F. (2024). Law Enforcement Strategies Against Money Laundering Through Cryptocurrency: Comparative Studies in Several Countries. International Conference on Cultural Policy and Sustainable Development (ICPSD 2024), Scharfman, J. (2024). Crypto Phishing and Spoofing Scams. In *The Cryptocurrency and Digital Asset Fraud Casebook, Volume II: DeFi, NFTs, DAOs, Meme Coins, and Other Digital Asset Hacks* (pp. 193-219). Springer.

Sabry, F., Labda, W., Erbad, A., Al Jawaheri, H., & Malluhi, Q. (2019). Anonymity and privacy in bitcoin escrow trades. In *18th ACM Workshop on Privacy in the Electronic Society (WPES)*. ACM. DOI: 10.1145/3338498.3358639

Sabry, F., Labda, W., Erbad, A., Al Jawaheri, H., & Malluhi, Q. (2020). Cryptocurrencies and artificial intelligence: Challenges and opportunities. *IEEE Access : Practical Innovations, Open Solutions*, *8*, 175856–175879. DOI: 10.1109/ACCESS.2020.3025211

Saferstein, R. (2004). *Criminalistics: An introduction to forensic science* (8th ed.). Pearson Prentice Hall.

Salah, K., Rehman, M. H. U., Nizamuddin, N., & Al-Fuqaha, A. (2019). Blockchain for AI: Review and open research challenges. *IEEE Access : Practical Innovations, Open Solutions*, *7*, 10127–10149. DOI: 10.1109/ACCESS.2018.2890507

Salisu, S., & Filipov, V. (2023). *Blockchain forensics: A modern approach to investigating cybercrime in the age of decentralisation.* Paper presented at the # PLACEHOLDER_PARENT_METADATA_VALUE#. DOI: 10.34190/iccws.18.1.947

Santana, C., & Albareda, L. (2022). Blockchain and the emergence of Decentralized Autonomous Organizations (DAOs): An integrative model and research agenda. *Technological Forecasting and Social Change*, *182*, 121806. DOI: 10.1016/j.techfore.2022.121806

Sapkale, Y. (2019, January 24). Aadhaar data breach largest in the world, says WEF's Global Risk Report and Avast. *Moneylife News & Views*. https://www.moneylife.in/article/aadhaar-data-breach-largest-in-the-world-says-wefs-global-risk-report-and-avast/56384.html

Sarbajna, R., Eick, C. F., & Laszka, A. (2023). *PhobosBC: A Blockchain-based Crowdsourced Post-disaster Mapping System and its Agent-based Simulation.* Paper presented at the Proceedings of the 6th ACM SIGSPATIAL International Workshop on GeoSpatial Simulation. DOI: 10.1145/3615891.3628016

Schär, F., & Gronde, F. (2021). Flash Loans and Decentralized Lending Protocols: An In-Depth Analysis. https://wwz.unibas.ch/fileadmin/user_upload/wwz/00_Professuren/Schaer_DLTFintech/Lehre/MA_Florian_Gronde_Flashloans-ohne_Appendix.pdf

Schär, F. (2021). Decentralized finance: On blockchain and smart contract-based financial markets. *Review - Federal Reserve Bank of St. Louis*, *103*(2), 153–174. DOI: 10.5451/unibas-ep86500

Scharfman, J. (2022). Operational Due Diligence on Cryptocurrency and Digital Asset Funds [Article]. *Journal of Alternative Investments*, *24*(3), 44–50. DOI: 10.3905/jai.2021.1.146

Schueffel, P. (2021). Defi: Decentralized finance-an introduction and overview. *Journal of Innovation Management*, *9*(3), I–XI. DOI: 10.24840/2183-0606_009.003_0001

SEC. (2017). *SEC V. RECOIN GROUP FOUNDATION, LLC, DRC: COMPLAINT WORLD INC. a/k/a DIAMOND RESERVE CLUB: and MAKSIM ZASLAVSKIY.* US Securities and Exchange Commission (SEC). Retrieved 4 February 2018 from https://www.sec.gov/litigation/complaints/2017/comp-pr2017-185.pdf

SEC. (2018). *SEC V. ARISEBANK, JARED RICE SR., and STANLEY FORD.* US Securities and Exchange Commission (SEC). Retrieved 4 February 2018 from https://www.sec.gov/litigation/complaints/2018/comp-pr2018-8.pdf

Senthuran, G., & Halgamuge, M. (2019). Prediction of cryptocurrency market price using deep learning and blockchain information: Bitcoin and Ethereum. In *Taylor & Francis* (pp. 349–364).

Senthuran, R., & Halgamuge, M. (2019). *Prediction of cryptocurrency market price using deep learning and blockchain information: Bitcoin and Ethereum.* Taylor & Francis. DOI: 10.1201/9780429674457-15

Sestino, A., Tuček, D., & Bresciani, S. (2024). The "dark side" and negative consequences of cryptocurrencies usage for unethical purposes as barriers to invest in Middle East and African (MEA) countries. *Journal of Small Business and Enterprise Development.*

Sgantzos, K., & Grigg, I. (2019). Artificial intelligence implementations on the blockchain: Use cases and future applications. *Future Internet, 11*(8), 170. DOI: 10.3390/fi11080170

Shah, D., & Zhang, K. (2014). Bayesian regression and bitcoin. In *Proceedings of the 52nd Annual Allerton Conference on Communication, Control, and Computing (Allerton)* (pp. 409–414). DOI: 10.1109/ALLERTON.2014.7028484

Sharma, D., Ghosh, R., Shri, C., & Khatter, D. (2024). Sentiments in the cryptocurrency market: an in-depth analysis of influential factors applying ISM-MICMAC and AHP [Article]. *Journal of Capital Markets Studies*. https://doi.org/DOI: 10.1108/JCMS-07-2024-0038

Sharma, M., & Kaur, M. (2022). A review of Deepfake technology: an emerging AI threat. *Soft Computing for Security Applications: Proceedings of ICSCS 2021*, 605-619.

Shekar, A., ... (2020, March 2). Duping buyers across India by posing as army officers on OLX: TN cops crack scam. *The News Minute*. https://www.thenewsminute.com/tamil-nadu/duping-buyers-across-india-posing-army-officers-olx-tn-cops-crack-scam-119709

Sherrod, J., Cory, K., & Caron, J. (2023, August 7). *Nigerian nationals extradited to U.S. for alleged role in sextortion ring, victim's mother speaks out*. FOX 17. Retrieved March 2, 2025, from https://www.fox17online.com/news/local-news/nigerian-nationals-extradited-to-u-s-for-alleged-role-in-sextortion-ring-victims-mother-speaks-out

Shevchuk, R., Lishchynskyy, I., Ciura, M., Lyzun, M., Kozak, R., & Kasianchuk, M. (2025). Application of Blockchain Technology in Emergency Management Systems: A Bibliometric Analysis. *Applied Sciences (Basel, Switzerland), 15*(10), 5405. DOI: 10.3390/app15105405

Shi, F. B., Sun, X. Q., Gao, J. H., Xu, L., Shen, H. W., & Cheng, X. Q. (2019). Anomaly detection in Bitcoin market via price return analysis [Article]. *PLoS One, 14*(6), e0218341. Advance online publication. DOI: 10.1371/journal.pone.0218341

Shin, E.-J., Kang, H.-G., & Bae, K. (2020). A study on the sustainable development of NPOs with blockchain technology. *Sustainability (Basel), 12*(15), 6158. DOI: 10.3390/su12156158

Shintate, T., & Pichl, L. (2019). Trend prediction classification for high frequency bitcoin time series with deep learning. *Journal of Risk and Financial Management, 12*(1), 17. DOI: 10.3390/jrfm12010017

Sholla, S., Naaz, S., Chishti, M. A., & Al-Turjman, F. (2021). Blockchain for sustainable and smart applications: Current trends, challenges, and future research directions. *Sustainable Cities and Society*, *72*, 103080. DOI: 10.1016/j.scs.2021.103080

Siemon, C., Rueckel, D., & Krumay, B. (2020). Blockchain technology for emergency response.

Sillaber, C., Waltl, B., Treiblmaier, H., Gallersdörfer, U., & Felderer, M. (2021). Laying the foundation for smart contract development: An integrated engineering process model. *Information Systems and e-Business Management*, *19*(3), 863–882. DOI: 10.1007/s10257-020-00465-5

Silverberg, K., French, C., & Ferenzy, D. (2018). *Initial Coin Offerings: The Frontier of Financing*. Institute of International Finance. Retrieved 3 March 2018 from https://www.iif.com/system/files/32370132_ico_background_final.pdf

Sinclair, S., & Peterson, M. (2022, October 12). *Mango Markets Mangled by Oracle Manipulation for $112M*. Retrieved from blockworks: https://blockworks.co/news/mango-markets-mangled-by-oracle-manipulation-for-112m

Singh, S. G. (2024, November 21). Bitcoin scam: The legality of cryptocurrencies in India. *Business Standard*. https://www.business-standard.com/finance/personal-finance/bitcoin-scam-the-legality-of-cryptocurrencies-in-india-explained-124112100977_1.html

Siu, G. A., Hutchings, A., Vasek, M., & Moore, T. (2022, November). Invest in crypto! In *An analysis of investment scam advertisements found in Bitcointalk. In 2022 APWG symposium on electronic crime research (eCrime)* (pp. 1–12). IEEE.

Sklaroff, J. M. (2017). Smart contracts and the cost of inflexibility. *U. Pa. L. Rev.*, *166*, 263.

Smith, M., & Tiwari, M. (2023). The implications of national blockchain infrastructure for financial crime. *Journal of Financial Crime, ahead-of-print*(ahead-of-print). https://doi.org/DOI: 10.1108/JFC-01-2023-0006

Smith, A., & Weismann, M. F. (2014). Are you ready for digital currency? *Journal of Corporate Accounting & Finance*, *26*(1), 17–21. DOI: 10.1002/jcaf.21999

Smith, D. (2024). *Money Laundering, Terrorist Financing and Virtual Assets*. Springer. DOI: 10.1007/978-3-031-59842-5

Smith, M. (2020). A modern approach to regulation: Integrating law, system architecture and blockchain technology in Australia'. *Australian Business Law Review, 48*(5), 460–465. https://sites.thomsonreuters.com.au/journals/2021/01/08/australian-business-law-review-update-vol-48-pt-5/

Smuts, N. (2019). What drives cryptocurrency prices?: An investigation of Google trends and Telegram sentiment. *Performance Evaluation Review, 46*(3), 131–134. DOI: 10.1145/3308897.3308955

Soldner, F., Plum, F., Kleinberg, B., & Johnson, S. D. (2024). From cryptomarkets to the surface web: Scouting eBay for counterfeits. *arXiv preprint arXiv:2406.05021.*

Sorell, T., & Whitty, M. (2019). Online romance scams and victimhood. *Security Journal, 32*(3), 342–361. DOI: 10.1057/s41284-019-00166-w

Sotiropoulou, A., & Ligot, S. (2019). Legal Challenges of Cryptocurrencies: Isn't It Time to Regulate the Intermediaries? *European Company and Financial Law Review, 16*(5), 652–676. DOI: 10.1515/ecfr-2019-0023

Sripathi, M., & Leelavati, T. (2024). The Fourth Industrial Revolution: A paradigm shift in healthcare delivery and management. *Digital Transformation in Healthcare 5.0, 1*, 67.

Steptoe & Johnson LLP. (2024, February 23). *In significant win for digital asset industry, the Fifth Circuit invalidates sanctions on Tornado Cash*. Steptoe & Johnson LLP. Retrieved February 24, 2025, from https://www.steptoe.com/en/news-publications/international-compliance-blog/in-significant-win-for-digital-asset-industry-the-fifth-circuit-invalidates-sanctions-on-tornado-cash.html

Stuhlmiller, L. (2013). *Mitigating virtual money laundering: An analysis of virtual worlds and virtual currencies* Utica College]. United States -- New York. https://search.proquest.com/docview/1449374093?accountid=26503

Stupp, C. (2019). August 30). Wall Street Journal: Fraudsters Used AI to Mimic CEO's Voice in Unusual Cybercrime Case. https://www.wsj.com/articles/fraudsters-use-aito-mimic-ceos-voice-in-unusual-cybercrime-case-11567157402

Subbian, R. G., & Gollapudi, P. K. Smart Contracts and Blockchain-The Next Frontier in Trustworthy P&C Insurance.

Sullivan, C., & Burger, E. (2017). E-residency and blockchain. *Computer Law & Security Review, 33*(4), 470–481. https://doi.org/https://doi.org/10.1016/j.clsr.2017.03.016. DOI: 10.1016/j.clsr.2017.03.016

Sun Yin, H., Langenheldt, K., Harlev, M., Mukkamala, R. R., & Vatrapu, R. (2019). Regulating cryptocurrencies: A supervised machine learning approach to de-anonymizing the Bitcoin blockchain. *Journal of Management Information Systems, 36*(1), 37–73. DOI: 10.1080/07421222.2018.1550550

Sunyaev, A., & Sunyaev, A. (2020). Distributed ledger technology. *Internet computing: Principles of distributed systems and emerging internet-based technologies*, 265-299.

Sureshbhai, P. N., Bhattacharya, P., & Tanwar, S., & Ieee. (2020). KaRuNa: A Blockchain-based Sentiment Analysis Framework for Fraud Cryptocurrency Schemes. In *2020 Ieee International Conference on Communications Workshops*. Ieee. <Go to ISI>://WOS:000607199300080 DOI: 10.1109/ICCWorkshops49005.2020.9145151

Survi. (2023). Unveiling the 2023 UPI scam in India: Stay secured. *Protegent360*. https://protegent360.com/blog/to-safeguard-the-data-of-enterprises-and-consumers-provide-robust-cyber-security-and-antivirus/?srsltid=AfmBOor-rJdrSnnFRwTWY_gOaNaw147Zrjcv-9GjmluIWYHIBBoTmNPe

Susilaningsih, L. E. D., & Indriayu, M. (2021). Financial Literacy in Student Financial Management Behavior in the Digital Age *Proceedings of the 4th International Conference on Learning Innovation and Quality Education*, Surakarta, Indonesia. https://doi.org/DOI: 10.1145/3452144.3453759

Symantec. (2003). *Internet security threat report*. https://symantec.com

Symantec. (2022). *Cryptojacking activity and trends report*. https://www.broadcom.com/company/newsroom/press-releases

Tadiparthi, R. (2024). RBI guidelines for UPI frauds in banks: Stay protected from UPI scams. *Paytm Blog*. https://paytm.com/blog/loan/repo-rate/rbi-guidelines-for-upi-frauds-in-banks/

Tandem Research. (2022). *AI on the ground: A snapshot of AI use in India*. https://images-production.authory.com/UrvashiAneja/AI-ON-THE-GROUND-A-SNAPSHOT-OF-AI-USE-IN-INDIA-1/fe06ba20-2bed-11ec-8805-7b8cab49e3f9.pdf

Tapscott, D., & Tapscott, A. (2017). How Blockchain Will Change Organizations. *MIT Sloan Management Review, 58*(2), 10.

Tay, R. S., & Chen, R. (2018). *Nonlinear time series analysis*. Wiley. DOI: 10.1002/9781119514312

Teichmann, F. M. J., & Falker, M. C. (2021). Cryptocurrencies and financial crime: Solutions from Liechtenstein [Article]. *Journal of Money Laundering Control, 24*(4), 775–788. DOI: 10.1108/JMLC-05-2020-0060

Teichmann, F. M. J., & Falker, M. C. (2021). Money laundering via cryptocurrencies - potential solutions from Liechtenstein [Article]. *Journal of Money Laundering Control, 24*(1), 91–101. DOI: 10.1108/JMLC-04-2020-0041

Thomas, J. (2019, December). A case study analysis of the Equifax data breach. https://www.researchgate.net/publication/337916068

Tidy, J. (2022, March 30). *Ronin Network: What a $600m hack says about the state of crypto.* Retrieved from bbc: https://www.bbc.com/news/technology-60933174

Tidy, J. (2025). *North Korean hackers cash out hundreds of millions from $1.5bn ByBit hack.* BBC. https://www.bbc.com/news/articles/c2kgndwwd7lo

Tiwari, S. (2024, November 29). Digital fear: How stock trading scams, investment frauds, digital arrest and threats from foreign lands are crippling. *Entrepreneur India.* https://www.entrepreneur.com/en-in/news-and-trends/digital-fear-how-stock-trading-scams-investment-frauds/483665

Tiwari, M., Gepp, A., & Kumar, K. (2019). The future of raising finance - a new opportunity to commit fraud: A review of initial coin offering (ICOs) scams. *Crime, Law, and Social Change.* Advance online publication. DOI: 10.1007/s10611-019-09873-2

Tiwari, M., Lupton, C., Bernot, A., & Halteh, K. (2024). The cryptocurrency conundrum: The emerging role of digital currencies in geopolitical conflicts. *Journal of Financial Crime, 31*(6), 1622–1634. DOI: 10.1108/JFC-12-2023-0306

Tiwari, M., Zhou, Y., Ferrill, J., & Smith, M. (2025a). Crypto Crashes: An examination of the Binance and FTX scandals and associated accounting challenges. *The British Accounting Review, 101584*, 101584. https://doi.org/https://doi.org/10.1016/j.bar.2025.101584. DOI: 10.1016/j.bar.2025.101584

Tiwari, M., Zhou, Y., Gilmour, P., & Bernot, A. (2025b). Confronting metacrime: Complexities, enforcement challenges, and regulatory pathways. *Law, Innovation and Technology, 17*(1), 1–18. DOI: 10.1080/17579961.2025.2469347

Toronto, C. E., & Remington, R. (2020). *A step-by-step guide to conducting an integrative review.* Springer. DOI: 10.1007/978-3-030-37504-1

Toulas, B. (2025). *New Apple CPU side-channel attacks steal data from browsers.* [online] BleepingComputer. Available at: https://www.bleepingcomputer.com/news/security/new-apple-cpu-side-channel-attack-steals-data-from-browsers/ [Accessed 5 Feb. 2025].

Transparency International Russia. (2023). *Anonymity for sale: The thriving black market of crypto-to-fiat mules.* https://ti-russia.org/wp-content/uploads/2023/10/epaycrypto_.pdf

TRM. (2025, January 09). *Squid Game Season 2: A Window Into Popular Culture and Crypto Scams.* Retrieved from TRM: https://www.trmlabs.com/post/squid-game-season-2-a-window-into-popular-culture-and-crypto-scams#:~:text=The%202021%20SQUID%20token%20scam,course%20of%20a%20few%20weeks

Trozze, A., Kamps, J., Akartuna, E. A., Hetzel, F. J., Kleinberg, B., Davies, T., & Johnson, S. D. (2022). Cryptocurrencies and future financial crime [Review]. *Crime Science, 11*(1), 35, Article 1. https://doi.org/DOI: 10.1186/s40163-021-00163-8

Trozze, A., Davies, T., & Kleinberg, B. (2021). Explaining prosecution outcomes for cryptocurrency-based financial crimes [Article; Early Access]. *Journal of Money Laundering Control, 17.* Advance online publication. DOI: 10.1108/JMLC-10-2021-0119

Tschorsch, F., & Scheuermann, B. (2016). Bitcoin and Beyond: A Technical Survey on Decentralized Digital Currencies. *IEEE Communications Surveys and Tutorials, 18*(3), 2084–2123. DOI: 10.1109/COMST.2016.2535718

Turner, A., & Irwin, A. S. M. (2018). Bitcoin transactions: A digital discovery of illicit activity on the blockchain. *Journal of Financial Crime, 25*(1), 109–130. https://doi.org/doi:10.1108/JFC-12-2016-0078. DOI: 10.1108/JFC-12-2016-0078

Turner, J. E. (2011). *Money laundering prevention: Deterring, detecting, and resolving financial fraud.* Wiley Online Library.

U.S. Department of Homeland Security. (n.d.). *Blockchain portfolio.* https://www.dhs.gov/science-and-technology/blockchain-portfolio

Underhill, J. (2018). *Initial coin offerings: Fraudsters use new technology to perpetrate old schemes.* ACFE Fraud Magazine. Retrieved 31 March 2018 from https://www.fraud-magazine.com/article.aspx?id=4295000887&Site=ACFEWEB

UNICEF. (2020). *UNICEF Innovation Fund: Blockchain 2020.* https://www.unicef.org/innovation/unicefinnovationfund/blockchain2020

Unit21. (n.d.-b). Tornado Cash: How it works & applicable sanctions. Unit21. Retrieved February 24, 2025, from https://www.unit21.ai/fraud-aml-dictionary/tornado-cash

Unit21.ai. (n.d.-a). Definition of financial crime and categories of financial crime. Retrieved January 29, 2025, from https://www.unit21.ai/fincrime-definition

United Nations Conference on Trade and Development. (n.d.). *Global report: Blockchain and its* implications for trade facilitation performance. https://unctad.org/publication/global-report-blockchain-and-its-implications-trade-facilitation-performance

United Nations Office on Drugs and Crime (UNODC). (2022). *Cryptocurrency investigation training program*. https://www.unodc.org/unodc/en/cybercrime/

United States Attorney's Office. Southern District of New York. (2024, April 24). Founders and CEO of cryptocurrency mixing service arrested and charged with money laundering and unlicensed money transmitting offenses. U.S. Department of Justice. Retrieved from https://www.justice.gov/usao-sdny/pr/founders-and-ceo-cryptocurrency-mixing-service-arrested-and-charged-money-laundering

United States Attorney's Office. Western District of Michigan. (2024, September 5). Ogoshi brothers sentenced to lengthy prison terms in sextortion scheme that resulted in death of teen. United States Department of Justice. Retrieved March 2, 2025, from https://www.justice.gov/usao-wdmi/pr/2024_0905_Ogoshi_Brothers_Sentenced

United States Code. 18 U.S.C. § 1341 (2025). Retrieved from https://www.law.cornell.edu/uscode/text/18/1341

United States Code. 18 U.S.C. § 1956 (2025). Retrieved from https://www.law.cornell.edu/uscode/text/18/1956

United States Department of the Treasury. (2022, August 8). U.S. Treasury sanctions notorious virtual currency mixer Tornado Cash. U.S. Department of the Treasury. Retrieved February 24, 2025, from https://home.treasury.gov/news/press-releases/jy0916

United States Securities and Exchange Commission. (n.d.). Ponzi scheme. Investor.gov. Retrieved March 2, 2025, from https://www.investor.gov/protect-your-investments/fraud/types-fraud/ponzi-scheme

Usman, N., Griffiths, M., & Alam, A. (2025). FinTech and money laundering: Moderating effect of financial regulations and financial literacy. *Digital Policy. Regulation & Governance*, *27*(3), 301–326. DOI: 10.1108/DPRG-04-2024-0068

Valencia, F., Gómez-Espinosa, A., & Valdés-Aguirre, B. (2019). Price movement prediction of cryptocurrencies using sentiment analysis and machine learning. *Entropy (Basel, Switzerland)*, *21*(6), 589. DOI: 10.3390/e21060589

van der Horst, M., Kho, R., Gadyatskaya, O., Mollema, M., Van Eeten, M., & Zhauniarovich, Y. (2025). *High Stakes, Low Certainty: Evaluating the Efficacy of High-Level Indicators of Compromise in Ransomware Attribution.* Paper presented at the Proceedings of the 34th USENIX Security Symposium (USENIX Sec).

Varma, R., & Kanaujiya, B. (2023). Case study of Saradha scam on Indian economy. *International Journal of Advanced Research in Science* [IJARSCT]. *Tongxin Jishu*, *3*(6).

Vaz, J., & Brown, K. (2020). Sustainable development and cryptocurrencies as private money. *Economia e Politica Industriale*, *47*(1), 163–184. DOI: 10.1007/s40812-019-00139-5

Verizon (2024a). 2024 Data Breach Investigations Report. [online] Verizon Business. Retrieved February 5, 2025, from: https://www.verizon.com/business/resources/reports/dbir

Verizon. (2024b). *2024 DBIR SMB infographic.* Verizon Business. Retrieved February 5, 2025, from https://www.verizon.com/business/resources/infographics/2024-dbir-smb-infographic.pdf

Verma, P., Srivastava, R., & Kumar, S. (2024). Blockchain Technology: Applications and Challenges. *Blockchain for IoT Systems*, 1-12.

Voice of America. (2024, February 5). *Deepfake scam video cost company $26 million, Hong Kong police say.* https://www.voanews.com/a/deepfake-scam-video-cost-company-26million-hong-kong-police-says/7470542.html

Voshmgir, S. (2025). *Token economy.* Token Kitchen, Labirinto Ecletico Unip LDA.

Wagner, J. (2019). Financial Education and Financial Literacy by Income and Education Groups. *Financial Counseling and Planning*, *30*(1), 132–141. DOI: 10.1891/1052-3073.30.1.132

Wang, F., & Zhou, X. (2023). Persuasive schemes for financial exploitation in online romance scam: An Anatomy on Sha Zhu pan ( ) in China. *Victims & Offenders*, *18*(5), 915–942. DOI: 10.1080/15564886.2022.2051109

Wang, H.-M., & Hsieh, M.-L. (2024). Cryptocurrency is new vogue: A reflection on money laundering prevention. *Security Journal*, *37*(1), 25–46. DOI: 10.1057/s41284-023-00366-5

Wang, J., Zhang, L., Xu, L., & Qian, X. (2024). The dynamic emotional experience of online fraud victims during the process of being defrauded: A text-based analysis. *Journal of Criminal Justice*, *94*, 102231. DOI: 10.1016/j.jcrimjus.2024.102231

Wang, X., Ma, J., Liang, Y., Ma, L., & Liu, P. (2023). The association between experiences of being defrauded and depressive symptoms of middle-aged and elderly people: A cross-sectional study in China. *Public Health*, *216*, 51–57. DOI: 10.1016/j.puhe.2023.01.002

Wang, Y. (2024). Do cryptocurrency investors in the UK need more protection? [Article]. *Journal of Financial Regulation and Compliance*, *32*(2), 230–249. DOI: 10.1108/JFRC-03-2023-0036

Wazid, M., Mishra, A. K., Mohd, N., & Das, A. K. (2024). A Secure Deepfake Mitigation Framework: Architecture, Issues, Challenges, and Societal Impact. *Cyber Security and Applications*, *2*, 100040. DOI: 10.1016/j.csa.2024.100040

Westerkamp, M. (2023). *Cross-blockchain smart contract interoperability*. Germany: Technische Universitaet Berlin. https://depositonce.tu-berlin.de/bitstreams/a0e4f4dc-abce-4c9a-938e-d37951dd1575/download

Westerlund, M. (2019). The emergence of deepfake technology: A review. *Technology Innovation Management Review*, *9*(11), 39–52. DOI: 10.22215/timreview/1282

Whelan, C. (2012). *Networks and national security: dynamics, effectiveness and organisation*. Routlege.

Whelan, C., Bright, D., & Martin, J. (2024). Reconceptualising organised (cyber) crime: The case of ransomware. *Journal of Criminology*, *57*(1), 45–61. DOI: 10.1177/26338076231199793

Whelan, C., Dupont, B., Harkin, D., Martin, J., Miccelli, M., & Villeneuve-Dubuc, M. P. (2024). Expertise integration in cybercrime policing: Exploring civilian career lifecycles. *Deviant Behavior*, •••, 1–18. DOI: 10.1080/01639625.2024.2357810

Willie, M. M. (2023). The role of organizational culture in cybersecurity: Building a security-first culture. *Journal of Research. Innovation and Technologies*, *2*(2 (4)), 179–198. DOI: 10.1051/e3sconf/202338907022

WIRED. (2021, November 02). *How a Squid Game Crypto Scam Got Away With Millions*. Retrieved from WIRED: https://www.wired.com/story/squid-game-coin-crypto-scam/

World Economic Forum. (2016). *The future of financial infrastructure*.

Wronka, C. (2022). Money laundering through cryptocurrencies - analysis of the phenomenon and appropriate prevention measures. *Journal of Money Laundering Control*, *25*(1), 79–94. DOI: 10.1108/JMLC-02-2021-0017

Wronka, C. (2023). Financial crime in the decentralized finance ecosystem: New challenges for compliance. *Journal of Financial Crime*, *30*(1), 97–113. DOI: 10.1108/JFC-09-2021-0218

Wronka, C. (2024). Crypto-asset activities and markets in the European Union: Issues, challenges and considerations for regulation, supervision and oversight. *Journal of Banking Regulation*, *25*(1), 84–93. DOI: 10.1057/s41261-023-00217-8

Wu, J., Lin, K., Lin, D., Zheng, Z., Huang, H., & Zheng, Z. (2023). Financial Crimes in Web3-Empowered Metaverse: Taxonomy, Countermeasures, and Opportunities. *IEEE Open Journal of the Computer Society*, *4*, 37–49. DOI: 10.1109/OJCS.2023.3245801

Wu, J., Liu, J., Chen, W., Huang, H., Zheng, Z., & Zhang, Y. (2022). Detecting Mixing Services via Mining Bitcoin Transaction Network with Hybrid Motifs [Article]. *IEEE Transactions on Systems, Man, and Cybernetics. Systems*, *52*(4), 2237–2249. DOI: 10.1109/TSMC.2021.3049278

Xia, P., Wang, H., Zhang, B., Ji, R., Gao, B., Wu, L., Luo, X., & Xu, G. (2020). Characterizing cryptocurrency exchange scams. *Computers & Security*, *98*, 101993. DOI: 10.1016/j.cose.2020.101993

Xidonas, P., Steuer, R., & Hassapis, C. (2020). Robust portfolio optimization: A categorized bibliographic review. *Annals of Operations Research*, *292*(1), 533–552. DOI: 10.1007/s10479-020-03630-8

Xie, Q., Tan, D., Zhu, T., Zhang, Q., Xiao, S., & Wang, J.. (2019, May). Chatbot application on cryptocurrency. In *Proceedings of the IEEE Conference on Computational Intelligence for Financial Engineering & Economics (CIFEr)* (pp. 1–8). DOI: 10.1109/CIFEr.2019.8759121

Xu, J., & Feng, Y. (2022). Reap the harvest on blockchain: A survey of yield farming protocols. *IEEE Transactions on Network and Service Management*, *20*(1), 858–869. DOI: 10.1109/TNSM.2022.3222815

Xu, J., Sun, G., Wu, S., Zhu, S., & Zhou, Y. (2024). Understanding health fraud offenders in China: An emotional labour perspective. *Asian Journal of Law and Society*, *11*(1), 54–69. DOI: 10.1017/als.2023.14

Yao, S. Y., Kong, X. R., Sensoy, A., Akyildirim, E., & Cheng, F. Y. (2021). Investor attention and idiosyncratic risk in cryptocurrency markets. *European Journal of Finance*. Advance online publication. DOI: 10.1080/1351847X.2021.1989008

Yazdinejad, A., Zolfaghari, B., Azmoodeh, A., Dehghantanha, A., Karimipour, H., Fraser, E., Green, A. G., Russell, C., & Duncan, E. (2021). A review on security of smart farming and precision agriculture: Security aspects, attacks, threats and countermeasures. *Applied Sciences (Basel, Switzerland)*, *11*(16), 7518. DOI: 10.3390/app11167518

Yeoh, P. (2017). Regulatory issues in blockchain technology. *Journal of Financial Regulation and Compliance*, *25*(2), 196–208. DOI: 10.1108/JFRC-08-2016-0068

Yin, S. H., & Vatrapu, R. (2017). A first estimation of the proportion of cybercriminal entities in the Bitcoin ecosystem using supervised machine learning. In 2017 IEEE International Conference on Big Data (Big Data) (pp. 3690–3699). IEEE. DOI: 10.1109/BigData.2017.8258365

Yiying, W., & Yeze, Z. (2019, March). Cryptocurrency price analysis with artificial intelligence. In *Proceedings of the 5th International Conference on Information Management (ICIM)* (pp. 97–101). DOI: 10.1109/INFOMAN.2019.8714700

Young, K. (2021). Cyber case study: Sony Pictures Entertainment hack. *CoverLink Insurance*. https://coverlink.com/case-study/sony-pictures-entertainment-hack/

Zaffaroni, E. (n.d.). *Blockchain and criminal law*. Pensamiento Penal. https://www.pensamientopenal.com.ar/system/files/Documento_Editado1686.pdf

Zetzsche, D. A., Arner, D. W., & Buckley, R. P. (2020). Decentralized finance. *Journal of Financial Regulation*, *6*(2), 172–203. https://academic.oup.com/jfr/advance-article-pdf/doi/10.1093/jfr/fjaa010/37064506/fjaa010.pdf. DOI: 10.1093/jfr/fjaa010

Zhang, J., & Chen, Z. (2024). Exploring Human Resource Management Digital Transformation in the Digital Age. *Journal of the Knowledge Economy*, *15*(1), 1482–1498. DOI: 10.1007/s13132-023-01214-y

Zhao, Q., Wang, Y., Yang, B., Shang, K., Sun, M., Wang, H., & Xin, H. (2023). A comprehensive overview of security vulnerability penetration methods in blockchain cross-chain bridges. *Authorea Preprints*, 76. https://doi.org/DOI: 10.22541/au.169760541.13864334/v1

Zhao, Y., Kang, X., Li, T., Chu, C. K., & Wang, H. (2022). Toward trustworthy defi oracles: Past, present, and future. *IEEE Access : Practical Innovations, Open Solutions*, *10*, 60914–60928. DOI: 10.1109/ACCESS.2022.3179374

Zheng, J., Lee, D. K., & Qian, D. (2023). An in-depth guide to cross-chain protocols under a multi-chain world. *World Scientific Annual Review of Fintech*, *1*, 2350003. DOI: 10.1142/S2811004823500033

Zhou, L., Diro, A., Saini, A., Kaisar, S., & Hiep, P. C. (2024). Leveraging zero knowledge proofs for blockchain-based identity sharing: A survey of advancements, challenges and opportunities. *Journal of Information Security and Applications*, *103678*, 103678. Advance online publication. DOI: 10.1016/j.jisa.2023.103678

Zhou, Y., Tiwari, M., Bernot, A., & Lin, K. (2024). Metacrime and Cybercrime: Exploring the Convergence and Divergence in Digital Criminality. *Asian Journal of Criminology*, *19*(3), 419–439. DOI: 10.1007/s11417-024-09436-y

Zhou, Y., Xu, B., Sun, I. Y., Zhang, Y., & Chang, L. Y. C. (2022). Examining Sexual Crime Severity in China: A General-Specific Model on Sex Offending Against Adults. *Sexual Abuse*, *34*(7), 830–856. DOI: 10.1177/10790632221112656

Zhou, Y., Xu, J., Wu, S., & Zhu, S. (2023). Health Fraud against the Elderly in China: The Perspective of Vulnerability Manipulation. *Victims & Offenders*, *18*(7), 1354–1372. DOI: 10.1080/15564886.2023.2211570

Zivot, E., & Wang, J. (2006). Nonlinear time series models. In *Modeling financial time series with S-PLUS* (pp. 653–712). Springer.

Zola, F., Eguimendia, M., Bruse, J. L., & Orduna Urrutia, R. (2019). Cascading machine learning to attack bitcoin anonymity. In *Proceedings of the IEEE International Conference on Blockchain* (pp. 154–167). DOI: 10.1109/Blockchain.2019.00011

About the Contributors

Leo S.F. Lin is a Senior Lecturer in Policing Studies at Charles Sturt University. He holds a PhD in International Development and Security Studies from the University of Southern Mississippi. Before joining Charles Sturt University, Dr. Lin served as an Assistant Professor and Visiting Lecturer at various higher education institutions, including the University of Malaya, the University of Glasgow, and Ming Chuan University. With 20 years of experience in the policing and security fields and numerous awards to his name, Dr. Lin is recognized for advancing education and research that strengthen law enforcement and public safety frameworks in crime prevention and emergency response.

***

Sina Ahmadi is a Lead Engineer at Block Inc., where he oversees global platform and networking infrastructure, focusing on cloud architecture and security. He is also a researcher with the National Coalition of Independent Scholars (NCIS), contributing to studies on AI, cybersecurity, and financial technologies. With extensive experience in infrastructure engineering and security optimization, Sina has authored multiple peer-reviewed publications in Cybersecurity, AI and networking. His expertise spans advanced fraud prevention, cloud security, and scalable infrastructure solutions, blending technical innovation with academic rigor to drive impactful outcomes.

Douglas M.C. Allan earned his PhD in Criminology from the Regulatory Institutions Network at the Australian National University. He is currently the Acting Head of the Australian Graduate School of Policing and Security at Charles Sturt University, managing a portfolio of undergraduate and postgraduate programs in law enforcement, national security, emergency management, law and financial crime. He has published in multiple areas, including education, financial crime, criminology and cybercrime.

Edward Danso Ansong is a Computer Scientist and Senior Lecturer at the Department of Computer Science, University of Ghana, Legon. He earned his PhD in Computer Science with a specialization in cybersecurity and intelligent systems. His academic portfolio includes teaching courses in computer networks, cybersecurity, and software engineering. He has published in areas including fraud detection, IoT security, and blockchain integration in digital systems. He has served as a supervisor for numerous postgraduate theses and is involved in curriculum development at the departmental level.

Duane Aslett earned his doctoral degree in law (LLD) from North-West University (NWU), South Africa, with a thesis on combating organized crime, and now serves as Associate Professor and Director of the Centre for Law and Justice at Charles Sturt University, Australia, where he coordinates the program with a focus on integrating practical and academic approaches to legal studies. His research interests include financial crime, corruption, money laundering, and organized crime. Dr Aslett's extensive career includes roles as an Inspector in the South African Police Service, Senior Public Prosecutor in the National Prosecuting Authority of South Africa, forensic investigator at PricewaterhouseCoopers, and leadership positions at NWU, including Program Leader of Forensic Accountancy and Director of Strategy in the Office of the Vice-Chancellor. Dr Aslett also served as researcher on the State Capture Commission in South Africa. In his spare time, he writes crime fiction, publishing novels and short stories in Afrikaans.

Rajni Bala is presently working as an associate professor in Chitkara Business School, Chitkara University, Punjab, India. She is having 16.4 years of teaching experience. She has worked with NIT, Kurukshetra, Maharishi Markandeshwar deemed to be University, Mullana and Mukand Lal National Group. She is having 25 research publications in her account indexed in Scopus and UGC care. She has presented a number of papers in various national and international conferences. She is having 4 patents and 3 copyrights in her account. She has delivered workshops on Writing Literature Review, Statistical Tools on Excel, Innovative technologies in education etc.

Vishal Jain is presently working as a Professor at the Department of Computer Science & Engineering, School of Engineering & Technology, Vivekananda Institute of Professional Studies - Technical Campus, New Delhi. Before that, he worked as Professor at Sharda University, Greater Noida and Associate Professor at Bharati Vidyapeeth's Institute of Computer Applications and Management (BVICAM),

New Delhi. He is associated with Kuala Lumpur University of Science and Technology (KLUST) (formerly known as Infrastructure University Kuala Lumpur (IUKL)), Malaysia, Lincoln University College, Malaysia and Research Institute of IoT Cybersecurity, Department of Electronic Engineering, National Kaohsiung University of Science and Technology, Taiwan for research oriented activities.

Preeti Jain is Assistant professor in Ajay Kumar Garg Institute of management , Ghaziabad, Uttar Pradesh and an accomplished academic and researcher with a Ph.D. in Commerce from CT University, and qualifications including UGC NET and an MBA from Lovely Professional University. she excels in communication, office automation, and data visualization tools. With a rich teaching background and numerous publications and patents, she has presented and published research on integrated marketing, sustainable development, and AI in finance. Dr. Jain has coordinated cultural events and academic programs at esteemed institutions and actively participates in workshops and FDPs on research methodology and innovation management.

Parveen Kumar is Assistant Professor, Department of Commerce, Chandigarh University, Mohali (Panjab), India. He holds a master degree in Commerce . He has also qualified UGC NET in Commerce. He has been teaching marketing, accounting and finance in several universities and has gained an experience of 5 years in Academics and teaching. He is Ph.D scholar and he has published 6 research papers and Book chapter in the leading journals and conferences (Scopus Indexed) and several other research papers in peer reviewed and UGC care journals.

Maral Mazjini holds a Ph.D. in Statistics and works as a Senior Scientist. Her research focuses on data modeling using dynamic mixture models, heavy-tailed distributions, AI and time-varying volatility structures. Her research combines theoretical development with real-world applications. Building on this foundation, her current work applies statistical and data science methodologies to support data-informed decision-making through trend analysis and AI. Her interests lie at the intersection of statistical theory and the applied use of data science and AI in studying complex, real-world data.

Geberew Tulu Mekonnen is a Lecturer at the School of Policing Studies at Charles Sturt University. He holds a PhD in Education from the University of Tasmania (UTAS), with a focus on the impact of the Bologna Process on Ethiopian higher education. Dr Mekonnen is engaged in criminology research, collaborating with colleagues on topics such as youth crime and education, cybercrime, cryptocurrencies, combating misinformation and disinformation, and deepfake technology. His broader academic contributions include publications on student learning and assessment, higher education governance, pedagogy, and leadership, reflecting his significant impact in these fields. Before joining Charles Sturt University, Dr Mekonnen held various roles at the University of Tasmania, including Sessional Academic Staff, Research Assistant, Research Outputs Officer, and Research Funding Officer. He also taught and conducted research at Addis Ababa University (AAU), Ethiopia. During his time at AAU, he served in administrative leadership positions, including Associate Dean for Undergraduate Programs, College Managing Director, and Program Coordinator.

Kwabena Owusu-Mensah is currently pursuing a PhD in the Department of Computer Science at the University of Ghana, Legon. His research focuses on developing an innovative framework to detect and prevent card-not-present (CNP) fraud by leveraging advanced machine learning techniques, Internet of Things (IoT) ecosystems, AI, and user behavioral analytics. In addition to this primary focus, he is engaged in scholarly investigations related to federated learning, privacy-preserving methodologies for fraud detection, and the implementation of real-time financial security systems. His academic background comprises extensive coursework and research in cybersecurity, fraud analytics, and system architecture tailored for financial institutions, positioning him as a knowledgeable contributor to the fields of cybersecurity and financial technology.

Eshan Singhal is a dedicated Research Scholar in Law at Dr. BhimRao Ambedkar University (DBRAU), Uttar Pradesh, India. With a strong academic foundation, he has authored and published several research papers in reputed journals and has actively participated in numerous national and international seminars and conferences. His research interests span constitutional law, criminal justice, and socio-legal issues. He is committed to contributing to the evolving landscape of legal scholarship in India. He strives to bridge the gap between academic research and practical legal reforms. He can be contacted at adv.eshansinghal277@gmail .com for academic or professional correspondence.

Sachin Sudan is an Associate Professor at MMDU, Mullana. He has experience of 15 years in teaching. My areas of expertise are marketing, consumer behavior, and branding strategies.

Milind Tiwari is a Senior Lecturer in Fraud and Financial Crime Studies at the Australian Graduate School of Policing and Security, Charles Sturt University. His research focuses on future crimes, food crime, money laundering, and other financial crimes. His publications appear in quality journals, including Computers in Human Behavior, British Accounting Review, and Asian Journal of Criminology.

Astrid Vachette is a lecturer and discipline lead in Emergency Management at the Australian Graduate School in Policing and Security, Charles Sturt University.

James Welch, Professor of criminal law at Alliance University, Anekal India; senior research consultant with Rabdan Academy's Security & Defense Institute (RSDI) at Rabdan Academy (RSDI); and senior researcher with IACS, is a seasoned professional with over 20 years of experience in law enforcement, intelligence, crisis and disaster management, and academia. Holding a Ph.D. from Leiden University and two master's degrees, his research spans forensic psychology, criminology, national security, international law and international relations. He has served in military and intelligence operations in Iraq and Afghanistan, instructed senior leaders at Rabdan Academy, and consulted for NATO and U.S. defense agencies. Dr. Welch's work combines theoretical rigor with practical applications in crisis management, policing, and intelligence. Notable publications include studies on drone warfare, crisis management, and AI's role in security. He has presented at international conferences on emerging threats and urban security dynamics, contributing significantly to both academic and strategic military discussions. Fluent in multiple languages, Dr. Welch remains passionate about applying his expertise to high-impact consulting and strategic advisory roles.

Winfred Yaokumah is a distinguished academic, researcher, and consultant specializing in information technology with a focus on cybersecurity, information assurance, and security governance. With a PhD in Information Technology (specializing in information assurance and cybersecurity), he has extensive expertise in cyber threat detection, risk management, and the development of secure information systems. His research portfolio comprises numerous peer-reviewed journal articles, book chapters, and conference proceedings that explore critical topics, including information security risk management and governance, cryptographic algorithms, network security, cyber ethics, and the application of machine learning in cyber defense.

Mladen Zecevic is a Lecturer at the School of Policing Studies, Charles Sturt University. He holds a Master of Education from Charles Sturt University. His work focuses on cybercrime and education.

You Zhou gained his PhD of criminology at Monash University. His research focuses on cybercrime, future crimes, cybercrime policing, juvenile violence, criminological theories, and mixed methods. His publications appear in quality journals, including Computers in Human Behavior, British Accounting Review, Crime & Delinquency, Victims & Offenders, and Asian Journal of Criminology.

Index

A

B

C

D

E

F

G

H

I

L

M

P

R

S

T

www.ingramcontent.com/pod-product-compliance
Lightning Source LLC
LaVergne TN
LVHW061525290926
849162LV00004B/667